The Art of Digital Video

John Watkinson

Focal Press
London & Boston

Focal Press
is an imprint of Butterworth Scientific

 PART OF REED INTERNATIONAL P.L.C.

First published 1990

© **John Watkinson, 1990**

British Library Cataloguing in Publication Data

Watkinson, John
  The art of digital video.
  1. Videorecording equipment. Equipment
  I. Title
  621.38833

ISBN 0-240-51287-1

Library of Congress Cataloging-in-Publication Data

Watkinson, John.
  The art of digital video/John Watkinson.
    p.   cm.
  Includes bibliographical references.
  ISBN 0-240-51287-1:
  1. Digital television.   I. Title.
  TK6678.W38   1990
  621.388—dc20   89-25740
                                        CIP

Photoset by Genesis Typesetting, Borough Green, Kent
Printed and bound by Hartnolls Ltd, Bodmin, Cornwall

Preface

There would be very little to document in the subject of digital video were it not for the persistence of those who overcame countless obstacles in order to make it happen.

It is not so long ago that many of the devices described in these pages existed only in the imagination of those who dreamed of a better way of conveying and processing video. This new approach would not be some refinement of existing technology, offering modest gains, but a totally different approach, which would wipe away existing problems and introduce dramatic opportunities.

It was not enough simply to have the dream, because dreams don't pay bills. It was necessary to implement the dream, and this would require the adoption of technologies which had previously little or no relevance to television: computation, laser optics, mass storage, simulation, error correction. Most of these disciplines were described in their own idiomatic terminology, and this in itself is a major obstacle to progress.

As yet there is no documented process which teaches us how to balance conflicting requirements of numerous disparate technologies to achieve a reliable end product. It can only be described as an art, and it has inspired the title of this book. Because there are so many disciplines involved, digital video is a fascinating and stimulating subject. It is a source of some regret that the intellectual content of modern digital video equipment generally exceeds that of the program material which it handles.

Digital video continues to develop, but it has reached a point where a book of this kind becomes feasible. The basic principles are largely agreed, there are real products with which to earn a living, and we now have standards for recording and interconnection of digital video. The picture quality obtained with these machines is of a high standard, but techniques which are yet to be widely applied can result in a further improvement within the existing line standards.

This book describes all of the essential theory of digital video and a great deal of the practice, but the subject is too great to attempt to include any history. The current position in High Definition is too fluid to document at the present time and has been consciously omitted except where general principles apply.

The range of disciplines to be covered is so great that this cannot be a conventional book. The need for understanding is too great for a book to assume a high academic level in all these subjects.

This book adopts the same approach as that used in *The Art of Digital Audio*. Every concept begins with the basic mechanism involved and defines its terminology. Wherever possible, explanations are given in plain English, equations being used as a last resort.

There are few stated facts, since these are easily forgotten. Instead there are reasons, arguments and mechanisms from which facts can be deduced. The approach works equally well from basic levels to advanced concepts, so there is also plenty in this book for the expert, and there are references for those who wish to go further.

Words have been carefully chosen to reduce the chances of misunderstanding, and where a misnomer is in common use, it will be identified.

A lot of care went into *The Art of Digital Audio*, but I was not prepared for the overwhelming support of the approach. It would be unthinkable to do anything different in this book.

Acknowledgements

For Anne

I must first thank David Kirk, who invited me to write a series on digital video for 'Broadcast Systems Engineering', which he then edited, and Ron Godwyn, who succeeded him. The response to this series provided the impetus to turn it into a book.

The publications of the Society of Motion Picture and Television Engineers and of the European Broadcasting Union have been extremely useful.

I am indebted to the many people who have found time to discuss complex subjects and to suggest reference works. Particular thanks go to David Lyon and Roderick Snell of Snell and Wilcox, Takeo Eguchi, Jim Wilkinson, David Huckfield and John Ive of Sony, Luigi Gallo of Accom, Graham Roe of Pro-Bel, Dave Trytko, Joe Attard, John Watney, Fraser Morrison and Ab Weber of Ampex, John Mallinson of CMRR San Diego, Roger Wood of IBM and John Baldwin.

Last but not least thanks to Margaret Riley of Focal Press for helping it along.

John Watkinson
Burghfield Common, England

Contents

Chapter 6 Digital magnetic and optical recording   226

Chapter 7 Error correction   275

Chapter 13 Digital audio with video   509

Index   575

Chapter 1

Why Digital?

1.1 The advantages of digital video

The first methods used in television transmission and recording were understandably analog, and the signal formats were essentially determined by the requirements of the cathode ray tube as a display, so that the receiver might be as simple as possible and be constructed with a minimum number of vacuum tubes. Following the development of magnetic audio recording during the Second World War, a need for television recording was perceived. This was due to the number of time zones across the United States. Without recording, popular television programmes had to be performed live several times so they could be seen at peak viewing time in each time zone. Ampex eventually succeeded in recording monochrome video in the 1950s, and the fundamentals of the Quadruplex machine were so soundly based that to this day analog video recorders still use rotating heads and frequency modulation.[1] Study of every shortcoming in the analog process has led to the development of some measure to reduce it, and current machines are capable of excellent performance. The point to appreciate, however, is that analog recording has become a mature technology and has almost reached limits determined by the laws of physics. The process of refinement produces increasingly small returns.

As there is now another video technology, and known as digital, the previous technology has to be referred to as analog. It is appropriate to begin with a comparison of the fundamental differences between these technologies.

In an analog system, information is conveyed by the infinite variation of some continuous parameter, such as the voltage on a wire or the strength of flux. When it comes to recording, the distance along the medium is a further analog of time. However much the signal is magnified, more and more detail will be revealed until a point is reached where the actual value is uncertain because of noise. A parameter can only be a true analog of the original if the conversion process is linear, otherwise harmonic distortion is introduced. If the speed of the medium is not constant there will not be a true analog of time and the result is known as timebase error.

It is a characteristic of an analog system that the degradations at the output are the sum of all the degradations introduced in each stage through which the signal has passed. This sets a limit to the number of stages a

1

signal can pass through before it becomes too impaired to be worth watching. Down at signal level, all impairments can be reduced to the addition of some unwanted signal such as noise or distortion, and timing instability such as group-delay effects and chroma phase errors. In an analog system, such effects can never be separated from the original signal; in the digital domain they can be eliminated.

Although it is possible to convey signals which have an arbitrary number of states, in most digital video systems, the information is in binary form. The signals sent have only two states, and change at predetermined times according to a stable clock. If the binary signal is degraded by noise, this will be rejected at the receiver, as the signal is judged solely on whether it is above or below some threshold. However, the signal will be conveyed with finite bandwidth, and this will restrict the rate at which the voltage changes. Superimposed noise can move the point at which the receiver judges that there has been a change of state. Time instability has this effect too. This instability is also rejected because, on receipt, the signal is reclocked by the stable clock, and all changes in the system will take place at the edges of that clock. Fig. 1.1 shows that, however many stages a binary signal passes through, it still comes out the same, only later. It is

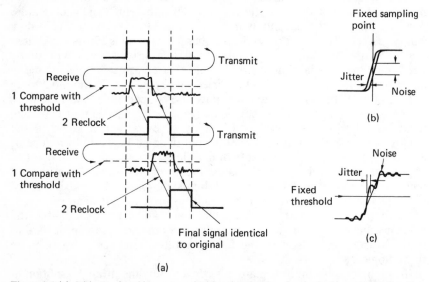

Figure 1.1 (a) A binary signal is compared with a threshold and reclocked on receipt, thus the meaning will be unchanged. (b) Jitter on a signal can appear as noise with respect to fixed timing. (c) Noise on a signal can appear as jitter when compared with a fixed threshold

possible to convey an analog waveform down such a signal path. That analog waveform has to be broken into evenly spaced time elements (a process known as sampling) and then each sample is expressed as a whole number, or integer, which can be carried by binary digits (bits for short). Fig. 1.2 shows that the signal path may convey sample values either in parallel on several wires, where each wire carries a binary signal representing a different power of two, or serially in one channel, at higher

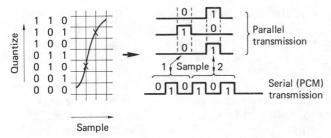

Figure 1.2 When a signal is carried in numerical form, either parallel or serial, the mechanisms of Figure 1.1 ensure that the only degradation is in the conversion processes

speed, a process called pulse code modulation (PCM). The only drawback of this scheme is that a single high-quality video channel requires about 200 million bits per second. Digital video only became viable when advances in high-density recording made such a data rate available at reasonable cost.

In simple terms, the signal waveform is conveyed in a digital recorder as if someone had measured the voltage at regular intervals with a digital voltmeter and written the readings in binary on a roll of paper. The rate at which these measurements are made and the accuracy of the meter now wholly determine the quality of the system, because once a parameter is expressed as discrete numbers, those numbers can be conveyed unchanged through a recording process. This dependence on the quality of conversion is the price paid to make quality independent of the signal path. As it is so critical to picture quality, a whole chapter of this book is dedicated to sampling and conversion. Since a digital system faithfully conveys the original analog waveform, it is equally feasible to digitize component or composite video signals. In the case of composite digital, there is complete freedom from differential gain error.

A magnetic head cannot know the meaning of signals which are passed through it, so there is no distinction at the head/medium interface between analog and digital recording. Thus a digital signal will suffer all the degradations that beset an analog signal: particulate noise, distortion, dropout, modulation noise, print-through, crosstalk and so on. However, there is a difference in the effect of these degradations on the meaning of the signals. As stated, digital recording uses a binary code, and the presence or absence of a flux change is the only item of interest. Provided that flux change can generate a playback pulse which is sensibly bigger than the noise, the numerical meaning will be unchanged by reasonable distortions of the waveform. In other words, a bit is still a bit, whatever its shape. This implies that the bits on the medium can be very small indeed and can be packed very close together; hence the required data rate is achievable. If the trivial example of the paper tape recording is pursued further, suppose that the tape upon which the voltages were written became crumpled up. If it were smoothed out, the numbers would still be legible and could be copied without error to a new piece of paper. By comparison, if a photograph is crumpled up, it will look like a crumpled-up photograph for evermore.

Large disturbances of the recording, such as dropout or severe interference, may cause flux changes to be missed, or simulate ones which did not exist. The result is that some of the numbers recorded will be incorrect. In numerical systems, provision of an error-correction system is feasible; in analog systems it is not. In PCM systems, corruption of high order bits can cause severe disturbance of the video waveform, and at the recording densities necessary to give economy of tape usage, a properly engineered error-correction system is absolutely essential to return the corrupted numbers to their original value. It is probably true to say that, without error-correction systems, digital video recording would not be economically feasible.

In the digital domain, signals can be easily conveyed and stored in electronic circuitry. Unavoidable speed variations in recorders cause the numbers to appear at a fluctuating rate. The use of a temporary store allows those numbers to be read out at constant rate, a process known as timebase correction. In this way, timebase errors and chroma phase errors can be eliminated. The rock-solid vector display of a composite digital recorder is uncanny at first. The C-format timebase corrector, which made professional helical scan recording possible without field segmentation, was one of the first major applications of digital video. Chapter 4 treats this subject in some detail. The ease with which delay is provided also allows phase-linear filters and interpolators to be created in a straightforward manner, because the group-delay problems of analog filters cannot occur. Filters can be constructed which work with mathematical precision and freedom from component drift and with a response that can be easily changed.

The main advantages of digital video can be summarized as follows (they are not in order of importance because this will change with the application):

* The quality of a digital video link is independent of the characteristics of the channel in a properly engineered system. Frequency response, linearity and noise are determined only by the quality of the conversion processes. In recorders there is complete freedom from moiré and other analog recording artifacts. The independence of the quality from the medium also means that a recorder will not display different picture or audio quality if different brands of tape are used, provided that they all have acceptable error rates.

* A digital recording is no more than a series of numbers, and hence can be copied through an indefinite number of generations without degradation. This implies that the life of a recording can be truly indefinite, because even if the medium begins to decay physically the sample values can be copied to a new medium with no loss of information.

* The use of error-correction techniques eliminates the effects of dropout. In consumer products, error correction can be used to advantage to ease the handling requirements.

* The use of timebase correction on replay eliminates timebase error and can be further used to synchronize more than one machine to sample accuracy, eliminating the need for lengthy timing-in processes.

* The use of digital recording and error correction allows the signal-to-noise ratio of the recorded tracks to be relatively poor. The tracks

can be narrow and hence achieve a saving in tape consumption despite the greater bandwidth. Professional analog recorders must use wide tape tracks to give extremely good first-generation quality which then allows several generations of dubbing.

* The advantages listed also apply to the audio channels of video recorders. It is natural to digitize both audio and video, so that much common circuitry can be used. The audio quality possible in a digital DVTR then exceeds that of a professional analog audio recorder, which could not be said for analog VTRs. The rigid timebase control prevents phase errors between channels, which is particularly important with the advent of stereo audio in television.

* It is possible to construct extremely precise and stable digital filters and equalizers with inherent phase linearity. Such devices need no adjustment, and so the cost of manufacture can be less than the analog equivalent. The adoption of digital filtering makes possible such devices as picture manipulators and other effects devices which, though complex, are extremely reliable.

1.2 The opportunities

Digital video does far more than merely compare favourably with analog. Its most exciting aspects are the tremendous possibilities which are denied to analog technology. Once in the digital domain, the original picture is just a series of numbers, and these can be stored, conveyed and processed in many and varied ways. The computer industry has spent decades perfecting machines to store, convey and process streams of numbers at high speed and at a cost which continues to fall. Computers can generate artificial images for computer-aided design systems and simulators. Work has been done on the improvement of resolution and the elimination of flicker and other artifacts for computer displays, and broadcast digital video can take full advantage of such techniques. Recordings can be stored on computer disk drives, magnetic or optical, whose radially moving heads allow rapid random access to the information. For animation or editing of video, this is far superior to waiting for tape recorders to shuttle and preroll, although the sheer data rate of digital video prevents current disk-based machines from making lengthy recordings. An edit can be effected by reading samples from two sources and fading or switching between them in digital circuitry. The edit can be simulated, so that the outcome can be assessed, and the edit points can be moved around at will until the result is satisfactory. The final edited version can be recorded on a different medium if necessary, leaving the source material intact.

The cable and satellite communications networks around the world are increasingly being used for digital transmission, and a packet of digital video information can pass through as easily as a telex message or a bank transaction. Provided the original numbers are fed in the correct order at the correct rate to the final destination, for conversion to a picture, it does not matter how they have been conveyed.

The worlds of digital video, digital audio, communication and computation are closely related, and that is where the real potential lies.

The time when television was a specialist subject which could evolve in isolation from other disciplines has gone – digital technology has made sure of that.

That technology allows processes which were virtually impossible in the analog domain. Modern effects machines produce manipulations which cannot be achieved in any other way. Standards conversion, graphics generation and paint systems rely heavily on digital technology.

1.3 Some typical machines outlined

Some outlines of possible digital video recorders follow to illustrate what is possible and to put the major chapters of this book into perspective.

Fig. 1.3 shows some of the ways in which a digital recording of component or composite video can be made, starting with the sampling and quantizing processes explained in Chapter 2. Once in digital form, the data are formed into blocks, and the encoding section of the error-correction system supplies additional bits designed to protect the data against errors. These blocks are then converted into some form of channel code which combines the data with clock information so that it is possible to identify how many bits were recorded even if several adjacent bits are identical. Chapter 6 deals with the extensive subject of digital recording.

The coded data are recorded on some medium, which can be optical or magnetic, disk or tape, rotary, moving or stationary head. Some media are erasable; some can only be recorded once. Videotape recording is almost universally done with rotary-head recorders. Stationary-head recorders cannot currently achieve the storage densities necessary for economic digital video recording, ' but advances in data reduction and head technology may change this position for consumer devices. Magnetic and optical disk drives are detailed in Chapter 12.

Upon replaying the recording of the hypothetical machine of Fig. 1.3, the errors caused by various mechanisms will be detected, corrected or concealed using the extra bits appended during the encoding process. Chapter 7 treats the subject of error correction as comprehensively as possible without becoming lost in the mathematics.

The replayed digital recording may be processed before being viewed again or re-recorded. Simple manipulations of digital video, such as gain control and mixing, are covered in Chapter 3; more advanced processes, such as digital filtering, standards conversion and effects, occupy Chapter 5.

The digital recorder and the digital mixer may well be two different units of different manufacture, and it is necessary to provide some standard interconnection between them in the digital domain. Chapter 8 details digital communications between equipment.

Digital video recorders were demonstrated in prototype form in the late seventies,[2] and as the analog recording technology of the time was composite, these early machines were also composite.

The first digital video recorder to reach the marketplace was, however a component machine which complied with the D-1 format. Technically

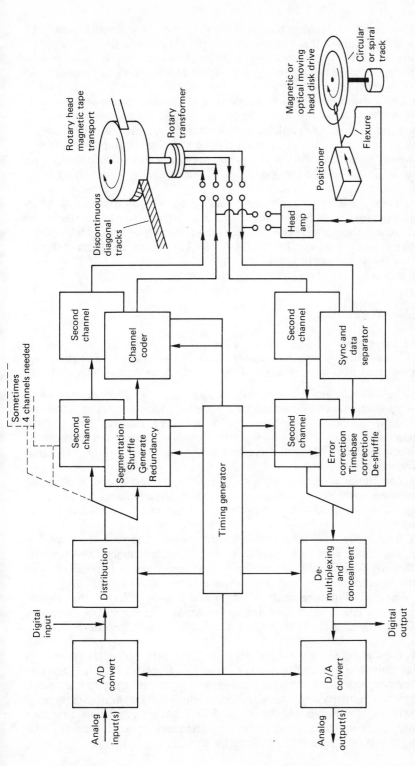

Figure 1.3 Basic digital video recording. The essential processes in digital recording do not change with the medium used except in detail. Data can be recorded on rotary head tape or magnetic or optical disk. Several parallel channels may be needed to handle the data rate in real time. This would not be necessary in the case of a still store.

speaking it was a tremendous achievement, but tape consumption was heavy, and although the component recording gave excellent quality, the machine could not readily be interfaced with the overwhelmingly composite world of broadcasting. The recent D-2 format is composite, and machines are fitted with converters so that they can directly replace analog recorders without any further expenditure. There is a direct analogy here with the first successful digital audio recorders. These units contained convertors, so that they could replace analog machines, and acted exactly like their analog predecessors, even having a similar layout of controls.

Chapter 9 details the mechanisms necessary for rotary-head tape recording, followed by Chapters 10 and 11 which deal respectively with the D-1 and D-2 digital formats.

The traditional neglect of audio quality in television has now been largely redressed, with the introduction of stereo sound in television broadcasting, the popularity of music video and such devices as CD-video, and digital audio tracks on DVTRs. Chapter 13 covers the subject of digital audio in the video environment.

1.4 Disadvantages

In this comparison of digital and analog technologies, the emphasis so far has been on the advantages of digital video. In the interests of fairness and truth we must also look at some of the problems of digital video.

(1) Digital recorders must use thin tape with a fine surface finish to allow the very-short-wavelength recordings needed. Contamination must be avoided at all costs. The tape tracks are very narrow, and greater mechanical stability is demanded from tape and transport to achieve reliable interchange. Digital recorders may be at a disadvantage in harsh environments.

(2) The signal quality of a digital format is chosen irrevocably at the design stage, and no improvement is then possible without fundamental change. This contrasts with the process of refinement observed in analog recorders.

(3) Inevitably, digital recorders are more complex than analog recorders, and this has implications for maintenance and repair. Faultfinding with traditional analog video techniques is impossible, and digital machines need computer-related approaches using diagnostic programs and signature analysis. It should not be inferred that digital machines are less reliable than analog machines. The biggest maintenance problem with digital video effects machines is that people break the joysticks!

(4) Digital filters have consistent performance, since there are no adjustments. If a filter contains a small ripple in its response, every filter to that design will have exactly the same ripple, at exactly the same frequency. Upon passing the signal through the same unit over several generations, the ripple will build up. Filter design must take this into account. Although a digital recorder may introduce no degradations to the signal, this is not quite true of digital processing.

References

1. GINSBURG, C.P., Comprehensive description of the Ampex video tape recorder. *SMPTE J.*, **66**, 177–182 (1957)
2. BALDWIN, J.L.E., Digital television recording – history and background. *SMPTE J.*, **95**, 1206–1214 (1986)

Conversion

The power of digital techniques is in storage without degradation and in complex processing and manipulations. If video is to take advantage of digital techniques, then means must be found to express the colour and movement of a real-life scene as a series of numbers. Once in the digital domain, degradations can be controlled, and so the conversion processes to and from the digital domain become the main sources of degradation. In the interests of quality, these processes deserve a great deal of attention and will form the main subjects of this chapter.

2.1 The discrete picture

At the moment it is not possible to convert directly from an image to the digital domain or vice versa. Generally cameras and displays are analog devices, and there is always an intermediate analog video stage at each end of the digital video chain. Frequently the digital domain is entered via an analog process originally intended as a broadcast standard. This inevitably compromises the quality which can be achieved. As new technologies emerge, this may not always be true.

To a human observer, a real scene appears continuous, whereas digital systems are, by definition, discrete, as are many aspects of analog television systems, particularly CCD cameras. At its most fundamental, a monochrome digital image is an array of points, generally rectangular, at each of which the brightness is stored as a number. The points are known as picture elements, generally abbreviated to pixels, although sometimes the abbreviation is more savage and they are known as pels. As shown in Fig. 2.1, the array will generally be arranged with an even spacing between pixels, which are in rows and columns. By placing the pixels close together, it is hoped that the observer will perceive a continuous image. Obviously the finer the pixel spacing, the greater will be the resolution of the picture, but the amount of digital data needed to store one picture will increase as the square of the resolution, and with it the costs. In this chapter the theoretical connection between resolution and pixel spacing will be examined, along with the reasons why it is seldom achieved in practice.

If it is desired to convey a coloured image, then each pixel is no longer a scalar brightness value, but a vector which describes in some way the

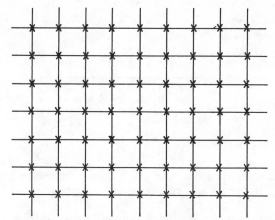

Figure 2.1 A picture can be stored digitally by representing the brightness at each of the above points by a binary number. For a colour picture each point becomes a vector and has to describe the brightness, hue and saturation of that part of the picture. Samples are usually but not always formed into regular arrays of rows and columns, and it is most efficient if the horizontal and vertical spacing are the same

brightness, hue and saturation of that point in the picture. The method which is in almost universal use at the camera is to use one sensor for each primary colour. Each sensor is fed by light of a different colour from an optical splitter block. Again the amount of data has increased, and with it the difficulty of implementation. It is not possible to represent accurately every colour which occurs naturally, because of the current lack of suitable display technology, and so there are further shortcomings in the reproduced image.

In order to produce moving pictures, the current approach is simply to provide a mechanism where the value of every pixel can be updated periodically. This effectively results in a three-dimensional array, where two of the axes are spatial and the third is temporal.

2.2 Sampling

Sampling is a way of expressing a continuous phenomenon by means of a periodic measurement. In television systems the input image which falls on the camera sensor will be continuous in time and continuous in two spatial dimensions corresponding to the height and width of the sensor. All three of these continuous dimensions will be sampled, as has been seen. There is a direct connection between the concept of temporal sampling, where the input changes with respect to time at some frequency and is sampled at some other frequency, and spatial sampling, where an image changes a given number of times per unit distance and is sampled at some other number of times per unit distance. The connection between the two is the process of scanning. Temporal frequency can be obtained by multiplying spatial frequency by the speed of the scan. Fig. 2.2 shows a hypothetical image sensor which has 1000 discrete sensors across a width of 1 cm. The spatial sampling rate of this sensor is thus 1000 per centimetre. If the

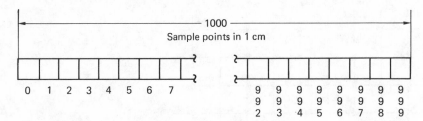

Figure 2.2 If the above spatial sampling arrangement of 1000 points per cm is scanned in one millisecond, the sampling rate will become 1 Megahertz

sensors are measured sequentially during a scan which takes 1 millisecond to go across the 1 cm width, the result will be a temporal sampling rate of 1 MHz.

Fig. 2.3(a) shows a waveform which has been sampled at a relatively high frequency, and intuitively it is clear that at this sampling rate the waveform has been preserved. Fig. 2.3(b) shows an example where the sampling rate is clearly inadequate. A phenomenon called *aliasing* has taken place, where a signal of a new frequency has replaced the original. Aliasing is commonly seen in film and television material, particularly when a stagecoach is being chased by Red Indians. The spoke passing frequency of the coach wheels exceeds the ability of the frame rate of the film camera (24 Hz) to follow them, and so the wheels can appear to be turning slowly or even backwards. This naturally confused the Indians, who went around saying 'How'?

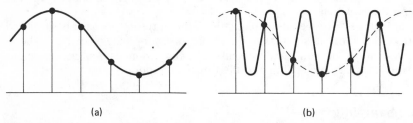

(a)   (b)

Figure 2.3 At (a), the sampling is adequate to reconstruct the original signal. At (b) the sampling rate is inadequate, and reconstruction produces the wrong waveform (dotted). Aliasing has taken place

Obviously aliasing can be prevented by sampling at a high frequency, but in practical systems bandwidth has to be paid for, and sampling at an unnecessarily high rate will cause problems when the information needs to be stored or transmitted. It is necessary to establish the precise connection between sampling rate and bandwidth.

Fig. 2.4 shows that sampling is essentially a process of modulation. The sampling waveform, which is a steady stream of narrow impulses, is amplitude modulated, or multiplied, by the baseband signal. Since the sampling waveform is impulsive rather than sinusoidal, its spectrum consists of the sampling rate and all of its harmonics. Multiplication causes sidebands, and these can be seen above and below the sampling frequency

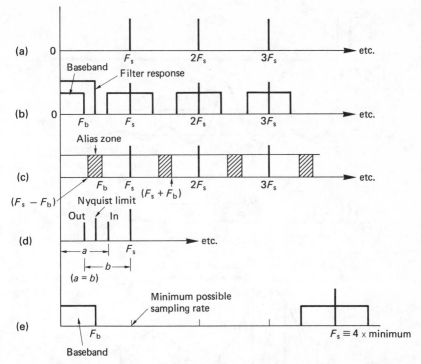

Figure 2.4 (a) Spectrum of sampling pulses. (b) Spectrum of samples. (c) Aliasing due to sideband overlap. (d) Beat-frequency production. (e) Oversampling

and each of the harmonics. In order to return to the continuous baseband signal it is necessary to use a low pass filter which rejects everything but the original spectrum.

Fig. 2.4 also shows the result when an excessive baseband spectrum enters a sampled system. The lower sideband of the sampling rate now overlaps the baseband, and no filter can determine whether energy in this area belongs to the baseband or the sideband. In particular, frequencies above half the sampling rate are heterodyned down to a new position the same distance below.

Fig. 2.4 shows that, in the extreme case, a rectangular baseband spectrum of one-half the sampling rate could be accommodated, and this is the conclusion of Shannon's sampling theory, also discovered in the Soviet Union by Kotelnikov.

Fig. 2.5 shows how it is possible to return to the continuous analog domain using a low-pass filter. The impulse response of a LPF which cuts off at one-half the sampling frequency is a $\sin x/x$ curve where the zero crossings are separated by the sampling period. This ensures that samples do not interfere with each other, since at the location of a given sample, the contributions from all other samples will be zero. The $\sin x/x$ impulses from all of the samples combine to produce a continuous waveform.

In sampled systems a low-pass filter is necessary before the sampling stage to prevent frequencies above half of the sampling rate entering the

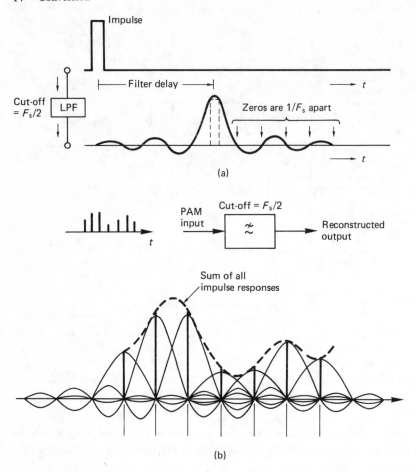

Figure 2.5 The impulse response of a low-pass filter which cuts off at $F_s/2$ has zeros at $1/F_s$ spacing which correspond to the position of adjacent samples, as shown in (b). The output will be a signal which has the value of each sample at the sample instant, but with smooth transitions from sample to sample

system. This will be called an *anti-aliasing* filter. A second identical filter will also be needed upon returning to the continuous domain, in order to reject the unwanted sidebands of the sampling. This will be called a *reconstruction* or *anti-image* filter.

The eye has a temporal filtering effect which is known as persistence of vision, and the phosphors of CRTs continue to emit light after the electron beam has passed. It might be thought that a temporal sampling rate (frame rate in progressive scan systems) which was high enough to make flicker invisible would be adequate, but in fact this is not the case, as will be seen when motion is discussed.

Since conventional analog video systems sample temporally and vertically, there will be two opportunities for aliasing to take place. Digital video is a three-dimensional sampling system, so aliasing can potentially occur in all three.

Whilst the maximum information capacity predicted by theory would be reached with filters which cut off at exactly half the sampling rate, such filters cannot be realized.

If an electrical filter is being used on a temporal signal, as the slope of the filter approaches infinity, so the group delay of the filter also approaches infinity. Realizable filters will have a finite slope, and so the sampling rate will always need to be raised above twice the baseband frequency by some factor which depends on the characteristics of the filter.

Where the input is a spatial spectrum, the filter must also be spatial rather than temporal, and so it cannot readily be implemented with electronics. However, the same restrictions apply to the achievable cut-off rate.

2.3 Aperture effect

The foregoing has discussed the effect of infinitely small sampling pulses, which are never achieved in practice. Whenever the sampling pulses at the input of a system, or the output pulses, have finite duration, the aperture effect is observed. This will also be seen in spatial sampling, where the sampling point has finite dimensions.

Fig. 2.6(a) shows a sampling system where the impulses have grown until they are as wide as the sample period. They can be considered to consist of an infinite number of narrow pulses. When the sample polarity alternates as shown, many of the positive pulses are cancelled by the negative pulses, and a loss occurs which clearly will not be observed at low frequencies. The resultant frequency response is shown in Fig. 2.6(b) where it will be seen to be a sin x/x curve with the first null at the sampling rate. This corresponds to a signal level of 0.64 of the LF level at half the sampling rate. Fig. 2.6(c) shows that there will be a family of responses according to the impulse width, becoming more linear as the impulse narrows. Dividing impulse width by the sample period gives the aperture ratio.

The aperture effect will show up in many aspects of television. Lenses have finite modulation transfer functions, such that a very small object becomes spread in the image. The image sensor will also have a finite aperture function. In tube cameras, the beam will have a finite radius and will not necessarily have a uniform energy distribution across its diameter. In CCD cameras, the sensor is split into elements which may almost touch in some cases. The element integrates light falling on its surface, and so will have a rectangular aperture. In both cases there will be a roll-off of higher spatial frequencies.

It is highly desirable to prevent spatial aliasing, since the result is visually irritating. In tube cameras the aliasing will be in the vertical dimension only, since the horizontal dimension is continuously scanned. Such cameras seldom attempt to prevent vertical aliasing. CCD sensors can, however, alias in both horizontal and vertical dimensions, and so an anti-aliasing optical filter is generally fitted between the lens and the sensor. This takes the form of a plate which diffuses the image formed by the lens. Such a device can never have a sharp cut-off nor will the aperture be rectangular. The aperture of the anti-aliasing plate is in series with the

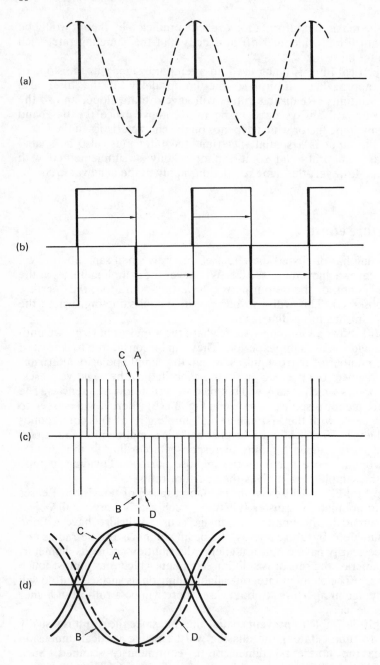

Figure 2.6(a) The mechanism of aperture effect which causes high-frequency losses when impulse has finite period. (a) Maximum-frequency sine wave in samples of zero duration. (b) Zero-order hold version of above (100% aperture). (c) Consider rectangular pulse as infinite number of delta functions. (d) Result of low-pass filtering some of above impulses. A cancels B completely. C cancels D partially

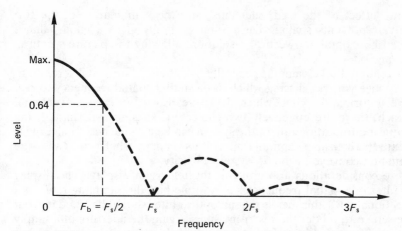

Figure 2.6(b) Frequency response with 100% aperture nulls at multiples of sampling rate. Area of interest is up to half sampling rate

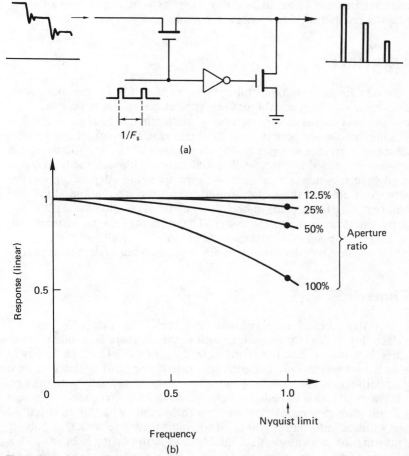

Figure 2.6(c) (a) Resampling circuit eliminates transients and reduces aperture ratio. (b) Response of various aperture ratios

aperture effect of the CCD elements, and the combination of the two effectively prevents spatial aliasing and generally gives a good balance between horizontal and vertical resolution, allowing the picture a natural appearance.

Conventional tube cameras generally have better horizontal resolution, and produce vertical aliasing which has a similar spatial frequency to real picture information, but which lacks realism. With a conventional approach, there are effectively two choices. If aliasing is permitted, the theoretical information rate of the system can be approached. If aliasing is prevented, realizable anti-aliasing filters cannot sharp-cut, and the information conveyed is below system capacity.

These considerations also apply at the television display. The display must filter out spatial frequencies above one-half the sampling rate. In a conventional CRT this means that an optical filter should be fitted in front of the screen to render the raster invisible. Again the aperture of a simply realizable filter would attenuate too much of the wanted spectrum, and so the technique is not used. The technique of spot wobble was most effective in reducing raster visibility in monochrome television sets without affecting horizontal resolution, and its neglect remains a mystery.

2.4 Kell effect

As noted, in conventional tube cameras and CRTs the horizontal dimension is continuous, whereas the vertical dimension is sampled. The aperture effect means that the vertical resolution in real systems will be less than sampling theory permits, and to obtain equal horizontal and vertical resolutions a greater number of lines is necessary. The magnitude of the increase is described by the so-called Kell factor,[1] although the term factor is a misnomer since it can have a range of values depending on the apertures in use and the methods used to measure resolution.[2] In digital video, sampling takes place in horizontal and vertical dimensions, and the Kell parameter becomes unnecessary. The outputs of digital systems will, however, be displayed on raster scan CRTs, and the Kell parameter of the display will then be effectively in series with the other system constraints.

2.5 Interlace

The terrestrial broadcast standards PAL, SECAM and NTSC use 2:1 interlace. Fig. 2.7(a) shows that, in such a system, there is an odd number of lines in a frame, and the frame is split into two fields. The first field begins with a whole line and ends with a half line, and the second field begins with a half line, which allows it to interleave spatially with the first field. The field rate is intended to determine the flicker frequency, whereas the frame rate determines the bandwidth needed, which is thus halved along with the information rate. Information theory tells us that halving the information rate must reduce quality, and so the saving in bandwidth is accompanied by a variety of effects. Fig. 2.7(b) shows the spatial/temporal sampling points in a 2:1 interlaced system. If an object has a sharp

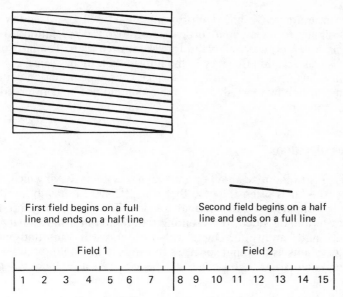

First field begins on a full
line and ends on a half line

Second field begins on a half
line and ends on a full line

Field 1

Field 2

| 1 | 2 | 3 | 4 | 5 | 6 | 7 | 8 | 9 | 10 | 11 | 12 | 13 | 14 | 15 |

There must be an odd number of lines in a frame

Figure 2.7(a) 2:1 Interlace

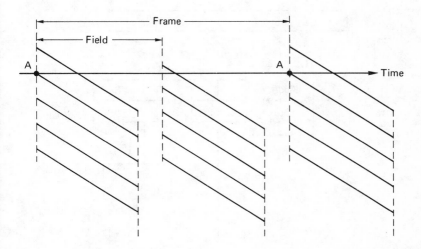

Figure 2.7(b) In an interlaced system, a given point A is only refreshed at frame rate, causing twitter on fine vertical detail

horizontal edge, it will be present in one field but not in the next. The refresh rate of the edge will be reduced to frame rate, 25 Hz or 30 Hz, and becomes visible as twitter. Whilst the vertical resolution of a test card is maintained with interlace, apart from the twitter noted, the ability of an interlaced standard to convey motion is halved. Tests[3] have shown that, all other things being equal, a 2:1 interlaced picture has to be viewed from almost twice as far away as a progressive scan picture in order to render the artifacts of scanning invisible. Unfortunately PAL, SECAM and NTSC were all designed to have equal vertical and horizontal resolution using a Kell parameter which was only valid for progressive scan. The horizontal resolution is wasted and efficiency in the information theory sense is poor. In the light of what is now known, interlace causes degradation roughly proportional to bandwidth reduction, and so should not be considered for any future standards.

2.6 Types of video

Whilst it is easy to theorize about optimal digital systems, having nice, neat arrays of pixels, it is often the case that a digital system has to interface with the real, imperfect, world of analog video. There are many different approaches to analog video, representing different compromises between performance and bandwidth. Digital video systems will often find one of the analog systems as an input, or need to produce an analog standard at the output, and so a knowledge of the nature of analog video is

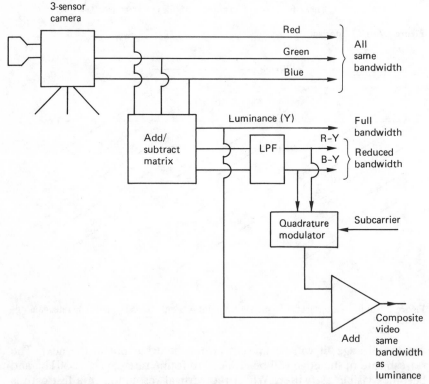

Figure 2.8 The major types of analog video. Red, Green and Blue signals emerge from the camera sensors, needing full bandwidth. If a luminance signal is obtained by a weighted sum of R, G and B, it will need full bandwidth, but the colour difference signals R−Y and B−Y need less bandwidth. Combining R−Y and B−Y into a subcarrier modulation scheme allows colour transmission in the same bandwidth as monochrome

indispensable in designing digital systems. The digital standards converter represents an extreme example where digital processing is simply a convenient tool to represent material shot in one analog format in a different one.

Fig. 2.8 shows some of the basic types of analog colour video. Each of these types can, of course, exist in a variety of line standards. Since practical colour cameras generally have three separate sensors, one for each primary colour, an RGB system will exist at some stage in the internal workings of the camera, even if it does not emerge in that form. RGB consists of three parallel signals each having the same spectrum, and is used where the highest accuracy is needed, often for production of still pictures. Examples of this are paint systems and in computer-aided design (CAD) displays. RGB is seldom used for real-time video recording; there is no standard RGB recording format for post production or broadcast, although the IBA did build an experimental analog RGB recorder. As the red, green and blue signals directly represent part of the image, this approach is known as component video.

Some saving of bandwidth can be obtained by using colour difference working. The human eye relies on brightness to convey detail, and much less resolution is needed in the colour information. R, G and B are matrixed together to form a luminance (and monochrome compatible) signal Y which has full bandwidth. The matrix also produces two colour difference signals, R–Y and B–Y, but these do not need the same bandwidth as Y; one-half or one-quarter will do depending on the application. Analog colour difference recorders such as Betacam and M II record these signals seperately. The D-1 format records 525/60 or 625/50 colour difference signals digitally. In casual parlance, colour difference formats are often called component formats to distinguish them from composite formats.

For colour television broadcast in a single channel, the NTSC, PAL and SECAM systems interleave into the spectrum of a monochrome signal a subcarrier which carries two colour difference signals of restricted bandwidth. The subcarrier is intended to be invisible on the screen of a monochrome television receiver. A subcarrier-based colour system is generally referred to as composite video, and the modulated subcarrier is called chrominance, universally abbreviated to chroma.

PAL and SECAM share the same scanning standard of 625/50, but the methods of conveying the colour are totally incompatible. NTSC scans at 525/59.94, but the colour system has a few things in common with PAL. All three standards use 2:1 interlace. Analog composite recorders include the B and C formats, and the D-2 format records PAL or NTSC digitally.

2.7 Spectrum of video

In video, sampling takes place in more than one dimension at once, and the resulting spectra can be complicated. It is well worth looking at the sampling spectra of analog video before the additional horizontal sampling of digital video takes place.

Some examples will now be given for different standards. Fig. 2.9(a)

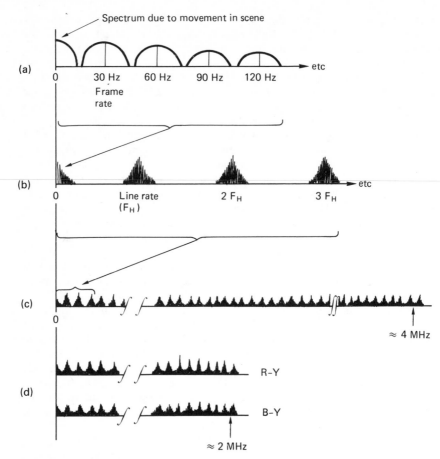

Figure 2.9 At (a) the spectrum of the scene movement is repeated in the upper and lower sidebands of the frame sampling and its harmonies. At (b) the spectrum of (a) is sampled vertically by the line rate and appears as lines with frame rate spacing around multiples of line rate. This spectrum continues to fill the system bandwidth as at (c) which could be a luminance, R, G, or B signal. In colour difference working, the luminance signal at (c) will be accompanied by two colour difference signals of approximately half the bandwidth, as at (d)

shows the spectrum due to sampling images at the US frame rate of 30 Hz. If the camera integrates incoming light over the frame period, as most do, there will be a temporal aperture effect which slopes off the spectrum. This spectrum is then itself sampled by the line scan process at 15 750 Hz, resulting in the combined spectrum of Fig. 2.9(b). This spectrum will repeat up to the allowable bandwidth of the video signal, as shown in Fig. 2.9(c). For component working, a camera will produce three signals having the same spectrum. In colour difference working one wideband luminance signal having the same spectrum as the components is accompanied by two colour difference signals which have the same spectral structure but whose overall bandwidth is less, as in Fig. 2.9(d).

For monochrome-compatible colour broadcasting, advantage is taken of the gaps in the spectra. In NTSC (National Television Systems

Committee), the two colour difference signals are used to generate reduced bandwidth signals which alternately phase-modulate a subcarrier. The subcarrier is suppressed to produce a chroma signal.

In order to allow the maximum perceived resolution with minimum bandwidth, the chroma phase was shifted slightly with respect to the horizontal, so that subcarrier phase demodulation would give a pair of signals known as I and Q (in-phase and quadrature). This placed the Q signal on the colour diagram axis to which the eye is least sensitive.

The chroma is given by:

$$I \sin F_{sc} + Q \cos F_{sc}$$

such that at 90° intervals, the chroma waveform represents I, Q, $-I$, $-Q$ repeatedly. If the receiver samples the chroma at the same intervals, but with the same phase shift, the two baseband colour difference signals can be restored.

The chroma modulation process takes the spectrum of the colour difference signals and produces upper and lower sidebands around the frequency of subcarrier. Since both colour and luminance signals have gaps in their spectra at multiples of line rate, it follows that if the subcarrier frequency is chosen to fall half-way between two of the harmonics of line rate, i.e. it is an odd multiple of half line rate, then the two spectra will interleave and share the same spectrum. In NTSC the subcarrier frequency is 227.5 times line rate. Fig. 2.10 shows that this frequency means that on successive lines the subcarrier will be phase inverted. The effect of the chroma added to luminance is to make the luminance alternately too dark or too bright. The phase inversion causes this effect to cancel over pairs of lines.

The existence of line pairs means that two frames or four fields must elapse before the same relationship between line pairs and frame sync repeats. When editing NTSC recordings, this four-field sequence must not be broken. If this rule is not followed, it is possible for a sudden inversion of subcarrier phase to occur at the edit point, which renders the signal unbroadcastable. Chapter 4 should be consulted to see how timebase correctors deal with this problem.

As the chroma of NTSC is suppressed carrier, it is necessary for the receiver to regenerate the carrier frequency so that it knows when to sample the chroma. This is done by broadcasting a portion of subcarrier, known as the burst, between the sync pulse and the active line. A phase-locked loop in the receiver will freewheel between bursts. The half line offset of the NTSC subcarrier means that if an oscilloscope is triggered from H-sync, normal and inverted bursts will appear superimposed on the trace.

Whilst the spectral interleaving of NTSC works fine for the video, there was a problem with the sound carrier. To prevent vision interference with the sound, the sound carrier of the 525/60 monochrome system had itself been placed at an odd multiple of half line rate, and so the addition of the chroma signal meant that chroma and sound could mutually interfere. The audio subcarrier frequency was standardized, and any change would have meant modifying every monochrome television set in the United States on the introduction of colour. The solution adopted was to contract the

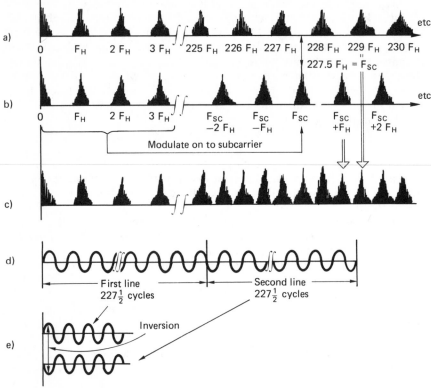

Figure 2.10 In NTSC, the luminance or monochrome spectrum is shown at (a). In (b) the colour difference spectrum is shifted up by modulating a subcarrier at 227.5 times line frquency. The spectra of the resulting chroma and the original luminance will then mesh as at (c). The half angle offset in Fsc results in a two-line sequence (d) where the first line ends on a half-cycle, and the second line chroma will be inverted with respect to the first as at (e)

spectrum of the video slightly by reducing the frame rate to 29.97 Hz. This made the line rate 15 734.25 Hz and the subcarrier frequency 3.5795 MHz. The small disparity between field rate and 60 Hz was of little consequence when it was introduced, but the development of the video recorder revealed a difficulty in synchronizing NTSC recordings to real time, which was alleviated by the invention of drop-frame time code. This allows a single count to count real time seconds and NTSC rate frames at the same time by having dropped frames, which do not exist in the video but which make the seconds count correct. The use of 29 February in the calendar has a similar effect.

The dependence of NTSC on the phase of subcarrier to convey colour accurately led to some difficulties in multipath reception conditions in high-rise districts, and to the somewhat unfair redefinition of the system title as Never Twice the Same Colour. In fact NTSC works well in the majority of other locations.

When the PAL (phase alternating line) system was being developed, it was decided that immunity to received phase errors should be a goal.

Fig. 2.11(a) shows how this was achieved. The two colour difference signals (U and V) are used to quadrature-modulate a subcarrier in a similar way as for NTSC, except that the phase of the V signal is reversed on alternate lines. The receiver must then reinvert the V signal in sympathy. If a phase error occurs in transmission, it will cause the phase of V to lead and lag alternately, as shown in Fig. 2.11(b). If the colour difference signals are

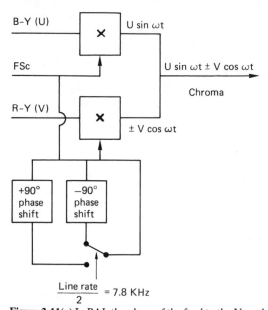

Figure 2.11(a) In PAL the phase of the feed to the V modulator is reversed of alternate lines

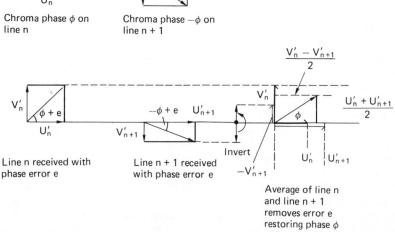

Figure 2.11(b) Top, chroma as transmitted. Bottom, chroma received with phase error. V is reversed on second line and the two lines are averaged, eliminating phase error, and giving a small saturation error

averaged over two lines, the phase error is eliminated and replaced with a small saturation error which is subjectively much less visible. This does, however, have a fundamental effect on the spectrum.

Fig. 2.12(a) shows the spectrum due to sampling at a frame rate of 25 Hz. The line rate sampling of 15 625 Hz then gives the spectrum of Fig. 2.12(b). The colour difference signals will have the same spectral structure, but less bandwidth. The $B-Y$ signal becomes U, but the $R-Y$ signal will be inverted on alternate lines to become $\pm V$. The inversion signal is a square wave at half line rate, and this effectively modulates the V signal at half line rate so that the V spectrum is divided by two, and so contains spectral entries at half line rate spacing. When U and V modulate the subcarrier, the spectrum of the chroma also contains energy at multiples of half line rate, and so spectral interleaving with a half cycle offset of subcarrier frequency will not work, as Fig. 2.12(c) shows. The solution is to adopt a subcarrier frequency with a quarter cycle per line offset. Multiplying the line rate by $283\frac{3}{4}$ allows the luminance and chrominance spectra to mesh as in Fig. 2.12(d).

The quarter cycle offset is fundamental to the elimination of phase errors, which PAL achieves, but it does cause some other effects which raise the complexity of implementation, leading to the retaliatory name of Problems Are Lurking. The receiver needs to know whether or not to invert V on a particular line, and this information is conveyed by swinging the phase of the burst plus and minus 135° on alternate lines. A damped PLL in the receiver will run at the average phase, i.e. subcarrier phase, but it will develop a half line rate phase error whose polarity determines the sense of V-switch.

The quarter cycle offset means that there are now line quartets instead of line pairs, and four frames or eight fields have to elapse before the same relationship of subcarrier to frame timing repeats. This restricts the way in which PAL recordings can be edited.

The quarter cycle offset also means that the line pair cancellation of NTSC is absent, and another means has to be found to achieve subcarrier visibility reduction. This is done by adding half frame rate to subcarrier frequency, such that an inversion in subcarrier is caused from one field to the next. Since in an interlaced system lines one field apart are adjacent on the screen, cancellation is achieved. The penalty of this approach is that subcarrier phase creeps forward with respect to H-sync at one cycle per frame. The eight-field sequence contains 2500 unique lines all having the subcarrier in a slightly different position. Observing burst on an H-triggered oscilloscope shows a stable envelope with a blurred interior. Measuring the phase of subcarrier with respect to sync requires specialist equipment or a great deal of determination. This is of little consequence for broadcasting, but it does raise the complexity of recorders and timebase correctors.

PAL-M and -N are unholy mixtures of PAL and NTSC which offer some of the advantages of PAL, but it is not necessary to detail them here since the digital implementation of both can be deduced from that of other formats.

SECAM (*sequentiel avec memoire*) is a composite system which sends the colour difference signals sequentially on alternate lines by *frequency-*

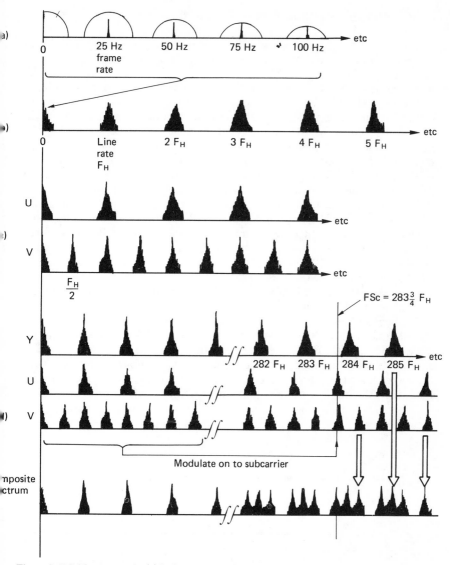

Figure 2.12 PAL spectra. At (a) is the spectrum due to sampling the image spectrum at the frame rate. This spectrum is in turn sampled at line rate, as in (b) which continues up to about 5.5 MHz. The V-switch process effectively reverses the polarity of V on alternate lines, so that two lines elapse before a cycle of V elapses instead of one line. This halves the spectral frequencies, as (c) shows. Clearly the ½ cycle offset of NTSC cannot be used in the presence of the half-line-rate energy in the V signal. Instead the subcarrier has a ¾ cycle offset, as (d) shows, and this allows the luminance and chroma to mesh as shown

modulating the subcarrier, which will have one of two different centre frequencies. Although it resists multipath transmission well, it cannot be processed because of the FM chroma. The idiosyncrasies of SECAM have led to the alternative name: *Système Essentiellement Contre les AMericains*.

2.8 Choice of sampling rate – component

If the reason for digitizing a video signal is simply to convey it from one place to another, then the choice of sampling frequency can be determined only by sampling theory and available filters. If, however, processing of the video in the digital domain is contemplated, the choices become smaller. In order to produce a two-dimensional array of samples which form rows and vertical columns, the sampling rate has to be an integral multiple of the line rate. This allows for the vertical picture processing necessary in special effects, telecine machines working on various aspect ratios, error concealment in recorders and standards conversion. Whilst the bandwidth needed by 525/59.94 video is less than that of 625/50, and a lower sampling rate might be used, practicality dictated that if a standard sampling rate for video components could be arrived at, then the design of standards converters would be simplified and digital recorders would operate at a similar data rate even though the frame rates would differ in different standards. This was the goal of CCIR Recommendation 601, which combined the 625/50 input of EBU Doc. Tech. 3246 and 3247 and the 525/59.94 input of SMPTE RP 125.

The result is not one sampling rate, but a family of rates based upon the carefully chosen frequency of 3.375 MHz.

Using four times this frequency (13.5 MHz) as a sampling rate produces 858 samples in the line period of 525/59.94 and 864 samples in the line period of 625/50. For lower bandwidths, the rate can be divided by three-quarters, one-half or one-quarter to give sampling rates of 10.125, 6.75 and 3.375 MHz respectively. If the lowest frequency is considered to be 1, then the highest is 4. For maximum quality RGB working, then three

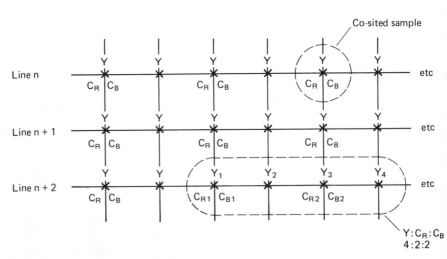

Figure 2.13 In CCIR-601 sampling mode 4:2:2, the line synchronous sampling rate of 13.5 MHz results in samples having the same position in successive lines, so that vertical columns are generated. The sampling rates of the colour difference signals CR, CB are one half of that of liminance i.e. 6.75 MHz, so that there are alternate Y only samples and co-sited samples which describe Y, CR and CB. In a run of four samples, there will be 4 Y samples, 2 CR samples and 2 CB samples, hence 4:2:2

parallel, identical sample streams would be required, which would be denoted by 4:4:4. Colour difference signals intended for post-production, where a wider colour difference bandwidth is needed, require 4:2:2 sampling for luminance, R–Y and B–Y respectively. 4:2:2 has the advantage that an integer number of colour difference samples also exist in both line standards. Fig. 2.13 shows the spatial arrangement given by 4:2:2 sampling. Luminance samples appear at half the spacing of colour difference samples, and half of the luminance samples are in the same physical position as a pair of colour difference samples, these being called co-sited samples. The D-1 recording format works with 4:2:2 sampling.

Where the signal is likely to be broadcast as PAL or NTSC, a standard of 4:1:1 is acceptable, since this still delivers a colour difference bandwidth in excess of 1 MHz. Where data rate is at a premium, 3:1:1 can be used and can still offer just about enough bandwidth for 525 lines. This would not be enough for 625 line working, but would be acceptable for ENG applications. The problem with the factors three and one is that they do not offer a columnar sampling structure, and so are not appropriate for processing systems.

Fig. 2.14(a) shows the spectrum which results from sampling 525/59.94 video at 13.5 MHz, and Fig. 2.14(b) shows the result for 625/50 video. Further details of CCIR 601 sampling can be found in Chapter 8.

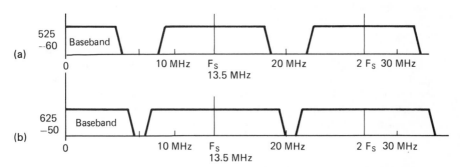

Figure 2.14 Spectra of video sampled at 13.5 MHz. At (a) the baseband 525/60 signal at left becomes the sidebands of the sampling rate and its harmonics. At (b) the same process for 625/50 signal results in a smaller gap between baseband and sideband because of the wider bandwidth of the 625 system. The same sampling rate for both standards results in a great deal of commonality between 50 Hz and 60 Hz equipment

2.9 Choice of sampling rate – composite

When composite video is to be digitized, the input will be a single waveform having spectrally interleaved luminance and chroma. Any sampling rate which allows sufficient bandwidth would convey composite video from one point to another. Indeed, 13.5 MHz is successfully used to sample PAL and NTSC, as will be seen in Chapter 5. However, if processing in the digital domain is contemplated, there will be less choice.

In many cases it will be necessary to decode the composite signal which will require some kind of digital filter. Whilst it is possible to construct

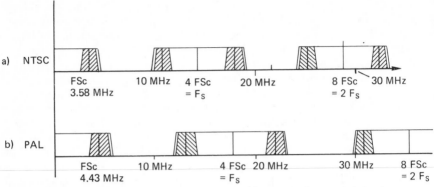

Figure 2.15 The spectra of NTSC at (a) and of PAL at (b) where both are sampled at four times the frequency of their respective subcarriers. This high sampling rate is unnecessary to satisfy sampling theory, and so both are oversampled systems. The advantages are in the large spectral gap between baseband and sideband which allows a more gentle filter slope to be employed, and in the relative ease of colour processing at a sampling rate related to subcarrier

filters with any desired response, it is a fact that a digital filter whose response is simply related to the sampling rate will be much less complex to implement. This is the reasoning which has led to the near universal use of four times subcarrier sampling rate. Fig. 2.15 shows the spectra of PAL and NTSC sampled at $4 \times F_{sc}$. It will be evident that there is a considerable space between the edge of the baseband and the lower sideband. This allows the anti-aliasing and reconstruction filters to have a more gradual cut-off, so that ripple in the passband can be reduced. This is particularly important for C-format timebase correctors and for D-2 composite digital recorders, since both are digital devices in an analog environment, and signals may have been converted to and from the digital domain many times in the course of production.

2.10 Motion and definition

Little has been said so far about the most fundamental sampling process, which is the frame rate. The choice of a frame rate is normally made simply on the basis of avoiding flicker, generally with the help (if it can be said to help) of interlace. The frame rates of film and television are very similar at 24, 25 and 30 Hz, and all use techniques to double the perceived rate. In film projectors the shutter is opened twice per frame; in broadcast video 2:1 interlace is used. In fact avoidance of flicker is not the criterion for choosing a frame rate – it is the accurate portrayal of motion.

Fig. 2.16 shows a camera pointing at a scene which for simplicity consists of 50 vertical bars. If this scene is stationary all modern video systems could resolve such large bars with ease. However, the camera is now slowly panned in a horizontal direction. Light falling on a given part of the camera sensor is now temporally modulated at the frequency with which the camera is scanning the bars. The very low frame rates chosen on a flicker basis offer a temporal bandwidth of less than half the frame rate, 12.5 Hz in

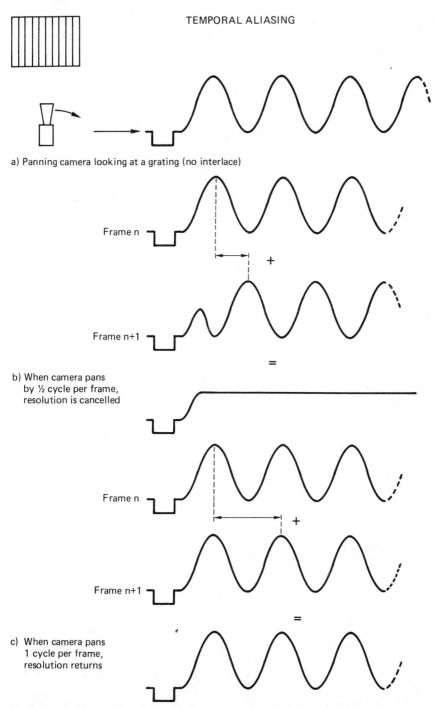

a) Panning camera looking at a grating (no interlace)

Frame n

+

Frame n+1

=

b) When camera pans
   by ½ cycle per frame,
   resolution is cancelled

Frame n

+

Frame n+1

=

c) When camera pans
   1 cycle per frame,
   resolution returns

Figure 2.16 (a) Panning Camera looking at a grating (no interlace). (b) When camera pans by ½ cycle per frame, resolution is cancelled. (c) When camera pans 1 cycle per frame, resolution returns

the case of PAL. In the example given, a temporal frequency of 12.5 Hz is reached by a pan speed which traverses the picture width in 4 seconds. At this slow speed, the large bars are completely blurred. If a greater number of bars were present in the scene, the allowable pan speed would be even less. Instead of panning, the camera could be stationary and an object could move in front of it. Above a very low speed, all detail in a moving object is lost because of the inadequate temporal sampling rate. In practice the temporal response of camera tubes is so poor that actual results will be worse than suggested here. CCD sensors do not suffer from lag, and so their temporal response will be determined by sampling theory.[4]

Objects do not suffer this degradation in real life. The eye can track a moving object, which remains in focus as it is followed. We can choose whether to look at the object or the background. When watching video this is not possible.

If the example of Fig. 2.16 is taken further, and the resolution of the scene is increased, the allowable speed of movement falls in proportion to the resolution, since the higher the static resolution of a scene, the higher will be the temporal frequencies produced when it moves. It is easy to demonstrate the effect with a to-and-fro zone plate.[5] This is an important result, because it casts grave doubts on the ability of so-called high-definition television standards to offer any meaningful improvement on real program material. An HDTV system having a bandwidth of, say, 30 MHz would offer movement portrayal five or six times worse than broadcast video, since the higher resolution is lost more readily by movement at the inadequate frame rates used. It appears that from theory and observation the only advantage of HDTV on moving images is to render the raster invisible, and this can be achieved by other means. Proper motion portrayal will require higher frame rates than are currently used.

2.11 Quantizing

Fig. 2.17 shows that the process of quantizing divides the voltage range up into quantizing intervals Q. These may be of differing size for particular applications, e.g. telephony, but in this case it becomes very difficult to process sample values arithmetically. Hence in most digital video and audio equipment all the quantizing intervals are the same, and the term *uniform quantizing* is applied. The term 'linear quantizing' will also be found, but this is a contradiction in terms.

Whatever the exact voltage of the input signal, the quantizer will express it as the number of the interval in which it falls. When that number arrives at the DAC, it will create the voltage corresponding to the centre of the interval. Quantizing thus makes errors, which cannot exceed $\pm \frac{1}{2}Q$. If the output of the DAC is resampled to avoid aperture effect, the impulses from the DAC can be compared with the impulses at the input sampling stage. The difference between the two will be an impulse train (Fig. 2.18) which can be thought of as an unwanted signal added by the quantizing process to a perfect signal. This is the quantizing error signal; it warrants considerable study since it has some unexpected characteristics.

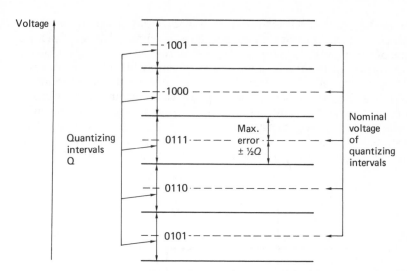

Figure 2.17 Quantizing. All voltages within a particular quantizing interval are assigned the same number, which corresponds to the voltage of the centre of the interval. The maximum quantizing error cannot exceed $\pm\frac{1}{2}Q$

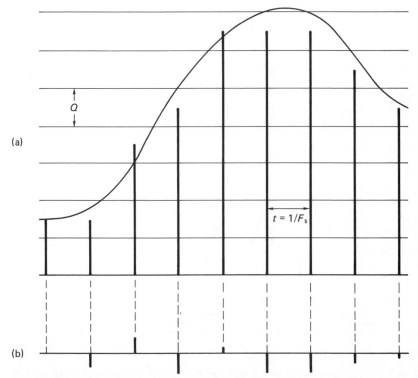

Figure 2.18 At (a) an arbitrary signal is represented to finite accuracy by PAM needles whose peaks are at the centre of the quantizing intervals. The errors caused can be thought of as an unwanted signal (b) added to the original

Where the input signal exercises the range of the quantizer and has a complex waveform such as that produced by a contrasty, detailed picture, the size of the quantizing error will be anywhere between $-\frac{1}{2}Q$ and $+\frac{1}{2}Q$ with uniform probability, as in Fig. 2.19. This probability density function should be contrasted with that of thermal noise in electronic components, which has a Gaussian shape. Since in this case the unwanted signal is uncorrelated with the information, it is appropriate to call it noise. However, the large signal case is the one where noise is of the least interest, since the presence of the signal masks noise. Nevertheless many treatments of quantizing proceed to make the simple connection between

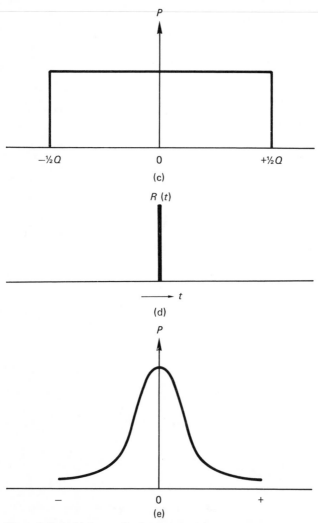

Figure 2.19 At (c) the amplitude of a quantizing error needle will be from $-\frac{1}{2}Q$ to $+\frac{1}{2}Q$ with equal probability. For large complex signals the autocorrelation function $R(t)$ has one spike as at (d), giving a uniform spectrum. Note, however, that white noise in analog circuits generally has Gaussian amplitude distribution, shown at (e)

the number of bits in the word,n, and the signal-to-noise ratio, namely $6.02n + 1.76\,\text{dB}$. There are two shortcomings to this simplistic approach. First, the noise power calculated has an infinite spectrum, and no account is taken of the effect of the reconstruction filter on this spectrum. Secondly, and much more importantly, the mathematics only holds if the probability density function of the quantizing error is uniform. At low levels, and particularly with spectrally pure or simple signals, the quantizing error ceases to be random and becomes a function of the input signal. Once an unwanted signal becomes a deterministic function of the wanted signal, it has to be referred to as distortion rather than noise. As the level of the analog input is reduced, the quantizing error becomes less random, and noise modulation occurs. Where more than one frequency is present in the input there will be intermodulation products.

The harmonics caused by these non-linear processes can alias with the sampling rate to produce anharmonic frequencies in the passband spectrum. Where the sampling rate is a multiple of the signal frequency, the effect is harmonic distortion. It is easy to demonstrate this phenomenon graphically (Fig. 2.20). The quantizing error has been determined from the signal and low-pass filtered by the reconstruction filter. Strong correlations between quantizing errors can be seen and the resultant harmonics of the signal are visible. This result is true for a perfect quantizer, and the effect can be demonstrated easily by temporarily disabling some of the low-order bits in a system, which is sometimes deliberately done for effect, as will be seen in Chapter 3.

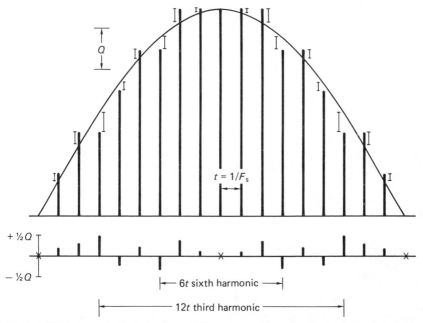

Figure 2.20 Mathematically derived quantizing error waveform for sine wave sampled at a multiple of itself. The numerous autocorrelations between quantizing errors show that there are harmonics of the signal in the error, and that the error is not random, but deterministic

In practice, it is difficult to obtain a perfectly deterministic quantizing error because of noise in the analog input signal.[6] This has a randomizing effect on the quantizing error, and reduces the distortion accordingly.[7] Fig. 2.21 shows that the effect is to smear the transfer function of the quantizer horizontally. Where the RMS noise voltage is one-third of a quantizing interval,[8] the quantizing error will be as random as the noise, and the quantizing process becomes perfectly linear. Another way of describing the effect is to say that the voltage of the input between quantizing intervals is conveyed in the duty cycle of the binary switching.

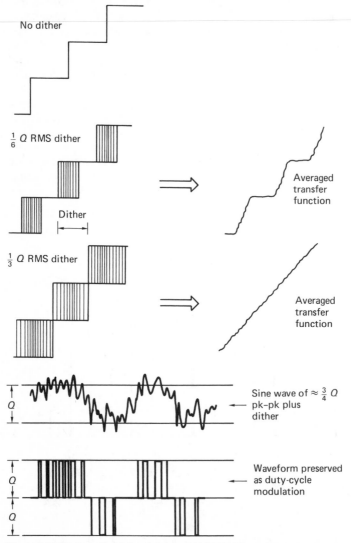

Figure 2.21 The use of wideband dither of ⅓Q RMS linearizes the transfer function and produces noise instead of distortion. This can be proved by time-averaging. Noise reduces with averaging: distortion would not

This randomizing technique is known as *dither*; in addition to linearizing the system it also defines the signal-to-noise ratio. If sufficient noise is not already superimposed on the input signal, a noise source can be built into the convertor. A diode can be used as a source of Gaussian noise. The probability density function of the dither is important. If rectangular PDF noise is created by connecting a digitally generated pseudo-random sequence to a DAC, the probability of the resultant quantizing error will be the combined probabilities of the dither and the undithered quantizing error. Since the pseudo-random generator output cannot be correlated with the undithered quantizing error, the combination of the two results in a triangular probability density function. The result will be slight noise modulation: the amplitude of the noise changes with signal amplitude, although the linearizing effect is unimpaired. If sufficient Gaussian dither is used to produce a linear system, namely $\frac{1}{3}Q$ RMS, the signal-to-noise ratio can easily be shown to be $6.02n$ dB. For most practical purposes, 6 dB per bit is an adequate assessment of signal to noise, but only if suitable dither is employed.

In an extension of the application of dither,[9] digitally generated dither is converted to the analog domain and added to the input signal prior to quantizing. That same digital dither is then subtracted from the digital quantizer output. The effect is that the transfer function of the quantizer is smeared diagonally (Fig. 2.22). The significance of this diagonal smearing is that the amplitude of the dither is not critical. However much dither is employed, the noise amplitude will remain the same. If dither of several quantizing intervals is used, it has the effect of making all the quantizing intervals in an imperfect convertor appear to have the same size.

The importance of correctly dithering a quantizer cannot be emphasized enough, since failure to dither irrevocably distorts the converted signal: there can be no process which will subsequently remove that distortion.

In principle a sample can be quantized into any number range desired, but it is convenient to use binary circuitry to handle and store the numbers, and accordingly quantizing ranges will always be some power of two. The appropriate range is hard to define since, as with any signal which will be assessed by a human being, results are subjective. It is tempting to take the signal-to-noise ratio of an equivalent analog system and divide by six to obtain the number of bits. Initially digital video machines used 8 bits, as do the D-1 and D-2 formats, but there is a trend today to go to 10 bits for some applications.

2.12 Filter design

The discussion so far has assumed that perfect anti-aliasing and reconstruction filters are used. Perfect filters are not available, of course, and because designers must use devices with finite slope and rejection, aliasing can occur, but it can be made less significant by raising the sampling frequency slightly. It is not easy to specify such filters, particularly the amount of stopband rejection needed. The amount of aliasing resulting would depend on, among other things, the amount of out-of-band energy in the input signal. Very little is known about the

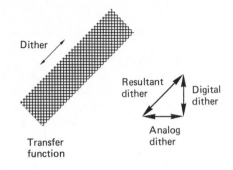

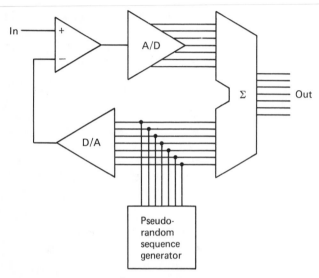

Figure 2.22 In this dither system, the dither added in the analog domain shifts the transfer function horizontally, but the same dither is subtracted in the digital domain, which shifts the transfer function vertically. The result is that the quantizer staircase is smeared diagonally as shown top left. There is thus no limit to dither amplitude, and excess dither can be used to improve differential linearity of the converter

energy in typical source material outside the usual frequency range. As a further complication, an out-of-band signal will be attenuated by the response of the anti-aliasing filter to that frequency, but the residual signal will then alias, and the reconstruction filter will reject it according to its attenuation at the new frequency to which it has aliased. To take the opposite extreme, if a camera were used which had no response at all above the video band, no anti-aliasing filter would be needed.

It would also be acceptable to bypass one of the filters involved in a copy from one digital machine to another via the analog domain, although a digital transfer is of course to be preferred.

The nature of the filters used has a great bearing on the subjective quality of the system. Entire books have been written about analog filters, and they will only be treated briefly here.

Fig. 2.23 shows the terminology used to describe the common, elliptic low-pass filter. These are popular because they can be realized with fewer components than other filters of similar response. It is a characteristic of these elliptic filters that there are ripples in the passband and stopband. In much equipment the anti-aliasing filter and the reconstruction filter will have the same specification, so that the passband ripple is doubled. Sometimes slightly different filters are used to reduce the effect.

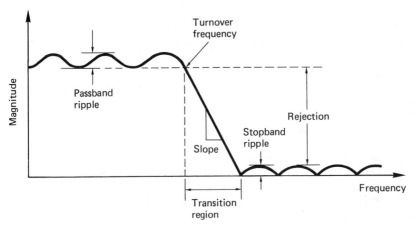

Figure 2.23 The important features and terminology of low-pass filters used for anti-aliasing and reconstruction

Active filters can simulate inductors using op-amp techniques, but they tend to suffer non-linearity at high frequencies where the falling open-loop gain reduces the effect of feedback. Active filters also can contribute noise, but this is not necessarily a bad thing in controlled amounts, since it can act as a dither source.

For video applications, the phase response of such filters must be linear. Since a sharp cut-off is generally achieved by cascading many filter sections which cut at a similar frequency, the phase responses of these sections will accumulate. The phase may start to leave linearity at only a half of the passband frequency, and near the cut-off frequency the phase error may be severe. Effective group delay equalization is necessary.

It is possible to construct a ripple-free phase-linear filter with the required stopband rejection, but it may be expensive in design effort and component complexity, and it might drift out of specification as components age. The money may be better spent in avoiding the need for such a filter. Much effort can be saved in analog filter design by using oversampling. Reference to Chapter 5 will show that digital filters are inherently phase linear and, using LSI, can be inexpensive to construct. The technical superiority of oversampling converters along with economics means that they will be increasingly used in the future, which is why the subject is more prominent here than the treatment of filter design.

2.13 Oversampling

Television systems have evolved from times when many of the freedoms of modern technology were not available. The terrestrial broadcast standards of today were designed to transmit a signal which could be fed to a CRT with the minimum processing. The number of lines in the camera, the number of lines in the broadcast standard and the number of lines in the display were all the same for reasons of simplicity, and performance fell short of that permitted by sampling theory. This need no longer be the case. Oversampling is a technique which allows sampled systems to approach theoretical performance limits more closely. It has become virtually universal in digital audio, since at the relatively low frequencies of audio it is easy to implement. It is only a matter of time before oversampling becomes common in video.

In the purest sense of the word, oversampling simply means using a sampling rate which is in excess of that required by sampling theory. By using a high sampling rate, the need for a steep-cut analog anti-aliasing filter is eliminated, but the higher sampling rate results in an unnecessarily high data rate. This is reduced to the desired sampling rate by a digital filter which can be designed for a sharper cut-off than an analog filter, whilst retaining phase linearity. The resulting sampling rate carries an information bandwidth which is closer to the theoretical limit. Oversampling can be applied to temporal or spatial sampling, so it can be used to overcome the difficulties involved in trying to prevent aliasing with optical filters.

Fig. 2.24(a) shows a temporal oversampling system, where the high sampling rate opens a wide gap between the baseband and the lower sideband. The analog anti-aliasing filter need only fall to the stopband response at half of the high sampling rate to prevent aliasing, and at the band edge of the baseband signal, attenuation will be minimal. Fig. 2.24(b) shows that the sampling rate is then reduced by a digital filter. In order to

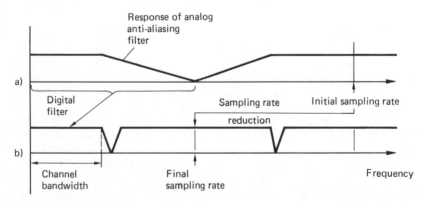

Figure 2.24 In a temporal oversampling system, the sampling rate is considerably higher than normal, and a gentle slope is adequate for the response of the anti-aliasing filter as shown at (a). Following sampling, the samples are digitally low pass filtered in a phase linear filter to the target channel bandwidth. The sampling rate can then be reduced without aliasing taking place. It is most convenient to use sampling rates which are integer multiples of the final sampling rate

prevent aliasing at the lower sampling rate the filter must incorporate a low-pass response. In the digital domain an optimal aperture function is more readily implemented, and so the resultant frequency response will be flatter.

Oversampling can be used in any of the three dimensions of digital video sampling, for either direction of conversion. Fig. 2.25(a) shows the circuit diagram of a typical analog reconstruction filter following a DAC, which would typically be used to return from the digital domain to raster-scanned analog. Following the low-pass filter is a phase correction network which is as complex as the filter itself. Fig. 2.25(b) shows an oversampling converter which increases the sampling rate in a digital interpolator before the DAC.[10] The resultant analog filter need not be so complex and will need less adjustment. Digital filters need no alignment and do not drift. As the cost of logic circuits continues to fall, it may become cheaper to implement oversampling converters, in addition to the improved performance gained. The example of Fig. 2.25 was in the horizontal direction. In order to apply oversampling in the vertical dimension, a camera with more lines than the target standard will be necessary. To produce 625 line video, a 1250 line camera would allow a two times vertical oversampling factor. The optical filter to prevent vertical aliasing will need to attenuate at half the vertical sampling rate, which is 625 lines, resulting in negligible attenuation at 312½ lines, the target resolution. The resultant lines of data are then digitally low-pass filtered in the vertical dimension to produce 625 line video having vertical resolution near to that theoretically attainable.

In tube cameras fitted with zoom lenses, the change of picture distortion as the lens zooms is compensated by distorting the shape of the raster. In CCD cameras the pixels are firmly fixed in the plane of the sensor and cannot be moved. Lens distortion can be removed from a CCD camera by using a two-dimensional digital interpolator.[11] The use of oversampling in such a camera would allow the digital interpolator to double as the low-pass filter for sampling rate reduction giving a high-performance cost-effective product.

Oversampling can also be used at the display end. The display monitor is made to run with typically twice as many lines as usual, but without changing the beam size. The aperture effect then renders the raster invisible. The incoming video is passed through a vertical interpolator which doubles the number of lines to produce an oversampled display. With an oversampling camera and display, Wendtland and Schröder[12, 13] measured a unity Kell parameter, which reinforces the view that the Kell parameter arises because of the aperture effect.

Since the use of oversampling allows a given line standard to approach the theoretical limits of resolution, there is an opportunity to upgrade existing broadcast standards by using oversampling cameras to originate higher-resolution material and oversampling receivers to display raster-free pictures. The 625/50 system is especially suitable, because it does not offer equal vertical and horizontal resolution owing to the use of a non-interlaced Kell parameter in its design. The poor vertical resolution which results has led the majority of television manufacturers to provide simple low-pass filters to reject subcarrier from luminance. The resulting bandwidth of about 3 MHz matches the vertical resolution. If two times

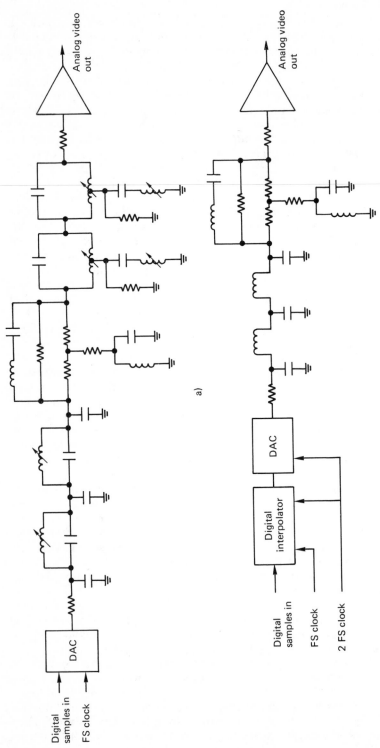

Figure 2.25 A conventional DAC and analog filter is shown at (a). It is complex and requires adjustment. At (b) a digital interpolator doubles the sampling rate supplied to the DAC so only a simple analog filter is required

vertical oversampling were to be used, the raster would be invisible and the vertical resolution might be increased by 30%. This could then be matched by the use of a comb filter to separate luminance and chroma to allow 5.5 MHz horizontal bandwidth.

Considerable improvement is also possible to NTSC using such techniques. In the Super NTSC system produced by Faroudja,[14] the camera is a progressive scan unit which feeds a vertical and temporal digital filter whose output is a 2:1 interlaced standard image but which lacks many of the motion artifacts and interlace twitter of a conventional camera. A 2:1 oversampling or line doubling monitor has also been designed to allow the best possible vertical resolution to be observed.

If a new standard is to be proposed, it should be realized that non-interlaced vertically oversampled video working at a Kell parameter of nearly unity gives about twice the vertical resolution of interlaced aperture-limited video. A 1250 line non-oversampling system would be working at a Kell parameter of no more than 0.64, so offering a vertical resolution of about 800 lines. Thus a 625 line progressive scan standard could offer about 70% of the vertical resolution of a 1250 line system. A 1250 line camera would make an excellent 625 line oversampling camera. The bandwidth saved by using 625 lines could be better used in raising the frame rate, since the higher the spatial resolution, the higher the temporal resolution must be to maintain detail in the presence of motion. As has been demonstrated, current HDTV proposals are deficient in this respect. The raising of the frame rate would reduce the occurrence of temporal aliasing and ease the design of standards converters.

2.14 Basic digital-to-analog conversion

There is only one way of obtaining an analog signal from PCM data at the frequencies of digital video. Essentially the input sample controls binary-weighted currents, and these are summed as shown in Fig. 2.26. In Fig. 2.26(b), the binary code is about to have a major overflow, and all the low-order currents are flowing. In Fig. 2.26(c), the binary input has increased by one, and only the most significant current flows. This current must equal the sum of all the others plus one least significant current to an accuracy of rather better than one least significant current. In this simple 4 bit example, the necessary accuracy is only one part in 16, but for an 8 bit system it would become one part in 256, or about 0.4%. This degree of accuracy can be achieved with care, and it must be maintained in the presence of ageing and temperature change.

To prevent interaction between the stages in weighted-current converters, the currents must be switched to ground or into the virtual earth by change-over switches. The on resistance of these switches is a source of error, particularly the MSB, which passes most current. A solution in monolithic converters is to fabricate switches whose area is proportional to the weighted current, so that the voltage drops of all the switches are the same. The error can then be removed with a suitable offset. The layout of such a device is dominated by the MSB switch since, by definition, it is as big as all the others put together.

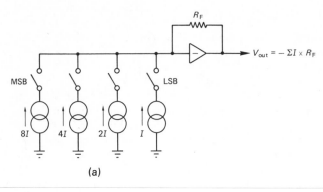

(a)

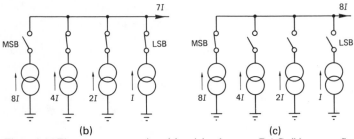

(b)   (c)

Figure 2.26 Elementary conversion: (a) weighted current DAC; (b) current flow with 0111 input; (c) current flow with 1000 input

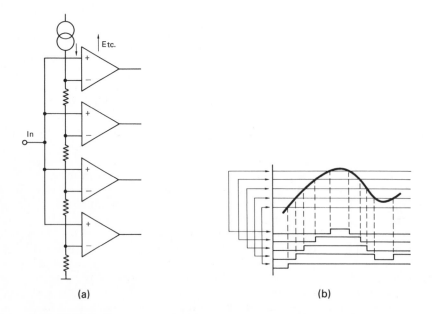

(a)   (b)

Figure 2.27 The flash converter. At (a) each quantizing interval has its own comparator, resulting in waveforms of (b). A priority encoder is necessary to convert the comparator outputs to a binary code.

2.15 Basic analog-to-digital conversion

The general principle of a quantizer is that different quantized voltages are compared with the unknown analog input until the closest quantized voltage is found. The code corresponding to this becomes the output.

The flash converter is probably the simplest technique available for PCM video conversion. The principle is shown in Fig. 2.27. The threshold

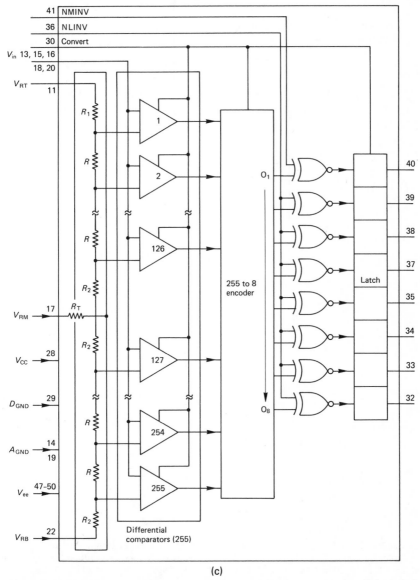

(c)

Figure 2.27 (*Continued*). Shown at (c) is a typical eight-bit flash converter primarily intended for video applications (Courtesy TRW.)

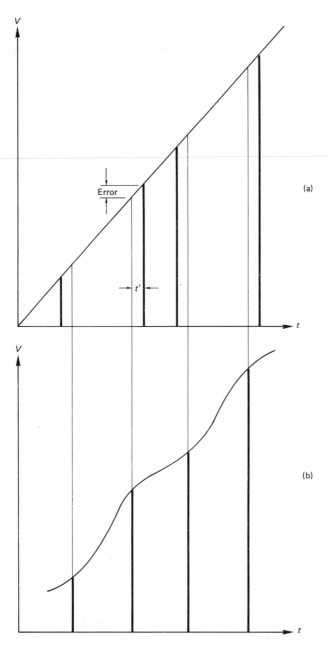

Figure 2.28 The effect of sampling timing jitter on noise, and calculation of the required accuracy for a sixteen-bit system. (a) Ramp sampled with jitter has error proportional to slope. (b) When jitter is removed by later circuits, error appears as noise added to samples

voltage of every quantizing interval is provided by a resistor chain which is fed by a reference voltage. This reference voltage can be varied to determine the sensitivity of the input. There is one voltage comparator connected to every reference voltage, and the other input of all of these is connected to the analog input. The input voltage determines how many of the comparators will have a true output. As one comparator is necessary for each quantizing interval, then, for example, in an 8 bit system there will be 255 binary comparator outputs, and it is necessary to use a priority encoder to convert these to a binary code. Although the device is simple in principle, it contains a lot of circuitry and can only be practicably implemented on a chip. The analog signal has to drive a lot of inputs, and a low-impedance driver is essential to avoid restricting the slewing rate of the input. The extreme speed of a flash converter is a distinct advantage in oversampling. Because computation of all bits is performed simultaneously, no analog track/hold circuit is required, and droop is eliminated. In fact the sampling process takes place on the binary comparator outputs after quantizing in a flash convertor. The clock which takes these samples must have very low jitter, with minimum skew between bits otherwise noise will be introduced. The mechanism is illustrated in Fig. 2.28, where a changing signal is being sampled. The mistiming due to clock jitter causes the wrong voltage to be sampled. The effect clearly rises with the rate of change of

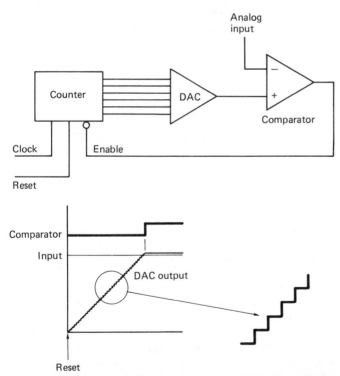

Figure 2.29 Simple ramp ADC compares output of DAC with input, Count is stopped when DAC output just exceeds input. This method, although potentially accurate, is much too slow for digital video

input voltage; therefore the amount of noise caused will depend on the spectrum of the input, making it a form of modulation noise. It is difficult to specify the clock jitter tolerance, since the worst-case assumptions demand an accuracy within about 100 ps!

2.16 Successive approximation

For applications which do not require such speed, such as digitizing the velocity error in TBCs, a reduction in component complexity can be achieved by quantizing serially. The most primitive method of generating different quantized voltages is to connect a counter to a DAC as in Fig. 2.29. The resulting staircase voltage is compared with the input and used to stop the clock to the counter when the DAC output has just exceeded the input. This method is painfully slow and is not used, as a much faster method exists which is only slightly more complex. Using successive approximation, each bit is tested in turn, starting with the MSB. If the input is greater than half range, the MSB will be retained and used as a base to test the next bit, which will be retained if the input exceeds three-quarters range and so on. The number of decisions is equal to the number of bits in the word, rather than the number of quantizing intervals, as in the previous example. A drawback of the successive approximation converter is that the least significant bits are computed last, when droop is at its worst. Fig. 2.30 shows that droop can cause a successive approximation converter to make a significant error under certain circumstances.

2.17 Imperfections of converters

ADCs and DACs have the same transfer function, since they are only distinguished by the direction of operation, and therefore the same terminology can be used to classify the shortcomings of both.

Fig. 2.31 shows the transfer functions resulting from the main types of converter error:

(a) *Offset error* A constant appears to have been added to the digital signal. This has a serious effect in video systems, since it causes black-level shifts. Offset error is sometimes cancelled by digitally sampling the converter output during blanking and feeding it back to the analog input as a small control voltage.

(b) *Gain error* The slope of the transfer function is incorrect. Since converters are referred to one end of the range, gain error causes an offset error. Severe gain errors will cause clipping.

(c) *Linearity* (also known as *integral linearity*). The deviation of the transfer function from a straight line (ignoring the quantizing steps). It has exactly the same significance as linearity in analog circuits, since if it is inadequate, harmonic distortion will be caused. Subclassifications of linearity which are used are *differential non-linearity*, which is the amount by which adjacent quantizing intervals differ in size, and *monotonicity*,

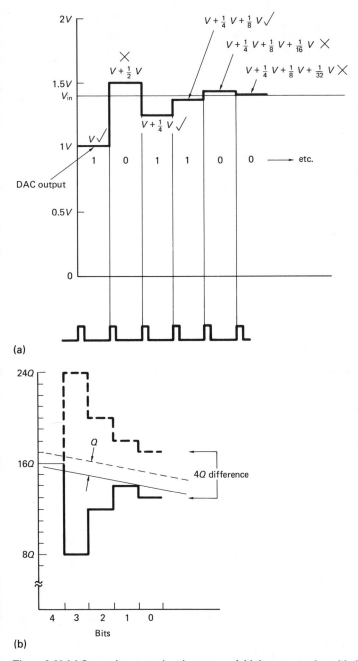

(a)

(b)

Figure 2.30 (a) Successive approximation tests each bit in turn, starting with the most significant. The DAC output is compared with the input. If the DAC output is below the input ($\sqrt{}$) the bit is made 1; if the DAC output is above the input ($\times$) the bit is made zero. (b) Two drooping track/hold signals (solid and dotted lines) which differ by one quantizing interval Q are shown here to result in conversions which are $4Q$ apart. Thus droop can destroy the monotonicity of a converter. Low-level signals (near the midrange of the number system) are especially vulnerable

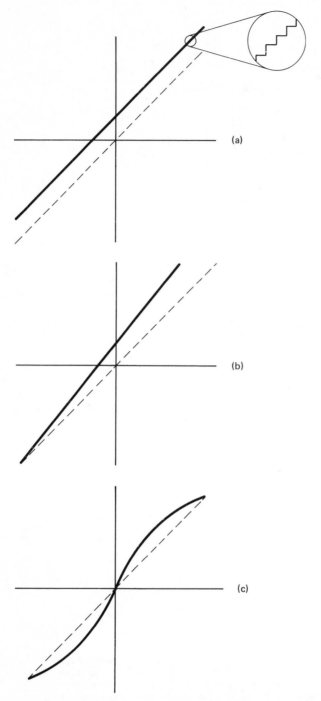

Figure 2.31 Main converter errors (solid line) compared with perfect transfer function (dotted line). These graphs hold for ADCs and DACs, and the axes are interchangeable; if one is chosen to be analog, the other will be digital

which is a special case of differential non-linearity. Non-monotonicity means that the output does not increase for an increase in input. Fig. 2.31 shows how this can happen. With a converter input code of 01111111 (127 decimal), the seven low-order current sources of the converter will be on. The next code is 10000000 (128 decimal), where only the eighth current source is operating. If the current it supplies is in error on the low side, the analog output for 128 may be less than that for 127. If a device has better than ½ Q linearity it must be monotonic.

(d) *Absolute accuracy* The difference between actual and ideal output for a given input. For video this is rather less important than linearity. For example, if all the current sources in a converter have good thermal tracking, linearity will be maintained, even though the absolute accuracy drifts.

References

1. KELL, R., BEDFORD, A. and TRAINER, M. A. An experimental television system, Part 2. *Proc. IRE*, **22**, 1246–1265 (1934)
2. HSU, S., The Kell factor: past and present. *SMPTE J.*, **95**, 206–214 (1986)
3. JESTY, L. C., The relationship between picture size, viewing distance and picture quality. *Proc. IEE*, **105B**, 425–439 (1958)
4. GURLEY, T. and HASLETT, C., Resolution considerations in using CCD imagers in broadcast quality cameras. *SMPTE J.*, **94**, 882–895 (1985)
5. FUKINUKI, T. and HIRANO, Y., The to-and-fro zone plate method for observing frequency characteristics in three dimensions. *SMPTE J.*, **95**, 899–902 (1986)
6. BENNETT, W. R., Spectra of quantized signals. *Bell Syst. Tech. J.*, **27**, 446–472 (1948)
7. GOODALL, W. M., Television by pulse code modulation. *Bell Syst. Tech. J.*, **30**, 33–49 (1951)
8. VANDERKOOY, J. and LIPSHITZ., S., Resolution below the least significant bit in digital systems with dither. *J. Audio Eng. Soc.*, **32**, 106–113 (1984)
9. ROBERTS, L. G., Picture coding using pseudo-random noise. *IRE Trans. Inf. Theor.*, **IT-8**, 145–154 (1962)
10. WILLIAMS, R. and PRATER, J., Digital filtering: the right stuff for video. *Electron. Syst. Des. Mag.*, Jan. 91–96 (1988)
11. LACOTTE, J. P., *et al.* Towards full quality CCD studio cameras: the last steps. Presented at the International Broadcasting Convention (Brighton, 1988), *IEE Conf. Publ. No. 293*, 156–169 (1988)
12. WENDTLAND, B. and SCHRÖDER, H., On picture quality of some television signal processing techniques, *SMPTE J.*, **93**, 915–922 (1984)
13. WENDTLAND, B. and SCHRÖDER, H., Signal processing for new HQTV systems. *SMPTE J.*, **94**, 182–189 (1985)
14. FAROUDJA, Y., Improving NTSC to achieve near AGB performance. *SMPTE J.*, **96**, 750–761 (1987)

Chapter 3

Digital video coding and processing

The conversion process expresses the analog input as a binary code. In this chapter the choice of code is shown to be governed by the requirements of digital signal processing, which is applied to the sample stream from a converter to perform in the digital domain the normal functions of vision mixers/switchers.

The subject of timebase correction introduced here is common in analog video recording and fundamental to digital recording. A brief introduction to binary arithmetic and logic is included for those who are approaching the subject for the first time.

3.1 Introduction to logic

The strength of binary logic is that the signal has only two states, and considerable noise and distortion can be tolerated before the state becomes uncertain. At every logical element, the signal is compared with a threshold and can thus can pass through any number of stages without being degraded. The two states of the signal when measured with an oscilloscope are simply two voltages, usually referred to as high and low. The actual voltage levels will depend on the type of logic chips in use and on the supply voltage used. Within logic, these levels are not of much consequence, and it is only necessary to know them when interfacing between different logic families or when driving external devices. The pure logic designer is not interested at all in these voltages, only in their meaning. Just as the electrical waveform from a camera represents picture brightness, so the waveform in a logic circuit represents the truth of some statement. As there are only two states, there can only be *true* or *false* meanings. The true state of the signal can be assigned by the designer to either voltage state. When a high voltage represents a true logic condition and a low voltage represents a false condition, the system is known as *positive logic*, or *high true* logic. This is the usual system, but sometimes the low voltage represents the true condition and the high voltage represents the false condition. This is known as *negative logic* or *low true* logic. Provided that everyone is aware of the logic convention in use, both work equally well.

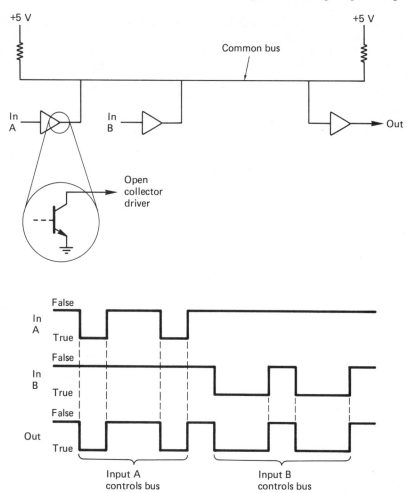

Figure 3.1 Using open-collector drive, several signal sources can share one common bus. If negative logic is used, the bus drivers turn off their output transistors with a false input, allowing another driver to control the bus. This will not happen with positive logic

Negative logic is often found in the TTL logic family, because in this technology it is easier to sink current to ground than to source it from the power supply. Fig. 3.1 shows that if it is necessary to connect several logic elements to a common bus so that any one can communicate with any other, an open collector system is used, where high levels are provided by pull-up resistors and the logic elements only pull the common line down. If positive logic were used, when no device was operating the pull-up resistors would cause the common line to take on an absurd true state, whereas if negative logic is used, the common line pulls up to a sensible false condition when there is no device using the bus. Whilst the open collector is a simple way of obtaining a shared bus system, it is limited in frequency of operation as a result of the time constant of the pull-up resistors charging the bus capacitance. In the so-called tri-state bus systems commonly used in digital video, there are both active pull-up and pull-down devices for speed (totem poles), but both devices will be disabled to a third state where the output assumes a high impedance, allowing some other driver to determine the bus state.

In logic systems, all complex devices can be configured from combinations of a few fundamental gates. It is not profitable to spend too much time arguing which are the really fundamental ones, since most can be made from combinations of others. Table 3.1 shows the important simple gates and their derivatives, and introduces the logical expressions to describe them, which can be compared with the truth-table notation. The figure also shows the important fact that when negative logic is used, the OR gate function interchanges with that of the AND gate. Sometimes

Table 3.1 The basic logic gates compared

Positive logic name	Boolean expression	Positive logic symbol	Positive logic truth table	Plain English
Inverter or NOT gate	$Q = \bar{A}$		$\begin{array}{c\|c} A & Q \\ \hline 0 & 1 \\ 1 & 0 \end{array}$	Output is opposite of input
AND gate	$Q = A \cdot B$		$\begin{array}{cc\|c} A & B & Q \\ \hline 0 & 0 & 0 \\ 0 & 1 & 0 \\ 1 & 0 & 0 \\ 1 & 1 & 1 \end{array}$	Output true when both inputs are true only
NAND (Not AND) gate	$Q = \overline{A \cdot B}$ $= \bar{A} + \bar{B}$		$\begin{array}{cc\|c} A & B & Q \\ \hline 0 & 0 & 1 \\ 0 & 1 & 1 \\ 1 & 0 & 1 \\ 1 & 1 & 0 \end{array}$	Output false when both inputs are true only
OR gate	$Q = A + B$		$\begin{array}{cc\|c} A & B & Q \\ \hline 0 & 0 & 0 \\ 0 & 1 & 1 \\ 1 & 0 & 1 \\ 1 & 1 & 1 \end{array}$	Output true if either or both inputs true
NOR (Not OR) gate	$Q = \overline{A + B}$ $= \bar{A} \cdot \bar{B}$		$\begin{array}{cc\|c} A & B & Q \\ \hline 0 & 0 & 1 \\ 0 & 1 & 0 \\ 1 & 0 & 0 \\ 1 & 1 & 0 \end{array}$	Output false if either or both inputs true
Exclusive OR (XOR) gate	$Q = A \oplus B$		$\begin{array}{cc\|c} A & B & Q \\ \hline 0 & 0 & 0 \\ 0 & 1 & 1 \\ 1 & 0 & 1 \\ 1 & 1 & 0 \end{array}$	Output true if inputs are different

schematics are drawn to reflect which voltage state represents the true condition. In the so-called intentional logic scheme, a negative logic signal always starts and ends at an inverting 'bubble'. If an AND function is required between two negative logic signals, it will be drawn as an AND symbol with bubbles on all the terminals, even though the component used will be a positive logic OR gate. Opinions vary on the merits of intentional logic.

If numerical quantities need to be conveyed down the two-state signal paths described here, then the only appropriate numbering system is binary, which has only two symbols, 0 and 1. Just as positive or negative logic could be used for the truth of a logical binary signal, it can also be used for a numerical binary signal. Normally, a high voltage level will represent a binary 1 and a low voltage will represent a binary 0, described as a 'high for a one' system. Clearly a 'low for a one' system is just as feasible. Decimal numbers have several columns, each of which represents a different power of ten; in binary the column position specifies the power of two. Fig. 3.2 shows some binary numbers and their equivalent in decimal. The radix point has the same significance in binary: symbols to the right of it represent one-half, one-quarter and so on. Binary is convenient for electronic circuits, which do not get tired, but numbers expressed in binary become very long, and writing them is tedious and error prone. The octal and hexadecimal notations are both used for writing binary since conversion is so simple. A binary number is split into groups of three or four digits starting at the least significant end, and the groups are individually converted to octal or hexadecimal digits. Since 16 different symbols are required in hexadecimal the letters A–F are used for the numbers above nine.

A number of binary digits or bits are needed to express a binary number. These bits can be conveyed at the same time by several signals to form a parallel system, which is most convenient inside equipment because it is fast, or one at a time down a single signal path, which is slower but convenient for cables between pieces of equipment because the connectors require fewer pins. When a binary system is used to convey numbers in this way, it can be called a digital system.

3.2 Binary codes

There are a wide variety of waveform types encountered in video and all of these can be successfully digitized. All that is needed is for the quantizing range to be a little greater than the useful voltage range of the waveform.

In monochrome, or in the luminance waveform of a component system, the useful waveform can only vary between black and white, since the syncs carry no information which cannot be recreated. However, if the quantizing range were set to exactly this range, a slightly excessive gain somewhere would cause clipping. In practice the quantizing range will be a little greater than the nominal signal range. This means that black level does not correspond to zero. In CCIR 601 it is 16_{10}. It is as if a constant of 16 had been added to every sample, and it gives rise to the term offset binary.

In order to deal with video waveforms which can go positive or negative,

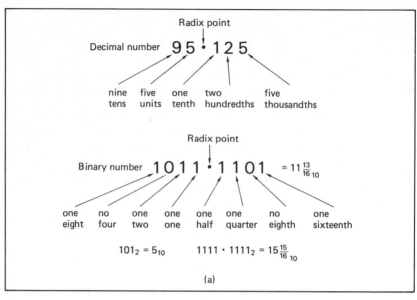

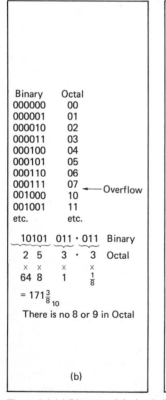

Figure 3.2 (a) Binary and decimal. (b) In octal, groups of three bits make one symbol 0–7. (c) In hex, groups of four bits make one symbol 0–F. Note how much shorter the number is in hex

such as colour difference signals, the offset is made one-half the number range of the converter. Effectively the quantizing range has been shifted so that positive and negative voltages in a real colour difference signal can be expressed by binary numbers which are only positive.

Composite video contains an embedded subcarrier, which has meaningful levels above white and below black. The quantizing range has to be extended to embrace the total possible excursion of luminance plus subcarrier. The resultant range is not far from the overall range of the signal, and it is sometimes useful to quantize the whole signal. This is particularly useful in PAL because the sampling points are locked to subcarrier and have a complex relationship to sync. Clearly in a composite system the offset value will be much greater than in a luminance convertor. The actual values used are detailed in Chapter 8.

The offset binary approach is perfectly acceptable where the signal has been digitized only for recording or transmission from one place to another, after which it will be converted back to analog. Under these conditions it is not actually necessary for the quantizing steps to be uniform, provided both ADCs and DACs are constructed to the same standard. In practice, it is the requirements of signal processing in the digital domain which make both non-uniform quantizing and offset binary unsuitable.

Fig. 3.3 shows that a colour difference signal voltage is referred to midrange. The level of the signal is measured by how far the waveform

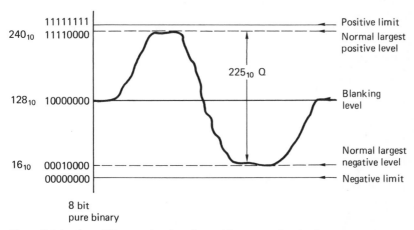

Figure 3.3 A colour difference signal can be positive or negative, but its value is always referred to blanking level, which cannot be zero in a pure binary system

deviates from midrange, and fading, gain and mixing all take place around midrange. It is necessary to add sample values from two or more different sources to perform the mixing function, and adding circuits assume that all bits represent the same quantizing interval so that the sum of two sample values will represent the sum of the two original analog voltages. In non-uniform quantizing this is not the case, and such signals cannot readily

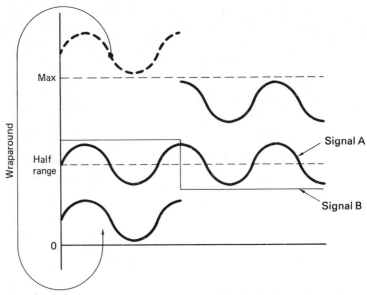

Figure 3.4 If two pure binary data streams are added to simulate mixing, offset or overflow will result

be processed. Fig. 3.4. shows that if two offset binary sample streams are added together in an attempt to perform digital mixing, the result will be an offset which may lead to an overflow. Similarly, if an attempt is made to fade by, say, 6 dB by dividing all of the sample values by two, Fig. 3.5 shows that a further offset results. The problem is that offset binary is referred to one end of the range. What is needed is a numbering system which operates symmetrically about the centre of the range.

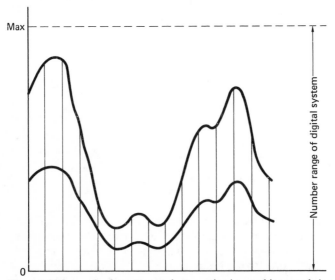

Figure 3.5 The result of an attempted attenuation in pure binary code is an offset. Pure binary cannot be used for digital video processing of colour difference signals

The two's complement system, which has this property, is commonly used for processing.

In two's complement, the upper half of the pure binary number range has been defined to represent negative quantities. If a pure binary counter is constantly incremented and allowed to overflow, it will produce all the numbers in the range permitted by the number of available bits, and these are shown for a 4 bit example drawn around the circle in Fig. 3.6. In two's complement, however, the number range this represents does not start at zero but on the opposite side of the circle. Zero is midrange, and all numbers with the most significant bit set are considered negative. Two's complement notation can also be considered as an offset binary code with the most significant bit inverted. This system allows two sample values to be added, where the result is referred to the system midrange; this is analogous to adding analog signals in an operational amplifier. A further asset of two's complement notation is that binary subtraction can be performed using only adding logic. The two's complement is added to perform a subtraction. This permits a significant saving in hardware complexity, since only carry logic is necessary and no borrow mechanism

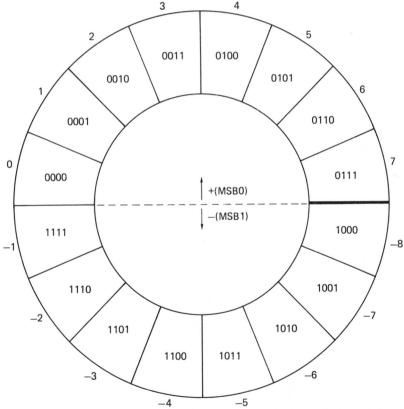

Figure 3.6 In this example of a four-bit two's complement code, the number range is from −8 to +7. Note that the MSB determines polarity

need be supported. For these reasons, two's complement notation is in common use in digital video processing.

Signals encoded according to CCIR 601 use offset binary, but fortunately the process of conversion to two's complement is simple; the most significant bit is inverted.

If a signed binary number is to be expressed as a negative number it is written down with leading zeros if necessary to occupy the wordlength of the system. All bits are then inverted, to form the one's complement, and one is added. To return to signed binary, if the most significant bit of the two's complement number is false, no action need be taken. If the most significant bit is set, the sign is negative, all bits are inverted, and one is added. Fig. 3.7 shows some examples of conversion to and from two's complement and illustrates how adding two's complement samples simulates the mixing process. Fig. 3.7 also illustrates the process of attenuating by 6 dB, dividing sample values in two's complement by two by shifting one place to the right. For positive numbers, this is easy; for

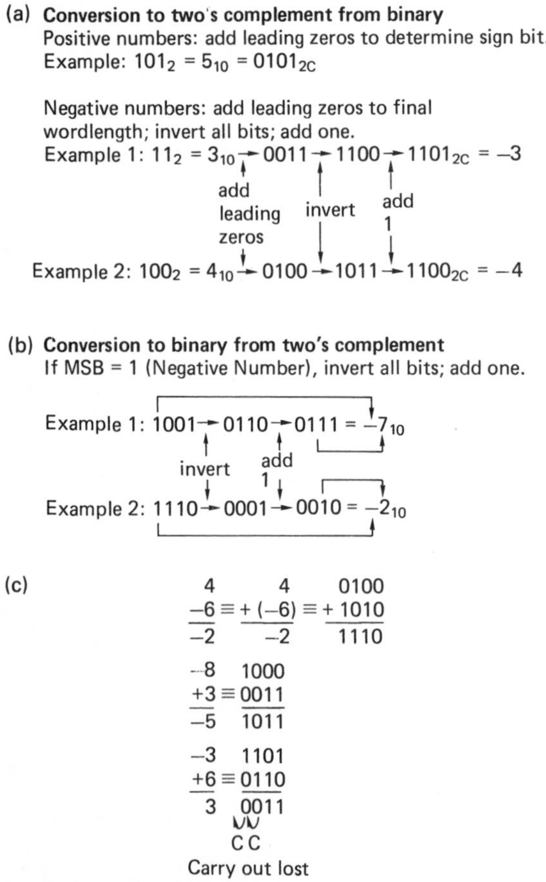

(a) **Conversion to two's complement from binary**
Positive numbers: add leading zeros to determine sign bit.
Example: $101_2 = 5_{10} = 0101_{2C}$

Negative numbers: add leading zeros to final
wordlength; invert all bits; add one.
Example 1: $11_2 = 3_{10} \to 0011 \to 1100 \to 1101_{2C} = -3$

add leading zeros   invert   add 1

Example 2: $100_2 = 4_{10} \to 0100 \to 1011 \to 1100_{2C} = -4$

(b) **Conversion to binary from two's complement**
If MSB = 1 (Negative Number), invert all bits; add one.

Example 1: $1001 \to 0110 \to 0111 = -7_{10}$

invert   add 1

Example 2: $1110 \to 0001 \to 0010 = -2_{10}$

(c)

$$
\begin{array}{r}
4 \\
-6 \\
\hline
-2
\end{array}
\equiv
\begin{array}{r}
+(-6) \\
\hline
-2
\end{array}
\equiv
\begin{array}{r}
0100 \\
+1010 \\
\hline
1110
\end{array}
$$

$$
\begin{array}{r}
-8 \\
+3 \\
\hline
-5
\end{array}
\quad
\begin{array}{r}
1000 \\
0011 \\
\hline
1011
\end{array}
$$

$$
\begin{array}{r}
-3 \\
+6 \\
\hline
3
\end{array}
\quad
\begin{array}{r}
1101 \\
0110 \\
\hline
0011 \\
\cup\cup \\
C\,C
\end{array}
$$

Carry out lost

Figure 3.7 (a) Binary to two's complement conversion. (b) Two's complement to binary. (c) Some examples.

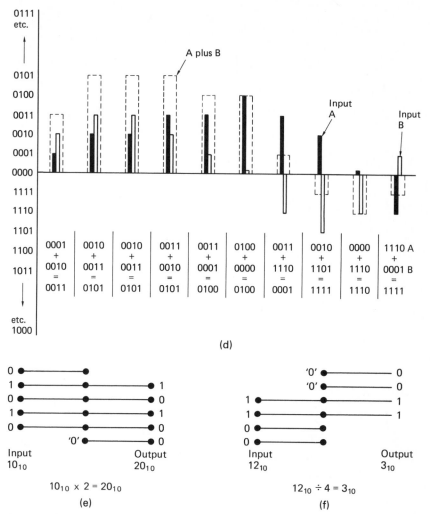

Figure 3.7 (*Continued*). (d) Using two's complement arithmetic, single values from two waveforms are added together with respect to midrange to give a correct mixing function. (e) Multiplication or (f) division by two by bit-shifting compounds to 6 dB gain change

negative numbers, the necessary shift to the right must carry in a one at the left of the number, not a zero. It should also be noted that in two's complement, if a radix point exists, numbers to the right of it are added. For example, 1100.1 is not −4.5, it is −4 + 0.5 = −3.5.

3.3 Binary adding

The circuitry necessary for adding binary numbers is shown in Fig. 3.8. Addition in binary requires 2 bits to be taken at a time from the same position in each word, starting at the least significant bit. Should both be

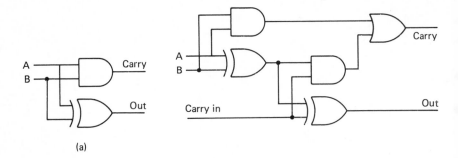

(a)

Data A	Bits B	Carry in	Out	Carry out
0	0	0	0	0
0	0	1	1	0
0	1	0	1	0
0	1	1	0	1
1	0	0	1	0
1	0	1	0	1
1	1	0	0	1
1	1	1	1	1

(b)

A MSB

B MSB

High when
A and B negative
but adder output
positive

High when
A and B positive
but adder output
negative

Adder
MSB

Input A

Two's
complement

Σ

Out

Input B

Maximum
positive
value

Maximum
negative
value

(c)

Figure 3.8 (a) Half adder; (b) full-adder circuit and truth table; (c) comparison of sign bits prevents wraparound on adder overflow by substituting clipping level

ones, the output is zero, and there is a carry out generated. Such a circuit is called a half adder, shown in Fig. 3.8(a), and is suitable for the least significant bit of the calculation. All higher stages will require a circuit which can accept a carry input as well as two data inputs. This is known as a full adder (Fig. 3.8(b)). Multibit full adders are available in chip form and have carry-in and carry-out terminals to allow them to be connected in parallel to operate on long wordlengths. Such a device is also convenient for producing the two's complement of a signed binary number, in conjunction with a set of inverters. The adder chip has one set of inputs grounded, and the carry in permanently held true, such that it adds one to the one's complement number from the inverter.

When mixing by adding sample values, care has to be taken to ensure that if the sum of the two sample values exceeds the number range the result will be clipping rather than wraparound. In two's complement, the action necessary depends on the polarities of the two signals. Clearly if one positive and one negative number are added, the result cannot exceed the number range. If two positive numbers are added, the symptom of positive overflow is that the most significant bit sets, causing an erroneous negative result, whereas a negative overflow results in the most significant bit clearing. The overflow control circuit will be designed to detect these two conditions and override the adder output. If the MSB of both inputs is zero, the numbers are both positive: thus if the sum has the MSB set, the output is replaced with the maximum positive code (0111 . . .). If the MSB of both inputs is set, the numbers are both negative, and if the sum has no MSB set, the output is replaced with the maximum negative code (1000 . . .). These conditions can also be connected to warning indicators. Fig. 3.8(c) shows this system in hardware. The resultant clipping on overload is sudden, and sometimes a PROM is included which translates values around and beyond maximum to soft-clipped values below or equal to maximum.

3.4 Digital fading and mixing

Fading is controlled in the digital domain by multiplying each sample value by some fixed coefficient. If that coefficient is less than one, fading will result; if it is greater than one, amplification can be obtained.

Multiplication in binary circuits is difficult. It can be performed by repeated adding, but this is too slow to be of any use. In fast multiplication, one of the inputs will be simultaneously multiplied by one, two, four, etc., by hard-wired bit shifting. Fig. 3.9 shows that the other input bits will determine which of these powers will be added to produce the final sum and which will be neglected. If multiplying by five, the process is the same as multiplying by four, multiplying by one, and adding the two products. This is achieved by adding the input to itself shifted two places. As the wordlength of such a device increases, the complexity increases exponentially, so this is a natural application for an integrated circuit. It is probably true that digital video processing would not have been viable without such chips.

In a digital vision mixer or switcher, the gain coefficients will originate in

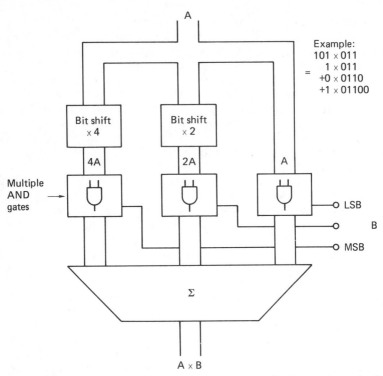

Figure 3.9 Structure of fast multiplier: The input A is multiplied by 1, 2, 4, 8 etc by the bit-shifting technique of Figure 3.8 (e). The digits of the B input then determine which multiples of A should be added together by enabling AND gates between the shifters and the adder. For long wordlengths, the number of gates required becomes enormous, and the device is best implemented in a chip

the hand-operated faders, but may also come from a pattern generator or from keying circuits. It is possible to obtain coefficients from an analog fader by feeding the end of the track with a stable DC voltage and digitizing the voltage on the wiper, but direct digital faders are also available. In these devices, a grating is moved with respect to several light beams, one for each bit of the coefficient. The interruption of the beams by the grating is monitored by photocells. It is not possible to encode such a grating in pure binary, as Fig. 3.10(a) shows that this generates transient false codes as a result of mechanical tolerances. The solution is to use a non-sequential binary code, where only one bit changes at a time between adjacent states. This approach avoids transients. One such code is the Gray code, shown in Fig. 3.10(b), which is used extensively in shaft encoders for machine control. The Gray code can be converted back to binary in a suitable PROM, available as a standard chip.

The luminance path of a simple component digital mixer is shown in Fig. 3.11. The CCIR 601 digital input is offset binary in that it has a nominal black level of 16_{10}, and a subtraction has to be made in order that fading will take place with respect to black. On a perfect signal, subtracting 16 would achieve this, but on a slightly out of range signal it would not. Since

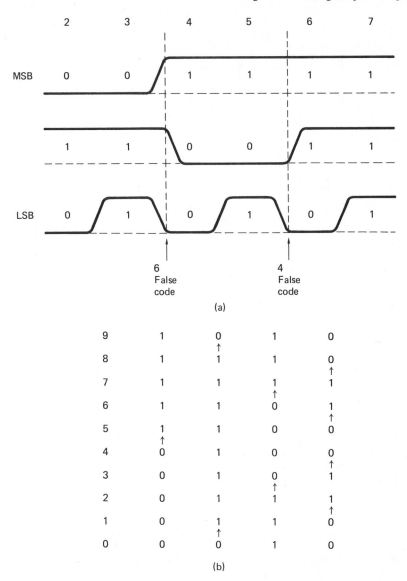

Figure 3.10 (a) Binary cannot be used for position encoders because mechanical tolerances cause false codes to be produced. (b) In Gray code, only one bit (arrowed) changes in between positions, so no false codes can be generated

the digital active line is slightly longer than the analog active line, the first sample should be blanking level, and this will be the value to subtract to obtain pure binary luminance with respect to black. This is the digital equivalent of black-level clamping. The two inputs are then multiplied by their respective coefficients and added together to achieve the mix. Peak limiting will be required as in Section 3.3, and then, if the output is to be to

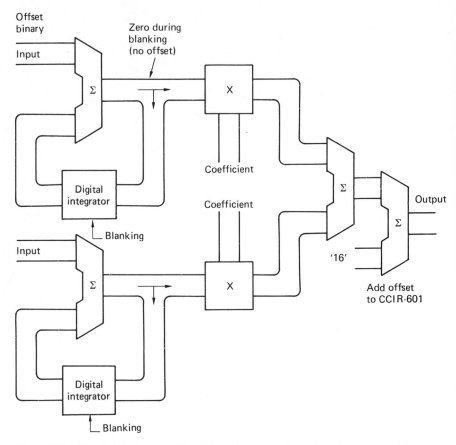

Figure 3.11 A simple digital mixer. Offset binary inputs must have the offset removed. A digital integrator will produce a counter-offset which is subtracted from every input sample. This will increase or reduce until the output of the subtractor is zero during blanking. The offset must be added back after processing if a CCIR-601 output is required

CCIR 601, 16_{10} must be added to each sample value to establish the correct offset. In most video applications, a crossfade will be needed, and a rearrangement of the crossfading equation allows one multiplier to be used instead of two, as shown in Fig. 3.12.

The colour difference signals are offset binary with an offset of 128_{10}, and again it is necessary to normalize these with respect to blanking level so that proper fading can be carried out. Since colour difference signals can be positive or negative, this process results in two's complement samples. Fig. 3.13 shows some examples.

In this form, the samples can be added with respect to blanking level. Following addition, a limiting stage is used as before, and then, if it is desired to return to the CCIR 601 standard, the samples must be converted from two's complement to offset binary.

In practice the same multiplier can be used to process luminance and colour difference signals. Since these will be arriving time-multiplexed at

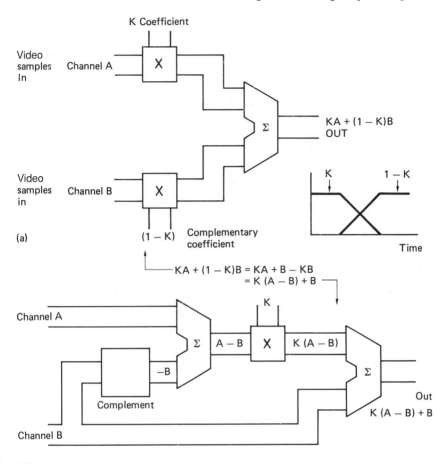

Figure 3.12 Crossfade at (a) requires two multipiers. Reconfiguration at (b) requires only one multiplier

27 MHz, it is only necessary to ensure that the correct coefficients are provided at the right time. Fig. 3.14 shows an example of part of a slow fade. As the co-sited samples C_B, Y and C_R enter, all are multiplied by the same coefficient K_n, but the next sample will be luminance only, so this will be multiplied by K_{n+1}. The next set of co-sited samples will be multiplied by K_{n+2} and so on. Clearly coefficients must be provided which change at 13.5 MHz. The sampling rate of the two inputs must be exactly the same, and in the same phase, or the circuit will not be able to add on a sample-by-sample basis. If the two inputs have come from different sources, they must be synchronized by the same master clock, and/or timebase correction must be provided on the inputs.

Some thought must be given to the wordlength of the system. If a sample is attenuated, it will develop bits which are below the radix point. For example, if an 8 bit sample is attenuated by 24 dB, the sample value will be shifted four places down. Extra bits must be available within the mixer to

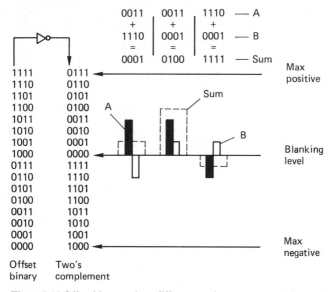

Figure 3.13 Offset binary colour difference values are converted to two's complement by reversing the state of the first bit. Two's complement values A and B will then add around blanking level

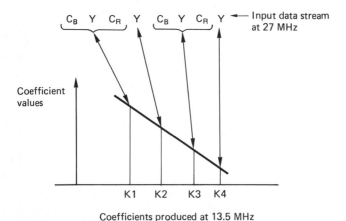

Coefficients produced at 13.5 MHz

Figure 3.14 When using one multiplier to fade both luminance and colour difference in a 27 MHz multiplex 4:2:2 system, one coefficient will be used three times on the co-sited samples, whereas the next coefficient will only be used for a single luminance sample

accommodate this shift. Digital vision mixers can have an internal wordlength of up to 16 bits. When several attenuated sources are added together to produce the final mix, the result will be a 16 bit sample stream. As the output will generally need to be of the same format as the input, the wordlength must be shortened. This must be done very carefully, as will be seen in Section 3.7.

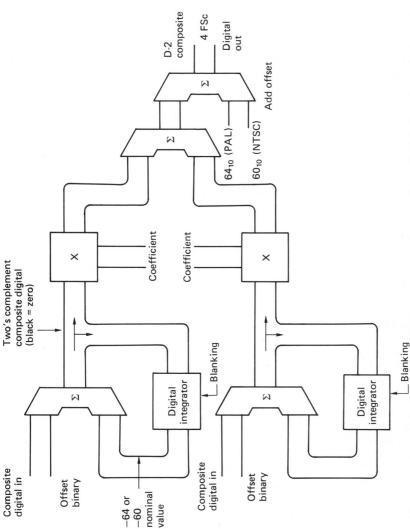

Figure 3.15 In a composite digital switcher, the samples also carry the subcarrier, and thus have meaning at levels below black. A larger offset, 60 or 64, is used than for components, and when this is subtracted a two's complement system is necessary to convey signals above or below black as positive or negative values which can then be faded without offsets resulting

It is possible to construct a digital composite switcher for NTSC or PAL which operates in much the same way as has been described for a colour difference channel above.

Fig. 3.15 shows that the black level to be subtracted will be numerically larger than for the luminance signal in a component system and may result in negative sample values which will need to be expressed in two's complement form before processing.

Clearly the adder which mixes the two channels can only produce a meaningful result if both input values are derived from samples which were taken at precisely the same phase relationship to subcarrier. The critical timing-in process of an analog composite switcher has been removed as far as the digital switcher is concerned, but the need for critical timing accuracy has not been eliminated – it has simply been moved to a different part of the system. A digital timebase corrector can be used to remove timing errors between input channels, but as it can only correct to the nearest sample, which is 90° in a $4F_{sc}$ system, it cannot remove errors due to the sampling clocks of the two channels having a different relationship to subcarrier. If the two channels have such a timing error, it can only be corrected in the digital domain by an interpolator of such complexity that it would be simpler to return to the analog domain for a solution. It is necessary to bear in mind that a composite digital recorder must have an input sampling clock which is accurately set to a standardized phase relationship with subcarrier, otherwise the recordings made cannot be mixed with others in the digital domain.

3.5 Concentrators/combiners

A concentrator or combiner is the name given to a special kind of digital switcher which is driven by a number of perspective effects machines. The illusion of a solid object can be created where each video input represents one face, often of a cube, but other shapes are possible.

Using the principle of transparency, images can be placed on the inside of a solid, and those at the rear can be seen through those at the front.

Transparency requires control of the amplitude of keying signals. Fig. 3.16 shows that a digital mixer is used, where the key signals are processed to become the coefficients for the mixer. The key processing is the most important aspect of the system, because it determines the realism of the final result. It is necessary to specify the priority of the images, that is to say which lies closest to the viewer, in the order A, B, C, D for a four-channel system. The priority determines the order in which the incoming key signals are processed. The goal of the key processor is to produce four coefficients which never sum to more than unity. In this way the output can be prevented from clipping.

On a pixel-by-pixel basis, the key signals are used to compute new coefficients. Suppose that the highest priority, or front, picture A has been given a transparency of 33%. This will result from a two-thirds amplitude key signal accompanying picture A. The key processor produces the A coefficient and also passes down to lower priority circuits the fact that two-thirds of the total permitted sum of coefficients has been used up. The

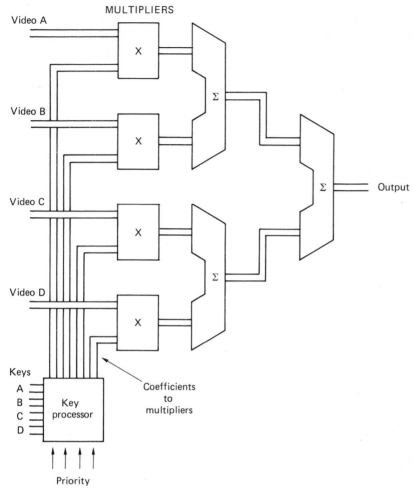

Figure 3.16 Transparency mixing requires one multiplication per input. The transparency of the highest priority input determines the gain given to lower priority inputs and so on

transparency of A is 33%, so only 33% of the brightness of the B picture can be added where A obscures B. Suppose that B also has a transparency of 33%, then light from picture C will be reduced to 33% of its original brightness passing through B, and reduced again by passing through A, so the coefficient needed will be about 11%. The process continues for as many channels of input as are available, plus a background value.

The coefficients then multiply their respective channels, and the products are summed to produce a single digital video stream carrying the final effect. Fig. 3.17 shows the effect on the key coefficients during a single raster line scan across a multilayer effect with transparency.

In some machines it is possible to make pictures in different planes intersect realistically. The position of the two planes in the Z axis is compared, and the picture with the lowest Z at a given pixel position will

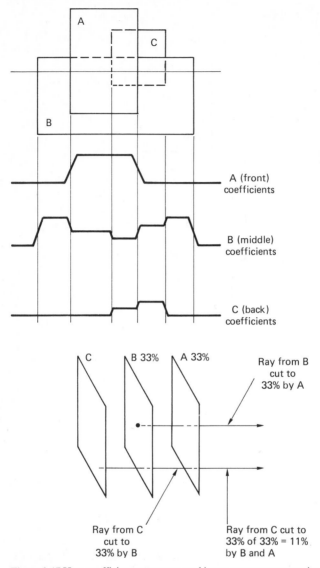

A (front)
coefficients

B (middle)
coefficients

C (back)
coefficients

C   B 33%   A 33%

Ray from B
cut to
33% by A

Ray from C
cut to
33% by B

Ray from C cut to
33% of 33% = 11%
by B and A

Figure 3.17 How coefficients are computed in transparency processing

get priority in the combiner. At the intersection point, priority will pass to the other picture. The transparencies allocated to both pictures will then be used to produce coefficients as before.

3.6 Blanking

It is often necessary to blank the ends of active line smoothly to prevent out-of-band signals being generated. This is usually the case where an effects machine has cropped the picture to fit inside a coloured border. The border will be generated by supplying constant luminance and colour difference values to the data stream. Blanking consists of sloping off the active line by multiplying the sample values by successively smaller coefficients until blanking is reached. This is easy where the sample values have been normalized so that zero represents black, but where the usual offset of 16_{10} is present, multiplication by descending coefficients will cause a black-level shift. The solution is to use a correction PROM which can be seen in Fig. 3.18. This is addressed by the multiplier coefficient and adds a suitable constant to the multiplier output. If the multiplier were to have a gain of one-half, this would shift the black level by eight quantizing intervals, and so the correction PROM would add eight to the output. Where the multiplier has fully blanked, the output will be zero, and the correction PROM has to add 16_{10} to the output.

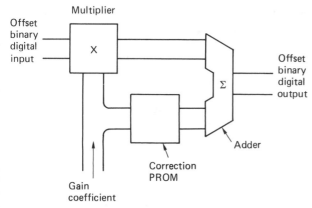

Figure 3.18 In order to fade an offset binary signal, a correction term from a PROM can be added to remove the level shift caused by fading

3.7 Digital dither

When a sample value is attenuated, the extra low-order bits made available preserve the resolution of the signal and the dither in the least significant bit which linearizes the system. If several such sample streams are added together, the random element in the low-order bits may now be some way below the least significant bit in the shortened word. If the word is simply truncated by ignoring the low-order bits below the desired wordlength, the result will be quantizing distortion, because the dither component has been removed. The wordlength of samples must be shortened so as to replace the lost dither, a process called digital dithering. A pseudo-random sequence generator is necessary, which is compared with the last bit to be retained and those below it. The comparison, as shown in Fig. 3.19, rounds up or down to yield the least significant bit of the shortened word, which has a linearizing random component. The probability density of the pseudo-random sequence is important. Vanderkooy and Lipshitz[1] found that uniform probability density produced noise modulation, in which the

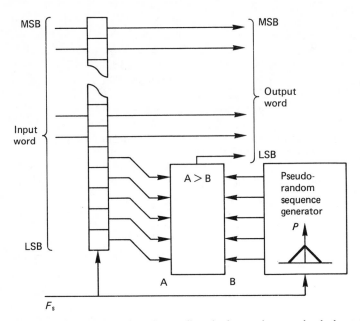

Figure 3.19 In order to shorten the wordlength of a sample correctly, the least significant bit must contain a random element to prevent quantizing distortion. By comparing the triangular probability pseudo-random sequence with the low-order bits, the resulting LSB contains information from those bits in the form of duty cycle modulation

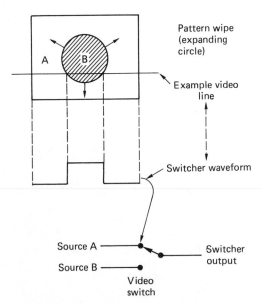

Figure 3.20 In a video switcher a pattern generator produces a switching waveform which changes from line to line and from frame to frame to allow moving pattern wipes between sources

amplitude of the random component varies as a function of the amplitude of the samples. A triangular probability density function obtained by adding together two pseudo-random sequences eliminated the noise modulation to yield a signal-independent white-noise component in the least significant bit. It is vital that such steps are taken when sample wordlength is to be reduced.

3.8 Keying

Keying is the process where one video signal can be cut into another to replace part of the picture with a different image. One application of keying is where a switcher can wipe from one input to another using one of a variety of different patterns. Fig. 3.20 shows that an analog switcher performs such an effect by generating a binary switching waveform in a pattern generator. Video switching between inputs actually takes place during the active line. In most analog switchers, the switching waveform is digitally generated and then fed to a DAC, whereas in a digital switcher, the pattern generator outputs become the coefficients supplied to the crossfader, which is sometimes referred to as a cutter. The switching edge must be positioned to an accuracy of a few nanoseconds, much less than the spacing of the pixels, otherwise slow wipes will not appear to move smoothly, and diagonal wipes will have stepped edges, a phenomenon known as ratcheting.

Positioning the switch point to sub-pixel accuracy is not particularly difficult, as Fig. 3.21 shows. A suitable series of coefficients can position the effective crossover point anywhere. The finite slope of the coefficients results in a brief crossfade from one video signal to the other. This soft keying gives a much more realistic effect than binary switchers, which often give a 'cut out with scissors' appearance. In some machines the slope of the crossfade can be adjusted to achieve the desired degree of softness.

3.9 Chroma keying

Another application of keying is to derive the switching signal by processing video from a camera in some way. By analysing colour difference signals, it is possible to determine where in a picture a particular colour occurs. When a key signal is generated in this way, the process is known as chroma keying, which is the electronic equivalent of matting in film.

In a 4:2:2 component system, it will be necessary to provide coefficients to the luminance crossfader at 13.5 MHz. Chroma samples only occur at half this frequency, so it is necessary to provide a chroma interpolator to raise the chroma sampling rate artificially. For chroma keying a simple linear interpolator is perfectly adequate. Intermediate chroma samples are simply the average of two adjacent samples. Fig. 3.22 shows how a multiplexed C_r, C_b signal can be averaged using a delay of two clocks.

As with analog switchers, chroma keying is also possible with composite digital inputs, but decoding must take place before it is possible to obtain

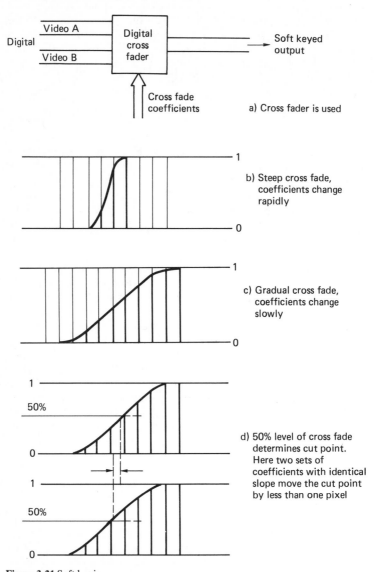

Figure 3.21 Soft keying

the key signals. The video signals which are being keyed will, however, remain in the composite digital format.

In switcher/keyers, it is necessary to obtain a switching signal which ramps between two states from an input signal which can be any allowable video waveform. Manual controls are provided so that the operator can set thresholds and gains to obtain the desired effect. In the analog domain, these controls distort the transfer function of a video amplifier so that it is no longer linear. A digital keyer will perform the same functions using logic circuits.

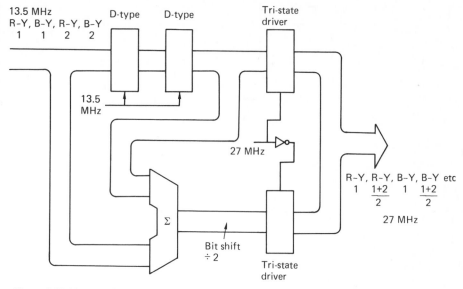

Figure 3.22 Alternate R–Y, B–Y samples can be averaged by a *two* sample delay and an adder. Output will then alternate between sample values and averaged sample values at 27 MHz. Demultiplexing the output will give two colour difference signals each at 13.5 MHz so that they can be used to produce coefficients at that rate to key luminance

Fig. 3.23(a) shows that the effect of a non-linear transfer function is to switch when the input signal passes through a particular level. The transfer function is implemented in a memory in digital systems. The incoming video sample value acts as the memory address, so that the selected memory location is proportional to the video level. At each memory location, the appropriate output level code is stored. If, for example, each memory location stored its own address, the output would equal the input and the device would be transparent. In practice, switching is obtained by distorting the transfer function to obtain more gain in one particular range of input levels at the expense of less gain at other input levels. With the transfer function shown in Fig. 3.23(b), an input level change from a to b causes a smaller output change, whereas the same level change between c and d causes a considerable output change.

If the memory is RAM, different transfer functions can be loaded in by the control system, and this requires multiplexers in both data and address lines as shown in Fig. 3.23(c).

In practice such a RAM will be installed in Y, C_r and C_b channels, and the results will be combined to obtain the final switching coefficients.

3.10 Simple effects

If a RAM of the type shown in Fig. 3.23 is inserted in a digital luminance path, the result will be *solarizing*, which is a form of contrast enhancement.

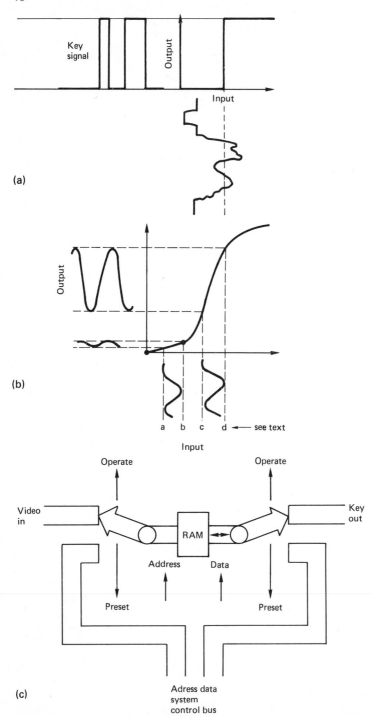

Figure 3.23 (a) A non-linear transfer function can be used to produce a keying signal. (b) The non-linear transfer function emphasizes contrast in part of the range but reduces it at other parts. (c) If a RAM is used as a flexible transfer function, it will be necessary to provide multiplexers so that the RAM can be preset with the desired values from the control system

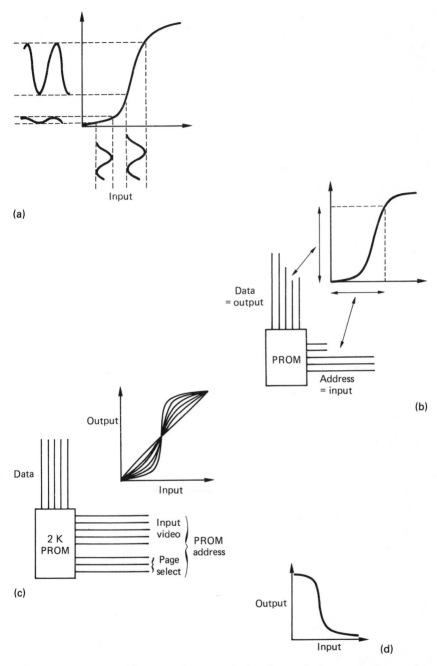

Figure 3.24 Solarization. (a) The non-linear transfer function emphasizes contrast in part of the range but reduces it at other parts. (b) The desired transfer function is implemented in a PROM. Each input sample value is used as the address to select a corresponding output valve stored in the PROM. (c) A family of transfer functions can be accommodated in a larger PROM. Page select affects the high order address bits. (d) Transfer function for luminance reversal

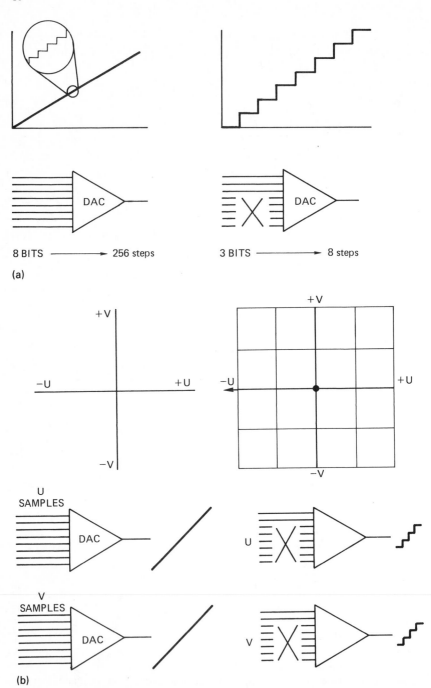

Figure 3.25 (a) In contouring, the least significant bits of the luminance samples are discarded, which reduces the number of possible output levels. (b) At left, the 8 bit colour difference signals allow 2^{16} different colours. At right, eliminating all but two bits of each colour difference signals allows only 2^4 different colours

Fig. 3.24 shows that a family of transfer functions can be implemented which control the degree of contrast enhancement. When the transfer function becomes so distorted that the slope reverses, the result is *luminance reversal*, where black and white are effectively interchanged. Solarizing can also be implemented in colour difference channels to obtain *chroma solarizing*. In effects machines, the degree of solarizing may need to change smoothly so that the effect can be gradually introduced. In this case the various transfer functions will be kept in different pages of a PROM, so that the degree of solarization can be selected immediately by changing the page address of the PROM. One page will have a straight transfer function, so the effect can be turned off by selecting that page.

In the digital domain it is easy to introduce various forms of quantizing distortion to obtain special effects. Fig. 3.25 shows that 8 bit luminance allows 256 different brightnesses, which to the naked eye appear to be a continuous range. If some of the low-order bits of the samples are disabled, then a smaller number of brightness values describes the range from black to white. For example, if 6 bits are disabled, only 2 bits remain, and so only four possible brightness levels can be output. This gives an effect known as *contouring* since the visual effect somewhat resembles a relief map.

When the same process is performed with colour difference signals, the result is to limit the number of possible colours in the picture, which gives an effect known as *posterizing*, since the picture appears to have been coloured by paint from pots. Solarizing, contouring and posterizing cannot be performed in the composite digital domain, owing to the presence of the subcarrier in the sample values.

Fig. 3.26 shows a latch in the luminance data which is being clocked at the sampling rate. It is transparent to the signal, but if the clock to the latch is divided down by some factor n, the result will be that the same sample value will be held on the output for n clock periods, giving the video waveform a staircase characteristic. This is the horizontal component of the effect known as *mosaicing*. The vertical component is obtained by feeding the output of the latch into a line memory, which stores one horizontally mosaiced line and then repeats that line m times. As n and m can be independently controlled, the mosaic tiles can be made to be of any size, and rectangular or square at will. Clearly the mosaic circuitry must be implemented simultaneously in luminance and colour difference signal paths. It is not possible to perform mosaicing on a composite digital signal, since it will destroy the subcarrier. It is common to provide a bypass route which allows mosaiced and unmosaiced video to be simultaneously available. Dynamic switching between the two sources controlled by a separate key signal then allows mosaicing to be restricted to certain parts of the picture.

3.11 Timebase correction

In Chapter 1 it was stated that a strength of digital technology is the ease with which delay can be provided. Accurate control of delay is the essence of timebase correction, necessary whenever the instantaneous time of arrival or rate from a data source does not match the destination. In digital

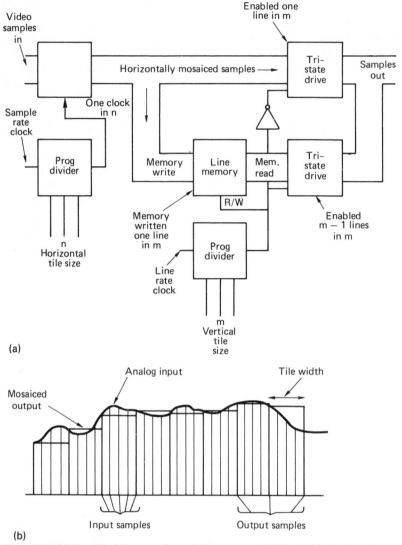

(a)

(b)

Figure 3.26 (a) Simplified diagram of mosaicing system. At left hand side, horizontal mosaicing is done by intercepting sample clocks. On one line in m, the horizontally mosaiced line becomes the output, and is simultaneously written into a one line memory. On the remaining (m−1) lines the memory is read to produce several identical successive lines to give the vertical dimensions of the tile. (b) In mosaicing, input samples are neglected, and the output is held constant by failing to clock a latch in the data stream for several sample periods. Heavy vertical lines here correspond to the clock signal occurring. Heavy horizontal line is resultant waveform

switchers, the various inputs will not necessarily be timed, and input timebase correctors are necessary to ensure phasing between channels.[2]

In magnetic tape recording, the destination will almost always have perfectly regular timing, namely the reference sampling rate generator, and one aspect of timebase correction consists of aligning jittery offtape signals with the stable reference. Rotary-head recorders suffer from impulsive jitter as a result of the heads striking the tape.

All digital video recorders, including disk drives, assemble data into blocks to facilitate editing and error correction as well as to permit head switching between blocks. Owing to the spaces between blocks, data arrive in bursts on replay, but must be fed to the output converters in an unbroken stream at the sampling rate. In this way, timing errors are rendered unmeasurable. An extension of the timebase correction concept is *time compression*, which is used in rotary-head machines to give more freedom in the mechanical design of the scanner. This will be treated in detail in Chapter 9.

In computer hard-disk drives, which are used in digital video still stores and paint systems, the data from the disk blocks arrive at a reasonably constant rate, but cannot necessarily be accepted at a steady rate by the logic because of contention for the use of buses and memory by the different parts of the system. In this case a further timebase corrector, usually referred to as a silo, is necessary.

Although delay is easily implemented, it is not possible to advance a data stream. Most real machines cause instabilities balanced about the correct timing: the output jitters between too early and too late. Since the information cannot be advanced in the corrector, only delayed, the solution is to run the machine in advance of real time. In this case, correctly timed output signals will need a nominal delay to align them with reference timing. Early output signals will receive more delay, and late output signals will receive less delay.

3.12 RAM timebase correction

There are three basic ways of obtaining delay in the digital domain: shift registers, memories and first-in–first-out devices (FIFOs).

The basic memory element in logic circuits is the latch, which is constructed from two gates and can be set or reset. A more useful variant is the D-type latch which remembers the state of the input at the time a separate clock either changes state for an edge-triggered device, or after it goes false for a level-triggered device. D-type latches are commonly available with four or eight latches to the chip. A shift register can be made by connecting them one after the other, so that data are delayed by the number of stages in the register.

Where large numbers of bits are to be stored, cross-coupled latches are less suitable because they are more complicated to fabricate inside integrated circuits than dynamic memory.

In large random access memories (RAMs), the data bits are stored as the presence or absence of charge in a tiny capacitor. The charge will suffer leakage, and the value would become indeterminate after a few milliseconds. Where the delay needed is less than this, decay is of no consequence, as data will be read out before they have had a chance to decay. Where longer delays are necessary, such memories must be refreshed periodically by reading the bit value and writing it back to the same place. Most modern RAM chips have suitable circuitry built in.

Large RAMs store thousands of bits, and it is clearly impractical to have a connection to each one. Instead, the desired bit has to be addressed before it can be read or written. The size of the chip package restricts the number of pins available, so that large memories use the same address pins more than once. The bits are arranged internally as rows and columns, and the row address and the column address are specified sequentially on the same pins. Fig. 3.27 shows some examples of different memory devices.

The shift-register approach and the memory approach to delay are very similar, as a shift register can be thought of as a memory whose address increases automatically when clocked. The data rate and the maximum

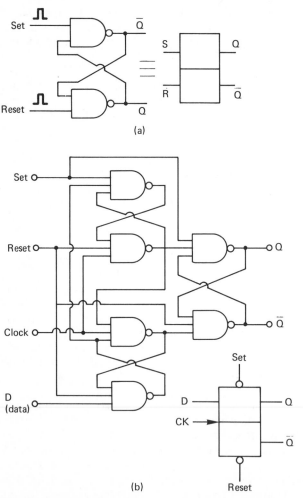

Figure 3.27 Digital semiconductor memory types. At (a), one data bit can be stored in a simple set–reset latch, which has little application because the D-type latch at (b) can store the state of the single data input when the clock occurs. These devices can be implemented with bipolar transistors of FETs, and are called static memories because they can store indefinitely. They consume a lot of power.

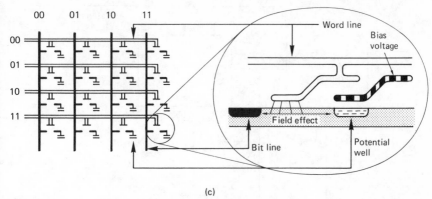

(c)

Figure 3.27 (*Continued*). At (c), a bit is stored as the charge in a potential well in the substrate of a chip. It is accessed by connecting the bit line with the field effect from the word line. The single well where the two lines cross can then be written or read. These devices are called dynamic RAMs because the charge decays, and they must be read and rewritten (refreshed) periodically

delay determine the capacity of the memory required. Fig. 3.28 shows that the addressing of the memory is by a counter that overflows endlessly from the end of the memory back to the beginning, giving the memory a ring-like structure. The write address is determined by the incoming data, and the read address is determined by the outgoing data. This means that the memory has to be able to read and write at the same time. The switching between read and write involves not only a data multiplexer but also an address multiplexer, as can be seen in Fig. 3.29. In general the arbitration between read and write will be done by signals from the stable side of the TBC, which in the case of digital recorder replay will be the read side. The stable side of the memory will read a sample when it demands, and the writing will be locked out for that period. The input data cannot be interrupted in many applications, however, so a small buffer silo is installed before the memory, which fills up as the writing is locked out and empties again as writing is permitted. Alternatively, the memory will be

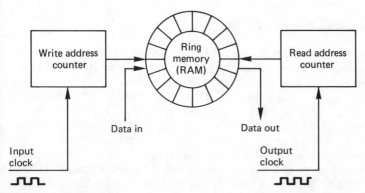

Figure 3.28 TBC memory is addressed by a counter which periodically overflows to give a ring structure. Memory allows read side to be non-synchronous with write side

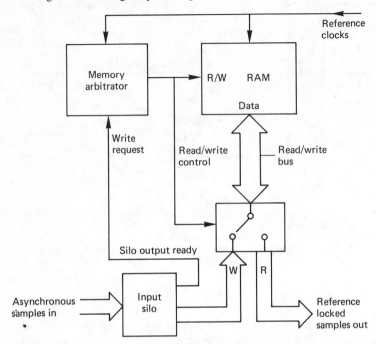

Figure 3.29 In a RAM-based TBC, the RAM is reference-synchronous, and an arbitrator decides when it will write. During reading, asynchronous input data backs up in the input silo, asserting a write request to the arbitrator. Arbitrator will then cause a write cycle between read cycles

split into blocks, such that when one block is reading a different block will be writing and the problem does not arise. In most digital video applications, the sampling rate exceeds the rate at which economically available RAM chips can operate. The solution is to arrange several video samples into one longer word, sometimes known as a superword, and to construct the memory so that it stores superwords in parallel.

3.13 FIFO timebase correction

Fig. 3.30 shows the operation of a FIFO chip, colloquially known as a silo because the data are tipped in at the top on delivery and drawn off at the bottom when needed. Each stage of the chip has a data register and a small amount of logic, including a data-valid or V bit. If the input register does not contain data, the first V bit will be reset, and this will cause the chip to assert 'input ready'. If data are presented at the input, and clocked into the first stage, the V bit will set, and the 'input ready' signal will become false. However, the logic associated with the next stage sees the V bit set in the top stage, and if its own V bit is clear, it will clock the data into its own register, set its own V bit, and clear the input V bit, causing 'input ready' to reassert, when another word can be fed in. This process then continues as the word moves down the silo, until it arrives at the last register in the chip.

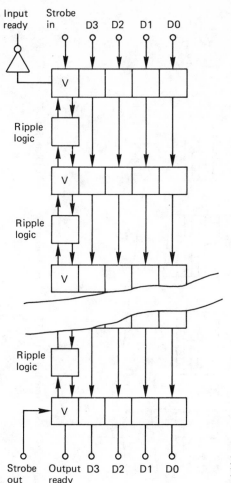

Figure 3.30 Structure of FIFO or silo chip. Ripple logic controls propagation of data down silo

The V bit of the last stage becomes the 'output ready' signal, telling subsequent circuitry that there are data to be read. If this word is not read, the next word entered will ripple down to the stage above. Words thus stack up at the bottom of the silo. When a word is read out, an external signal must be provided which resets the bottom V bit. The 'output ready' signal now goes false, and the logic associated with the last stage now sees valid data above and loads down the word when it will become ready again. The last register but one will now have no V bit set, and will see data above itself and bring that down. In this way a reset V bit propagates up the chip while the data ripple down, rather like a hole in a semiconductor going the opposite way to the electrons. Silo chips are usually available in four bit wordlengths, but can easily be connected in parallel to form superwords. Silo chips are asynchronous, and paralleled chips will not necessarily all work at the same speed. This problem is easily overcome by 'anding'

88

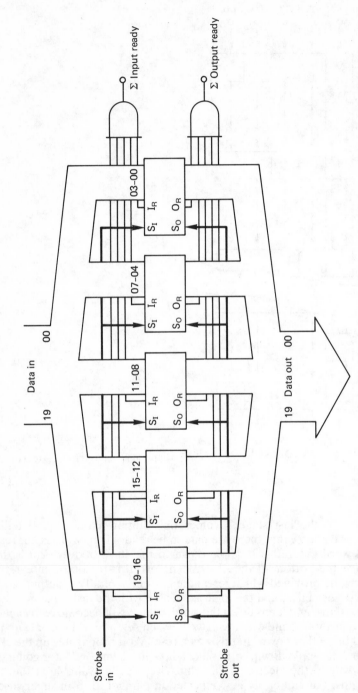

Figure 3.31 In this example, a twenty-bit wordlength silo is made from five parallel FIFO chips. The asynchronous ripple action of FIFOs means that it is necessary to 'and' together the ready signals

together all of the input-ready and output-ready signals and parallel-connecting the strobes. Fig. 3.31 shows this mode of operation.

When used in a hard-disk system, a silo will allow data to and from the disk, which is turning at constant speed. When reading the disk, Fig. 3.32(a) shows that the silo starts empty, and if there is bus contention, the silo will start to fill. Where the bus is free, the disk controller will attempt to empty the silo into the memory. The system can take advantage of the interblock gaps on the disk, containing headers, preambles and redundancy, for in these areas there are no data to transfer and there is some breathing space to empty the silo before the next block. In practice the silo need not be empty at the start of every block, provided it never becomes full before the end of the transfer. If this happens some data are lost and the function must be aborted. The block containing the silo overflow will generally be re-read on the next revolution. In sophisticated systems, the silo has a kind of dipstick and can interrupt the CPU if the data get too deep. The CPU can then suspend some bus activity to allow the disk controller more time to empty the silo.

When the disk is to be written, as in Fig. 3.32(b), a continuous data stream must be provided during each block, as the disk cannot stop. The

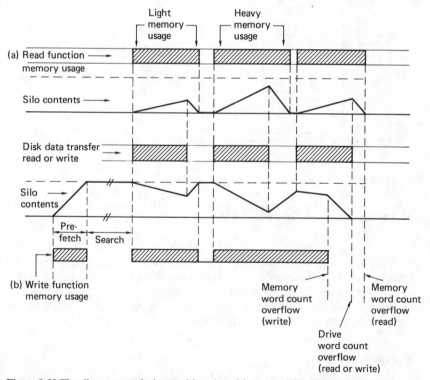

Figure 3.32 The silo contents during read functions (a) appear different from those during write functions (b). In (a)., the control logic attempts to keep the silo as empty as possible; in (b) the logic prefills the silo and attempts to keep it full until the memory word count overflows

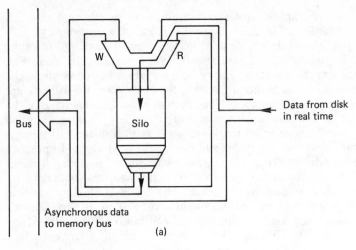

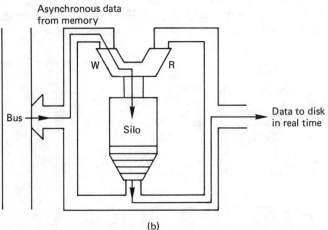

Figure 3.33 In order to guarantee that the drive can transfer data in real time at regular intervals (determined by disk speed and density) the silo provides buffering to the asynchronous operation of the memory access process. At (a) the silo is configured for a disk read. The same silo is used at (b) for a disk write

silo will be prefilled before the disk attempts to write, and the disk controller attempts to keep it full. In this case all will be well if the silo does not become empty before the end of the transfer. Fig. 3.33 shows the silo of a typical disk controller with the multiplexers necessary to put it in the read data stream or the write data stream.

References

1. VANDERKOOY, J. and LIPSHITZ, S.P., Digital dither. Presented at the 81st Audio Engineering Society Convention (Los Angeles, 1986), preprint 2412(c-8)
2. NASSE, D., GRIMALDI, J.L. and CAYET, A., An experimental all-digital television center. *SMPTE J.*, **95**, 13–19 (1986)

Chapter 4

The C-format timebase corrector

The C-format uses analog recording and yet it virtually has to be regarded as a digital format because it would not have been feasible without the support of digital processing circuitry with which it was designed to work. This chapter looks in detail at the digital aspects of C-format, with enough detail of the analog recording process to define the task of the digital circuits.

4.1 Introduction to C-format

The first broadcast video recorders were Quadruplex, using a transverse scanning head which wrote tracks across 2 inch wide tape. It was not possible to fit a whole field into one track, so the recording was segmented, and switching from one head to the other took place several times in each field, during the horizontal blanking period. The unsupported tape length of a transverse scan machine is very small, and timebase error was reduced by extremely good mechanical design, which actually compensated for the head radius changing as the tips wore. The residual errors could be corrected by an analog variable delay using varicap diodes (also known as varactors). The Quadruplex format was a tremendous achievement by Ampex; it is difficult today to imagine a world without video recording. It was not long before users began demanding more operational features. Audio recorders offer confidence replay and work at varying speeds; why not video recorders?

Confidence replay was extremely difficult in Quadruplex because the extra heads could not then be accommodated in the very small scanner. Variable speed in video can only refer to the speed of the image; the field rate must remain the same. In order to run at variable speed, a video recorder would have to omit or repeat fields on tape so that the output field rate could remain stable. With the segmented recording of Quadruplex, omitting or repeating fields would have been a mechanical nightmare, although it was done experimentally.

To obtain a wide speed range with the technology of the day, it was necessary to have one tape track contain one video field. Within the available recorded wavelength limits, this meant a track much longer than the width of 2 inch tape. The solution was to use helical scan, where the tracks make an acute angle with the edge of the tape.

The track containing one field turned out to be very long, nearly 18 in, and to keep the scanner reasonably compact the tape was wrapped around it almost completely, so that a complete revolution of the scanner wrote a single field in a single track. Using the so-called Omega wrap, the head will be out of contact with the tape briefly, while it traverses the gap between the pins which guide the tape in and out of the scanner. This is known as the *vertical or format dropout* and is timed to coincide with the vertical blanking period. Vertical synchronizing pulses can easily be recreated from reference signals, and so the storage of the vertical interval is optional in C-format. Where vertical sync storage is implemented, a second sync-only head is installed in the scanner 30° behind the video head. This is positioned such that it records in an area between the control track and audio 3. Fig. 4.1 shows the resultant pattern on the tape and includes the linear audio and control tracks.[1] The scanner turns against the direction of tape travel, so that the head-to-tape speed is the vector sum of the scanner peripheral velocity and the tape linear velocity. Similarly the angle of the tape tracks is a function of the drum geometry and the tape speed. The scanners of most C-format machines have three video heads set at 120° spacing. The first of these is a flying erase head which will be needed for editing. Next comes the record head, followed by the confidence replay head. All three are positioned in the scanner at slightly different heights, such that they traverse the same track in sequence.

During playback the capstan and scanner servos must phase-lock to an external reference, so that offtape video can be timed to the reference. This means that correctly timed playback can only take place at normal speed. Furthermore, the head will only trace the tape tracks if the scanner and capstan turn with a fixed relationship.

Owing to the long tape tracks, small tension and dimensional changes due to temperature and humidity differences can cause changes in the effective length of the field. Although these are minute in percentage terms, they can become enormous when measured in degrees of subcarrier, which is important as C-format records the composite PAL signal. These instabilities are far greater on C-format than they were for quadruplex and beyond the range of a varicap delay. Variable speed operation changes the head-to-tape speed which exaggerates the problem. It is probably true to say that without the digital timebase corrector, the C-format would not be viable.

4.2 Track following

Track following is a means of actively controlling the relationship between the replay head and the track so that the track is traced more accurately than it would be by purely mechanical means.

This can be applied to systems operating at normal speed, in order to allow interchange at higher recording densities, but in C-format track following is an option, and satisfactory interchange can be achieved without it. Track following in C-format was developed to allow variable speed operation. The principle has various names: Ampex call it automatic scan tracking (AST)[2], Sony use the term dynamic tracking (DT), and Hitachi use Hitachi scan tracking (HST).

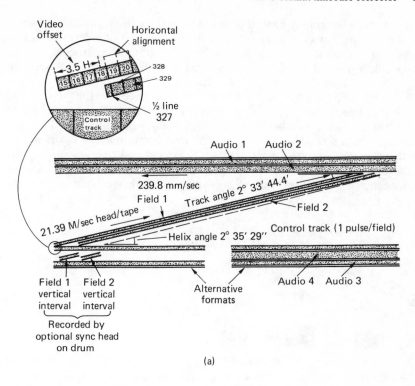

(a)

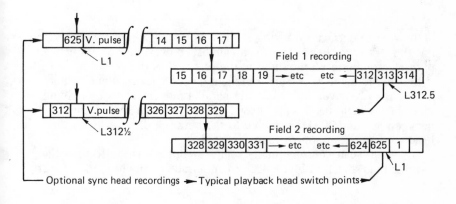

(b)

Figure 4.1 (a) shows essentials of PAL C-format. Tape is guided round drum at helix angle, but movement of tape against drum rotation causes track angle to be slightly smaller than helix angle. Tape speed is chosen to give video offset of 3.5 lines, which gives horizontal alignment condition (inset). Vertical interval storage is optional and a fourth audio track is an alternative.

Where optional sync. head is used, vertical interval is recorded separately (b), with overlap. Effect of interlace is to record two types of field. Two-field sequence repeats endlessly. Addition of chrominance to interlace sequence causes sequence to extend

Essentially the replay head is able to move along the scanner axis, which is at right angles to the tape track, and it forms part of a position servo, requiring a position error signal to drive it. It is interesting to compare the track-following system of a video recorder with the systems developed for disk which are described in Chapter 12.

Fig. 4.2 shows three relationships of the head to the track, and corresponding signal output. Analog video recorders use FM recording to cater for the wide bandwidth of the baseband video signal and to give immunity to head contact variations. The waveforms in Fig. 4.2 correspond to the RF envelope of the FM carrier. Case (a) and case (c) display the same output, although the tracking error has the opposite sense. Simple processing of the RF level only gives the magnitude of the error, not the sense.

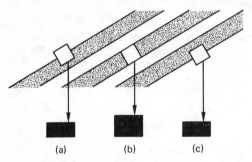

Figure 4.2 Effect of tracking error on playback signal. Signal amplitude in (a) and (c) is identical, despite sense of tracking error. Maximum signal occurs with correct alignment as in (b)

In order to extract a tracking error, a wobble or dither is superimposed on the tracking head, which is almost universally positioned by a piezoelectric bimorph mounted in the scanner, as shown in Fig. 4.3.

In order to avoid zenith error preventing good head-to-tape contact, the head has to be given an essentially parallel movement by combining two bimorphs which bend in opposite directions. An AC component of between 400 and 700 Hz is added to the bimorph drive, which causes the head to execute an approximate sinusoid.

One field scan contains many cycles of dither. The effect on the RF envelope, as shown in Fig. 4.4, is an amplitude modulation of the carrier,

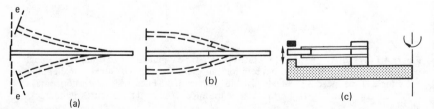

Figure 4.3 Simple single bimorph at (a) changes head contact angle e. At (b) compound bimorph closely approximates parallel action. Tracking head mounted on video drum is shown at (c)

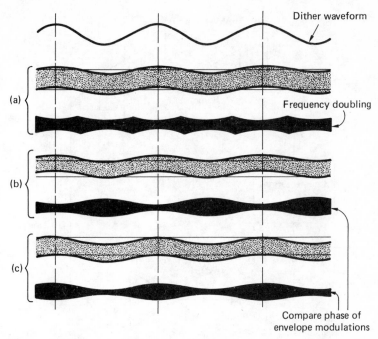

Dither waveform

(a)

Frequency doubling

(b)

(c)

Compare phase of
envelope modulations

Figure 4.4 Top, dither waveform which causes head to oscillate across track. At (a) is optimum alignment, showing frequency doubling in r.f. envelope. With head above track centre, as in (b), r.f. amplitude increases as head reaches lowest point, whereas reverse applies in case (c)

which has little effect on the video, owing to the insensitivity of the FM system to amplitude effects. Fig. 4.4(a) shows that the effect of dither on a correctly aligned head is a frequency doubling in the RF envelope. Fig. 4.4(b) and Fig. 4.4(c) show the effect of the head off track. Both cases appear similar, but the phase of the envelope modulation is different and can be used to extract the sense of the tracking error.

In Fig. 4.5 the RF is detected to obtain a level, which is fed to a phase-sensitive rectifier whose reference is the dither drive signal. The output of the phase-sensitive rectifier is a tracking error signal which contains both magnitude and sense (and rather a lot of harmonics of dither) which can be fed back to the bimorph drive circuit to cancel the error.

As the mass of the track-following head and the compliance of the bimorph form a mechanically resonant system, frequency of operation must be below resonance, and damping is required. Damping is provided by positional feedback from the bimorph. A break is formed in the electrodes on the surface of the bimorph which apply the electric field for deflection, and the small electrode which is isolated in this way becomes a sense strip which generates a deflection signal used for damping and for feedback during the vertical interval when the head loses contact with the tape.

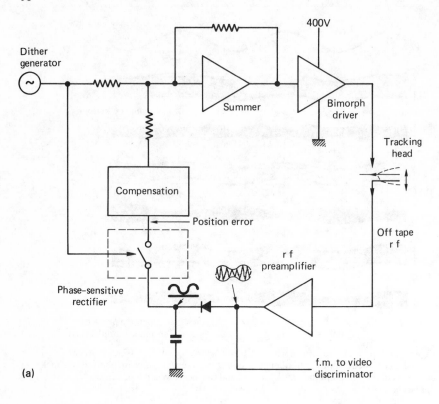

(a)

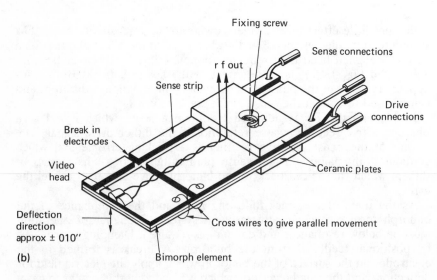

(b)

Figure 4.5 Phase-sensitive rectifier in (a) extracts tracking from r.f. envelope. Position feedback from sense strip provides damping. At (b), break in electrode plating isolates sense strip on bimorph, isolating two sections of element which bend in oposition due to cross wire connections

If the recorder is playing at normal speed, the long-term position of the bimorph will be neutral. If the tape is made to run at slightly less than normal speed, the scanner cannot change speed because it must provide output at field rate. The tracking servo will cause the head to bend down the scanner axis further and further as it attempts to follow tracks which are not arriving fast enough. Conversely, if the tape runs slightly fast, the bimorph will bend up the scanner axis to follow the tracks which are passing too quickly.

In both cases, the situation cannot continue indefinitely. To allow continuous operation it is necessary to make the head jump as it crosses the format dropout, to reduce the deflection. When running slow, the jump will be one-track pitch back, such that from time to time a field will be played twice to maintain output field rate, whereas when running fast the jump will be forwards, so that a field will be missed periodically. The more the speed differs from unity, the more often such jumps will need to take place. Fig. 4.6 shows several examples of jumping and also shows the drive signals which will be sent to the bimorph (neglecting the dither signal). Note the dipulses which are necessary to accelerate and decelerate the head during the jump.

It is possible to stop the tape completely and still maintain output. In this case the bimorph can be made to follow one field continuously by making a one-track reverse jump during the format dropout, using the drive

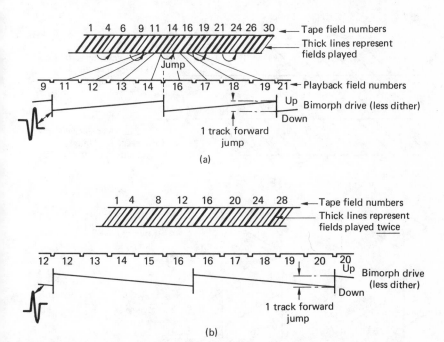

Figure 4.6 Tape at (a) moving at 125% normal speed: to maintain field rate, four out of every five tracks are played, with single-track jump every four. Slope of bimorph drive signal is positive: negative steps are where head jumps down to skip one track. At (b), tape moves at 80% of forward speed: every fourth track played twice using single-track reverse jump. Slope of bimorph drive is negative, with positive jumps to repeat one track

waveform shown in Fig. 4.7(a). An alternative is to repeat one complete frame, where a reverse jump of two tracks takes place every two fields. If the tape is reversed at normal speed, the head can still follow the tracks, but has to make a two-track reverse jump every revolution.

From Fig. 4.7 it can be seen that the waveforms needed for −1× and +3× speeds are the inverse of one another. This is because +1× speed is obtained by transport geometry, and the −1× and +3× speeds represent an equal departure from it. This should be examined in the context of head-to-tape speed. Because the scanner peripheral velocity is the

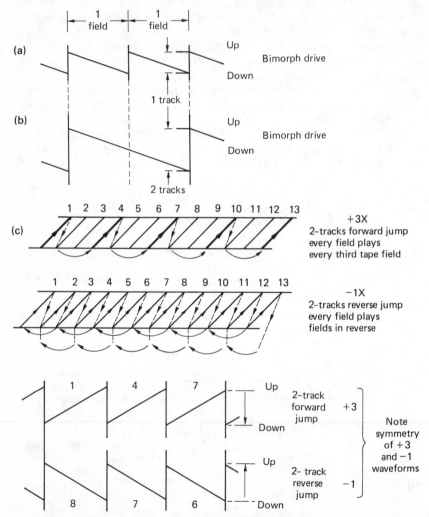

Figure 4.7 Still-field mode at (a) repeats one field endlessly. With tape stationary, one-track reverse jump is needed once per field. Still-frame mode at (b) repeats two fields endlessly. Two-track reverse jump once per frame. Depending on where tape stops, d.c. component may be needed. (c) Single-track advance is obtained by normal tape movement. Two-track jump forwards adds to give ×3 speed: two-track backwards subtracts to give −1 speed

dominant factor, stopping or reversing the tape only reduces the head-to-tape speed slightly. Similarly doubling or tripling the linear tape speed only slightly increases the head-to-tape speed. Note that in C-format the scanner turns against the direction of tape travel. In some formats, the scanner turns with tape travel, and many of the effects described here will be reversed.

When the tape speed exceeds certain limits, the bimorph does not have enough physical travel to stay on one track for a complete revolution of the scanner. In this case jumping must also take place during the visible part of the scan, and guard band noise between tracks will be present in the playback signal during the jump. There is no disturbance to H-sync phase caused by in-field track switching, because the C-format, like most video formats, is designed so that H-pulses on adjacent tracks are aligned. This is achieved by choosing a linear tape speed which causes a 3.5 line shift between tracks in 625/50 and a 2.5 line shift in 525/60. The half line component removes the effects of interlace on the H/V-sync relationship, permitting the horizontal alignment condition. It is this constraint which results in video recorders having rather strange linear tape speeds.

One revolution of the scanner can now play back segments of various tracks to build up a field. This will be beyond the speed range where a broadcast-quality picture might be needed, for example in shuttle. The picture is imperfect but better than no picture.

The track following head is in a scanner of 67.31 mm diameter, turning at field rate, which means it experiences a pull of between 700 and 1000 times the force of gravity, which tries to oppose the deflection of the bimorph. The large deflections needed for variable speed operation mean that several hundred volts of drive will be needed by the bimorph.

Using feedback alone is not adequate for variable speed track following, since an appreciable tracking error will be necessary to produce the large deflections needed. This problem can be eliminated by combining the feedback system with feedforward.

For any linear tape speed, it is possible geometrically to calculate the slope of the deflection ramp needed to keep the head on track. Fig. 4.6 and Fig. 4.7 show that the slope is proportional to the deviation from normal speed, i.e. the slope is zero at normal speed, and the slope at 3× speed is equal and opposite to the slope at −1× speed. The capstan circuit can determine the speed deviation, and if this is fed to an integrator, a predicted deflection signal can be obtained.[3] The feedback system has now only to correct for differences between the actual and predicted tracking, so the tracking error will be independent of the deflection. Fig. 4.8 shows details of the system.

Stability criteria for a dither-based servo are somewhat complex. The tracking error is essentially sampled at the dither frequency by a phase-sensitive rectifier.[4] Sampling theory states that there will be no information above one-half the sampling frequency. It is essential to filter the tracking error to get rid of the dither harmonics, otherwise there would be interference with the real dither. Filtering is difficult in servo systems, because all real filters introduce delay, and this corresponds to a phase shift which could cause instability.

The approach generally used is to make the dither frequency an odd

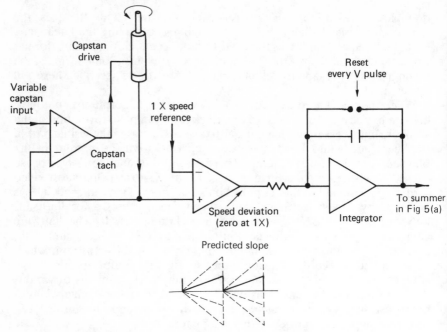

Figure 4.8 Circuit arrangement shows feedforward signal predicting slope of bimorph drive derived from capstan speed deviation

multiple of half the scanner frequency, so that the dither is antiphase in successive fields. Fig. 4.9 shows that the tracking error spectrum will interleave the dither spectrum, so that a comb filter can recover the tracking error and reject the dither harmonics. The comb filter needs a delay of one revolution between inputs, so that over two revolutions the tracking error adds and the dither cancels. Clearly 625/50 machines will need a different dither frequency to 525/60 machines.

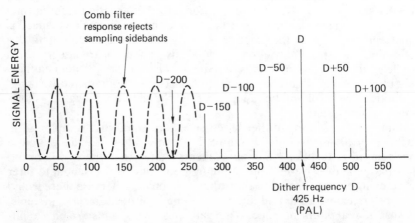

Figure 4.9 Correct choice of dither frequency enables interleaving of tracking-error spectrum and sampling

To complete the track-following mechanism, the jumping system must be added. To reduce jerkiness in the picture, the jumps should be as small as possible. To give broadcastable pictures, the jump should only occur at the format dropout. From stationary to +2× speed, single-track jumps are sufficient, varying in frequency from never at normal speed to once per field at 2× speed, where every other field is played back. This variation is infinite, so it is not trivial to calculate where to jump. In general a jump will be made if it will result in the magnitude of the deflection becoming smaller. Thus from still to 2× speed, a jump will be made if the deflection exceeds ½ track at the end of a field. This will cause the displacement to become ½ track in the opposite sense, and if that tape speed is maintained the deflection will reduce before increasing again to cause a further jump. Between +2× and +3× speeds and between still and −1× speed, it will be necessary to make a sequence of single- and two-track jumps. A single-track jump will always be made, but if the displacement exceeds one track at the end of the current field, a two-track jump will be made.

Owing to the format dropout, the whole of the the vertical interval is not recorded on the main video track, so vertical detection has to be done by locating the equalizing pulses which are at the end of the track. These are relatively narrow, and one might be missed in the case of a dropout. The VTR contains a phase-locked loop which predicts where the vertical interval will be and validates its detection. If a head jump takes place, the offset between the start point of successive tracks has to be allowed for, and the phase of the loop needs to be updated by 3.5 lines (625/50) or 2.5 lines (525/60).

4.3 Instabilities in C-format

Mixing in composite video is only possible provided that all sources are synchronized to within about 5° of subcarrier, which is about 3 ns in PAL. A field in PAL has a duration of 20 ms, so the stability demanded is given by

$$\frac{3 \times 10^{-9}}{20 \times 10^{-3}} \times 100\% = 0.000\,015\%$$

No mechanism can approach such tolerances, so timebase correction is mandatory in C-format even at normal speed.

Instabilities in C-format are actually greater than in the Quadruplex system because of the long tracks. Video tape has a plastics backing, which has a relatively high coefficient of expansion and also changes its dimensions in response to humidity changes. It is also flexible, so track length can be changed by variations in tape tension.

Tension, temperature and humidity changes produce relatively stable changes in offtape signal frequency, as does slow-motion operation at a fixed speed. However, the rotating video and sync heads impact the tape six times per field and cause shock waves to travel along the tape. The effect of these is that the head-to-tape speed experiences a superimposed AC component which causes the chroma phase to oscillate about the correct value. These disturbances are referred to as velocity errors, even though they are caused by tape accelerations. The effect can also be observed when the tape speed is changed in slow motion.

When portable recorders are carried whilst running, any rotation of the machine about the scanner axis can cause timing errors. Owing to scanner inertia, the scanner stays in the same phase relative to the earth after the recorder has moved, until the scanner servo can rephase it. As there are 312.5 lines (PAL) or 262.5 lines (NTSC) in one scanner revolution, one degree of scanner lag can cause nearly a line of timing error. These inertial errors are generally and again erroneously referred to as gyroscopic errors.

Videotape also suffers from dropouts, which do not of themselves change timing, but can result in timing problems. In particular the loss of a burst due to dropout renders meaningless the whole of the chroma on the current line. This has to be compensated in the timebase corrector.

If variable-speed playback is employed, the demands on the timebase corrector become more extreme, and the line period changes significantly from standard. It is possible to calculate the line period for any given linear tape speed by some tedious geometry, but there is in fact a much simpler method which is derived from an understanding of how the track jumping works.

Consider a C-format machine playing at +2× speed. There will be a one-track jump every scanner revolution, but the scanner speed remains locked to field rate.

In 625/50, an extra 3.5 lines can be fitted into the rotational period of the scanner, because of the 3.5 line offset of the start points of the tracks. If the normal line period is T_h, the new line period T'_h will be given by

$$T'_h = \frac{T_h \times 312.5}{312.5 + 3.5} \ \mu s$$

In 525/60 the expression becomes:

$$T'_h = \frac{T_h \times 262.5}{262.5 \times 2.5} \ \mu s$$

Fig. 4.10 shows the effect of a variety of speeds on the video line for 625/50. The change in head-to-tape speed changes the apparent frequency of the FM carrier, and consequently the levels and amplitudes of the playback video will change. The percentage change tracks the change in line rate.

Track jumping in variable speed causes fields to be omitted or repeated, and this destroys interlace and the subcarrier sequence of the composite recording. The recreation of interlace and the subcarrier sequence, the correction of the time compression/expansion of the field timing and the restoration of correct video levels are major additional functions of a timebase corrector intended for variable-speed working.

4.4 Basic timebase correction

The fundamental principle of all timebase correctors is to introduce a controlled delay in the signal path which opposes timing errors due to

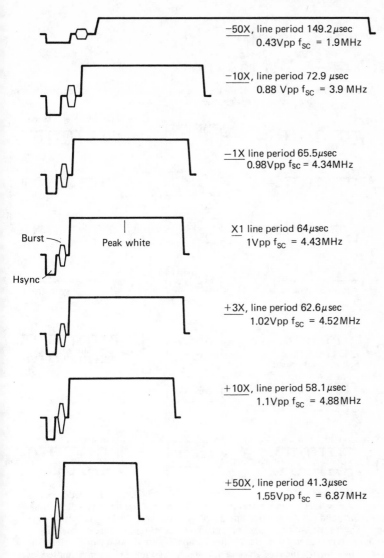

-50X, line period 149.2 µsec
0.43Vpp f_{SC} = 1.9MHz

-10X, line period 72.9 µsec
0.88 Vpp f_{SC} = 3.9 MHz

-1X line period 65.5µsec
0.98Vpp f_{SC} = 4.34MHz

X1 line period 64µsec
1Vpp f_{SC} = 4.43MHz

+3X, line period 62.6µsec
1.02Vpp f_{SC} = 4.52MHz

+10X, line period 58.1µsec
1.1Vpp f_{SC} = 4.88MHz

+50X, line period 41.3µsec
1.55Vpp f_{SC} = 6.87MHz

Figure 4.10 The effect of a variety of tape speeds on a PAL recording

replay. Analog delay is difficult, whereas binary data can be delayed indefinitely in RAM without degradation. In a digital timebase corrector, the unstable analog video input is digitized so that it can be delayed, then converted back to stable analog. The conversion processes were described in Chapter 2.

All of the timing errors mentioned in the previous section can be broken down into three basic categories which are shown in Fig. 4.11. Instabilities will cause the timing of the replay signal to fluctuate ahead of and behind the reference timing. Clearly a timebase corrector cannot advance an offtape video signal – it can only delay. The video recorder synchronizes to

A tv picture containing vertical bars as shown here will be generated by repeating the monochrome lines shown in (a), (b) & (c)

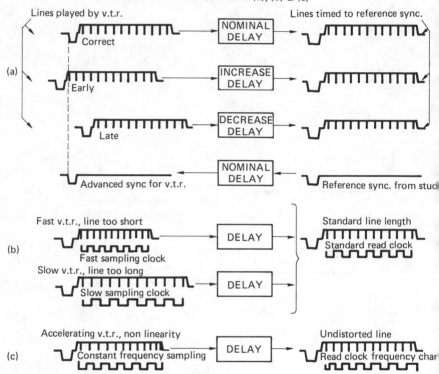

Figure 4.11 Three fundamental timebase corrections. At (a), the v.t.r. is advanced from reference, and correctly timed output lines are returned to reference timing by a delay equal to the advance. Early and late lines are compensated by changing the delay. At (b), off-tape lines are sampled by a clock which changes proportionally to off-tape line frequency. Line period errors are removed in this way. Shown at (c) is non-linearity due to tape acceleration which is removed by swinging the read clock in the same way (Burst and chroma omitted for clarity.)

an advanced reference, which leads station reference by a nominal value as shown in Fig. 4.11(a). The timebase corrector then delays the replay signal by the nominal value. If the replay timing is advanced by instabilities, the delay is increased; if it is retarded, the delay will be reduced. To obtain a symmetrical correction range, known as the *window*, the advance should be one-half of the maximum delay that the timebase corrector can introduce, which clearly is proportional to the amount of memory it contains.

Where the line has the wrong period, as at (b), it can be corrected by producing a sampling clock known as the *write clock* whose frequency is proportional to head-to-tape speed. As a result, the line will be converted into the same number of samples irrespective of the line period. When the samples are read from memory at the correct rate, the proper line length results.

The third mechanism is the correction of velocity errors which occur when the head-to-tape speed changes significantly during the video line. At (c), the tape speed increases and compresses the end of the line. In most timebase correctors, the write clock remains constant in frequency throughout the line, and the phase of the read clock is modified to achieve *velocity compensation*. There are several ways in which this can be done. The exception to this principle is the Ampex Zeus, which functions in a different way and will be treated separately.

In practice all three of the processes described will be taking place simultaneously.

The basic components of a simple timebase corrector are shown in Fig. 4.12. These must include:

(a) The offtape sampling rate, or write clock, must be locked to offtape signals, starting in a repeatable place on each line and dividing the line into a constant number of samples, irrespective of line period.

(b) A sample store, which introduces a delay which can vary up to its maximum capacity.

(c) Reference sampling rate or *read clock* generator, producing a clock which reads samples out of the memory, spacing them out to give the standard line length.

(d) Some form of velocity compensation to accommodate instabilities within the line.

(e) A colour framing or vertical lock system which takes care of the vertical timing of the system so that the first line of an input video frame' becomes the first line of the output video frame.

4.5 Generating the write clock

The most critical timing parameter in composite video is chroma phase. This can only be made stable if the write clock is generated from offtape subcarrier and the read clock is generated from reference. The only part of the composite video signal which conveys subcarrier phase is the burst, so write and read clocks in PAL and NTSC timebase correctors are derived from it. In SECAM, the chroma is frequency modulated, and chroma phase is no more critical than horizontal phase. In SECAM timebase correctors, the clocks are derived from horizontal sync.

Fig. 4.13 shows the write clock generator of a typical TBC. The offtape burst is used to phase-lock an oscillator which runs at $4 \times F_{sc}$, which is convenient because PAL burst swing can be eliminated by comparing with adjacent cycles of $4 \times F_{sc}$ which are 90° of subcarrier apart. More precisely, *burst crossings* (the points where a positive-going burst voltage cuts through blanking voltage) are used. The chroma stability of a good TBC is determined entirely by the signal-to-noise ratio of the offtape burst, since burst noise can move the position of crossings and cause chroma

106

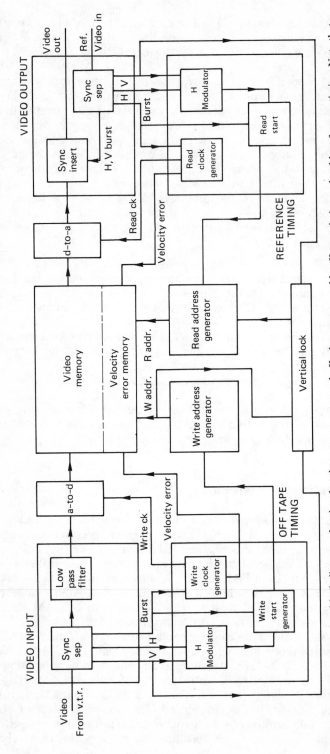

Figure 4.12 Simplified t.b.c. block diagram, showing that the memory acts as a buffer between unstable off-tape timing and stable reference timing. Note that the dropout compensator and the varispeed colour processor have been omitted as these functions can be performed at various different places

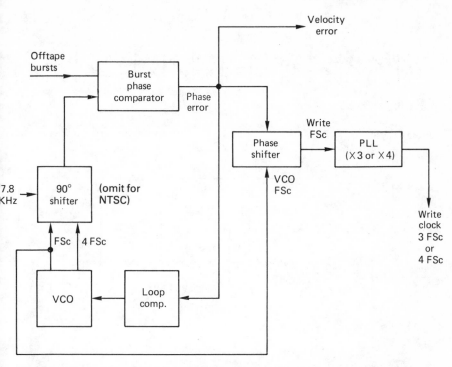

Figure 4.13 Production of write clock from offtape bursts. The phase comparator produces a phase error between the VCO and offtape subcarrier, which drives a phase shifter to make Write FSc have the same phase as offtape subcarrier at the beginning of the line. The phase error also becomes the velocity error for the end of the previous line

phase jitter. This is the reason why C-format records burst with double amplitude and attenuates on playback.

The phase-locked oscillator can only make a phase comparison once per line when there is a new burst, and if the head-to-tape speed changes during the line, there will be a phase error between the PLO and the next burst because of the lag of the phase-locked loop. The phase error is measured and used for two purposes. First, it represents the difference between the PLO phase and the subcarrier phase at the end of the previous line. This is the velocity error, and it will be stored along with the samples for the line. Secondly, the error represents the phase error between the PLO and the subcarrier phase at the beginning of the new line. This is used to control a phase shifter between the PLO and the write clock or generator. Clearly in order to track a swinging burst and to deal with the quarter cycle offset of PAL subcarrier from one line to the next, a PLO running at $4 \times F_{sc}$ is desirable, but this does not necessarily mean that the sampling rate has to be $4 \times F_{sc}$. Numerous successful timebase correctors have been made which sampled at $3 \times F_{sc}$, with a corresponding economy in memory requirements. Now that memory prices have fallen, the cost of the memory is no longer a dominant factor in the design of the machine, and all modern designs use $4 \times F_{sc}$. Where digital manipulation of the signal is anticipated, $4 \times F_{sc}$ sampling becomes mandatory.

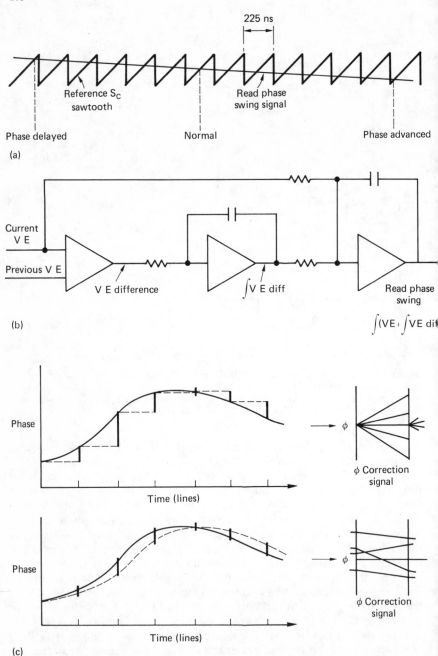

225 ns

Reference S_C
sawtooth

Read phase
swing signal

Phase delayed

Normal

Phase advanced

(a)

Current
V E

Previous V E

V E difference

∫V E diff

Read phase
swing

$\int (VE + \int VE \, dif$

(b)

Phase

Time (lines)

φ

φ Correction
signal

Phase

Time (lines)

φ

φ Correction
signal

(c)

Figure 4.14 (a) Phase correction ramp shifts crossings in a FSc rate sawtooth. (b) Using a double integrator, a curved phase correction signal can be obtained for second order velocity compensation. (c) Comparison of two methods of velcomp. At top, write clock phase (shown dotted) is reset to offtape phase (solid line) at beginning of every line. Correction ramp (right) always starts at zero. At bottom, write clock is from a lagging VCO, and phase error at beginning and end of line are used for continuous correction

In the system described, the write clock always begins the line in the correct phase, and velocity errors will only cause an error at the end of the line. When the line of samples is read from the memory, the velocity error parameter is used to swing the phase of the read clock to cancel the velocity error. Fig. 4.14(a) shows that this can be done by using a sawtooth signal at subcarrier frequency and comparing it with a ramp whose period is one line and whose amplitude is the velocity error. The output of this phase modulator is then fed to a phase-locked loop which multiplies it by the appropriate factor to obtain the read clock. Since the write clock was phase corrected at the beginning of each line, the ramp will commence from zero and slope up or down according to the sense and size of the velocity error. This produces a piecewise linear approximation to the correct phase. Using a double integrator circuit shown in Fig. 4.14(b) it is possible to use the difference between successive velocity errors to generate a curved correction waveform, which is known as second-order velocity compensation.[5]

An alternative method of velocity compensation, used in certain Ampex timebase correctors, is to dispense with the phase shifter between the burst-locked PLO and the write clock. The burst-locked PLO then runs at $4 \times F_{sc}$ and generates the write clock directly. When the head-to-tape speed changes, the PLO will phase lag, and the write clock with it. The phase lag measured at any burst will be used as the velocity error at the end of the previous line, as before, but will also be used as the velocity error at the start of the next line. In order to phase-correct a line, the correction voltage must now swing from one value to another, as shown in Fig. 4.14(c). This method allows the phase shifter in the write clock generator to be eliminated and allows a softer locking PLO to be used with a potential reduction in jitter.

Fig. 4.15 shows that the presence of velocity errors in the preceding systems means that the sampling phase has no fixed relationship with the chroma signal. It is virtually impossible to decode the chroma in the digital

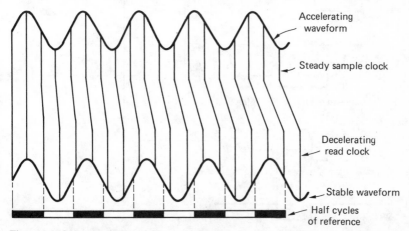

Figure 4.15 In conventional velocity compensation, the real clock is phase swung to correct the phase error on sampling. This works well for an analogue output but the phase between samples and chroma becomes arbitrary

domain, because a chroma decoder needs to sample exactly every 90° of subcarrier, and this was not how the samples in the timebase corrector were taken.

4.6 Velocity compensation in Zeus

In the Ampex Zeus it was specifically intended to use a digital colour processor to obtain the highest possible slow-motion quality, and a different form of velocity compensation is necessary to permit samples with a fixed relationship to offtape subcarrier to be made in the presence of velocity errors.[6] If the write clock phase is to be made to track the offtape subcarrier phase instabilities, it is necessary to use information from the burst before and after the line of interest. As the burst at the end of the current line will not be available until after the line has passed, a one-line delay is necessary. In the Zeus video processor, a CCD delay is used, which is a sampled analog device running at 27 MHz. The bandwidth and noise performance of this delay are engineered to be in excess of the constraints set by the sampling and quantizing parameters of the machine, so it is essentially transparent.

As Fig. 4.16 shows, the delay is actually slightly longer than one line, and an analog switch allows the delay to be bypassed briefly, so that part of the sync pulse is replaced by the burst from the end of the line which has been

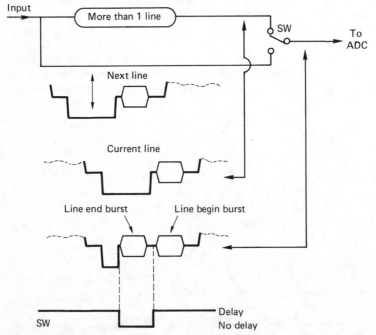

Figure 4.16 Using a delay of a little over one line, it is possible to switch the delay out momentarily so that the current burst and the next burst appear side by side. Both are digitized to compute the velocity error over the line

advanced by omitting the delay. This signal is fed to the ADC, which makes it available to the memory and to the sampling clock control circuits.

The effect of sampling the burst with a four times subcarrier clock is to produce a repeating set of four sample values which reveal the phase relationship between the clock and the burst in rectangular coordinates. In practice there will be noise on the burst, but by adding together the sets of sample values from several cycles, and dividing by the number of cycles acquired, a noise-free determination of the coordinates can be made. The actual phase relationship can be expressed in angular terms by some trigonometrical calculations. By successively processing the two bursts coming from the analog switch, it is possible to compute the current phase error in the sampling clock, i.e. the amount by which the clock phase needs to be changed to sample correctly the beginning of the line and to compute what the phase error will be when the end of the line is reached. In order to get into lock, it is necessary to know the approximate clock frequency needed. This is obtained by timing the period between horizontal sync pulses. The sampling clock is obtained from a digital frequency synthesizer, which is essentially the digital equivalent of a voltage-controlled oscillator, but which has no drift or tolerance mechanisms and thus needs no initial or periodic adjustments. The equivalent of the VCO control voltage is the digital burst phase errors.

There is very little time between the end of the second burst and the start of the active line, and so the digital burst phase filters and phase measuring circuitry must work very fast indeed.

When the speed of the tape is varied, the line period will also vary, and the length of the delay must be adjusted to suit. This is achieved automatically by clocking the CCD delay from the digital synthesizer. If the tape speed were to increase, the first sign of this would be that the advanced (undelayed) burst would have a phase lead relative to the sampling clock, whereas the delayed burst would not. This would cause the synthesizer to speed up the clock to cancel the phase lead over the line. The raised clock frequency would then make the delay period correct for the next line and so on. In this way the sampling clock tracks offtape subcarrier over the speed range where colour is provided. As with all phase-locked loops, the damping has to be critically set to the best compromise between jitter and speed of response. In a sampled system, the response cannot exceed half the line rate, and so the synthesizer is damped so that it cannot produce frequency changes more rapidly than that during sampling of the active line.

An advantage of this method of clock generation is that the ADC is contained within the loop, because it is the digital samples which are used to control the clock. Phase errors due to drift in the converter or component tolerances are thus eliminated, along with corresponding adjustments.

4.7 Starting in the right place

Some time has been spent describing the control of the write clock frequency and phase, but it is just as important to ensure that sampling commences in a consistent place on each line of each frame. Clearly the position of the first sample in a line must be on one cycle or another of the sampling clock. The edge of the picture is, however, defined by the sync pulse leading edge, and the TBC has to resolve the conflict of sampling at a fixed relationship to H-sync in order to keep the edge of the picture straight with the need to sample at a multiple of subcarrier. In NTSC this is relatively easy, owing to the simple relationship between subcarrier and sync, but in the PAL system it becomes an exceedingly difficult task because of the complex relationship of subcarrier and sync. It is vital to understand the structure of composite video systems in some detail if the intricacies of C-format TBCs are to be appreciated, and a brief description is included here.

In NTSC the subcarrier frequency is an odd multiple of half line rate, so that there will be two different types of line: those which begin with the subcarrier in phase, and those which begin with the subcarrier out of phase. Since two will not divide into 525, there will be two types of frame where the subcarrier in one is inverted with respect to that in the other. If a horizontally triggered oscilloscope is used to examine NTSC burst, the normal and inverted phases can be seen. There will be two different relationships between horizontal sync and a positive burst crossing. The position of the first sample on the line is determined by the circuit of Fig. 4.17.

A sync stripper detects the 50% point of horizontal sync and triggers a fixed delay and a short variable delay in series. The end of these delays will coincide with the approximate centre of the burst. The incoming burst is turned into a square wave by slicing around the midpoint. Since there are

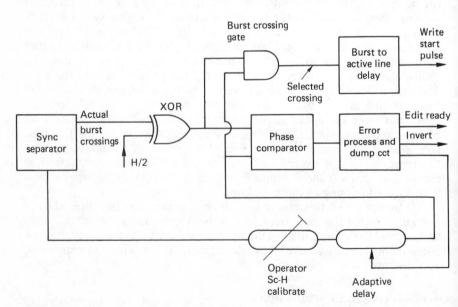

Figure 4.17 NTSC Write Start generator compensates for line by line burst inversion using XOR gate, and consistently select the same burst crossing on every line. Phase error corrects adaptive delay to minimize prediction error

two relationships of burst crossing to horizontal, the burst is simply inverted on alternate lines. The first selectively inverted burst crossing after the end of the delay period becomes the basis for the start of sampling. It is only necessary to count a fixed number of cycles of write clock from that point to determine when the first sample should be stored. The end of the delay from horizontal sync should be exactly half-way between burst crossings to give maximum immunity to offtape jitter, and for a given delay period this will only be true for one value of ScH (subcarrier to horizontal) phase. A phase comparator measures the relationship between the end of the delay and the burst crossings, and drives an indicator. The operator can then adjust the variable delay to calibrate the TBC for the ScH phase of the tape being played. In some machines the phase error adjusts the delay directly.

In PAL, the eight-field sequence comes about because of the quarter cycle offset of subcarrier against line rate. There are 283¾ cycles of subcarrier in one line, which means that four lines must pass before the same relationship occurs between subcarrier and H-sync. The odd number of lines in a frame necessary for interlace mean that four frames must

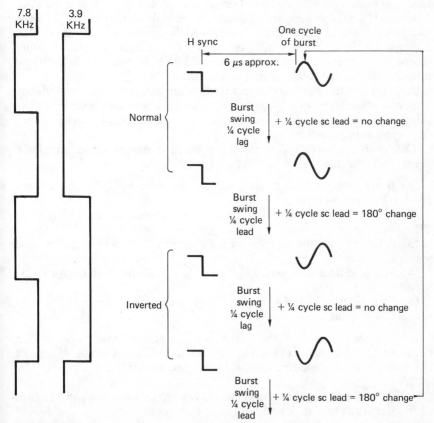

Figure 4.18 Quarter-cycle subcarrier/H relationship and burst swing combine to give four-line sequence

elapse before the four-line sequence assumes the same relationship with vertical. Unlike NTSC which has a half cycle offset, PAL does not naturally have good cancellation of subcarrier on the screen. This is achieved by the addition of 25 Hz to the subcarrier frequency, which causes the subcarrier on a given line to be antiphase with the subcarrier on the line in the next field which will be physically adjacent on the interlaced display. Although this 25 Hz component achieves its goal, it also drives TBC designers to distraction because instead of having four different relationships of subcarrier to horizontal there are now 2500!

Since the TBC will use offtape burst crossings to generate both write clock and the start pulse, it is necessary to follow what the burst does with respect to horizontal. Owing to the quarter cycle offset, the subcarrier phase advances by 90° from line to line, but the burst swings forward 90° on one line and back 90° on the next to convey the state of V-switch. This means that the burst swing will alternately cancel or double the subcarrier phase advance, giving two lines with the same burst to sync relationship followed by two lines with an inverted burst to sync relationship. Fig. 4.18 shows that these four lines repeat at 3.9 kHz and contain two complete cycles of V-switch which runs at 7.8 kHz. It is absolutely vital that these four types of line are never mixed up, and to ensure that this is so all PAL TBCs have a memory capacity which is a multiple of four lines. The least significant 2 bits of the memory address are then automatically identical to 7.8 and 3.9 kHz. Where a TBC contains a frame store to permit picture freeze this approach is not possible, and a 2 bit line-type tag will be added to every line as it enters the memory instead.

The effect of the 25 Hz component is that the subcarrier moves along the line towards sync by one cycle every frame. The absolute position of the subcarrier cannot be determined because it depends on the ScH phase of the tape being played back.

The problems involved in tracking burst crossings are summarized below, prior to the somewhat involved solutions.

(1) Burst swing causes burst crossings to move by 112 ns relative to H-sync between line pairs.

(2) 25 Hz offset causes burst crossings to advance towards H-sync by 225 ns per frame.

(3) Absolute position of burst crossing depends on ScH phase of tape which can drift.

(4) Absolute time from sync to burst crossing will vary with head-to-tape speed.

(5) Four-field edits will cause the burst crossings to jump 112 ns with respect to H-sync.

In the presence of all of the above mechanisms, the TBC must select a consistent burst crossing in each line of the eight-field sequence. If it picks the wrong crossing, the line involved will appear displaced horizontally by ±225 ns.

Fig. 4.19 shows that the solution to these problems lies in a combination of feedforward, feedback and human intervention.

The position of a burst crossing on a given line will be predicted, and the next actual crossing will be used to generate the start pulse. In addition, the

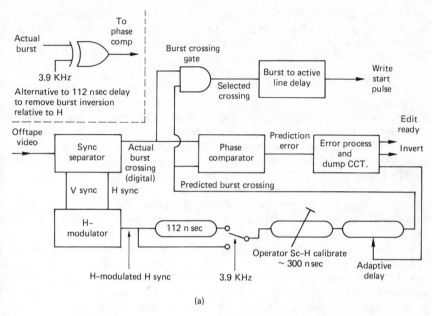

(a)

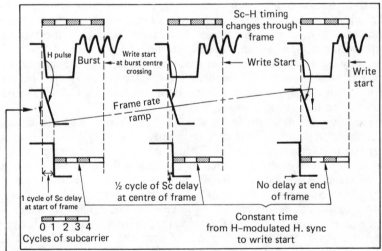

Frame rate ramp at normal speed.
In still field, it will be field rate ramp.
In slow motion, a combination of both.

(b)

Figure 4.19 (a) Write Start Pulse generator resolves conflict between subcarrier and H-syne. Burst inversion is removed by XOR gate (shown inset) or compensated by switched 112 nsec delay. H modulator (shown detailed in (b)) removes effect of 25 Hz subcarrier component. (b) Since the 25 Hz component of subcarrier causes burst centre crossings to advance towards H-sync at one cycle per frame, the write start point has to jump one cycle every frame to keep the horizontal position of the picture constant. The use of H-modulation converts the steady phase advance to a once-per-frame step of one cycle, which takes place during vertical blanking. The write start point will now be unambiguous through the frame. Note that burst inversion is neglected in the diagram

accuracy of the prediction is measured and used to correct the prediction for following lines. By displaying the accuracy of the prediction, an operator can adjust the centre point of the system so that maximum ScH drift and offtape jitter can be tolerated.

In the figure, H-sync is separated from the offtape video and is made to follow the 25 Hz component of subcarrier by subjecting it to a delay which is modulated by the position of the line in the frame. Incoming H-pulses are fed to an integrator which gives the leading edge a rise time of 225 ns or one cycle of subcarrier. A second integrator produces a sawtooth of the same amplitude, but whose period is one frame. A comparator changes state when the H-rate ramp crosses the frame-rate ramp. The effect is to delay H-sync pulses by 225 ns at the beginning of a frame, falling to zero delay at the end of the frame. The four line sequences now have a stable relationship to the H-modulated sync. If the head jumps, the frame-rate ramp will have to jump in sympathy with it, in order to keep the H-modulator working properly.

In order to target a particular burst crossing, the H-modulated sync pulse is delayed by the time between sync and the centre of the burst. This delay is affected by four factors. First, the head-to-tape speed programs the delay so that it still finds the centre of the burst when the line period changes in variable-speed operation. Secondly, a delay of 112 ns is switched in and out at 3.9 kHz to follow the burst inversion every pair of lines. Thirdly, an operator adjustment changes the delay over a range of about one cycle to calibrate the system to the ScH phase of the tape. Fourthly, an adaptive delay affects the timing. When correctly set up, the predicted signal will occur exactly half-way between two burst crossings, and the second of those crossings will be used to generate the start pulse. By predicting exactly between crossings, the greatest amount of jitter (±112 ns) can be tolerated before the wrong crossing is chosen.

A phase comparison is made between the prediction and the actual crossings, and the phase error is used to modify the fourth delay in such a way that the prediction gets better. Clearly if the operator increases the delay in the third stage, this feedback mechanism will reduce the delay in the fourth stage. An indicator, usually labelled *edit ready* is illuminated when the phase comparison shows that the prediction is half-way between the burst crossings. The operator simply changes the delay whenever a different tape is to be played until the indicator illuminates. If the indicator is not on, it suggests that in the presence of jitter the TBC could pick the wrong burst crossing on some lines and horizontally tear the picture. If the TBC is properly calibrated, it will only remain in this state if the ScH phase of the tape is constant. If there is any ScH drift, eventually the adaptive delay will find itself changing to centre the prediction between burst crossings. After a whole cycle of drift, the adaptive action would mean that the start pulse would move by 225 ns. If this process were allowed to continue indefinitely, the picture would slowly wind itself off the screen. In practice, the control signal to the adaptive delay is measured, and when it exceeds $\pm$ one cycle of delay, the control signal is clamped back to zero during the vertical interval, which forces the system to pick a burst crossing one cycle away, recentring the prediction system and causing a one-cycle hop in the picture. The process is called *dumping*.

When a four-field edit occurs, the subcarrier will be inverted suddenly, and the prediction will find itself on top of a burst crossing instead of between two. To prevent a ragged picture caused by noise and jitter moving the start pulse between two burst crossings, the system must rapidly recognize the situation and put half a cycle of delay in the prediction. On the next four-field edit it must take out the delay. It thus needs a bistable memory of the system state, and this is sometimes displayed as an indicator labelled *invert*. Because the prediction is moved by half a cycle when invert is on, the TBC is actually edit ready when it is showing invert status.

Using the above mechanisms, samples can be put into memory in a consistent way. Because H-sync was displaced to align it with the subcarrier, the picture in the memory will be slightly rhombic, but this is of no consequence, because identical circuitry, including an H-modulator, is necessary on the read side of the memory to generate a read clock from reference subcarrier and to generate a read start pulse from targeted reference burst crossings. The picture distortion caused by H-modulating the input sync is cancelled by H-modulating output sync.

Fig. 4.12 showed a simple TBC which would only work at normal speed. It is interesting to follow the actions of such a TBC following editing on a tape to be replayed. If a colour-framed edit is made, it will pass the TBC unnoticed. However, if an edit to only four-field accuracy is made (two fields in NTSC), this will result in the subcarrier being inverted relative to H. This cannot be allowed to happen on the output, which must convey an unbroken subcarrier sequence. The only solution is to move the video waveform along the line by 112 ns such that the subcarrier phase will align to reference. As the waveform is composite, this unavoidably causes a shift in the picture content. If an inverting edit accompanies a scene change, the shift will not be noticeable, but if the edit is used to shorten a still scene, it will be most irritating. If a two-field accurate edit is made in PAL, the incoming signal will have the wrong sense of V-switch relative to reference and a quarter cycle phase error. The only solution is to change the TBC delay by one whole line, which corrects the sense of V-switch and the quarter cycle offset simultaneously. Clearly there will be a vertical movement in the picture. Since it is quite difficult in modern equipment to perform a two-field edit, TBCs tend to view a reversal of burst swing with deep suspicion until it has been consistently wrong for several lines. This prevents unnecessary correction taking place if a burst suffers a partial dropout or extreme jitter, but it does mean that when an error takes place the output will have complementary colours until the vertical shift is made. These horizontal and vertical shifts are inherent in a composite system, and a simple TBC can do nothing better.

4.8 Colour processing

When variable speed is used, the C-format recorder cannot change its scanner speed, because this determines field rate. If the tape speed is too low, some tape tracks have to be repeated to maintain field rate, whereas if the tape speed is too high, some tracks need to be skipped. The effect of a head jump is that the subcarrier sequence is randomly broken. A TBC of normal speed only would have to move the picture every which way to attempt to keep the output subcarrier continuous in the presence of these input jumps. The resulting picture would be unwatchable. If variable speed is to be used, or if it is proposed to play non-colour-framed edits without shifts, then it is necessary to decode the discontinuous incoming subcarrier to baseband and re-encode it to continuous reference phase. The unit which does this job is called the colour processor. The colour processor can be positioned in a number of places. It can go before the memory, as in most Ampex TBCs, or after the memory as in Sony TBCs and the Ampex Zeus.

In conventional TBCs the colour processor is an analog circuit which will separate luminance and chrominance with a simple low-pass filter in the luminance channel and a bandpass filter in the chroma channel. The resulting luminance bandwidth will be noticeably less than usual. In NTSC there are only two line types, and the colour processor simply has to invert the subcarrier selectively before adding it back to the luminance.

In PAL, as usual, the solution is more complex. Chroma is filtered from luminance as before, but the chroma signal will then be decoded to U and V baseband signals. This can only be done if a local subcarrier phased to the suppressed subcarrier of the offtape chroma signal is available. Head jumps in the VTR will cause sudden jumps in the offtape subcarrier phase which the decoder must follow. This is helped by the VTR which sends signals to the TBC telling it what has happened. These signals are also needed by the H-modulator so that it can produce the frame- or field-rate ramps.

In Ampex TBCs the signals describe the direction and magnitude of track jumps, and the TBC computes what must have happened to the subcarrier, whereas in Sony TBCs the VTR computes what must have happened to the subcarrier and sends a signal which tells the TBC how much the four-line sequence has jumped as a result. If the reference line has the opposite V-switch sense to the input line, the baseband V signal will be inverted before both are fed to a chroma encoder running from reference subcarrier. If the colour processor comes after the memory this reference subcarrier is easily obtained. If the colour processor comes before the memory the reference subcarrier is not quite what is needed. The encoder requires a subcarrier which will be the same as reference *after* the memory delay. This is provided by using the two least significant bits of the memory write line address (7.8 and 3.9 kHz) to drive a phase shifter which runs from the write clock divided by four. This provides an encoder subcarrier which has the correct relationship to H-sync for the type of line which is currently being sampled. The reduction in luminance bandwidth is unfortunate, but it is paralleled in the vertical direction because if a single-track jump is performed by the VTR head, the playback will be out of interlace. The half-line timing shift of an odd field relative to an even field will be automatically taken care of, since the TBC write circuits will wait until a sync pulse and a burst herald a new line. In some TBCs no further action is taken except to colour-process the wrong field to give it the correct subcarrier phase, and to pretend it is the right field. When a single-track jump takes place, this results in small vertical picture shifts known as the hops. Some VTRs such as the VPR-3 have the ability to delay track jumps until sufficient head deflection has built up to permit a two-track jump. The picture will thus never be out of interlace, but if there are moving objects in the picture, the two-track jump can sometimes be perceived to cause sudden changes in their position, a phenomenon known as the jerks. A third alternative is to interpolate between available line samples to form a synthetic intermediate line when the VTR is out of interlace. This can cause a reduction in vertical resolution (known as the fuzzies) which comes and goes as the playback goes in and out of interlace. There was until recently no alternative to the hops, the jerks or the fuzzies, but this changed with the advent of the Ampex Zeus which must be the definitive C-format TBC. As has been described, in the Zeus velocity compensation is performed by swinging the write clock phase so that all samples are made with consistent phasing relative to subcarrier despite changes in head-to-tape speed. It is now possible to use an entirely digital colour processor.

4.9 Colour processing in Zeus

The separation of luminance and chrominance in the digital domain need not entail any sacrifice in luminance bandwidth, because a comb filter can be used. The one-line delays needed, which would be a nuisance in analog form, are conveniently achieved using RAM. Only when vertical colour changes cause the comb to fail to mesh will the system resort to a lower quality of Y/C separation from a digital bandpass filter. The digital chroma is then rephased to reference before being added to the digital luminance signal. The colour processor thus has a performance which is determined only by the composite video system. The problem of what to do when the VTR is out of interlace is solved by a sophisticated vertical interpolator.

The digital colour processor of a PAL Zeus will now be described, beginning with the functions it has to perform, which result from the structure of the PAL signal. As has been explained, the quarter cycle offset of PAL subcarrier results in four different line types. The task of the colour processor is to take one of the four line types from the input field and make it into the necessary line type for the field being output. The presence of the V-switch on alternate lines which gave PAL its name complicates this process.

Fig. 4.20(a) shows that, from line to line, the phase of U advances 90° as a result of the quarter cycle offset, and the phase of V alternately leads and lags U. Fig. 4.20(b) shows that if chroma is sampled on the U and V axes the result of these two effects is that, from one line to the next, the chroma samples represent different sequences of U and V. The shift to the right of the U sample due to the quarter cycle offset can be seen. It is not immediately obvious how one line of chroma could be made into another with this approach.

The solution adopted in the Zeus, and in D-2, is to sample at 45° to the U and V axes, i.e. in phase with the burst. Fig. 4.20(c) shows that, when this is done, the samples represent $U \times \cos 45 + V \times \cos 45$ etc. If everything is normalized by dividing by $\cos 45$, the samples become $U+V$, $-U+V$, etc.

If it is required to convert a line into the next line type, having the

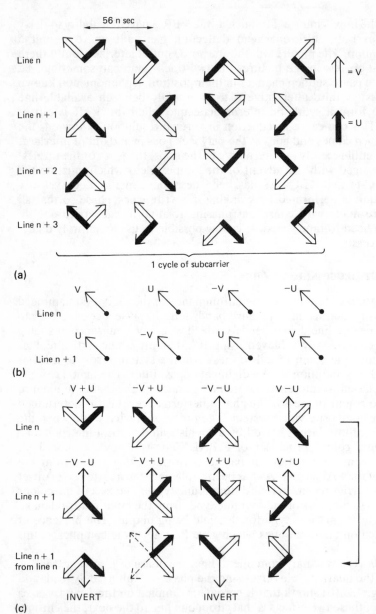

56 n sec

Line n

Line n + 1

Line n + 2

Line n + 3

= V

= U

1 cycle of subcarrier

(a)

Line n

Line n + 1

(b)

Line n

Line n + 1

Line n + 1
from line n

INVERT   INVERT

(c)

Figure 4.20 (a) The combined effects of V-switch quarter-cycle offset in PAL cause the above relative phases of U and V from line to line, in a four line sequence which only repeats after four frames. (b) If a sampling system takes samples on the U and V axes, it results in the samples having the values shown here. It is not then possible to convert from one line type to the next because, for example, V cannot be processed to become U and so on. (c) If sampling is performed with sample phase between U and V axes (thin arrow) the samples represent sums and differences of the two signals (cosine term neglected). It will be seen that line n can be made into line n + 1 by inverting the samples when U and V have the same sign. When the sample is made, phase information is lost and only amplitude is known. For this reason, the non-inverted samples phase mirror (dotted arrow) because the phase is determined in the context of adjacent samples

opposite sense of V-switch, this can be done by inverting the samples where U and V have different polarities, but not where they have the same polarity.

If the difference is two lines, the only requirement is to invert the whole chroma waveform, as V-switch is the same after two lines, and there have been two quarter cycle offsets of subcarrier making 180°. This selective chroma inversion will be the only processing necessary in NTSC.

If the difference is three lines, an inversion combined with V-switch reversal is needed, and this can simply be done by inverting samples where U and V have the same polarity and not where the polarity is different.

As Zeus has a frame store, the memory line address does not specify the line type, so a line-type parameter is entered into the memory, along with the offtape video samples for the line, and is available when the line is read out. The required line type is available by decoding the ScH phase of the station reference input, and by comparing the two line types the conversion to be performed by the colour processor can be determined. The chroma must be separated from the luminance signal before the colour processor can operate, and this is done by a digital filter. A combination of chroma band-pass and comb filtering is used. The comb filter gives good separation of sidebands, but fails when there are vertical chroma phase changes in the picture. The chroma phases at the beginning, centre and end of the delays are monitored by a correlator, and when the comb filter fails to mesh, the bandpass signal alone is used. The filtered chroma signal is then subtracted from the composite signal to give digital luminance. Once chroma and luminance are separated, a digital chroma gain control can be incorporated simply by passing the chroma samples through a multiplier.

Owing to the use of interlace, the head jumps may result in an odd field being played when an even field is needed, and vice versa. The vertical picture movement which results from outputting the wrong field can be completely removed by vertical interpolation.

The output raster and the input raster are shifted slightly so that neither input field aligns with either output field. By using memory to produce three delays of one line each, samples representing four points in a vertical line on the input field are simultaneously available to a four-point FIR filter. If the output field is to be the same as the input field, the phase of the interpolator will be such that the sample value for a line ¼ of the way down from an input line will be computed. If the opposite type of field is required, the order of the coefficients to the FIR filter will be reversed such that a line ¾ of the way down from an input line will be computed. Fig. 4.21 illustrates how this process results in the image staying at the same vertical position on the screen irrespective of the relation of input and output fields.[7]

The luminance conveys the subjective resolution, and so the vertical chroma interpolation can be done with a simpler filter having only one line of delay to give two points.

In this way the output picture in slow motion has the same bandwidth as in colour-framed operation, and there are no other artifacts to show that the picture has been processed. As the colour processing is so transparent, it is possible to use it at normal speed, such that non-colour-framed edits can be played back without jumps.

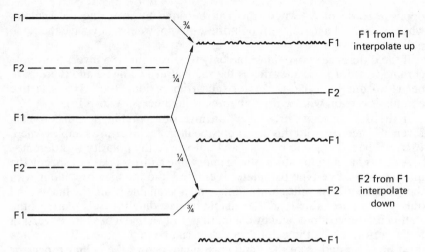

Figure 4.21 Vertical interpolation of either output field from either input field using a half line shift means that output resolution is not changed whether VTR is interlaced or not, and ·vertical movement is eliminated

A word of caution, however: once a tape with non-colour-framed edits has been played through a conventional TBC, the edits are forced to be colour framed by shifting the picture. If a master tape with non-framed edits is dubbed through a conventional TBC and the copy played on a Zeus, the edits will still hop whether or not Zeus is in decode mode. It is possible to tell if a tape is an edit master or a dub by watching for ScH meter movement at cuts, especially where there is a shift. If the meter is unchanged when a shift is observed, the tape is probably a dub.

4.10 Memory control

The memories of C-format timebase correctors have been constructed in numerous ways, including RAM and shift registers. Memory addressing falls into two distinct areas, one of which is the control of the sample address within the line, the other being the control of the line address within the memory.

Owing to the high sampling rates of digital video, interleaving is almost always necessary to allow individual devices to operate more slowly. The degree of interleaving will depend upon the speed of the device, the chosen sampling rate and the speed range of the TBC, since at forward shuttle speeds the sampling rate virtually doubles.

Fig. 4.22(a) shows the memory arrangement of the Ampex TBC-2, an early C-format unit. Bipolar shift registers are used with six-way interleaving to support a sampling rate of $3 \times F_{sc}$. The Sony BVT-2000P, a contemporary of the TBC-2, uses 256 word RAMs with a factor of eight rate reduction to allow a sampling rate of $4 \times F_{sc}$ to be used. Individual devices will be working at the same speed in these two machines.

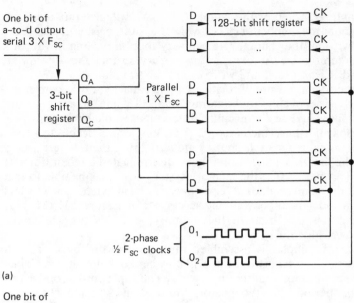

One bit of
a-to-d output
serial 3 × F_{SC}

(a)

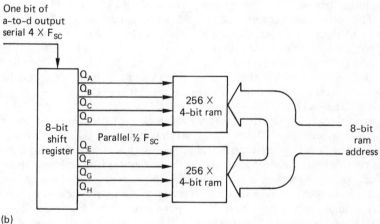

One bit of
a-to-d output
serial 4 × F_{SC}

(b)

Figure 4.22 (a) Shift register memory of Ampex TBC-2 was 3 to 1 bit rate reduction in shift register and further 2 to 1 reduction by interleaving dual register with two phase clock. (b) RAM memory of Sony BVT-2000 uses one stage 8 to 1 bit rate reduction. 256 location RAMs store bits for a pair of lines – good for storage density, but has a side effect of making the window smaller. Note that a and b are repeated 8 times to store 8 bit A/D output

Since memory devices always have a capacity which is some power of two, interleaving has been used to choose the number of samples stored in a line without unnecessarily complex addressing methods or a waste of memory capacity. For example, the six 128 bit shift registers of Fig. 4.22(a) store 1 bit from a total of 768 samples in one line. At $3 \times F_{sc}$ in PAL this allows a stored period of $768 \times 75\,\text{ns} = 57.6\,\text{ns}$. Clearly a $4 \times F_{sc}$ device will require 1024 samples to store the same period. The full line period is not necessary, since only active line need be stored.

A counter is needed to control both RAM and shift-register storage. In both cases, the counter is enabled by the start pulse at the beginning of active line and is clocked by the sampling clock. It will generate the RAM address or count the number of clocks which the shift register needs. When memory is written, the counter rate can vary, but on reading it will come from stable references. A selector is necessary so that the appropriate clock is used. Clearly read and write cannot be simultaneous.

When memory chips were of relatively small capacity, it was convenient to assign a given set of chips to the storage of one TV line. At any one time, one set of chips would be writing and a different set would be reading. Now that chip capacities have increased, it is no longer practicable to have a separate set of chips for each line. In modern TBCs there is just a large RAM and the individual lines can only be discriminated by their different addresses. This means that the memory system now must be able to read and write at the same time, or at least appear to be able to do so. The high rate of digital video is still beyond the access rate of economic RAM chips, so interleaving is still used in the memory, but this time to enable simultaneous read/write.

A number of samples is assembled into a *superword* by a serial to parallel register. The superword rate will now be the sampling rate divided by the number of samples in the superword. The superword period is now divided into a period when the memory can read and a period when it can write. The switching between read and write functions involves both address and data multiplexers, and arbitration. In general, the memory timing will be locked to stable reference clocks, and when the memory is being read the write process is locked out. A small buffer silo is installed before the memory which allows the write process to be interrupted by reading and accommodates the difference betwen stable read clocks and unstable write clocks.

For variable-speed operation, the write clock rate will vary. At lower than normal speeds, the data rate falls, so that not every write period will be used. Clearly at higher than normal speeds this approach cannot be used. The solution is then to subdivide the superword period into three time slots, one for reading and two for writing if necessary. Thus at low rates the silo may not have a superword ready when a write period occurs, whereas at high rates it may have two superwords ready. Fig. 4.23 shows the general arrangement of an arbitrating RAM and shows the input silo. In some machines, such as the Ampex TBC-6, the silo performs timebase correction to the nearest superword, whereas in the Zeus the silo has a four-line capacity and corrects to the nearest line, leaving the main memory to correct timing in integer line steps.

4.11 Memory line addressing

The functions of the memory line addressing system can be summarized as follows:

(1) Updates write line address at offtape H-rate and read line address at reference H-rate.

(2) Ensures that the two line types of NTSC or the four line types of PAL are never interchanged.

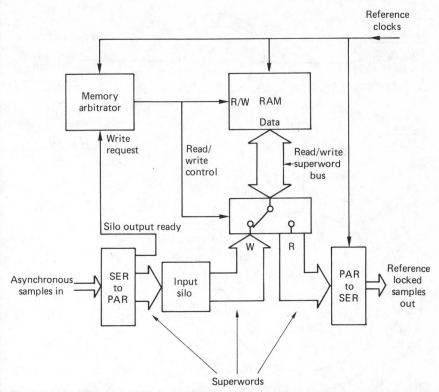

Figure 4.23 In a RAM-based TBC, the RAM is reference synchronous, and an arbitrator decides when it will read and when it will write. During reading, asynchronous input data backs up in the input silo, asserting a write request to the arbitrator. Arbitrator will then cause a Write Cycle between Read Cycles

(3) Ensures that the first line of an offtape field becomes the first line of a reference field irrespective of the time difference between these events. This is known as *vertical locking*.

(4) Caters for additional modes of the VTR, such as confidence replay and E-E (electronics-to-electronics mode, bypassing record and play heads).

Fig. 4.24 shows that the memory address continually overflows from the highest to the lowest, giving the memory the structure of a ring. In PAL machines, there will always be a multiple of four lines in the memory, so that the 3.9 and 7.8 kHz sequences are unbroken at the overflow, and the least significant 2 bits of the line address then convey the state of these two signals. At normal speed, when playback is colour framed, the correct sequence will be obtained in some machines by resetting these bits whenever a colour frame pulse is seen in the control track, which will be once every four frames. In NTSC there are only two line types, and correct operation can be obtained by resetting the LSB of the line address when a colour frame flag is seen every two fields. Under these conditions the read and write addresses will remain opposite one another in the ring memory unless a 'gyroscopic' error is encountered.

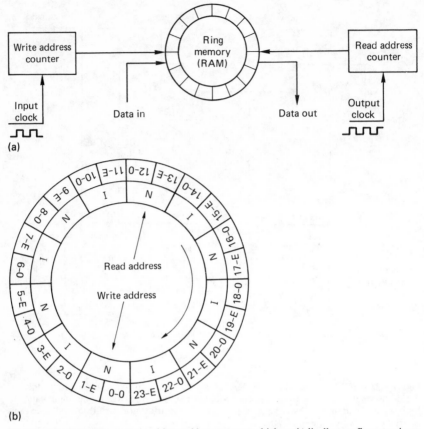

Figure 4.24 (a) TBC memory is addressed by a counter which periodically overflows to give a Ring Structure. Memory allows read side to be non-synchronous with write side. (b) Ring memory structure of 24 line TBC. Note the subdivision into 4 line blocks in order to cater for the PAL 4 line sequence. N = Normal Burst. I = Inverted Burst (3.9 KHz). O/E = odd/Even V switch (7.8 KHz)

At varying speeds, track jumps will break the line sequence, but fortunately it is possible to compute the discontinuity from the number of tracks jumped.

As has been explained, the read address and write address increment at different rates in varispeed. To quantify this phenomenon, it is necessary to return to the tape format itself. Fig. 4.25 shows a view across a PAL C-format tape. Owing to the horizontal alignment condition, a line perpendicular to the tracks will intersect precisely 85 tracks at points which are successively 3.5 lines further along. In NTSC the shift is only 2.5 lines, and there are approximately 100 tracks across the tape.

In both cases, upward movement of the track-following head is the equivalent of an advance, and downward movement the equivalent of a delay, relative to scanner phase. When the tape is moving at a steady but non-normal speed, the head must follow a ramp to stay on track, which causes a steady growth in timing error, until a jump causes a step timing

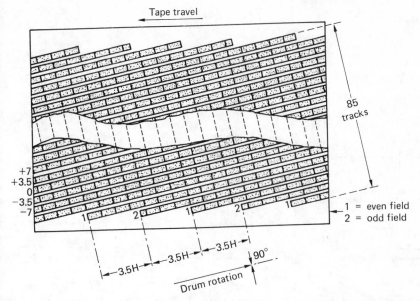

Figure 4.25 PAL C-format tape has 85 parallel tracks at any one perpendicular, with a 3.5 H timing shift between each. The 0.5 H term cancels the effect of interlace and H pulses in all tracks are aligned. The timing error in variable speed will be obtained by multiplying the head deflection (in tracks) by 3.5 H. Eg. +½ track deflection = 1.75 H advance

shift. Clearly the step timing shifts caused by jumps must be exactly equal and opposite to the gradual timing changes due to deflection of the head.

Some examples will now be given. At just below normal speed, the head will occasionally have to make a reverse jump in order to repeat a field. This has the effect of suddenly advancing replay timing by 3.5 or 2.5 lines. Over the subsequent fields, the timing error will slowly drift back until another jump takes place. Conversely, at just above normal speed, the occasionally skipped field will cause a sudden 3.5 or 2.5 line delay, which will slowly advance again. In both cases the timing errors stay within 3.5 or 2.5 lines, giving an indication of the amount of memory that a TBC might need to perform that function and, incidentally, illustrating that to obtain the same speed range, a PAL TBC needs a larger memory than an NTSC machine.

At a speed of +3×, the VTR plays back every third field by performing a two-track jump at every revolution of the scanner. The head ramps up the scanner axis as the track is followed, causing a steady rate of timing advance, and jumps down, giving a step delay of seven lines (PAL) or five lines (NTSC). Fig. 4.26 shows the overall timing sequence in a PAL machine, including the delay of the TBC. The field begins 3.5 lines late, but finishes 3.5 lines early. As the field proceeds, the write address gets closer to the read address, but during the vertical interval the write address stops incrementing for a longer period as a result of the time compression of the field, allowing the read address to move away again. Ideally, the read and write addresses will be at their maximum separation half-way

128

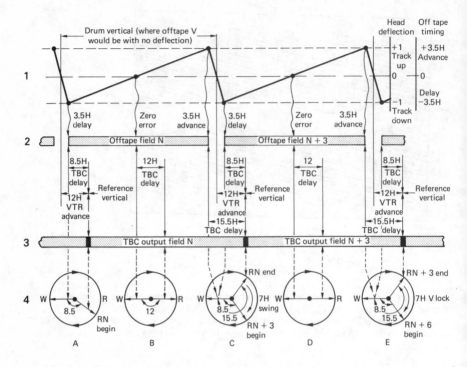

Figure 4.26 Composite timing diagram for v.t.r. and t.b.c. running at +3× speed. t.b.c. has 24 line memory, requiring 12-line v.t.r. advance. Line 1 shows both head deflection and the effect on office-tape timing, since these are directly related. At 3×, the v.t.r. head performs a two-track jump every drum revolution, playing every third field. Line 2 shows the time compression of the offtape fields owing to the raised head/tape speed. Line 3 shows the t.b.c. output which has restored the fields to reference timing. Line 4 shows the relative address relationships in the t.b.c. at different times A, B, C, D and E. It does not show absolute addresses. Example A, At the beginning of a field, head is deflected 1 track down, and offtape timing is 3½H behind drum timing (lines 1 and 2). Since reference is 12 lines behind drum timing, the t.b.c. requires a delay of 12 − 3½ = 8½ lines, and line 4 shows the memory read address 8½ lines behind the write address. Example B, Midfield, with no head deflection or timing error the t.b.c. delay of 12 lines matches the drum advance. Example C, End of field N, head deflected 1 track up, offtape timing if 3½H ahead of drum timing (lines 1 and 2) t.b.c. requires a delay as 12 + 3½ = 15½ lines. During the field, the raised head/tape speed has caused the write address to swing from an 8½ line advance to a 15½ line advance. At the end of the field, the write address stops advancing, and the head jumps to find field N + 3. However, Read address keeps advancing as t.b.c. completes the output field. When 7 lines have been output, Read address will be at RN + 3, coincident with the start of offtape field N + 3, thus the new field is commenced with the same address relationship as example A. The Write Address begins to advance again, and the first write address of the new field is stored in the V-lock memory. 8½ lines later, the read address will have advanced to where the first line was stored, coincident with reference vertical, and coincidence is ensured because the read address will be jammed to the write address in the V-lock memory. Example D is as for B, and E is as for C. Note that this example has assumed optimum timing. In real life, there would be an uncertainty of 3½H in the offtape timing, owing to the random tape/drum phase with an unlocked capstan. Note also that the format dropout has been neglected for simplicity

through the field, when head deflection is zero and the TBC delay is equal to the VTR advance.

In these examples, there has always been sufficient memory in the TBC to allow the write timing to lead and lag the nominal advance. It is usually only necessary to guarantee this condition over the full field variable-speed range of the VTR, generally $-1\times$ to $+3\times$. Beyond this range, the track-following head may need to jump during the field, and the picture will not be of broadcast quality. A picture will still be necessary in order to locate edit points, for example. At these higher speeds, the memory may not be large enough to accommodate the swings in write timing, as they will be bigger than the correction window. At high forward speeds the write address catches up with the slower read address before the end of the field, causing an effect known as a *write overload*. In fast reverse, the read address catches up the slower write address, causing a *read overload*.

These overloads are handled with varying degrees of sophistication. The simplest approach is to blank the video output until the addresses have passed one another. This causes horizontal black bars in the picture and vertical shifts below each bar. In fast forward the write address passes the read address, and thus overwrites lines which have not been read. A number of lines equal to the memory capacity are omitted from the picture, and lines lower down move up to fill the space. In fast reverse the same number of lines will be repeated instead of omitted.

A more satisfactory approach is to cross-couple the address generators so that they each know if they are about to increment to a line address which will cause an overload. In that case the increment cannot be performed. Clearly it is not acceptable simply to hold the same line address, as this would destroy the line-type sequence. In NTSC the line address can be decremented instead of being incremented, and in PAL three can be subtracted instead of adding one to the line address, so that in both cases the sequence of line types is unbroken.

The effect of this kind of overload handling is that in fast forward the write address occasionally steps back instead of forward, overwriting previous lines and causing a small vertical contraction in the picture. Read overloads cause the read address to step back, resulting in small areas being read twice and causing a vertical expansion. These small vertical effects are much more acceptable than the severe shifts and black bars of the simple system.

The Sony BVT-2000 PAL TBC had an interesting form of overload handling at lower shuttle speeds. If an overload occurred, the address did not step back three, but only one, causing a two-line error in the line-type sequence and making the chroma in the subsequent lines inverted. In this machine the colour processor was after the memory, and so it could be made to correct the chroma inversion due to the overload. The vertical disturbances were then only two lines instead of four.

4.12 Vertical locking

The apparently simple goal of ensuring that the top of the field appears at the top of the picture can be complicated to achieve in practice.

The operation in colour-framed mode will be considered first. The TBC generates advanced syncs for the VTR to use as a reference, so a colour frame flag will be detected by the VTR colour framer slightly ahead of the same event being generated in the reference system of the TBC. The control track of the tape also contains colour frame flags, and in this mode the capstan system acts as a colour frame flag phase comparator, changing the phase of tape motion until flags from tape coincide with advanced reference flags. The tape will be travelling at exactly normal speed. All the TBC has to do is to introduce a delay nominally equal to the advance, to correct small errors. Since the tape playback is colour framed, the colour processor will be bypassed.

Consider a TBC having a 16 line memory. If the write line address is reset to zero at the first line in an offtape colour frame and then allowed to count lines, the next time that the line address of zero will occur at the first line of a frame will be 16 frames later, after the addresses have counted around the ring 625 times in PAL or 525 times in NTSC. Clearly 16 frames after a colour frame is another colour frame. Vertical locking is achieved by resetting the write line address to zero at a colour frame once every 16 frames. On the same colour frame, the read line address is also set to zero, and this is also repeated every 16 frames. In practice, once lock is achieved, these resets simply force the addresses to values to which they have already counted naturally, but the mechanism is vital in order to get into lock the first time.

In this way, a given line type at the top of an offtape field will emerge from a colour-framed timebase corrector as the same line type at the top of an output field.

In variable speed, colour framing is destroyed, and the colour processor must be in circuit. If the colour processor is before the memory, the memory can remain colour framed, because the colour processor will use the memory address to calculate the line type it has to generate, and it can compute the incoming line type from the track-jumping information supplied by the VTR. If the colour processor is after the memory, the memory cannot readily be colour framed, since it has to accept whatever line type comes offtape. In this case the write circuits compute how far out of sequence the line is, and store that along with the samples in the memory. On reading the memory the colour processor can then decide what to do with the chroma. Since the line address no longer carries colour framing information, periodic resetting of the address will no longer work, and a different mechanism is necessary. Fig. 4.27 shows that a latch is provided whose input is the write address. The latch is clocked when offtape vertical is generated at the beginning of a track. A few lines later, reference vertical will occur, and at this point the contents of the latch will be forced into the read address generator, so that it must find the top of the field.

In E-E mode the output timing of the VTR is the same as that of the signal fed to the VTR, with a small delay due to modulating and demodulating. No advance is possible, and as the TBC can only introduce delay, vertical lock cannot be achieved. The closest which the TBC can manage is to delay the output by four lines (PAL) or two lines (NTSC) so the correct line type emerges. The effect is that the picture shifts down the screen slightly.

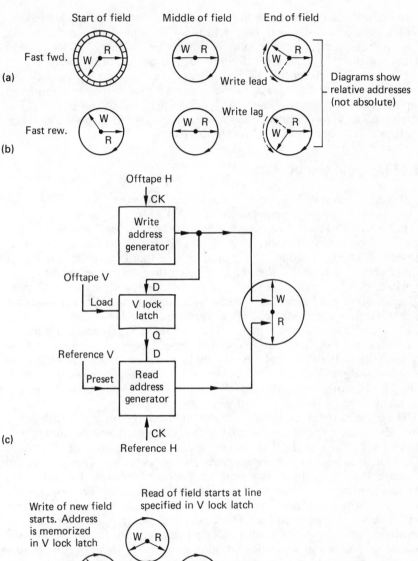

(a) Fast fwd.

Start of field   Middle of field   End of field

Write lead

Write lag

Diagrams show
relative addresses
(not absolute)

(b) Fast rew.

Offtape H

CK

Write
address
generator

Offtape V

Load

V lock
latch

D

Q

W

R

Reference V

Preset

Read
address
generator

D

CK

(c)

Reference H

Write of new field
starts. Address
is memorized
in V lock latch

Read of field starts at line
specified in V lock latch

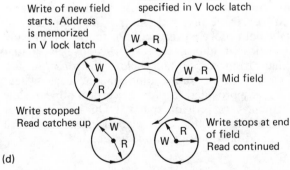

Mid field

Write stopped
Read catches up

Write stops at end
of field
Read continued

(d)

Figure 4.27 Read and write relationship at higher speeds. At high forward speed (a) the write address starts one field delayed and finishes advanced in relation to drum phase. In reverse (b) write address starts advanced. V-lock in (c) remembers write address of first time and (d) shows that, at high speed, write starts late, ending early, close to read. V-lock causes read to find first address of next field

In confidence replay, the replay signal is one-third of a field behind the timing of the record signal, owing to the 120° angle between the heads. Clearly this timing error is beyond the correction window of a TBC, and so it cannot provide a station reference locked output. The solution is to generate a new reference close enough to the confidence replay timing to bring the offtape timing within the window. The output in confidence replay must be monitored using the syncs on the TBC output signal. If it is attempted to view confidence replay on a monitor fed with station syncs, there will be a one-third field roll in the picture.

4.13 Dropout compensation

Although it has nothing to do with timebase correction *per se*, TBCs also incorporate dropout compensation (DOC). Most C-format recorders monitor the RF level on replay and can assert a logic level which is sent to the TBC during a dropout. The dropout compensator, like the colour processor, can be fitted in the digital domain either before the memory or after. The advantage of fitting the DOC after the memory is that the circuit works at constant clock rates irrespective of tape speed, and thus dropout compensation will be available over a wide speed range. The disadvantage is that it is necessary to store the position of dropouts in the memory so that they can be corrected on readout. This is often done by reserving one of the codes in the digital video to specify a dropout. For example, in an 8 bit system, the code FF hex (all ones) might be reserved, and the ADC output is digitally clipped such that it can only produce sample values from 00 to FE. The FF code passes through the memory like a valid sample, but can be recognized by the DOC during memory read.

The principle of all dropout concealment is that signals from nearby lines are substituted to produce a signal which is a reasonable approximation to that which is missing. In PAL this substitution is quite difficult because of the four-line sequence. Samples from the previous line cannot be used because they have the wrong state of V-switch and would give colours complementary to those needed. Samples from two lines away have inverted chroma but the correct sense of V-switch. A digital Y/C separator and inverter can be used to provide inverted chroma video for dropout compensation. If a digital colour processor is used, this function is already available. A more sophisticated alternative to the above is spatial compensation, where data from above and below the dropout are interpolated to give a more accurate substitution. In the Zeus, where vertical interpolation is already provided to prevent vertical hops in slow motion, the additional circuitry to provide spatial DOC is minimal. If dropouts occur in the same line position over several lines, the spatial averaging will be defeated and previous line mode will be used.

4.14 Output processing

Once the dropout compensation, colour processing and vertical interpolation are completed, the chroma and luminance can be recombined in an adder and the functions of the processing amplifier can be undertaken.

These include black clipping, to prevent luminance going blacker than black level, black level and pedestal adjusment, the reinsertion of syncs and burst at the desired ScH phase, and a chroma phase control. In most TBCs, all of these processes are carried out in the analog domain after the DAC, but in Zeus these are all carried out in the digital domain prior to the DAC, with resultant stability and freedom from periodic adjustment. A further advantage of the all-digital approach is that all parameters are set in output ports of a control microprocesor, and this makes remote control very easy. The TBC is controlled from the control panel of the VTR by a serial link to the microprocessor.

4.15 Variable-speed recording

So far the topic has been the reproduction of recordings which were themselves made at normal speed. This section deals with making a C-format recording at the wrong speed. The result of a variable-speed recording must still be a standard C-format tape which contains the normal subcarrier sequence.

Fig. 4.28 shows that in PAL, if successive fields are not recorded, then there are a restricted number of speeds which can be used, such as ⅑

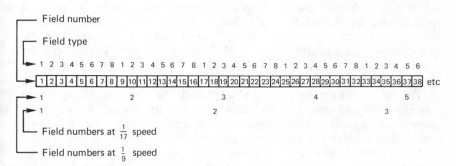

Figure 4.28 To maintain the eight-field sequence, only certain speeds can be used, two examples of which are shown here. The speeds available can be obtained from the expression $1/(8n + 1)$ where n is an integer

and ¹⁄₁₇ of normal, since only these speeds offer the correct field sequence. If any other speeds are required, it will be necessary to adopt one of two approaches. A colour processor can be placed before the recorder to convert the incoming field into the one which the recorder needs next, or an agile composite encoder must be used with a component input. In both cases interlace may not be achieved, and some form of vertical interpolation would be necessary to obtain an interlaced recording.

In the BVH-2500 built by Sony, recording actually takes place with the tape moving at the wrong speed.[8]

The track pattern on the tape cannot be made standard with a fixed record head, and so a deflecting head is necessary. Deflecting the head causes timing errors and means that a small part of the track end cannot be accessed by the record head.

The record head is mounted on a bimorph assembly, and it has to carry its own erase head. The deflection system is unable to read the tape track, because it is recording, so the deflection system can only use mechanical feedback from a deflection sensor on the bimorph. The system relies heavily on feedforward which predicts the slope of the head deflection ramp from the tape speed and the DC level of the ramp from the control track phase.

This allows the record head to trace a standard track. The timing errors due to head deflection must be compensated by installing a timebase corrector before the recording circuits. The TBC is controlled by the same feedforward mechanism which deflects the head, since this is related to the timing error. Thus the error in head-to-tape speed due to recording at the wrong speed is exactly matched by the TBC which produces the video to be recorded at an equally wrong speed. Owing to the constraints of colour framing, recording can only take place at certain speeds as has been described.

4.16 Multigen

Multigen is a method of simply displaying the results of multiple generations of recording using one C-format VTR and a timebase corrector. It has been developed by Ampex and is implemented on the VPR-3/Zeus combination. The VPR-3 has confidence replay and the ability to insert the Zeus after the replay channel, or before the record channel – the so-called preprocess mode.

The process begins by playing a tape which contains colour bars. These are digitized and stored in the Zeus memory. By placing the VPR-3 in preprocess mode, the Zeus memory can then be read to produce an analog video signal which can be recorded again. This recording is then played back into the Zeus which has resumed its normal configuration, only to revert to preprocess mode to make another generation of recording. As a result it is possible in a very short time to display a tenth-generation signal from the Zeus framestore. The results of all the adjustments in the loop are effectively magnified, so that each adjustment can be made more precisely. Other equipment such as switchers can be included in the loop and adjusted to the same degree of precision. Using this system, 23 generations in NTSC and 18 generations in PAL have been reported.[9]

References

1. Basic system and transport geometry parameters for 1-inch 'Type-C' video tape recording. *ANSI* C98-18M (1979)
2. HATHAWAY, R. and RAVIZZA, R., Development of the Ampex auto scan tracking (AST) system. *SMPTE J.*, **89**, 931–934 (1980)
3. SAKAMOTO, H. *et al.*, *US Patent* no. 4,287,538 (Sept. 1981)
4. RAVIZZA, R., *US Patent* no. 4,163,993 (Aug. 1979)

5. KAMATH, B.Y., *US Patent* no. 4,321,619 (Mar. 1982)
6. MORRISON, E.F., Technical advances in type-C picture processing. Presented at 127th SMPTE Technical Conference (Los Angeles, 1985), paper no. 127–128
7. CROLL, M.G., The general design of a digital still storage system for use with an electronic rostrum colour camera. *BBC Res. Dep. Rep.* no. 1980/3
8. FUJIWARA, S., SAKAMOTO, H. and SARAFIAN, S., Delta-T adds new dimension to Type-C recording. Presented at SMPTE Conference (Nov. 1983)
9. SALTER, M., Improved analog video recording. *Broadcast Syst. Eng.*, **13**, no. 8, 72–74 (1987)

Chapter 5
Advanced digital processing

Chapter 3 dealt with the important basics of multiplication, addition and delay, for these are the foundation of all digital filtering. In this chapter, the use of digital filters for oversampling, composite decoding, standards conversion and special effects will be explained.

5.1 Phase linearity

One of the strengths of digital signal processing is that filtering can be performed with stable binary logic instead of the inductors and capacitors needed for analog filters. In analog filtering, the frequency response is usually the most quoted parameter, followed by the phase response and the impulse response. These last two are the most difficult to get right in an analog filter.

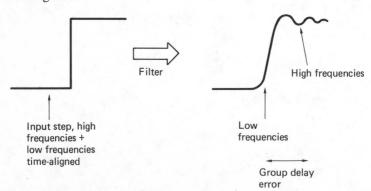

Figure 5.1 Group delay time displaces signals as a function of frequency

Fig. 5.1 shows that impulse response testing tells a great deal about a filter. In a perfect filter, all frequencies should experience the same time delay; this is the group delay. If not, there is a group-delay error. As an impulse contains an infinite spectrum, a filter fed with an impulse will separate the different frequencies in time if it suffers from group-delay error. Group-delay error is particularly unacceptable in video, because it causes the different frequencies in a sharp edge to appear at different places across the screen.

136

A pure delay will cause a phase shift proportional to frequency, and a filter with this characteristic is said to be phase linear. The impulse response of a phase linear filter is symmetrical. If a filter suffers from group delay error it cannot be phase linear. It is almost impossible to make a phase-linear analog filter, and many filters have a group-delay equalization stage following them which is often as complex as the filter itself. In the digital domain it is reasonably straightforward to make a phase-linear filter, and phase equalization becomes unnecessary. Because of the sampled nature of the signal, whatever the response at low frequencies may be, all digital channels act as low-pass filters cutting off at the Nyquist limit, or half the sampling frequency.

5.2 FIR and IIR filters compared

Filters can be described in two main classes, as shown in Fig. 5.2, according to the nature of the impulse response. Finite-impulse response (FIR) filters are always stable and, as their name suggests, respond to an impulse once, as they have only a forward path. In the temporal domain, the time for which the filter responds to an input is finite, fixed and readily established. The same is therefore true about the distance over which an FIR filter responds in the spatial domain.

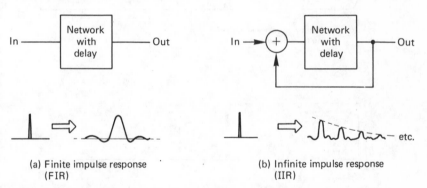

(a) Finite impulse response   (b) Infinite impulse response
     (FIR)   (IIR)

Figure 5.2 A FIR filter (a) responds only to an input, whereas the output of an IIR filter (b) continues indefinitely rather like a decaying echo

Most filters intended for video use fall into this category. Infinite-impulse response (IIR) filters respond to an impulse indefinitely and are not necessarily stable, as they have a return path from the output to the input. For this reason they are also called recursive filters. Digital noise reducers and effects units which generate trails employ recursive filters, and these applications will be treated at the end of this chapter.

5.3 FIR filters

An FIR filter works by graphically constructing the impulse response for every input sample. It is first necessary to establish the correct impulse

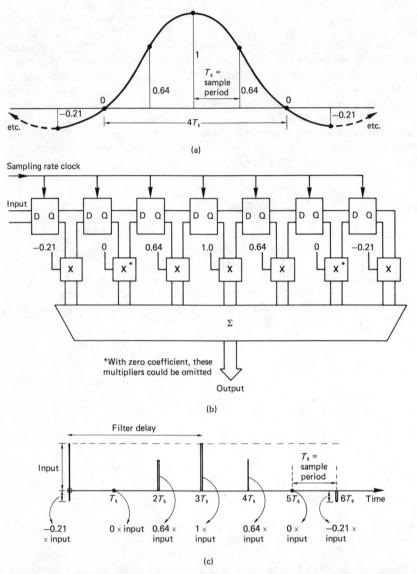

(a)

(b)

(c)

Figure 5.3 (a) The impulse response of an LPF is a $\sin x/x$ curve which stretches from −infinity to +infinity in time. The ends of the response must be neglected, and a delay introduced to make the filter causal. (b) The structure of an FIR LPF. Input samples shift across the register, and at each point are multiplied by different coefficients. (c) When a single unit sample shifts across the circuit of Figure 5.3 (b), the impulse response is created at the output as the impulse is multiplied by each coefficient in turn

response. Fig. 5.3(a) shows an example of a low-pass filter which cuts off at ¼ of the sampling rate. The impulse response of a perfect low-pass filter is a $\sin x/x$ curve, where the time between the two central zero crossings is the reciprocal of the cut-off frequency. According to the mathematics, the waveform has always existed and carries on for ever. The peak value of the output coincides with the input impulse. This means that the filter is not causal, because the output has changed before the input is known. Thus in all practical applications it is necessary to truncate the extreme ends of the impulse response, which causes an aperture effect, and to introduce a time delay in the filter equal to half the duration of the truncated impulse in order to make the filter causal. As an input impulse is shifted through the series of registers in Fig. 5.3(b), the impulse response is created, because at each point it is multiplied by a coefficient as in Fig. 5.3(c). These coefficients are simply the result of sampling and quantizing the desired impulse response. Clearly the sampling rate used to sample the impulse must be the same as the sampling rate for which the filter is being designed. In practice the coefficients are calculated, rather than attempting to sample an actual impulse response, although this would be possible if a particular analog filter had to be duplicated in the digital domain. The coefficient wordlength will be a compromise between cost and performance. Because the input sample shifts across the system to create the shape of the impulse response, the configuration is also known as a transversal filter. In operation with real sample streams, there will be several consecutive sample values in the filter registers at any time in order to convolve the input with the impulse response.

Simply truncating the impulse response causes an abrupt transition from input samples which matter and those which do not. This aperture effect results in a tendency for the response to peak just before the cut-off frequency. This peak is known as Gibb's phenomenon; it causes ripples in both passband and stopband.[1,2] As a result, the length of the impulse which must be considered will depend not only on the frequency response, but also on the amount of ripple which can be tolerated. If the relevant period of the impulse is measured in sample periods, the result will be the number of points needed in the filter.

Fig. 5.4 compares the performance of filters with different numbers of points. A typical digital video FIR filter may need eight points.

Rather than simply truncate the impulse response in time, it is better to make a smooth transition from samples which do not count to those that do. This can be done by multiplying the coefficients in the filter by a window function which peaks in the centre of the impulse. Fig. 5.5 shows some different window functions and their responses. Clearly the

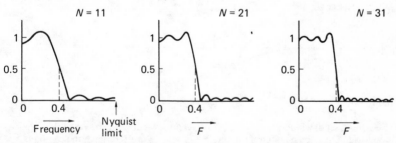

Figure 5.4 The truncation of the impulse in an FIR filter caused by the use of a finite number of points (N) results in ripple in the response. Shown here are three different numbers of points for the same impulse response. The filter is an LPF which rolls off at 0.4 of the fundamental interval (Courtesy *Philips Technical Review*)

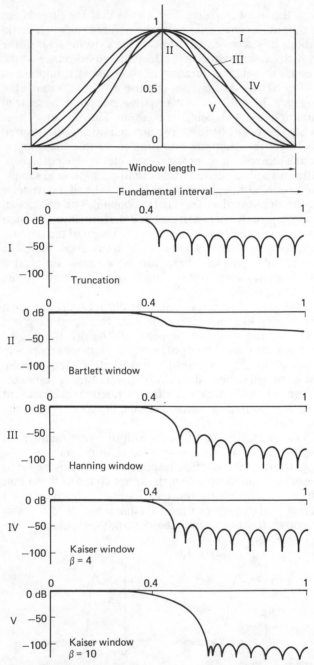

Figure 5.5 The effect of window functions. At top, various window functions are shown in continuous form. Once the number of samples in the window is established, the continuous functions shown here are sampled at the appropriate spacing to obtain window coefficients. These are multiplied by the truncated impulse response coefficients to obtain the actual coefficients used by the filter. The amplitude responses I–V correspond to the window functions illustrated (Responses courtesy *Philips Technical Review*)

rectangular window is the same as truncation, and the response is shown at I. A linear reduction in weight from the centre of the window to the edges characterizes the Bartlett window II, which trades ripple for an increase in transition region width. At III is shown the Hanning window, which is essentially a raised cosine shape. Not shown is the similar Hamming window, which offers a slightly different trade-off between ripple and the width of the main lobe. The Blackman window introduces an extra cosine term into the Hamming window at half the period of the main cosine period, reducing Gibb's phenomenon and ripple level, but increasing the width of the transition region. The Kaiser window is a family of windows based on the Bessel function, allowing various trade-offs between ripple ratio and main lobe width. Two of these are shown in IV and V. The drawback of the Kaiser windows is that they are complex to implement.

Filter coefficients can be optimized by computer simulation. One of the best-known techniques used is the Remez exchange algorithm, which converges on the optimum coefficients after a number of iterations.

In the example of Fig. 5.6, the low-pass filter of Fig. 5.3 is shown with a Bartlett window. Acceptable ripple determines the number of significant

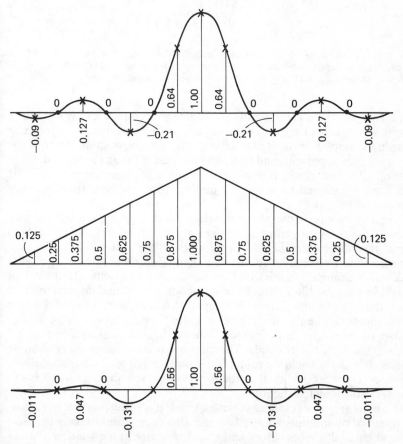

Figure 5.6 A truncated sin x/x impulse (top) is multiplied by a Bartlett window function (centre) to produce the actual coefficients used (bottom)

sample periods embraced by the impulse. This determines in turn both the number of points in the filter and the filter delay. As the impulse is symmetrical, the delay will be half the impulse period. The impulse response is a $\sin x/x$ function, and this has been calculated in the figure. The $\sin x/x$ response is next multiplied by the window function to give the windowed impulse response. If the coefficients are not quantized finely enough, it will be as if they had been calculated inaccurately, and the performance of the filter will be less than expected. Fig. 5.7 shows an example of quantizing coefficients. Conversely, raising the wordlength of the coefficients increases cost.

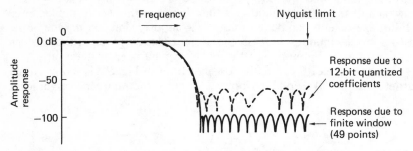

Figure 5.7 Frequency response of a 49-point transversal filter with infinite precision (solid line) shows ripple due to finite window size. Quantizing coefficients to 12 bits reduces attenuation in the stopband (Responses courtesy *Philips Technical Review*)

The FIR structure is inherently phase linear because there is rigid time control as a result of the way samples are shifted through the filter. The individual samples in a digital system do not know in isolation what frequency they represent, and they can only pass through the filter at a rate determined by the clock. Because of this inherent phase linearity, an FIR filter can be designed for a specific impulse response, and the frequency response will follow.

The frequency response of the filter can be changed at will by changing the coefficients. A programmable filter only requires a series of PROMs to supply the coefficients; the address supplied to the PROMs will select the response. The frequency response of a digital filter will also change if the clock rate is changed, so it is often less ambiguous to specify a frequency of interest in a digital filter in terms of a fraction of the fundamental interval rather than in absolute terms. This approach also helps in spatial filters where the fundamental interval is a spatial frequency of one-half the number of pixels per unit distance. The configuration shown in Fig. 5.3 serves to illustrate the principle. The units used on the diagrams are sample periods, but these could be replaced by pixel spacings for a spatial filter. The response is proportional to these periods or spacings, and so it is not necessary to use actual figures.

Where the impulse response is symmetrical, it is often possible to reduce the number of multiplications, because the same product can be used twice, at equal distances before and after the centre of the window. This is known as folding the filter. A folded filter is shown in Fig. 5.8.

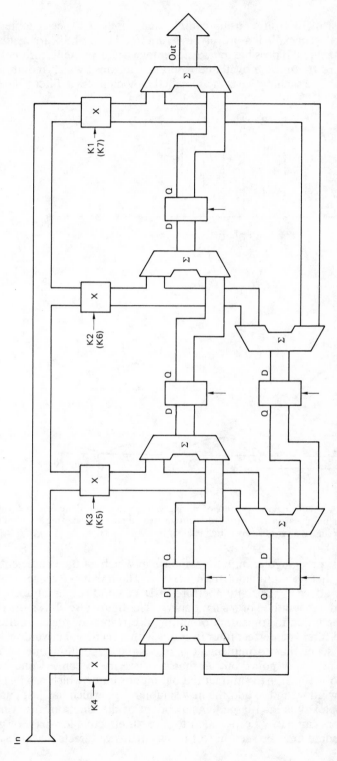

Figure 5.8 A seven-point folded filter for a symmetrical impulse response. In this case K1 and K7 will be identical, and so the input sample can be multiplied by either in one multiplier, and the product fed into the output shift system in two different places. The centre coefficient K4 appears once. In an even-numbered filter the centre coefficient would also be used twice

The cost of FIR filters using complicated impulse shapes is sometimes prohibitive, especially if a prototype is required before LSIs are available. In this case it is still possible to take advantage of the phase linearity of FIR filters by restricting the available responses to those which require little hardware. One such device is the so-called moving-average filter (Fig. 5.9),

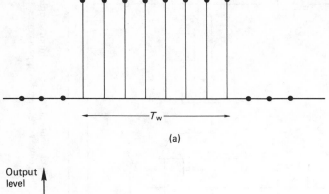

(a)

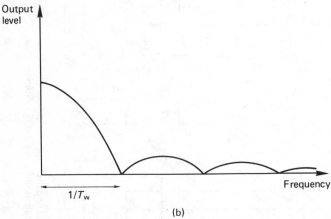

(b)

Figure 5.9 At (a) the impulse response of moving average filter has all coefficients equal to one, so no multipliers are necessary. (b) The frequency response of a moving average filter is the familiar sin x/x curve of an aperture function

which has a rectangular impulse response in which all the coefficients are unity, so that no multipliers are necessary. The moving-average filter has the same effect as the finite aperture in DACs and results in a response which is the magnitude of a sin x/x curve. The figure also shows the origin of the ripple due to truncation of an impulse response, since, in effect, a truncated filter is a perfect filter in series with a rectangular window filter. It might seem that to implement a moving-average filter one adder is required for every point, but all that is necessary to convert one output value into the next is to subtract the old input sample which has just gone past the window and to add the new sample value which has just entered. The complexity is then largely independent of the length of the window. Such filters can easily be cascaded to give an effective low-pass response and can sometimes be seen in soft focus circuits of effects machines.

5.4 The need for sampling-rate conversion

The topic of sampling-rate conversion has become increasingly important as the use of digital video equipment becomes more common. In digital video, the sampling rate takes on many guises. When analog video is sampled in real time, the sampling rate is temporal, but where pixels form a static array, the sampling rate is a spatial frequency. Many of the circumstances in which a change of either kind of sampling rate is necessary are set out here.

(1) Standards converters need to change two of the sampling rates of the video they handle, namely the temporal frame rate and the vertical line spacing, which is in fact a spatial sampling frequency. Standards converters working with composite digital signals will also need to change the sampling rate along the line since it will be a multiple of the appropriate subcarrier frequency.

(2) Different sampling rates exist today for different purposes. Most component digital devices sample at 13.5 MHz, using the 4:2:2 format, but other variations are possible, such as 3:1:1. Component machines sample at a multiple of the subcarrier frequency of their line standard. Rate conversion allows material to be exchanged freely between such formats. For example, the output of a D-1 recorder at 13.5 MHz may be digitally converted to $4 \times F_{sc}$ for use as input to a D-2 recorder.

(3) To take advantage of oversampling converters, an increase in sampling rate is necessary for DACs and a reduction in sampling rate is necessary for ADCs. In oversampling, the factors by which the rates are changed are simpler than in other applications.

(4) In effects machines, the size of the picture will be changed without the pixel spacing being changed. This is exactly the opposite of the standards converter, which leaves the picture size unchanged and changes the pixel spacing.

Sampling-rate conversion can sometimes be effected by returning to the analog domain. A DAC is connected to an ADC. In order to satisfy the requirements of sampling theory, there must be a low-pass filter between the two with response one-half of the lower sampling rate. In reality this is seldom done, because all practical machines have anti-aliasing filters at their analog inputs and anti-image filters at their analog outputs. Connecting one machine to another by the analog sockets therefore includes one unnecessary filter in the chain. Since analog filters are seldom optimal, there will be a degradation caused by rate converting through the analog, particularly in the area of phase response. The increase in noise due to an additional quantizing stage and additional double exposure to clock jitter is not beneficial. Clearly it is only possible to make an analog connection if the line standards are identical. Methods of sampling-rate conversion in the digital domain are necessary and will be described here.

5.5 Categories of rate conversion

There are three basic but related categories of rate conversion, as shown in Fig. 5.10. The most straightforward (a) changes the rate by an integer

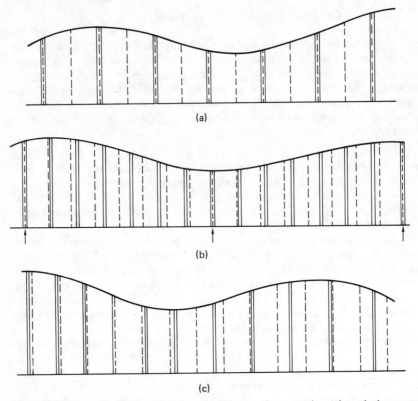

Figure 5.10 Categories of rate conversion. (a) Integer ratio conversion, where the lower-rate samples are always coincident with those of the higher rate. There are a small number of phases needed. (b) Fractional ratio conversion, where sample coincidence is periodic. A larger number of phases is required. Example here is conversion from 50.4 kHz to 44.1 kHz (8/7). (c) Variable ratio conversion, where there is no fixed relationship, and a large number of phases are required

ratio, up or down. The timing of the system is thus simplified because all samples (input and output) are present on edges of the higher-rate sampling clock. Such a system is generally adopted for oversampling converters. In oversampling, the exact sampling rate immediately adjacent to the analog domain is not critical and will be chosen to make the filters easier to implement.

Next in order of difficulty is the category shown at (b) where the rate is changed by the ratio of two small integers. Samples in the input periodically time-align with the output. Such devices can be used for converting from $4 \times F_{sc}$ to $3 \times F_{sc}$, in the vertical processing of standards converters, or between the various rates of CCIR 601.

The most complex rate-conversion category is where there is no simple relationship between input and output sampling rates, and indeed they are allowed to vary. This situation shown at (c) is known as variable-ratio conversion. The time/space relationship of input and output samples is arbitrary, and independent clocks are necessary. This problem will be met in effects machines which zoom or rotate images.

5.6 Integer-ratio conversion

As the technique of integer-ratio conversion is used almost exclusively for oversampling in digital video it will be discussed in that context. Sampling-rate reduction by an integer factor is dealt with first.

Fig. 5.11(a) shows the spectrum of a typical sampled system where the sampling rate is a little more than twice the analog bandwidth. Attempts to reduce the sampling rate by simply omitting samples, a process known as decimation, will result in aliasing, as shown in Fig. 5.11(b). Intuitively it is obvious that omitting samples is the same as if the original sampling rate was lower. In order to prevent aliasing, it is necessary to incorporate low-pass filtering into the system where the cut-off frequency reflects the new, lower, sampling rate. An FIR-type low-pass filter could be installed, as described earlier in this chapter, immediately prior to the stage where samples are omitted, but this would be wasteful, because for much of its time the FIR filter would be calculating sample values which are to be discarded. The more effective method is to combine the low-pass filter with the decimator so that the filter only calculates values to be retained in the output sample stream. Fig. 5.11(c) shows how this is done. The filter

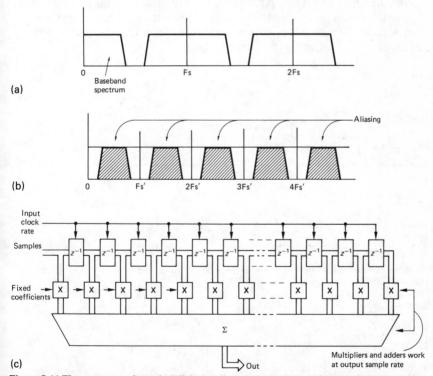

Figure 5.11 The spectrum of a typical digital audio sample stream at (a) will be subject to aliasing as in (b) if the baseband width is not reduced by an LPF. At (c) an FIR low-pass filter prevents aliasing. Samples are clocked transversely across the filter at the input rate, but the filter only computes at the output sample rate. Clearly this will only work if the two are related by an integer factor

makes one accumulation for every output sample, but that accumulation is the result of multiplying all relevant input samples in the filter window by an appropriate coefficient. The number of points in the filter is determined by the number of *input* samples in the period of the filter window, but the number of multiplications per second is obtained by multiplying that figure by the *output* rate. If the filter is not integrated with the decimator, the number of points has to be multiplied by the input rate. The larger the rate-reduction factor the more advantageous the decimating filter ought to be, but this is not quite the case, as the greater the reduction in rate, the longer the filter window will need to be to accommodate the broader impulse response.

When the sampling rate is to be increased by an integer factor, additional samples must be created at even spacing between the existing ones. There is no need for the bandwidth of the input samples to be reduced since, if the original sampling rate was adequate, a higher one must also be adequate.

Fig. 5.12 shows that the process of sampling-rate increase can be thought of in two stages. First the correct rate is achieved by inserting samples of zero value at the correct instant, and then the additional samples are given meaningful values by passing the sample stream through a low-pass filter which cuts off at the Nyquist frequency of the original sampling rate. This filter is known as an interpolator, and one of its tasks is to prevent images of the lower input-sampling spectrum from appearing in the extended baseband of the higher-rate output spectrum.

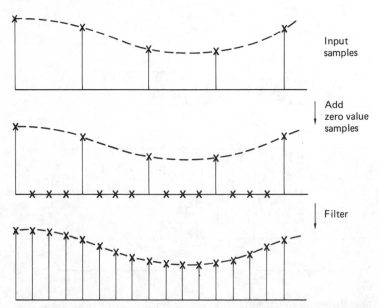

Figure 5.12 In integer ratio sampling, rate increase can be obtained in two stages. First zero value samples are inserted to increase the rate, and then filtering is used to give the extra samples real values. The filter necessary will be an LPF with a response which cuts off at the Nyquist frequency of the input samples

How do interpolators work? Remember that, according to Nyquist, all sampled systems have finite bandwidth. An individual digital sample value is obtained by sampling the instantaneous voltage of the original analog waveform, and because it has zero duration it must contain an infinite spectrum. However, such a sample can never be seen in that form because of the reconstruction process, which limits the spectrum of the impulse to the Nyquist limit. After reconstruction, one infinitely short digital sample actually represents a $\sin x/x$ pulse whose central peak width is determined by the response of the reconstruction filter and whose amplitude is proportional to the sample value. This implies that, in reality, one sample value has meaning over a considerable timespan, rather than just at the sample instant. In the spatial domain, one can consider that a pixel has meaning over a considerable distance, in two dimensions in a still frame, in three in moving video. If this were not true, it would be impossible to build an interpolator or standards converter.

As in rate reduction, performing the steps separately is inefficient. The bandwidth of the information is unchanged when the sampling rate is increased; therefore the original input samples will pass through the filter unchanged, and it is superfluous to compute them. The combination of the two processes into an interpolating filter minimizes the amount of computation.

As the purpose of the system is purely to increase the sampling rate, the filter must be as transparent as possible, and this implies that a linear phase configuration is mandatory, suggesting the use of an FIR structure. Fig. 5.13 shows that the theoretical impulse response of such a filter is a $\sin x/x$ curve which has zero value at the position of adjacent input samples. In

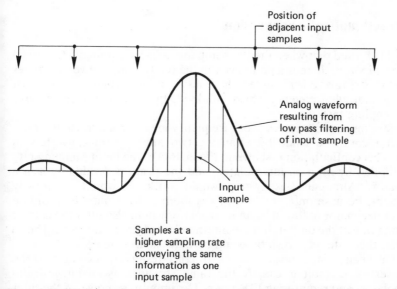

Figure 5.13 A single sample results in a $\sin x/x$ waveform after filtering in the analog domain. At a new, higher, sampling rate, the same waveform after filtering will be obtained if the numerous samples of differing size shown here are used. It follows that the values of these new samples can be calculated from the input samples in the digital domain in an FIR filter

practice this impulse cannot be implemented because it is infinite. The impulse response used will be truncated and windowed as described earlier. To simplify this discussion, assume that a sin$x$/x impulse is to be used. To see how the process of interpolation works, recall the principle of the reconstruction filter described in Chapter 2. The analog voltage is returned to the time-continuous state by summing the analog impulses due to each sample. In a digital interpolating filter, this process is duplicated.[3]

If the sampling rate is to be doubled, new samples must be interpolated exactly half-way between existing samples. The necessary impulse response is shown in Fig. 5.14; it can be sampled at the *output* sample period and quantized to form coefficients. If a single input sample is multiplied by each of these coefficients in turn, the impulse response of that sample at the new sampling rate will be obtained. Note that every other coefficient is zero, which confirms that no computation is necessary on the existing samples; they are just transferred to the output. The intermediate sample is computed by adding together the impulse responses of every input sample in the window. The figure shows how this mechanism operates. If the sampling rate is to be increased by a factor of four, three sample values must be interpolated between existing input samples. Fig. 5.15 shows that it is only necessary to sample the impulse response at one-quarter the period of input samples to obtain three sets of coefficients which will be used in turn. In hardware-implemented filters, the input sample which is passed straight to the output is transferred by using a fourth filter phase where all coefficients are zero except the central one which is unity.

5.7 Fractional-ratio conversion

Fig. 5.11 showed that when the two sampling rates have a simple fractional relationship m/n, there is a periodicity in the relationship between samples in the two streams. It is possible to have a system clock running at the least common multiple frequency which will divide by different integers to give each sampling rate.

The existence of a common clock frequency means that a fractional-ratio converter could be made by arranging two integer-ratio converters in series. This configuration is shown in Fig. 5.16(a). The input sampling rate is multiplied by m in an interpolator, and the result is divided by n in a decimator. Although this system would work, it would be grossly inefficient, because only one in n of the interpolator's outputs would be used. A decimator followed by an interpolator would also offer the correct sampling rate at the output, but the intermediate sampling rate would be so low that the system bandwidth would be quite unacceptable.

As has been seen, a more efficient structure results from combining the processes. The result is exactly the same structure as an integer-ratio interpolator, and requires an FIR filter. The impulse response of the filter is determined by the lower of the two sampling rates, and as before it prevents aliasing when the rate is being reduced, and prevents images when the rate is being increased. The interpolator has sufficient coefficient

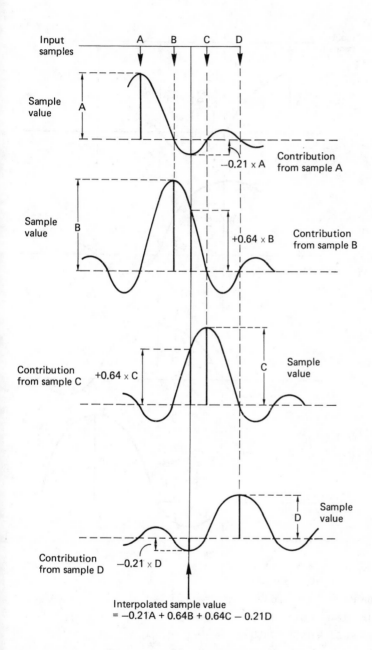

Figure 5.14 A two times oversampling interpolator. To compute an intermediate sample, the input samples are imagined to be sin x/x impulses, and the contributions from each at the point of interest can be calculated. In practice, rather more samples on either side need to be taken into account

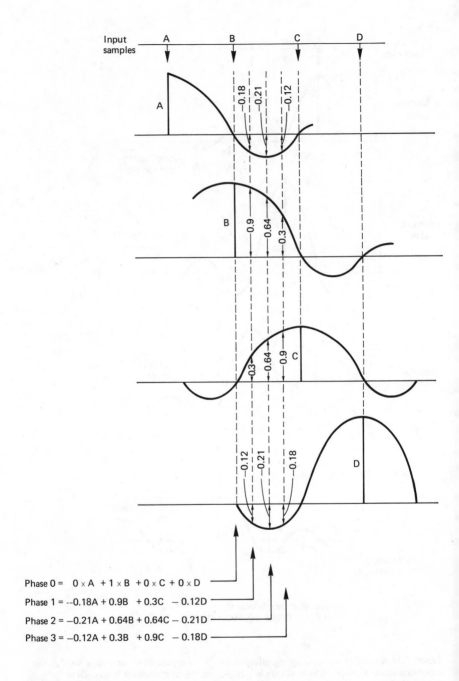

Input samples

Phase 0 =   0 × A + 1 × B   + 0 × C + 0 × D
Phase 1 = −0.18A + 0.9B   + 0.3C − 0.12D
Phase 2 = −0.21A + 0.64B + 0.64C − 0.21D
Phase 3 = −0.12A + 0.3B   + 0.9C − 0.18D

Figure 5.15 In 4× oversampling, for each set of input samples, four phases of coefficients are necessary, each of which produces one of the oversampled values

phases to interpolate *m* output samples for every input sample, but not all of these values are computed; only interpolations which coincide with an output sample are performed. It will be seen in Fig. 5.16(b) that input samples shift across the transversal filter at the input sampling rate, but interpolations are only performed at the output sample rate. This is possible because a different filter phase will be used at each interpolation. Conversion of this kind can be used when changing between 525 line and 625 line systems, as both standards represent fixed vertical sampling rates which have a ratio of 21:25.

5.8 Variable-ratio conversion

In the previous examples, the sample rate of the filter output had a constant relationship to the input, which meant that the two rates had to be

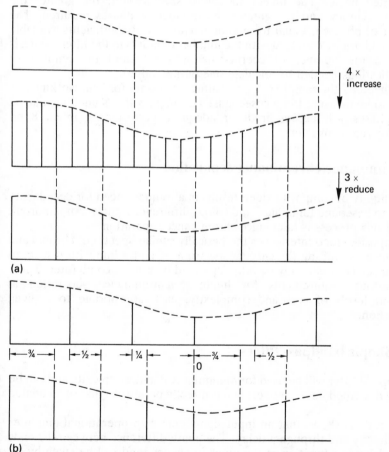

(a)

(b)

Figure 5.16 At (a), fractional ratio conversion of ¾ in this example is by increasing to 4× input prior to reducing by 3×. The inefficiency due to discarding previously computed values is clear. At (b), efficiency is raised since only needed values will be computed. Note how the interpolation phase changes for each putput. Fixed coefficients can no longer be used

phase locked. This is an undesirable constraint in some applications, including image manipulators. In a variable-ratio converter, values will exist for the points at which input pixels were sampled, but it is necessary to compute what the pixel values would have been at absolutely any position between available pixels. The general concept of the interpolator is the same as for the fractional-ratio converter, except that an infinite number of filter phases is necessary. Since a realizable filter will have a finite number of phases, it is necessary to study the degradation this causes. The desired continuous time or distance axis of the interpolator is quantized by the phase spacing, and a pixel value needed at a particular time or position will be replaced by a value for the nearest available filter phase. The number of phases in the filter therefore determines the accuracy of the interpolation. The effects of calculating a value for the wrong time or position are identical to sampling with jitter, in that an error occurs proportional to the slope of the signal. The result is program-modulated noise. The higher the noise specification, the greater the desired accuracy and the greater the number of phases required. The number of phases is equal to the number of sets of coefficients available and should not be confused with the number of points in the filter, which is equal to the number of coefficients in a set (and the number of multiplications needed to calculate one output value).

In Chapter 2 the sampling jitter accuracy necessary for 8 bit working was shown to be measured in picoseconds. This implies that something like 32 filter phases will be required for adequate performance in an 8 bit sampling-rate converter.

5.9 Luminance/chrominance separation

The ubiquity of composite video results in a frequent need for decoders to return to baseband luminance and colour difference signals. An important part of this process is luminance/chrominance separation.

Composite video interleaves the basically similar spectra of chroma and luminance by shifting the chroma spectrum by half a line with respect to luminance. They can only be fully separated by using a comb filter. There are various requirements for luminance/chrominance separation at different levels of cost and complexity, each appropriate to a given application.

5.10 Simple bandpass filters

This type of filter will be used for minimum cost and complexity and can be readily described because operation is directly parallel to that of an analog filter.

Fig. 5.17(a) shows that an input signal enters an operational amplifier both directly and through a delay. The phase difference between the ends of the delay is a function of the input frequency, and will be given by:

$$\frac{\text{delay period}}{\text{signal period}} \times 360°$$

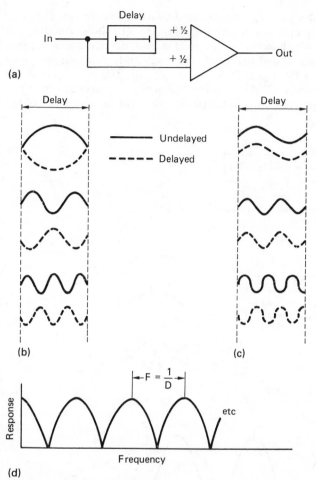

(a)

(b)

(c)

(d)

Figure 5.17 Simple comb filter at (a) has delay in one input of adder. At some frequencies, (b) delay causes cancellation, whereas at others (c) delayed and undelayed signals are in phase. Frequency response shown at (d)

The op-amp output is the vector sum of the two inputs:

$$\tfrac{1}{2}V_{in} + \tfrac{1}{2}V_{in} \sin T$$

where T is the phase angle between the inputs. When the delay period exceeds the signal period, the phase shift exceeds 360°, and clearly subtracting 360° or multiples thereof does not change the vector sum. There will thus be a series of signal periods all of which will have the same gain. The frequency response becomes repetitive, hence the term comb filter. Fig. 5.17(b) shows several frequencies, all of which suffer complete cancellation because of effective inversion by the delay, and Fig. 5.17(c) shows frequencies which give unity gain because the delay is an integer multiple of the signal period. Fig. 5.17(d) shows the overall frequency response, which has a rectified cosine shape. Note that the peak spacing is at the reciprocal of the delay period.

A sharper response peak can be obtained by using two delays, as in Fig. 5.18(a). The op-amp now has three inputs. Fig. 5.18(b) shows the situation where a frequency which suffers a 180° shift in each delay is applied. Since the twice-delayed signal and the input signal will add, they must be given half as much gain as the signal from the centre tap. The op-amp thus has weighted gains of $+\frac{1}{4}$, $-\frac{1}{2}$ and $+\frac{1}{4}$. The frequency response shown in Fig. 5.18(d) is a cosinusoid, again with the peaks spaced at the reciprocal of the delay.

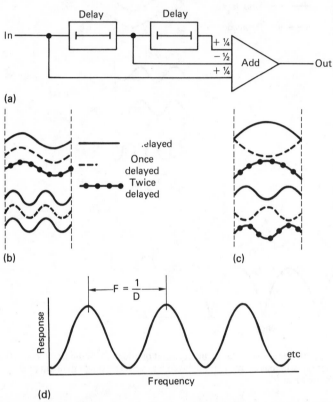

(a)

(b)

(c)

(d)

Figure 5.18 Two-delay comb filter at (a). In (b) certain frequencies suffer 360° shift in one delay, but since once-delayed signal has twice the weighting there is cancellation. At (c) is 180° resultant phase shift in one delay, removed by inverting input, permitting unity gain. Response at (d) is cosinusoid

Fig. 5.19 shows a relative of the two-delay filter of Fig. 5.18. The difference is that the weights and phases of all the inputs are the same at $\frac{1}{3}$. When the input frequency suffers a phase shift of 120°, there will be complete cancellation. Again the system acts as a comb filter with a response shown in Fig. 5.19(b) where the first null is at the reciprocal of the delay.

Transferring to the digital domain, signal voltage is represented by a binary number, delay is achieved using latches or RAM, and the operational amplifier is replaced by an adder. Fig. 5.20 shows the digital

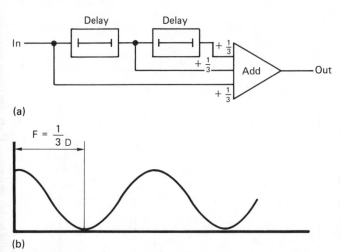

Figure 5.19 Comb filter working on 120° delays to give cancellation. Response at (b). Nulls are 1/3D, 1D, etc

equivalent of Fig. 5.18. The constraint in this kind of filter is that the delay periods can only be integer multiples of the sampling period. As the delay period is intimately related to the frequency response, the desired response and the sampling rate largely determine the filter configuration. It is important to remember that there is also an upper limit to the frequency response due to the fact that it is a sampled system.

Fig. 5.18 and Fig. 5.20. show filters where a phase shift of 180° is necessary at the null frequency. This phase shift is readily achieved in a $4 \times F_{sc}$ system by using two sample periods of delay. Fig. 5.19 showed a filter which needed 120° of phase shift, and this is readily obtained by a one-sample delay in a $3 \times F_{sc}$ system. Fig. 5.21 shows a digital filter based on this principle. Since division by three is difficult in binary, a close approximation is obtained by multiplying by 85 (64 + 16 + 4 + 1) and dividing by 256, since all of these factors can be obtained by shifting.

The $4 \times F_{sc}$ filter of Fig. 5.20 has a gain peak at subcarrier frequency, and the output will be chroma. To obtain luminance, output values are subtracted from input values, with a compensating delay.

5.11 Advanced composite decoders

In effects units, any change in picture size changes the spectrum of the signal. Where the input is composite, it is paramount that residual chroma in the luminance is minimal before manipulation, so that it does not result in moiré fringes. As the Y/C separation is in the main video path of such machines, it must be of high quality. Since the spectral interleave of a composite signal is primarily on multiples of line rate, it follows that delays of one line are necessary in the comb filter, so that the frequency response peaks will be at multiples of F_h. Fig. 5.22 shows a simple line comb filter. Although this device has a good spectral response, promising to give

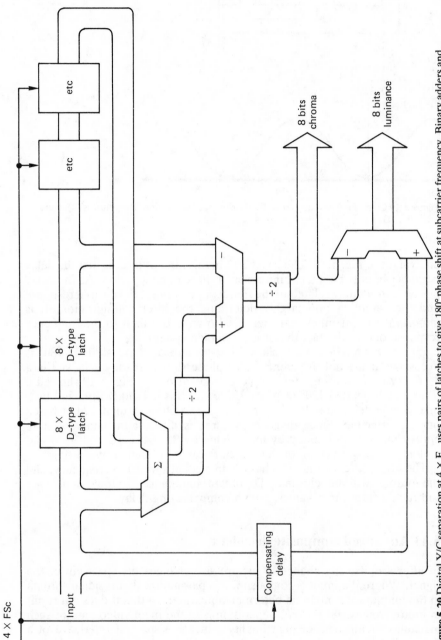

Figure 5.20 Digital Y/C separation at $4 \times F_{sc}$ uses pairs of latches to give 180° phase shift at subcarrier frequency. Binary adders and dividers give weighting of $+\frac{1}{4}$, $-\frac{1}{4}$, $+\frac{1}{4}$ to three samples. Chroma output is subtracted from the input to give luminance. There is only one

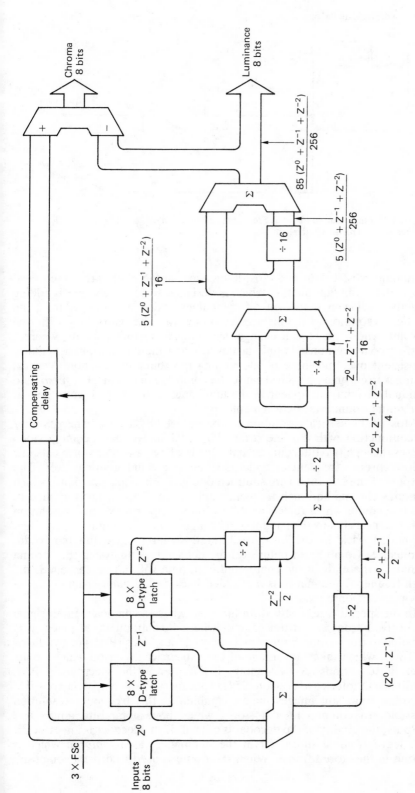

Figure 5.21 $3 \times F_{sc}$ Y/C separation approximates closely to divide by 3 of Fig. 5.19

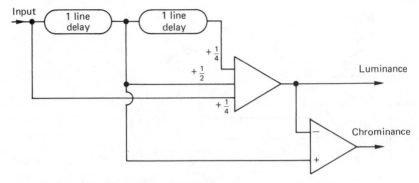

Figure 5.22 Simple line comb filter. Frequency response is ideal, but there are practical shortcomings explained in the text

minimum cross-colour and cross-luminance, in fact there are some snags. First, the summing junction which is designed to reject chroma is adding together adjacent points on different lines and is actually reducing the vertical resolution of the picture. Secondly, the filter is working with real chroma whose phase can change according to picture content, whereas perfect comb response is only achieved when the chroma phase remains consistent over the three points feeding the summing junction. Vertical changes in chroma phase will cause the comb to fail to cancel or *mesh*, and residual chroma will appear in the luminance as a series of white dots at horizontal boundaries between colours.

Most of the vertical resolution can be restored by using a bandpass filter in conjunction with the line comb. Fig. 5.23 shows that incoming video passes through two filters in parallel. One is a low-pass filter which cuts just below chroma frequencies and the other is a band limiting filter. The outputs of the two filters are subtracted to give a bandpass response which contains chroma and high-frequency luminance. This signal is applied to the line comb, which rejects chroma without impairing vertical resolution at frequencies below the bandpass. The high-frequency luminance can then be added back to the low-pass filtered signal to give full bandwidth luminance. Comb mesh failure can be detected by analysing the chroma signals at the ends of the comb, and if chroma will not be cancelled, the high-frequency luminance is not added back to the main channel, and a low-pass response results.

In the special case of still store filtering, where a composite input signal is received from a rostrum camera where no motion takes place, it is possible to use a comb filter with a delay of four fields (PAL) or two fields (NTSC), which takes advantage of the subcarrier inversion which occurs over those periods. As was shown in Chapter 2, the spectrum of PAL continues to interleave down to 25 Hz spacing, and the long delay possible in video from still images makes combing at this frequency resolution possible. In component still stores which have composite inputs and outputs, the quality of the decoder is critical. If the decoder is imperfect, it will leave residual subcarrier in the luminance, as a *footprint* which is frozen in the stored frame. When the frame is used to drive a composite

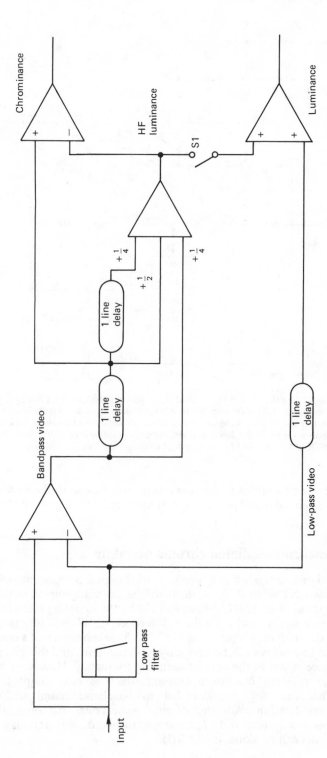

Figure 5.23(a) A more complex line comb filter where the line comb works on bandpass video to reduce the loss of vertical resolution. HF luminance is added back to low-pass signal to restore luminance bandwidth. If comb fails to mesh due to vertical chroma phase change, switch S1 opens to prevent chroma breaking through into luminance bandwidth is reduced

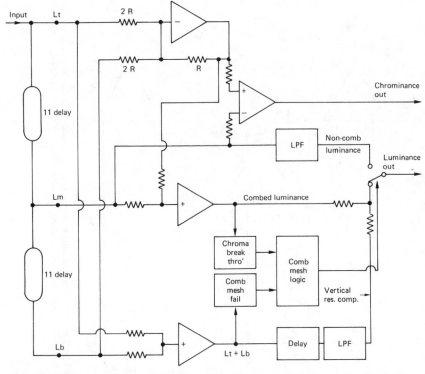

Figure 5.23(b) Rearranging the filter of Fig. 5.23(a) in this way eliminates a delay line by restoring vertical resolution a different way. Vertical resolution compensation is achieved by taking signals from top and bottom of the delays and adding them back to luminance via a low pass filter shown bottom right. In the digital domain, replace operational amplifiers with adders, delays with RAM. Low pass filters will be FIR types as described

encoder, the frozen footprint in the frame store will beat with the moving subcarrier of the encoder and produce low-frequency flickering of coloured areas.

5.12 Line synchronous digital chroma decoding

Where the goal of a subsystem is to produce 4:2:2 digital component video from a composite NTSC or PAL input, it will be advantageous to sample the composite input at 13.5 MHz,[4] since this will be the sampling rate of the output luminance signal, and the colour difference signals will ultimately be sampled at one-half of this rate. The use of 13.5 MHz means that a comb filter using one-line delays will be very easy to implement, and this gives a digital luminance signal at the correct sampling frequency. However, this filter will also produce composite chroma which is also sampled at 13.5 MHz. This can only be decoded to baseband luminance by synchronous rectification with the original subcarrier. Although the operation of such a system at $4 \times F_{sc}$ is straightforward, it is not easy to visualize how this can be done at 13.5 MHz.

To follow the action of a line synchronous demodulator it is necessary to return to the fundamental way in which the analog equivalent would work, and then to duplicate this action in the digital domain. The operation of a synchronous rectifier in the analog domain is to regenerate a sinusoidal subcarrier signal from burst and then to multiply the chroma by this signal, which will, after low-pass filtering, produce the $B-Y$ signal. Performing a similar process with a quadrature reference will produce the $R-Y$ signal. In the analog domain all of these signals are continuous, but the same process can be carried out in the sampled domain, whether or not the sampling rate is subcarrier synchronous.

If a subcarrier synchronous system is used, then the samples of the subcarrier will fall at regular positions on the sinusoid, and the coefficients by which the chroma needs to be multiplied become unity and zero, which simplifies circuitry tremendously. However, if the sampling is asynchronous, it is necessary to create digital values which truly represent a subcarrier sampled in the same instantaneous phase as the input chroma.

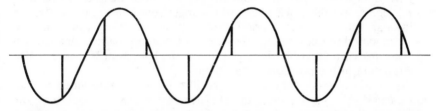

Figure 5.24 A subcarrier of 4.43 MHz sampled at 13.5 MHz. It will be seen that the sample values are variable, and need to be expressed by a multi-bit sample. Such a sample stream can be used to demodulate composite video which has been sampled at 13.5 MHz

As Fig. 5.24 shows, this results in values which need to represented by a multibit parameter to give the necessary accuracy. These parameters must then be digitally multiplied by the chroma samples to obtain one of the colour difference signals, which will be rich in subcarrier frequency harmonics. A straightforward low-pass FIR filter can be given a response tailored to the appropriate bandwidth and can double as the decimator which reduces the sampling rate to 6.75 MHz. A second system which generates samples corresponding to a quadrature subcarrier will yield the other colour difference signal.

The system results in 27 million multiplications per second being necessary, which is rather less than the number which would be necessary to convert to sample rate from $4 \times F_{sc}$ to 13.5 MHz. An application of such a system may be in a DVE which has 4:2:2 internal processing, but which requires to have an analog component input, one example of this being the Ampex ADO 100.

5.13 Converting 625/50 4:2:2 to D-2 PAL composite digital

This conversion can be performed in the digital domain quite readily, and since the chroma bandwidth of the component input is greater than that of the composite output, there need be no loss of quality.

The main issues to be addressed are:

(1) Reducing the chroma bandwidth to the 1.3 MHz allowed for composite.

(2) Converting the sampling rate of the colour difference signals to $4 \times F_{sc}$ and creating a digital representation of quadrature-modulated subcarrier with V-switch.

(3) Converting the sampling rate of luminance from 13.5 MHz to $4 \times F_{sc}$ and adding the subcarrier.

(4) Scaling the numerical sample values since quantizing intervals of luminance, colour difference and composite signals are all of different sizes (see Chapter 8).

(5) Generating sync and burst.

The most complex issue in this conversion is clock generation and timing, since the sampling rate of composite digital reflects the 25 Hz offset of PAL subcarrier. One line contains slightly more than 1135 cycles of $4 \times F_{sc}$ clock, and the clock phase will change from line to line so that an additional four samples periods (one cycle of subcarrier) can be accommodated in one frame. The phase of the interpolations needed will vary not just as a function of the position in the line, as in NTSC, but also as a function of the position in the frame.

The timing system of the converter will need to recreate video timing, and it can do this by obtaining the H-synchronous 27 MHz clock from the CCIR 601 digital input and using the synchronizing patterns to determine the position in the line and frame. Fig. 5.25 shows how the output sampling rate is generated. Input 27 MHz is divided down by 1728 to produce line rate, which is synchronized by the *SAV* signal (see Chapter 8), and this is then used as the input to a phase-locked loop which multiplies by 1135. The resultant frequency is exactly 100 Hz too low, and input field rate will be multiplied by two to obtain 100 Hz. This can conveniently be done by addressing a PROM with a line count in the frame and storing four cycles of a waveform in the PROM over a range of 625 locations. A modulator

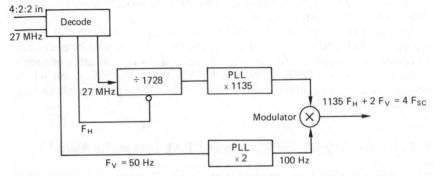

Figure 5.25 Since PAL subcarrier is given by $283\frac{3}{4} F_H + F_{v/2}$, then multiplying this expression by four gives $4F_{sc} = 1135 F_H + 2F_v$. Both frequencies are produced from the 4:2:2 decoder and phase locked loops. Adding in a modulator results in $4F_{sc}$

can then be used to mix the frequencies and generate $4 \times F_{sc}$. The ScH phase of the clock is determined by the phase of the 100 Hz component. Alternatively a direct synthesis approach may be used, where a phase accumulator adds the equivalent of the number of degrees of subcarrier in a CCIR 601 sample period at each input clock, and so produces a representation of subcarrier. The $4 \times F_{sc}$ clock is then divided by four in two different dividers. Combining the output of these dividers in various ways allows the generation of a subcarrier frequency square wave for generation of the U component and a quadrature square wave for generation of the V component. These waveforms will be phased by presetting the dividers once every eight fields.

There is only one signal in composite digital, which is at a sampling rate of $4 \times F_{sc}$. Accordingly the sampling rates of the luminance and colour difference signals of the 4:2:2 input must all be raised to this sampling rate by interpolation, before it is possible to create a composite signal.

Reduction of the chroma bandwidth and sampling-rate conversion from 6.75 MHz to $4 \times F_{sc}$ can be achieved in the same process. Since the new sampling rate is higher than the luminance sampling rate of 13.5 MHz, no bandwidth reduction of luminance is needed.

Three parallel sampling-rate converters will be needed, and these must have a considerable amount of coefficient storage, because the phase of PAL subcarrier-derived samples constantly slips with respect to the phase of the H-derived 4:2:2 sampling clock. As the colour difference signals have yet to suffer the V-switch inversion, it is only necessary at this stage to consider the relative phases of $4 \times F_{sc}$ and $864 \times F_h$. There will be an integer number of cycles N_{4sc} of $4 \times F_{sc}$ in one frame, given by

$$N_{4sc} = (625 \times 283.75)4 + 4 = 709\,379$$

In the same period there will also be an integer number of cycles of 13.5 MHz, N_y, given by:

$$N_y = 625 \times 864 = 540\,000$$

It will be possible to determine the relative phase of any cycle of $4 \times F_{sc}$ and any cycle of 13.5 MHz from the position in the frame. A PROM addressed by line count will be able to provide the starting phase for each line, and then a sample count along the line can modify the phase by a constant amount for each interpolation. Fortunately the phase has only to be calculated once, since it can be used by the luminance and both the colour difference interpolators. As the colour difference signals are at half the luminance sampling rate, one interpolator could be multiplexed to process both colour difference signals alternately.

The luminance interpolator will use coefficients which produce a frequency response of 5.75 MHz. There will then be no loss of luminance resolution. The frequency responses of the colour difference interpolators will be much lower, in order to tailor the U and V spectra to that permitted in PAL.

There are now three sample streams, Y,U and V, all running at $4 \times F_{sc}$ and all using offset binary code. Multiplexers are used to insert blanking values outside the active line.

166

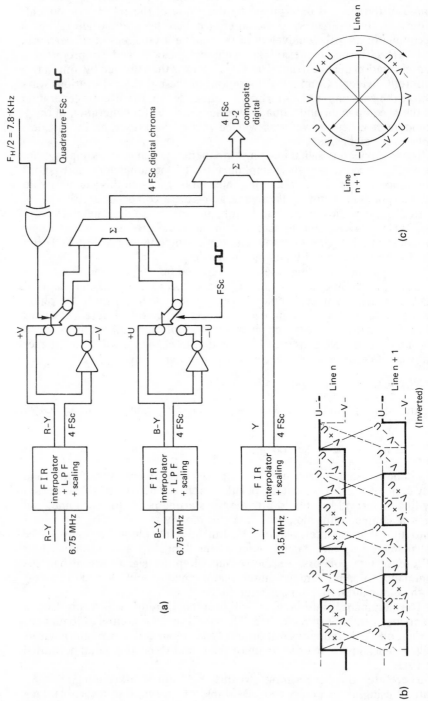

Figure 5.26 4:2:2 to D–2 PAL conversion requires all 3 components to be raised to 4F_{sc} sampling rate before generating digital chroma with V-switch using selectors running at F_{sc} and quadrature F_{sc} as in (a). Waveforms of the selectors are shown in (b) for two successive lines where effect of V-switch

The colour difference signals are next converted to two's complement, and a normal and an inverted version of both are made available to a pair of multiplexers. The U and $-U$ multiplexer is switched by the subcarrier rate square wave, and the V and $-V$ multiplexer is switched by a quadrature square wave which is inverted from one line to the next to obtain the characteristic V-switch of PAL. The outputs of the two multiplexers are next added together, and Fig. 5.26 shows that this results in the digital sampled equivalent of chroma, with samples taken at burst phase as the D-2 format specifies. The slanting vertical lines in the figure show the quarter cycle offset from one line to the next, with U and $\pm V$ superimposed. For each sample period, the relative polarities of U and V are shown. The effect of V-switch can be seen, because although the U signal advances one sample (90°) per line, the inversion of V causes the V signal to lag one sample per line.

The result of this process is not quite D-2 digital chroma, because the gain is incorrect. The digital modulation process simply added and subtracted U and V at the sample points, whereas a conventional analog modulator would have produced the sum of $U\cos 45$ plus $V\cos 45$ at these points. A further point is that the quantizing intervals of D-1 and D-2 are a different size.

It is necessary to scale the magnitude of the chroma samples by multiplying by a factor which is $\cos 45$ multiplied by the ratio of the quantizing structures. It is worth remembering that the quantizing intervals of luminance and colour difference are not the same size (see Chapter 8). In this way a maximum value colour difference signal will result in maximum amplitude chroma.

The interpolated luminance will also need scaling, since the quantizing intervals are a different size, and the offset value corresponding to blanking level is different between D-1 and D-2. Luminance in D-1 ranges from 16_{10} to 235_{10}, whereas PAL D-2 luminance ranges from 64_{10} to 211_{10}. Since the scale factor never changes, scaling is most conveniently performed in PROM. The input value forms the PROM address, and the PROM contains the scaled value as data at that address.

The scaled chroma and luminance can now be added numerically. This is easy since they are both sample streams at the same sampling rate. It is only necessary to add syncs digitally, and the output can be converted to balanced ECL drive and fed to the 25 pin D-type connector.

Sync generation is messy in D-2 PAL because the sampling rate is not H-coherent. Sync values will change from line to line as the sampling clock slides towards sync by four samples per frame. Since the unit described has a luminance interpolator which is unemployed during blanking, it is probably easiest to regenerate syncs from the H-synchronous 27 MHz input timing, and then pass them through the interpolator to produce syncs at $4 \times F_{sc}$. This needs some care, since the quantizing range of the interpolator only goes from black to white to give the best noise performance, whereas syncs go below black. The simple solution is to generate positive-going syncs for interpolation and invert them afterwards. The same procedure can be used for burst envelope generation by producing envelope values at 6.75 MHz and passing them through the colour difference interpolators.

5.14 Converting 525/59.94 4:2:2 to D-2 NTSC composite digital

This conversion is more straightforward than the PAL conversion, because of the simple subcarrier frequency of NTSC.

The main issues to be addressed are:

(1) Reducing the chroma bandwidth to that allowed for composite.

(2) Converting the sampling rate of the colour difference signals to $4 \times F_{sc}$ and creating a digital representation of quadrature-modulated subcarrier.

(3) Converting the sampling rate of luminance from 13.5 MHz to $4 \times F_{sc}$ and adding the subcarrier.

(4) Scaling the numerical sample values since quantizing intervals of luminance, colour difference and composite signals are all different (see Chapter 8).

(5) Generating sync and burst, with the burst at a phase shift of 57° to the sampling structure.

The timing system of the converter will need to recreate video timing, and it can do this by obtaining the H-synchronous 27 MHz clock from the CCIR 601 digital input and using the synchronizing patterns to determine the position in the line and frame. Fig. 5.27 shows how the output sampling

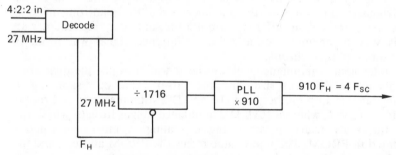

Figure 5.27 Generating NTSC sampling rate from 4:2:2 digital input requires division to line rate followed by multiplication. This is simpler than for PAL because NTSC subcarrier is line locked. Sine $F_{sc} = 227.5 F_H$, then $4F_{sc} = 910 F_H$

rate is generated. Input 27 MHz is divided down by 1716 to produce line rate, which is synchronized by the *SAV* signal (see Chapter 8), and this is then used as the input to a phase-locked loop which multiplies by 910 to generate $4 \times F_{sc}$. The $4 \times F_{sc}$ clock is then divided by four in two different dividers. Combining the output of these dividers in various ways allows the generation of a subcarrier frequency square wave, for generation of the $R-Y$ component, and a quadrature square wave for generation of the $B-Y$ component. These waveforms will be phased by presetting the dividers once every four fields.

There is only one signal in composite digital, which is at a sampling rate of $4 \times F_{sc}$. Accordingly the sampling rates of the luminance and colour difference signals of the 4:2:2 input must all be raised to this sampling rate by interpolation, before it is possible to create a composite signal.

Reduction of the chroma bandwidth and sampling-rate conversion from 6.75 MHz to $4 \times F_{sc}$ can be achieved in the same process, but even though the new sampling rate is slightly higher than the luminance sampling rate of 13.5 MHz, the bandwidth needed in the interpolator will be that of NTSC.

Three parallel sampling-rate converters will be needed, and the coefficients can be obtained by considering the relative phases of $4 \times F_{sc}$ and $858 \times F_h$. Since both frequencies repeat at line rate, it is only necessary to have one set of coefficients, and these will serve for every line. As the colour difference signals are at half the luminance sampling rate, one interpolator could be multiplexed to process both colour difference signals alternately.

The frequency responses of the colour difference interpolators will be much lower, in order to tailor the $R-Y$ and $B-Y$ spectra to those permitted in NTSC.

There are now three sample streams, $Y, R-Y$ and $B-Y$, all running at $4 \times F_{sc}$ and all using offset binary code. Multiplexers are used to insert blanking values outside the active line, and the colour difference signals can additionally have a burst envelope inserted.

The colour difference signals are next converted to two's complement, and a normal and an inverted version of both are made available to a pair of multiplexers. The multiplexer which switches between $R-Y$ and its complement is driven by a subcarrier rate square wave, and the multiplexer which switches between $B-Y$ and its complement is driven by a quadrature square wave.

The outputs of the two multiplexers are next added together, and Fig. 5.28 shows that this results in the digital sampled equivalent of chroma, with samples taken at the correct phase as the D-2 format specifies. Note that this is not burst phase in NTSC.

The result of this process is not quite D-2 digital chroma. The gain is incorrect because the quantizing intervals of D-1 and D-2 are a different size. It is necessary to scale the magnitude of the chroma samples by multiplying by an appropriate factor. It is worth remembering that the quantizing intervals of luminance and colour difference are not the same size (see Chapter 8). In this way a maximum value colour difference signal will result in maximum amplitude chroma.

The interpolated luminance will also need scaling, since the quantizing intervals are a different size and the offset value corresponding to blanking level is different between D-1 and D-2. Luminance in D-1 ranges from 16_{10} to 235_{10}, whereas NTSC D-2 luminance ranges from 60_{10} to 200_{10}. Scaling is most conveniently performed in PROM. The input value forms the PROM address, and the PROM contains the scaled value as data at that address.

The scaled chroma and luminance can now be added numerically. This is easy since they are both sample streams at the same sampling rate. It is only necessary to add syncs digitally, and the output can be converted to balanced ECL drive and fed to the 25 pin D-type connector. Since the subcarrier is line synchronous, syncs are easily generated by a PROM addressed by the sample count along the line.

As will be seen in Chapter 8, there is a 57° phase shift between D-2 samples and NTSC subcarrier. This requires some caution when generating

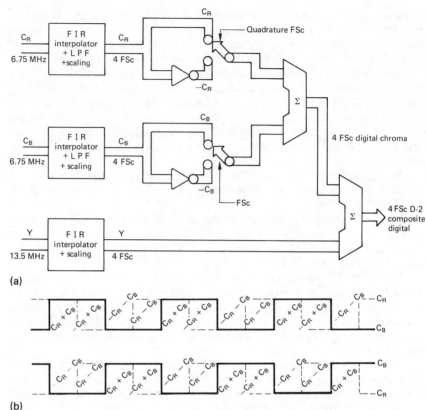

(a)

(b)

Figure 5.28 4:2:2 to D-2 NTSC conversion requires all 3 components to be raised to $4F_{sc}$ sampling rate before generating digital chroma using selectors running at F_{sc} and quadrature F_{sc} as in (a). Waveforms of the selectors are shown in (b) for two successive lines where the 2-line sequence of NTSC and the line by line chroma inversion can be seen. Note that D-2 NTSC does not sample on subcarrier axes, but on colour difference axes 57 degrees away

burst, since NTSC burst is a portion of subcarrier. Burst at any phase can be generated simply by feeding appropriate constants to the colour difference signals prior to modulating, but a more accurate method exists. Since burst has a standard amplitude and phase, and D-2 has standardized quantizing intervals, it follows that burst samples can be calculated allowing for the 57° shift. If a sampling clock is used to generate values of 83_{10}, 74_{10}, 37_{10} and 46_{10} in endless sequence, the result will be correctly phased subcarrier. This will automatically invert from one line to the next, since there are 910 samples per line, which gives a remainder of two when divided by four. Burst values can easily be stored in PROM, along with diminished values to allow the ends of the envelope to be shaped.

5.15 Delays in digital filters

All of the conversion devices described in the preceding paragraphs require phase-linear filters, and these cannot be implemented without causing a delay equal to one-half the window period. In particular, comb filters will delay the video by one or two lines. This makes it difficult to synchronize equipment on both sides of the converter. Where a converter is free standing, one side will have to be the timing reference, and the other side cannot therefore be synchronized. In the case of a D-1 to D-2 converter, or vice versa, the source will often be a DVTR, whose output timing can be controlled. Fig. 5.29 shows that the converter takes a reference feed on the output side and synchronizes its output signals to that reference. It then produces an advanced reference which leads the station reference by the processing delay. This advanced reference is fed to the DVTR. The DVTR then provides video ahead of reference, which when delayed by the converter will be synchronous with station reference.

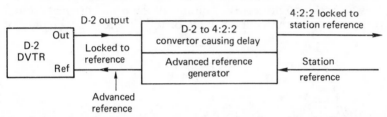

Figure 5.29 Since sampling rate convertor must be phase linear they must have symmetrical impulse responses and will cause a delay to the signal. Practical convertors will incorporate an advanced reference generator which advances the source by an amount equal to the convertor delay

An alternative solution is to incorporate a frame store in the unit, which will increase the delay from a few lines to an entire frame. Input and output can then be timed together. Where the converter forms part of a DVE, the delay will be added to the overall delay of the effects transforms, which will total an integer number of frames, achieving the same effect.

5.16 Planar digital video effects

One can scarcely watch television nowadays without becoming aware of picture manipulation. Flips, tumbles, spins and page turn effects, perspective rotation, and rolling the picture on to the surface of a solid are all commonly seen. In all but the last mentioned, the picture remains flat, hence the title of this paragraph. Non-planar manipulation requires further complexity which will be treated in due course.

Effects machines which manipulate video pictures are close relatives of the machines which produce computer-generated images.[5] Computer-generated images require enormous processing power, and even with state-of-the-art CPUs the time needed to compute a single frame is several orders of magnitude too long to work with real-time video. Video effects machines, then, represent a significant technical achievement, because they have only a field period to complete the processing before another field comes along. General purpose processors are usually too slow for effects work, and most units incorporate dedicated hardware to obtain sufficient throughput. Owing to the advanced technology used in these machines, the reader should be aware that many of the techniques described here are patented. The processing must be done extremely rapidly, and this implies high current consumption and the generation of heat. A typical DVE may consume several hundred amps from the 5 volt rail and contain over a thousand integrated circuits.

5.17 Mapping

The principle of all video manipulators is the same as the technique used by cartographers for centuries. Cartographers are faced with a continual problem in that the earth is round and paper is flat. In order to produce flat maps, it is necessary to project the features of the round original on to a flat surface. Fig. 5.30 shows an example of this. There are a number of

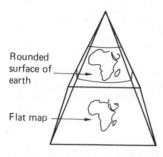

Rounded surface of earth

Flat map

Figure 5.30 Map projection is a close relative of video effects units which manipulate the shape of pictures

different ways of projecting maps, and all of them must by definition produce distortion. The effect of this distortion is that distances measured near the extremities of the map appear further than they actually are. Another effect is that *great circle routes* (the shortest or longest path between two places on a planet) appear curved on a projected map. The type of projection used is usually printed somewhere on the map, a very common system being that due to Mercator. Clearly the process of mapping involves some three-dimensional geometry in order to simulate the paths of light rays from the map so that they appear to have come from the curved surface. Video effects machines work in exactly the same way.

   The distortion of maps means that things are not where they seem. In timesharing computers, every user appears to have their own identical address space in which their program resides, despite the fact that many different programs are simultaneously in the memory. In order to resolve this contradiction, memory management units are constructed which add a constant value to the address which the user thinks they have (the *virtual address*) in order to produce the *physical address*. As long as the unit gives each user a different constant, they can all program in the same virtual address space without one corrupting another's programs. Because the program is no longer where it seems to be, the term of mapping was introduced. The address space of a computer is one dimensional, but a video frame expressed as rows and columns of pixels can be considered to

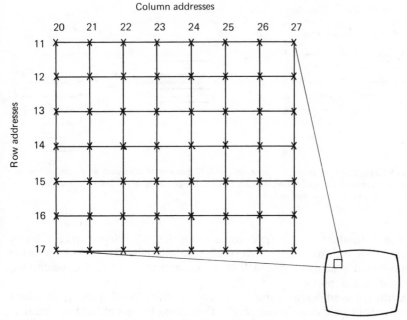

Figure 5.31 The entire TV picture can be broken down into uniquely addressable pixels

have a two-dimensional address as in Fig. 5.31. Video manipulators work by mapping the pixel addresses in two dimensions.

5.18 De-interlacing

All manipulators must begin with an array of pixels, in which the columns must be vertical. This can only be easily obtained if the sampling rate of the incoming video is a multiple of line rate, as is done in CCIR 601. Composite video cannot be used directly, because the phase of the subcarrier would become meaningless after manipulation. If a composite video input is used, it must be decoded to baseband luminance and colour difference, so that in actuality there are three superimposed arrays of samples to be processed, one luminance, and two colour difference. Most modern DVEs use CCIR 601 sampling, so digital signals conforming to this standard could be used directly, from, for example, a D-1 format recorder or a hard-disk recorder.

There are two main types of effects machines: those which are field based and those which are frame based. The former are more cost conscious, the latter are more quality conscious.

Fig. 5.32(a) shows an example of a field-based manipulator, such as the Ampex ADO 1000. In this example, the size of the picture is to be doubled. The information from lines on a given input field will appear on every other output line, and the lines in between will have to be produced by interpolation. In Fig. 5.32(b) a frame-based machine, such as the ADO 2000 or 3000, is performing the same operation. Here, the lines necessary

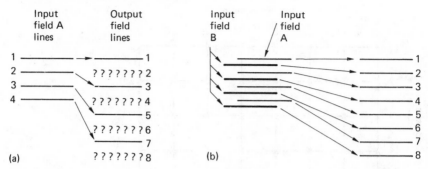

Figure 5.32 (a) In a field based machine, interpolation becomes necessary when size of the picture is increased. (b) In a frame based machine, the presence of the second input field allows greater vertical resolution

for the magnified output field come from the other input field. Clearly there is an improvement in vertical resolution to be gained by using frame-based machines, but it will be seen that there is a considerable increase in complexity.

A frame-based machine must produce a de-interlaced frame from which every output field can choose pixels. Producing frames at field rate sounds rather like getting something for nothing, but this is not exactly what happens. In practice, at a given field time, the lines of that field will be available, and between them will be placed the lines from the previous (most recent) field. Fig. 5.33 shows that, at each new field, a new pair of fields will be combined to make a frame. Unfortunately it is not possible to

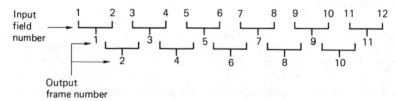

Figure 5.33 Frames are produced at field rate by combining the latest pair of fields

use the information from two different fields directly. Fig. 5.34 shows a scene in which an object is moving. When the second field of the scene leaves the camera, the object will have assumed a different position from the one it had in the first field, and the result of combining the two fields to make a de-interlaced frame will be a double image. This effect can easily be demonstrated on any video recorder which offers a choice of still field or still frame. Stationary objects before a stationary camera, however, can be de-interlaced perfectly. Frame-based machines must use motion sensing so that de-interlacing can be disabled when movement occurs and interpolation used instead. Motion sensing implies comparison of one picture with the next. If interpolation is only to be used in areas where there is movement, it is necessary to test for motion over the entire frame. Motion

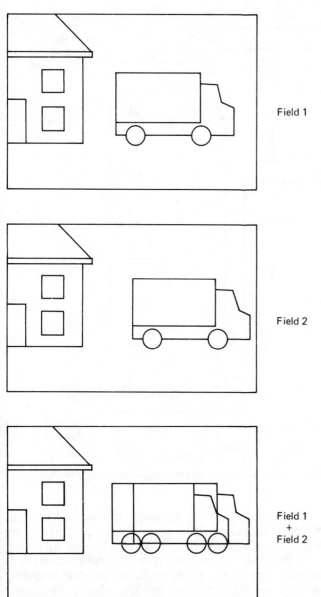

Field 1

Field 2

Field 1
+
Field 2

Figure 5.34 Moving object will be in a different place in two successive fields and will produce a double image

can be detected by comparing the luminance value of a given pixel with the value of the same pixel two fields earlier. As two fields are to be combined, and motion can occur in either, then the comparison must be made between two odd fields and two even fields. Thus four fields of memory are needed to perform motion sensing correctly. The luminance from four fields requires about a megabyte of storage. In practice the speed of

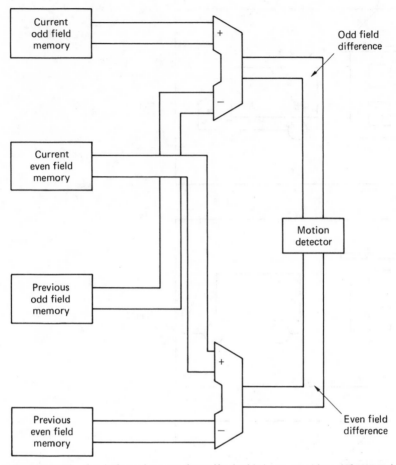

Figure 5.35 The circuit shown here can detect if a double image would result from motion

operation required makes it difficult for memories to read and write at once, so that five fields of memory will sometimes be needed, and at any one time, one will be writing a new field and four will be reading earlier fields for motion sensing. Fig. 5.35 shows how the motion sensing is performed. One subtractor compares pixels in the most recent odd field with the same pixels in the odd field before that, whereas the other subtractor compares the most recent even field with the even field before that. Clearly, in order to work in real time, the subtractions must each be done at the sampling rate, and so there will be 27 million subtractions per second taking place for the purpose of detecting motion alone. The differences from the subtractors can have many values – from zero with a noise-free still input to maximum when a cut to black takes place. At some point a decision must be made to abandon pixels from the previous field, which are in the wrong place due to motion, and to interpolate them from adjacent lines in the current field. Switching suddenly in this way is visible to the naked eye, and there is a more sophisticated mechanism which can be used. In Fig. 5.36, two fields are shown, separated in time. Interlace can be seen by following lines from pixels in one field, which pass between pixels in the other field. If there is no movement, the fact that the two fields are separated in time is irrelevant, and the two can be superimposed to make a frame array. When there is motion, pixels from above and below the unknown pixels are added together and divided by two, to produce interpolated values. If both of these mechanisms work all the time, a better quality picture results if a crossfade is made between the two based on the amount of motion. A suitable digital crossfader was shown in Chapter 3.

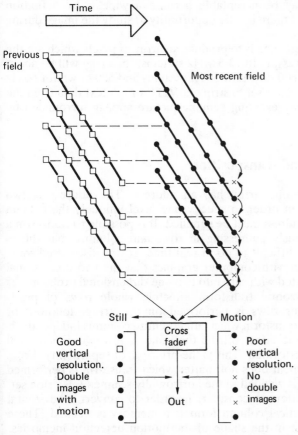

Figure 5.36 Pixels from the most recent field (●) are interpolated spatially to form low vertical resolution pixels (x) which will be used if there is excessive motion, pixels from the previous field (□) will be used to give maximum vertical resolution. The best possible de-interlaced frame results

At some motion value, or some magnitude of pixel difference, the loss of resolution due to a double image is equal to the loss of resolution due to interpolation. That amount of motion should result in the crossfader arriving at a 50/50 setting. Any less motion will result in a fade towards both fields and any more motion in a fade towards the interpolated values.

Using crossfading, the transition from high-resolution areas to low-resolution areas is gradual, and hard to see. In any case the eye is accustomed to moving objects appearing less sharp than stationary objects on television, because of the marginal field rates used. As the resolution of the eye is much worse for changes in colour than it is for changes in brightness, de-interlacing is not generally necessary for the colour difference signals. Clearly the additional cost and complexity of a frame-based processor is not trivial, but this is justified for post-production work, where the utmost quality is demanded. Where an effects unit is used to increase the range of wipe patterns in an on-air video switcher, a field-based system may be acceptable because a wipe is by definition transient in nature, and there is little opportunity to study the image during the wipe.

The effect of de-interlacing is to produce an array of pixels which are the input data for the processor. In 13.5 MHz systems, the array will be about 750 pixels across, and 600 down for 50 Hz systems and 500 down for 60 Hz systems. Most machines are set to strip out VITC or teletext data from the input, so that pixels representing genuine picture appear surrounded by blanking level.

5.19 Separability and transposition

Every pixel in the frame array has an address. The address is two dimensional, because in order to specify one pixel uniquely the column address and the row address must be supplied. It is possible to transform a picture by simultaneously addressing in rows and columns, but this is complicated and very difficult to do in real time. It was discovered some time ago in connection with computer graphics that the two-dimensional problem can be converted with care into two one-dimensional problems.[5,6] Essentially, if a horizontal transform affecting whole rows of pixels independently of other rows is performed on the array, followed or preceded by a vertical transform which affects entire columns independently of other columns, the effect will be the same as if a two-dimensional transform had been performed. This is the principle of separability. From an academic standpoint, it does not matter which transform is performed first. In a world which is wedded to the horizontally scanned television set, there are practical matters to consider. In order to convert a horizontal raster input into a vertical column format, a memory is needed. These memories already exist in the shape of the motion detection memories. Fig. 5.37 shows a simplified TV standard where there are exactly 750 samples per line. As the first line of a field enters, it will be put into addresses 0 to 749. As the second line of the frame appears, it will be put in addresses 750 to 1499 and so on. If subsequently a small accumulator is arranged to provide addresses which are given by $n \times 750 + k$, where n goes from zero upwards, if $k = 0$ the addresses 0, 750, 1500, 2250, etc. will be generated, which correspond to the first column of pixels. If k is increased to 1, the addresses 1, 751, 1501, 2251, etc. will be generated, which correspond to the second column of pixels. In order to de-interlace two fields A and B, the two address accumulators would need to be

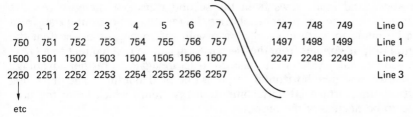

0	1	2	3	4	5	6	7		747	748	749	Line 0
750	751	752	753	754	755	756	757		1497	1498	1499	Line 1
1500	1501	1502	1503	1504	1505	1506	1507		2247	2248	2249	Line 2
2250	2251	2252	2253	2254	2255	2256	2257					Line 3

etc

Figure 37 Pixels are written into a memory in the order of address counting a line at a time. If the read address is given by (n × 750)+k, for each value of k, a different column will be read by increasing n. For example k=4, addresses will be 4, 754, 1504, 2254 etc. This transposes the incoming raster to a vertical scan format

synchronized so that they alternated. The effect would then be to provide a single column of pixels in the sequence A0, B0, A750, B750, A1500, B1500, etc. Where there is motion, an alternate pixel stream would be selected, which would be A0, A0/2 + A750/2, A750, A750/2 + A1500/2, A2250, etc., which contains no B field data. The average of two successive pixels can be obtained using an adder which has its two inputs connected one at each side of a pixel delay latch.

The process of writing rows and reading columns in a memory is called transposition. Clearly two stages of transposition are necessary to return to a horizontal raster output, as shown in Fig. 5.38. The vertical transform must take place between the two transposes, but the horizontal transform could take place before the first transpose or after the second one. In practice the horizontal transform cannot be placed before the first transpose, because it would interfere with the de-interlace and motion-sensing process. The horizontal transform is placed after the second

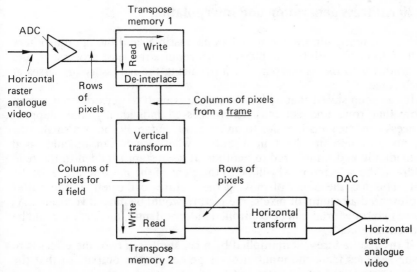

Figure 5.38 Two transposing memories are necessary, one before and one after the vertical transform

transpose and reads rows from the second transpose memory. As the output of the machine must be a horizontal raster, the horizontal transform can be made to work in synchronism with reference H-sync, so that the digital output samples from the H-transform can be taken direct to a DAC to become analog video with standard structure again. A further advantage is that the real-time horizontal output is one field at a time. The preceding vertical transform need only compute array values which lie in the next field to be needed at the output.

It is not possible to take a complete column from a memory until all of the rows have entered. The presence of the two transposes in a DVE results in an unavoidable delay of one frame in the output image. Some DVEs can manage greater delay. The effect on lip-sync may have to be considered. It is not advisable to cut from the input of a DVE to the output, since a frame will be lost, and on cutting back a frame will be repeated.

In a composite environment, the delay due to effects units has some implications. Video from a colour-framed VTR playing back through an effects machine will appear late relative to time code, so edits made on it will look different to the same edit made without the effects unit if there is movement in the scene. The delay through an effects unit does not affect colour framing, however, because a decoder is installed before the transforms and an encoder after. The colour framing of the effects machine output will then be determined entirely by the reference colour black fed to the output encoder.

Because of the decode/encode the VTR does not actually need to be colour framed, provided it is frame synchronized, and if an associated editor has the facility to override the automatic colour framing, then edits can be made to frame accuracy.

5.20 Address generation and interpolation

There are many different manipulations possible, and the approach here will be to begin with the simplest, which require the least processing, and to graduate to the most complex, introducing the necessary processes at each stage.

It has been stated that address mapping is used to perform transforms. Now that rows and columns are processed individually, the mapping process becomes much easier to understand. Fig. 5.39 shows a single row of pixels which are held in a buffer where each can be addressed individually and transferred to another. If a constant is added to the read address, the selected pixel will be to the right of the place where it will be put. This has the effect of moving the picture to the left. If the buffer represented a column of pixels, the picture would be moved vertically. As these two transforms can be controlled independently, the picture could be moved diagonally.

If the read address is multiplied by a constant, say two, the effect is to bring samples from the input closer together on the output, so that the picture size is reduced. Again independent control of the horizontal and vertical transforms is possible, so that the aspect ratio of the picture can be

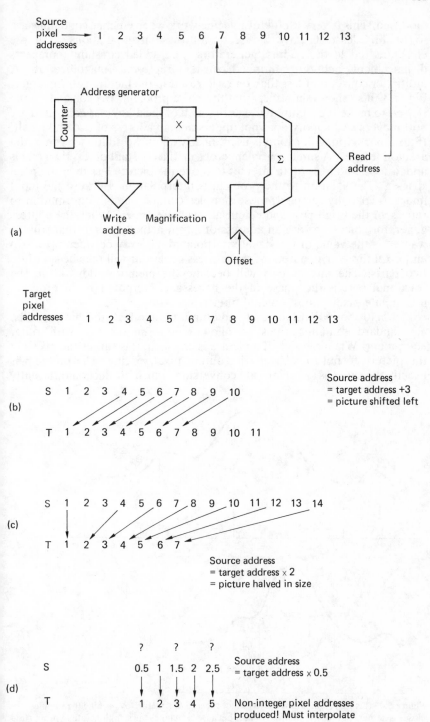

Figure 5.39 Address generation is the fundamental process behind transforms

modified. This is very useful for telecine work when cinemascope films are to be broadcast. Clearly the secret of these manipulations is in the constants fed to the address generators. The added constant represents displacement, and the multiplied constant represents magnification. A multiplier constant of less than one will result in the picture getting larger. Fig. 5.39 also shows, however, that there is a problem. If a constant of 0.5 is used to make the picture twice as big, half of the addresses generated are not integers. A memory does not understand an address of two and a half! If an arbitrary magnification is used, nearly all of the addresses generated are non-integer. A similar problem crops up if a constant of less than one is added to the address in an attempt to move the picture less than the pixel spacing. The solution to the problem is interpolation. Because the input image is spatially sampled, those samples contain enough information to represent the brightness and colour all over the screen. When the address generator comes up with an address of 2.5, it actually means that what is wanted is the value of the signal interpolated half-way between pixel two and pixel three. The output of the address generator will thus be split into two parts. The integer part will become the memory address and the fractional part is the phase of the necessary interpolation. In order to interpolate pixel values a digital filter is necessary.

Fig. 5.40 shows that the input and output of an effects machine must be at standard sampling rates to allow digital interchange with other equipment. When the size of a picture is changed, this causes the pixels in the picture to fail to register with output pixel spacing. The problem is exactly the same as sampling-rate conversion, which produces a differently

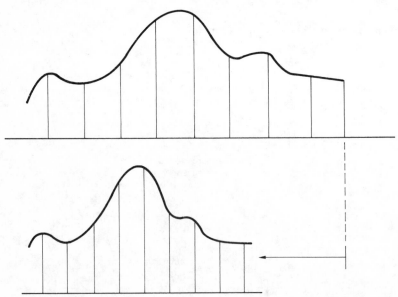

Figure 5.40 It is easy, almost trivial, to reduce the size of a picture by pushing the samples closer together, but this is not often of use, because it changes the sampling rate in proportion to the compression. Where a standard sampling rate output is needed, interpolation must be used

spaced set of samples which still represent the original waveform. One pixel value actually represents the peak brightness of a two-dimensional intensity function, which is the effect of the modulation transfer function of the system on an infinitely small point. As each dimension can be treated separately, the equivalent in one axis is that the pixel value represents the peak value of an infinitely short impulse which has been low-pass filtered to the system bandwidth. The waveform is that of a $\sin x/x$ curve, which has value everywhere except at the centre of other pixels. In order to compute an interpolated value, it is necessary to add together the contribution from all relevant samples, at the point of interest. Each contribution can be obtained by looking up the value of a unity $\sin x/x$ curve at the distance from the input pixel to the output pixel to obtain a coefficient, and multiplying the input pixel value by that coefficient. The process of taking several pixel values, multiplying each by a different coefficient and summing the products can be performed by the FIR (finite impulse response) configuration described earlier. The impulse response of the filter necessary depends on the magnification. Where the picture is being enlarged, the impulse response can be the same as at normal size, but as the size is reduced, the impulse response has to become broader (corresponding to a reduced spatial frequency response) so that more input samples are averaged together to prevent aliasing. The coefficient store will need a two-dimensional structure, such that the magnification and the interpolation phase must both be supplied to obtain a set of coefficients. The magnification can easily be obtained by comparing successive outputs from the address generator.

The number of points in the filter is a compromise between cost and performance, eight being a typical number for high quality. As there are two transform processes in series, every output pixel will be the result of 16 multiplications, so there will be 216 million multiplications per second taking place in the luminance channel alone for a 13.5 MHz sampling-rate unit. The quality of the output video also depends on the number of different interpolation phases available between pixels. The address generator may compute fractional addresses to any accuracy, but these will be rounded off to the nearest available phase in the digital filter. The effect is that the output pixel value provided is actually the value a tiny distance away and has the same result as sampling clock jitter, which is to produce program-modulated noise. The greater the number of phases provided, the larger will be the size of the coefficient store needed. As the coefficient store is two dimensional, an increase in the number of filter points and phases causes an exponential growth in size and cost. The filter itself can be implemented readily with fast multiplier chips, but one problem is accessing the memory to provide input samples. What the memory must do is to take the integer part of the address generator output and provide simultaneously as many adjacent pixels as there are points in the filter. This problem is usually solved by making the memory from several smaller memories with an interleaved address structure, so that several pixel values can be provided from one address.

Fig. 5.41(a) shows one way in which this can be done. The incoming memory write address is split into two sections. The three low-order bits are decoded successively to enable one out of eight RAMs which are fed

184

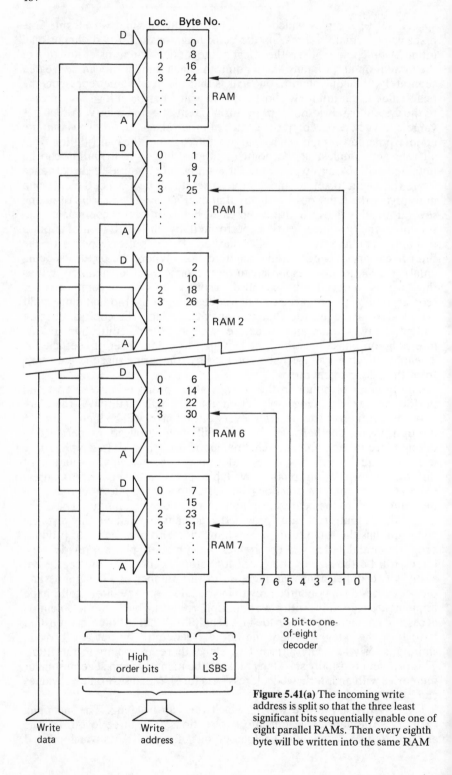

Figure 5.41(a) The incoming write address is split so that the three least significant bits sequentially enable one of eight parallel RAMs. Then every eighth byte will be written into the same RAM

185

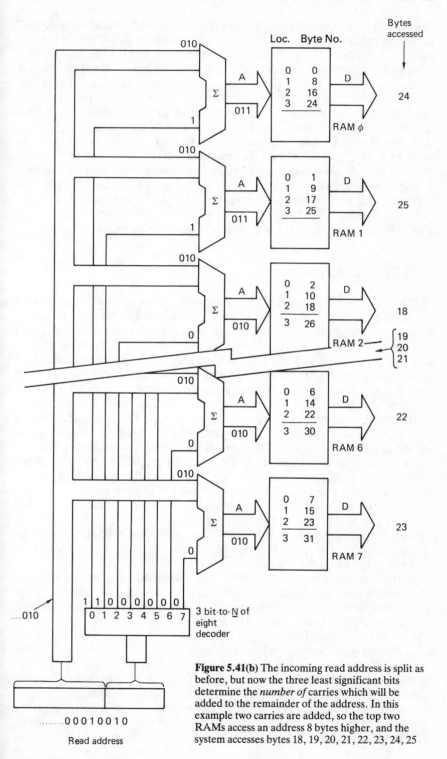

Figure 5.41(b) The incoming read address is split as before, but now the three least significant bits determine the *number of* carries which will be added to the remainder of the address. In this example two carries are added, so the top two RAMs access an address 8 bytes higher, and the system accesses bytes 18, 19, 20, 21, 22, 23, 24, 25

the remainder of the address bits in parallel. The result of this arrangement is that samples 0 through 7 are written in location 0 of successive RAMs, samples 8 through 15 are written in location 1 of the RAMs, and so on.

In order to read the memories, a different addressing configuration is used. The read address comes from the address generator and is split into two sections as before. The most significant bits are fed in parallel to all RAMs, but each RAM is furnished with an adder which allows the address to be increased by one. The least significant bits are also treated in a different manner. They decide *how many* of the addresses will be incremented. Fig. 5.41(b) lists the result for a series of input addresses. In each case, providing one *source address* produces eight adjacent sample values simultaneously. The correct sample numbers are produced, but they suffer an end-around rotation of position. As each one is to be fed to one point of a parallel FIR filter, this does not matter, provided that the coefficients fed to the filter are given the same rotation.

5.21 Skew and rotation

It has been seen that adding a constant to the source address produces a displacement. It is not necessary for the displacement constant to be the same throughout the frame. If the horizontal transform is considered, as in Fig. 5.42(a), the effect of making the displacement a function of line address is to cause a skew. Essentially each line is displaced a different amount. The necessary function generator is shown in simplified form in Fig. 5.42(b), although it could equally be realized in a fast CPU with appropriate software.

It will be seen that the address generator is really two accumulators in series, where the first operates once per line to calculate a new offset which grows linearly from line to line, and the second operates at pixel rate to calculate source addresses from the required magnification. The initial state of the second accumulator is the offset from the first accumulator.

If two skews, one vertical and one horizontal, are performed in turn on the same frame, the result is a rotation as shown in Fig. 5.42(c). Clearly the skew angle parameters for the two transforms must be in the correct relationship to obtain pure rotation. Additionally the magnification needs to be modified by a cosine function of the rotation angle to counteract the stretching effect of the skews.

In the horizontal process, the offset will change once per line, whereas in the vertical process, the offset will change once per column. For simplicity, the offset generators are sometimes referred to as the *slow* address generators, whereas the accumulators which operate at pixel rate are called the *fast* address generators.

Unfortunately skew rotations cannot approach 90°, because the skew parameter goes to infinity, and so a skew rotate is generally restricted to rotations of ±45°. This is not a real restriction, since the apparatus already exists to turn a picture on its side. This can be done readily by failing to transpose in one of the memories. There will no longer be two cancelling transposes, so the picture will be turned through 90° when it emerges. Although the failure to transpose could be at either of the memories if only

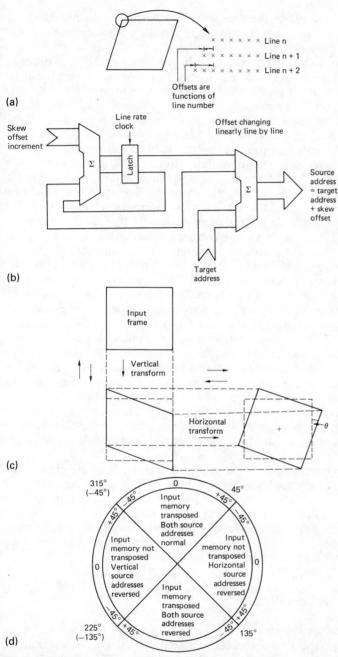

(a)

(b)

(c)

(d)

Figure 5.42 (a) Skew is achieved by subjecting each line of pixels to a different offset (b) The hardware necessary to perform a skew where the left hand accumulator produces the offset which increases every line, and the right hand accumulator adds it to the address. (c) A z-axis rotate is performed using a pair of skews in succession. The magnification of each transform must also change from unity to cos θ because horizontal and vertical components of distances on the frame reduce as the frame turns. (d) The four modes necessary for a complete z-axis rotation using skews. Switching between modes at the vertical interval allows a skew range of ±45° (outer ring) to embrace a complete revolution in conjunction with memory transposes which exchange rows and columns to give 90° changes

this effect is required, in practice it cannot be at the second memory, because this would put both transforms in series on the same axis, so that any other manipulation in addition to the rotate could only be done in one axis. The failure to transpose has to be in the input memory, in order to keep the horizontal and vertical transforms at right angles. Using the input memory causes a small problem when motion is detected. When turning the picture 90°, the input memory is read in rows, as it is written, but the readout is treated as a column. In order to de-interlace under these conditions, whole lines must be read from the A and B field memories alternately and treated as columns by the vertical transform. If there is motion, entire lines must be interpolated from the A memory. The first line would be A0, A1, A2, etc., but the next line would be A0/2 + A750/2, A1/2 + A751/2, A2/2 + A752/2, etc., and the line after that would be A750, A751, A752, etc. This is a different interpolation process to that shown earlier, and the de-interlacer must be told that there has been a failure to transpose. To obtain the correct interpolation, the delay in the pixel averager has to be increased from one pixel to one line.

Fig. 5.42(d) shows how continuous rotation can be obtained. From −45° to +45°, normal skew rotation is used. At 45°, during the vertical interval, the memory transpose is turned off, causing the picture to be flipped 90° and laterally inverted. Reversing the source address sequence cancels the lateral inversion, and at the same time the skew parameters are changed from +45° to -45°. In this way the picture passes smoothly through the 45° barrier, and skew parameters continue to change until 135° (90° transpose + 45° skew) is reached. At this point, three things happen, again during the vertical interval. The transpose is switched back on, re-orienting the picture, the source addresses are both reversed, which turns the picture upside down, and a skew rotate of −45° is applied, returning the picture to 135° of rotation, from which point motion can continue. The remainder of the rotation takes place along similar lines which can be followed in the diagram.

The rotation described is in the Z axis, i.e. the axis coming out of the source picture at right angles. Rotation about the other axes is rather more difficult, because to perform the effect properly, perspective is needed. In simple machines, there is no perspective, and the effect of rotation is as if viewed from a long way away. These non-perspective pseudo-rotations are achieved by simply changing the magnification in the appropriate axis as a cosine function of the rotation angle.

5.22 Perspective rotation

In order to follow the operation of a true perspective machine, some knowledge of perspective is necessary. Stated briefly, the phenomenon of perspective is due to the angle subtended to the eye by objects being a function not only of their size but also of their distance. Fig. 5.43 shows that the size of an image on the rear wall of a pinhole camera can be increased either by making the object larger or bringing it closer. In the absence of stereoscopic vision, it is not possible to tell which has happened. The pinhole camera is very useful for the study of perspective and has

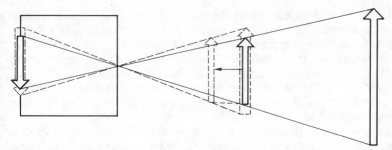

Figure 5.43 The image on the rear of the pinhole camera is identical for the two solid objects shown because the size of the object is proportional to distance, and the subtended angle remains the same. The image can be made larger (dotted) by making the object larger or moving it closer

indeed been used by artists for that purpose. The clinically precise perspective of Canaletto paintings was achieved through the use of the camera obscura (darkened room in Latin).[7]

It is sometimes claimed that the focal length of the lens used on a camera changes the perspective of a picture. This is not true: perspective is only a function of the relative positions of the camera and the subject. Fitting a wide-angle lens simply allows the camera to come near enough to keep dramatic perspective within the frame, whereas fitting a long-focus lens allows the camera to be far enough away to display a reasonable-sized image with flat perspective.[8]

Since a single eye cannot tell distance unaided, all current effects machines work by simply producing the correct subtended angles which the brain perceives as a three-dimensional effect. Fig. 5.44 shows that, to a single eye, there is no difference between a three-dimensional scene and a two-dimensional image formed where rays traced from features to the eye intersect an imaginary plane. This is exactly the reverse of the map projection shown in Fig. 5.30 and is the principle of all perspective manipulators.

The case of perspective rotation of a plane source will be discussed first. Fig. 5.44 shows that when a plane input frame is rotated about a horizontal

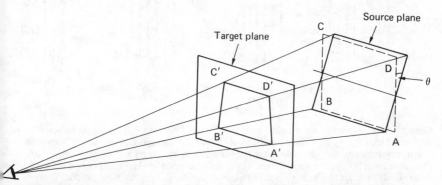

Figure 5.44 In a planar rotation effect the source plane ABCD is the rectangular input picture. If it is rotated through the angle θ, ray tracing to a single eye at left will produce a trapezoidal image A'B'C'D' on the target. Magnification will now vary with position on the picture

axis, the distance from the top of the picture to the eye is no longer the same as the distance from the bottom of the picture to the eye. The result is that the top and bottom edges of the picture subtend different angles to the eye, and where the rays cross the target plane, the image has become trapezoidal. There is now no such thing as the magnification of the picture. The magnification changes continuously from top to bottom of the picture, and if a uniform grid is input, after a perspective rotation it will appear non-linear as the diagram shows.

As the two axes of the picture are transformed consecutively, it can be seen in Fig. 5.45(a) that the first process will be a vertical transform which is non-linear. The address generator produces a function or series of addresses which is curved, which will be seen in Fig. 5.45(b) to produce the desired distortion. The vertical process is followed by the horizontal process where each line or row of pixels has the same magnification, but

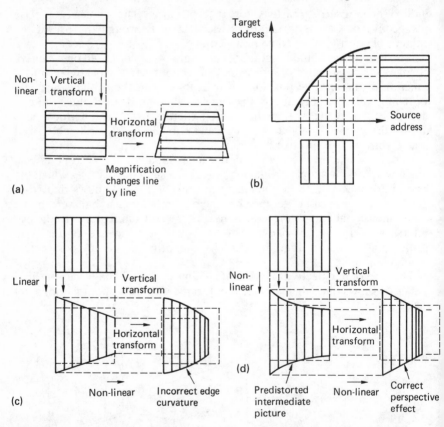

Figure 5.45 (a) A perspective rotation consists of a non-linear vertical transform followed by a horizontal transform where the magnification is linear but changes line by line (b) Non-linear transforms require a curved relationship between source and target address (c) How not to perform a rotation about a vertical axis. The non-linear horizontal process distorts the vertical process. (d) In order to give correct manipulation, the vertical process must produce columns which will be the correct length for the position the horizontal process will put them in. This implies that the vertical transform knows what the horizontal transform will do and pre-distorts accordingly. The non-linear horizontal transform then cancels the distortion

the magnification changes from one line to the next. The result is the desired trapezoidal shape with the correct non-linearity, which the eye takes to be a rotation of the source, even though the image never leaves the plane of the monitor. Rotation about a vertical axis will now be considered. Again this results in a trapezoidal picture, but now the non-linearity appears in the horizontal transform. Fig. 5.45(c) shows that if the vertical and horizontal transforms are performed in that order, the non-linear horizontal transform causes an unwanted distortion – the edges of the picture become curved. This is a fundamental problem of separating the axes, and some thought is necessary to provide a solution. Fig. 5.45(d) shows that the problem is caused by the vertical process moving a given pixel vertically by what appears to be the correct distance, whereas it should move the pixel so that it will be at the correct vertical position *after* it has been horizontally transformed. In other words, the vertical process must predistort the intermediate image in such a way that the non-linear horizontal process will cancel the predistortion to give the correct overall transform.

The above process implies that the vertical transform must be exactly aware of what the horizontal transform will do. This is no problem because both transforms are computed from high-level commands put in to the system by the operator, but it does require some care to supply the transform parameters to the processors at the correct time, because the horizontal transform cannot begin until the vertical transform is completed, owing to the presence of the transpose memory. This means that the transform parameters for the horizontal processor will need to be supplied one field later than the parameters for the vertical process. Fig. 5.46 shows how the field shift in the parameters relates to the progress of fields through a machine.

Real time field no	n	n + 1	n + 2	n + 3	n + 4
Field being written to input memory	n *	n + 1	n + 2	n + 3	n + 4
Vertical transform	n − 1	n *	n + 1	n + 2	n + 3
Horizontal transform	n -- 2	n − 1	n *	n + 1	n + 2
Odd field parameters		Vert *	Horiz *	Vert	Horiz
Even field parameters	Vert	Horiz	Vert	Horiz	

Figure 5.46 Timing chart showing how the transform parameters are supplied at the correct time. For a field which arrives at time n it can be read from input memory at field n + 1 where the vetical transform will take place. The horizontal transform will take place in the next field. In order to have matching transform parameters, the vertical parameters must be supplied one field ahead of the horizontal parameters (Follow asterisk for progress of field n)

The address generators for perspective operation are necessarily complex, and a careful approach is necessary to produce the complex calculations at the necessary speed.[9] Fig. 5.47 shows a section through a transform where the source plane has been rotated about an axis perpendicular to the page. The mapping or ray tracing process must produce a straight line from every target pixel (corresponding to where an output value is needed) to locate a source address (corresponding to where an input value is available). Moving the source value to the target performs the necessary transform.

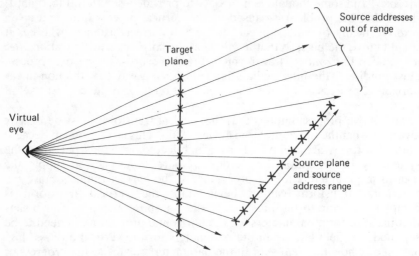

Figure 5.47 A rotation of the source plane along with a movement away from the observer is shown here. The system has to produce pixel values at the spacing demanded by the output. Thus a ray from the eye to each target pixel is produced to locate a source pixel. Since the chances of exactly hitting a source pixel are small, the need for interpolation is clear. If the source plane is missed, this will result in an out-of-range source address, and a background value will be substituted

Clearly it is possible to compute any source address from the target address and a knowledge of the geometry of the system. This will take several minutes with a pocket calculator, making liberal use of trigonometric functions. The DVE must compute the source address in 75 ns, and no known computer can perform the calculation at that speed. The solution is to split the problem into two parts. For a given position of the source plane in space, all of the angles except that of the ray being traced become constants, and therefore the trigonometrical functions of those angles also become constants. A general purpose computer can work out what the constants are for a given source orientation in less than a field period, and these constants are then used by the slow and fast address generators which execute much simpler equations at line/column and pixel rate.

The derivation of the address generator equations is high-cholesterol mathematics which can be found in Newman and Sproull[6] and in the ADO patent.[9] For the purposes of this chapter, an understanding of the result can be had by considering the example of Fig. 5.48.

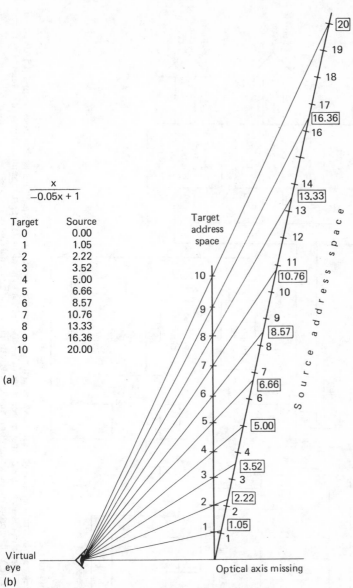

$$\frac{x}{-0.05x + 1}$$

Target	Source
0	0.00
1	1.05
2	2.22
3	3.52
4	5.00
5	6.66
6	8.57
7	10.76
8	13.33
9	16.36
10	20.00

(a)

(b)

Figure 5.48 (a) The above equation calculates the source address for each evenly spaced target address from 0 to 10. All numbers are kept positive for simplicity, so only one side of the picture is represented here. (b) The ray tracing diagram corresponding to the calculations of (a). Following a ray from the virtual eye through any target pixel address will locate the source addresses calculated

In this figure, successive integer values of x have been used in a simple source address calculation equation which contains a division stage. The addresses produced form a non-linear sequence and will be seen to lie on a rotated source plane. The actual equations necessary for a planar transform are shown in Fig. 5.49 along with the block diagram of one

194

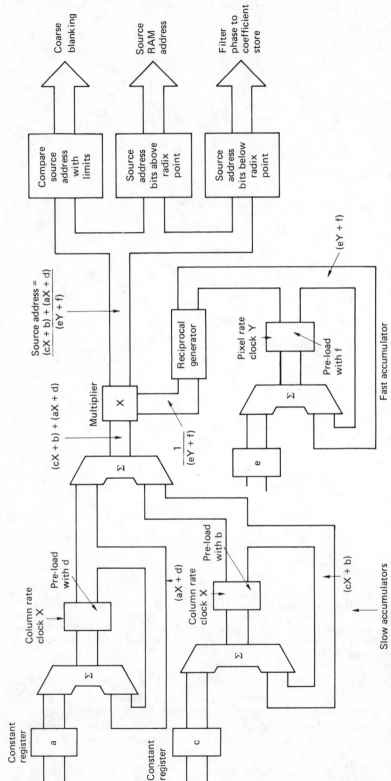

Figure 5.49(a) Hardware block diagram of vertical address generator. Accumulators on left operate once per column. When latch is clocked, preloaded value d (or b) is added to constant a (or c) once more, hence (aX + d) or (cX + b) is calculated. Fast accumulator produces a new denominator by clocking at pixel rate Y. Reciprocal of denominator is multiplied by numerator to give final source address

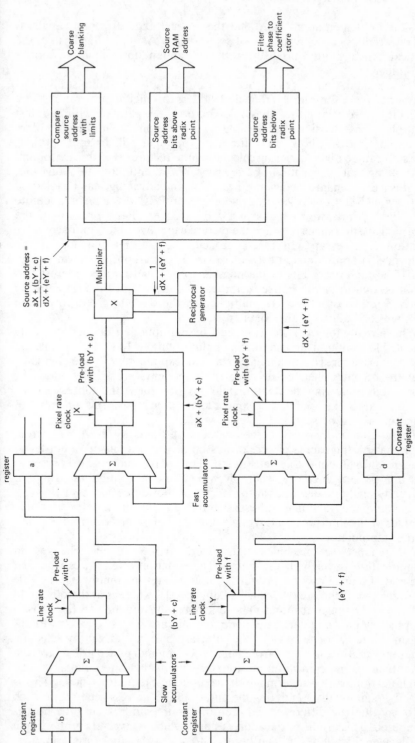

Figure 5.49(b) Hardware block diagram to implement horizontal equation. Slow accumulators are pre-loaded with constants c and f at the beginning of each field and calculate a new value $(bY + c)$ or $(eY + f)$ every line. Fast accumulators are preloaded with the values from the slow accumulators at the start of every line, then revert to constant registers a, d

possible implementation. Note that the vertical and horizontal equations are different because of the use of separability. As Fig. 5.45 showed, the vertical transform must predistort if the subsequent horizontal transform is non-linear.

The accumulation stages of the address generator are quite straightforward, as these are simply repeated adders or digital integrators. The difficulty arises with the division. There is no parallel with the fast multiplier. Fast division is impossible, as all divisions are in the form of an experiment, to see how many times one number will fit into another. Division can be made easier by calculating the reciprocal of the divisor and multiplying. The calculation of a reciprocal is, admittedly, still a division, but it is a division into a constant, i.e. unity, and advantage can be taken of PROMs. For short wordlengths, the reciprocal PROM will be of moderate size, but address wordlengths in DVEs are very large because of the enormous virtual space in which the picture can move, and a more complex solution is necessary. In this approach, the transfer function of the reciprocal is approximated by a piecewise linear graph, as shown in Fig. 5.50. The high-order bits of the number to be inverted now address two PROMs, one to give a coarse reciprocal and one to give the slope of the curve. The low-order bits are multiplied by the slope to give a correction term which is added to the coarse reciprocal.

Where really long wordlengths must be multiplied or divided, the only practicable solution is to use floating point notation. In floating point, the numbers are expressed as a mantissa and an exponent. Only the mantissae need to be multiplied or divided; the exponents are simply added or subtracted. Following the floating point division stage, the addresses must be returned to fixed point. The source address then performs a number of functions as can be seen in Fig. 5.49.

The source address will be compared with limits to see if a ray from target has hit the source picture or missed it. If it has missed, a border or background value must be substituted. The source address also passes to the interpolator memory where it will access a contiguous group of (typically) eight pixels. The low-order bits of the source address below the radix point (the fractional address) determine the position between source samples of the interpolated target pixel, and so these bits control the phase of the interpolator.

All perspective machines must work with dynamic changes in magnification throughout the frame. The situation often arises where at one end of a pixel row the magnification is greater than unity and the FIR filter has to interpolate between available pixels, whereas at the other end of the row the magnification will be less than unity and the FIR filter has to adopt a low-pass and decimate mode to eliminate excessive pixels without aliasing. The characteristics of the filter are changed at will by selecting different coefficient sets from pages of memory according to the instantaneous magnification at the centre of the filter window. The magnification can be determined by computing the address slope. This is done by digitally differentiating the output of the address generator, which is to say that the difference between one source address and the next is computed. This produces the address slope, which is inversely proportional to the magnification, and can be used to select the appropriate impulse

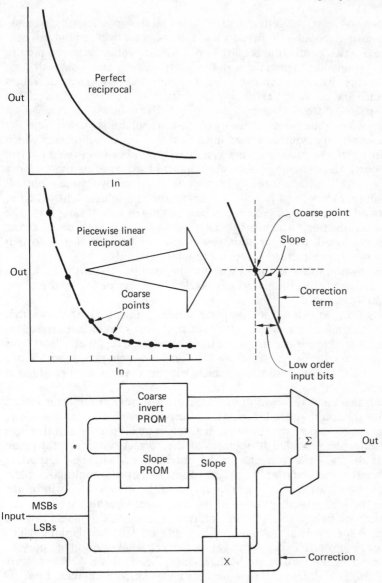

Figure 5.50 Piecewise linear reciprocal calculator

response width in the interpolator. The interpolator output is then a transformed image.

5.23 DVE backgrounds

When an effects unit reduces the size of the picture, it is necesary to control what happens in the area between the edge of the picture and the edge of the screen. At least, the system must ensure that this area defaults to black, but it is usually possible to insert some kind of plain background instead. There are two conflicting requirements. The transition between picture and background has to pass through the interpolator so that a smooth edge results. This will be achieved by switching to background values (luminance and colour differences in the respective processing channels) in source space before the interpolator. Fig. 5.51(a) shows the mechanism necessary. When the source memory of the interpolator is loaded from the transpose memory, sample values must pass through a multiplexer which can switch between picture samples and background values from a control system port. The switching points are obtained by comparing the memory addresses with limit addresses which are also provided by a system port. If the memory address falls outside the limits, the multiplexer will switch to background values and the result will be a column or row of samples in the interpolator memory which has background values at both ends. If the picture is cropped, the limit addresses are simply brought closer, so that more of the source picture is replaced by background.

The transition to background will now be manipulated with the source picture and can be positioned to sub-pixel accuracy according to the phase of the interpolator.

This is not, however, the complete solution. Fig. 5.51(b) shows that when the magnification becomes very small, the background area in source space must tend towards infinite size if the screen is to be filled. Clearly this is impossible. In order to allow background generation without a restriction on the magnification which will be used, a further stage is necessary.

The arrangement is shown in Fig. 5.51(c). A further multiplexer inserts an identical background value *after* the interpolator. This device is working in target space, and so can only switch at target pixel spacing, but this is of no consequence provided it operates at the correct time. Several pixels away from the source picture, the interpolator will be outputting background values, and as the result of interpolating a continuous plain area is the same as sampling it, the output of the interpolator will be the same as the background value, and the switch can operate invisibly. The two processes, before and after the interpolator, are called fine and coarse blanking respectively and should not be confused with the blanking which is necessary to return background values to black level smoothly to prevent out-of-band signals with bright backgrounds. Clearly this is only necessary in the horizontal domain. It is sometimes called smooth blanking to avoid confusion. Fig. 5.51(d) shows the sequence of events in a horizontal line output from a DVE. At the beginning of the line the smooth blanker slowly releases so that a gradual transition to background takes place. The background values have come from the coarse blanker after the interpolator. As the line proceeds, the output of the transform address generator will fall within the range of the interpolator memory, and meaningful samples will begin to come from the interpolator. These will be numerically identical to the coarse blanking value, because they have come from the fine blanking multiplexer via the interpolator. It is now possible to switch invisibly to the interpolator output. The picture/background transition will thus have come through the interpolator. At the opposite

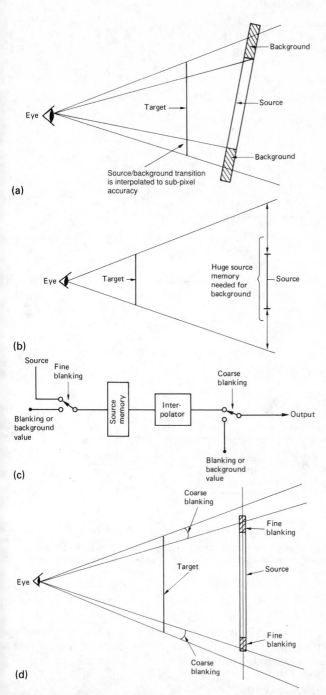

Figure 5.51 (a) Source/background transition is interpolated to sub-pixel accuracy. (b) At small magnifications the memory needed in source space to hold background values becomes very large. (c) Two multiplexers are necessary to insert background before and after the interpolator. (d) Coarse blanking multiplexer is switched in before the fine blanking in source space runs out at the ends of the address sequence

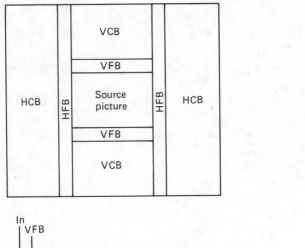

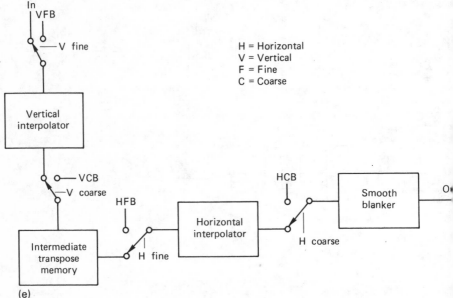

(e)

Figure 5.51 (*Continued*). (e) The position of the four blanking multiplexers in the vertical and horizontal processes, and the position on the screen of the contributions from each when the picture size is greatly reduced

edge of the picture, the return transition will be similarly treated. Shortly after this, the interpolator output will again be identical to the coarse blanking value, and a second invisible switch will be made to coarse background. At the end of active line, the smooth blanker will gradually fade the background value to black.

With a reduced size picture it is possible to see the origin of sample values in different parts of the screen (Fig. 5.51(e)), and this is one of the most powerful tools available for locating the position of a failure in a DVE.

5.24 Non-planar effects

The basic approach to perspective rotation of plane pictures has been described, and this can be extended to embrace transforms which make the source picture appear non-planar. Effects in this category include rolling the picture on to the surface of an imaginary solid such as a cylinder or a cone. Fig. 5.52 shows that the ray tracing principle is still used, but that the relationship between source and target addresses has become much more complex. The problem is that when a source picture can be curved, it may

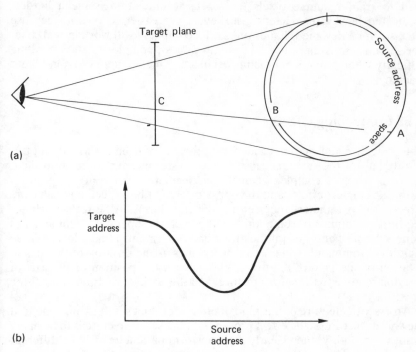

(a)

(b)

Figure 5.52 (a) To produce a rolled up image for a given target pixel address C, there will be two source addresses A and B. Pixel data from A and B must be added with weighting dependent on the transparency of the nearer pixel to produce the pixel value to be put on the target plane at C. (b) Transfer function for a rolling up transform. There are two source addresses for every target address, hence the need for target accumulation

be put in such an attitude that one part of the source can be seen through another part. This results in two difficulties. First the source address function needs to be of higher order, and secondly the target needs to be able to accept and accumulate pixel data from two different source addresses, with weighting given to the one nearer the viewer according to the transparency allocated to the picture. Transparency was discussed in Chapter 3.

The high-order address functions needed for non-planar images cannot be readily implemented in fast hard-wired accumulators, because too much hardware would be needed. A fast CPU will be needed to generate these address sequences in real time. It is possible, but difficult, to go from high-level operator commands to transform parameters in real time, as is done in Sony's System G. In other non-planar machines, it is usually necessary to design the effect without seeing it, in high-level language, and then compile the high-level program into machine code which the transform processors can then use as microcode at a later time. Where the picking of source pixels to perform the transform is in a software-driven CPU, accumulation with transparency in target space is relatively easy if the CPU is fast enough, because only a few extra microinstructions will be necessary to include the accumulation, but where dedicated hardware is used to tranfer source pixels to target, accumulation is much harder. Dedicated hardware machines, however, are easier to operate because effects can be designed 'hands on' as the compilers will work in real time. For these reasons there is a large jump in cost, complexity and operating difficulty when going from planar perspective manipulators to non-planar machines.

5.25 Controlling effects

The basic mechanism of the transform process has been described, but this is only half of the story, because these transforms have to be controlled. There is a lot of complex geometrical calculation necessary to perform even the simplest effect, and the operator cannot be expected to calculate directly the parameters required for the transforms. All effects machines require a computer of some kind, with which the operator communicates using keyboard entry or joystick/trackball movements at high level. These high-level commands will specify such things as the position of the axis of rotation of the picture relative to the viewer, the position of the axis of rotation relative to the source picture, and the angle of rotation in the three axes.

An essential feature of this kind of effects machines is fluid movement of the source picture as the effect proceeds. If the source picture is to be made to move smoothly, then clearly the transform parameters will be different in each field. The operator cannot be expected to input the source position for every field, because this would be an enormous task. Additionally, storing the effect would require a lot of space. The solution is for the operator to specify the picture position at strategic points during the effect, and then digital filters are used to compute the intermediate positions so that every field will have different parameters.

The specified positions are referred to as knots, nodes or keyframes, the first being the computer graphics term. The operator is free to enter knots anywhere in the effect, and so they will not necessarily be evenly spaced in time, i.e. there may well be different numbers of fields between each knot. In this environment it is not possible to use conventional FIR-type digital filtering, because a fixed impulse response is inappropriate for irregularly spaced samples.

Interpolation of various orders is used ranging from zero-order hold for special jerky effects through linear interpolation to cubic interpolation for very smooth motion. The algorithms used to perform the interpolation are known as splines, a term which has come down from shipbuilding via computer graphics.[10] When a ship is designed, the draughtsman produces hull cross-sections at intervals along the keel, whereas the shipyard needs to recreate a continuous structure. The solution was a lead-filled bar, known as a spline, which could be formed to join up each cross-section in a smooth curve, and then used as a template to form the hull plating.

The filter which does not ring cannot be made, and so the use of spline algorithms for smooth motion sometimes results in unintentional overshoots of the picture position. This can be overcome by modifying the filtering algorithm. Spline algorithms usually look ahead beyond the next knot in order to compute the degree of curvature in the graph of the parameter against time. If a break is put in that parameter at a given knot, the spline algorithm is prevented from looking ahead, and no overshoot will occur. In practice the effect is created and run without breaks, and then breaks are added later where they are subjectively thought necessary.

It will be seen that there are several levels of control in an effects machine. At the highest level, the operator can create, store and edit knots, and specify the times which elapse between them. The next level is for the knots to be interpolated by spline algorithms to produce parameters for every field in the effect. The field frequency parameters are then used as the inputs to the geometrical computation of transform parameters which the lowest level of the machine will use as microinstructions to act upon the pixel data. Each of these layers will often have a separate processor, not just for speed, but also to allow software to be updated at certain levels without disturbing others.

5.26 Digital standards conversion

The interchange of video program material between line standards has been necessary because of the unfortunate number of different broadcast standards in use throughout the world. Standards conversion is relatively difficult, and it is only recently that the quality obtained has approached theoretical limits with the adoption of complex digital techniques. It will be shown here that the maximum performance achievable is rather poor, not because of any lack of understanding, but as a direct consequence of the fundamental shortcomings of broadcast television which are exaggerated by standards conversion.

Frame-based systems sample the changes of the image with respect to time. The sampling rate is the frame rate in a non-interleaved system. The input scene should not then change more often than one cycle per two frames, or aliasing will take place. In practice the camera has no control over the scene, and aliasing is inevitable on fast-moving objects such as helicopter rotors and stagecoach wheels, and for less obvious reasons on slow-moving fine detail.

As was explained in Chapter 2, once a sampled system has aliased, the effects can never be removed, because the alias frequencies cannot be distinguished from genuine information at the same frequency. Standards converters have great difficulty with aliased signals, and as these occur frequently on real video due to the rather inadequate frame rates, too much should not be expected from the converter as it is making the best of a bad job.

The bandwidth required by a television signal is obtained by multiplying the number of cycles of resolution in a line by the number of lines in a frame, and then by the frame rate. If similar vertical and horizontal resolution is assumed, bandwidth increases as the square of the resolution for a given frame rate. The adoption of interlace was claimed to allow the apparent picture rate to be higher than the frame rate. The apparent picture rate or field rate determines the visibility of flicker. With interlace, sending half the picture twice as often allows the bandwidth to be halved without producing flicker. Since only half of the necessary information is sent, information theory alone will tell us not to expect great things. Interlace is a form of temporal oversampling at the expense of spatial resolution. The effect of interlace on still scenes is invisible, because spatially adjacent lines in different fields combine to give full resolution. On moving scenes the image in successive fields will be different, and full resolution is not available. In the vertical axis, the vertical frequency will be one-half the spatial line frequency in a field, or one-quarter the spatial line frequency of the complete picture. The presence of interlace compounds the effect of an already inadequate field rate, making standards conversion doubly difficult.

Fig. 5.53 shows that a television signal in a certain line standard represents a series of two-dimensional images. A different line standard could have a different number of lines and a different number of frames per second. For colour broadcasts, the modulation method used to carry the colour information could also be different. The task of the standards converter is to transfer the moving image from one signal structure to the other as faithfully as possible.

Conversion from one colour modulation system to another is relatively easy. Conversion between different numbers of lines per frame is relatively straightforward, but conversion between different frame rates is very difficult indeed, particularly in the presence of interlace and with the unavoidable aliasing in real pictures.

The handling of colour information in standards conversion is generally to decode the composite input to form separate luminance and colour difference signal channels. These are then passed to three similar baseband standards converters, although the performance of the colour difference channels would not need to be so high. Following the conversion, the output signals would then be re-encoded into the appropriate composite form. This approach is necessary because the transforms needed for spatial and temporal interpolation of the image would destroy the phase and thus the meaning of any subcarrier. The decoding can be considered separately from the conversion process. As there are many different types of colour modulation methods, a multi-standard converter will necessarily be complex. The colour decoding and encoding techniques may be analog or digital, and the digital techniques have already been discussed in this chapter. Where conversion between NTSC and PAL or SECAM is considered, the signal bandwidth cannot exceed the 4.2 MHz of NTSC, so there is little point in attempting to decode PAL luminance above the subcarrier frequency. Low-pass filtering is often used to obtain luminance, which means that any residual subcarrier footprint is unlikely to cause beats in the other standard.

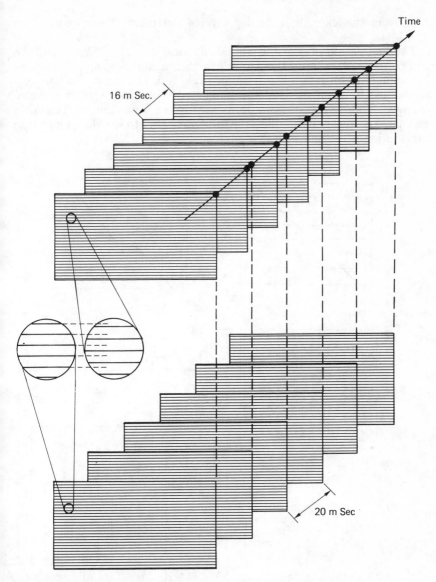

Figure 5.53 The basic problem of standards conversion. The line spacing is easy to accommodate. The field spacing is not

As the composite decoding takes place prior to the standards conversion proper, it is relatively straightforward to insert a digital signal according to CCIR 601 which bypasses the composite decoder and the analog-to-digital converters. It is also feasible to incorporate the D-2 to 4:2:2 decoder described earlier in this chapter to allow the input section to be entirely digital. The digital output of the standards conversion process could then be output according to CCIR 601, but in the alternative line standard.

Clearly in this case the sampling rate of the machine will need to be 13.5 MHz.

The line period of 625/50 is almost identical to that of 525/60, and the consequence of assuming them to be exactly the same is a minute change of horizontal magnification which can be neglected. The number of lines in a field must be changed, and the number of fields per second must be changed. These processes can be consecutive or simultaneous. The latter may yield hardware economies, the former is easier to visualize, and so the explanation will begin with that approach.

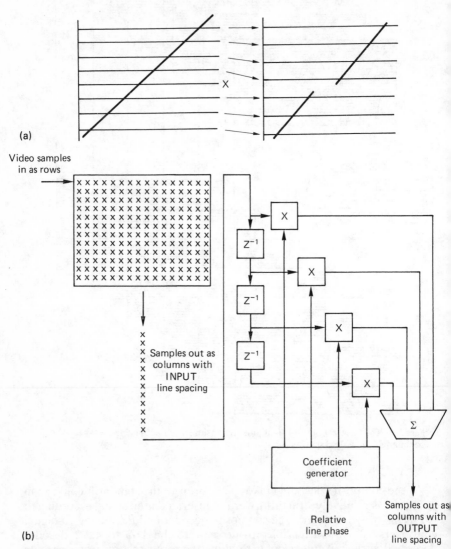

Figure 5.54 (a) Omitting or repeating lines in standards conversion causes discontinuities on diagonal detail. (b) The conversion of line spacing is by vertical FIR filtering on columns of pixels

In order to change the number of lines in a field, interpolation is necessary in a vertical direction. The difference in line spacing between 625/50 and 525/60 is such that there are 21 different relationships between the lines. It is not possible to throw away lines or repeat lines, as this results in steps on diagonal edges, as shown in Fig. 5.54. The figure also shows that columns of pixels are fed to a digital filter which has a low-pass response cutting off at the vertical spatial frequency of half the line spatial frequency. The necessary phase-linear characteristic is supplied by using the FIR (finite-impulse response) structure which has been described. Because there are many different line relationships, a different set of coefficients corresponding to a different offset of the impulse is necessary for each phase of interpolation.

In a standards converter, the magnification is fixed by the relationship between the number of active lines in the two standards. Production of the best resolution requires a de-interlaced frame as input, but it is not always necessary to de-interlace the incoming fields separately prior to filtering. Fig. 5.55 shows that it is possible to supply alternate points in the FIR filter from columns of pixels in alternate fields. In this case the vertical frequency of the input is doubled, and the impulse response of the filter is sharpened in order to obtain maximum vertical resolution. Unfortunately

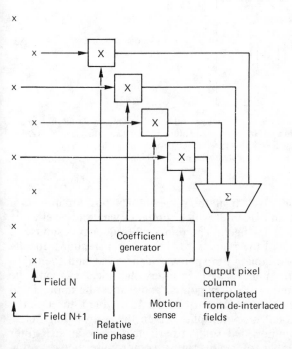

Figure 5.55 Information from both fields can be used to improve vertical resolution when there is little motion. When motion occurs, the filter impulse response must broaden, as samples from one of the fields will be neglected, and vertical resolution falls

the presence of movement in the images means that if successive fields are superimposed a double image results. It is necessary to use motion detection by comparing successive frames as has been described. When there is motion in the area of the picture being processed, the pixels from the field farthest away in time are neglected by setting the coefficients fed to every other filter point to zero. The impulse response of the filter must also be broadened to account for the lack of resolution on the input. The coefficient store will thus have a two-dimensional structure, where one dimension is the repeating vertical phase relationship of the lines and the other is the amount of motion detected.[11]

As has been noted, the conversion of field rate is difficult. Fig. 5.56 shows that it is not possible to omit or repeat frames because this results in jerky movement. It is again necessary to interpolate, this time temporally.

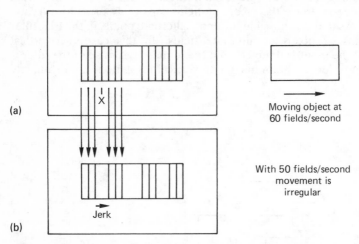

Figure 5.56 At (a) a rectangular object is moving smoothly to the right, and 7 superimposed fields are shown in the frame in a 60 Hz system. If an attempt is made to convert to 50 HZ by omitting fields, as at (b) there will be jerky movement where the image moves a greater distance due to the omission. This is subjectively highly disturbing

In temporal interpolation, pixels from the same physical position in several frames form the input to an FIR filter which computes what the pixel value in between frames would have been. The temporal frequency response of the filter must be one-half of the frame rate of the slower standard. Ideally the filter should have a frequency response which is flat and then falls steeply at the cut-off frequency. In FIR filters this ideal can only be realized with a large number of filter points, and it must be appreciated that for every point in the filter there must be a field of video stored in the machine, and an additional fast multiplier. Even the use of four fields, which is increasingly common, is less than perfect, because an FIR filter with such a small number of points must compromise between the conflicting requirements of stopband rejection and rate of roll-off. As the filter is designed to suppress the unwanted field rate in the information spectrum, stopband rejection is important. The symptom of insufficient stopband rejection would be beats between the two field rates modulating the brightness. Since this is highly objectionable, the rate of roll-off is generally sacrificed instead, which means that the temporal frequency response of the converter is impaired.

The use of separate processes for vertical and temporal filtering requires more hardware, such as a further memory to buffer the two processes. It is usual to combine both processes into one and construct a two-dimensional digital filter. In the analog domain, such a device would be unthinkable; in the digital domain it is much easier to construct than to describe.

Fig. 5.57 shows that the input to a two-dimensional filter can be considered to be pixels in columns whose height represents distance up the tube face, spaced apart by the period between fields. Owing to interlace, the pixels in odd fields have a vertical displacement relative to the pixels in even fields. Assuming a typical value of four filter points in each dimension, four pixels from four fields are combined to produce one output pixel by providing each input pixel with a coefficient by which it is multiplied before adding the products. The output pixel will have a temporal and spatial phase which determines what the coefficients must be.

Fig. 5.58 shows that if the temporal impulse response is considered first, an interpolated pixel value is obtained by computing the time at which the pixel is needed in relation to the time of available fields. In 525/60 to 625/50 conversion, input spacing will be 16.7 milliseconds and output spacing will be 20 milliseconds. The time determines the filter phase, which has the effect of shifting the impulse response of the filter through time to allow a greater contribution from near fields and a smaller contribution from far fields.

The vertical phase of the desired pixel in relation to the available pixels will then determine the vertical phase of the filter. The sum of the four coefficients used in a given field column will equal the (imaginary) coefficient of a one-dimensional temporal filter at that field.

Where the difference between successive frames is very small, this can be assumed to be due to random noise, and broadening the impulse response has the effect of reducing the noise.

It is not practicable to optimize the action of such a device for all material, because good performance on noisy inputs may result in unnatural removal of rain and reflections on water in normal video inputs. It is usual to provide an operator control so that the motion sensing can be made more or less active according to the subject matter.

Where the difference between pixels in successive frames is large, this must be due to motion, and it will be necessary to modify the two-dimensional impulse response to prevent multiple images. Essentially what happens is that the coefficients for fields which contain movement are reduced, so their contribution to the output pixel becomes smaller, and the coefficients fed to remaining fields increase to compensate.

With considerable complexity, it is possible to construct a correlator which attempts to find similarities between one frame and the next frame which has been subject to a series of displacements. Where the movement of the image is equal and opposite to the displacement, correlation will be high between the two, and the distance and direction of image movement can then be established. If the movement of the image between two frames is known, then the moving area can be shifted to the position it would have occupied at the time an output field is required, and it can then be used as an input to the filter. This allows higher resolution to be achieved, but the complexity of circuitry required is formidable, as it must of course work in real time.

5.27 Character generators

The simplest form of screen presentation of alphanumerics is the ubiquitous visual display unit (VDU) which is frequently necessary to control computer-based systems. The mechanism used for character generation in such devices is very simple and thus makes a good introduction to the subject.

In VDUs there is no grey scale, and the characters are formed by changing the video signal between two levels at the appropriate place in the line. Fig. 5.59 shows how a character is built up in this way and also illustrates how easy it is to obtain the reversed video used in some wordprocessor displays to simulate dark characters on white paper. Also shown is the method of highlighting single characters or words by using localized reverse video.

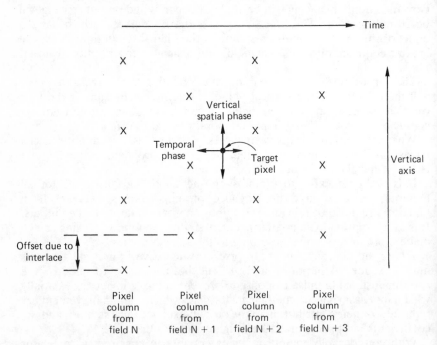

Figure 5.57(a) In a two-dimensional digital filter, columns from several fields form the input, and the target pixel phase vertically and temporally controls the coefficients. The structure of the filter is exactly that of a FIR filter, only the sources of information cause the two-dimensional effect

211

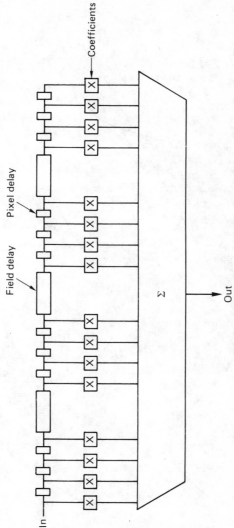

Figure 5.57(b) Rearrangement of 2-D FIR filter into temporal domain illustrates how the impulse response spreads over many fields because of the low temporal frequency response of television systems. Note that input is pixel columns

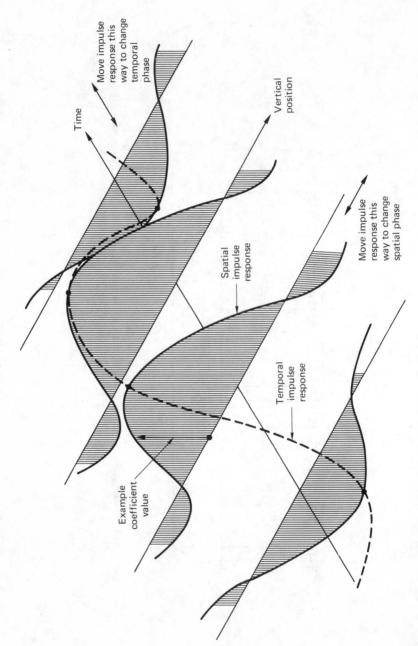

Figure 5.58 Two-dimensional impulse response. See text for details

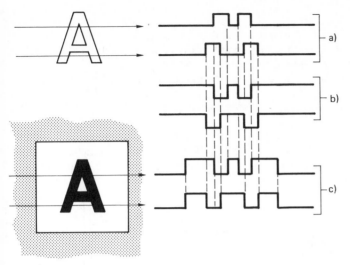

Figure 5.59 Elementary character generation. At (a), white on black waveform for two raster lines passing through letter A. At (b), black on white is simple inversion. At (c), reverse video highlight waveforms

Fig. 5.60 is a representative character generator, as might be used in a VDU. The characters to be displayed are stored as ASCII symbols in a RAM, which has one location for each character position on each available text line on the screen. Each character must be used to generate a series of dots on the screen which will extend over several lines. Typically the characters are formed by an array of five dots by nine. In order to convert from the ASCII code to a dot pattern, a ROM is programmed with a conversion. This will be addressed by the ASCII character, and the column and row addresses in the character array, and will output a high or low (bright or dark) output.

As the VDU screen is a raster-scanned device, the display scan will begin at the left-hand end of the top line. The first character in the ASCII RAM will be selected, and this and the first row and column addresses will be sent to the character generator, which ouputs the video level for the first pixel. The next column address will then be selected, and the next pixel will be output. As the scan proceeds, it will pass from the top line of the first character to the top line of the second character, so that the ASCII RAM address will need to be incremented. This process continues until the whole video line is completed. The next line on the screen is generated by repeating the selection of characters from the ASCII RAM, but using the second array line as the address to the character generator. This process will repeat until all of the video lines needed to form one row of characters are complete. The next row of characters in the ASCII RAM can then be accessed to create the next line of text on the screen and so on.

The character quality of VDUs is adequate for the application, but is not satisfactory for high-quality broadcast graphics. The characters are monochrome, have a fixed simple font, fixed size and no grey scale, and their sloping edges have the usual stepped appearance because of the lack of grey scale. This stepping of diagonal edges is sometimes erroneously called aliasing. Since it is not a result of inadequate sampling rate, but a result of quantizing distortion, the use of the term is wholly inappropriate.

In a broadcast graphics unit, the characters will be needed in colour and in varying size. Different fonts will be necessary, and additional features such as solid lines around characters and drop shadows are desirable. The complexity and cost of the necessary hardware is much greater than in the previous example.

In order to generate a character in a broadcast machine, a font and the character within that font are selected. The characters are actually stored as key signals, because the only difference between one character and

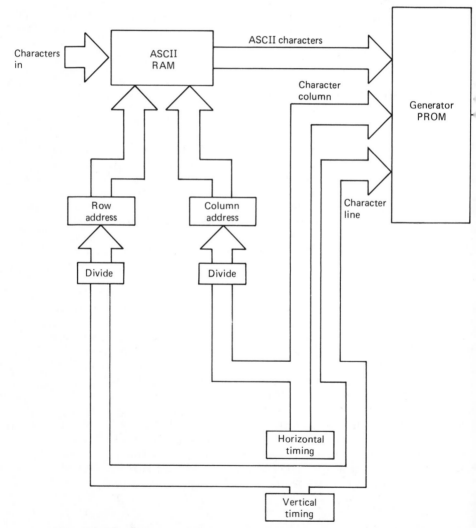

Figure 5.60 Simple character generator produces characters as rows and columns of pixels. See text for details

another in the same font is the shape. A character is generated by specifying a constant background colour and luminance, and a constant character colour and luminance, and using the key signal to cut a hole in the background and insert the character colour. This is illustrated in Fig. 5.61. The problem of stepped diagonal edges is overcome by giving the key signal a grey scale. The grey scale eliminates the quantizing distortion

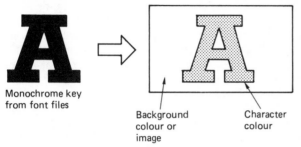

Monochrome key
from font files

Background
colour or
image

Character
colour

Figure 5.61 Font characters only store the shape of the character. This can be used to key any coloured character into a background

responsible for the stepped edges. The edge of the character now takes the form of a ramp, which has the desirable characteristic of limiting the bandwidth of the character generator output. Early character generators were notorious for producing out-of-band frequencies which drove equipment further down the line to distraction and in some cases would interfere with the sound channel on being broadcast. Fig. 5.62 illustrates how in a system with grey scale and sloped edges, the edge of a character can be positioned to sub-pixel resolution, which completely removes the stepped effect on diagonals.

In a powerful system, the number of fonts available will be large, and all of the necessary characters will be stored on disk drives. Some systems,

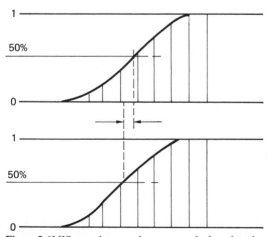

Figure 5.62 When a character has a ramped edge, the edge position can be moved in sub-pixel steps by changing the pixel values in the ramp

such as the Ampex ESS-3, allow users to enter their own fonts using a rostrum camera. A frame grab is performed, but the system can be told to file the image as a font character key signal rather than as a still frame. This approach allows infinite flexibility if it is desired to work in Kanji or Cyrillic and allows European graphics to be done with all necessary umlauts, tildes and cedillas.

In order to create a character string on the screen, it is necessary to produce a key signal which has been assembled from all of the individual character keys. The keys are usually stored in a large format to give highest quality, and it will be necessary to reduce the size of the characters to fit the available screen area. The size reduction of a key signal in the digital domain is exactly the same as the zoom function of an effects machine, requiring FIR filtering and interpolation, but again it is not necessary for it to be done in real time, and so less hardware can be used. The key source for the generation of the final video output is a RAM which has one location for every screen pixel. The position of the characters on the screen is controlled by changing the addresses in the key RAM into which the size-reduced character keys are written.

The keying system necessary is shown in Fig. 5.63. The character colour and the background colour are produced by latches on the control system bus, which output continuous digital parameters. The grey scale key signal

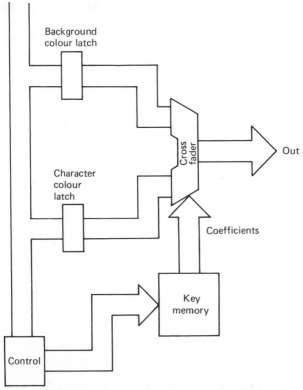

Figure 5.63 Simple character generator using keying. See text for details

obtained by scanning the key memory is used to provide coefficients for the digital crossfader which cuts between background and character colour to assemble the video signal in real time.

If characters with contrasting edges are required, an extra stage of keying can be used. The steps described above take place, but the background colour is replaced by the desired character edge colour. The size of each character key is then increased slightly, and the new key signal is used to cut the characters and a contrasting border into the final background.

Most character generators are based on a frame store which refreshes the dynamic output video. The Ampex ALEX has moved on from this technology and allows an unparalleled freedom of control over characters and symbols. It probably represents the state of the art in such devices and so is detailed here.

Fig. 5.64 shows some of the effects which can be achieved. The symbols which make up a word can move on and turn with respect to the plane in which they reside as a function of time in any way individually or together. Text can also be mapped on to an arbitrarily shaped line. The angle of the characters can follow a tangent to the line or can remain at a fixed angle regardless of the line angle.

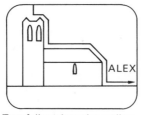

Independent motion of characters   Text follows irregular outlines

Figure 5.64 The individual characters of a word can be independently controlled, or the entire word can be positioned as a unit in the Alex graphics generator

By controlling the size of planes, characters or words can appear to zoom into view from a distance and recede again. Rotation of the character planes off the plane of the screen allows the perspective effects to be seen. Rotating a plane back about a horizontal axis by 90° will reduce it to an edge-on line, but lowering the plane to the bottom of the screen allows the top surface to be seen, receding into the distance like a road. Characters or text strings can then roll off into the distance, getting smaller as they go. In fact the planes do not rotate, but a perspective transform is performed on them.

Since characters can be moved without restriction, it will be possible to make them overlap. Either one can be declared to be at the front, so that it cuts out the other, but if desired the overlapping area can be made a different colour to either of the characters concerned. If this is done with care, the overlapping colour will give the effect of transparency. In fact colour is attributed to characters flexibly so that a character may change colour with respect to time. If this is combined with a movement, the colour will appear to change with position. The background can also be allocated a colour in this way, or the background can be input video. Instead of filling characters with colour on a video background, the characters, or only certain characters, or only the overlapping areas of characters, can be filled with video.

There are eight planes on which characters can move, and these are assigned a priority sequence so that the first one is essentially at the front of the screen and the last one is at the back. Where no character exists, a plane is transparent, and every character on a plane has an 8 bit transparency figure allocated to it. When characters on two different planes are moved until they overlap, the priority system and the transparency parameter decide what will be seen. An opaque front character will obscure any character behind it, whereas using a more transparent parameter will allow a proportion of a character to be seen through one in front of it. Since characters have 8 bit accuracy, all transparency effects are performed without degradation, and character edges always remain smooth, even at overlaps. Clearly the character planes are not memories or frame stores, because perspective rotation of images held in a frame stores in real time in this way would require vast amounts of processing power. Instead, ALEX computes the contents of output fields in real time. Every field is determined individually, so it is scarcely more difficult to animate by making successive fields different.

ALEX makes use of techniques used in computer-generated images. In a 32 bit computer a symbol or character exists not as an array of pixels but as an outline, rather as if a thin wire frame had been made to fit the edge of the symbol. The wire frame is described by a set of mathematical expressions. The operator positions the wire frame in space and turns it to any angle. The computer then calculates what the wire frame will look like from the viewing position. Effectively the shape of the frame is projected on to a surface which will become the TV screen. The principle is shown in Fig. 5.65 and will be seen to be another example of mapping. If drop or

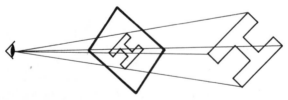

Figure 5.65 Perspective effects result from mapping or projecting the character outline on to a plane which represents the screen

plane shadows are being used, a further projection takes place which determines how the shadow of the wire frame would fall on a second plane. The only difference here between drop and plane shadows is the angle of the plane the shadow falls on. If it is parallel to the symbol frame, the result is a drop shadow. If it is at right angles, the result is a plane shadow.

Since the wire frame can be described by a minimum amount of data, the geometrical calculations needed to project on to the screen and shadow planes are quick and are repeated for every symbol. This process also reveals where overlaps occur within a plane, since the projected frames will cross each other. This computation takes place for all planes. The positions of the symbol edges are then converted to a pixel array in a field-interlaced raster scan. Because the symbols are described by 8 bit pixels, edges can be positioned to sub-pixel accuracy. An example is shown in Fig. 5.66. The pixel sequence is now effectively a digital key signal, and the priority and transparency parameters are now used to reduce the amplitude of a given key when it is behind a symbol on a plane of higher priority which has less than 100% transparency.

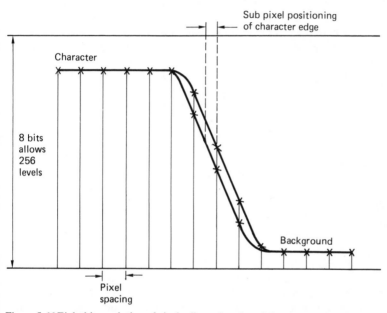

Figure 5.66 Eight bit resolution of pixels allows the edge of characters to be placed accurately independent of the sampling points. This offers smooth character edges

The key signals then pass to a device known as the filler which is a fast digital mixer which has as inputs the colour of each character and the background, whether colour or video. On a pixel-by-pixel basis, the filler crossfades between different colours as the video line proceeds. The crossfading is controlled by the key signals. The output is three data streams – red, green and blue. The output board takes the data and converts them to the video standard needed, and the result can then be seen.

5.28 Graphic art/paint systems

In graphic art systems, there is a requirement for disk storage of the generated images, and some art machines incorporate a still store unit, whereas others can be connected to a separate one by an interface. Disk-based stores are discussed in Chapter 12. The essence of an art system is that an artist can draw images which become a video signal directly with no intermediate paper and paint. Central to the operation of most art systems is a digitizing tablet, which is a flat surface over which the operator draws a stylus. The tablet can establish the position of the stylus in vertical and horizontal axes. One way in which this can be done is to launch ultrasonic pulses down the tablet, which are detected by a transducer in the stylus. The time taken to receive the pulse is proportional to the distance to the stylus. The coordinates of the stylus are converted to addresses in the frame store which correspond to the same physical position on the screen. In order to make a simple sketch, the operator specifies a background parameter, perhaps white, which would be loaded into every location in the frame store. A different parameter is then written into every location addressed by movement of the stylus, which results in a line drawing on the screen. The art world uses pens and brushes of different shapes and sizes to obtain a variety of effects, one common example being the rectangular pen nib where the width of the resulting line depends on the angle at which the pen is moved. This can be simulated on art systems, because the address derived from the tablet is processed to produce a range of addresses within a certain screen distance of the stylus. If all of these locations are updated as the stylus moves, a broad stroke results.

If the address range is larger in the horizontal axis than in the vertical axis, for example, the width of the stroke will be a function of the direction of stylus travel. Some systems have a sprung tip on the stylus which connects to a force transducer, so that the system can measure the pressure the operator uses. By making the address range a function of pressure, broader strokes can be obtained simply by pressing harder. In order to simulate a set of colours available on a palette, the operator can select a mode where small areas of each colour are displayed in boxes on the monitor screen. The desired colour is selected by moving a screen cursor over the box using the tablet. The parameter to be written into selected locations in the frame RAM now reflects the chosen colour. In more advanced systems, simulation of airbrushing is possible. In this technique, the transparency of the stroke is great at the edge, where the background can be seen showing through, but reduces to the centre of the stroke. A read modify write process is necessary in the frame memory, where background values are read, mixed with paint values with the appropriate transparency, and written back. The position of the stylus effectively determines the centre of a two-dimensional transparency contour, which is convolved with the memory contents as the stylus moves.

Individual users of paint systems will tend to use a certain subset of the huge range of possibilities in order to give all of their work a common style. Where a number of users share the same system, a saving in time can be obtained if each user can immediately restore his or her favourite parameters from some storage medium instead of having to key then in each time. Some paint systems have a small floppy disk or tape cartridge drive with which the user can insert his or her own commonly used parameters, which are usually known as a palette.

When a frame is being drawn on an art system, the movement and pressure of each stroke of the stylus is stored along with the colour selected. The frame can be redrawn at any time simply by executing once more the list of stylus movements. This means that if a mistake is made, the effect of the latest action can be erased by executing every movement except the last. The frame will then be restored to the exact conditions before the mistake was made. It is also possible to edit the list to eliminate certain strokes.

Once the frame is completed, it exists in two forms. One is the list of strokes which make up the frame, and the other is the video frame itself held in the frame store. Either or both can be stored. The video frame can be stored in a general purpose still store which may be part of the paint system or which may be a separate unit.

The storage requirements for the video frame will be greater, but since it is a standard frame it can be stored in a variety of ways on standard digital video equipment such as hard disks or a DVTR. This will enable rapid access to the frame in the future, but once stored in this way it cannot readily be edited.

If the list of strokes is stored, the storage requirement is quite small, but the list is not a standard video frame and can only be stored and interpreted by the paint system which generated it. If the frame is required to be seen, the list must be executed each time, which is a much slower process than retrieval of the frame from a still store. However, the list can be changed at will, so if it may be necessary to edit the frame in the future it makes sense to store the list in the paint system.

5.29 Recursive filtering for noise reduction

The basic principle of all video noise reducers is that there is a certain amount of correlation between the video content of successive frames, whereas there is no correlation between the noise content.

A basic recursive device is shown in Fig. 5.67. There is a frame store which acts as a delay, and the output of the delay can be fed back to the input through an attenuator, which in the digital domain will be a multiplier. In the case of a still picture, successive frames will be identical and the recursion will be large. This means that the output video will actually be the average of many frames. If there is movement of the image, it will be necessary to reduce the amount of recursion to prevent the generation of trails or smears. Probably the most famous examples of recursion smear are the television pictures sent back of astronauts walking on the moon. The received pictures were very noisy and needed a lot of averaging to make them viewable. This was fine until the astronaut moved. The technology of the day did not permit motion sensing.

DVEs which are frame based have motion sensing as part of the de-interlace system. Large motion values discontinue the use of the second field. The same motion parameter can also be used for noise reduction. When numerical differences between frames are very small, they will be due to noise, and noise reduction can be obtained by adding half of the difference between frames to the most recent frame. The motion parameter is fed to a PROM, which outputs noise-correction values for small differences, but which outputs zero values for all larger differences. The ADO-2000 and 3000 incorporate such a device.

In advanced noise reducers, motion measurement is used to determine

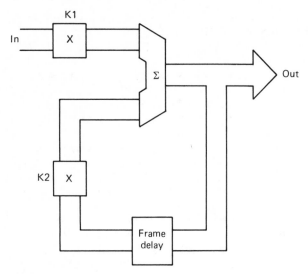

Figure 5.67 A basic recursive device feeds back the output to the input via a frame store which acts as a delay. The characteristics of the device are controlled totally by the values of the two coefficients K1 and K2 which control the multipliers

where moving objects have gone from one frame to the next. This is a similar process to the correlation used in some standards converters. An object which has moved a short distance from one frame to the next can be averaged by moving the picture content from the previous frame by the same distance using interpolation. Averaging can then take place without loss of resolution.

5.30 Recursive filtering for effects

The principle of recursion can be used for certain special effects, and a suitable frame store is often added at the output of a DVE so that the recursive effects are available superimposed on existing effects, giving a larger range of possibilities.

DVEs often move the source picture around the screen, and in this mode the use of recursion as an effect is the most useful. Adding a decaying trail which follows a moving picture is relatively easy. The presence of a frame store allows the current output frame and the previous output frame to be simultaneously available. A suitable switcher similar to the combiner described in Chapter 3 will allow both to be seen on the screen, with the older image having lower priority and only visible where the more recent image has moved. The combiner output then becomes the next input to the frame store, so that one frame later three overlapping images will be seen. This process can continue indefinitely, as the structure used is that of an infinite-impulse response filter. In practice the gain of the recursive signals will be less than unity, so that the brightness of the trailing images decays exponentially.

The incorporation of a random number generator allows sparkles to be generated in the recursive data.

It is also possible to use a target frame store to make a collage. The recursion is set to unity gain, and the input to the DVE switches between sources as the image moves rapidly. Each input picture will appear in sequence across the screen.

With unity recursion, the input can be removed and the output will remain, but if the recursion factor is minutely reduced, the frozen frame will gradually fade.

5.31 Data reduction and transform coding

The data rates resulting from conventional video digitizing are quite high, and although recorders have been developed which store the signals in this form, they will remain exclusively in the professional domain for the foreseeable future. If digital video recording is to be made available to the consumer, tape consumption will need to be reduced considerably, and one way of doing this is to use data reduction, often in the form of transform coding.

The transform itself does not achieve any reduction of data, but simply presents the information in a form where it is easier to perform the actual reduction.

The Fourier transform is well known and can be used to illustrate the principle. To convey a sine wave in a digital system requires a constant stream of samples, whereas in the Fourier domain a sine wave is a single event which can be totally described by two parameters, amplitude and phase. Any waveform can be analysed to find its components and described by their amplitudes and phases. In theory, it would be possible to produce the Fourier transform of a video signal and to achieve considerable data reduction by storing the transform. In practice an enormous amount of computation would be necessary to obtain the Fourier transform.

A relative of the discrete fourier transform is the discrete cosine transform (DCT). In the DCT, there are a number of discrete frequencies available as before, but they all have the same phase, i.e. the phase parameter of the DFT is absent. This dramatically simplifies the transform process, so that it becomes possible to implement a DCT with a reasonable amount of hardware. Fig. 5.68 shows an example of the different coefficients of a DCT for an 8 × 8 pixel array (courtesy Philips Research), and adding these together in different proportions will give any original pixel array. The coefficients with many small squares represent the higher two-dimensional spatial frequencies, and these will be absent or of small value in large areas of typical video, because of motion blurring, or simply plain, undetailed areas before the camera. Additionally the eye is less able to resolve the higher spatial frequencies. The different coefficients are thus weighted so that those conveying low frequencies are given more gain than those conveying high frequencies. The weighted coefficients are then compared with thresholds, and those which fail to exceed the threshold are

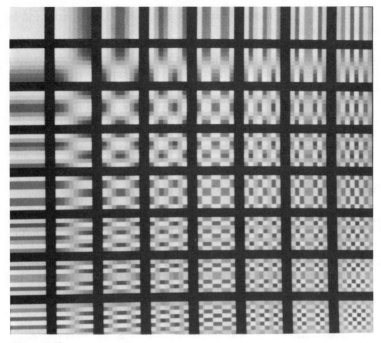

Figure 5.68

simply not recorded, because their absence represents a trivial departure from the overall picture content.

The coefficients which are to be retained can be quantized in a non-linear fashion to reduce the number of bits needed to convey the coefficient. In this way blocks containing rapid transients will have large coefficients which are coarsely quantized, whereas gradually varying areas will use small quantizing intervals to prevent contouring. In real video the amount of detail will vary, and so the amount of coefficient data to be recorded would vary. This causes practical difficulties, and to obtain a constant data rate the system is designed to raise the thresholds to cut down the data rate when presented with frames with overall high spatial frequencies.

An experimental machine built by Philips[12] used these techniques to reduce the data rate to about one-fifth of normal, so that a digital VCR could be made using an 8 mm cassette.

References

1. VAN DEN ENDEN, A.W.M. and VERHOECKX, N.A.M. Digital signal processing: theoretical background. *Philips Tech. Rev.*, **42**, 110–144, (1985)
2. MCCLELLAN, J.H., PARKS, T.W. and RABINER, L.R., A computer program for designing optimum FIR linear-phase filters. *IEEE Trans. Audio Electroacoust.*, **AU-21**, 506–526 (1973)

3. CROCHIERE, R.E. and RABINER, L.R., Interpolation and decimation of digital signals – a tutorial review. *Proc. IEEE*, **69**, 300–331 (1981)

4. CLARKE, C.K.P., High quality decoding for PAL inputs to digital YUV studios. *BBC Res. Dep. Rep.* RD 1982/12

5. AIRD, B., Three dimensional picture synthesis. *Broadcast Syst. Eng.*, **12** no. 3, 34–40 (1986)

6. NEWMAN, W.M. and SPROULL, R.F., *Principles of Interactive Computer Graphics* Tokyo: McGraw-Hill (1979)

7. GERNSHEIM, H., *A Concise History of Photography*, London: Thames and Hudson, pp. 9–15 (1971)

8. HEDGECOE, J., *The Photographer's Handbook*, London: Ebury Press, pp. 104–105 (1977)

9. BENNETT, P., *et al.*, Spatial transformation system including key signal generator. *US Patent* no. 4,463,372 (1984)

10. DE BOOR, C., *A Practical Guide to Splines*, Berlin: Springer, 1978

11. BEANLAND, D., ISIS. *Int. Broadcast Eng.*, **20** no. 229, 40–43 (1989)

12. BORGERS, S.M.C., *et al.*, An experimental digital VCR with 40 mm drum, single actuator and DCT based bit-rate reduction. *IEEE Trans. Consum. Electron.*, **CE-34** no. 3, 597–605 (1988)

Chapter 6

Digital magnetic and optical recording

Although the physics of the record/replay process is unaffected by the meaning attributed to signals, the techniques used in digital recording are rather different from those found in analog recording, although often the same phenomenon shows up in a different guise. In this chapter the fundamentals of digital magnetic and optical recording are treated along with the necessary coding methods.

6.1 Magnetic recording

In analog recording, the characteristics of the medium affect the signal recorded directly, whereas by expressing a signal in binary numerical form by sampling and quantizing, the quality becomes independent of the medium. The dynamic range required no longer directly decides the track width needed. In digital circuitry there is a great deal of noise immunity because the signal can only have two states, which are widely separated compared with the amplitude of noise. In digital magnetic recording there are also only two states of the medium, N–S and S–N, but paradoxically the noise immunity is much reduced. As noise immunity is a function of track width, reduction of the working SNR of a digital track allows the same information to be carried in a smaller area of the medium, improving economy of operation. It also increases the random error rate, but as an error-correction system is already necessary to deal with dropouts, it is simply made to work harder.

It is interesting to compare tape consumption between analog and digital machines where possible. In professional video recording, the analog C-format transports 1 inch tape at 230 mm/s, whereas the D-2 composite digital recorder uses ¾ inch tape at only 130 mm/s. In digital recording narrower tracks are to be expected, and steps must be taken to register the heads accurately with the tracks by appropriate mechanical design and improved edge straightness in the tape.

6.2 Head noise and head-to-tape speed

There are several important sources of replay noise in a magnetic recorder, which will be examined later in this chapter. One of these is the noise from the head. All components with resistance generate noise according to their temperature, and the replay head is no exception. If a given recording exists on a tape, a better SNR will be obtained by moving the head relative to the tape at a higher speed, since the head noise is constant and the signal induced is proportional to speed. This is one reason why rotary-head recorders offer better packing density than stationary-head recorders. The other reason is much more obvious. A rotary-head machine determines track spacing by linear tape speed, whereas stationary heads are difficult to fabricate with narrow spacing between tracks. In digitizing a video waveform, there has been an exchange in the importance of SNR and bandwidth. The bandwidth of a digital channel always exceeds the bandwidth of the original analog signal, but the extra bandwidth is only required with poor SNR. This explains the paradox that greater bandwidth is needed but less tape is used. As in analog recording, the rotating head can be used to obtain high bandwidth without excessively short tape wavelengths and at moderate linear tape speed. A further advantage of rotary-head machines is that, by changing the scanner geometry, the best compromise can be reached between bandwidth and SNR. Fig. 6.1 shows that, in the same area of tape, two different recordings can be made. The

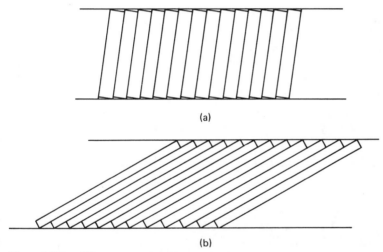

(a)

(b)

Figure 6.1 Two different rotary-head formats having the same tape consumption but different characteristics

first has a lower head-to-tape speed because the tracks are shorter, but better SNR because they are wider. The second has higher bandwidth because of the longer tracks, but these tracks are narrower. In the absence of head noise, the information capacity of both formats would be the same. Where head noise is a factor, the second format will be superior. The lower limit to track width is generally set by the ability to register a head with adequate precision, and sometimes track-following servos are necessary to achieve the highest densities without sacrificing the ability to interchange a recording between machines. Another technique is to use azimuth recording which gives some protection from residual tracking error. The comparison of tape consumption between the D-2 and the C-format is even more dramatic because of the adoption of azimuth recording.

Whether the machine is stationary or rotary head, the recorded wavelengths must be kept short to conserve tape in the direction of the track. Very short wavelengths can only be replayed with consistent intimate contact between the head and the medium, so that the surface finish of the medium must be of the highest order. The roughness of the tape backcoat must be limited to prevent the back of one layer embossing an adjacent magnetic layer when the tape is wound on a spool. Digital tape has a thin coating, because thickness loss prevents flux from a thick coat being of much use at short wavelengths and because a thin coating is less prone to self-demagnetization. The thin coat needs high-energy particles to allow useful replay signals with reduced magnetic volume. The backing material, or substrate, is relatively thin to allow the tape to accommodate head irregularities without losing contact, but print-through is not an issue in digital recording. A happy consequence of the use of thin tape is that more can be accommodated in a given cassette, but it does require careful transport design to avoid damage. Transports are considered in Chapter 9.

6.3 Basic digital magnetic recording

The basic principle of digital magnetic recording is remarkably simple. Since it is intended that the medium should have only two states, the record waveform will typically be a current whose direction reverses but whose magnitude remains constant, as in Fig. 6.2. To provide the best SNR

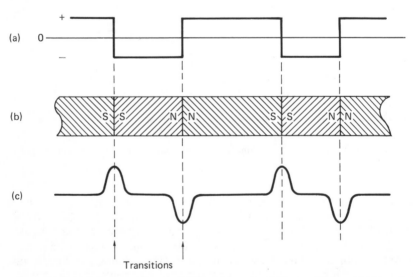

Figure 6.2 Basic digital recording. At (a) the write current in the head is reversed from time to time, leaving a binary magnetization pattern shown at (b). When replayed, the waveform at (c) results because an ouput is only produced when flux in the head changes. Changes are referred to as transitions

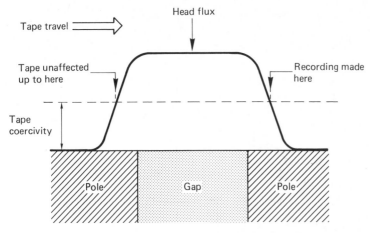

Figure 6.3 The recording is actually made near the trailing pole of the head where the head flux falls below the coercivity of the tape

on replay, the current required is a little less than that needed to saturate the tape, as saturation causes fringing fields around the head and crosstalk in adjacent tracks. In recent machines, the record current may be produced in an analog amplifier which has a response which corrects for losses in the record-head material at high frequencies. The tape encounters a strength of flux which increases and then decreases as it passes the head. The recording is actually made near the trailing pole of the head, as shown in Fig. 6.3, where the flux from the head falls below the coercive force needed to change the state of the particles. The steeper the flux gradient on the trailing pole, the shorter the wavelength which can be recorded. This is generally obtained with a relatively wide gap. Bias is unnecessary in digital recording because linearity is not a goal.

6.4 Fixed heads

The construction of a bulk ferrite multitrack head is shown in Fig. 6.4, where it will be seen that space must be left between the magnetic circuits to accommodate the windings. Track spacing is improved by putting the windings on alternate sides of the gap. The parallel close-spaced magnetic circuits have considerable mutual inductance and suffer from crosstalk. This can be compensated when several adjacent tracks record together by cross-connecting antiphase feeds to the record amplifiers.

Using thin-film heads, the magnetic circuits and windings are produced by deposition on a substrate at right angles to the tape plane, and as seen in Fig. 6.5 they can be made very accurately at small track spacings. Perhaps more importantly, because the magnetic circuits do not have such large parallel areas, mutual inductance and crosstalk are smaller allowing a higher practical track density.

Whereas most replay heads are inductive and generate an output which is the differential of the tape flux, there is another, less common device

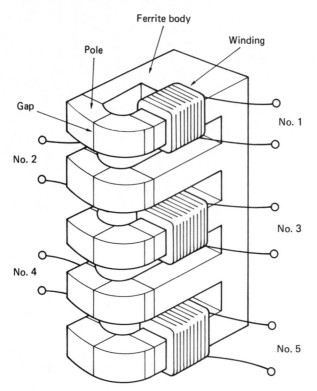

Figure 6.4 A typical multitrack ferrite head. Windings are placed on alternate sides to save space, but parallel magnetic circuits have high crosstalk

known as the magnetoresistive head. In this device, use is made of the Hall effect, where an applied magnetic field causes electrons passing down a semiconductor to bunch together so that they experience higher resistance. The strength of flux is measured directly by the head, but it is not sensitive to polarity, and it is usually necessary to incorporate a steady biasing field into the head, so that the reversing flux from the tape is converted to a unidirectional changing flux at the sensor. Such heads have a noise advantage over inductive heads at very low tape speeds, but a separate head is required for recording. At the time of writing there is no stationary-head DVTR because the storage densities achieved are considerably better with rotary heads, but improvements in data reduction techniques and magnetoresistive head technology could make a consumer device feasible.

6.5 Flying heads in disk drives

Disk drives permanently sacrifice storage density in order to offer rapid access. The use of a flying head with a deliberate air gap between it and the medium is necessary because of the high medium speed, but this causes a

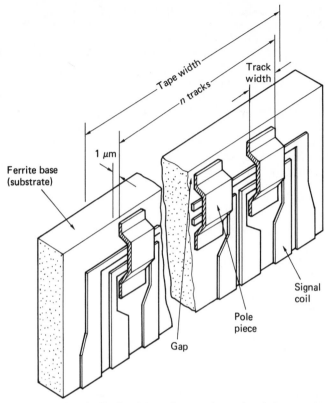

Figure 6.5 The thin-film head shown here can be produced photographically with very small dimensions. Flat structure reduces crosstalk

severe separation loss which restricts the linear density available. The air gap must be accurately maintained, and consequently the head is of low mass and is mounted flexibly.

The aerohydrodynamic part of the head is known as the slipper; it is designed to provide lift from the boundary layer which changes rapidly with changes in flying height. It is not initially obvious that the difficulty with disk heads is not making them fly, but making them fly close enough to the disk surface. The boundary layer travelling at the disk surface has the same speed as the disk, but as height increases it slows down owing to drag from the surrounding air. As the lift is a function of relative air speed, the closer the slipper comes to the disk, the greater the lift will be. The slipper is therefore mounted at the end of a rigid cantilever sprung towards the medium. The force with which the head is pressed towards the disk by the spring is equal to the lift at the designed flying height. Because of the spring, the head may rise and fall over small warps in the disk. It would be virtually impossible to manufacture disks flat enough to dispense with this feature. As the slipper negotiates a warp it will pitch and roll in addition to rising and falling, but it must be prevented from yawing, as this would cause an azimuth error. Downthrust is applied to the centre of pressure by a spherical thrust button, and the required degrees of freedom are supplied by a thin flexible gimbal. The slipper has to bleed away surplus air in order to approach close enough to the disk, and holes or grooves are usually provided for this purpose in the same way that tyres have grooves to take away water on wet roads.

Fig. 6.6 shows how disk heads are made. The magnetic circuit of disk heads was originally assembled from discrete magnetic elements. As the gap and flying height became smaller to increase linear recording density, the slipper was made from ferrite and became part of the magnetic circuit. This was completed by a small C-shaped ferrite piece which carried the coil. In thin-film heads, the magnetic circuit and coil are both formed by deposition on a substrate which becomes the rear of the slipper.

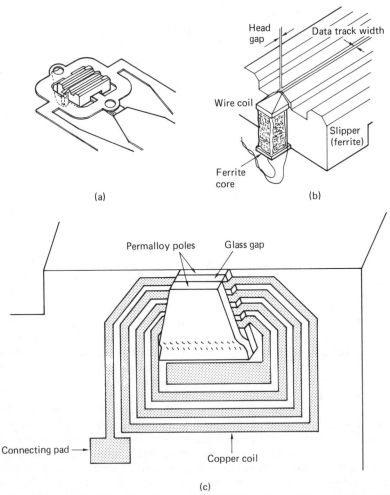

Figure 6.6 (a) Winchester head construction showing large air bleed grooves. (b) Close-up of slipper showing magnetic circuit on trailing edge. (c) Thin film head is fabricated on the end of the slipper using microcircuit technology

In a moving-head device it is not practicable to position separate erase, record and playback heads accurately. Erase is by overwriting, and reading and writing are carried out by the same head. The construction of disk drives is described in Chapter 12.

6.6 Playback

When a digital recording is replayed, the output of the head will be a differentiated version of the record waveform, because the head only responds to the rate of change of flux.

The initial task of the replay circuits is to reconstruct the record waveform. The amplitude of the signal is of no consequence; what matters is the time at which the write current, and hence the flux stored on the medium, reverses. This can be determined by locating the peaks of the replay impulses. At high data rates this can conveniently be done by differentiating the signal and looking for zero crossings. Fig. 6.7 shows that this results in noise between the peaks. This problem is overcome by the

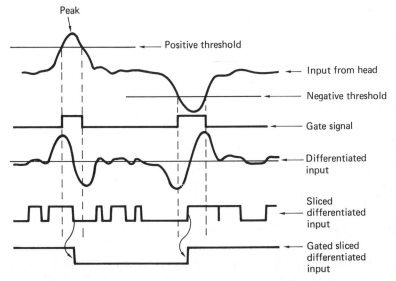

Figure 6.7 Gated peak detection rejects noise by disabling the differentiated output between transitions

gated peak detector, where only zero crossings from a pulse which exceeds the threshold will be counted. This method is almost universally used in digital video and in disk drives whereas at the relatively low data rates of floppy disks and in digital audio the record waveform can also be restored by integration, which opposes the differentiation of the head as in Fig. 6.8.[1]

There are a number of details which must be added to this simplistic picture in order to appreciate the real position. Fig. 6.9 shows that the

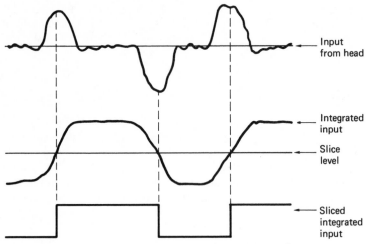

Figure 6.8 Integration method for re-creating write-current waveform

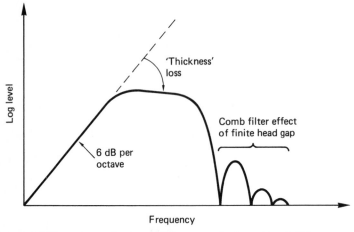

Figure 6.9 The major mechanisms defining magnetic channel bandwidth

differentiating effect of the replay process causes the head output initially to rise at 6 dB per octave from a DC response of zero. Although a high-frequency recording can be made throughout the thickness of the medium, the flux deep within the medium cannot couple with the replay head at short wavelengths, so as recorded wavelength falls, a thinner and thinner layer near the surface remains responsible for the replay flux.[2] This is called thickness loss, although it is a form of separation loss, and it causes a loss of 6 dB per octave, which cancels the differentiating effect to give a region of constant frequency response. The construction of the head results in the same action as that of a two-point transversal filter, as the two poles of the head see the tape with a small delay interposed due to the finite gap. As expected, the head response is like a comb filter with the well-known nulls where flux cancellation takes place across the gap. Clearly the smaller the gap the shorter the wavelength of the first null. This contradicts the requirement of the record head to have a large gap. In quality analog recorders, it is the norm to have different record and replay heads for this reason, and the same is sometimes true in digital recording.

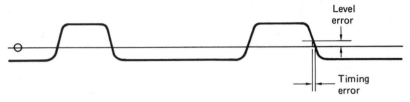

Figure 6.10 A DC offset can cause timing errors

Fig. 6.10 shows that when an uneven duty cycle is recorded, there are a number of problems. The lack of DC response causes a level shift. Combined with the finite rate of change of voltage, the shift can cause timing errors unless care is taken to slice the signal about its own centre. The finite gap in the replay head causes closely spaced flux reversals to interfere with one another, which causes peak shift distortion (also known as intersymbol interference or pulse crowding) and tends to reduce the asymmetry of the waveform, again causing timing errors. The mechanism responsible for peak shift is shown in Fig. 6.11(a). The results of two independent and opposite transitions passing the head are shown, and summing these gives the result of replaying two close together. Interaction between the two transitions reduces the amplitude of the signal and moves the peaks apart. Avoidance of peak shift requires equalization of the channel,[3] and this can be done by a network after the replay head, termed an equalizer or pulse sharpener,[4] as in Fig. 6.11(b), or before the record head, where it is called precompensation, as in Fig. 6.11(c). Both of these techniques use transversal filtering to oppose the inherent transversal effect of the head. By way of contrast, it will be seen later that partial response replay takes advantage of intersymbol interference and indeed depends on it.

6.7 Azimuth recording and rotary heads

Conventional magnetic recorders record the transitions on the tape track at right angles to the edge of the track, and Fig. 6.12 shows that it is necessary to leave so called guard bands between tracks to allow some tracking error without causing crosstalk from adjacent tracks. These guard bands represent wasted tape.

Fig. 6.13(a) shows that, in azimuth recording, the transitions are laid down at an angle to the track by using a head which is tilted. Machines using azimuth recording must always have an even number of heads, so that adjacent tracks can be recorded with opposite azimuth angle. The two track types are usually referred to as A and B. Fig. 6.13(b) shows the effect of playing a track with the wrong type of head. The playback process suffers from an enormous azimuth error. The effect of azimuth error can

236

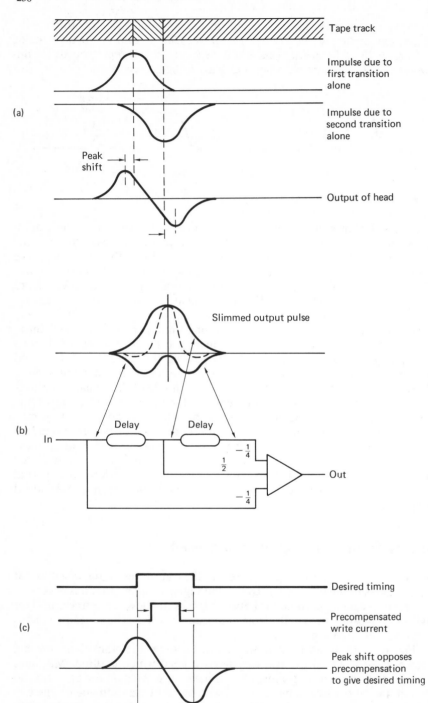

Figure 6.11 (a) Peak shift distortion can be reduced by (b) equalization in replay, or (c) precompensation

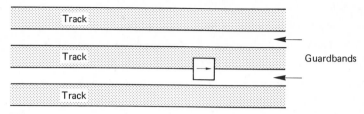

Figure 6.12 In conventional recording, a space or guard band must be left between tracks so that if a head is misaligned, the output signal simply reduces instead of becoming a composite signal from two tracks. The guard bands represent unused tape

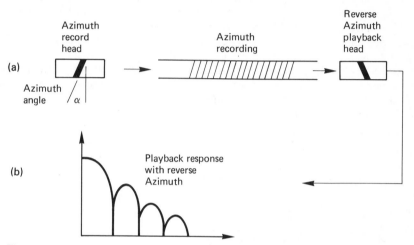

Figure 6.13 In azimuth recording (a), the head gap is tilted. If the track is played with the same head, playback is normal, but the response of the reverse azimuth head is attenuated (b)

be understood by imagining the tape track to be made from many identical parallel strips. In the presence of azimuth error, the strips at one edge of the track are played back with a phase shift relative to strips at the other side. At some wavelengths, the phase shift will be 180°, and there will be no output, while at other wavelengths, especially long wavelengths, some output will reappear. The effect is rather like that of a comb filter and serves to attenuate crosstalk due to adjacent tracks. Since no tape is wasted between the tracks, efficient use is made of the tape. The term guard-band-less recording is often used instead of, or in addition to, the term azimuth recording. The failure of the azimuth effect at long wavelengths is a characteristic of azimuth recording, and it is necessary to ensure that the spectrum of the signal to be recorded has a small low-frequency content.

In digital recording there is often no separate erase process, and erasure is achieved by overwriting with a new waveform. When a rotary-head machine uses overwriting in conjunction with azimuth recording, the recorded tracks can be made rather narrower than the head pole simply by reducing the linear speed of the tape so that it does not advance so far between sweeps of the rotary heads. This can be seen in Fig. 6.14. The same head can be used for replay, even though it is wider than the tracks. It

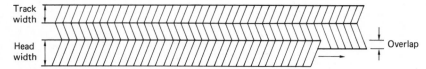

Figure 6.14 In azimuth recording, the tracks can be made narrower than the head pole by overwriting the previous track

can be seen from Fig. 6.15 that there will be crosstalk from tracks at both sides of the home track, but this crosstalk is attenuated by azimuth effect. The amount by which the head overlaps the adjacent track determines the spectrum of the crosstalk, since it changes the delay in the azimuth comb-filtering effect. More importantly, the signal-to-crosstalk ratio becomes independent of tracking error over a small range, because as the head moves to one side the loss of crosstalk from one adjacent track is balanced by the increase of crosstalk from the track on the opposite side. This phenomenon allows for some loss of track straightness and for the residual error which is present in all track-following servo systems.

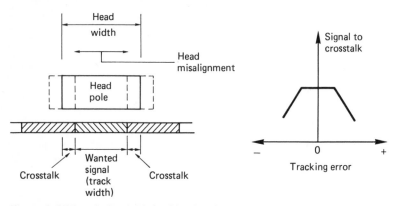

Figure 6.15 When the head pole is wider than the track, the wanted signal is picked up along with crosstalk from the adjacent tracks. If the head is misaligned, the signal-to-crosstalk ratio remains the same until the head fails to register with the whole of the wanted track

The azimuth angle used has to be chosen with some care. The greater the azimuth angle, the less will be the crosstalk, but the effective writing speed is the head-to-tape speed multiplied by the cosine of the azimuth angle. A further smaller effect is that the tape is anisotropic because of particle orientation. Noise due to the medium, head or amplifier is virtually unaffected by the azimuth angle, and there is no point in reducing crosstalk below the noise. The value of $\pm15°$ used in D-2 causes a loss of less than 1 dB due to the apparent reduction in writing speed.

6.8 Equalization

In practice there are difficulties in providing correct equalization at all times. Tape surface asperities and substrate irregularities cause variations in the intimacy of head contact, which changes the response at high frequencies much more than at low frequencies, thereby undermining any fixed equalization. In disk drives, the varying radius of the tracks results in a linear density variation of about two to one. The presence of the air film causes severe separation loss, and peak shift distortion is a major problem. The flying height of the head varies with the radius of the disk track, and it is difficult to provide accurate equalization of the replay channel because of this. The write current is often controlled as a function of track radius so that the changing reluctance of the air gap does not change the resulting record flux. Equalization is used on recording in the form of precompensation, which moves recorded transitions in such a way as to oppose the effects of peak shift. Optimum equalization is difficult under dynamic conditions, although an adaptive equalizer can be made which uses the timing errors caused by poor equalization to change the response. This approach is used in the Ampex D-2 machines.

In most of the above, a clearer picture has been obtained by studying the impulse response of devices than from the frequency response, and this follows from the impulsive nature of digital techniques.

6.9 Types of optical disk

The principles of laser disks will now be described, based on an introduction to optical physics.

There are numerous types of optical disk, which have different characteristics.[5] There are, however, three broad groups which can be usefuly compared.

(1) The Laservision/Compact Disc/CD-Video/CD-ROM disk is an example of a read-only laser disk, which is designed for mass duplication by stamping. These disks cannot be recorded.

Fig. 6.16 shows that the information layer of CD/LV is an optically flat mirror upon which microscopic bumps are raised. A thin coating of aluminium renders the layer reflective. When a small spot of light is focused on the information layer, the presence of the bumps affects the way in which the light is reflected back, and variations in the reflected light are detected to read the disc. The height of the bumps in the mirror surface has to be one-quarter of the wavelength of the light used, so that light reflected from a bump has travelled half a wavelength less than light reflected from the mirror surface, and will be out of phase with it. This results in destructive interference in light returning to the source, and the light will escape, in any direction where constructive interference allows, as a diffraction pattern primarily along a disc radius. Effectively a bump scatters light, reducing the amount of reflected light. Fig. 6.16 also illustrates the very small dimensions involved, which demand the utmost cleanliness in manufacture.

(2) Some laser disks can be recorded, but once a recording has been made it cannot be changed or erased. These are usually referred to as write-once-read-many (WORM) disks. The general principle is that the disk contains a thin layer of metal; on recording, a powerful laser melts spots on the layer. Surface tension causes a hole to form in the metal, with

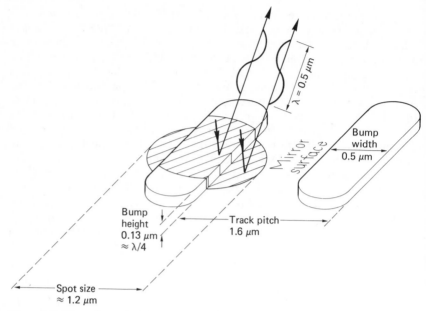

Figure 6.16 CD readout principle and dimensions. The presence of a bump causes destructive interference in the reflected light

a thickened rim around the hole. Subsequently a low-power laser can read the disk because the metal reflects light, but the hole passes it through. Clearly once a pattern of holes has been made, it is permanent.

(3) Erasable optical disks have essentially the same characteristic as magnetic disks, in that new and different recordings can be made in the same track indefinitely, but there is usually a separate erase cycle needed before a new recording can be made since overwrite is not generally possible. To contrast with systems such as the Compact Disc, which requires considerable processing after the write stage before reading is possible, such systems are called direct-read-after-write (DRAW) disks.

6.10 Optical theory

All of these technologies are restricted by the wave and quantum nature of light and depend heavily on certain optical devices such as lasers, polarizers and diffraction gratings. These subjects will be outlined here.

The wave theory of light suggests that a plane wave advances because an infinite number of point sources can be considered to emit spherical waves which will only add when they are all in the same phase. This can only occur in the plane of the wavefront. Fig. 6.17 shows that, at all other angles, interference between spherical waves is destructive.

When such a wavefront arrives at an interface with a denser medium, the velocity of propagation is reduced; therefore the wavelength in the medium becomes shorter, causing the wavefront to leave the interface at a different angle (Fig. 6.18). This is known as refraction. The ratio of

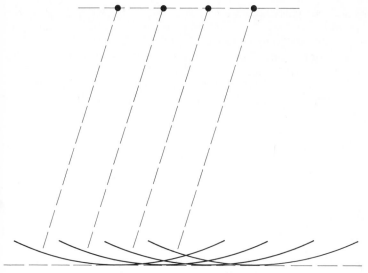

Figure 6.17 Plane-wave propagation considered as infinite numbers of spherical waves

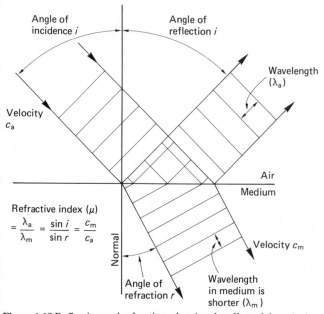

Figure 6.18 Reflection and refraction, showing the effect of the velocity of light in a medium

velocity *in vacuo* to velocity in the medium is known as the refractive index of that medium; it determines the relationship between the angles of the incident and refracted wavefronts. Reflected light, however, leaves at the same angle to the normal as the incident light. If the speed of light in the medium varies with wavelength, incident white light will be split into a rainbow spectrum leaving the interface at different angles. Glass used for chandeliers and cut glass is chosen for this property, whereas glass for optical instruments will be chosen to have a refractive index which is as constant as possible with changing wavelength.

When a wavefront reaches an aperture which is small compared with the wavelength, the aperture acts as a point source, and the process of diffraction can be observed as a spherical wavefront leaving the aperture as in Fig. 6.19. Where the wavefront passes through a regular structure,

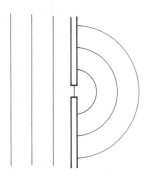

Figure 6.19 Diffraction as a plane wave reaches a small aperture

known as a diffraction grating, light on the far side will form new wavefronts wherever radiation is in phase, and Fig. 6.20 shows that these will be at an angle to the normal depending on the spacing of the structure and the wavelength of the light. A diffraction grating illuminated by white light will produce a rainbow spectrum at each side of the normal. To obtain a fixed angle of diffraction, monochromatic light is necessary.

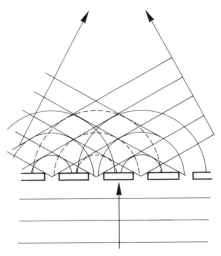

Figure 6.20 In a diffraction grating, constructive interference can take place at more than one angle for a single wavelength

For a given wavelength, the greater the spatial frequency of the grating (bars per unit of distance) the greater will be the angle of diffraction. A corollary of this effect is that the more finely detailed an object is, the greater the angle over which light must be collected to see the detail. The light-collecting angle of a lens shown in Fig. 6.21 is measured by the

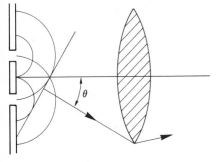

Figure 6.21 Fine detail in an object can only be resolved if the diffracted wavefront due to the highest spatial frequency is collected by the lens. Numerical aperture (NA) = sin θ, and as θ is the diffraction angle it follows that, for a given wavelength, NA determines resolution

numerical aperture (NA), which is the sine of the angle between the optical axis and the wavefront carrying the finest detail in the image. All lenses thus act as spatial filters which cut off at a spatial frequency limited by NA. The response is known as the modulation transfer function (MTF). Light travelling on the axis of a lens is conveying the average brightness of the image, not the detail, as this is conveyed in the more oblique light collected at the rim of the lens. Lenses can fall short of their theoretical MTF because of shortcomings in manufacture. If a lens is made accurately enough, a wavefront which has passed through it will have the same phase over its entire area. Where wavefront aberrations have a variance of less than the square of the wavelength divided by 180, the lens is said to meet the Maréchal criterion, which essentially means that the performance of the lens is as good as it is going to get because it is now diffraction limited rather than tolerance limited.

When a diffraction-limited lens is used to focus a point source on a plane, the image will not be a point owing to the exclusion of higher spatial frequencies by the finite numerical aperture. The resulting image is in fact the spatial equivalent of the impulse response of a low-pass filter and results in a diffraction pattern known as an Airy pattern, after Sir George Airy, who first quantified the intensity function. It is the dimensions of the Airy pattern which limit the density of all optical media, since it controls the minimum size of features that the laser can produce or resolve. The only way a laser disk could hold more data would be if the working wavelength could be reduced, since this would reduce the size of the spot.

By the same argument, it is not much use trying to measure the pit dimensions of a laser disk with an optical microscope. It is necessary to use an electron microscope to make measurements where conventional optics are diffraction limiting.

6.11 The laser

The semiconductor laser is a relative of the light-emitting diode (LED). Both operate by raising the energy of electrons to move them from one valence band to another conduction band. Electrons which fall back to the valence band emit a quantum of energy as a photon whose frequency is proportional to the energy difference between the bands. The process is described by Planck's law:

Energy Difference E $= h \times f$

Where H is Planck's constant and equal to 6.6262×10^{-34} joules s.

For gallium arsenide, the energy difference is about 1.6 eV, where 1 eV is 1.6×10^{-19} joules. Using Planck's Law, the frequency of emission will be

$$f = \frac{1.6 \times 1.6 \times 10^{-19}}{6.6262 \times 10^{-34}} \text{ Hz}$$

The wavelength will be c/f where 8 c is the velocity of light and equal to 3 × 10^8 m/s:

$$\text{Wavelength} = \frac{3 \times 10^8 \times 6.6262 \times 10^{-34}}{2.56 \times 10^{-19}} \text{ m.}$$

$$= 780 \text{nm.}$$

In the LED, electrons fall back to the valence band randomly, and the light produced is incoherent. In the laser, the ends of the semiconductor are optically flat mirrors, which produce an optically resonant cavity. One photon can bounce to and fro, exciting others in synchronism, to produce coherent light. This can result in a runaway condition where all available energy is used up in one flash. In injection lasers, an equilibrium is reached between energy input and light output, allowing continuous operation. The equilibrium is delicate, and such devices are usually fed from a current source. To avoid runaway when a temperature change disturbs the equilibrium, a photosensor is often fed back to the current source. Such lasers have a finite life and become steadily less efficient. The feedback will maintain output, and it is possible to anticipate the failure of the laser by monitoring the drive voltage needed to give the correct output.

6.12 Polarization

In natural light, the electric field component will be in many planes. Light is said to be polarized when the electric field direction is constrained. The wave can be considered as made up from two orthogonal components. When these are in phase, the polarization is said to be linear. When there is a phase shift between the components, the polarization is said to be elliptical, with a special case at 90° called circular polarization. These types of polarization are contrasted in Fig. 6.22.

To create polarized light, anisotropic materials are convenient. Polaroid material, invented by Edwin Land, is vinyl which is made anisotropic by stretching it while hot. This causes the long polymer molecules to line up along the axis of stretching. If the material is soaked in iodine, the molecules are rendered conductive and short out any electric field component along themselves. Electric fields at right angles are unaffected; thus the transmission plane is at right angles to the stretching axis.

Stretching plastics can also result in anisotropy of refractive index; this effect is known as birefringence. If a linearly polarized wavefront enters

Polarization

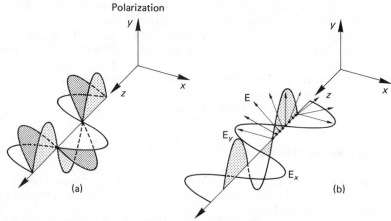

Figure 6.22 (a) Linear polarization: orthogonal components are in phase. (b) Circular polarization: orthogonal components are in phase quadrature

such a medium, the two orthogonal components propagate at different velocities, causing a relative phase difference proportional to the distance travelled. The plane of polarization of the light is rotated. Where the thickness of the material is such that a 90° phase change is caused, the device is known as a quarter-wave plate. The action of such a device is shown in Fig. 6.23. If the plane of polarization of the incident light is at 45° to the planes of greatest and least refractive index, the two orthogonal components of the light will be of equal magnitude, and this results in circular polarization. Similarly, circularly polarized light can be returned to

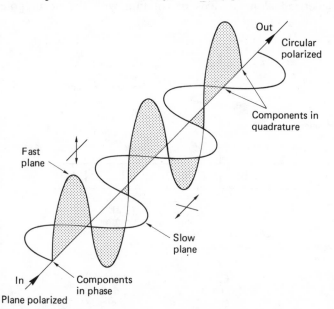

Figure 6.23 Different speed of light in different planes rotates the plane of polarization in a quarter-wave plate to give a circular-polarized output

the linearly polarized state by a further quarter-wave plate. Rotation of the plane of polarization is a useful method of separating incident and reflected light in a laser pickup. Using a quarter-wave plate, the plane of polarization of light leaving the pickup will have been turned 45°, and on return it will be rotated a further 45°, so that it is now at right angles to the plane of polarization of light from the source. The two can easily be separated by a polarizing prism, which acts as a transparent block to light in one plane, but as a prism to light in the other plane.

6.13 Thermomagneto-optics

A relatively recent and fascinating field is the use of magneto-optics,[6] also known more fully as thermomagneto-optics, for data storage where the medium can be re-recorded.

Writing in a DRAW device makes use of a thermomagnetic property possessed by all magnetic materials, which is that above a certain temperature, known as the Curie temperature, their coercive force becomes zero. This means that they become magnetically very soft and take on the flux direction of any externally applied field. On cooling, this field orientation will be frozen in the material, and the coercivity will oppose attempts to change it. There are unfortunately relatively few materials which have a suitably low Curie temperature. Compounds of terbium and gadolinium have been used, and one of the major problems to be overcome is that almost all suitable materials from a magnetic viewpoint corrode very quickly in air.

Fig. 6.24 shows how a DRAW disk is written. If the disk is considered to be initially magnetized along its axis of rotation with the north pole

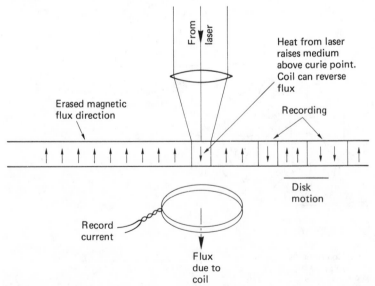

Figure 6.24 The thermomagneto-optical disk uses the heat from a laser to allow a magnetic field to record on the disk

upwards, it is rotated in a field of the opposite sense, produced by coils, which is weaker than the room-temperature coercivity of the medium. The coils will therefore have no effect. A laser beam is focused on the medium as it turns, and a pulse from the laser will momentarily heat a very small area of the medium past its Curie temperature, whereby it will take on a reversed flux as a result of the presence of the field coils. This reversed-flux direction will be retained indefinitely as the medium cools. The storage medium is thus clearly magnetic, but the writing mechanism is the heat produced by light from a laser; hence the term thermomagneto-optics. The advantage of this writing mechanism is that there is no physical contact between the writing head and the medium. The distance can be several millimetres, some of which is taken up with a protective layer to prevent corrosion. In prototypes this layer is glass, but it is expected that commercially available DRAW disks will be plastic.

The laser beam will supply a relatively high power for writing, since it is supplying heat energy. For reading, the laser power is reduced, such that it cannot heat the medium past the Curie temperature, and it is left on continuously. Readout depends on the so-called Kerr effect, or the related Faraday effect, which are both a rotation of the plane of polarization of light due to a magnetic field. The name of the effect depends on whether transmitted or reflected light is of interest. The magnetic areas written on the disk will rotate the plane of polarization of incident polarized light to two different planes, and it is possible to detect the change in rotation by passing the reflected light through a further polarizing screen. The light whose plane of polarization is more nearly parallel with the transmission plane of the screen will pass more easily than the light whose plane of polarization is rotated away from the transmission plane, and a photosensor will detect an intensity change which recreates the write waveform. The readout signal is very small, since the Kerr effect is subtle. The plane of polarization is rotated only a fraction of a degree in typical devices, which makes the replay signal prone to noise. In order to change a recording, it must first be erased. The laser is set to the power level required for writing, but the coils adjacent to the disk are fed with a reversed current to that used in the write process. As the laser scans the old recording, the heat raises the track above its Curie temperature and causes it to take on the direction of the applied field, which is that of the erased state. The coil current is then set back to the write direction, and the disk track can be rewritten with laser pulses as before. The erase process is necessary because the write process can only set the magnetic state. It cannot reset it.

Experimental recordable Compact Discs have been made based on this principle.[6–8]

6.14 Optical readout

The information layer of an optical disc is read through the thickness of the disc. Fig. 6.25 shows that this approach causes the readout beam to enter and leave the disc surface through the largest possible area. The actual dimensions of CD are shown in the figure. Despite the minute spot size of

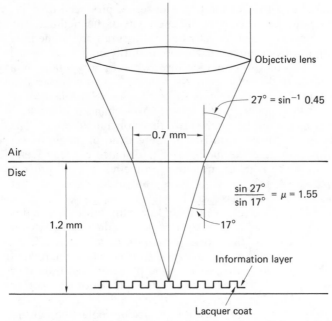

Figure 6.25 The objective lens of a CD pickup has a numerical aperture (NA) of 0.45; thus the outermost rays will be inclined at approximately 27° to the normal. Refraction at the air/disk interface changes this to approximately 17° within the disk. Thus light focused to a spot on the information layer has entered the disk through a 0.7 mm diameter circle, giving good resistance to surface contamination

about 1.2 µm diameter, light enters and leaves through a 0.7 mm diameter circle. As a result, surface debris has to be three orders of magnitude larger than the readout spot before the beam is obscured. The size of the entry circle is a function of the refractive index of the disc material, the numerical aperture of the objective lens and the thickness of the disc. The method of readout through the disc thickness tolerates surface scratches very well. Most optical disks are in fact made from two disks sandwiched together with the two information layers on the inside.

Continuing the example of CD, the specified wavelength of 780 nm and the numerical aperture of 0.45 results in an Airy function where the half-power level is at a diameter of about 1 µm. The first dark ring will be at about 1.9 µm diameter. As the illumination follows an intensity function, it is really meaningless to talk about spot size unless the relative power level is specified. The analogy is quoting frequency response without dB limits.

Allowable crosstalk between tracks then determines the track pitch. The first ring outside the central disc carries some 7% of the total power and limits crosstalk performance. The track spacing is such that with a slightly defocused beam and a slight tracking error, crosstalk due to adjacent tracks is acceptable. Since aberrations in the objective will increase the spot size and crosstalk, the CD specification requires the lens to be within the Maréchal criterion. Clearly the numerical aperture of the lens, the wavelength of the laser, the refractive index and thickness of the disc, and the height and size of the bumps must all be simultaneously specified.

The cutter spot size determines the reader spot size, and this in turn determines the shortest wavelength along the track which can be resolved. If the track velocity is specified, the wavelength limit becomes a frequency limit. The optical cut-off frequency is that frequency where the amplitude of modulation replayed from the disc has fallen to zero, and it is given by

$$F_c = \frac{2NA}{\text{wavelength}} \times \text{velocity}$$

The minimum linear velocity of CD is 1.2 m/s, giving a cut-off frequency of

$$F_c = \frac{2 \times 0.45 \times 1.2}{780 \times 10^{-9}} = 1.38\,\text{MHz}$$

Fig. 6.26 shows that the frequency response falls linearly to the cut-off and that actual measurements are only a little worse than the theory predicts. Clearly, to obtain any noise immunity, the maximum operating frequency must be rather less than the cut-off frequency.

The construction of laser disk drives is detailed in Chapter 12.

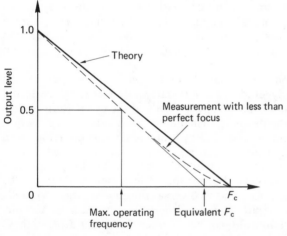

Figure 6.26 Frequency response of laser pickup. Maximum operating frequency is about half of cut-off frequency F_c

6.15 Shortcomings of recording channels

This chapter has outlined the basic physics of various recording processes, and introduced numerous shortcomings and restrictions from which real recording channels will suffer. Now these shortcomings will be categorized, and coding methods to overcome them will be described.

Noise in the channel causes uncertainty about the voltage of the reproduced signal. Jitter causes uncertainty about the time at which a particular event occurred. The frequency response of the channel then places an overall limit on the spacing of events in the channel. Particular emphasis must be placed on the interplay of bandwidth, jitter and noise, which will be shown here to be the key to the design of a successful channel code.

In laser recording, the interference readout process will respond down to DC, but usually the low-frequency portion of the channel is required by the focus and tracking mechanisms, and DC-free channel codes will still be necessary. The high-frequency response is governed by the modulation transfer function of the optics, which is normally limited by the numerical aperture of the objective and the linear speed of the track. The frequency response of a laser recorder falls to zero at the cut-off frequency and, unlike magnetic recording, never rises again.

6.16 Jitter windows

Fig. 6.27 shows several possibilities for a complete digital recording channel. The reconstituted waveform at the output of this channel will now be a replica of the timing of the record signal, with the addition of time uncertainty in the position of the edges due to noise, jitter and dubious equalization. In the same way that binary circuits reject noise by using two voltage levels which are spaced further apart than the uncertainty due to noise, digital recording combats time uncertainty by using events, known as transitions, at multiples of some basic time period, which is larger than the typical time uncertainty. Fig. 6.28 shows how this jitter rejection mechanism works.

As digital transitions occur at multiples of a basic period, an oscilloscope, which is triggered on random data, will show an eye pattern if connected to the output of the equalizer. Study of the eye pattern reveals how well the coding used suits the channel.[9] Noise closes the eyes in a vertical direction, and jitter closes the eyes in a horizontal direction, as in Fig. 6.29. In the centre of the eyes, at regular intervals, the receiver must make binary decisions about the state of the signal, high or low. If the eyes remain sensibly open, this will be possible. Clearly more jitter can be tolerated if there is less noise, and vice versa. Information theory usually only takes account of SNR and bandwidth when assessing channel capacity. Magnetic and optical recorder channels will never achieve these capacities because of jitter.

It is not possible to record data directly on to the medium, because in real data continuous ones and continuous zeros can occur and, as shown in Fig. 6.30, this is effectively a DC component of the source data. Alternate ones and zeros represent the other extreme, a frequency of half the bit rate, which is known as the Nyquist rate. Magnetic recorders will not respond to DC, nor is it possible to discriminate between successive identical bits in a channel subject to time instability.

Both of these problems can be solved with a suitable channel code, which will combine a clock with the data prior to recording, in a way which reduces the DC content and permits separation of adjacent symbols on replay. Fig. 6.31 shows that a channel coder is necessary prior to the record

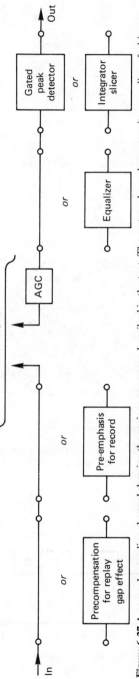

Figure 6.27 A general recording channel showing the various processes described in the text. The system shown here permits recording of a binary waveform

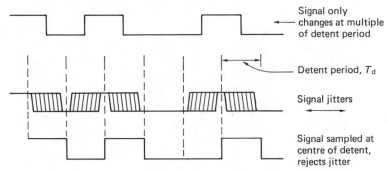

Figure 6.28 A certain amount of jitter can be rejected by changing the signal at multiples of the basic detent period T_d

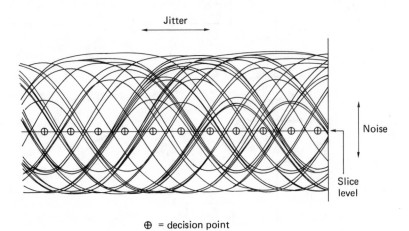

⊕ = decision point

Figure 6.29 At the decision points, the receiver must make binary decisions about the voltage of the signal, whether it is above or below the slicing level. If the eyes remain open, this will be possible in the presence of noise and jitter

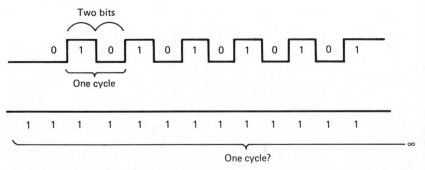

Figure 6.30 The extreme cases of real data. Alternate ones and zeros gives the highest Nyquist rate (= half bit rate). Continuous ones (or zeros) gives DC. Real data fill the spectrum from DC to Nyquist rate

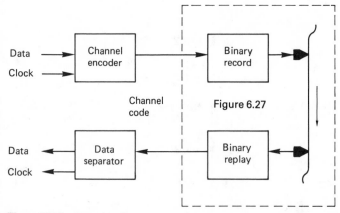

Figure 6.31 In channel coding, the input data and clock are combined into a single waveform called the channel code. On replay the channel code is restored to the original data stream by the data separator

stage and that a decoder, known as a data separator, is necessary after the replay stage.

Some codes eliminate DC content entirely, which is advantageous for rotary-head recording. Some codes can reduce the channel bandwidth needed by lowering the upper spectrum limit. This permits higher linear density, but usually at the expense of jitter rejection. A code with a narrow spectrum has a number of advantages. The reduction in asymmetry will reduce peak shift, and data separators can lock more readily where the possible frequencies are fewer. In theory, the narrower the spectrum, the less noise, but excessive noise filtering can ruin the equalization, nullifying any gain.

A convenient definition of a channel code (for there are certainly others) is: 'A method of modulating real data such that they can be reliably received despite shortcomings of a real channel, while making maximum economic use of the channel capacity'.

The storage density of data recorders has steadily increased as a result of improvements in medium and transducer technology, but modern storage densities are also a function of improvements in channel coding. Fig. 6.32(a) shows how linear density improvements due to channel coding alone have occurred and introduces one of the fundamental parameters of a channel code, the density ratio (DR). One definition of density ratio is that it is the worst-case ratio of the number of data bits recorded to the number of transitions in the channel. It can also be thought of as the ratio between the Nyquist rate of the data and the frequency response of the channel. When better hardware is available to increase the capacity of a channel, the use of a higher density ratio code multiplies the capacity further. It should be appreciated that many of the codes described in this chapter are protected by patents and that non-optimal codes are often devised to avoid the need to pay royalties on a patented code.

The basic time periods of the recorded signal are called positions or detents, in which the recorded flux will be reversed or stay the same

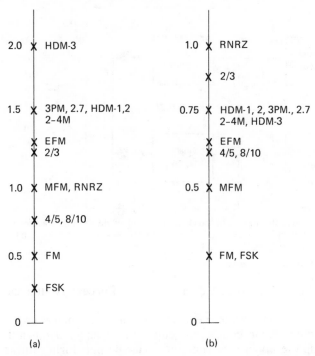

Figure 6.32 (a) Comparison of codes by density ratio; (b) comparison of codes by figure of merit. Note how 4/5, 2/3, 8/10 + RNRZ move up because of good jitter performance; HDM-3 moves down because of jitter sensitivity

according to the state of a channel bit which describes the detent. The symbol used for the units of channel time is T_d. Channel coding is the art of converting real data into channel bits. It is important to appreciate that the convention in coding is that a channel bit one represents a flux change, whereas a zero represents no change. This is confusing because the input data only change where successive bits differ. The differentiating action of magnetic playback has a lot to do with these conventions.

As jitter is such an important issue in digital recording, a parameter has been introduced to quantify the ability of a channel code to reject time instability. This parameter, the jitter window, also known as the window margin or phase margin (T_w), is defined as the permitted range of time over which a transition can still be received correctly, divided by the data bit-cell period (T).

Since equalization is often difficult in practice, a code which has a large jitter margin will sometimes be used with short recorded wavelengths because it resists the effects of peak shift distortion. Such a code may achieve a working density better than a code with a higher density ratio but poor jitter performance.

A more realistic comparison of code performance will be obtained by taking into account both density ratio and jitter margin. This is the purpose of the figure of merit (FoM), which is defined as DR $\times$ T_w. Fig. 6.32(b) shows a comparison of codes by FoM.

255

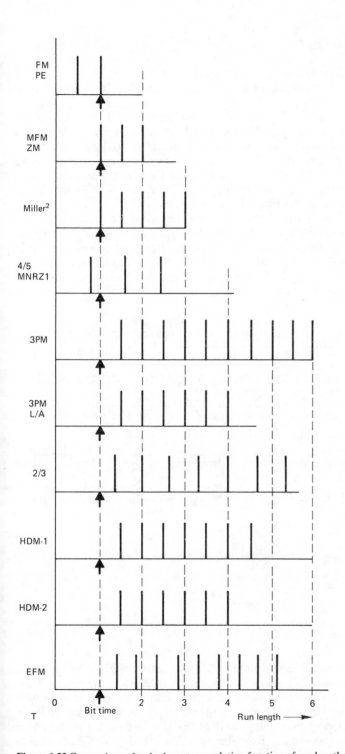

Figure 6.33 Comparison of codes by autocorrelation function of run length

6.17 Simple codes

Some actual codes will now be examined.

The essence of channel coding is to convert real data into channel bits. Since the time quantizing is linear, channel codes lend themselves to convenient comparison by analysis of the autocorrelation function. In autocorrelation, a signal is delayed and multiplied by itself. When the delay is swept, a graph is obtained of the product versus delay, known as the autocorrelation function. Most of the parameters of a code can be read from the autocorrelation function at a glance, whereas the more common use of the code spectrum makes this more difficult. Fig. 6.33 shows the autocorrelation functions of a number of codes.

The adoption of FM in analog recorders permitted the recording of DC levels for instrumentation and video. When a binary signal is fed to a frequency modulator, the result is frequency shift keying (FSK) shown in Fig. 6.34(a). This is inherently DC free and suits radio transmission and rotary-head recorders. FSK has a poor density ratio and has been superseded by more recent codes.

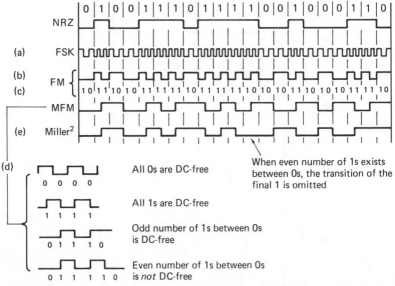

Figure 6.34 Evolution from FSK to Miller^2. Note that although Miller^2 is DC-free T_{max} and L_c are worse than MFM

The limiting case of FSK is binary FM (also known as Manchester code) shown in Fig. 6.34(b). This was the first practical self-clocking binary code. It is DC free and very easy to encode and decode. It remains in use today where recording density is not of prime importance, for example in single-density floppy disks and in SMPTE/EBU time code for professional audio and video recorders. It is also specified for the AES/EBU digital audio interconnect standard which transmits audio serially down cables.

In FM there is always a transition at the bit-cell boundary which acts as a clock. For a data one, there is an additional transition at the bit-cell centre. Fig. 6.34(c) shows that each data bit is represented by two channel bits. For a data zero, they will be 10, and for a data one they will be 11. Since the first bit is always one, it conveys no information and is responsible for the density ratio of only one-half. Since there can be two transitions for each data bit, the jitter window can only be half a bit, and the FoM resulting is only 0.25. The high clock content of FM does, however, mean that data recovery is possible over a wide range of speeds; hence the use for time code.

In MFM the highly redundant clock content of FM was reduced by the use of a phase-locked loop in the receiver which could flywheel over missing clock transitions. This technique is implicit in all the more advanced codes. The bit-cell centre transition on a data one was retained, but the bit-cell boundary transition is now only required between successive zeros. There are still two channel bits for every data bit, but adjacent channel bits will never be one, doubling the minimum time between transitions and giving a DR of 1. Clearly the coding of the current bit is now influenced by the preceding bit. The maximum number of prior bits which affect the current bit is known as the constraint length L_c, measured in data-bit periods. For MFM $L_c = T$. Another way of considering the constraint length is that it assesses the number of data bits which may be corrupted if the receiver misplaces one transition. If L_c is long, all errors will be burst errors.

MFM doubled the density ratio compared with FM without changing the jitter performance; thus the FoM also doubles. It was adopted for many rigid disks at the time of its development and remains in use on double-density floppy disks. It is not, however, DC free. Fig. 6.34(d) shows how MFM can have DC content, and that in Miller^2 code the DC content is eliminated by a slight increase in complexity. Wherever an even number of ones occurs between zeros, the transition at the last one is omitted. This creates an additional entry in the autocorrelation function because T_{max} has increased. Miller^2 code is used in the D-2 composite digital video format.[6, 10, 11]

A similar performance is given by zero modulation but with an increase in complexity.[6, 12]

6.18 Group codes

Further improvements in coding rely on converting patterns of real data to patterns of channel bits with more desirable characteristics using a conversion table known as a codebook. If a data symbol of m bits is considered, it can have 2^m different combinations. As it is intended to discard undesirable patterns to improve the code, it follows that the number of channel bits n must be greater than m. The number of patterns which can be discarded is $2^n - 2^m$. One name for the principle is group code recording (GCR), and an important parameter is the code rate, defined as

$$\text{Code rate } R = \frac{m}{n}$$

It will be evident that the jitter window T_w is numerically equal to the code rate, and so a code rate close to unity is desirable. The choice of patterns which are used in the codebook will be those which give the desired balance between clock content, bandwidth and DC content.

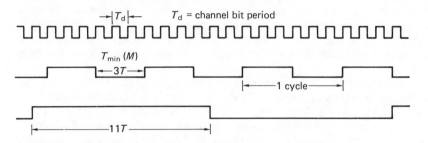

Figure 6.35 A channel code can control its spectrum by placing limits on $T_{min}(M)$ and T_{max} which define upper and lower frequences. Ratio of T_{max}/T_{min} determines asymmetry of waveform and predicts DC content and peak shift

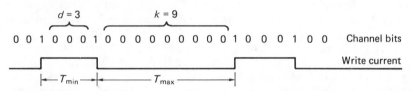

Figure 6.36 Channel-bit convention is that a 1 represents a transition. Parameters d and k are the number of zeros between ones. d = min, k = max. Clearly T_{min}, T_{max} are greater than d, k by one channel-bit period

In Fig. 6.35 it is shown that the upper spectral limit can be made to be some fraction of the channel-bit rate according to the minimum distance between ones in the channel bits. This is known as T_{min}, also referred to as the minimum transition parameter M, and in both cases is measured in data bits T. It can be obtained by multiplying the number of channel detent periods between transitions by the code rate. Unfortunately, codes are measured by the number of consecutive zeros in the channel bits, given by the symbol d, which Fig. 6.36 shows is always one less than the number of detent periods. In fact T_{min} is numerically equal to the density ratio.

$$T_{min} = M = DR = \frac{(d + 1) \times m}{n}$$

It will be evident that choosing a low code rate could increase the density ratio, but it will impair the jitter window. The figure of merit is

$$FoM = DR \times T^w = \frac{(d + 1) \times m^2}{n^2}$$

since $T_w = m/n$

Fig. 6.35 also shows that the lower spectral limit is influenced by the maximum distance between transitions T_{max}. This is also obtained by multiplying the maximum number of detent periods between transitions by the code rate. Again, codes are measured by the maximum number of zeros between channel ones, k, and so

$$T_{max} = \frac{(k+1) \times m}{n}$$

and the maximum/minimum ratio P is

$$P = \frac{k+1}{d+1}$$

The length of time between channel transitions is known as the run length. Another name for this class is the run-length-limited (RLL) codes.[13] Since m data bits are considered as one symbol, the constraint length L_c will be increased in RLL codes to at least m. It is, however, possible for a code to have run-length limits without it being a group code.

In practice, the junction of two adjacent channel symbols may violate run-length limits, and it is necessary to create a further codebook of symbol size $2n$ which converts violating codes to acceptable codes. This is known as merging and follows the golden rule that the substitute $2n$ symbol must finish with a pattern which eliminates the possibility of a subsequent violation. These patterns must also differ from all other symbols.

Substitution may also be used to different degrees in the same nominal code to allow a choice of maximum run length, e.g. 3PM.[14] The maximum number of symbols involved in a substitution is denoted by r.[6,15,16] There are many RLL codes and the parameters d, k, m, n and r are a way of comparing them.

Sometimes the code rate forms the name of the code, as in 2/3, 8/10 and EFM; at other times the code may be named after the d, k parameters, as in 2,7 code.

Various examples will be given which illustrate the principles involved. 4/5 code uses 16 out of 32 possible channel symbols to represent the data.

Table 6.1 The codebook of 4/5 code. Maximum number of zeros (k) is two; thus T_{max} is $4(k+1)/5 = 2.4$ bits. Adjacent ones are permitted: thus DR $= 4/5$.

Data		
Decimal	Binary	Channel bits
0	0000	11001
1	0001	11011
2	0010	10010
3	0011	10011
4	0100	11101
5	0101	10101
6	0110	10110
7	0111	10111
8	1000	11010
9	1001	01001
10	1010	01010
11	1011	01011
12	1100	11110
13	1101	01101
14	1110	01110
15	1111	01111

The criterion for 4/5 was high clock content to give immunity to jitter, without a great sacrifice of DR.[17] The codebook is shown in Table 6.1. Each one in the code represents a flux reversal, and there are never more than three channel bits (2.4 data bits) of time between clock edges ($k = 2$). This permits a simple AGC system to be used in the read circuits. As codes had to be rejected to achieve the main criterion, the remaining codes have to be accepted; thus the minimum run length is only 1 bit, as adjacent ones are allowed in the codebook ($d = 0$). The code is thus described as 0,1,4,5,1. $L_c = 4T$, and the density ratio is given by

$$DR = \frac{(d + 1) \times m}{n} = 0.8$$

The spectrum needed is thus 1.25 times that of the data, but there can be no merging violations, and an extremely good window margin T_w of 0.8 is obtained, giving an FoM of 0.64.

This code was used by the IBM 6250 BPI tape format and represented an improvement factor of nearly four over the 1600 BPI phase-encoded (PE) system which preceded it. The FoM was better than PE by a factor of more than 2½, thus reducing the improvements needed to the head and tape.

Fig. 6.37(a) shows an optimized code which also illustrates the process of merging. This is a 1,7,2,3,2 code known as 2/3. It is designed to have a large window to resist peak shift in disk drives, along with a good density

Data	Code
0 0	1 0 1
0 1	1 0 0
1 0	0 0 1
1 1	0 1 0

(a)

Data	Illegal code	Substitution
0 0 0 0	1 0 1 1 0 1	1 0 1 0 0 0
0 0 0 1	1 0 1 1 0 0	1 0 0 0 0 0
1 0 0 0	0 0 1 1 0 1	0 0 1 0 0 0
1 0 0 1	0 0 1 1 0 0	0 1 0 0 0 0

(b)

Figure 6.37 2/3 code. At (a) two data bits (m) are expressed as three channel bits (n) without adjacent transitions ($d=1$). Violations are dealt with by substitution.

$$DR = \frac{(d+1)m}{n} = \frac{2 \times 2}{3} = 1.33$$

Adjacent data pairs can break the encoding rule; in these cases substitutions are made, as shown at (b)

ratio.[18] In 2/3 code, pairs of data bits create symbols of three adjacent channel bits. For bandwidth reduction, all codes with adjacent ones are eliminated. This halves the code spectrum, and the density ratio improves accordingly:

$$DR = \frac{(d+1) \times m}{n} = \frac{2 \times 2}{3} = 1.33$$

In Fig. 6.37(b), the effect of some data combinations will be code violations. Thus pairs of three channel-bit symbols are replaced with a new six channel-bit symbol. L_c is thus $4T$, the same as for 4/5 code. The jitter window is given by

$$T_w = \frac{m}{n} = \frac{2}{3} T$$

and the FoM is

$$\frac{2}{3} \times \frac{4}{3} = \frac{8}{9}$$

This is an extremely good figure for an RLL code, and is some 10% better than the FoM of 3PM[19] and 2,7.

In order to reduce the complexity of encoding logic, it is common in GCR to computer-optimize the relationship between data patterns and code patterns so that the conversion can be performed in a programmed logic array.

6.19 CCIR-656 serial video code

This code was developed to allow serial communication of digital component video sampled in 4:2:2 form. The communication may be with coaxial cable or a fibre-optic link. In each case it is desirable to limit the DC content of the code to prevent jitter due to shift of the baseline. The code is an 8,9 group code, where 8 bits of data, in fact a video sample, are converted to 9 channel bits. In this code a channel zero represents a low level and a channel one represents a high level, a different approach to group coding descriptions for recording. There are 512 combinations in 9 bits, and these are selected to have either five or four zeros in each symbol to reduce DC content. Unfortunately there are not 256 combinations of 9 bits having this characteristic – there are only 213, and so there will be 43 combinations which cannot be encoded in this way. These must be encoded in channel symbols which may have 6 bits in one state and 3 in the other, which clearly are not DC free. In practice, such symbols have a complementary symbol, which has opposite DC content, so for each of these 43 symbols there will be a positive DC content version and a negative DC content version. These alternative symbols can be seen in Fig. 6.38 which is the codebook for the CCIR 8,9 code. When symbols are encoded, the channel symbol is checked for DC content. If it is normal, the symbol is transmitted. If the symbol has DC content, it is transmitted, but the fact is recorded in a latch. When the next symbol having DC content is detected,

8B	9B	$\overline{9B}$	8B	9B	$\overline{9B}$	8B	9B	$\overline{9B}$	8B	9B	$\overline{9B}$	8B	9B	$\overline{9B}$	8B	9B
00	0FE	101	2C	1AC		58	099		84	0D5		B0	11A		DC	131
01	027		2D	057		59	166		85	12A		B1	0E9		DD	0DC
02	1D8		2E	09B		5A	09B		86	095		B2	116		DE	127
03	033		2F	059		5B	164		87	16A		B3	02E		DF	0E2
04	1CC		30	1A6		5C	09D		88	0B5		B4	1D1		E0	123
05	037		31	05B		5D	162		89	14A		B5	036		E1	0E4
06	1C8		32	05D		5E	0A3		8A	09A		B6	1C9		E2	11D
07	039		33	1A4		5F	15C		8B	165		B7	03A		E3	0E6
08	1C6		34	065		60	0A7		8C	0A6		B8	1C5		E4	11B
09	03B		35	19A		61	158		8D	159		B9	04E		E5	0E8
0A	1C4		36	069		62	025	1DA	8E	0AC		BA	1B1		E6	119
0B	03D		37	196		63	0A1	15E	8F	153		BB	05C		E7	0EC
0C	1C2		38	026	1D9	64	029	1D6	90	0AE		BC	1A3		E8	117
0D	14D		39	08C	173	65	091	16E	91	151		BD	05E		E9	0F2
0E	0B4		3A	02C	1D3	66	045	1BA	92	02A	1D5	BE	1A1		EA	113
0F	14B		3B	098	167	67	089	176	93	092	16D	BF	066		EB	0F4
10	1A2		3C	032	1CD	68	049	1B6	94	04A	1B5	C0	199		EC	10D
11	0B6		3D	0BE	141	69	085	17A	95	094	16B	C1	06C		ED	076
12	149		3E	034	1CB	6A	051	1AE	96	0A8	157	C2	193		EE	10B
13	0BA		3F	0C2	13D	6B	08A	175	97	0B7	148	C3	06E		EF	0C7
14	145		40	046	1B9	6C	0A4	15B	98	0F5	10A	C4	191		F0	13C
15	0CA		41	0C4	13B	6D	054	1AB	99	0BB	144	C5	072		F1	047
16	135		42	04C	1B3	6E	0A2	15D	9A	0ED	112	C6	18D		F2	1B8
17	0D2		43	0C8	137	6F	052	1AD	9B	0BD	142	C7	074		F3	067
18	12D		44	058	1A7	70	056		9C	0EB	114	C8	18B		F4	19C
19	0D4		45	0B1		71	1A9		9D	0D7	129	C9	07A		F5	071
1A	129		46	14E		72	05A		9E	0DD	122	CA	189		F6	198
1B	0D6		47	0B3		73	1A5		9F	0DB	124	CB	08E		F7	073
1C	125		48	14C		74	06A		A0	146		CC	185		F8	18E
1D	0DA		49	0B9		75	195		A1	0C5		CD	09C		F9	079
1E	115		4A	06B		76	096		A2	13A		CE	171		FA	18C
1F	0EA		4B	194		77	169		A3	0C9		CF	09E		FB	087
20	0B2		4C	06D		78	0A9		A4	136		D0	163		FC	186
21	02B		4D	192		79	156		A5	0CB		D1	0B8		FD	0C3
22	1D4		4E	075		7A	0AB		A6	134		D2	161		FE	178
23	02D		4F	18A		7B	154		A7	0CD		D3	0BC		FF	062
24	1D2		50	08B		7C	0A5		A8	132		D4	147			
25	035		51	174		7D	15A		A9	0D1		D5	0C6			
26	1CA		52	08D		7E	0AD		AA	12E		D6	143			
27	04B		53	172		7F	152		AB	0D3		D7	0CC			
28	1B4		54	093		80	155		AC	12C		D8	139			
29	04D		55	16C		81	0AA		AD	0D9		D9	0CE			
2A	1B2		56	097		82	055		AE	126		DA	133			
2B	053		57	168		83	1AA		AF	0E5		DB	0D8			

Figure 6.38 Code book for CCIR 8, 9 code. Some 9 bit symbols have excessive D.C. content, and a complemented version $\overline{9B}$ also exists. Normal and complemented symbols are used alternately to control D.C. *See* Figure 6.39

the existence of the bit in the latch causes the symbol to be inverted and the latch to be reset.

This procedure results in symbols having DC content to be sent with alternate polarity, as the example of Fig. 6.39 shows.

Decoding is simpler, because there is a direct relationship between 9 bit codes and 8 bit data. Since this code is not strictly DC free, it is described as a low disparity code. More details of the 8/9 interconnect can be found in Chapter 8.

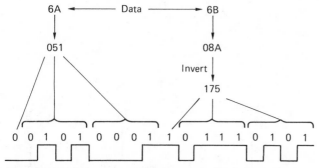

Figure 6.39 In this example, the symbol on the left results in a code symbol having six zeros, which has negative D.C. content. The next symbol which has a D.C. content will be inverted as shown so that the D.C. content is cancelled

6.20 Tracking signals

For recorders with active track-following systems, it is possible to bury low-frequency tracking tones within digital data. A group code is used, where for each data group several valid channel groups exist, each having a different DC content. By choosing a group not only from the data to be recorded but also to produce the desired DC level, it is possible to generate a low frequency from the sequence of DC levels used.[20] This can be filtered from the data frequencies used. Different tones are buried in adjacent tracks to allow a tracking error to be generated.

As an alternative, if an analog record amplifier is used, the analog tracking tones are linearly added to the channel coded data to produce a composite signal for recording.

6.21 Randomized NRZ and 10 bit serial video code

Genuine data are unsuitable for direct recording, because, as has been seen, they have an undefined maximum run length, T_{max}, which gives severe problems with clock recovery, AGC and DC content. In other respects, however, raw data have potential because the density ratio of unity is combined with the extremely good jitter window, which is also unity, to give an FoM of 1, which is higher than the best group codes.

It is possible to convert raw data into a channel code in a non-redundant fashion by performing a modulo-2 (XOR) addition with a pseudo-random sequence. As Fig. 6.40(a) shows, the result of this process is that T_{max} is drastically reduced. Obviously the same pseudo-random sequence must be provided on replay, synchronized to the data, if there is to be correct recovery. In practice the system cannot accept truly random data, since if by chance the data are identical to the pseudo-random sequence, the system breaks down. The probability of such an occurrence is low, and the error-correction system would deal with it. The so-called randomized NRZI coding is used in D-1 component digital video recorders, since the pseudo-random sequence reduces the DC content of the waveform, which

264

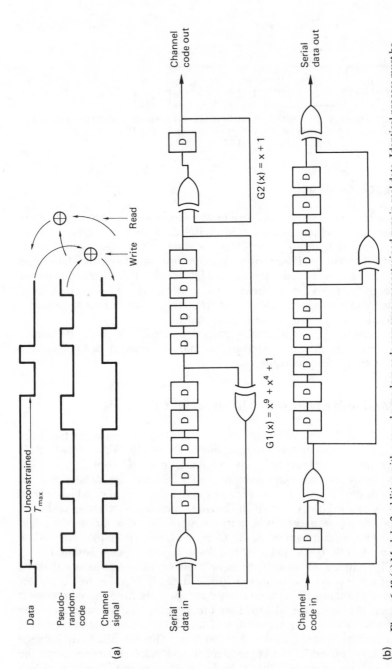

Figure 6.40 (a) Modulo-2 addition with a pseudo-random code removes unconstrained runs in real data. Identical process must be provided on replay. (b) Convolutional randomizing encoder, at top, transmits exclusive-or of three bits at a fixed spacing in the data. One bit delay, far right, produces channel transitions from data ones. Decoder, below, has opposing one bit delay to return from transitions to data levels, followed by an opposing shift register which exactly reverses the coding process

is essential as the format requires a rotary transformer in the channel. The randomizing in D-1 is clearly block based, since this matches the block structure on tape. Where there is no obvious block structure, convolutional or endless randomizing can be used. This is the approach used in the scrambled serial digital video interconnect, which allows composite or component video of up to 10 bit wordlength to be sent serially.

Fig. 6.40(b) shows that in convolutional randomizing a channel bit is the exclusive-or of a number of data bits at a fixed spacing, which is implemented with a shift register. This has the same effect as block randomizing, in that long runs are broken up and the DC content is reduced, but it has the advantage over block randomizing that no synchronizing is required. The original data can be obtained by a second shift register with the exclusive-or gates connected in a reverse pattern. Clearly the system will take a few clock periods to produce valid data after commencement of transmission; this is no problem on a permanent wired connection where the transmission is continuous.

Further details of the scrambled serial code can be found in Chapter 8.

6.22 Partial response

It has been stated that the head acts as a transversal filter, because it has two poles. In addition the output is differentiated, so that the head may be thought of as a $(1 - D)$ impulse response system, where D is the delay which is a function of the tape speed and gap size. It is this delay which results in intersymbol interference. Conventional equalizers attempt to oppose this effect and succeed in raising the noise level in the process of making the frequency response linear. Fig. 6.41 shows that the frequency response necessary to pass data with insignificant peak shift is a bandwidth of half the bit rate, which is the Nyquist rate. In Class IV partial response, the frequency response of the system is made to have nulls at DC and at the

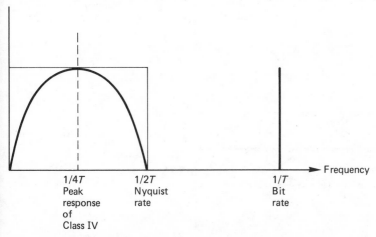

Figure 6.41 Class IV response has spectral nulls at DC and the Nyquist rate, giving a noise advantage, since magnetic replay signal is weak at both frequencies in a high-density channel

Nyquist rate. This is achieved by an overall impulse response of $(1 - D^2)$, where D is now the bit period. There are a number of ways in which this can be done.

If the head gap is made equal to one bit, the $(1 - D)$ head response may be converted to the desired response by the use of a $(1 + D)$ filter, as in Fig. 6.42(a).[21] Alternatively, a head of unspecified gapwidth may be connected to an integrator, and equalized flat to reproduce the record current waveform before being fed to a $(1 - D^2)$ filter as in Fig. 6.42(b).[22]

The result of both of these techniques is a ternary signal. The eye pattern has two sets of eyes as in Fig. 6.42(c).[23] When slicing such a signal, a smaller amount of noise will cause an error than in the binary case.

The treatment of the signal thus far represents an equalization technique and not a channel code. However, to take full advantage of Class IV partial

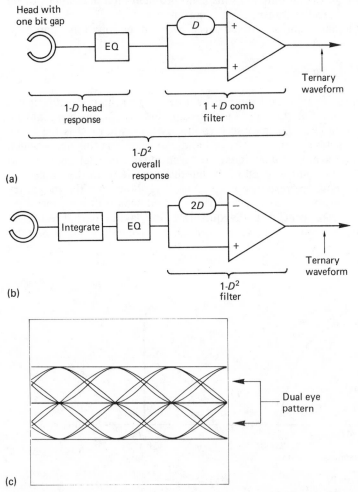

Figure 6.42 (a), (b) Two ways of obtaining partial response. (c) Characteristic eye pattern of ternary signal

response, suitable precoding is necessary prior to recording, which does then constitute a channel-coding technique. This precoding is shown in Fig. 6.43(a). Data are added modulo-2 to themselves with a 2 bit delay. The effect of this precoding is that the outer levels of the ternary signals, which represent data ones, alternate in polarity on all odd bits and on all even bits. This is because the precoder acts like two interleaved 1 bit delay circuits, as in Fig. 6.43(b). As this alternation of polarity is a form of redundancy, it can be used to recover the 3 dB SNR loss encountered in slicing a ternary eye pattern. Viterbi decoding[24] can be used for this purpose. In Viterbi decoding, each channel bit is not sliced individually;

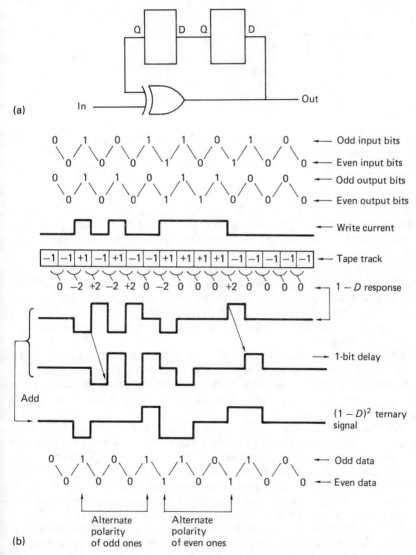

Figure 6.43 Class IV precoding at (a) causes redundancy in replay signal as derived in (b)

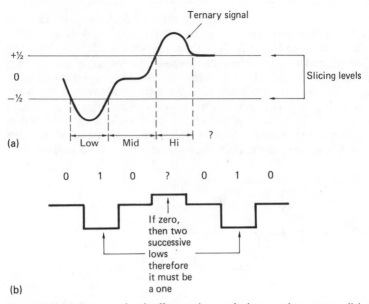

Figure 6.44 (a) A ternary signal suffers a noise penalty because there are two slicing levels. (b) The redundancy is used to determine the bit value in the presence of noise. Here the pulse height has been reduced to make it ambiguous 1/0, but only 1 is valid as zero violates the redundancy rules

the slicing decision is made in the context of adjacent decisions. Fig. 6.44 shows a replay waveform which is so noisy that, at the decision point, the signal voltage crosses the centre of the eye and the slicer alone cannot tell whether the correct decision is an inner or an outer level. In this case, the decoder essentially allows both decisions to stand, in order to see what happens. A symbol representing indecision is output. It will be seen from the figure that as subsequent bits are received, one of these decisions will result in an absurd situation, which indicates that the other decision was the right one. The decoder can then locate the undecided symbol and set it to the correct value.

Clearly a ternary signal having a dual eye pattern is more sensitive than a binary signal, and it is important to keep the maximum run length $T_{\max}$ small in order to have accurate AGC. The use of pseudo-random coding along with partial response equalization and precoding is a logical combination.[25]

Another way of using the information content of a ternary signal is to have the three states determine the amount by which a multilevel parameter changes from one channel bit to the next. A chart of this parameter versus channel symbols is called a trellis, as in Fig. 6.45. In trellis coding, the record signal is precoded so that only certain paths through the trellis are valid, and others must represent errors, which can be corrected by deducing the most likely path from the received path.[26] There is then no distinction between the channel code and the error-correction system. Viterbi decoding and trellis coding are primarily applicable to channels with random errors due to Gaussian statistics, and they cannot

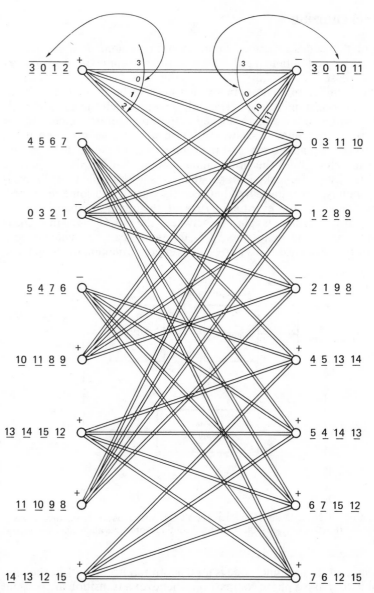

Figure 6.45 An example of trellis coding. The eight states of the trellis represent a three-bit symbol ($2^3 = 8$). From any starting state, there are four possible destinations according to a four-bit (0–15) symbol from the channel

cope with burst errors. In a head-noise-limited system, however, the use of a Viterbi detector could increase the power of an error-correction system by relieving it of the need to correct random errors due to noise. The error-correction system could then concentrate on correcting burst errors unimpaired. The significance of this statement will become clearer upon referring to Chapter 8.

6.23 Synchronizing

In most of the codes described here, an improvement in some desired parameter has been obtained either by a sacrifice of some other parameter or by an increase in complexity. Often it is the clock content which suffers, so that the number of channel bits which have to be measured between transitions becomes quite large. The only way in which the channel code can be decoded is to use a phase-locked loop to regenerate the channel-bit clock. A fixed-frequency clock would be of no use, because even if the medium could be made to move at the right speed for the channel-bit rate to match the clock rate, the instantaneous errors due to jitter would be insuperable. In phase-locked loops, the voltage-controlled oscillator is driven by a phase error measured between the output and some reference, such that the oscillator eventually runs at the same frequency as the reference. If a divider is placed between the VCO and the phase comparator, as in Fig. 6.46, the VCO frequency can be made to be a multiple of the reference. This also has the effect of making the loop more

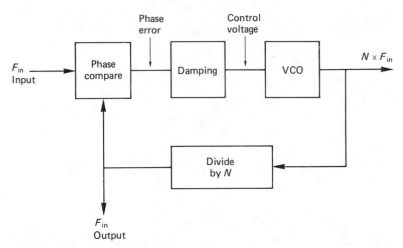

Figure 6.46 A typical phase-locked loop where the VCO is forced to run at a multiple of the input frequency. If the input ceases, the output will continue for a time at the same frequency until it drifts

heavily damped. If a channel code is used as a reference to a PLL, the loop will be able to make a phase comparison whenever a transition arrives, but when there are channel zeros between transitions, the loop will flywheel at the last known frequency and phase until it can rephase at a subsequent transition. In this way, cycles of the VCO can be counted to measure the number of channel zeros between transitions and hence to decode the information. Fig. 6.47 illustrates this mechanism.

Clearly data cannot be separated if the PLL is not locked, but it cannot be locked until it has seen transitions for a reasonable period. The solution is to precede each data block with a pattern of transitions whose sole purpose is to provide a timing reference for synchronizing the phase-locked loop. This pattern is known as a preamble. In MFM, the preamble will

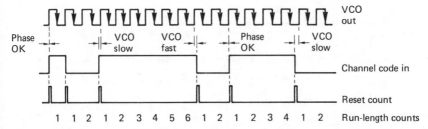

Figure 6.47 In order to reconstruct the channel patterns, a phase-locked loop is fed with the channel code, and freewheels between transitions, correcting its phase at each one. Counting the VCO edges (↓) between transitions reconstructs the channel bits. If the medium changes speed, the VCO will track. If the maximum run length is too long, the VCO will not be able to phase correct often enough, and may miscount channel bits in the presence of jitter

usually be the result of encoding all zeros, which is a square wave at the bit rate. In high-density recording, the preamble may be some simple fraction of the bit rate to avoid the attenuation of the highest frequencies when the PLL is attempting to lock. In magnetic recording there is almost always a postamble at the end of the data block. Again a few zeros are recorded after the real data. When magnetic heads are turned off at the end of a write, there is often a transient which corrupts the last bits written. The postamble can be damaged in this way without consequence. Another reason for a postamble is to enable a block to be read backwards. This is often done in computer magtapes to shorten access time. Time code has to be legible in either direction and at varying speeds. Some channel codes are designed to work backwards, such as phase encoding, 4/5GCR, zero modulation and FM. For reverse reading, the postamble will be the same length as the preamble; otherwise it will be much shorter.

Once the PLL has locked to the preamble, a data stream and a clock will emerge from the data separator. It is then vital to know at what point in the data stream the preamble finishes and the actual data commences. In serial recording, words are recorded one after the other, one bit at a time, with no spaces in between, so that although the designer knows that a block contains, say, 24 words of 8 bits each, the medium simply holds 192 bits in a row. If the exact position of the first bit is not known, then it is not possible to put all the bits in the right places in the right words. The effect of sync slippage is devastating, because a 1 bit disparity between the data-bit count and the bit stream will corrupt every word in the block, which is just as bad as a massive dropout.[27]

The synchronization of the data separator and the synchronization to the block format are two distinct problems, and they are often solved separately. At the end of the preamble, a so-called sync pattern may be inserted. This is a pattern which is identical for every block; it will be recognized by the replay circuitry and used to reset the bit count through the block. By counting bits from the sync pattern and dividing by the wordlength, the replay circuitry will be able to determine the position of the boundaries between words. The sync pattern must be chosen with care, so that a bit or bits in error does not cause sync to be recognized in the wrong place. Such a pattern is designed to be as different as possible to

272   Digital magnetic and optical recording

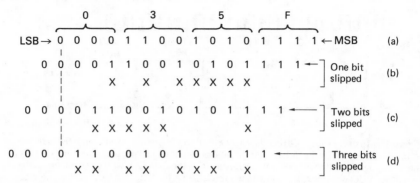

Figure 6.48 A synchronizing pattern having a low autocorrection is shown here at (a). In (b), the pattern is one bit from synchronization, and fails to match in seven places (shown as X). In (c) the pattern is two bits away from synchronization, and fails to match in six places. At (d) the pattern is three bits away from synchronization, and fails in eight places.

Owing to the large number of differences when the pattern shifts, there is a much reduced probability of an error reading the pattern causing false synchronization. The pattern shown is used in the D-1 format DVTR for both audio and video data blocks

itself however many places it is shifted, which is the same as saying it has a low autocorrelation. A good example of a low-autocorrelation sync pattern is that used in the D-1 format DVTR, which is 30F5 hex, or 0000110010101111. Fig. 6.48 shows how many differences are caused for different false sync states, which helps to ensure that only the correct timing is recognized.

In group codes and run-length-limited codes, it is possible to combine the function of preamble and sync pattern by producing a transition pattern at the start of the block which contains timing to phase the channel-bit rate PLL, but which contains run lengths which violate the limits. There is no way that these run lengths will be interpreted as data, but they can be detected by the replay circuitry. Such techniques are used in the CCIR serial video format (see Chapter 8) and the AES/EBU digital audio interconnect (see Chapter 13), and are illustrated in Fig. 6.49.

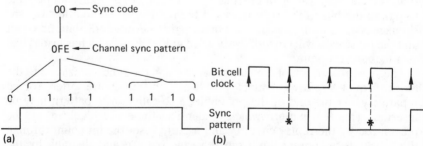

Figure 6.49 Synchronization by Run Length Violation. In the 8/9 code of CCIR serial interface, the sync code 00 results in a channel pattern having a run-length of seven bits, which cannot occur in any other data combination. 00 is disallowed in video data. At (b) the AES/EBU audio interface uses FM code which *must* have a transition on every bit cell clock. One of the possible sync patterns is shown here to violate the code at points *

Where reading in both directions is required, a reverse sync pattern will be placed between the data and the postamble. In SMPTE/EBU time code, the sync pattern is asymmetrical, so that the read circuitry can tell which way the tape is moving without any other source of information.

References

1. DEELEY, E.M., Integrating and differentiating channels in digital tape recording. *Radio Electron. Eng.*, **56**, 169–173 (1986)
2. MEE, C.D., *The Physics of Magnetic Recording*, Amsterdam: Elsevier–North-Holland (1978)
3. JACOBY, G.V., Signal equalization in digital magnetic recording. *IEEE Trans. Magn.*, **MAG-11**, 302–305 (1975)
4. SCHNEIDER, R.C., An improved pulse-slimming method for magnetic recording. *IEEE Trans. Magn.*, **MAG-11**, 1240–1241 (1975)
5. BOUWHUIS, G. *et al.*, *Principles of Optical Disc Systems,* Bristol: Adam Hilger (1985)
6. OHR, S., Magneto-optics combines erasability and high-density storage. *Electron. Des.*, 11 July 1985, 93–100
7. SCHOUHAMER IMMINK, K.A. and BRAAT, J.J.M., Experiments towards an erasable Compact Disc digital audio system. Presented at 73rd Audio Engineering Society Convention (Eindhoven, 1983), preprint 1970(E2)
8. KURAHASHI, A. *et al.*, Development of an erasable magneto-optical digital audio recorder. Presented at 79th Audio Engineering Society Convention (New York, 1985), preprint 2296(A-1)
9. NAKAJIMA, H., *et al.*, *Digital Audio Technology*, Blue Ridge Summit, PA: TAB Books, pp. 150–152, (1983)
10. MALLINSON, J.C. and MILLER, J.W., Optimum codes for digital magnetic recording. *Radio Electron. Eng.*, **47**, 172–176 (1977)
11. MILLER, J.W., DC-free encoding for data transmission system. *US Patent* no. 4,027,335 (1977)
12. PATEL, A.M., Zero-modulation encoding in magnetic recording. *IBM J. Res. Dev.*, **19**, 366–378 (1975)
13. TANG, D.T., Run-length-limited codes. IEEE International Symposium on Information Theory (1969)
14. COHN, M. and JACOBY, G., Run-length reduction of 3PM code via lookahead technique. *IEEE Trans. Magn.*, **MAG-18**, 1253–1255 (1982)
15. HORIGUCHI, T. and MORITA, K., On optimisation of modulation codes in digital recording. *IEEE Trans. Magn.*, **MAG-12**, 740–742 (1976)
16. FRANASZEK, P.A., Sequence state methods for run-length limited coding. *IBM J. Res. Dev.*, **14**, 376–383 (1970)
17. TAMURA, T. *et al.*, A coding method in digital magnetic recording. IEEE Trans. Magn., **MAG-8**, 612–614 (1972)
18. JACOBY, G.V. and KOST, R., Binary two-thirds-rate code with full word lookahead. *IEEE Trans. Magn.*, **MAG-20**, 709–714 (1984)
19. JACOBY, G.V., A new lookahead code for increased data density. *IEEE Trans. Magn.*, **MAG-13**, 1202–1204 (1977)
20. SCHOUHAMER IMMINK, K.A., Signal to noise ratio of pilot tracking tones embedded in binary coded signals. *IEEE Trans. Magn.* **MAG-24**, (1988)
21. YOKOYAMA, K., Digital video tape recorder. *NHK Technical Monograph*, no. 31 (Mar. 1982)
22. COLEMAN, C.H. *et al.*, High data-rate magnetic recording in a single channel. *J. IERE*, **55**, 229–236 (1985)

23. KOBAYASHI, H., Application of partial-response channel coding to magnetic recording systems. *IBM J. Res. Dev.*, **14**, 368–375 (1970)
24. FORNEY, G.D. JR, The Viterbi algorithm. *Proc. IEEE*, **61**, 268–278 (1973)
25. WOOD, R.W. and PETERSEN, D.A., Viterbi detection of class IV partial response on a magnetic recording channel. *IEEE Trans. Commun.*, **34**, 454–461 (1986)
26. WOLF, J.K. and UNGERBOECK, G., Trellis coding for partial response channels. Center for Magnetic Recording Research, University of California, San Diego.
27. GRIFFITHS, F.A., A digital audio recording system. Presented at 65th Audio Engineering Society Convention (London, 1980), preprint 1580(C1)

Chapter 7

Error correction

The subject of error correction is almost always described in mathematical terms by specialists for the benefit of other specialists. Such mathematical approaches are quite inappropriate for a proper understanding of the concepts of error correction and only become necessary to analyse the quantitative behaviour of a system. The description below will use the minimum possible amount of mathematics, and it will then be seen that error correction is, in fact, quite straightforward.

7.1 Sensitivity of message to error

Before attempting to specify any piece of equipment, it is necessary to quantify the problems to be overcome and how effectively they need to be overcome. For a digital recording or transmission system the causes of errors must be studied to quantify the problem, and the sensitivity of the destination to errors must be assessed. In computers there is tremendous sensitivity to errors in instructions. In audio and video, the sensitivity to errors must be subjective. In both, the effect of a single bit in error depends upon the significance of the bit. If the least significant bit of a sample is wrong, the chances are that the effect will be lost in the noise. Conversely, if a high-order bit is in error, a massive transient will be added to the sound or picture waveform. The effect of uncorrected high-order errors in PCM video is to produce dots in the picture, which will be visible as bright dots in dark areas and vice versa. The effect of errors in delta modulation is much smaller, because every bit has the same significance and the information content of each bit is low.

If the error rate demanded by the destination cannot be met by the unaided channel, some form of error handling will be necessary. In some circumstances a delta-modulated system can be used with no error correction, but this is generally impossible in PCM.

7.2 Error mechanisms

Since digital data can be conveyed in many different ways, each having its own error mechanisms, it follows that there will be different approaches to protection of data. In addition, the kind of use to which a piece of equipment is put will make some error-protection schemes more practical than others.

Inside equipment, where data are conveyed in binary on wires, the noise resistance can be designed such that to all intents and purposes there will be no errors. For transmission between equipment, there will be less control of the electromagnetic environment, and interference may corrupt binary data on wires, but not in optical fibres. Such interference will generally not correlate with the data. For long-distance transmission by wire there will be the effects of lightning and switching noise in exchanges to combat.

In MOS memories the datum is stored in a tiny charge well which acts as a capacitor, and natural radioactive decay of the chip materials can produce alpha particles which have enough energy to discharge a well, resulting in a single-bit error. This only happens once every 30 years or so in a given chip, but when a great many chips are assembled to form a large memory for a computer, the probability rises to one error every few minutes.

In magnetic recording, there are many more mechanisms available to corrupt data, from mechanical problems such as media dropout and poor head contact, to Gaussian thermal noise in replay circuits and heads. In optical media the equivalent of dropout in manufacture is contamination of the optical layer by dust before it is sealed. In replay, surface contamination from fingerprints and birefringence in the transparent medium distort and diffuse the laser beam so that the reflected light pattern cannot be discerned.

Despite the difference in operating principle, magnetic recorders and optical media have similar effects when the corruption of data is studied. There are large isolated corruptions, called error bursts, where numerous bits are corrupted all together in an area which is otherwise error free, and there are random errors affecting single bits or symbols. In the discussion of channel coding in Chapter 6 it was noted that, wherever group codes are used, a single corruption in a group renders meaningless all of the data bits in that group. Thus single-bit errors are much less common in group-coded data.

Whatever the mechanism, the result will be that the received data will not be exactly the same as those sent. Sometimes it is enough to know that there has been an error, if time allows a retransmission to be arranged. This is quite feasible for telex messages, but quite inappropriate for digital audio or video, which work in real time.

7.3 Error handling

Fig. 7.1 shows the broad subdivisions of error handling. The first stage might well be called error avoidance and includes such measures as creating bad block files in hard disks, placing digital audio blocks at the centre of the tape in D-1 format, and rewriting on a read-after-write error in computer tapes. Following these moves, the data are entrusted to the channel, which causes whatever corruptions it feels like. On receipt of the

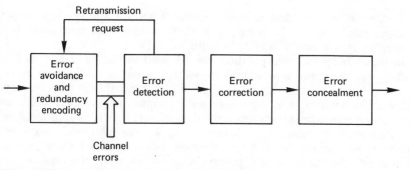

Figure 7.1 The major processes in an error-handling system

data the occurrence of errors is first detected, and this process must be extremely reliable, as it does not matter how fast the retry mechanism, how effective the correction or how good the concealment algorithm, if it is not known that they are necessary! The detection of an error then results in a course of action being decided. In a bidirectional link, a retransmission could be requested. In a critical financial computer, reference to the backup file may be requested. In computer disk drives the detection of a read error frequently results in a retry. The disk is turning at typically 3600 rev/min and repeatedly presents the same data to a fixed head, making a retry very easy. Disk drives will also verify the data integrity of a new disk, and any blocks containing dropouts will be allocated to a hypothetical file which makes them appear to be already used. The computer will never write on them. The computer magnetic tape transports read the tape as it is being written, and if an error is detected the transport will commonly reverse to the beginning of the block, erase a short length of tape, and try again. These are luxuries not available to digital audio or video recorders. The chore of verifying a tape before use would be unacceptable, and in any case there is no guarantee that new tape defects will not arise in use. The non-contact rigid disk is much more consistent in this respect. It is reasonable to expect that the error handling of digital audio and video equipment will be more complex than that of computer equipment.

7.4 Interpolation

Although audio and video recorders are at a disadvantage with respect to computer recorders in that they cannot preformat and verify the medium, and there is no time for retries, they have the advantage that there is a certain amount of redundancy in the information conveyed. If an error cannot be corrected, then it can be concealed. In audio systems, if a sample is lost, it is possible to obtain an approximation to it by interpolating between adjacent values. Momentary interpolations in music are not serious, but sustained use of interpolation restricts bandwidth and can cause aliasing if high frequencies are present. In advanced systems, a spectral analysis of the sound is made, and if sample values are not available, samples having the same spectral characteristics are inserted.

This concealment method is quite successful because the spectral shape changes relatively slowly in music. If there is too much corruption for concealment, the only course is to mute.

In video recorders interpolation can be used in the same way as for audio, but there are additional possibilities, such as taking data from adjacent lines, or from a previous field. Video concealment is a complex subject which will be dealt with later in this chapter. In general, if use is to be made of concealment on replay, the data must generally be reordered or shuffled prior to recording. To take a simple example, odd-numbered samples are subject to a delay whereas even-numbered samples are undelayed. On playback, this process must be reversed. If a gross error occurs on the tape, following the reverse shuffle this will be broken into two separate error zones, one of which has corrupted odd samples and the other of which has corrupted even samples. Interpolation is then possible if the power of the correction system is exceeded.

7.5 Noise and probability

Whilst it is generally stated that inside a piece of logic circuitry the binary signal is always greater than the noise, so that there will be no errors, the same is not true in high-density recording. To see why, it is necessary to look at the characteristics of noise.

Noise is random, and although under given conditions the noise power in a system may be constant, this value only determines the heat that would be developed in a resistive load. In digital recording, it is the instantaneous voltage of noise which is of interest, since it is a form of interference which could alter the state of a binary signal if it were large enough. Unfortunately it cannot be predicted; indeed if it could the interference could not be called noise. Noise can only be quantified statistically, by measuring or predicting the likelihood of a given noise amplitude.

Fig. 7.2 shows a graph relating the probability of occurrence to the amplitude of noise. The noise amplitude increases away from the origin along the horizontal axis, and for any amplitude of interest the probability

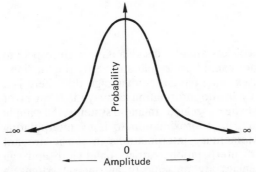

Figure 7.2 The probability of occurrence of noise of a given amplitude falls as that amplitude increases, but never reaches zero, as a consequence, however good signal-to-noise ratio may be, errors will still occur

of that noise amplitude occurring can be read from the curve. The shape of the curve is known as a Gaussian distribution, which crops up whenever the overall effect of a large number of independent phenomena is considered. Magnetic recording depends on superimposing some average magnetism on vast numbers of magnetic particles.

If it were possible to isolate an individual noise-generating microcosm of a tape or a head on the molecular scale, the noise it could generate would have physical limits owing to the finite energy present. The noise distribution might then be rectangular as shown in Fig. 7.3(a), where all amplitudes below the physical limit are equally likely. If the combined effect of two of these microcosms is considered, clearly the maximum amplitude is now doubled, because the two effects can add, but since the two effects are uncorrelated, they can also subtract, so the probability is no longer rectangular, but becomes triangular as in Fig. 7.3(b). Probability falls to zero at peak amplitude because the chances of two independent mechanisms reaching their peak value with the same polarity at the same time are understandably small.

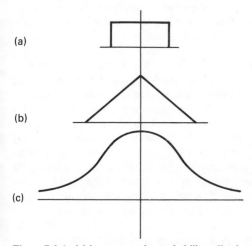

(a)

(b)

(c)

Figure 7.3 At (a) is a rectangular probability; all values are equally likely, but between physical limits. At (b) is the sum of two rectangular probabilities, which is triangular and at (c) is the Gaussian cuve which is the sum of an infinite number of rectangular probabilities

If the number of mechanisms summed together is now allowed to increase without limit, the result is the Gaussian curve shown in Fig. 7.3(c), where it will be seen that the curve has no limit, because it is just possible that all mechanisms will simultaneously reach their peak value together, although the chances of this happening are incredibly remote.

Some conclusions can be drawn from the Gaussian distribution of noise. First, it is not possible to make error-free digital recordings, because however high the signal-to-noise ratio of the recording, there is still a small but finite chance that the noise can exceed the signal. Measuring the signal-to-noise ratio of a channel establishes the noise power, which determines the width of the noise distribution curve relative to the signal amplitude. When in a binary system the noise amplitude exceeds the signal amplitude, a bit error will occur. Knowledge of the shape of the Gaussian curve allows the conversion of signal-to-noise ratio into bit error rate (BER). It can be predicted how many bits will fail owing to noise in a given recording, but it is not possible to say which bits will be affected.

The logical reaction to this statement is to decide that error correction is necessary.

Error correction works by adding some bits to the data which are calculated from the data. This creates an entity called a codeword which spans a greater length of time than one bit alone. The statistics of noise mean that whilst one bit may be lost in a codeword, the loss of the rest of the codeword due to noise is highly improbable. As will be described later in this chapter, codewords are designed to be able to correct totally a finite number of corrupted bits. The greater the timespan over which the coding is performed, the greater will be the reliability achieved, although this does mean that an encoding delay will be experienced on recording, and a similar delay on reproduction. Shannon[1] discovered that a message can be sent to any desired degree of accuracy provided that it is spread over a sufficient timespan. Engineers have to compromise, because an infinite delay in the recovery of an error-free signal is not acceptable.

Having decided that error correction is necessary, it is then only a small step to put it to maximum use. All error correction depends on adding bits to the original message, and this of course increases the number of bits to be recorded, although it does not increase the information recorded. It might be imagined that error correction is going to reduce storage capacity, because space has to be found for all the extra bits. Nothing could be further from the truth. Once an error-correction system is used, the signal-to-noise ratio of the channel can be reduced, because the raised BER of the channel will be overcome by the error-correction system. Reduction of SNR by 3 dB in a magnetic tape track can be achieved by halving the track width, provided that the system is not dominated by head noise. This doubles the recording density, making the storage of the additional bits needed for error correction a trivial matter. In short error correction is not a nuisance to be tolerated, but a vital tool needed to maximize the efficiency of recorders. High-density recording would not be possible without it.

Although the foregoing is true, error-correction systems must be able to handle burst errors due to dropouts as well as random errors due to noise.

7.6 Parity

The error detection and correction processes are closely related and will be dealt with together here. The actual correction of an error is simplified tremendously by the adoption of binary. As there are only two symbols, 0 and 1, it is enough to know that a symbol is wrong and the correct value is obvious. Fig. 7.4 shows a minimal circuit required for correction once the bit in error has been identified. The exclusive–OR gate shows up extensively in error correction and the figure also shows the truth table. One way of remembering the characteristics of this useful device is that

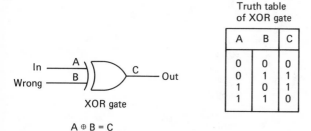

Truth table
of XOR gate

A	B	C
0	0	0
0	1	1
1	0	1
1	1	0

A ⊕ B = C

Figure 7.4 Once the position of the error is identified, the correction process in binary is easy

there will be an output when the inputs are different. Inspection of the truth table will show that there is an even number of ones in each row (zero is an even number) and so the device could also be called an even parity gate.

Parity is a fundamental concept in error detection. In Fig. 7.5, the example is given of a 4 bit data word which is to be protected. If an extra bit is added to the word which is calculated in such a way that the total number of ones in the 5 bit word is even, this property can be tested on receipt. The generation of the parity bit in Fig. 7.5 can be performed by a number of the ubiquitous XOR gates configured into what is known as a parity tree. In the figure, if a bit is corrupted, the received message will be seen no longer to have an even number of ones. If two bits are corrupted, the failure will be undetected. This example can be used to introduce much of the terminology of error correction. The extra bit added to the message carries no information of its own, since it is calculated from the other bits. It is therefore called a redundant bit. The addition of the redundant bit gives the message a special property, i.e. the number of ones is even. A message having some special property irrespective of the actual data content is called a codeword. All error correction relies on adding redundancy to real data to form codewords for transmission. If any corruption occurs, the intention is that the received message will not have the special property; in other words if the received message is not a codeword there has definitely been an error. If the received message is a codeword, there probably has not been an error. The word 'probably' must be used because the figure shows that 2 bits in error will cause the received message to be a codeword, which cannot be discerned from an error-free message. If it is known that generally the only failure mechanism in the channel in question is loss of a single bit, it is *assumed* that receipt of a codeword means that there has been no error. If there is a probability of two error bits, that becomes very nearly the probability of failing to detect an error, since all odd numbers of errors will be detected, and a 4 bit error is much less likely. It is paramount in all error-correction systems that the protection used should be appropriate for the probability of errors to be encountered. An inadequate error-correction system is actually worse than not having any correction. Error correction works by trading probabilities. Error-free performance with a certain error rate is achieved at the expense of performance at higher error rates. Fig. 7.6 shows the effect of an error-correction system on the output error rate for a given raw, or input,

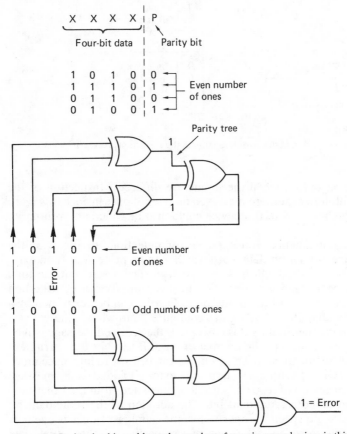

Figure 7.5 Parity checking adds up the number of ones in a word using, in this example, parity trees. One error bit and odd numbers of errors are detected. Even numbers of errors cannot be detected

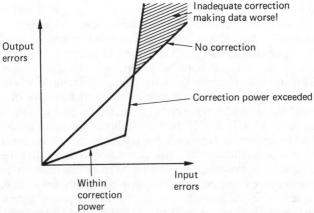

Figure 7.6 An error correction system can only reduce errors at normal error rates at the expense of increasing errors at higher rates. It is most important to keep a system working to the left of the knee in the graph

error rate. It will be seen that there is a characteristic knee in the graph. If the expected raw error rate has been misjudged, the consequences can be disastrous. Another result demonstrated by the example is that we can only guarantee to detect the same number of bits in error as there are redundant bits.

7.7 Wyner–Ash code

Despite its extreme simplicity, the principle of parity can be used to make an effective digital audio error-correcting scheme. In the Wyner–Ash code employed in some early BBC work,[2] four tape tracks were required to convey one digital audio channel, which reduced the linear speed of the tape and reduced the impact of a dropout on the data. Fig. 7.7(a) shows that alternate tracks carried data and parity bits computed from running pairs of data bits. With this mechanism, data-track errors always cause an even number of parity failures, and Fig. 7.7(b) shows an example of how such an error can be corrected. Parity-track errors, however, cause single parity failures, which can be neglected, as in Fig. 7.7(c). Whilst this technique was successful, it requires an overhead of 100% redundancy, which implies that tape consumption must suffer. Such a code could not be considered for digital video but is included here as an illustration. Codes which need less overhead are inevitably more complex, however.

7.8 Product code

In the example of Fig. 7.5, the error was detected but it was not possible to say which bit was in error. Even though the code used can only detect errors, correction is still possible if a suitable strategy is used. Fig. 7.8 shows the use of a product code, also known as a crossword code. The data are formed into a two-dimensional array, with parity taken on rows and columns. If a single bit fails, one row check and one column check will fail, and the failing bit can be located at the intersection of the two failing checks. Although 2 bits in error confuse this simple scheme, using more complex coding in a two-dimensional structure is very powerful, and further examples will be given throughout this chapter.

7.9 Hamming code

In a one-dimensional code, the position of the failing bit can be determined by using more parity checks. In Fig. 7.9, the four data bits have been used to compute three redundancy bits, making a 7 bit codeword. The four data bits are examined in turn, and each bit which is a one will cause the corresponding row of a generator matrix to be added to an exclusive–OR sum. For example, if the data were 1001, the top and bottom rows of the matrix would be XORed. The matrix used is known as an identity matrix, because the data bits in the codeword are identical to the data bits to be conveyed. This is useful because the original data can be stored

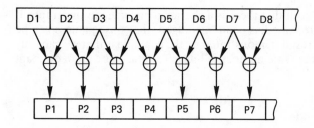

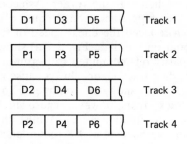

(a)

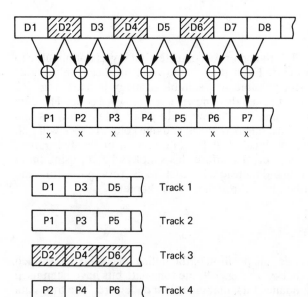

(b)

Figure 7.7 In the Wyner–Ash coding illustrated here, there is 100% overhead due to the additional parity symbols. The data and parity are distributed over the tape tracks, as shown in (a). At (b) a burst error in a data track causes continuous parity errors as shown, and correction can be performed. For example D2 = D1 ⊕ P1 etc

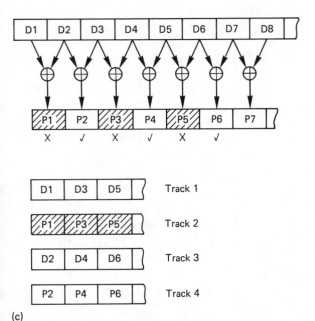

(c)

Figure 7.7 (*Continued*) At (c) a burst error in a parity track causes alternate parity errors, which can be ignored

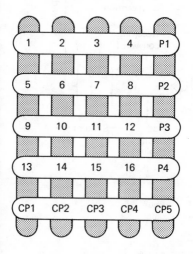

Figure 7.8 A crossword parity-check system. Horizontal checks are made by P1, P2, etc, and cross parity checks on columns are made by CP1, CP2, etc. If, for example, bit 10 were in error, it would be located by CP2 and P3 intersecting

unmodified, and the check bits are simply attached to the end to make a so-called systematic codeword. Almost all digital recording equipment uses systematic codes. The way in which the redundancy bits are calculated is simply that they do not all use every data bit. If a data bit has not been included in a parity check, it can fail without affecting the outcome of that check. The position of the error is deduced from the pattern of successful and unsuccessful checks in the check matrix. This pattern is known as a syndrome.

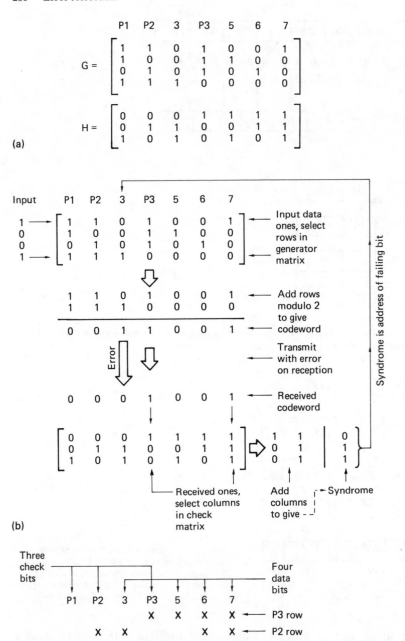

Figure 7.9 (a) The generator and check matrices of a Hamming code. The data and check bits are arranged as shown because it causes the syndrome to be the binary address of the failing bit. (b) An example of Hamming-code generation and error correction. (c) Another way of looking at Hamming code is to say that the rows of crosses in this chart are calculated to have even parity. If bit 3 fails, parity check P3 is not affected, but parity checks P1 and P2 both include bit 3 and will fail

In the figure the example of a failing bit is given. Bit three fails, and because this bit is included in only two of the checks, there are two ones in the failure pattern, 011. As some care was taken in designing the matrix pattern for the generation of the check bits, the syndrome, 011, is the address of the failing bit. This is the fundamental feature of the Hamming codes due to Richard Hamming.[3] The performance of this 7 bit code word can be assessed. In 7 bits there can be 128 combinations, but in four data bits there are only 16 combinations. Thus out of 128 possible received messages, only 16 will be codewords, so if the message is completely trashed by a gross corruption, it will still be possible to detect that this has happened 112 times out of 127, as in these cases the syndrome will be non-zero (the 128th case is the correct data). There is thus only a probability of detecting that all of the message is corrupt. In an idle moment it is possible to work out, in a similar way, the number of false codewords which can result from different numbers of bits being assumed to have failed. For less than 3 bits, the failure will always be detected, because there are three check bits. Returning to the example, if 2 bits fail, there will be a non-zero syndrome, but if this is used to point to a bit in error, a miscorrection will result. From these results can be deduced another important feature of error codes. The power of detection is always greater than the power of correction, which is also fortunate, since if the correcting power is exceeded by an error it will at least be a known problem and steps can taken to prevent any undesirable consequences.

A Hamming code is used to protect the timing reference signals in video sampled to CCIR 601, and details of this can be found in Chapter 8.

7.10 Hamming distance

It is useful at this point to introduce the concept of Hamming distance. This is the minimum number of bits that must be changed in any codeword without turning it into another codeword. Clearly if errors corrupt a codeword so that it is no longer a codeword, it will definitely be detectable and possibly correctable. If errors convert one codeword into another, it will not even be detected.

Fig. 7.10 shows Hamming distance diagrammatically. A 3 bit codeword is used with two data bits and one parity bit. With 3 bits, a received code could have eight combinations, but only four of these will be codewords. The valid codewords are shown in the centre of each of the discs, and these will be seen to be identical to the rows of the truth table in Fig. 7.4. At the perimeter of the discs are shown the received words which would result from a single-bit error, i.e. they have a Hamming distance of 1. It will be seen that the same received word (on the vertical bars) can be obtained from a different single-bit corruption of any three codewords. It is thus not possible to tell which codeword was corrupted and so, although all single-bit errors can be detected, correction is not possible. This diagram should be compared with that of Fig. 7.11, which is a Venn diagram where there is a set in which the MSB is 1 (upper circle), a set in which the middle bit is 1 (lower left circle) and a set in which the LSB is 1 (lower right circle). Note that in crossing any boundary only one bit changes, and so each

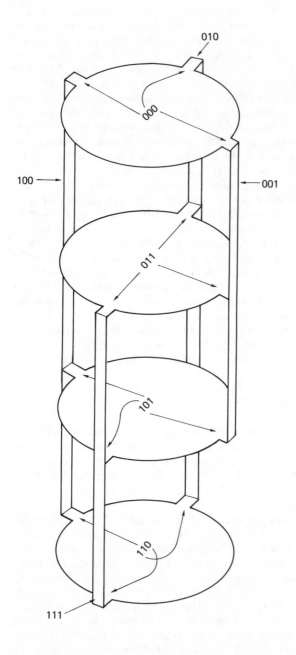

Figure 7.10 Hamming distance of two. The disk centres contain codewords. Corrupting each bit in turn produces the distance one values on the vertical members. In order to change one codeword to another, two bits must be changed, so the code has a Hamming distance of two

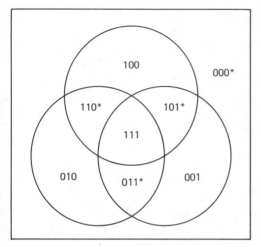

Figure 7.11 Venn diagram shows a one bit change crossing any boundary which is a Hamming Distance of one. Compare with Figure 7.10. Codewords marked*

boundary represents a Hamming distance change of one. The four codewords of Fig. 7.10 are repeated here, and it will be seen that single-bit errors in any codeword produce a non-codeword, and so single-bit errors are always detectable.

Correction is possible if the number of non-codewords is increased by increasing the number of redundant bits. This means that it is possible to spread out the actual codewords in Hamming distance terms.

Fig. 7.12(a) shows a distance 2 code, where there is only one redundancy bit, and so half of the possible words will be codewords. There will be non-codewords at distance 1 which can be produced by altering a single bit in either of two codewords. In this case it is not possible to tell what the original codeword was in the case of a single-bit error.

Fig. 7.12(b) shows a distance 3 code, where there will now be at least two non-codewords between codewords. If a single-bit error occurs in a codeword, the resulting non-codeword will be at distance 1 from the original codeword. This same non-codeword could also have been produced by changing 2 bits in a different codeword. If it is known that the failure mechanism is a single bit, it can be *assumed* that the original codeword was the one which is closest in Hamming distance to the received bit pattern, and so correction is possible. If, however, our assumption about the error mechanism proved to be wrong, and in fact a 2 bit error had occurred, this assumption would take us to the wrong codeword, turning the event into a 3 bit error. This is an illustration of the knee in the graph of Fig. 7.6, where if the power of the code is exceeded it makes things worse.

Fig. 7.12(c) shows a distance 4 code. There are now three non-codewords between codewords, and clearly single-bit errors can still be corrected by choosing the nearest codeword. Double-bit errors will be detected because they result in non-codewords equidistant in Hamming

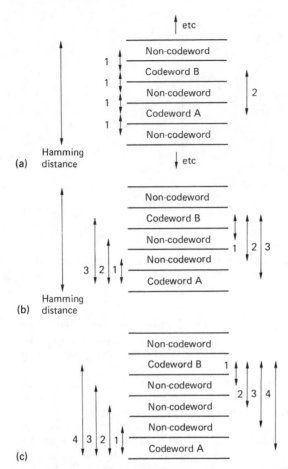

Figure 7.12 (a) Distance 2 code, non-codewords are at distance 1 from *two* possible codewords so it cannot be deduced what the correct one is. (b) Distance 3 code, non-codewords which have *single-bit errors* can be attributed to the nearest codeword. Breaks down in presence of double-bit errors. (c) Distance 4 code, non-codewords which have single-bit errors can be attributed to the nearest codeword, AND double bit errors form *different* non-codewords, and can thus be detected but not corrected

terms from codewords, but it is not possible to say what the original codeword was.

Fig. 7.13 shows a more complex arrangement of the 16 possible combinations of 4 bits. Travelling along any of the ties between discs is the equivalent of a Hamming distance of 1. The equivalent Venn diagram is shown in Fig. 7.14. At this point the Venn diagram no longer shows the whole story, because although there is still a Hamming distance of 1 when crossing a boundary, some of the areas have only three sides, so not all possible changes are shown, and it is necessary to add magic tunnels, whose length is a Hamming distance of 1, to allow all single-bit changes to be followed.

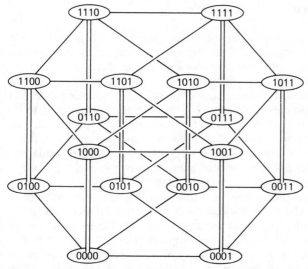

Figure 7.13 Hamming Distance diagram for four bits. Each bond between the disks is unit Hamming Distance

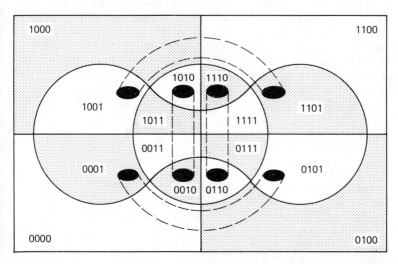

Figure 7.14 Modified Venn Diagram which also shows Hamming distance. A Hamming distance of one can be obtained by crossing any one boundary, or by travelling down a magic tunnel

Unfortunately, attempts to draw more complex Hamming distance diagrams for longer wordlengths result in a real mess, because the number of tunnels needed rises sharply. It is, however, possible to draw Venn diagrams to almost any number of bits,[4] which will show Hamming distance in a restricted sense.

7.11 Applications of Hamming code

The Hamming codes are used in computer memories where the failure mechanism is that of single bits. The efficiency in terms of storage needed is not very good in the simple example of Fig. 7.9, as three check bits are needed for only four data bits. Since the failing bit is determined using a binary split mechanism, it follows that doubling the amount of data will only require one extra check bit, provided that the number of errors to be detected remains the same. Thus for the smallest proportion of redundancy, long codewords should be used. In computer memories these codewords are typically four or eight data bytes in length, plus redundancy. A drawback of long codewords for computer memory applications is that if it is required to change only one byte in the memory, the whole word has to be read, corrected, modified, encoded and stored again – a so-called read modify write cycle. The codes for computer memories will generally have an extra check bit which allows the occurrence of a double-bit error always to be detected but not corrected. If this happens, the syndrome will be the address of a bit which is outside the data word. Such codes are known as SECDED (single-error-correcting double-error-detecting) codes. The Hamming distance of these codes is one greater than the equivalent SEC (single-error-correcting) code.

The correction of 1 bit is of little use in the presence of burst errors, but a Hamming code can be made to correct burst errors by using interleaving. Fig. 7.15 shows that if several codewords are calculated beforehand and woven together as shown before they are sent down the channel, then a burst of errors which corrupts several bits will become a number of single-bit errors in separate codewords upon de-interleaving. Interleaving is used extensively in digital recording and will be discussed in greater detail later in this chapter.

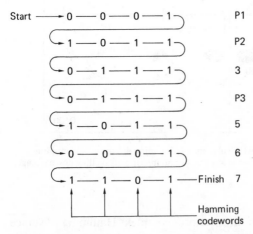

Figure 7.15 The vertical columns of this diagram are all codewords generated by the matrix of Figure 7.9 which can correct a single-bit error. If these words are recorded in the order shown, a burst error of up to four bits will result in one single-bit error in each codeword, which is correctable. Interleave requires memory, and causes delay. Deinterleave requires the same

7.12 Cyclic codes

The implementation of a Hamming code can be made very fast using parity trees, which is ideal for memory applications where access time is increased by the correction process. However, in most video applications, the data are stored serially, such as on a magnetic or optical track, and it is desirable to use relatively large data blocks to reduce the amount of the medium devoted to preambles, addressing and synchronizing. Where large data blocks are to be handled, the use of a lookup table or tree has to be abandoned because it would become impossibly large. The principle of generator and check matrices will still be employed, but they will be matrices which can be generated algorithmically. The syndrome will then be converted to the bit(s) in error not by looking them up, but by solving an equation.

Where data can be accessed serially, simpler circuitry can be used because the same gate will be used for many XOR operations. Unfortunately the reduction in component count is only paralleled by an increase in the difficulty of explaining what takes place.

The circuit of Fig. 7.16 is a kind of shift register, but with a peculiar feedback arrangement which leads it to be known as a twisted-ring counter. If seven message bits A–G are applied serially to this circuit, and each one of them is clocked, the outcome can be followed in the diagram. As bit A is presented and the system is clocked, bit A will enter the left-hand latch. When bits B and C are presented, A moves across to the

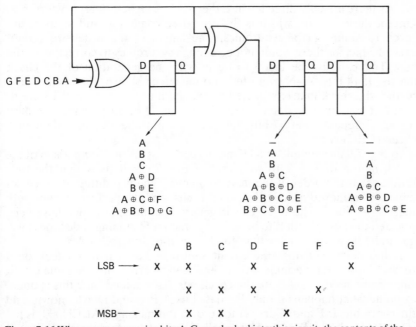

Figure 7.16 When seven successive bits A-G are clocked into this circuit, the contents of the three latches are shown for each clock. The final result is a parity-check matrix

right. Both XOR gates will have A on the upper input from the right-hand latch, the left one has D on the lower input and the right one has B on the lower input. When clocked, the left latch will thus be loaded with the XOR of A and D, and the right one with the XOR of A and B. The remainder of the sequence can be followed, bearing in mind that when the same term appears on both inputs of an XOR gate, it goes out, as the XOR of something with itself is nothing. At the end of the process, the latches contain three different expressions. Essentially, the circuit makes three parity checks through the message, leaving the result of each in the three stages of the register. In the figure, these expressions have been used to draw up a check matrix. The significance of these steps can now be explained. The bits A B C and D are four data bits, and the bits E F and G are redundancy. When the redundancy is calculated, bit E is chosen so that there are an even number of ones in bits A B C and E; bit F is chosen such that the same applies to bits B C D and F, and similarly for bit G. Thus the four data bits and the three check bits form a 7 bit codeword. If there is no error in the codeword, when it is fed into the circuit shown, the result of each of the three parity checks will be zero and every stage of the shift register will be cleared. If a bit in the codeword is corrupted, there will be a non-zero result. For example, if bit D fails, the check on bits A B D and G will fail, and a one will appear in the left-hand latch. The check on bits B C D F will also fail, and the centre latch will set. The check on bits A B C E will not fail, because D is not involved in it, making the right-hand bit zero. There will be a syndrome of 110 in the register, and this will be seen from the check matrix to correspond to an error in bit D. Whichever bit fails, there will be a different 3 bit syndrome which uniquely identifies the failed bit. As there are only three latches, there can be eight different syndromes. One of these is zero, which is the error-free condition, and so there are seven remaining error syndromes. The length of the codeword cannot exceed 7 bits, or there would not be enough syndromes to correct all of the bits. This can also be made to tie in with the generation of the check matrix. If 14 bits, A–N, were fed into the circuit shown, the result would be that the check matrix repeated twice, and if a syndrome of 101 were to result, it could not be determined whether bit D or bit K failed. Because the check repeats every 7 bits, the code is said to be a cyclic redundancy check (CRC) code.

In Fig. 7.9 an example of a Hamming code was given. Comparison of the check matrix of Fig. 7.16 with that of Fig. 7.9 will show that the only difference is the order of the matrix columns. The two different processes have thus achieved exactly the same results, and the performance of both must be identical. This is not true in general, but these examples have been selected to allow parallels to be seen. In practice Hamming code blocks will generally be much smaller than the blocks used in CRC codes.

It has been seen that the circuit shown makes a matrix check on a received word to determine if there has been an error, but the same circuit can also be used to generate the check bits. To visualize how this is done, examine what happens if only the data bits A B C and D are known, and the check bits E F and G are set to zero. If this message, ABCD000, is fed into the circuit, the left-hand latch will afterwards contain the XOR of A B C and zero, which is of course what E should be. The centre latch will contain the XOR of B C D and zero, which is what F should be and so on. This process is not quite ideal, however, because it is necessary to wait for three clock periods after entering the data before the check bits are available. Where the data are simultaneously being recorded and fed into the encoder, the delay would prevent the check bits being easily added to the end of the data stream. This problem can be overcome by slightly modifying the encoder circuit as shown in Fig. 7.17. By moving the position

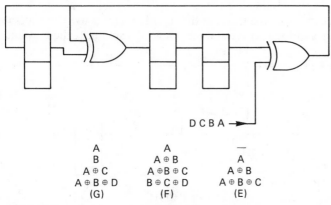

	G	F	E
	A	A	—
	B	A ⊕ B	A
	A ⊕ C	A ⊕ B ⊕ C	A ⊕ B
	A ⊕ B ⊕ D	B ⊕ C ⊕ D	A ⊕ B ⊕ C

Figure 7.17 By moving the insertion point three places to the right, the calculation of the check bits is completed in only four clock periods and they can follow the data immediately. This is equivalent to premultiplying the data by x^3

of the input to the right, the operation of the circuit is advanced so that the check bits are ready after only four clocks. The process can be followed in the diagram for the four data bits A B C and D. On the first clock, bit A enters the left two latches, whereas on the second clock, bit B will appear on the upper input of the left XOR gate, with bit A on the lower input, causing the centre latch to load the XOR of A and B and so on.

The way in which the correction system works has been described in engineering terms, but it can be described mathematically if analysis is contemplated.

Just as the position of a decimal digit in a number determines the power of ten (whether that digit means one, ten or a hundred), the position of a binary digit determines the power of two (whether it means one, two or four). It is possible to rewrite a binary number so that it is expressed as a list of powers of two. For example, the binary number 1101 means $8 + 4 + 1$ and can be written:

$$2^3 + 2^2 + 2^0$$

In fact, much of the theory of error correction applies to symbols in number bases other than 2, so that the number can also be written more generally as

$$x^3 + x^2 + 1 \quad (2^0 = 1)$$

which also looks much more impressive. This expression, containing as it does various powers, is of course a polynomial, and the circuit of Fig. 7.16

which has been seen to construct a parity-check matrix on a codeword, can also be described as calculating the remainder due to dividing the input by a polynomial using modulo-2 arithmetic. In modulo-2 there are no borrows or carries, and addition and subtraction are replaced by the XOR function, which makes hardware implementation very easy. In Fig. 7.18 it will be seen that the circuit of Fig. 7.16 actually divides the codeword by a polynomial which is

$$x^3 + x + 1 \quad \text{or} \quad 1011$$

This can be deduced from the fact that the right-hand bit is fed into several lower-order stages of the register at once. Once all the bits of the message

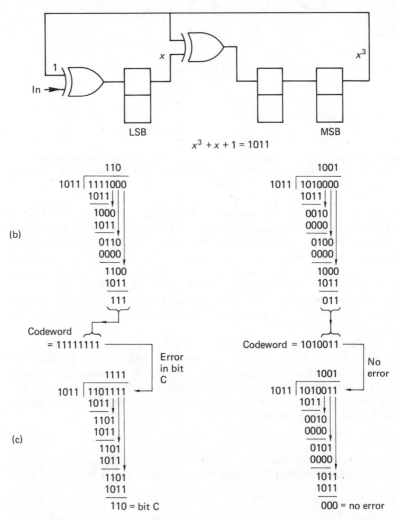

Figure 7.18 Circuit of Figure 7.16 divides by $x^3 + x + 1$ to find remainder. At (b) this is used to calculate check bits. At (c) left, there is an error, non-zero syndrome 110 points to bit C. At (c) right, zero syndrome, no error

have been clocked in, the circuit contains the remainder. In mathematical terms, the special property of a codeword is that it is a polynomial which yields a remainder of zero when divided by the generating polynomial. If an error has occurred it is considered that this is due to an error polynomial which has been added to the codeword polynomial. If a codeword divided by the check polynomial is zero, a non-zero syndrome must represent the error polynomial divided by the check polynomial. Some examples of modulo-2 division are given in Fig. 7.18 which can be compared with the parallel computation of parity checks according to the matrix of Fig. 7.16.

The process of generating the codeword from the original data can also be described mathematically. If a codeword has to give zero remainder when divided, it follows that the data can be converted to a codeword by adding the remainder when the data are divided. Generally speaking the remainder would have to be subtracted, but in modulo-2 there is no distinction. This process is also illustrated in Fig. 7.18. The four data bits have three zeros placed on the right-hand end to make the wordlength equal to that of a codeword, and this word is then divided by the polynomial to calculate the remainder. The remainder is added to the zero-extended data to form a codeword. The modified circuit of Fig. 7.17 can be described as premultiplying the data by x^3 before dividing.

It is also interesting to study the operation of the circuit of Fig. 7.16 with no input. Whatever the starting condition of the 3 bits in the latches, the same state will always be reached again after seven clocks, except if zero is used. The states of the latches form an endless ring of non-sequential numbers called a Galois field after the French mathematical prodigy Evariste Galois who discovered them. The states of the circuit form a maximum length sequence because there are as many states as are permitted by the wordlength. As the all-zero case is disallowed, the length of a maximum length sequence generated by a register of m bits cannot exceed (2^m-1) states. This figure will also be the length of the codeword in simple cyclic codes. The Galois field, however, includes the zero term. It is interesting to explore the bizarre mathematics of Galois fields which use modulo-2 arithmetic (exclusively!). Familiarity with such manipulations is useful when studying more advanced codes.

As the circuit of Fig. 7.16 divides the input by the function $F(x) = x^3 + x + 1$, and there is no input in this case, the operation of the circuit has to be described by

$$x^3 + x + 1 = 0$$

Each 3 bit state of the circuit can be described by combinations of powers of x, such as

$$x^2 = 100$$

$$x = 010$$

$$x^2 + x = 110, \text{ etc.}$$

To avoid confusion, the 3 bit state of the field will be called a, which is a primitive element.

Now,

$$a^3 + a + 1 = 0$$

In modulo 2,

$$a + a = a^2 + a^2 = 0$$
$$a = x = 010$$
$$a^2 = x^2 = 100$$
$$a^3 = a + 1 = 011$$
$$a^4 = a \times a^3 = a(a + 1) = a^2 + a = 110$$
$$a^5 = a^2 + a + 1 = 111$$
$$a^6 = a \times a^5 = a(a^2 + a + 1)$$
$$= a^3 + a^2 + a = a + 1 + a^2 + a$$
$$= a^2 + 1 = 101$$
$$a^7 = a(a^2 + 1) = a^3 + a$$
$$= a + 1 + a = 1 = 001$$

In this way it can be seen that the complete set of elements of the Galois field can be expressed by successive powers of the primitive element. Note that the twisted-ring circuit of Fig. 7.16 simply raises a to higher and higher powers as it is clocked; thus the seemingly complex multibit changes caused by a single clock of the register become simple to calculate using the correct primitive and the appropriate power.

CRC codes are of primary importance for detecting errors, and several have been standardized for use in digital communications. The most common of these are:

$$x^{16} + x^{15} + x^2 + 1 \quad \text{(CRC–16)}$$

$$x^{16} + x^{12} + x^5 + 1 \quad \text{(CRC–CCITT)}$$

Integrated circuits are available which contain all the necessary circuitry[5] to generate and check redundancy. A representative chip is the Fairchild 9401 which will be found in a great deal of digital audio equipment and in floppy-disk drives, because it implements the above polynomials in addition to some others. A feature of the chip is that the feedback register can be configured to work backwards if required. The required polynomial is selected by a 3 bit control code, as shown in Fig. 7.19. The desired code is implemented by enabling different feedback connections kept in a ROM. The data stream to be recorded is clocked in serially, with the control signal CWE (check word enable) true. At the end of the data, this signal is made false, and it turns off the feedback, so that the device behaves as an ordinary shift register and the check bits can be clocked out of the Q output and appended to the recording. Upon playback, the entire codeword is clocked into the device with CWE true, and at the end of the codeword, if the register contains all zeros the error output will be false, whereas if the syndrome is non-zero it will be true.

The output of such a chip is binary; either there was an error or (with high probability) there was not. There is no indication where the error was. Nevertheless, an effective error-correction system can be made using a product or crossword code. An example of this is the error-correction system of the Sony PCM-1610/1630 unit used for Compact Disc mastering.

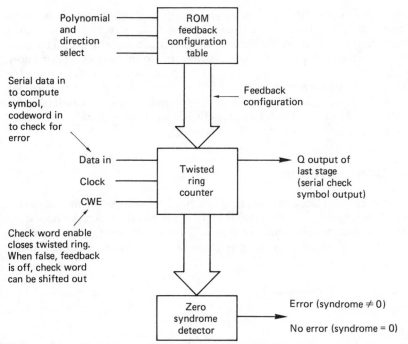

Figure 7.19 Simplified block by CRC chip which can implement several polynomials, and both generate and check redundancy

Fig. 7.20 shows that, in this system, two sets of three audio samples have a CRCC added to form codewords. Three parity words are generated by taking the exclusive–OR of the two sets of samples, and a CRCC is added to this also. If an error occurs in one sample, the CRC for the codeword containing that sample will fail, and *all* samples in the codeword are deemed to be in error. The sample can be corrected by taking the

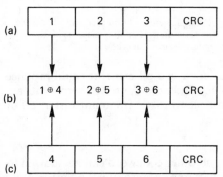

Figure 7.20 The simple crossword code of the PCM 1610/1630 format. Horizontal codewords are cyclic polynomials; vertical codewords are simple parity. Cyclic code detects errors, and acts as erasure pointer for parity correction. For example, if word 2 fails, CRC (a) fails, and 1, 2, and 3 are all erased. the correct values are computed from (b) and (c) such that:

$$1 = (1{\oplus}4){\oplus}4 \qquad 2=(2{\oplus}5){\oplus}5 \qquad 3=(3{\oplus}6){\oplus}6$$

exclusive–OR of the other samples and the parity words. The error detector simply serves as a pointer to a separate correction mechanism. This technique is often referred to as correction by erasure. The error detector erases the samples which are in error, so that the corrector knows which ones to correct. If the error is in the parity words, no action need be taken. It will be seen that there is 100% redundancy in this simple format, but the unit is intended to record digital audio with a standard video recorder, whose bandwidth is predefined, so there would be no saving involved in using a code with less overhead.

7.13 Burst correction

The concept of Hamming distance has been introduced in the context of single-bit correction. However, it can be extended to explain how more than 1 bit can be corrected. In Fig. 7.21 the example of 2 bits in error is given. If a codeword 4 bits long suffers a single-bit error, it could produce

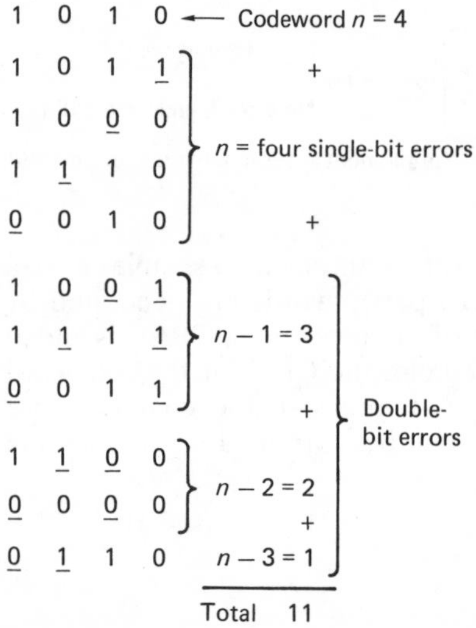

Figure 7.21 Where double-bit errors occur, the number of patterns necessary is $(n - 1) +$ $(n - 2) + (n - 3) + \ldots$ etc. Total necessary is $1 + n + (n - 1) + (n - 2) + (n - 3) + \ldots$ etc. Example here is of four bits, and all possible patterns up to Hamming distance of 2 are shown (errors underlined)

one of four different words. If it suffers a two-bit error, it could produce one of $3 + 2 + 1$ different words as shown in the figure (the error bits are underlined). The total number of possible words of Hamming distance 1 or 2 from a 4 bit codeword is thus

$$4 + 3 + 2 + 1 = 10$$

If the 2 bit error is to be correctable, no other codeword can be allowed to become one of this number of error patterns because of a 2 bit error of its own. Thus every codeword requires space for itself plus all possible error patterns of Hamming distance 2 or 1, which is 11 patterns in this example. Clearly there are only 16 patterns available in a 4 bit code, and thus no data can be conveyed if 2 bit protection is necessary.

The number of different patterns possible in a word of n bits is

$$1 + n + (n\text{-}1) + (n\text{-}2) + (n\text{-}3) + \ldots$$

and this pattern range has to be shared between the ranges of each codeword without overlap. For example, an 8 bit codeword could result in $1 + 8 + 7 + 6 + 5 + 4 + 3 + 2 + 1 = 39$ patterns. As there are only 256 patterns in 8 bits, it follows that only 256/39 pieces of information can be conveyed. The nearest integer below is six, and the nearest power of two below is four, which corresponds to two data bits and six check bits in the 8 bit word. The amount of redundancy necessary to correct *any* 2 bits in error is large, and as the number of bits to be corrected grows, the redundancy necessary becomes enormous and impractical. A further problem is that the more redundancy is added, the greater the probability of an error in a codeword. Fortunately, in practice errors occur in bursts, as has already been described, and it is a happy consequence that the number of patterns that result from the corruption of a codeword by *adjacent* 2 bit errors is much smaller.

It can be deduced that the number of redundant bits necessary to correct a burst error is twice the number of bits in the burst for a perfect code. This is done by working out the number of received messages which could result from corruption of the codeword by bursts of from 1 bit up to the largest burst size allowed, and then making sure that there are enough redundant bits to allow that number of combinations in the received message.

Some codes, such as the Fire code due to Philip Fire,[6] are designed to correct single bursts in the codeword, whereas later codes, such as the B-adjacent code due to Bossen,[7] could correct two bursts. The Reed–Solomon codes (Irving Reed and Gustave Solomon)[8] have the extremely useful feature that the number of bursts which are correctable can be chosen at the design stage by the amount of redundancy.

7.14 Fire code

The operation of a Fire code will now be illustrated. A data block has deliberately been made small for the purposes of illustration in Fig. 7.22(a). The matrix for generating parity bits on the data is shown beneath the block. In each horizontal row of the matrix, the presence of an X means that the data bit in that column has been counted in a parity check. The five rows result in five parity bits which are appended to the data. The simple circuit needed to generate this checkword is also shown. The same codeword corrupted by three errors is shown in Fig. 7.22(b). The matrix check now results in a different check code. An exclusive–OR between the original and the new checkwords gives the error syndrome. Fig. 7.22(c) shows a different error condition which results in the same syndrome, an ambiguity which must be resolved. The method of doing this which is fundamental to Fire code follows. The definition of a burst of length b bits is that the first and last bits must be wrong, but the intervening $b-2$ bits may or may not be wrong. As the presence of a one in a syndrome shows there is a bit in error, another way of stating this is that a burst syndrome of length b cannot contain more than $b-2$ zeros between the ones. If the

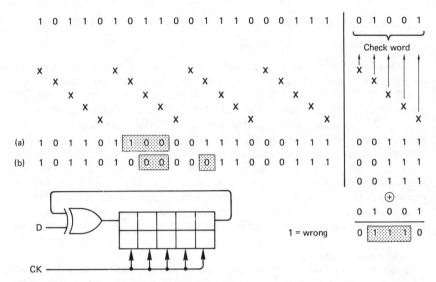

Figure 7.22 This matrix develops a burst-detecting code with circuit shown. On reading, the same encoding process is used, and the two checkwords are XOR-gated. Two examples of error bursts shown (a, b) give the same syndrome; this ambiguity is resolved by the technique of Figure 7.23

number of check bits used to correct a burst of length b is increased to $2b-1$, then a burst of length b can be unambiguously defined by shifting the syndrome and looking for $b-1$ successive zeros. Since the burst cannot contain more than $b-2$ zeros, the $b-1$ zeros must lie outside the burst. Fig. 7.23 gives an example of the process and shows that the number of shifts necessary to put the $b-1$ zeros at the left-hand side of the register is equal to the distance of the burst edge from the previous $n \times (2b-1)$th bit boundary. The b right-hand bits will be the burst pattern, and if the received bits are inverted wherever a one appears in this pattern, correction will be achieved. Obviously if the burst exceeds b bits long, the $b-1$ contiguous zeros will never be found and correction is impossible. Using this approach alone, it is not possible to determine what the value of n is. The burst has been defined, but its location is not known. To locate the burst requires the use of a cyclic polynomial code described earlier. A burst-correcting Fire code is made by combining the expression for the burst-defining code with the expression for the burst-locating polynomial. If the burst-locating polynomial appends an m bit remainder to the data, the checkword will consist of $m + 2b-1$ bits, and the codeword length n becomes

$$n = (2^m - 1) \times (2b - 1) \text{ bits}$$

Fig. 7.24 shows the synthesis of a Fire code from the two parts, with the polynomial expressions for comparison with the necessary hardware. During writing, k serial data bits are shifted into the circuit, and $n-k$ check bits are shifted out to give a codeword of length n. On reading, the codeword is shifted into the same circuit and should result in an all-zero

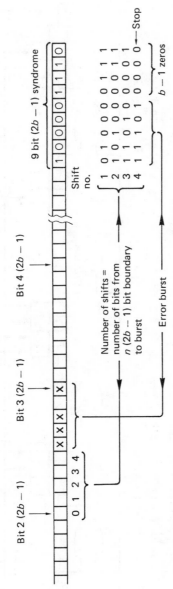

Figure 7.23 Burst of length b bits can only contain $b - 2$ zeros, so $b - 1$ zeros cannot be in a burst. By shifting the syndrome until $b - 1$ zeros are detected, the burst is defined unambiguously. The number of shifts needed gives the positon of the burst relative to the previous $n(2b - 1)$th bit boundary. In this example $b = 5$, hence $2b - 1 = 9$ and the boundaries referred to will be at bits 9, 18, 27, etc. A burst of up to nine bits can be detected but not corrected. Only the nature of the burst is defined by this process; its position has to be determined independently

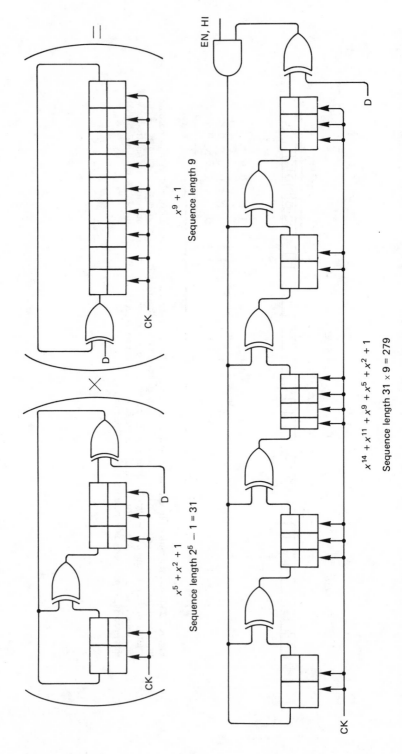

$x^5 + x^2 + 1$

Sequence length $2^5 - 1 = 31$

$x^9 + 1$

Sequence length 9

$x^{14} + x^{11} + x^9 + x^5 + x^2 + 1$

Sequence length $31 \times 9 = 279$

EN, HI

Figure 7.24 Derivation of Fire code from two fundamental expressions, together with encoding circuits. From the codeword length of 279 bits, 14 are check bits, making this a (279, 265) code

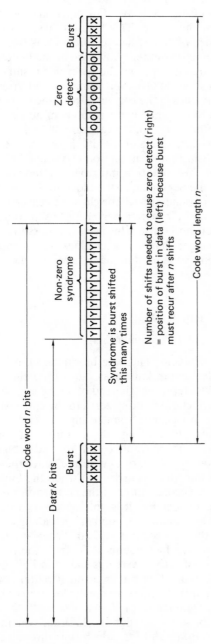

Figure 7.25 Owing to the characteristics of Galois fields, syndrome Y is simply the error burst which has been shifted a number of times equal to the number of bits from the burst to the end of the code word. As the field repeats every n shifts, it is only necessary to shift the syndrome and count the number of shifts necessary to give a zero detect condition. This number is equal to the position of the burst in the data. If no zero condition is found, then the burst is longer than b and cannot be corrected. It is, however, important to detect uncorrectable errors. The example can detect all bursts up to the length of the checkword $n - k$; beyond this a statistical element is introduced

syndrome if there has been no error, as in Fig. 7.25. If there is a non-zero syndrome, there has been an error. As all data blocks are recorded as codewords, the effect of the actual data on the check circuit is to give a zero remainder. The only effect on the syndrome is due to the errors. Any non-zero syndrome represents the exclusive–OR function of what the data should have been and what they were. This function has, however, been shifted an unknown number of times. The error burst is one state of a Galois field and the syndrome is another. Any state of the Galois field can be reached from any other by shifting, so if the syndrome is shifted, sooner or later the error burst will show up. The only remaining question is how it will be recognized. The only ones in the correct state of the Galois field will be those representing the burst, and they will be confined to the last b stages of the register. All other stages of the register will be zero. Owing to the highly non-sequential nature of Galois fields, there is no possibility of $n-k-b$ contiguous zeros being found in any other state. The number of shifts required to arrive at this condition must be counted, because it is equal to the distance from the beginning of the block to the burst. In most Fire code applications, the parameter b will be chosen to exceed the typical burst size of the channel, and the parameter m is chosen to achieve the desired probability of undetected error. This usually results in a codeword of enormous size, much longer than the data blocks used on most disk drives. For example, the Fire code used in many IBM disk drives uses the polynomial

$$(x^{21} + 1) (x^{11} + x^2 + 1)$$

which gives a codeword of length

$$(2^{11} - 1) \times 21 = 42987 \text{ bits (42955 data bits)}$$

In practice this is not a problem. The data block can be made shorter than the codeword by a technique known as puncturing the code. The actual data and the check bits represent the end of a long codeword which begins with zeros. As the effect of inputting zeros to the checkword circuit during a write is to cause no change, puncturing the code on writing requires no special action. On reading, by a similar argument, the syndrome generated will be as if the whole codeword had been recorded, except that the leading zeros are, of course, error free, since they were not recorded. Thus the shift count which is arrived at when the burst appears represents the bit count from the beginning of the codeword, not from the beginning of the real data. In practice, it is only necessary to employ an additional shift counter. This counts the number of leading zeros which were not recorded, when the syndrome is shifted. When it overflows, it enables a second shift counter, which counts shifts from the beginning of the data. The block diagram of such a system is shown in Fig. 7.26. There are two outputs from the circuit: first the error-burst pattern, which will contain a one for every bit in error, and secondly the location of the start of the burst in bits from the beginning of the block.

An alternative is to construct a slightly different version of the twisted-ring counter for syndrome shifting, which runs through the Galois field backwards. With punctured codes, this will perform correction faster. A faster correction still in Fire code can be obtained using the so-called

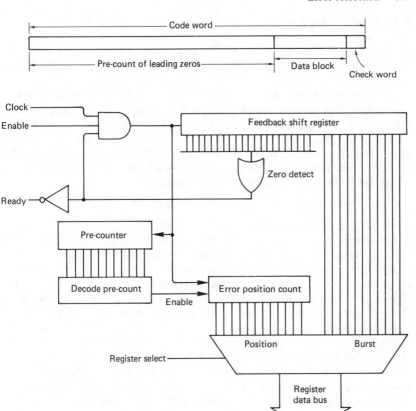

Figure 7.26 Error-correction hardware where data block is smaller than the codeword length. When a non-zero syndrome is detected after a read, the leading zeros in the codeword which precede the data are counted by the precounter. When the precount satisfies the decoder, error-position counter is enabled, which gives error position relative to the start of data when zero condition is detected. This disables the shifting and raises the ready bit

Chinese-remainder theorem. Instead of dividing the codeword by the full polynomial, it is simultaneously divided by the factors of the polynomial instead. If there is an error, the burst-pattern syndrome is shifted first to locate the burst pattern at the end of the register. The registers containing the other factors can then be shifted until their contents are the same as the burst pattern, when the number of shifts each needs can be used to find the burst position. In addition to allowing the use of conveniently sized blocks, puncturing a code can also be employed to decrease the probabilities of undetected error or miscorrection. Clearly, if part of a codeword is not recorded it cannot contain errors!

Whilst Fire code was discovered at about the same time as the superior Reed–Solomon codes, it was dominant in disk drives until recently because it is so much easier to implement in circuitry. All that is needed is a handful of XOR gates, latches and counters or, more recently, one chip.

7.15 B-adjacent code

In the B-adjacent code, used in consumer digital audio adaptors conforming to the EIAJ format, two bursts can be corrected. The mechanism is shown in Fig. 7.27 and operates as follows.

Six words of 14 bits, A–F, are made into a codeword by the addition of two redundancy words, P and Q. The P word is a simple exclusive–OR sum of A–F, but the calculation of Q is more complex. The circuit of Fig. 7.27(a) is supplied with each data word in turn and clocked, so that after six clocks the Q word has been calculated. The effect of the circuit of Fig. 7.27(a) is actually to perform the matrix transform of Fig. 7.27(b). If the transform is given by T, then Q will be given by

$$Q = T^6A \oplus T^5B \oplus T^4C \oplus T^3D \oplus T^2E \oplus TF$$

where $\oplus$ is modulo-2 addition.

The words A–F and P and Q form a codeword and are recorded. On replay, a separate mechanism determines which symbols in the codeword contain errors by the erasure method noted earlier in this chapter. For the purposes of this discussion, it is assumed that words A and C are in error. The readback words are all fed into a similar circuit to the encoder. Since the codeword has the characteristic that it gives zero remainder when fed into the check circuit, it follows that the syndrome left in the check circuit in the case of an error is a function of the error alone. If words A and C are in error, the P section of the syndrome SP will be the exclusive–OR of the two errors, EA + EC. The Q section of the syndrome SQ will be the exclusive–OR sum of the A word error multiplied by the sixth power of the transform T and the C word error multiplied by the fourth power of T:

$$SP = EA \oplus EC \qquad\qquad\qquad (7.1)$$

$$SQ = T^6EA \oplus T^4EC \qquad\qquad\qquad (7.2)$$

Dividing through Eqn. 7.2 by T^4 gives

$$T^{-4}SQ = T^2EA \oplus EC$$

Adding SP to both sides of Eqn.7.3 gives

$$SP \oplus T^{-4}SQ = T^2EA \oplus EC \oplus SP$$

But SP = EA $\oplus$ EC, therefore

$$\begin{aligned}SP \oplus T^{-4}SQ &= T^2EA \oplus EC \oplus EA \oplus EC \\ &= T^2EA \oplus EA \\ &= (1 + T^2)EA\end{aligned}$$

Therefore

$$EA = \frac{SP \oplus T^{-4}SQ}{1 + T^2}$$

and EC follows from Eqn. 7.1.

It is thus only necessary to process the Q syndrome in a reverse transform according to the positions of the errors in the codeword in order to correct both errors.

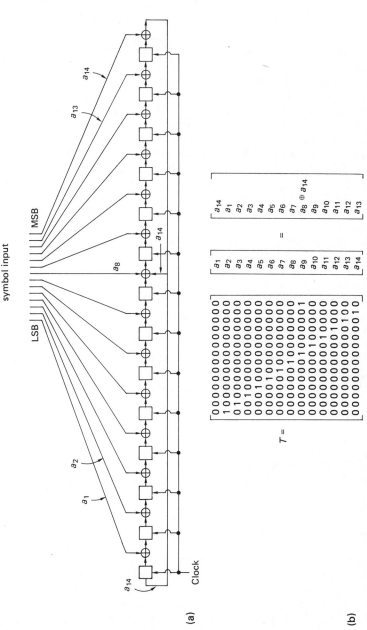

Figure 7.27 B-adjacent encoding; the circuit at (a) is presented with the input symbols sequentially, and each one is clocked. The feedback connections cause the circuit to execute the transform T shown in (b) at each clock. After several clocks, the register will contain the sum of each symbol multiplied by successively higher powers of T

7.16 Reed–Solomon code

In the B-adjacent code, data are assembled into words for the purpose of burst correction. This is implicit in the operation of the Reed–Solomon codes.

The concept of the Galois field has been introduced earlier in this chapter in conjunction with Fire code. In Fire code, the error-burst pattern becomes one state of a Galois field, the syndrome becomes another, but the data bits are all still individually treated. In the Reed–Solomon codes, data bits are assembled into words, or symbols, which become elements of the Galois field upon which the code is based. The number of bits in the symbol determines the size of the Galois field, and hence the number of symbols in the codeword. A symbol size of eight is commonly used because it fits in conveniently with 16 bit audio samples, 8 bit video samples and byte-oriented computers. It is also highly appropriate for the Compact Disc and RDAT, since the EFM and 8/10 channel codes are group codes which can suffer up to 8 bits in error if a single channel bit is corrupted. A Galois field with 8 bit symbols has a maximum sequence length of $2^8 - 1 = 255$. As each symbol contains 8 bits, the code word will be: $255 \times 8 = 2040$ bits long.

As further examples, 5 bit symbols could be used to form a codeword 31 symbols long, and 3 bit symbols would form a codeword seven symbols long. This latter size is small enough to permit some worked examples and will be used further here.

In Section 7.12 it was shown that the circuit of Fig. 7.16 generated a Galois field when clocked with no input. The primitive element a will do this when raised to sequential powers. In Reed–Solomon coding, each symbol will be multiplied by some power of such a primitive element. It is necessary to construct hardware which will perform this multiplication. Fig. 7.28 shows some examples, and Table 7.1 shows that a truth table can be drawn up for a Galois field multiplier by simply adding the powers of the inputs.

For example:

$$a^2 = 100,\ a^3 = 011,\ \text{so } 100 \times 011 = a^5 = 111$$

Note that the results of a Galois multiplication are quite different from binary multiplication. Because all products must be elements of the field, sums of powers which exceed seven wrap around by having seven subtracted:

$$a^5 \times a^6 = a^{11} = a^4 = 110$$

It has been stated that the effect of an error is to add an error polynomial to the message polynomial. The number of terms in the error polynomial is the same as the number of errors in the codeword. In a simple CRC system, the effect of the error is detected by ensuring that the codeword can be divided by a polynomial. In the Reed–Solomon codes, several errors can be isolated by ensuring that the codeword will divide by a number of first-order polynomials. If it is proposed to correct for a number of symbols in error given by t, the codeword must be divisible by $2t$

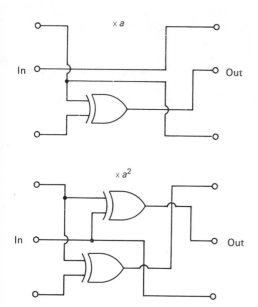

Figure 7.28 Some examples of GF multiplier circuits

Table 7.1 The truth table for Galois field multiplication of GF (2^3). $F(x) = x^3 + x + 1$. Primitive element $a = 010$.

Element: Bits:	0 000	a 010	a^2 100	a^3 011	a^4 110	a^5 111	a^6 101	$a^7 = 1$ 001
0 000	0 000	0 000	0 000	0 000	0 000	0 000	0 000	0 000
a 010	0 000	a^2 100	a^3 011	a^4 110	a^5 111	a^6 101	1 001	a 010
a^2 100	0 000	a^3 011	a^4 110	a^5 111	a^6 101	1 001	a 010	a^2 100
a^3 011	0 000	a^4 110	a^5 111	a^6 101	1 001	a 010	a^2 100	a^3 011
a^4 110	0 000	a^5 111	a^6 101	1 001	a 010	a^2 100	a^3 011	a^4 110
a^5 111	0 000	a^6 101	1 001	a 010	a^2 100	a^3 011	a^4 110	a^5 111
a^6 101	0 000	1 001	a 010	a^2 100	a^3 011	a^4 110	a^5 111	a^6 101
$a^7 = 1$ 001	0 000	a 010	a^2 100	a^3 011	a^4 110	a^5 111	a^6 101	1 001

different polynomials of the form $(x + a^n)$ where n takes all values up to $2t$. a is the primitive element discussed earlier.

Fig. 7.29, Fig. 7.30 and Table 7.2 show some examples of Reed–Solomon coding processes. The Galois field of Fig. 7.16 has been used, and the primitive element $a = 010$ from Table 7.1 will be used. Five symbols of 3 bits each, A–E, are the data, and two redundant symbols, P and Q, will be

Input data	A	101	a^6A = 111	a^2A = 010
	B	100	a B = 011	a^3B = 111
	C	010	a^2C = 011	a^6C = 001
	D	100	a^5D = 001	a^4D = 101
	E	111	a^3E = 010	a E = 101
Check symbols	P	100 ←	—— 100	100
	Q	100 ←		

Codeword	A	101	a^7A = 101
	B	100	a^6B = 010
	C	010	a^5C = 101
	D	100	a^4D = 101
	E	111	a^3E = 010
	P	100	a^2P = 110
	Q	100	a Q = 011

$S_0 = \overline{000}$ $S_1 = \overline{000}$ ← Both syndromes zero

Figure 7.29 Five data symbols A–E are used as terms in the generator polynomials derived in Appendix 7.1 to calculate two redundant symbols P and Q. An example is shown at the top. Below is the result of using the codeword symbols A–Q as terms in the checking polynomials. As there is no error, both syndromes are zero

7	A	101	a^7A = 101
6	B	100	a^6B = 010
5	C	010	a^5C = 101
4	D'	101	a^4D' = 011 ←
3	E	111	a^3E = 010
2	P	100	a^2P = 110
1	Q	100	a Q = 011
	$S_0 =$	$\overline{001}$	$S_1 = \overline{110}$

$\dfrac{S_1}{S_0} = \dfrac{a^4}{1} = a^4$

$k = 4$

$D' + S_0 = 101 + 001$
$D = 100$

7	A	101	a^7A = 101
6	B	100	a^6B = 010
5	C'	110	a^5C = 100 ←
4	D	100	a^4D = 101
3	E	111	a^3E = 010
2	P	100	a^2P = 110
1	Q	100	a Q = 011
	$S_0 =$	$\overline{100}$	$S_1 = \overline{001}$

$\dfrac{S_1}{S_0} = \dfrac{1}{a^2} = \dfrac{1}{a^2} \times \dfrac{a^5}{a^5} = a^5$

$k = 5$

$C' + S_0 = 110 + 100$
$C = 010$

7	A'	111	a^7A = 111 ↖
6	B	100	a^6B = 010
5	C	010	a^5C = 101
4	D	100	a^4D = 101
3	E	111	a^3E = 010
2	P	100	a^2P = 110
1	Q	100	a Q = 011
	$S_0 =$	$\overline{010}$	$S_1 = \overline{010}$

$\dfrac{S_1}{S_0} = \dfrac{a}{a} = 001 = a^7$

$k = 7$

$A' + S_0 = 111 + 010$
$A = 101$

Figure 7.30 Three examples of error location and correction. The number of bits in error in a symbol is irrelevant; if all three were wrong, S_0 would be 111, but correction is still possible

Table 7.2 When the position of errors is known by some other means, two errors can be corrected for the same amount of redundancy. The technique is to set the symbols in error to zero, as shown, and calculate what they should have been. This gives the name of erasure correction to the system.

A	101	$a^7A =$	101
B	100	$a^6B =$	010	$S_0 = C \oplus D$
C	000	$a^5C =$	000
D	$\overline{000}$	$a^4D =$	$\overline{000}$	$S_1 = a^5 C \oplus a^4D$
E	$\overline{111}$	$a^3E =$	$\overline{010}$
P	100	$a^2P =$	110
Q	$\underline{100}$	$a\ Q =$	011
S_0	$=110$	$S_1\ =$	$\overline{000}$

$S_1 = a^5S_0 \oplus a^5D \oplus a^4D = a^5S_0 \oplus D$

$\therefore D = S_1 \oplus a^5S_0 = 000 \oplus 100 = \underline{100}$

$S_1 = a^5C \oplus a^4C \oplus a^4S_0 = C \oplus a^4S_0$

$\therefore C = S_1 \oplus a^4S_0 = 000 \oplus 010 = \underline{010}$

used because this simple example will locate and correct only a single symbol in error. It does not matter, however, how many bits in the symbol are in error.

The two check symbols are solutions to the following equations:

$$A \oplus B \oplus C \oplus D \oplus E \oplus P \oplus Q = 0$$

$$a^7A \oplus a^6B \oplus a^5C \oplus a^4D \oplus a^3E \oplus a^2P \oplus aQ = 0$$

By some tedious mathematics, which are shown for reference in Appendix 7.1, it is possible to derive the following expressions which must be used to calculate P and Q from the data in order to satisfy the above equations. These are:

$$P = a^6A \oplus aB \oplus a^2C \oplus a^5D \oplus a^3E$$

$$Q = a^2A \oplus a^3B \oplus a^6C \oplus a^4D \oplus aE$$

In Fig. 7.29 the redundant symbols have been calculated. In order to calculate P, the symbol A is multiplied by a^6 according to the Table 7.1, B is multiplied by a, and so on, and the products are added modulo-2. A similar process is used to calculate Q. The entire codeword now exists and can be recorded. In Fig. 7.29 it is also demonstrated that the codeword satisfies the checking equations.

Upon replaying the information, two checks must be made on the received message to see if it is a codeword. This is done by calculating syndromes using the following expressions, where the prime implies the received symbol which is not necessarily correct:

$$S_0 = A' \oplus B' \oplus C' \oplus D' \oplus E' \oplus P' \oplus Q'$$
(This is in fact a simple parity check.)

$$S_1 = a^7A' \oplus a^6B' \oplus a^5C' \oplus a^4D' \oplus a^3E' \oplus a^2P' \oplus aQ'$$

In Fig. 7.30 three examples of errors are given, where the erroneous symbol is marked with a dash. As there has been an error, the syndromes

S_0 and S_1 will not be zero. The syndrome calculation is performed with Table 7.1 as before.

The parity syndrome S_0 determines the error bit pattern, and the syndrome S_1 is the same error bit pattern, but it has been raised to a different power of a dependent on the position of the error symbol in the block. If the position of the error is in symbol k, then

$$S_0 \times a^k = S_1$$

Hence

$$a^k = \frac{S_1}{S_0}$$

The error symbol can be located by multiplying S_0 by various powers of a (which is the same as multiplying by successive elements of the Galois field) until the product is the same as S_1. The power of a necessary is known as the locator, because it gives the position of the error. The process of finding the error position by experiment is known as a Chien search.[9] Once the locator has identified the erroneous symbol, the correct value is obtained by adding S_0 (the corrector) to it.

In the examples of Fig. 7.30, two redundant symbols have been used to locate and correct one error symbol. If the positions of errors are known by some separate mechanism (see cross-interleaving, Section 7.18), the number of symbols which can be corrected is equal to the number of redundant symbols. In Table 7.2 two errors have taken place, and it is known that they are in symbols C and D. Since S_0 is a simple parity check, it will reflect the modulo-2 sum of the two errors. Hence:

$$S_0 = EC \oplus ED$$

The two errors will have been multiplied by different powers in S_1, such that

$$S_1 = a^5EC \oplus a^4ED$$

It is possible to solve these two equations, as shown in the figure, to find EA and EB, and the correct value of the symbol will be obtained by adding these correctors to the erroneous values. It is, however, easier to set the values of the symbols in error to zero, and the correct values are then found more simply as shown in Table 7.2. This setting of symbols to zero gives rise to the term erasure.

The necessary circuitry for encoding the examples given is shown in Fig. 7.31. The P and Q redundancy is computed using suitable Galois field multipliers to obtain the necessary powers of the primitive element according to Table 7.1. In Fig. 7.32 the circuitry for calculating the syndromes is shown. The S_0 circuit is a simple parity checker which produces the modulo-2 sum of all symbols fed to it. The S_1 circuit is more subtle, because it contains a Galois field multiplier in a feedback loop, such that early symbols fed in are raised to higher powers than later symbols because they have been recirculated through the Galois field (GF) multiplier more often. It is possible to compare the operation of these circuits with the examples of Fig. 7.29, Fig. 7.30 and Table 7.2 to confirm that the same results are obtained.

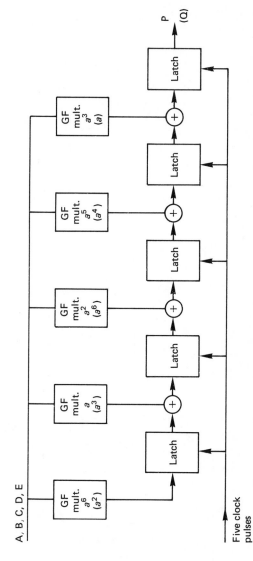

315

A, B, C, D, E

P
(Q)

Five clock
pulses

Figure 7.31 If the five data symbols of Figure 7.23 and Table 7.2 are supplied to this circuit in sequence, after five clocks, one of the check symbols will appear at the output. Terms without brackets will calculate P, bracketed terms calculate Q

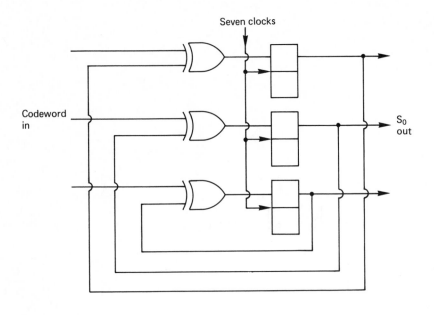

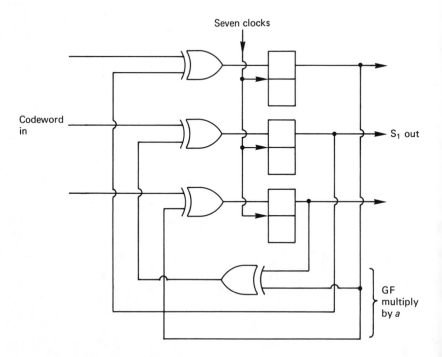

Figure 7.32 Circuits for parallel calculation of syndromes S_0, S_1. S_0 is a simple parity check. S_1 has a GF multiplication by a in the feedback, so that A is multiplied by a^7, B is multiplied by a^6 etc, and all are summed to give S_1

Where two symbols are to be corrected without the help of erasure pointers, four redundant symbols are necessary, and the codeword polynomial must then be divisible by

$$(x + a^0)(x + a^1)(x + a^2)(x + a^3)$$

Upon receipt of the message, four syndromes must be calculated, and the two error patterns and their positions are determined by solving four simultaneous equations. This generally requires an iterative procedure, and a number of algorithms have been developed for the purpose.[7, 10–12] Clearly a double-error-correcting Reed–Solomon (R–S) code will be capable of four-symbol correction if erasure pointers are available. Such techniques are very powerful, because the amount of overhead necessary can be made quite small without sacrificing output error rate. The D-1 and D-2 digital video formats, Compact Disc, RDAT and the Mitsubishi stationary-head digital audio formats use erasure techniques with Reed–Solomon coding extensively. The primitive polynomial commonly used with GF (256) is

$$x^8 + x^4 + x^3 + x^2 + 1$$

The larger GFs require less redundancy, but the computational problem increases. LSI chips have been developed specifically for R–S decoding for D-1, D-2 and for other formats.[13]

7.17 Interleaving

The concept of bit interleaving was introduced in connection with a single-bit correcting code to allow it to correct small bursts. With burst-correcting codes such as Reed–Solomon, bit interleave is unnecessary. In most channels, particularly high-density recording channels used for digital video, the burst size may be many bytes rather than bits, and to rely on a cyclic code alone to correct such errors would require a lot of redundancy. The solution in this case is to employ word interleaving, as shown in Fig. 7.33(a). Several codewords are encoded from input data, yet these are not recorded in the order they were input, but are physically reordered in the channel, so that a real burst error is split into smaller bursts in several codewords. The size of the burst seen by each codeword is now determined primarily by the parameters of the interleave, and Fig. 7.34 shows that the probability of occurrence of bursts with respect to the burst length in a given codeword is modified. The number of bits in the interleave word can be made equal to the burst-correcting ability of the code in the knowledge that it will be exceeded only very infrequently.

There are a number of different ways in which interleaving can be performed. Fig. 7.35 shows that in block interleaving, words are reordered within blocks which are themselves in the correct order. This approach is attractive for digital video cassette recorders, such as D-1 and D-2, because the blocks fit into the segmented frame structure of the television waveform, and editing is easy. The block interleave is achieved by writing samples into a memory in sequential address locations from a counter, and reading the memory with non-sequential addresses from a sequencer. The

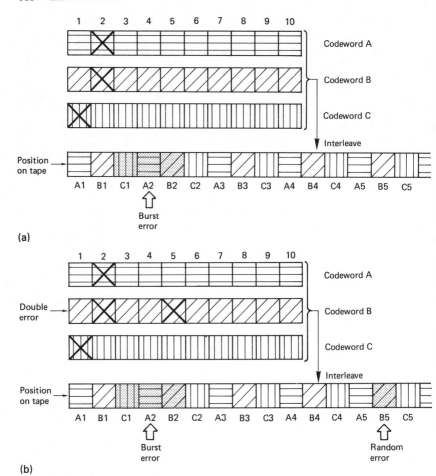

Figure 7.33 At (a), interleave controls the size of burst errors in individual code words, but at (b) the system falls down when a random error occurs adjacent to a burst

effect is to convert a one-dimensional sequence of samples into a two-dimensional structure having rows and columns.

Fig. 7.36 shows that, in convolutional interleaving, the interleave process is endless. Samples are assembled into short blocks, and then each sample is individually delayed by an amount proportional to the position in the block. Clearly rows cannot be practically assembled in an endless process, as they would be infinitely long, so convolutional interleave produces diagonal codewords. It is possible for a convolutional interleave to continue from track to track in rotary-head systems. Convolutional interleave requires some caution in editing.

A combination of the two techniques above is shown in Fig. 7.37, where a convolutional code is made to have finite size by making it into a loop. This is known as a block-completed convolutional code and is found in the digital audio blocks of the Video 8 format. The effect of the interleave can be maintained in block-completed interleave provided the block is large

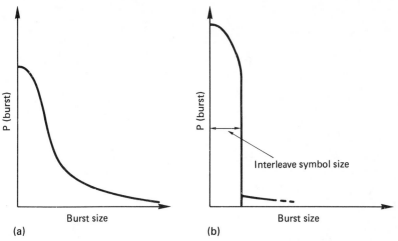

Figure 7.34 (a) The distribution of burst sizes might look like this. (b) Following interleave, the burst size within a codeword is controlled to that of the interleave symbol size, except for gross errors which have low probability

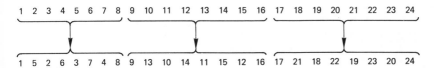

Figure 7.35 In block interleaving, data are scrambled within blocks which are themselves in the correct order

enough compared with the interleave parameters, but this requires a large interleave memory.

Rotary-head recorders naturally interleave spatially on the tape. Fig. 7.38 shows that a single, large tape defect becomes a series of small defects owing to the geometry of helical scanning.

7.18 Cross-interleaving

In the presence of burst errors alone, the system of interleaving works very well, but it is known that in many channels there are also uncorrelated errors of a few bits due to noise. Fig. 7.33(b) shows that a noise error in the vicinity of a burst error will cause two errors in one codeword, which may not be correctable. The solution to this problem is to use a system where codewords are formed both before and after the interleave process. In block interleaving this results in a product code, whereas in convolutional interleaving the result is known as cross-interleaving.[14] Many of the characteristics of these systems are similar. Fig. 7.39(a) shows a cross-interleave system where several errors have taken place. In one row there are two errors, which are beyond the power of the codeword to

320

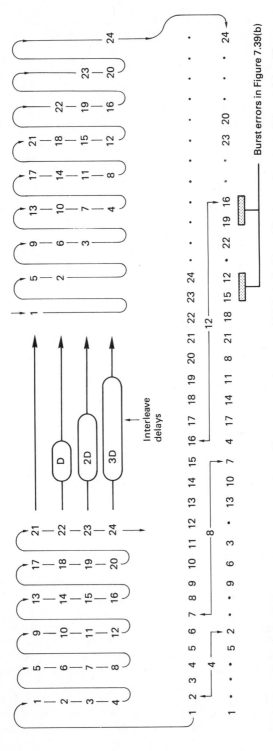

Figure 7.36 In convolutional interleaving, samples are formed into a rectangular array, which is sheared by subjecting each row to a different delay. The sheared array is read in vertical columns to provide the interleaved output. In this example, samples will be found at 4, 8 and 12 places away from their original order

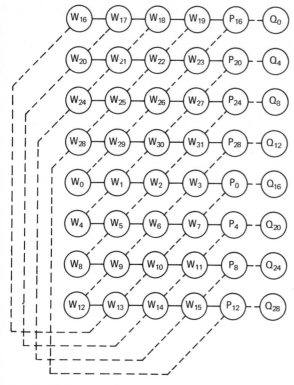

Figure 7.37 In block-completed convolutional interleave some diagonal codewords wrap around the end of the block. This requires a large memory and causes a longer deinterleaving delay

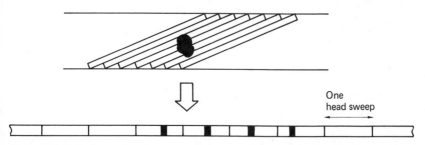

Figure 7.38 Helical-scan recorders produce a form of mechanical interleaving, because one large defect on the medium becomes distributed over several head sweeps

correct, and on two diagonals the same is true. However, if a diagonal has two errors, a row will generally only have one. This one error can be corrected, which means that one ·of the two errors in the diagonal disappears, and so the diagonal codeword can correct it. This then means that there will be only one error in the next row and so on. Random errors in the vicinity of bursts can now be corrected.

In fact, the power of cross-interleaving and product codes goes beyond the ability to deal with real-life errors. The fact that there is a

1, 2, 3, 4 and P1 form a codeword

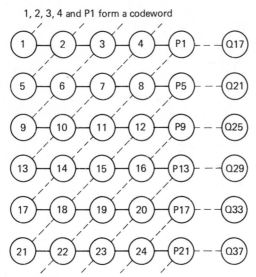

17, 14, 11, 8, P1 and Q17 form a
cross-codeword.

(a)

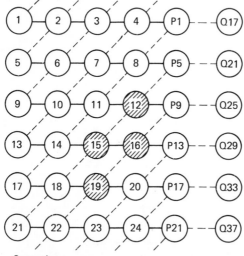

Correction sequence
P9 corrects 12, which enables Q21 to correct 15.
With 15 correct, P13 corrects 16.
P17 corrects 19.

(b)

Figure 7.39 (a) In cross-interleaving, codewords are formed on data before interleaving (1, 2, 3, 4, P1), and after convolutional interleaving (21, 18, 15, 12, P5, Q21). Compare with Figure 7.36. (b) Multiple errors in one codeword will become single errors in another. If the sequence shown is followed, then all the errors can be corrected. In this example, error samples 12, 15, 16 and 19 are due to two bursts in the convolutional interleave of Figure 7.36

two-dimensional structure allows the position of an error to be discovered because it will be at the intersection of two codewords. If the position of the error can be established geometrically, then it is not necessary to find it by using a code which needs redundancy. The overhead required for a product code is actually less than any other system for a given performance, because the detection of an error in one codeword before de-interleave can be used to generate erasure pointers which help a further codeword after de-interleave. The combination of codewords with interleaving in several dimensions yields an error-protection strategy which is truly synergistic, in that the end result is more powerful than the sum of the parts. Needless to say, the technique is used extensively in digital vide recording systems.

7.19 Error correction in D-1 and D-2

The interleave and error-correction systems will now be discussed. Fig. 7.40 shows a conceptual block diagram of the system used in both formats which differ in detail rather than in principle.

Both D-1 and D-2 use a product code formed by producing Reed-Solomon codewords at right angles across an array. The array is formed in a memory, and the layout used in D-2 (PAL) can be seen in Fig. 7.41. Incoming samples (bytes) are written into the array in columns. Each column is then made into a codeword by the addition of 4 bytes of redundancy, whereas D-1 has only 2 bytes. These are the outer codewords. Each row of the array is then formed into six inner codewords by the addition of 8 bytes of redundancy to each. In order to make a recording, the memory is read in rows, and two inner codewords fit into one block along the track. Every block in an eight-field sequence is given a unique header address. This process continues until the entire array has been laid on tape to form a segment. The process then repeats for the other record head pair. In D-1 the process is similar except that the inner codewords only have four check bytes. Writing the memory in columns and reading in rows achieves the necessary interleave.

On replay, a combination of random errors and burst errors will occur. Data will come from tape in the sequence of the inner codewords. In D-2 each of these has 8 bytes of redundancy, so it would be possible to locate and correct up to 4 bytes in error in the codeword. This, however, is not done, because it is better to limit the correction power to 3 bytes and use the remaining redundancy to decrease the probability of miscorrection. In this way, random errors are corrected with a high degree of confidence. Errors exceeding 3 bytes cause the entire inner codeword to be declared corrupt, and it is written into the appropriate row of the de-interleave array as all zeros, with error flags set. D-1 is restricted to correcting up to 2 bytes. When all of the rows of the array are completed, it is possible to begin processing the columns. A burst error on tape which destroys one or more inner codewords will result in single-byte errors with flags in many different outer codewords. The presence of the error flags means that the outer code does not need to compute the position of the errors, so the full power of the outer code redundancy is available for correction. The four

324

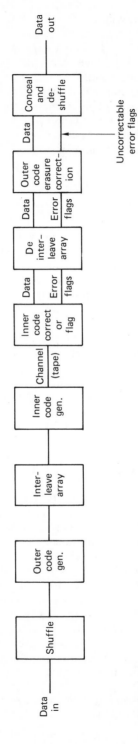

Figure 7.40 Block diagram of error correction strategy of DVTR. See text for details

325

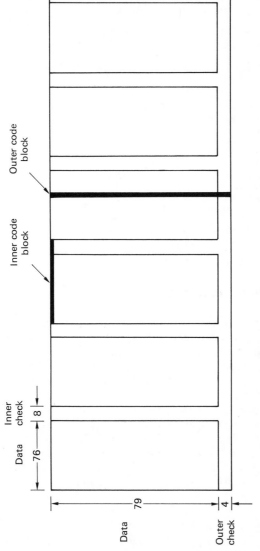

Figure 7.41 Video Product-Block Reed-Solomon Code Structure for D-2 DVTR

redundancy bytes of D-2 can correct four error bytes as compared with two error bytes in D-1. The process of using error flags to assist a code is called erasure. It will be evident that enormous damage must be done to the tape track before 4 bytes are corrupted in a single outer codeword, which gives high resistance to dropouts and tape scratches. The error-correction strategy of D-2 is more powerful than that of D-1, but this is as it should be since D-2 has a higher recording density. Table 7.3 compares the main error-correction parameters of D-1 and D-2.[15]

Table 7.3 Comparison of error correction coding system parameters

Parameter	D-2	D-1
Inner block symbol size	8 *bits*	8 *bits*
Inner block size, data	76^2	60
Inner block size, check	8	4
Video outer block symbol size	8 *bits*	8 *bits*
Video outer block size, data	79	30
Video outer block size, check	4	2
Video product block interleave depth	6 *inner blocks*	10 *inner blocks*
Correctable video burst	≤ 2064	≤ 1340
Audio outer block symbol size	8 *bits*	4 *bits*
Audio outer block size, data	8	7 *nibbles*
Audio outer block size, check	4	3 *nibbles*
Audio product block interleave depth	1 *inner block*	1 *inner block*
Correctable audio burst[3]	≤ 344	≤ 198

Notes: 1. Table values in bytes unless otherwise indicated.
2. Inner block size does not include identification pattern.
3. Without utilizing duplication of audio data.

7.20 Concealment and shuffle

In the event of a gross error, correction may not be possible and some bytes may be declared uncorrectable. In this case the errors must be concealed by interpolation from adjacent samples. Owing to the regular structure of the product code block, uncorrectable burst errors would show up as a regular pattern of interpolations on the screen. The eye is extremely good at finding such patterns, so the visibility is higher than might be expected. The solution to this problem is to perform a two-dimensional pseudo-random shuffle on the video samples before generating the product code. The reverse shuffle is performed on replay. The positions of interpolated samples arising from an uncorrected error now form a pseudo-random pattern with much decreased visibility.

The D-1 and D-2 formats will be discussed in more detail in Chapters 10 and 11.

Appendix 7.1 Calculation of Reed–Solomon generator polynomials

For a Reed–Solomon codeword over $GF(2^3)$, there will be seven three-bit symbols. For location and correction of one symbol, there must be two redundant symbols P and Q, leaving A–E for data.

The following expressions must be true, where a is the primitive element of $x^3 + x + 1$ and + is XOR throughout.

$$A + B + C + D + E + P + Q = 0 \tag{1}$$
$$a^7A + a^6B + a^5C + a^4D + a^3E + a^2P + aQ = 0 \tag{2}$$

Dividing eq. (2) by a:

$a^6A + a^5B + a^4C + a^3D + a^2E + aP + Q = 0 = A + B + C + D + E + P + Q$

Cancelling Q, and collecting terms:

$(a^6 + 1)A + (a^5 + 1)B + (a^4 + 1)C + (a^3 + 1)D + (a^2 + 1)E = (a + 1)P$

Using Table 7.1 to calculate $(a^n + 1)$, e.g. $a^6 + 1 = 101 + 001 = 100 = a^2$

$a^2A + a^4B + a^5C + aD + a^6E = a^3P$

$a^6A + aB + a^2C + a^5D + a^3E = P$ $\hspace{2cm}$ (3)

Multiply eq. (1) by a^2 and equating to eq. (2):

$a^2A + a^2B + a^2C + a^2D + a^2E + a^2P + a^2Q = 0$

$\hspace{1.5cm} = a^7A + a^6B + a^5C + a^4D + a^3E + a^2P + aQ$

Cancelling a^2P and collecting terms (remember $a^2 + a^2 = 0$):

$(a^7 + a^2)A + (a^6 + a^2)B + (a^5 + a^2)C + (a^4 + a^2)D + (a^3 + a^2)E = (a^2 + a)Q$

Adding powers according to Table 7.1, e.g. $a^7 + a^2 = 001 + 100 = 101 = a^6$:

$a^6A + B + a^3C + aD + a^5E = a^4Q$

$a^2A + a^3B + a^6C + a^4D + aE = Q$

References

1. SHANNON, C.E., A mathematical theory of communication. *Bell Syst. Tech. J.*, **27**, 379 (1948)

2. BELLIS, F.A., A multichannel digital sound recorder. Presented at the Video and Data Recording Conference (Birmingham, England), *IERE Conf. Proc.*, no. 35, 123–126 (1976)

3. HAMMING, R.W., Error-detecting and error-correcting codes. *Bell Syst. Tech. J.*, **26**, 147–160 (1950)

4. EDWARDS, A.W.F., Venn diagrams for many sets. *New Sci.*, **1646**, 51–56 (1989)

5. PETERSON, W. and BROWN, D., Cyclic codes for error detection. *Proc. IRE*, 228–235 (1961)

6. FIRE, P., A class of multiple-error correcting codes for non-independent errors. *Sylvania Reconnaissance Systems Lab. Rep.*, RSL-E-2 (1959)

7. BOSSEN, D.C., B-adjacent error correction. *IBM J. Res. Dev.*, **14**, 402–408 (1970)

8. REED, I.S. and SOLOMON, G., Polynomial codes over certain finite fields. *J. Soc. Ind. Appl. Math.*, **8**, 300–304 (1960)

9. CHIEN, R.T., CUNNINGHAM, B.D. and OLDHAM, I.B., Hybrid methods for finding roots of a polynomial – with application to BCH decoding. *IEEE Trans. Inf. Theory.*, **IT–15**, 329–334 (1969)

10. BERLEKAMP, E.R., *Algebraic Coding Theory*, New York: McGraw-Hill (1967). Reprint edn: Laguna Hills, CA: Aegean Park Press (1983)

11. SUGIYAMA, Y. *et al.*, An erasures and errors decoding algorithm for Goppa codes. *IEEE Trans. Inf. Theory*, **IT–22** (1976)

12. PETERSON, W.W. and WELDON, E.J., *Error Correcting Codes*, 2nd edn, Cambridge, MA: MIT Press (1972)

13. *Ampex Data Sheets* V5125 and V5126, Ampex Data Systems Division, Redwood City, CA

14. DOI, T.T., ODAKA, K., FUKUDA, G. and FURUKAWA, S., Crossinterleave code for error correction of digital audio systems. *J. Audio Eng. Soc.*, **27**, 1028 (1979)

15. BRUSH, R., Design considerations for the D-2 PAL composite DVTR. Presented at 7th IERE Video, Audio and Data Recording Conference (York, 1988), *IERE Publ*, no. 79, 141–148 (1988)

Chapter 8

Digital Video Interconnects

Since digital video equipment is supplied by a variety of manufacturers, there is a need for a standardized interconnect so that units may communicate in the digital domain. This chapter discusses the interconnects possible for component and composite digital video.

8.1 Introduction

Of all the advantages of digital recording applied to video the most important of these for production work is the ability to record through multiple generations without quality loss. Effects machines perform transforms on images in the digital domain which remain impossible in the analog domain. For the highest-quality post-production work, digital interconnection between such items as switchers, recorders and effects machines is highly desirable to avoid the degradation due to repeated conversion and filtering stages.

In 4:2:2 sampling according to CCIR 601, the luminance is sampled at 13.5 MHz, which is line synchronous to both broadcast line rates, and the two colour difference signals are sampled at one-half that frequency. Composite digital machines sample at four times subcarrier. All of the signals use 8 or 10 bit resolution. Video converters universally use parallel connection, where all bits of the pixel value are applied simultaneously to separate pins. Rotary-head digital recorders lay data on the tape serially, but within the circuitry of the recorder; parallel presentation is in the majority, because it allows slower, and hence cheaper, memory chips to be used for interleaving and timebase correction. The Reed–Solomon error correction depends upon symbols assembled from several bits at once. Digital effects machines and switchers universally operate upon pixel values in parallel using fast multiplier chips.

Bearing all of this in mind, there is a strong argument for parallel connection, because the video naturally appears in the parallel format in typical machines. All that is necessary is a set of suitable driver chips, running at an appropriate sampling rate, to send video down cables having separate conductors for each bit of the sample and clocks to tell the receiver when to sample the bit values. The cost in electronic components is very small, and for short distances this approach represents the optimum

328

solution. An example would be where it is desired to dub a digital recording from one machine to another standing beside it.

Parallel connection has drawbacks too; these come into play when longer distances are contemplated. A multicore cable is expensive, and the connectors are physically large. It is difficult to provide good screening of a multicore cable without it becoming inflexible. More seriously, there are electronic problems with multicore cables. The propagation speeds of pulses down all of the cores in the cable will not be exactly the same, and so, at the end of a long cable, some bits may still be in transition when the clock arrives while others may have begun to change to the value in the next pixel. In the presence of crosstalk between the conductors, and reflections due to suboptimal termination, the data integrity eventually becomes marginal.

Where it is proposed to interconnect a large number of units with a router, that device will be extremely complex because of the number of parallel signals to be handled.

The answer to these problems is the serial connection. All of the digital samples are multiplexed into a serial bit stream, and this is encoded to form a self-clocking channel code which can be sent down a single channel. Skew caused by differences in propagation speed cannot then occur. The bit rate necessary is of the order of 200 Mbits/s, but this is easily accommodated by coaxial cable. Provided suitable equalization and termination is used, it may be possible to send such a signal over cables intended for analog video. A similar approach was pioneered in digital audio by the AES/EBU serial interface, which allowed digital audio to be transmitted down existing twisted-pair analog cabling.

The cabling savings implicit in such a system are obvious, but the electronic complexity of a serial interconnect is much greater, as high-speed multiplexers or shift registers are necessary at the transmitting end, and a phase-locked loop, data separator and deserializer are needed at the receiver to regenerate the parallel signal needed within the equipment. Although this increased complexity raises cost, it has to be offset against the saving in cabling. The availability of specialized chips will speed the acceptance of serial transmission.

A distinct advantage of serial transmission is that a matrix distribution unit is more easily realized. Where numerous pieces of video equipment need to be interconnected in various ways for different purposes, a crosspoint matrix is an obvious solution. With serial signals, only one switching element per signal is needed, whereas in a parallel system, a matrix would be unwieldy. A serial system has a potential disadvantage that the time distribution of bits within the block has to be closely defined, and, once standardized, it is extremely difficult to increase the wordlength if this is found to be necessary. The CCIR 8 bit system suffered from this problem and has been supplanted by a new serial standard which incorporates two extension bits which can be transmitted as zero in 8 bit applications, but allows 10 bit use if necessary. In a parallel interconnect, the word extension can be achieved by adding extra conductors alongside the existing bits, which is much easier.

The third interconnect to be considered uses fibre-optics. The advantages of this technology are numerous: the bandwidth of an optical fibre is staggering, as it is determined primarily by the speed of the light source and sensor, and it is possible to multiplex many digital TV signals down one cable, although the cost of the multiplexing circuitry would preclude this except for long distances. The optical transmission is immune to electromagnetic interference from other sources, nor does it contribute any. The cable can be made completely from insulating materials, so that ground loops cannot occur.

Drawbacks of fibre-optics are few. They do not like too many connectors in a given channel, as the losses at a connection are much greater than with an electrical plug and socket. It is preferable for the only breaks in the fibre to be at the transmitting and receiving points. For similar reasons, fibre-optics are less suitable for distribution, where one source feeds many destinations. The familiar loop-through connection of analog video is just not possible. The bidirectional open-collector or tri-state buses of electronic systems cannot be implemented with fibre-optics, nor is it easy to build a crosspoint matrix.

8.2 Component digital parallel interfacing

In 4:2:2 component digital video, luminance Y is sampled at 13.5 MHz, and the colour difference signals C_r and C_b are each sampled at 6.75 MHz.[1] Fig. 8.1(a) shows that this results in alternate co-sited samples and luminance-only samples. Multiplexing the colour difference samples into one channel then gives two channels both having a 13.5 MHz rate. If these are then interleaved, the entire signal can be carried as a 27 MHz parallel data stream. The word order will be:

C_b, Y, C_r, Y, etc.

In order to demultiplex the samples unambiguously, the first sample in an active line is always C_b.

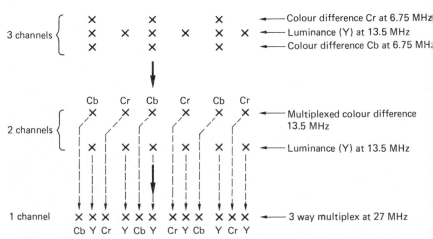

Figure 8.1 The colour difference sampling rate is one half that of luminance, but there are *two* colour difference signals Cr and C_b hence the colour difference data rate is equal to the luminance data rate, and a 27 MHz interleaved format is possible in a single channel

The sampling rate of 4:2:2 was chosen to allow an integer number of sample periods in the line periods of both 625/50 and 525/59.94 standards. The sampling rate is obtained from input video sync using a phase-locked loop which multiplies by 864 or 858. Since both of these numbers are even, the colour difference signals at half the sampling rate of luminance will also have an integer number of samples per line and will also form columns as in Fig. 8.1(b).

It is not necessary to digitize sync in component systems, since the sampling rate itself is derived from sync. The only useful data are generated during the active line. All that is necessary is to standardize the position of active line in terms of a sample count from sync.

Fig. 8.2 shows that in 625 line systems, the control system will wait for 132 sample periods before enabling the sampled output, and then 720 Y samples, 360 C_r samples and 360 C_b samples will be taken. A further 12 sample periods will elapse before the next sync edge, making $132 + 720 + 12 = 864$ sample periods.

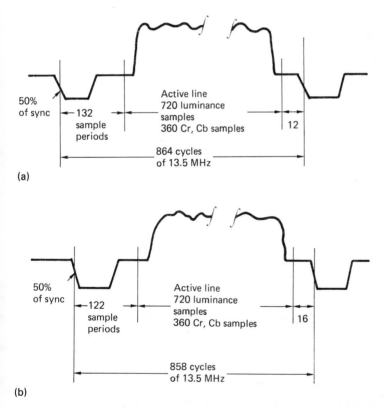

Figure 8.2 (a) In 625 line systems to CCIR-601, with 4:2:2 sampling, the sampling rate is exactly 864 times line rate, but only the active line is sampled, 132 sample periods after sync. (b) In 525 line systems to CCIR-601, with 4:2:2 sampling, the sampling rate is exactly 858 times line rate, but only the active line is sampled, 122 sample periods after sync. Note active line contains exactly the same quantity of data as for 50 Hz systems

In 525 line systems, the controller waits 122 sample periods before taking the same number of samples of active line. There will then be a further 16 sample periods before the next sync edge, making $122 + 720 + 16 = 858$ sample periods. The identical number of samples at an identical rate in both standards simplifies standards conversion. As the colour difference signals are multiplexed with the luminance at 27 MHz, there will be 1440 samples sent during the active line period.

In addition to specifying the position of active samples on the line, it is necessary to standardize the relationship between the gain of the analog video signals and the numerical range of the digital video so that all machines will interpret the numerical data in the same way.

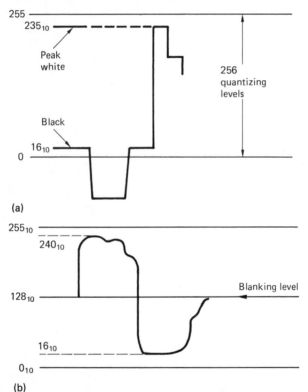

(a)

(b)

Figure 8.3 (a) The luminance signal fits into the quantizing range with a little allowance for excessive gain, here black is at 16_{10} and peak white is at 235_{10}. The sync pulse goes outside the quantizing range but this is of no consequence as it is not transmitted. (b) The colour difference signals use offset binary where blanking level is 128_{10}, and the peaks occur at 16_{10} and 240_{10} respectively

Fig. 8.3 shows how the Y signal fits into the quantizing range of an 8 bit system. Black is at a nominal level of 16_{10} and peak white is reached at 235_{10}. This allows some latitude for out-of-range signals.

The colour difference signals use offset binary, where 128_{10} is considered to be blanking level. The limits are reached at 16_{10} and 240_{10} respectively, again giving some latitude for excessive level. Note that the extreme levels of all zeros and all ones are reserved and cannot be allowed to result from video waveforms. These values are used for synchronizing in the interface. It will be seen that the Y signal fits into 220 quantizing intervals and the colour difference signals fit into 225 levels. This does not cause any difficulty, as the reference voltages of the respective converters are simply set to that ratio, and the correct gain can be obtained when the signal returns to the analog domain in the future. It will be necessary to allow for this difference if 4:2:2 is converted digitally to some other standard.

Since the analog sync pulses are not conveyed, the interface must produce an equivalent. Horizontal and vertical timing for the destination are provided by synchronizing patterns.

Immediately before the start of active video is the SAV (start of active video) pattern, and immediately after is the EAV (end of active video) pattern. These unique patterns occur on every line, and continue through the vertical interval.

Each synchronizing pattern consists of four samples. The first sample value is all ones and the next two are all zeros. These codes are reserved and cannot appear in active video, so there is no possibility of the receiver interpreting video as a spurious sync pattern. The fourth sample in each sync pattern is a data byte, which contains three data bits, H, F and V. These bits are protected by four redundancy bits which form a Hamming codeword for the purpose of correcting errors. The subject of Hamming code was treated in Chapter 7.

It will be seen in Fig. 8.4(a) that the data bits have the following meanings:

H is used to distinguish between SAV, where it is set to 0, and EAV, where it is set to 1.

F defines the state of interlace and is 0 during the first field and 1 during the second field. F is only allowed to change at EAV.

V is 1 during vertical blanking, and 0 during the active part of the field. It can only change at EAV.

Fig. 8.4(b) shows the relationship of the sync patterns to 625 line timing, and below can be seen the equivalent for 525 lines. In 625 lines, there will be 288 active lines in both fields, whereas in 525 lines, there are 244 active lines in field one and 243 lines in field two.

Since only the active line is transmitted, there is spare transmission

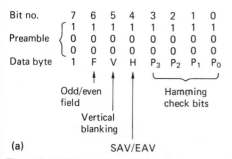

(a)   SAV/EAV

Figure 8.4(a) The four byte synchronizing pattern which precedes and follows every active line sample block has this structure

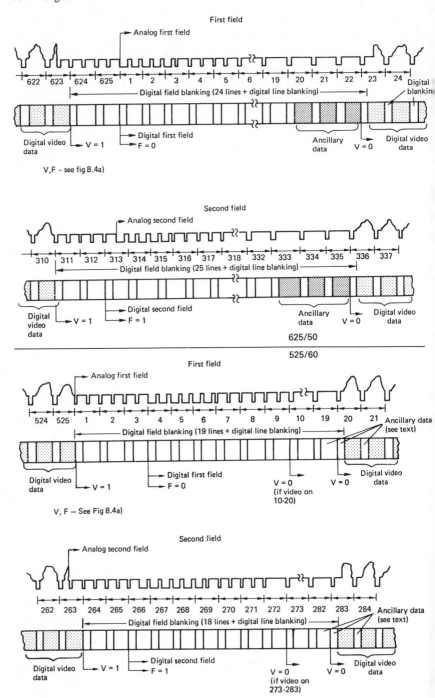

Figure 8.4 (*Continued*) (b) The relationships between analog video timing and the information in the digital timing reference signals for 625/50 (above) and 525/60 (below)

capacity in the interface. The two line standards differ considerably on how this is used. In 625 lines, only the active line period may be used on lines 20 to 22 and 333 to 335[2]. Lines 20 and 333 are reserved for equipment self-testing. In each case 1440 bytes may be conveyed per line. In 525 lines, ancillary data may be placed anywhere there is no video, either during horizontal blanking, vertical blanking or both.[3]

Since the all-ones and all-zero values are reserved for synchronizing, the ancillary data cannot be allowed to assume those values. Only 7 bits of the word can be ancillary data because the eighth bit is redundancy which makes the whole word odd parity. Since all zeros and all ones are both even parity, the accidental generation of sync is precluded. At the time of writing, the remainder of the ancillary data format had not been defined.

The electrical interface is the same as for D-2, and is described in Section 8.6.

8.3 Composite digital interface

Composite digital samples at four times the subcarrier frequency, and so there will be major differences between the standards. Unlike 4:2:2, which only transmits the active line, the composite digital interface is continuously operating and transmits syncs and burst as well, so there is no ancillary data option.[4] The PAL and NTSC versions of the composite digital interface will be described separately. The electrical interface is identical to that of the 4:2:2 standard and is described in Section 8.6.

8.4 PAL composite digital interface

In composite video, chroma phase is of paramount importance, and in PAL, the composite digital interface samples at $4 \times F_{sc}$ with sample phase aligned with burst phase. PAL burst swing results in burst phases of $\pm 135°$, and samples are taken at these phases and at $\pm 45°$, precisely half-way between the U and V axes. Chapter 4 showed how this was useful for colour processing.

The quantizing range of digital PAL is shown in Fig. 8.5. Note that the whole of the analog signal fits into the range. This is necessary because chroma can go above white or below black. In an 8 bit system, blanking level will be 64_{10}.

Fig. 8.6 shows how the sampling clock may be derived. The incoming sync is used to derive a burst gate, during which the samples of burst are analysed. If the clock is correctly phased, the sampled burst will give values of 95_{10}, 64_{10}, 32_{10}, 64_{10}, repeated, whereas if a phase error exists, the values at the burst crossings will be above or below 64_{10}. The difference between the sample values and blanking level can be used to drive a DAC which controls the sampling VCO. In this way any phase errors in the ADC are eliminated, because the sampling clock will automatically servo its phase to be identical to digital burst. Burst swing causes the burst-peak and burst-crossing samples to change places, so a phase comparison is always

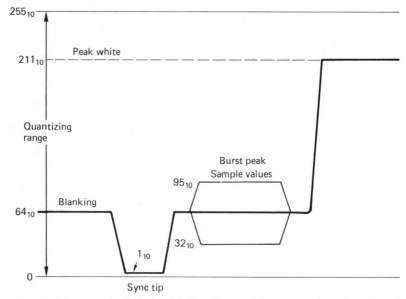

Figure 8.5 The composite PAL signal fits into the quantizing range as shown here. Note that there is sufficient range to allow the instantaneous voltage to exceed that of peak white in the presence of saturated bright colours. Values shown are decimal equivalents in a ten or eight bit system. In a ten bit system the additional two bits increase resolution, not magnitude, so they are below the radix point and the decimal equivalent is unchanged. D-2 PAL samples in phase with burst, so the values shown are on the burst peaks and are thus also the values of the envelope

possible during burst. The sample numbers are also shown in Fig. 8.6, sample zero always being at the start of active line.

In PAL, the subcarrier frequency contains a 25 Hz offset, and so $4 \times F_{sc}$ will contain a 100 Hz offset. The sampling rate is not h-coherent, and the sampling structure is not orthogonal. As subcarrier is given by

$$F_{sc} = 283\frac{3}{4} \times F_h + 25\,\text{Hz}$$

there will be 1135 samples per line, with an additional four sample periods spread over the frame, making a total of 709 379 samples per frame.

Since sampling is not h-coherent, the position of sync pulses will change relative to the sampling points from line to line. The relationship can also be changed by the ScH phase of the analog input. Zero ScH is defined as coincidence between sync and zero degrees of subcarrier phase at line one of field one. Since composite digital samples on burst phase, not on subcarrier phase, the definition of zero ScH will be as shown in Fig. 8.6, where it will be seen that two samples occur at exactly equal distances either side of the 50% sync point. If the input is not zero ScH, the samples conveying sync will have different values. It will be seen in Chapter 11 that this is not a problem because the D-2 DVTR does not record sync and will regenerate zero ScH syncs on replay. It is most important that samples are

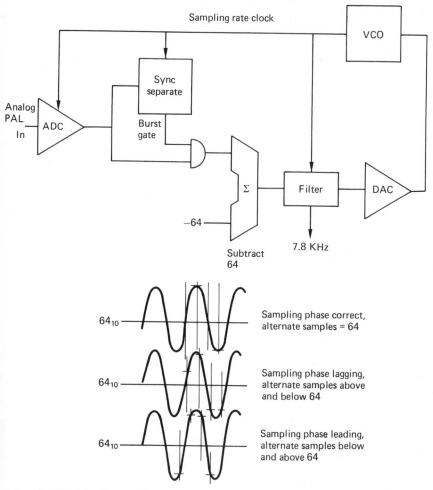

Figure 8.6 Obtaining the sampling clock in PAL D-2. The values obtained by sampling burst are analysed. When phase is correct, burst will be sampled at zero crossing and sample value will be 64_{10} or blanking level. If phase is wrong, sample will be above or below blanking. Filter must ignore alternate samples at burst peaks and shift one sample every line to allow for burst swing. It also averages over several burst crossings to reduce jitter. Filter output drives DAC and thus controls sampling clock VCO

taken exactly at the points specified, since any residual phase error in the sampling clock will cause the equivalent of a chroma phase error when the samples are added to other samples in a switcher.

8.5 NTSC composite digital interface

Although they have some similarities, PAL and NTSC are quite different when analysed at the digital sample level.

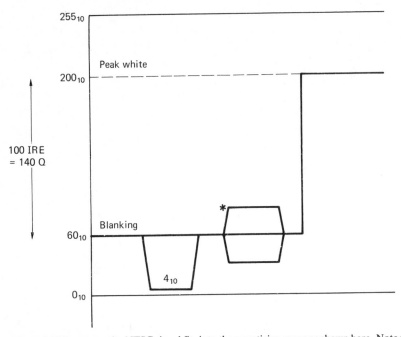

Figure 8.7 The composite NTSC signal fits into the quantizing range as shown here. Note that there is sufficient range to allow the instantaneous voltage to exceed peak white in the presence of saturated, bright colours. Values shown are decimal equivalents in a ten or eight-bit system. In a ten-bit system the additional two bits increase resolution, not magnitude, so they are below the radix point and the decimal equivalent is unchanged. *Note that unlike PAL, NTSC D-2 does not sample on burst phase and so values during burst are not shown here. See Figure 8.8 for burst sample details

Fig. 8.7 shows how the NTSC waveform fits into the quantizing structure. Blanking is at 60_{10} in an 8 bit system, and peak white is at 200_{10}, so that 1 IRE unit is the equivalent of $1.4Q$.

Subcarrier in NTSC has an exact half line offset, so there will be an integer number of cycles of subcarrier in two lines. F_{sc} is simply $227.5 \times F_h$, and as sampling is at $4 \times F_{sc}$, there will be $227.5 \times 4 = 910$ samples per line period, and the sampling will be orthogonal.

As with PAL, the sampling phase is chosen to facilitate decoding in the digital domain. In NTSC there is a phase shift of 57° between subcarrier and the $B-Y$ axis, and burst is simply a piece of the subcarrier waveform. Composite digital NTSC does not sample in phase with subcarrier/burst, but at 57°, 147°, 237° and 327° of subcarrier, exactly as an NTSC decoder would. As a result, filtering off luminance will leave chroma samples which contain alternately $B-Y$ and $R-Y$.

Fig. 8.8 shows how this approach works in relation to sync and burst. Zero ScH is defined as zero degrees of subcarrier at the 50% point on sync, but the 57° sampling phase means that the sync edge is actually sampled 25.6 ns ahead of, and 44.2 ns after the 50% point. Similarly, when the burst is reached, the phase shift means that burst-sample values will be 46_{10}, 83_{10}, 74_{10} and 37_{10} repeating. The phase-locked loop which produces the

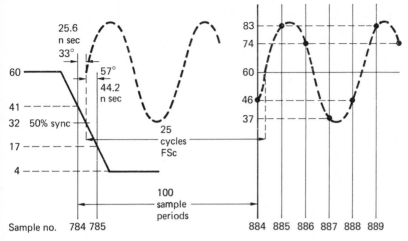

Figure 8.8 NTSC D-2 Sc-H phase. Sampling is not performed in phase with burst, but on the R-Y and B-Y axes to aid decoding. Since in NTSC there is a phase angle of 57° between subcarrier and B-Y, this will also be the phase at which burst samples are taken. If Sc-H is zero, then phase of subcarrier taken at 50% sync will be zero. 25 cycles or 100 samples later, during burst, the sample values shown here will be obtained

sampling clock will digitally compare the samples of burst with the values given here. Since it is not sampling burst at a zero crossing, the slope will be slightly less, so the gain of the phase error detector will also be less and more prone to burst noise than in the PAL process. The phase error can, however, be averaged over several burst samples to overcome this problem.

The diagram shows sample numbers which, as for PAL, start at zero at the beginning of the active line. Again, if the analog input does not have zero ScH phase, the sync pulse values will change, but burst values will not. The D-2 recorder does not record sync and will regenerate zero ScH syncs on replay.

8.6 The parallel electrical interface

The same electrical and mechanical interface is used for 4:2:2 and composite working,[3-5] although clearly it is not possible to connect one to the other directly. Each signal in the interface is carried by a balanced pair using ECL drive levels. As Fig. 8.9 shows, there are eight signal pairs and two spares, so that a 10 bit word can be accommodated. The spare signals are used to add bits at the least significant end of the word. A separate clock and a number of grounding and shielding pins complete the connection. A 25 pin D-type connector to ISO 2110-1980 is specified. Equipment always has female connectors, cables always have male connectors. Connector latching is by screw locks, with suitable posts provided on the female connector.

Pin no.	Function		Pin no.	Function	
1	Clock +		14	Clock −	
2	System ground		15	System ground	
3	Data 7 (MSB) +		16	Data 7 (MSB) −	
4	Data 6 +		17	Data 6 −	
5	Data 5 +		18	Data 5 −	
6	Data 4 +		19	Data 4 −	
7	Data 3 +		20	Data 3 −	
8	Data 2 +		21	Data 2 −	
9	Data 1 +		22	Data 1 −	
10	Data 0 +		23	Data 0 −	
11	Data −1 + ⎫ Ten-bit		24	Data −1 − ⎫ Ten-bit	
12	Data −2 + ⎭ systems only		25	Data −2 − ⎭ systems only	
13	Cable shield				

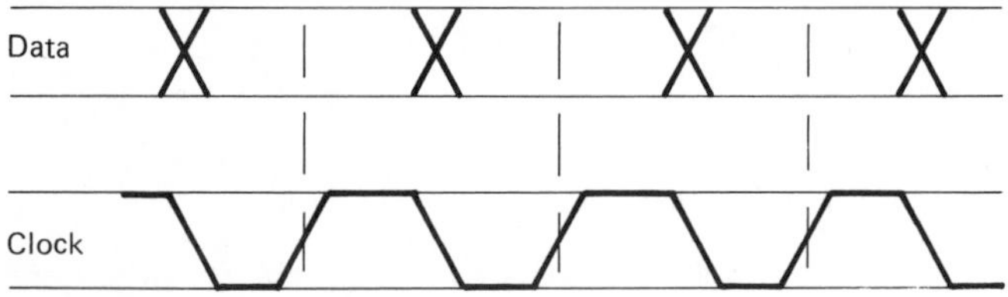

Figure 8.9 In the parallel interface there is capacity for ten bit words plus a clock where each signal is differential. In eight bit systems DATA −1 and DATA −2 are not used. Clock transition takes place in the centre of a data bit cell as shown below

Fig. 8.9 also shows the relationship between the clock and the data. A positive-going clock edge is used to sample the signal lines after the level has settled between transitions. In 4:2:2, the clock will be line synchronous 27 MHz, irrespective of the line standard, whereas in composite digital the clock will be four times the frequency of PAL or NTSC subcarrier.

8.7 Component serial interfaces

These serial interfaces allows transmission of 4:2:2 component digital over 75Ω coaxial cable. There are two alternative approaches which are not compatible. The CCIR standard [5,6] uses a form of group coding requiring lookup tables to convert each 8 bit sample into a 9 bit code for transmission, and to reconvert on reception.

Group coding is a channel code, and the 8/9 code of this interface was described in Chapter 6. Longer wordlengths are not possible in this standard.

Fig. 8.10 shows the major components necessary in a serial link. Parallel input data at 27 MHz to CCIR 601/RP125 having 8 bit wordlength are used to address a PROM, or gate array, which is programmed to output a unique 9 bit channel pattern for each 8 bit input. These channel patterns are parallel loaded into a shift register, which is clocked at nine times the input data rate. This 243 MHz clock is produced from the input word clock in a phase-locked loop. The serial data are sent to a driver and on to the coaxial cable.

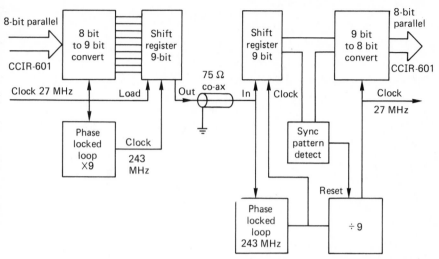

Figure 8.10 The major components necessary for a CCIR standard 8-bit serial link. Incoming data bytes are converted to 9-bit symbols which are clocked out of a shift register serially by a 243 MHz clock obtained from input 27 MHz. On reception a 243 MHz PLL locks to the data and produces a clock. When the sync pattern is seen, the divide by 9 counter is re-phased to correctly grab 9-bit symbols from the shift register which are then re-converted to 8 bits

The receiver has a number of tasks. First, it must lock to the bit rate of the transmission and generate a local 243 MHz clock in a phase-locked loop. This is made easier by the use of 9 bit channel patterns, since these will have more frequent transitions than would be present in raw data. Secondly, the beginning of the 9 bit sequence must be identified, so that the channel patterns are correctly presented for decoding. This is done by detecting the all-zero preamble in the timing reference bytes. These are coded to a 9 bit channel pattern which is unique in that it contains a run length of 7 bits without a transition (011111110 or 100000001) which cannot occur in any valid data code. The receiver can detect this pattern with a decoder which is connected to the parallel outputs of the shift register. When the sync pattern is detected, it will reset a divide-by-nine counter which runs from the received bit rate and clocks 9 bit channel patterns into the decoding PROM or gate array. This 27 MHz clock will also become the parallel word clock.

The receiver may also then detect the timing reference signals and check the validity of the Hamming coded data.

8.8 Scrambled serial interface

The CCIR serial interface is defined only for component signals and only supports 8 bit wordlength.

The alternative approach described here has been developed to allow up to 10 bit samples of component or composite digital video to be communicated serially.[7]

342

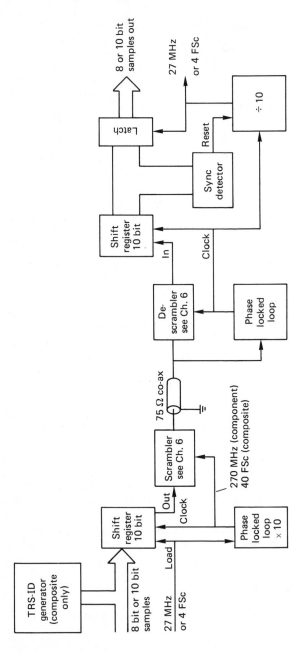

Figure 8.11 Major components of a serial scrambled link. Input samples are converted to serial form in a shift register clocked at ten times the sample rate. The serial data are then scrambled for transmission. On reception, a phase locked loop re-creates the bit rate clock and drives the de-scrambler and serial to parallel conversion. On detection of the sync pattern, the divide-by-ten counter is re-phased to correctly load parallel samples into the latch. For composite working the bit rate will be 40 times subcarrier, and a sync pattern generator (top left) is needed to inject TRS-ID into the D-2 data stream – see Figure 8.12 for TRS-ID detail

Scrambling, or pseudo-random coding, uses the concepts introduced in Chapter 6. The serial interface uses convolutional coding, which is simpler to implement in a cable installation because no separate synchronizing of the randomizing is needed.

The components necessary for a component serial link are shown in Fig. 8.11. Parallel data according to CCIR 601/RP125 having a wordlength of up to 10 bits form the input. These are fed to a 10 bit shift register which is clocked at ten times the input rate, or 270 MHz. If there are less than 10 bits in the input words, the missing bits are forced to zero for transmission. The serial data from the shift register are then passed through the scrambler, which produces the exclusive–OR of a given bit and 2 bits which are five and nine clocks ahead. This is followed by another stage, which converts channel ones into transitions. The resulting signal can be fed down 75 Ω coaxial cable using BNC connectors.

The receiver must generate a bit clock at 270 MHz from the input signal, and this clock drives a circuit which simply reverses the scrambling at the transmitter. The first stage returns transitions to ones, and the second stage is a mirror image of the encoder which reverses the exclusive–OR calculation to output the original data. It is necessary to obtain word synchronization, and this is done by detecting the all-ones and all-zero patterns in the timing reference signal. On detection, a divide-by-ten circuit is reset, and this will clock words out of the shift register at the correct times, to become the output word clock.

For composite working, the input will be up to 10 bit words at $4F_{sc}$. The D-2 composite digital parallel interconnect is, however, continuous, as syncs and burst are carried as well as active line, so there is no equivalent of the timing reference signal of 4:2:2. It is necessary to create one, so that the reciever can get into word synchronization on the serial data.

This signal is called TRS-ID and consists of five words which are inserted just after the leading edge of video sync. The first four are for synchronizing and are a single word of all ones, followed by three words of all zeros. The fifth word is for identification and carries line and field numbering information shown in Fig. 8.12. In PAL the field numbering will go from zero to seven, whereas in NTSC it will only reach three.

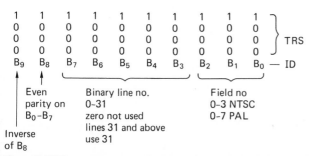

Figure 8.12 The contents of the TRS-ID pattern which is added to the transmission during the horizontal sync pulse just after the leading edge. The field number conveys the composite colour framing field count, and the line number carries a restricted line count intended to give vertical positioning information during the vertical interval. This count saturates at 31 for lines of that number and above

It is also possible to merge four channels of digital audio with the scrambled serial interface, and this is described in Chapter 13.

References

1. CCIR Recommendation 601-1
2. EBU Doc. Tech. 3246
3. SMPTE RP 125
4. Ampex Corporation, Ampex digital format for video and audio tape recording of composite video signals using 19 mm type D-2 cassette (1988)
5. CCIR Recommendation 656
6. EBU Doc. Tech. 3247
7. Proposed American National Standard, Serial digital interface for 10 bit 4:2:2 component and NTSC composite digital signals

Chapter 9

Rotary-head Tape Transports

There is more to digital video recording than electronics. It depends heavily on mechanical engineering of the highest quality and several extraordinarily accurate servo systems. This chapter looks at the techniques necessary to build and control a rotary-head transport.

9.1 Why rotary heads?

The helical scan tape deck has more in common with the helicopter than just the geometrical terminology. The rotary-head recorder is to the fixed-head recorder what the rotary-winged flying machine is to the fixed-wing machine.

In both cases the rotary machine is more complex, more expensive, consumes more power, needs more maintenance and adjustment, and makes more noise than its fixed counterpart. If these were our only criteria, this comparison would amount to a condemnation. The truth of the matter is that all of these characteristics have to be accepted in order to obtain one particular attribute which cannot be obtained in any other way. In the case of the helicopter, the ability to stop dead in mid-air is vital for many applications. In the case of the helical recorder, the attribute obtained is the ability to record exceptional bandwidths with high density and to replay at varying speed. If these are the requirements, there is no competition from simpler hardware. The problems have to be overcome by matching each one with the appropriate mechanical design, materials and control systems.

The attractions of the helical recorder are that the head-to-tape speed and hence bandwidth are high, whereas the linear tape speed is not. The space between tracks is determined by the linear tape speed, not by multitrack head technology. Chapter 6 showed how rotary-head machines make better use of the tape area, particularly if azimuth recording is used. The high head speed raises the frequency of offtape signals, and since output is proportional to frequency, playback signals are raised above head noise even with very narrow tracks.

9.2 Helical geometry

Fig. 9.1 shows the two fundamental approaches to helical scan. In the rotating upper drum system, one or more heads are mounted on the periphery of a revolving drum or scanner. The fixed base of the scanner carries a helical ramp in the form of a step (see inset) or, for greater wear resistance, a hardened band which is suitably attached. Alternatively, both top and bottom of the scanner are fixed and the headwheel turns in a slot between them. Both approaches have advantages and disadvantages. The rotating upper drum approach is simpler to manufacture than the fixed upper drum, because the latter requires to be rigidly and accurately cantilevered out over the headwheel. The rotating part of the scanner will produce an air film which raises its effective diameter. The rotor will thus need to be made slightly smaller than the lower drum, so that the tape sees a constant diameter as it rises up the scanner. There will be plenty of space inside the rotor to install individually replaceable heads.

The fixed upper drum approach requires less power, since there is less air resistance. The headwheel acts as a centrifugal pump and supplies air to the periphery of the slot where it lubricates both upper and lower drums, which are of the same diameter. This approach gives head contact which is more consistent over the length of the track, but it makes the provision of replaceable heads more difficult, and it is generally necessary to replace the entire headwheel as an assembly.

In both cases, a pair of fixed guides, known as the entry and exit guides, lead the tape to and from the ramp. The tape may wrap around the scanner by various amounts. Some early machines used a complete circuit around the scanner which led the tape to cross itself in the so-called Alpha wrap. The C-format uses almost a complete circuit of the scanner where the tape turns sharply around the entrance and exit guides in the shape of an Omega. The tape may only pass half-way around the scanner in a U-shape, hence the name U-matic. The total angle of scanner rotation for which the heads touch the tape is called the *wrap angle*.

The scanner can rotate either with or against the direction of linear tape motion; turning against is more common in professional machines. It will be evident that as the tape is caused to climb up the scanner axis by the ramp, it actually takes on the path of a helix. The head rotates in a circular path, and so will record diagonal tracks across the width of the tape. So it is not really the scanning which is helical, it is the tape path. If the tape is stationary, the head will constantly retrace the same track, and the angle of the track can be calculated by measuring the rise of the tape along the scanner axis and the circumferential distance over which this rise takes place. The latter can be obtained from the diameter of the scanner and the wrap angle. The tangent of the *helix angle* is given by the rise over the distance. It can also be obtained by measuring the distance along the ramp corresponding to the wrap angle; this dimension will give the sine of the helix angle.

When the tape moves, the angle between the tracks and the edge of the tape will not be the helix angle. Fig. 9.2 shows how this occurs. When the head contact commences, the tape will be at a given location, but when the head contact ceases, the tape will have moved a certain linear distance. To

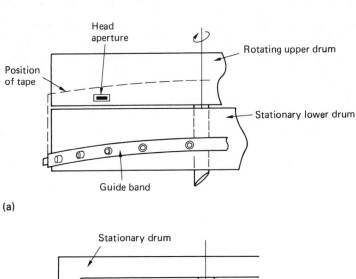

(a)

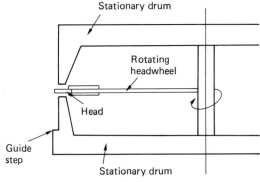

(b)

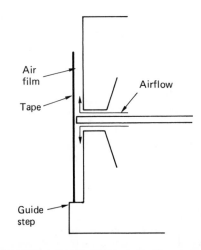

(c)

Figure 9.1 (a) Rotating top type scanner. The upper drum is slightly smaller than the lower drum due to the air film it develops. Helical band guides lower edge of tape. (b) Stationary top scanner, where headwheel rotates in a slot between upper and lower drums. (c) Airflow in stationary top scanner. Headwheel acts as a centrifugal pump, producing air film between tape and drums

obtain the *track angle* it is necessary to take into account the tape motion.

The length of the track resulting from scanning a stationary tape, which will be at the helix angle, can be resolved into two distances at right angles as shown in Fig. 9.2. One of these is across the tape width while the other is along the length of the tape. The tangent of the helix angle will be the ratio of these lengths. If the length along the tape is corrected by adding or subtracting the distance the tape moves during one scan, depending upon whether tape motion aids or opposes scanner rotation, the new ratio of the lengths will be the tangent of the track angle. In practice this process will often be reversed, because it is the track angle which is standardized, and the transport designer has to find a helix angle which will produce it.

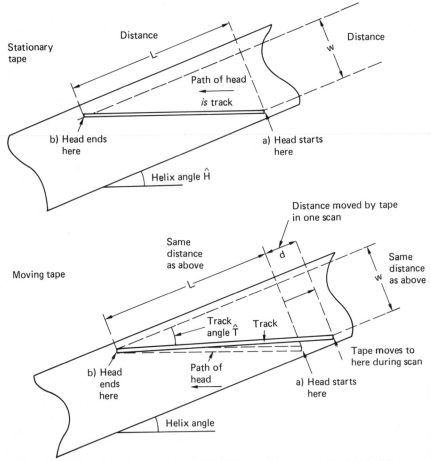

Figure 9.2 When the tape is moving the track laid down will be at an angle which is different from the helix angle, because the tape is in a different place at the end of the scan than at the beginning. Track length can be considered as two components L and w for stationary case, and L + d and w for moving case.

Hence $\dfrac{w}{L} = \tan \hat{H}$ and $\dfrac{w}{L + d} = \tan \hat{T}$

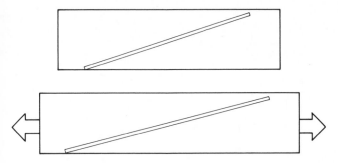

Figure 9.3 Tape is flexible, so change of tension will result in change of length. This causes a change in track angle known as skew shown exaggerated here

Provided that the tape linear speed and scanner speed remain the same, the theoretical track angle will remain the same. In practice this will only be the case if the tape tension is constant. Fig. 9.3 shows that if the back tension changes, the effective length of the tape will also change, and with it the track angle, a phenomenon known as *skew*. All helical scan recorders need some form of tape tension servo to maintain the tape tension around the scanner constant irrespective of the size of the pack on the supply hub. In practice, tension servos can only control the tension of the tape entering the scanner. Since there will be friction between the tape and the scanner, the tape tension will gradually increase between the entrance and exit guides, and so the tape will be extended more towards the exit guide. When the tape subsequently relaxes, it will be found that the track is actually curved. The ramp can be made to deviate from a theoretical helix to counteract this effect, or all scanners can be built to the same design, so that effectively the track curvature becomes part of the format. Another possibility is to use some form of embedded track-following system, or a system like azimuth recording which tolerates residual tracking errors.

When the tape direction reverses, the sense of the friction in the scanner will also reverse, so the back tension has to increase to keep the average tension the same as when going forward.

When verifying the track angle produced by a new design, it is usual to develop a tape which it has recorded with magnetic fluid and take measurements under a travelling microscope. With the very small track widths of digital recorders, it is usually necessary to compensate for skew by applying standard tension to the tape when it is being measured, or by computing a correction factor for the track angle from the modulus of elasticity of the tape.

The *track pitch* is the distance, measured at right angles to the tracks, from a given place on one track to the same place on the next. The track pitch is a function of the linear tape speed, the head passing frequency and the helix angle. It can be seen in Fig. 9.4 that the linear speed and the helix angle determine the rise rate up the scanner axis, and the knowledge of the rotational period of the scanner will allow the rise in one revolution to be calculated. If the rise is divided by the number of active heads on the scanner, the result will be the track pitch. If everything else remains equal,

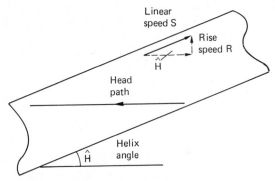

Figure 9.4 The linear speed of the tape S can be resolved into the speed of the tape along the scanner axis which is the rise speed R. R = S sinĤ. Dividing the Rise Speed by the Head Passing Frequency gives the track pitch. Head passing frequency is simply the number of heads multiplied by the scanner rotational frequency. Thus track pitch is proportional to tape speed

the track pitch is proportional to the linear tape speed. Note that the track angle will also change with tape speed.

Fig. 9.5 shows that in guard band recording, the track pitch is equal to the width of the track plus the width of the guard band. The track width is determined by the width of the head poles, and the linear tape speed will be high enough so that the desired guard band is obtained.

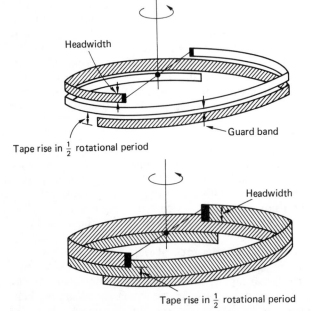

Figure 9.5 (a) Where tape rise is more than head width, a guard band between the tracks results. (b) Where tape rise is less than head width, overwrite takes place and the tracks are narrower than the heads. Shown here for 2 headed scanner, the minimum configuration for azimuth recording

In azimuth recording the reverse situation is used. The head width is greater than the track pitch, so that the tape does not rise far enough for one track to clear the previous one. Part of the previous track will be overwritten, so that the track width and the track pitch become identical.

The length of the track laid on the tape is a function of the scanner diameter and the wrap angle. Fig. 9.6 shows a number of ways in which the same length of track can be put on the tape.

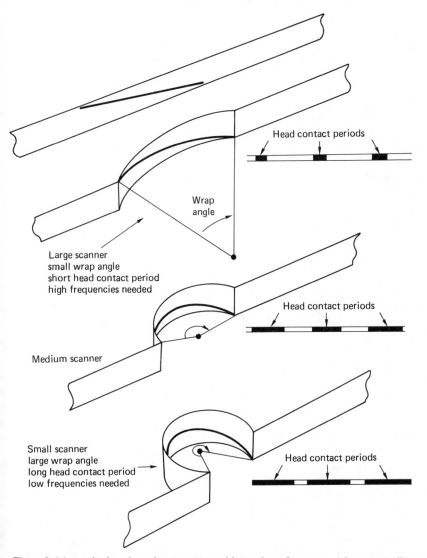

Figure 9.6 A standard track can be put on tape with a variety of scanners. A large wrap allows the lowest frequencies at the head but increases complexity of threading mechanism and increases tape path friction. The helix angle will be different in each case in order to match the tape rise speed to the head peripheral speed – giving the same track angle

A small scanner with a large wrap angle works just as well as a large scanner with a small wrap angle. If the tape speed, and hence the track rate, is constant, and for the purposes of this comparison the number of heads on the scanners remains constant, the heads on the smaller scanner will take a longer time to traverse the track than the heads on the larger scanner. This means that the helix angle will need to be different so that the same track angle is achieved in all cases. In practice, a larger scanner can be used to mount more heads which work in turn, so that the scanner speed will then be less than before. Alternatively the space inside the larger scanner may be used to incorporate track-following heads. Another advantage of the large scanner is that the reduced wrap angle is easier to thread up. A small scanner is attractive for a portable machine since it is compact and requires less power. The greater wrap angle has to be accepted.

The different scanner sizes in the example of Fig. 9.6 traced standard tracks in different periods of time, as shown in the diagram. In analog recorders such as the C-format and U-matic, the time period had to be one television field so that the television waveform could be directly fed to the heads, and design of the scanner was extremely inflexible.

Using time compression, the actual duration of the head sweep and the real time in the recording which it represents are independent. The principle can be used in both analog and digital recorders. Component camcorders time-compress the colour difference signals to record both sequentially on one track. Consumer machines such as Betamovie and Compact VHS use time compression so that real-time video can be recorded with a smaller than usual scanner for portable applications.

In the digital domain there is even more freedom. The video frame is expressed by a given number of samples, and as long as these appear on replay in the right sequence, their actual position in the recording or the exact time at which they were recorded is of no consequence. Clearly the record and replay processes must complement one another.

9.3 Segmentation

The number of bits to be recorded for one field will be a direct result of the sampling scheme chosen. The minimum wavelength which can be reliably recorded will then determine the length of track that is necessary.

With 4:2:2 sampling, and allowing for redundancy and the presence of the digital audio, there will be about 4.5 Mbits in one field for 50 Hz and about 3.75 Mbits for 60 Hz. With $4 \times F_{sc}$ composite sampling, the figures will be about 3 Mbits and 2 Mbits per field respectively.

Since current wavelengths are restricted to about $0.9 \mu m$ (which records 2 bits) then the track lengths needed will be about 2 metres for 4:2:2 and 1 metre for composite (50 Hz) or about 1.7 metres and 1.1 metres (60 Hz). Clearly no one in their right mind is going to design a scanner large enough to put the whole of one field on one track. A further consideration is that current head technology does not permit operation at a high enough frequency to pass all the data through one head. Eddy current losses in the head get worse at high frequencies.

The solution to both problems is *segmentation* where the data for one field are recorded in a number of head sweeps. With segmentation it is easy to share the data between more than one head. In the D-1 format four heads are necessary, whereas in D-2 two heads are necessary, and the formats reflect these restrictions.

With segmentation, the contents of a field can be divided into convenient-sized pieces for recording. This allows the width of the tape to be chosen. If the tape is wide, then tracks of a given length can be placed at a greater angle to the edge of the tape, and so the tape will move more slowly for a given track rate. This means that the effective rewinding time will be reduced because a given recording will occupy a shorter length of tape. Taken to extremes, this would result in very wide tape on small reels.

This is not the only criterion, however. A wide tape needs a physically larger scanner assembly and requires greater precision in guidance. It is seldom possible to engineer a tape transport with total precision, so the tape will always be expected to accommodate small inaccuracies by flexing. The stiffness of the tape against bending in its own plane is proportional to the moment of inertia of its cross-section. This rises as the cube of tape width. The selection of a narrower tape will ease transport accuracy requirements slightly. The final factor to be considered is the recording density. A high-density recording requires less tape area per unit time, and so the effective rewinding speed will be proportional to the recording density. Consideration of these factors led to the choice of ¾ inch wide tape for the digital video cassette. The choice was basically between that and 1 inch tape, since the choice of a non-standard width would have unnecessarily raised the cost of the medium as existing slitters could not have been used.

Having chosen the tape width, the number of segments per field can be established. A large number of short, steep tracks will give the same overall track length as a smaller number of long, shallow tracks. For normal speed operation, there is little difference between the two approaches, but for variable speed, the smaller the number of segments the better, since the magnitude of head jumps will be reduced.

The actual segmentation techiques used in D-1 and D-2 will be discussed in the appropriate chapters.

9.4 Head configurations

There is some freedom in the positioning of heads in the scanner. Fig. 9.7 shows a scanner which carries four heads spaced evenly around the periphery. All of the heads are at the same height on the scanner axis, which means that they would all pass the same point in space as the scanner rotates.

One revolution of such a scanner would lay down four evenly spaced tracks on the tape and would play them back equally well. With a wrap angle of 180°, two heads would be in contact with the tape at any one time, and so the data rate of an individual head will be half the total.

If it is necessary to play back at variable speed, each of the heads will need to be movable and will need to be individually controlled, so the cost

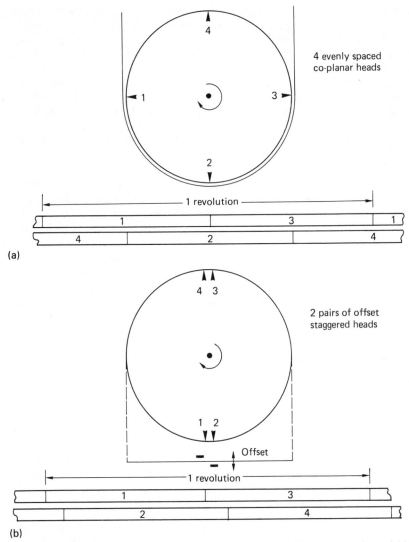

(a)

(b)

Figure 9.7 (a) Evenly spaced heads in a single plane require individual actuators for variable speed. (b) Two of the heads are slid along the tape track to give pairs of offset-staggered heads. Same tape format results if signal timing to heads is suitably modified

of implementation will be rather high. An alternative approach is shown in Fig. 9.7(b) where the heads are mounted in pairs at 180°. The same tape format can be recorded, provided that the heads in each pair are mounted in different planes. The separation between the head planes depends on the track pitch and the angular separation between the heads. If this geometry is correct, the same format will result, but the time at which the various tracks are laid down will be different, as the figure shows. No problem will arise provided that the record and reproduce electronics are designed to expect to transfer data at the appropriate time. The main advantage of this approach is that there is now only a requirement for two head positioners, which is a great improvement over four. The elimination of two head positioners is a great simplification of the scanner, but it means that one of the advantages of azimuth recording is lost.

Consider an azimuth recording scanner with four evenly spaced heads. The track width depends on the scanner speed and the linear tape speed, since this determines the amount by which one head overwrites the track of the previous head. Clearly all tracks will have the same width. In D-2 it is necessary to have different scanner speeds in PAL and NTSC, yet the tape speed remains the same, requiring the tracks to become narrower. With four evenly spaced heads, this would be achieved by simply changing the scanner speed. However, if two pairs of heads are to be used, changing the scanner speed results in an asymmetrical overwrite pattern, where there will be alternating narrow and wide tracks. For this reason the PAL and NTSC D-2 machines using head pairs will need different head assemblies with slightly different offset between the heads in the pair. Since there will be other differences between PAL and NTSC machines due not least to their respective chroma systems, this is a small loss.

The stagger between the heads is necessary whether the heads are intended for azimuth recording or guard band recording. In both cases the head is physically larger than the track it writes, owing to the poles being milled away in the area of the gap. It is not possible to put the heads side by side without a large guard band resulting. Fig. 9.8 shows that staggering the heads allows the guard band to be any size, even negative in azimuth applications.

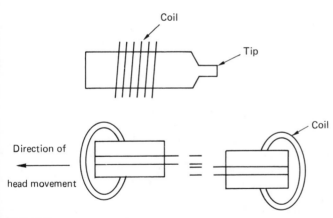

Figure 9.8

Since the diagonal tracks will begin in slightly different places along the tape, it is possible to stagger the heads by the same amount so that both heads will transfer data from their respective tracks at an identical time. The bit error rate from the trailing head of a staggered head pair is generally slightly worse than that of the leading head because it is working in the shock wave pattern set up by the first head and flies over any particles of debris which the first head loosens.

9.5 The basic rotary-head transport

Fig. 9.9 shows the important components of a rotary-head helical scan tape transport. There are four servo systems which must correctly interact to obtain all modes of operation: two reel servos, the scanner servo and the capstan servo. The capstan and reel servos together move the tape, and the scanner servo moves the heads. For variable-speed operation a further servo system will be necessary to deflect the heads.

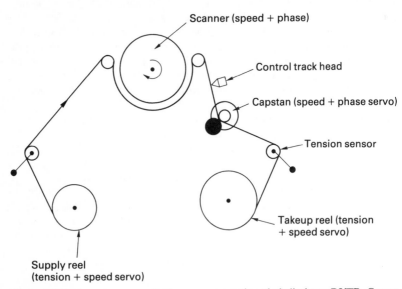

Figure 9.9 The four servos essential for proper operation of a helical scan DVTR. Cassette based units will also require loading and threading servos, and for variable speed a track following servo will be necessary

There are two approaches to capstan drive – those which use a pinch roller and those which do not. In a pinch roller drive, the tape is held against the capstan by pressure from a resilient roller which is normally pulled towards the capstan by a solenoid. The capstan only drives the tape over a narrow speed range, generally the range in which broadcastable pictures are required. Outside this range, the pinch roller retracts, the tape will be driven by reel motors alone, and the reel motors will need to change their operating mode.

In a pinch-roller-less transport, the tape is wrapped some way around a relatively large capstan to give a good area of contact. A drilled capstan connected to a suction pump can also be used to obtain extra adhesion. The tape is always in contact with the capstan, irrespective of operating mode, and so the reel servos never need to change mode. A large capstan has to be used to give sufficient contact area and to permit high shuttle speed without excessive motor rev/min. This means that at play speed it will be turning slowly and must be accurately controlled and free from cogging. A multipole ironless-rotor pancake-type brush motor is often used, or a sinusoidal-drive brushless motor.

The simplest operating mode to consider is the first recording on a blank tape. In this mode, the capstan will rotate at constant speed and drive the tape at the linear speed specified for the format. The scanner must rotate at a precisely determined speed, so that the correct number of tracks per unit distance will be laid down on the tape. Since in a segmented recording each track will be a constant fraction of a television field, the scanner speed must ultimately be determined by the incoming video signal to be recorded. To take the example of a PAL D-2 recorder having two record-head pairs, eight tracks or four segments will be necessary to record one field, and so the scanner must make exactly two complete revolutions in one field period, requiring it to run at 100 Hz. In the case of NTSC D-2, there are six tracks or three segments per field, and so the scanner must turn at one and a half times field rate, or a little under 90 Hz. The phase of the scanner depends upon the time delay necessary to shuffle and interleave the video samples, which was seen to be necessary in Chapter 7. This will be at least one segment.

9.6 Controlling motor speed

In various modes of operation, the capstan and/or the scanner will need to have accurate control of their rotational speed. During crash record, the capstan must run at an exact and constant speed. When the scanner is first started, it must be brought to the correct speed before phase lock can be attempted. The principle of speed control commonly used will be examined here.

Fig. 9.10(a) shows that the motor whose speed is to be controlled is fitted with a toothed wheel or slotted disc. For convenience, the number of slots will usually be some power of two. A sensor, magnetic or optical, will produce one pulse per slot, and these will be counted by a binary divider. A similar counter is driven by a reference frequency. This may often be derived by multiplying the input video field rate in a phase-locked loop. The operation of a phase-locked loop was described in Chapter 6.

The outputs of the two counters are taken to a full adder, whose output drives a DAC which in turn drives the motor. The bias of the motor amplifier is arranged so that a DAC code of one-half of the quantizing range results in zero drive to the motor, and smaller or larger codes will result in forward or reverse drive.

If the count in the tacho divider lags behind the count in the reference divider, the motor will receive increased power, whereas if the count in the tacho divider leads the count in the reference divider, the motor will experience reverse drive, which slows it down. The result is that the speed of the motor is exactly proportional to the reference frequency. In principle the system is a phase-locked loop, where the voltage-controlled oscillator has been replaced by a motor and a frequency-generating (FG) wheel.

9.7 Phase-locked servos

In a DVTR the rotational phase of the scanner and capstan must be accurately controlled. In the case of the scanner, the phase must be

358

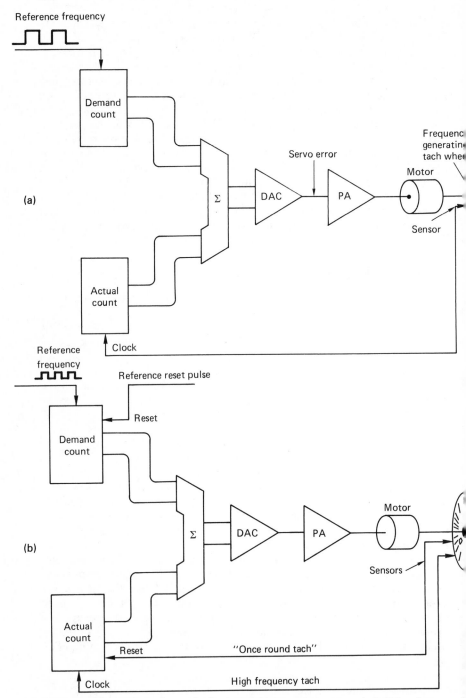

Figure 9.10 (a) Motor speed control using frequency generator on motor shaft. Pulses from F.G. are compared with pulses from reference to derive servo error. (b) An additional sensor resets the actual count once per revolution, so it counts motor phase angle. Demand count is reset by reference timing. Thus motor phase is locked to reference

controlled so that the heads reach the beginning of a track at a time which is appropriate to the station reference video fed to the machine.

A slightly more complex version of the speed control system of Fig. 9.10(a) is required, as will be seen in Fig. 9.10(b). In addition to a toothed wheel or slotted disc, the motor carries a reference slot which produces a rotational phase reference commonly called *once-round tach*. This reference presets the tach divider, so that the tach count becomes an accurate binary representation of the actual angle of rotation.

A similar divider is fed by a reference clock as before and preset at appropriate intervals. The reference clock has the same frequency as the tooth-passing frequency of the tacho at normal speed. In a PAL D-2 machine which needs two scanner rotations per field, the counter will need to be preset twice per field, or, more elegantly, the counter will have an additional high-order bit which does not go to the adder, and then it can be preset once per field, since disconnection of the upper bit will cause two repeated counts of half a field duration each, with an overflow between.

The adder output will increase or decrease the motor drive until the once-round tach occurs exactly opposite the reference preset pulse, because in this condition the sum of the two inputs to the adder is always zero.

The binary count of the tach counter can be used to address a rotation phase PROM. This will be programmed to generate signals which enable the different sectors of the recorded format to be put in the correct place on the track. For example, if it is desired to edit one audio channel without changing any other part of a recording, the record head must be enabled for a short period at precisely the correct scanner angle. The scanner phase PROM will provide the timing information needed.

When the tape is playing, the phase of the control track must be locked to reference segment phase in order to achieve accurate tracking. Fig. 9.11 shows that a similar configuration to the scanner servo is used, but there is no once-round tach on the capstan wheel. Instead, the tach counter is reset by the segment pulses obtained by replaying the control track. Since the speed of the control track is proportional to the capstan speed, resetting the tach count in this way results in a count of control track phase. The reference counter is reset by segment rate pulses, which can be obtained from the scanner, and so the capstan motor will be driven in such a way that the phase error between control track pulses and reference pulses is minimized. In this way the rotary heads will accurately track the diagonal tracks.

During an assemble edit, the capstan will phase-lock to control track during the preroll, but must revert to constant speed mode at the in-point, since the control track will be recorded from that point. This transition can be obtained by simply disabling the capstan tach counter reset, which causes the system to revert to the speed control servo of Fig. 9.10.

9.8 Tension servos

It has been shown that tape tension control is critical in helical scan machines, primarily to ensure interchange and the correct head contact. Tension control will also be necessary for shuttle.

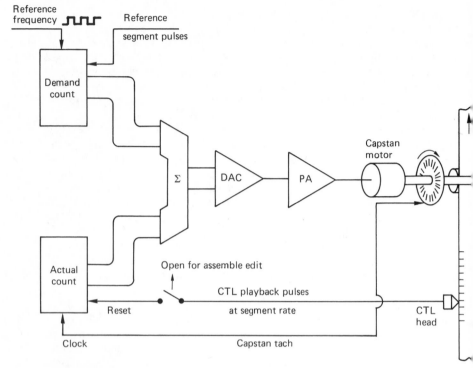

Figure 9.11 If the encoder counter is reset by CTL pulses, it will count linear tape phase, i.e. distance between CTL pulses. Controlling demand counter from reference segment pulses phase locks tape CTL track to segment rate resulting in correct tracking. At an assemble edit the reset is disabled and the capstan servo makes a smooth transition to the velocity control mode of Figure 9.10(a)

Fig. 9.12 shows a typical back tension control system. A swinging guide called a tension arm is mounted on a position sensor which can be optical or magnetic. A spring applies a force to the tension arm in a direction which would make the tape path longer. The position sensor output is connected to the supply reel motor amplifier which is biased in such a way that when the sensor is in the centre of its travel the motor will receive no drive. The polarity of the system is arranged so that the reel motor will be driven in reverse when the spring contracts. The result is that the reel motor will apply a reverse torque which will extend the spring as it attempts to return the tension arm to the neutral position. If the system is given adequate loop gain, a minute deflection of the arm will result in full motor torque, so the arm will be kept in an essentially constant position. This means that the spring will have a constant length, and so the tape tension will be constant. Different tensions can be obtained by switching offsets into the feedback loop, which result in the system null being at a different extension of the spring.

The error in the servo will only be small if the reel can accelerate fast enough to follow tape motion. In a machine with permanent capstan engagement, the capstan can accelerate much faster than the reels can. If

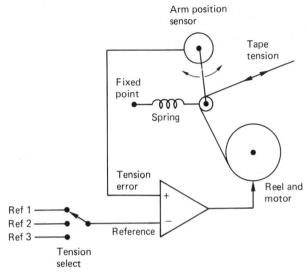

Figure 9.12 Tension servo controls reel motor current so that motor extends sprung arm. Sensor determines extension of spring and thus tape tension

not controlled, this would lead to the tension arm moving to one or other end of its travel, resulting in tape stretch, or a slack loop which will subsequently snatch tight with the same results. A fixed acceleration limit on the capstan servo would prevent the problem, but it would have to be set to allow a full reel on a large-size cassette to keep up. The motion of a small cassette with vastly reduced inertia would be made artificially ponderous. The solution is to feed back the displacement of the tension sensors to the capstan servo. If the magnitude of the tension error from either tension arm is excessive, the capstan acceleration is cut back. In this way the reels are accelerated as fast as possible without the tension becoming incorrect.

In a cassette-based recorder, the tension arms usually need to be motorized so that they can fit into the mouth of the cassette for loading and pull tape out into the threaded position. It is possible to replace the spring which provides tape tension with a steady current through the arm motor. By controlling this current, the tape tension can be programmed.

9.9 Tape-remaining sensing

It is most important in a cassette to prevent the tape running out at speed. The tape is spliced to a heavy leader at each end, and this leader is firmly attached to the reel hub. In an audio cassette, there is sufficient length of this leader to reach to the other reel, and so the impact of a run-off can be withstood. This approach cannot be used with a video cassette, because the heavy leader cannot be allowed to enter the scanner, as it would damage the rotating heads.

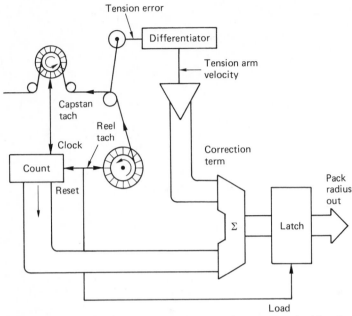

Figure 9.13 Tape remaining is calculated by comparing capstan tach with reel tach. If tension arm is moving, tape speed at reel and capstan will be different, so correction term from tension arm sensor is added.

Pinch roller type transports disengage the capstan in shuttle, and so the timer roller tacho would be used instead

The transport must compute the tape remaining in order to prevent running off at speed. This will be done by measuring the linear speed of the tape and comparing it with the rotational speed of the reel. The linear speed will be the capstan speed in a permanent capstan drive transport, while a timer roller will be necessary in a pinch-roller-type transport. The rotational speed of the reels will be obtained from a frequency generator on the reel motors. Fig. 9.13 shows a simple method of computing the tape remaining. FG pulses from the capstan cause a counter to increment. When a reel FG pulse occurs, the count will be transferred to a latch, and the counter will be reset. When the reel is full, there will be many capstan FG pulses between reel FG pulses, but as the radius of the tape pack falls, the count transferred to the latch will also fall. It will be possible to determine the limit count from a knowledge of the capstan and reel hub diameters and the number of teeth on their generators. The latch count is not quite the pack radius, because if the tension arm is moving as a result of an acceleration, the linear speed of the tape at the capstan will not be the same as the linear speed at the reel. To prevent false shutdowns when accelerating near the end of the tape, the tension arm signal is differentiated to give an arm velocity signal, and this can be digitized and used to produce a correction factor for the radius parameter.

To prevent run-off, the reel pack radius of the reel which is unwinding profiles the allowable shuttle speed, so that as the pack radius falls, the tape speed falls with it. Thus when the tape finally runs out, it will be travelling at very low speed, and the photoelectric sensor which detects the leader will be able to halt the transport without damage.

9.10 Brushless DC motors

The reliability of digital circuitry is of little consequence if a breakdown is caused by the failure of an associated mechanical component. Video recorders, including digital video recorders, are a complex alliance of mechanical, magnetic and electronic technology, and the electronic wizardry has to be matched by some good mechanical engineering. As the cost of electronics falls, it becomes possible to replace certain mechanical devices cost-effectively, and there is an impetus to do this if a wear mechanism can be eliminated. The brushless motor is one such device. The conventional DC brush motor is ubiquitous, and life would be infinitely less convenient without it, for it allows reasonable efficiency, a wide speed range, reversing and relatively compact size. The weak point of all motors of this kind is the brush/commutator system, which serves to distribute current to the windings which are in the best position relative to the field to generate torque. There is a physical wear mechanism, and the best brush material developed will still produce a conductive powder which will be distributed far and wide by the need to have airflow through the motor for cooling. The interruption of current in an inductive circuit results in sparking, which can cause electrical interference and erosion of the brushes and commutator. The brushless motor allows all of the benefits of the DC motor, without the drawbacks of commutation.

Fig. 9.14 shows that a brushless motor is not unlike a normal motor turned inside out. In a normal motor, the field magnet is stationary and the

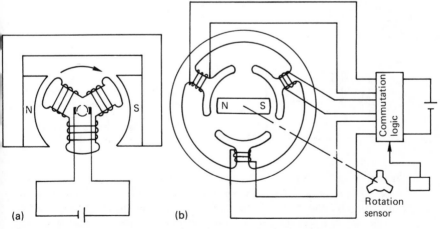

Figure 9.14 At (a) a conventional brush motor has rotating windings. Current is fed through stationary brushes and commutation is automatic. At (b) the motor has been turned inside-out, the magnet revolves and the windings are now stationary so they can be directly connected to an electronic commutating circuit. The rotation sensor on the magnet shaft tells the commutator when to switch

windings rotate. In a brushless motor, the windings are stationary and the magnet rotates. The stationary windings eliminate the need to supply current to the rotor, and with it the need for brushes. The commutating action is replaced by electronic switches. These need to be told the rotational angle of the shaft, a function which is intrinsic in the conventional commutator. A rotation sensor performs this function.

Fig. 9.15 shows the circuit of a typical brushless motor. The three-phase winding is driven by six switching devices, usually power FETs. By switching these on in various combinations, it is possible to produce six resultant field directions in the windings. The switching is synchronized to the rotation of the magnet, such that the magnetic field of the rotor always finds itself at right angles to the field from the windings and so produces the most torque. In this condition the motor will produce the most back EMF, and the normal way of adjusting the rotation sensor is to allow the motor to run on no load and to adjust the angular sensor position mechanically until the motor consumes minimum current.

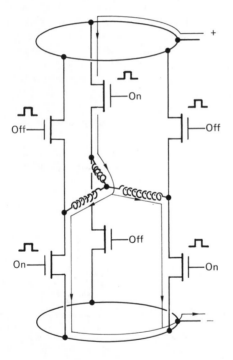

Figure 9.15 Circuit of a brushless D.C. motor is basically a three-phase bridge. Six different flux directions can be obtained by switching combinations of FETs. One example is shown

The rotating magnet has to be sufficiently powerful to provide the necessary field, and in early brushless motors it was heavy, which gave the motor a high inertial time constant. Whilst this was of no consequence in steady speed applications, it caused problems in servos. The brushless servo motor was basically waiting for high-energy permanent magnets, which could produce the necessary field without excessive mass. These rare earth magnets are currently more expensive than the common ferrite magnet, and so the first applications of brushless motors have been in machines where the motor cost is a relatively small proportion of the high overall cost and where reliability is paramount. Professional recorders come into this category. Down time for brush replacement and labour costs eclipse the cost of the brushes. The scanner motor of a video recorder in a modern post-production suite has to run at speed hour after hour, day after day, and is a natural application of a brushless motor.

The development of the power FET also helped brushless motors, since all DC motors regenerate, which is to say that when the torque opposes the direction of rotation, the current reverses. FETs are not perturbed by current direction, whereas bipolar devices were at best inefficient or would at worst fail in the presence of reverse current. Power FETs can handle currents which would destroy brush gear, and so large transient accelerations are easily obtained, overcoming the inertia of the rotating magnet.

A typical brushless motor appears to the drive amplifier just like a normal DC motor. It has only two power terminals, has back EMF, and will regenerate. The only major difference is the way that reversing is achieved. Brush motors reverse by reversing drive polarity, whereas brushless motors reverse by changing the phase of the commutation.

The number of motor poles directly influences the complexity of the switching circuitry, and brushless motors tend to have relatively few poles. Conventional motors suffer from cogging or a cyclic variation in torque, and those with few poles suffer most. Whilst it is of little consequence in a scanner motor which runs at high speed and has the inertia of the scanner to smooth out rotation, it can be important in direct drive capstan motors, which turn at low speed and have low inertia.

Many transports retain multipole brush motors for the capstan, but it is possible to construct a cogging-free motor. The commutation circuit is no longer switching, but consists of a number of analog amplifiers which will feed the motor with sinusoidal waveforms in fixed phase relationships. In the case of a two-phase motor, this will be two waveforms at 90°, for a three-phase motor, it will be three waveforms at 120°.

The drive signals for the amplifiers are produced by a number of rotation sensors, which directly produce analog sinusoids. These can conveniently be Hall effect sensors which detect the fields from rotating magnets.

9.11 Switched-mode motor amplifiers

The switched-mode motor amplifier has much in common with the switched-mode power supply, since both have the same objectives, namely an increase in electrical efficiency through reduced dissipation, and reduction in size and weight. In studio-based machines reduced dissipation will help to increase reliability, whereas in portable machines the efficiency is paramount since existing battery technology is still a handicap.

The linear amplifier must act as a variable resistance, and so current flowing through it will cause heat to be developed. Linear amplifiers are particularly inefficient for driving tape reel motors, since to obtain fast shuttle speed the supply voltage must be high, and this means that when the machine plays, the reels are turning slowly and the motor voltage will be very small, so that most of the power supply voltage has to be dropped by the amplifier, which is extremely inefficient. Some transports using linear motor amplifiers will program a switched-mode power supply to provide just enough voltage for the instantaneous requirements, helping to raise efficiency.

The principle of a switched-mode amplifier is quite simple. The current is controlled by an electronic switch which is either fully on or fully off. In both cases dissipation in the switch is minimal. The only difficulty consists of providing a variable output despite the binary switching. This will be done by a combination of duty cycle control and filtering.

Fig. 9.16 shows a typical switched-mode motor amplifier. It consists of a normal bridge configuration with a number of additional components, a pair of inductors and a current sense resistor in series with the motor, and a number of reverse-connected flywheel diodes.

If it is desired to make current flow through the motor from left to right, then field-effect transistors T_1 and T_4 will be turned fully on. Owing to the presence of the inductors, the current through the motor increases gradually, and when the desired current is reached, transistor T_1 is switched off. The current flowing in the inductive circuit must continue flowing, and it will do so through D_3, as shown in (b). Greater efficiency will be obtained if T_3 is then switched on, as the forward drop of the diode is then bypassed. Transistor T_4 is then switched off, and the current loop will be blocked, causing the flux in the inductors to decay and raising their terminal voltage. This will result in current flowing through D_2 back to the power supply. Greater efficiency will be obtained if T_2 is turned on. The current is now being opposed by the power supply and will decay. After a short time, transistor T_2 must be switched off, and transistor T_4 will be switched on again. In this way, the current rises and falls about the desired value. If the switching rate is made high, the variations in current will be small with respect to the average current. The inertia of the motor will in any case prevent any mechanical response at the switching frequency. It will be noted that during this process current flowed in reverse through two of the transistors, requiring the use of field-effect devices.

Clearly if current flowing from right to left is required, the bridge switching will change over, but the principle remains the same.

The torque generated by the motor is proportional to the current, and torque can be applied with or against rotation. For example, when the transport is in play mode, the take-up motor is turning in the same direction as its torque, whereas the supply motor is providing back tension and is turning against its torque. In this case, the motor EMF will cause current to flow in the flywheel circuit, and the switching will take energy out of the current flywheel back to the power supply. This is the principle of regenerative braking. If the motor is being turned by the tape, it will generate, and a current will flow as shown in (c). The current will rise gradually owing to the presence of the inductors. When the current reaches the value needed to give the correct back tension, T_3 will be switched off, and the flywheel current will find itself blocked. The result will be a flux collapse causing the inductors to raise their terminal voltage until a current path is found. When the voltage exceeds the power supply voltage, current will flow in D_1, back to the supply. Again greater efficiency will be

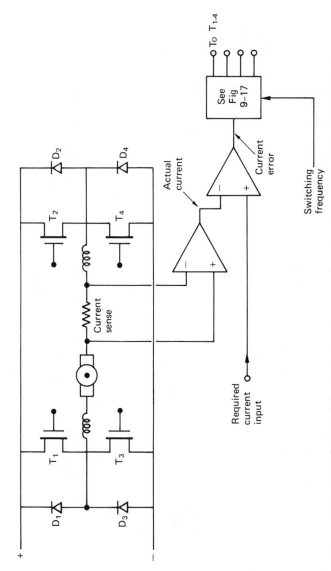

Figure 9.16 General arrangement of switched-mode power amplifier. Devices T_1–T_4 are Power FETs which are on or off. Inductors in series with motor inductance limit rate of change of current.

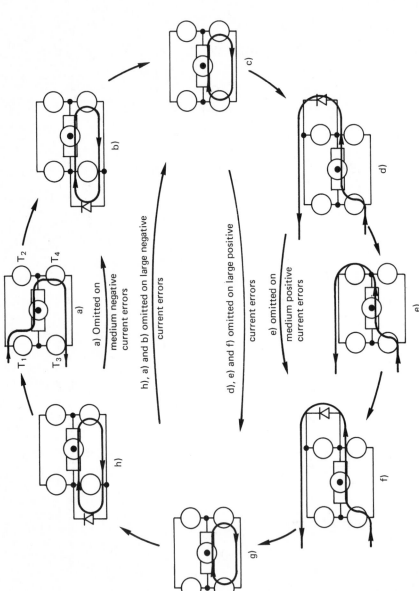

Figure 9.16 (*Continued*). Switching sequence begins at (a) with current building up, a transitional phase (b) a
~~flexical phase (c) transitional phase (d) and at (e) the system regenerates, or opposes the power supply. This~~

obtained if T_1 is switched on, since the diode drop is bypassed. Since the power supply voltage is opposing the motor EMF, the current will fall, and when it has fallen sufficiently, T_1 will be switched off and T_3 will be switched on again.

The switching sequence of the transistors is important, since turning on the wrong pair will short out the power supply! One method of controlling the switching is to produce a current error by comparing the current sensed with the desired current. The current error then changes the DC level of a triangle wave, which is compared with four thresholds, each of which controls one of the transistors. Fig. 9.17 shows the switching sequence which results. Note that when the current error is zero, the system alternates equally between opposing and assisting the current, and so there is no change.

A motor which is producing back tension will return power to the supply, which will be used by the motor which is taking up, and by the scanner motor. If the machine is braking from a high shuttle speed, both reel motors may together produce more power than the rest of the machine can use, and the power supply voltage will rise. In AC-powered machines, it is necessary to shunt the supply with a resistor in this condition, whereas in battery-powered machines, the regenerative current simply recharges the battery. Clearly a power failure in shuttle is no problem, for as long as the reels are being decelerated, power is generated. This can be augmented if necessary by decelerating the scanner.

9.12 The digital video cassette

The D-1 and D-2 formats use the same mechanical parts and dimensions in their respective cassettes, even though the kind of tape and the track pattern are completely different.

The main advantages of a cassette are that the medium is better protected from contamination whilst out of the transport, and that an unskilled operator or a mechanical elevator can load the tape.

It is not true that cassettes offer any advantage for storage except for the ease of handling. In fact a cassette takes up more space than a tape reel, because it must contain two such reels, only one of which will be full at any one time. In some cases it is possible to reduce the space needed by using flangeless hubs and guiding liner sheets as is done in the Compact Cassette and RDAT, or pairs of hubs with flanges on opposite sides, as in U-matic. Whilst such approaches are acceptable for consumer and industrial products, they are inappropriate for the digital video cassette, because as a professional unit it will be expected to wind at high speeds in automation and editing systems. Accordingly the digital cassette contains two fully flanged reels side by side. The use of a cassette causes a further drawback which is that it is not as easy to provide a range of sizes as it is with reels. Simply putting smaller reels in a cassette with the same hub spacing does not produce a significantly smaller cassette. The only solution is to specify different hub spacings for different sizes of cassette. This gives the best volumetric efficiency for storage, but it does mean that the transport must be able to reposition the reel drive motors if it is to play more than one size of cassette.

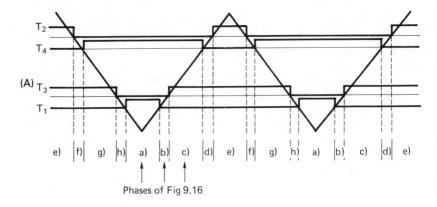

Phases of Fig 9.16

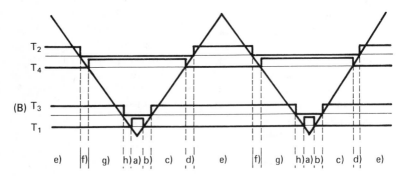

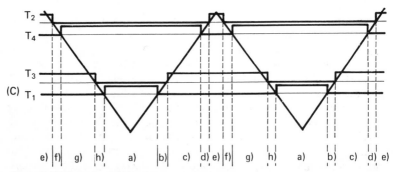

Figure 9.17 The power FETs of Figure 9.16 are switched by comparing the current error with a sawtooth signal produced from the switching frequency. Four offset voltages are added to the current error, and four comparators are used, one for each power device. The offsets are constant, so all four current errors move together.

At (A) above, the current error is zero, so the switching is symmetrical because time period (a) has the same length as time period (e) and the current is neither increased or reduced. At (B) the current error is negative, and phase (a) is very short whereas phase (e) is much longer, thus current reduces because the motor is regenerating. At (C) the current error is positive and phase (a) is now longer than phase (e) so current increases. If the current error increases further, some phases will no longer take place. An inverse of the error in (C) will result in phase (e) disappearing since (d) and (f) are identical. Further increase will cause (d), (e) and (f) to disappear giving the sequence a, b, c, g, h, ...

If the small, medium and large digital video cassettes are placed in a stack with their throats and tape guides in a vertical line, the centres of the hubs will be seen to fall on a pair of diagonal lines going outwards and backwards. This arrangement was chosen to allow the reel motors to travel along a linear track in a machine which accepts more than one size.

The D-1 format is somewhat pushed to get playing time, and the large-size cassette was the largest size which could be accommodated in a transport which would still fit in a 19 inch rack. This cassette will hold 1300

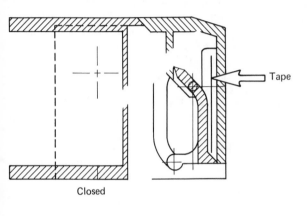

Closed

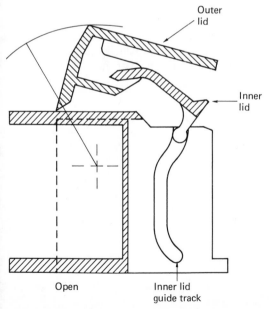

Open

Figure 9.18 When the cassette lid is closed, both sides of the tape are protected by covers. As the outer lid swings up on a pivot, the inner lid is guided around the back of the tape by a curved track

metres of 16μm tape or 1750 metres of 13μm tape. The medium-size cassette holds about half of these amounts, and the small cassette holds 190 metres or 250 metres.

All three sizes of cassette have basically the same structure, and detail differences will be noted. The cassette has a double-door arrangement shown in Fig. 9.18. When the cassette is removed, both sides of the tape in the throat are covered. The inner door is guided by a curved track. The door extends to the edges of the small and medium cassettes, but this is unnecessary on the large cassette. The door has a lock which prevents accidental opening, and this is released by a pin when the cassette enters the transport. The lock release mechanism is as near the edge of the small cassette as possible, but it cannot be in the same place on the medium cassette, as it would foul the tape path to the larger reel. Three lock release pins are needed, one for each size, and the larger cassettes need dummy slots which clear the pins used by the smaller sizes.

The cassettes also have hub locks which prevent unwanted rotation in storage or transit. On the larger two sizes, the lock is released by a lever operated by the act of opening the door. There is insufficient room for this mechanism on the small cassette, and so the brake is released by a central post in the transport.

The cassettes are designed for front or side loading, and so have guiding slots running at right angles. Most studio recorders are front loading, whereas many automated machines use side loading. The front-loading guide groove is centrally positioned and the threading throat forms a lead-in to it, helping to centralize the smaller cassettes in a loading slot which will accept a large cassette.

A number of identification holes are provided in the cassettes which are sensed by switches on the transport. Four of these are coding holes which are in the form of break-off tabs which will be set when the cassette is made, and four of them are resettable user holes which can be controlled with a screwdriver. Table 9.1 shows the significance of the coding and user holes.

Table 9.1 (a) Manufacturers' coding holes (0 = tab removed). (b) User Holes (0 = tab removed)

(a) Holes 1 and 2 shall be used in combination to indicate tape thickness according to the following logic table:	Holes 3 and 4 shall be used to indicate the coercivity of the magnetic recording tape.
Hole number: 1 2	Hole number: 3 4
0 0 = 16 μm tape	0 0 = Class 850
0 1 = 13 μm tape	0 1 = Undefined/reserved
1 0 = Undefined/reserved	1 0 = Undefined/reserved
1 1 = Undefined/reserved	1 1 = Undefined/reserved

(b) When a "0" state exists, the user holes shall identify the following conditions:

1. Total record lock out
   (audio/video/cue/time code/control track)
2. Reserved and undefined
3. Reserved and undefined
4. Reserved and undefined

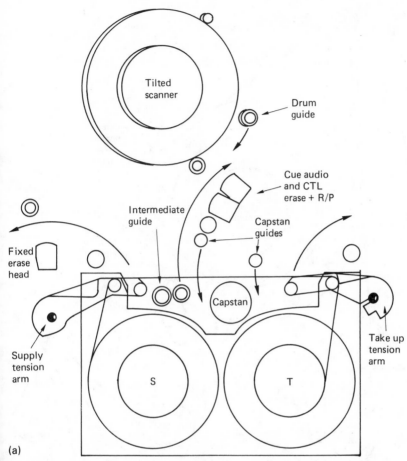

Figure 9.19 (a) Ampex D-2 transport with cassette just lowered onto drive hubs. Note permanently engaged capstan in cassette throat

Areas are specified for the positioning of labels, and these are recessed to prevent fouling of elevators or guides. Automated machines will use the end location for a bar code which can be read by the elevator while the cassette is stacked.

9.13 Threading the tape

The sequence of operations when a cassette is inserted in the machine will be followed.

In many machines, all three cassette sizes can be used without any adjustment. The operator simply pushes the cassette into the aperture in the machine. The smaller sizes are guided into the centre of the aperture by a central slot with a tapered lead-in. The presence of the cassette is sensed optically, or by switches, and by the same means the machine can decide which size of cassette has been inserted. The cassette is drawn into the machine horizontally by motor-driven tractor belts which are positioned

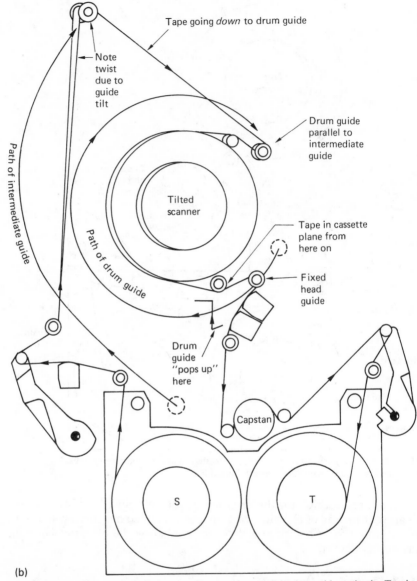

(b)

Figure 9.19 (*Continued*) (b) Fixed headguide swings out, and capstan guides swing in. Tension arms extend. Then drum and intermediate guides complete scanner wrap.

If the scanner guides are not operated, tape can be transported past stationary heads for timecode striping or pre-positioning tape without scanner wear

such that all sizes of cassette can be gripped. Alternatively the cassette fits into a cage which is driven by a toothed rack.

As the hub spacing differs between cassette sizes, the transport automatically moves the sliding reel motors to the correct position. In the case of a small cassette, the hub locks are released when the central guide

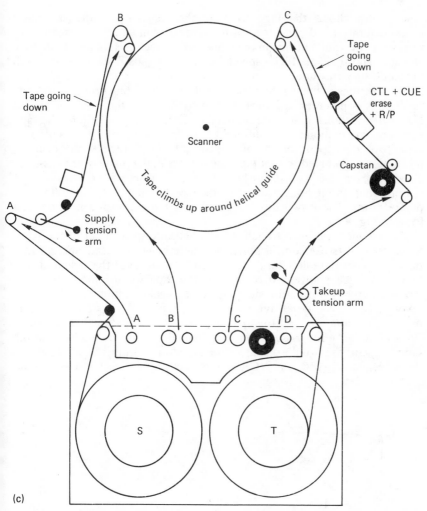

Figure 9.19 (*Continued*) (c) In the Sony D-1 transport an extended wrap is used, and guides move on both sides of the scanner to create the wrap. Tape begins the helix below the cassette plane and ends the scan above it. This contrasts with the Ampex approach where the tape begins the helix far below the cassette plane and ends in the cassette plane

reaches the end of the cassette slot and pushes the brake lever at the end of the horizontal travel into the machine. In all sizes, the final part of horizontal travel unlocks the cassette door. The cassette elevator is then driven downwards. The door is opened, and in the medium and large sizes this releases the hub brakes. The opened cassette is then lowered on to the reel motors, and locating dowels on the transport register the cassette body. The several guides and tension arms are positioned so that the throat of the cassette drops over them with the front run of tape between them and the head drum. In the Ampex VPR-300 transport the permanently engaged capstan also fits inside the casstte throat. A short movement of the tape guides allows the tape to wrap the capstan and the stationary timecode/erase head. This is known as coplanar mode, which means that the tape path is still entirely in the plane of the tape reels. In this mode tape can be shuttled at high speed, and it is possible to erase and timecode-stripe without causing wear to the rotary-head assembly.

For functions involving the rotary heads, the threading process proceeds further. It is inherent in helical scan recorders that the tape enters and leaves the head drum at different heights. In C-format recorders, the tape reels are simply mounted at different heights, but this is not possible in a cassette if it is to be of reasonable size. In the VPR-300 the drum is positioned and angled so that tape leaving it is in the plane of the cassette. Tape entering the head drum has to be moved out of the plane of the cassette first. In the Sony transports, the tape is manipulated on both sides of the drum. These two threading methods are contrasted in simplified form in Fig. 9.19.

Various methods exist to achieve the helical displacement of the tape. Some transports use conical posts, but these have the disadvantages that there is a considerable lateral force against the edge of the tape and that they cannot be allowed to revolve or the tape would climb off them. Angled pins do not suffer side force, but again cannot be allowed to revolve. In the VPR-300, the tape in the plane of the cassette is slightly twisted on a long run and then passes around a conventional guide which causes it to leave the cassette plane at an angle. A second guide set at the same angle as the drum axis passes the tape to the drum.[1] Fig. 9.20 shows the principle. As with any VCR, the guides start inside the cassette and

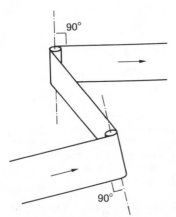

Figure 9.20 Two rollers or air lubricated cylinders can be used to change the plane in which a tape runs without producing an edge force. A slight twist is induced in the tape path between the rollers

move to various positions as threading proceeds. As the VPR-300 is designed for rapid threading and unthreading without tape damage, particular care was taken to ensure that the tape path geometry is perfect not just when threaded, but at all times during the threading process. There are two guides which primarily control threading the tape around the drum. The drum guide moves in a circular path on a threading ring, which rotates concentric with the drum. This guide begins its motion on the wrong side of the tape, but as the threading ring turns, the guide pops up and engages the back of the tape. Then as the threading ring rotates further, the guide is slowly lowered along the drum axis at the correct rate by a cam, such that the tape is laid on to the drum at the helix angle. When the drum guide reaches the end of its travel, its supporting shaft comes up against a fixed V-block which positions it repeatably. It is held in contact with the block by a solenoid.

The intermediate guide is designed to move away from the cassette as the drum guide proceeds around the threading ring, and the tilt angle of this guide, which imparts the tape twist, is changed as it moves so that a cylindrical wrap is always maintained. This guide is mounted on three V-shaped rollers which are preloaded outwards and ride in a matching slot in the deck plate. The tilt of the guide is controlled by a spherical roller on an extension of the guide shaft, which bears against a cam profile below the guide track. The principle is shown in Fig. 9.21. All of the cam profiles which achieve these operations were computer generated.

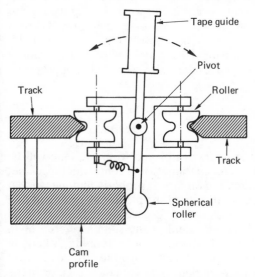

Figure 9.21 The spherical roller and cam profile tilt the tape guide axis to the correct angle as threading proceeds. Tape geometry can then be perfect at all points in the threading

Since the total guide wrap angle of cassette transports inevitably amounts to several revolutions, tension buildup is often a problem. In this transport, all tape guides are lubricated by compressed air, except for the tilting threading guide, which is a roller. The drum guide has to travel a long distance, and it is difficult to provide a permanent air supply. The air feed is through the solenoid locking arm, so that air supply becomes available when the tape is fully threaded. The air film lubrication system has shown itself to be highly successful on the VPR-3.

The VPR-300 transport has much in common with the ACR-225 transport and is based on a massive casting which is CNC machined. The other major component is a substantial cast bridge holding fixed heads and guides.

9.14 Operating modes of a digital recorder

The digital video recorder is expected to do much more than record and replay in a modern installation. The main operating modes will be examined here, followed by the more obscure modes.

In *crash record* the tape is either blank or is considered to be blank, and no reference will be made to any previous information on the tape. As with analog video recorders, if a crash recording is made in the middle of an existing recording, the playback will lose lock at the transition. In this mode the full width erase head will be active, and the entire tape format will be laid down, including audio blocks and control track.

There are a fixed number of segments in a field, and so the scanner speed will be locked to incoming video. The scanner phase will be determined by the delay needed to shuffle and encode the data in a segment. Owing to the encoding delay, the recording heads on the scanner will begin tracing a segment some time after the beginning of the input field. The capstan will simply rotate at constant speed, driving the tape at the speed specified in the format. As the rotating heads begin a diagonal track, a segment pulse will be recorded in the control track. Once per field, the segment pulse will be accompanied by a field pulse. In composite machines, there will also be a colour frame pulse recorded at appropriate intervals.

9.15 Framed playback

In framed playback, the number of frames played from the tape will be equal to the number of station reference frames. In a component machine, framing requires that the segmentation on tape is properly undone, so that the first segment in a field arrives at the top of the picture monitor and that the interlace sequence is synchronous with reference, so that an odd field comes from tape when there is an odd field in the station reference. In composite systems, the framing will become colour framing, where in addition to correct segmentation and interlace framing the offtape field will be the same type of field in the four- or eight-field sequence as exists in the reference.

The error correction and de-interleaving processes on replay require a finite time in which to operate, and so the transport must play back segments ahead of real time, in the same way that analog machines play back ahead of real time for timebase correction purposes. The scanner speed will be synchronous with reference, and the scanner phase will be determined by the decoding delay.

The capstan system will be responsible for tracking and framing and will need to vary the speed of the tape until framing is achieved. It will then vary the phase of the tape to optimize tracking.

The capstan and tape form part of a phase-locked loop where the phase of the control track pulses are compared with reference pulses. In order to achieve framing, the phase comparison must be between reference frame pulses and offtape frame pulses in a component machine, and between reference colour frame pulses and offtape colour frame pulses in a composite machine. In this way the linear motion of the tape is phased such that reference and offtape framing are the same. The capstan speed must vary during this part of the lock-up sequence, and the picture may be temporarily degraded unless the machine has provision for operating at non-normal speed.

Once framing is achieved, the capstan will switch to a different mode in order to obtain accurate tracking. The phase comparison will now be between offtape segment pulses and pulses generated by the rotation of the scanner. If the phase error between these is used to modify the capstan drive, the error can be eliminated, since the capstan drives the tape which produces the control track segment pulses. Eliminating this timing error results in the rotating heads following the tape tracks properly. Artificially delaying or advancing the reference pulses from the scanner will result in a tracking adjustment.

9.16 Assembly editing

In an assemble edit, new material is appended to an existing recording in such a way that the video timing structure continues unbroken over the edit point. In a component recording, this timing will be the synchronizing pulses, whereas in a composite recording the subcarrier phase will also need to be continuous.

The recording will begin at a vertical interval, and it will be necessary to have a preroll in order to synchronize tape and scanner motion to the signal to be recorded. The procedure during the preroll is similar to that of framed playback, except that the input video timing is used. The goal of the preroll process is to ensure that the record head is at the beginning of the first segment in a field exactly one encode delay after the beginning of the desired field in the input video signal. At this point the record head will be turned on, and in D-1 machines this will automatically enable the flying erase heads; D-2 machines will erase by overwrite, so no erase is needed. After the assemble point, there will not necessarily be a control track, and the capstan must smoothly enter constant speed mode without a disturbance to tape motion. The control track will begin to record in a continuation of the phase of the existing control track. This process will then continue indefinitely until halted.

9.17 Insert editing

An insert differs from an assemble in that a short part of a recording is replaced by new material somewhere in the centre. An insert can only be made on a tape which has a continuous control track, because the in- and out-point edits must both be synchronous. The preroll will be exactly as for an assemble edit, and the video record process will be exactly the same, but the capstan control will be achieved by playing back the control track at all times, so that the new video tracks are laid down in exactly the same place as the previous recording. At the out-point, the record heads will be turned off at the end of the last segment in a field.

9.18 Tape speed offset

One of the most useful features of a production recorder is the ability to operate at variable speed. The variable speed modes of the VPR-300 are TSO (tape speed offset), slow motion/jog and shuttle.

In TSO, the speed is only changed by a maximum of 15% from normal in order to trim a programme to fit a broadcast time slot. Clearly the audio must be fully recovered, and so no replay head jumping is permissible. The speed of the entire transport is changed by changing the transport timing reference with respect to station reference. The drum and the capstan change speed in proportion so that the heads still follow the helical tracks properly. All of the audio blocks are recovered, and full-quality digital audio is output. Owing to the speed change, the audio sampling rate will not be exactly 48 kHz, and a digital pitch changer or sampling-rate converter can be used if necessary. Clearly the offtape field rate will no longer match reference, and the difference is accommodated by a framestore/timebase corrector, which is written at offtape speed and read at reference speed. Fields will occasionally be skipped or repeated as TBC addresses lap one another.

In slow motion or jog, the track-following head system comes into operation. Variable-speed operation differs considerably between D-1 and D-2 formats and is dealt with in the respective chapters.

References

1. RYAN, D.M., Mechanical considerations in the design of a digital video cassette recorder. Presented at International Broadcasting Convention (Brighton, 1988), *IEE Conf. Publ.* **293**, 387–390

Chapter 10

The D-1 colour difference DVTR format

The D-1 format allows recording of digital colour difference signals sampled in 4:2:2 format according to CCIR601. In this chapter the tape format which results will be seen to be determined by the conflicting requirements of a powerful error correction and concealment strategy and the need to be able to view pictures in shuttle.

10.1 Introduction

The D-1 format was designed to record transparently the digital data resulting from sampling 625/50[1] or 525/60[2] colour difference video at 13.5 MHz for luminance and at 6.75 MHz for C_r and C_b. Details of this form of sampling have been given in Chapters 2 and 8 and are not repeated here. Along with the digital video, four independent channels of digital audio can also be recorded, and a detailed explanation of the audio aspects can be found in Chapter 13. As with all VTRs, timecode recording is implemented for the purpose of editing control and synchronization to other devices.

The quality of a properly engineered digital recorder is determined only by the conversion processes, and since these are laid down in CCIR601, the D-1 format has only to demonstrate an acceptable bit error rate and it can be considered to introduce no further degradation to the signals it handles. Accordingly a proper discussion of the D-1 format must be based upon the strategies necessary to record the digital data as transparently as possible, since this has a major bearing on the design.

If it were only necessary to be able to record and play back in a single line standard, the design of a DVTR would be relatively easy. The D-1 format, however, must be available in two line standards with as much mechanical and electrical commonality as possible for economic and practical reasons, and it must be possible to observe a reasonable picture in shuttle and a full-quality picture over a moderate range of speeds. It is these requirements which have largely dictated the approach taken to the format of D-1.

10.2 Data rate, segmentation and the control track

The data rate of D-1 can be directly deduced from the CCIR601 standard. In every active line, 720 luminance samples and 360 of each type of colour difference sample are produced, making a total of 1440 samples per line. In 625/ 50, lines 11–310 and lines 324–623 are recorded, making 300 lines per field, or 1500 lines per second. In 525/60, lines 14–263 and lines 276–525 are recorded, making 250 lines per field, which results in the same data rate of 1500 lines per second.

In both cases the video data rate will be 1500 × 1440 Bytes/s, or 2.16 megabytes/s. The actual bit rate recorded will be in excess of the video data rate to take into account the redundancy, the audio and identification codes. Further track space will be required to accommodate preambles and synchronizing patterns.

In Chapter 9 it was shown that the data content of a field is so great that it precludes the use of a field-per-scan format with currently achievable wavelengths; the tracks would simply be too long and segmentation is the only answer. Similarly the data rate is too great for a single head to handle. The head to tape speed would be extremely high, leading to contact problems, and losses in the head would be intolerable with the head technology at the time of the D-1 design. Accordingly D-1 assumes that two heads are working in parallel in order to halve the instantaneous data rate seen by each, and so a segment becomes a *pair* of tape tracks. In the D-1 transports designed by Sony, two head pairs are installed on opposite sides of the scanner, and an extended tape wrap is used with a relatively small scanner to allow the use of time expansion (see Chapter 9) to reduce further the instantaneous data rate seen by the heads. Other head configurations are possible, since the format only specifies the track pattern.

As the fields in the two line standards contain 300 and 250 lines, it makes a good deal of sense for each segment or track pair to record the highest common multiple, 50 lines, such that a field will comprise either six or five segments. The segment rate will then be 300 Hz in both standards, and since the scanner in the Sony transport has two pairs of heads, it will turn at 150 revolutions per second. The transport can be mechanically identical in the two line standards. It should be appreciated that in fact the field rate of the 525 line system is 59.94 Hz, and so the scanner speed (and hence the capstan speed) will be 0.1% slower in the 525 line version. This is of no real consequence to the format, except for some very small dimensional changes, and for simplicity will not be mentioned again in this chapter.

As far as the heads are concerned, D-1 is a two-channel format, since it is possible with recent head technology to make a two-headed scanner turning at segment rate. However, this is not the only consideration.

If the error-correction system is working within its correcting power, there will be an uncorrupted stream of data which can be used to recreate the picture directly. However, in the real world, tape dropouts of a size which may exceed the correction power can occur, albeit infrequently, debris may reduce the efficiency of head contact, and ultimately a head may become clogged. In these cases it will be necessary to use concealment to produce replacements for the lost data by interpolation. This will only be possible if the recorded samples are distributed around the tape surface in a way which causes large contiguous physical defects to result in many single samples being lost over a large area of the picture, since adjacent samples can then be used to obtain a concealed value by interpolation. If only two data channels are used, then an uncorrectable error in one channel would result in half of the data being uncorrectable, whereas increasing the number of data channels to four results in only one quarter of data being uncorrectable, and concealment would then be much more

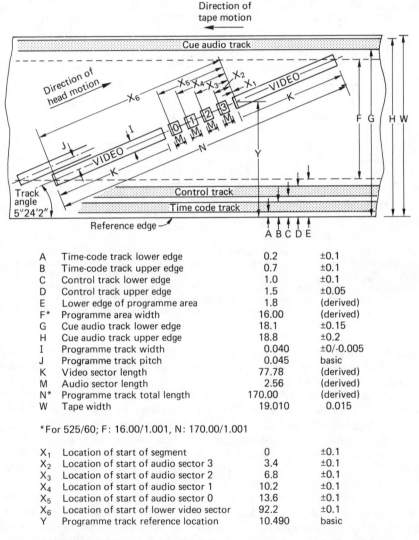

A	Time-code track lower edge	0.2	±0.1
B	Time-code track upper edge	0.7	±0.1
C	Control track lower edge	1.0	±0.1
D	Control track upper edge	1.5	±0.05
E	Lower edge of programme area	1.8	(derived)
F*	Programme area width	16.00	(derived)
G	Cue audio track lower edge	18.1	±0.15
H	Cue audio track upper edge	18.8	±0.2
I	Programme track width	0.040	±0/-0.005
J	Programme track pitch	0.045	basic
K	Video sector length	77.78	(derived)
M	Audio sector length	2.56	(derived)
N*	Programme track total length	170.00	(derived)
W	Tape width	19.010	0.015

*For 525/60; F: 16.00/1.001, N: 170.00/1.001

X_1	Location of start of segment	0	±0.1
X_2	Location of start of audio sector 3	3.4	±0.1
X_3	Location of start of audio sector 2	6.8	±0.1
X_4	Location of start of audio sector 1	10.2	±0.1
X_5	Location of start of audio sector 0	13.6	±0.1
X_6	Location of start of lower video sector	92.2	±0.1
Y	Programme track reference location	10.490	basic

All dimensions in mm

Figure 10.1(a) The track dimensions of D-1. Note that the segment begins at X_1 after the audio blocks

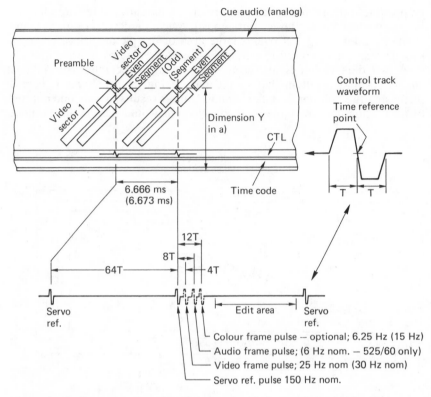

Figure 10.1(b) The arrangement of the D-1 control track. Servo pulses coincide with the beginning of an even segment after the audio blocks. The next segment has no control track pulse, and so the pulses repeat at drum rotation rate for a four headed machine. Additional pulses locate the top segment in a frame and record optional colour framing (see text). The value T is 1⁄64 the time taken for four tracks to pass. Values shown are for 625/50, with 525/60 values in brackets. 525/50 also has audio frame pulse described in Chapter 13

effective[3]. In the case of a four-headed scanner, which all current machines use, then one head can fail completely and a subjectively acceptable picture can still be obtained.

The four channels might have been created by placing one channel in each track over two segments. This approach would work for the 625 line format, but would cause difficulty in the 525 line format because there are then an odd number of segments in the field, and the data for one field could not be divided by four without an enormous increase in complexity. The solution was to divide the tape tracks in half lengthways to form two video *sectors*, such that there are then four sectors in a segment.

Fig. 10.1(a) shows that the resulting tracks consist of pairs of sectors containing the video data, and the four audio channels are carried in smaller sectors between them. The audio is then in the centre of the tape, where the better data reliability compensates for the fact that the audio blocks must be interleaved over a smaller area. As a further measure, all audio sectors are recorded twice with a different head and in a different sector location for each version. Fig. 10.1(a) also shows that there are three linear tracks in addition to the slant tracks.

A control track is used to drive the capstan in replay and in the various edit modes as was explained in Chapter 9. As this is a segmented format, the control track contains pulses which occur every two segments as in Fig. 10.1(b). This is the equivalent of once per scanner rotation in a four headed machine, and so these will be at 150 Hz at normal speed. The segment is considered to begin after the audio blocks at the centre of the track; in fact the servo pulse coincides with the end of the preamble on the video sector.

Once per frame, a second pulse is recorded. This frame pulse accompanies every sixth servo pulse for 625 lines, every fifth servo pulse for 525 lines. There is no field pulse, since in 525 line working it would have to occur in between the servo pulses.

It will be seen in Chapter 13 that interaction between the audio sampling rate and the 525 line frame rate produces a five-frame sequence, and this is recorded in a third control track pulse. Finally, if the component input has come from a decoded composite signal, the colour framing flag of that composite signal can optionally be recorded. If a residual subcarrier footprint exists in the component recording, it can be cancelled out if the coder/decoder combination is reversible (see chapter 5) and if the recording is colour framed to a subsequent composite modulator.

The cue audio track is designed to permit audio to be heard over a wide speed range, since all machines, especially portable machines, will not necessarily be able to recover the digital audio from the slant tracks at all times. The recording is analog with conventional bias and is not intended to be of high quality.

The timecode track has had two possible implementations. In original proposals the length of track corresponding to one frame is divided so two independent timecodes can be recorded[4]. This would allow the timecode of source material to be conveyed in an edited version which would have its own contiguous timecode. In the actual D-1 standard, the timecode is essentially identical to the existing EBU/SMPTE timecodes used on other video products.

10.3 Distribution

As stated, the segment begins after the audio blocks, with sectors zero and one, and continues on the next pair of tracks with sectors two and three. This arrangement ensures that in a four-headed machine data from each segment is distributed over all four heads. Fig. 10.2 shows the relationship between sector number and head number. Heads zero and one begin the track by playing sectors two and three of an odd segment, and continue through the audio sectors to play sectors zero and one of the next segment. If head one should clog, sector one will be lost in even-numbered segments, whereas sector three will be lost in odd-numbered segments. Similarly if head two clogs, sector two in even-numbered segments and sector zero in odd-numbered segments will be lost. It will be seen that this

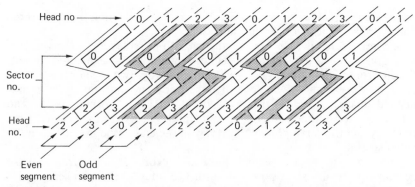

Figure 10.2 Sector distribution within a segment. In even segments, sector number equals head number, whereas in odd segments (shown shaded) head zero exchanges with head two and head one exchanges with head three. If, for example, head one were to clog, sector one would be lost in even segments whereas sector three would be lost in odd segments. In the absence of this arrangement, a clogged head would lose half of every other segment, which would be harder to conceal

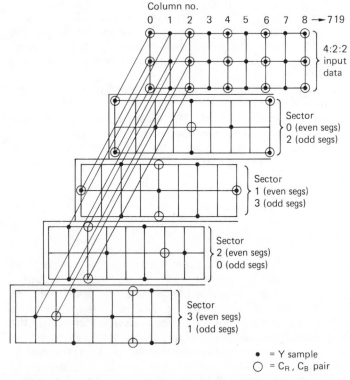

Figure 10.3(a) Distribution of the input 4:2:2 data over four parallel channels is performed as shown here. The criterion is the best concealment ability in case of the loss of one or more channels

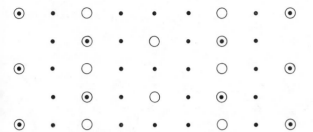

Figure 10.3(b) The result of combining the channels when data from sector 1 is lost. Spatial interpolation can be used to restore picture content

Figure 10.3(c) When sectors 0 and 1 are both lost both Y and C_R, C_B are still available at half the normal sampling rate and so effective concealment is still possible

alternation between odd and even segments is reflected in the data distribution over the four sectors.

Fig. 10.3(a) shows how the data from 50 video lines are distributed over the four sectors of a segment[5]. The distribution is complicated by the fact that the video data consist of pixels which are alternately co-sited Y, C_r, C_b samples and Y-only samples. The goal of the distribution strategy is to permit the best concealment possible in the case of lost sectors, and Fig. 10.3(b) also shows the samples which will be lost if one sector is unrecoverable. Horizontal or vertical interpolation is possible to conceal the missing samples. Fig. 10.3(c) shows the result if two sectors are lost. Samples of both luminance and colour difference are still available at one-half of the original sampling rates of each, and so a reduced bandwidth picture can still be produced.

10.4 Video mapping

In binary PCM systems, the samples consist of a number of bits, in this case 8, which each determine whether a particular power of two should be present in the output level. An 8 bit system has 256 quantizing intervals, and an error in the least significant bit of a sample results in an error of one of these levels, whereas an error in the most significant bit results in an error of 128 levels, or half of the signal range. If the two most significant bits are considered, the maximum possible error will be 192 levels, but the largest errors will result if the sample value is near the end of the range, as shown in Fig. 10.4(a).

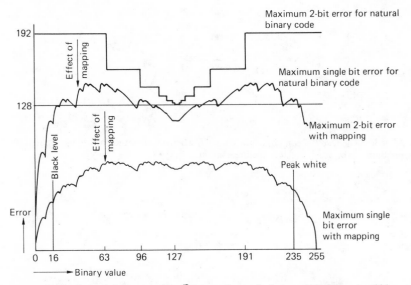

Figure 10.4(a) A single bit error will cause a maximum deviation of 128Q in natural binary, but this is reduced to the lower line by mapping. A double bit error will cause a maximum deviation of 128 + 64 = 192Q, and the effect of mapping on this magnitude of error is also shown

		Least significant four bits														
Input	0	1	2	3	4	5	6	7	8	9	A	B	C	D	E	F
0	00	80	40	20	10	08	04	02	01	C0	A0	90	88	84	82	81
1	60	50	48	44	42	41	30	28	24	22	21	18	14	12	11	0C
2	0A	09	06	05	03	E0	D0	C8	C4	C2	C1	B0	A8	A4	A2	A1
3	98	94	92	91	8C	8A	89	86	85	83	70	68	64	62	61	58
4	54	52	51	4C	4A	49	46	45	43	38	34	32	31	2C	2A	29
5	26	25	23	1C	1A	19	16	15	13	0E	0D	0B	07	F0	E8	E4
6	E2	E1	D8	D4	D2	D1	CC	CA	C9	C6	C5	C3	B8	B4	B2	B1
7	AC	AA	A9	A6	A5	A3	9C	9A	99	96	95	93	8E	8D	8B	87
8	78	74	72	71	6C	6A	69	66	65	63	5C	5A	59	56	55	53
9	4E	4D	4B	47	3C	3A	39	36	35	33	2E	2D	2B	27	1E	1D
A	1B	17	0F	F8	F4	F2	F1	EC	EA	E9	E6	E5	E3	DC	DA	D9
B	D6	D5	D3	CE	CD	CB	C7	BC	BA	B9	B6	B5	B3	AE	AD	AB
C	A7	9E	9D	9B	97	8F	7C	7A	79	76	75	73	6E	6D	6B	67
D	5E	5D	5B	57	4F	3E	3D	3B	37	2F	1F	FC	FA	F9	F6	F5
E	F3	EE	ED	EB	E7	DE	DD	DB	D7	CF	BE	BD	BB	B7	AF	9F
F	7E	7D	7B	77	6F	5F	3F	FE	FD	FB	F7	EF	DF	BF	7F	FF

Most significant four bits (row label, vertical)

Figure 10.4(b) The mapping table. This will need to be reversed on playback

Essentially some bits are more important than others in PCM systems. An uncorrected least significant bit would probably go unnoticed on real programme material, whereas an uncorrected most significant bit would result in an obvious dot contrasting with the surrounding picture area. The eye is most sensitive to such errors where the background is dark, i.e. the numerical values of the samples involved are small, and yet it is in exactly this region that the double-bit error is the greatest[6].

Mapping is a process which is designed to reduce the dominance of the most significant bits. Incoming video samples to be recorded are fed to a lookup table which translates each 8-bit value to a different 8-bit value. The reverse process takes place on replay, and in the absence of errors, the original data are restored perfectly. However, if 1 or 2 bits of the mapped sample are wrong, the incorrect value which results from the reverse mapping process will have an error which is considerably smaller.

Fig. 10.4(a) shows that the result of mapping is to reduce the actual error magnitude when bit errors occur. If the error-correction system is working properly, this is of no consequence, but it was included because it was felt that portable machines might be made which had full record circuitry, but which had confidence replay without error correction to reduce power consumption and size. In this case, mapping would result in a real improvement in subjective quality. Developments in LSI technology mean that full error correction is now possible even in portable machines, so this feature is in fact unnecessary, and it has no parallel in the D-2 format.

The mapping table is shown in Fig. 10.4(b). This is most commonly implemented in a PROM. An example is shown to illustrate the reduction in error magnitude achieved.

Only active line video samples are mapped.

10.5 Constraints on the error-correction strategy

The error-correction strategy of DVTRs is a difficult subject because there are conflicting requirements. It was shown in Chapter 7 that interleaving is essential to break up large physical bursts into smaller errors in many different codewords. It is simplest if the interleaving structure is regular, so that a product code can be implemented on the rows and columns of blocks of data. Unfortunately, if such a simple scheme is overwhelmed by an excess of errors, the uncorrectable samples will appear in regular rows or columns on the picture and concealment will be less effective because the eye can perceive more easily the regular structure.

An irregular interleave, known as a *shuffle*, can be designed to disperse contiguous errors on the tape track over large distances in two dimensions on the screen, and the concealment is then more effective[7].

Shuffling over an entire field or frame contradicts the requirement for picture in shuttle, and the shuffle has to be limited to segment size.

In shuttle, the helical scan process breaks down because the tape speed is no longer proportional to the scanner speed, and the tape tracks are pulled across the head path so that the recovery of entire sectors is impossible. A picture of some sort is required in shuttle to aid the rapid location of wanted material on the tape, although the quality criteria can be relaxed considerably since such a picture would never be broadcast.

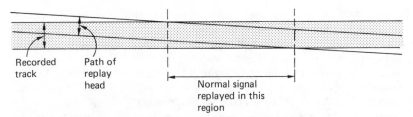

Recorded
track

Path of
replay
head

Normal signal
replayed in this
region

Figure 10.5 The replay head is slightly narrower than the recorded track, and so a short length of track is replayed normally when the heads cross tracks in shuttle. A sync block is made shorter than the length of track which can be recovered at the highest shuttle speed

Fig. 10.5 shows that in shuttle the path of a head crosses tape tracks obliquely. If the replay head is slightly narrower than the record head, which is usually the case, the replay signal can be of sufficient quality for a reasonable time when the head is within the track boundaries. The sectors are broken up into short elements called *sync blocks* which are smaller than the length of track which can be recovered at typical shuttle speeds. There are 160 sync blocks in a sector, 720 in a segment. Each sync block contains two entire Reed–Solomon codewords, and so it is possible to tell if the sync block was correctly recovered or not, without reference to any other part of the track.

If a sync block is read correctly, it is used to update a frame store which refreshes the picture monitor. Sync blocks which are not read correctly are prevented from updating the frame store, so if concealment cannot be used, the previous data are used again. It is preferable to use concealment, since excessive stale data causes trails on movement. The displayed picture in shuttle will thus be a mixture of information from more or less recent fields off tape. Since alternate pixels in a colour difference DVTR consist of three components, it is important that all three components of given pixels are in the same sync block, otherwise it is not possible to update the frame store properly. Updating the luminance without the colour difference, or updating one colour difference value and not the other, would produce some peculiar effects. This places a further constraint on the way in which samples can be distributed across the tape surface.

At certain tape speeds, the rotation of the heads will beat with the passage of tape tracks such that some parts of the sectors are never or rarely recovered. The framestore is not updated, and the screen continues to be refreshed with stale data which is no longer representative of the picture at that position on the tape. The problem of stale data in shuttle is reduced if the shuffle used has a *random dispersion*, but this then contradicts the requirements of good concealment at normal speeds, since a random shuffle implies that uncorrected errors can be clustered on the monitor screen, making concealment more difficult than if they were subject to a *maximum dispersion* shuffle.

Finally it is necessary to consider the implementation of an interleaving/shuffling scheme. Picture samples have a two-dimensional picture address, and shuffle is achieved by address mapping (see Chapter 5). An overcomplicated address generator will raise the cost of the hardware needed to implement the format.

10.6 Interleaving for shuttle

The samples from the distributor of Fig. 10.3 are recorded quite independently in four different sectors, and so each will store one-quarter of the total. As a result, following the distributor, each line consists of 360 samples, 180 of luminance and 90 of each type of colour difference sample. As each segment contains 50 lines, one sector will contain 50 × 360 = 18 000 samples. These will be assembled into a *sector array*, and codewords will be formed in rows and columns through the array. Incoming samples will be made into codewords which are written into the array in columns. The array is then read in rows, and the rows are formed into further codewords which are written on tape as sync blocks. On replay, the process is reversed. Fig. 10.6 shows that codewords are generated on columns

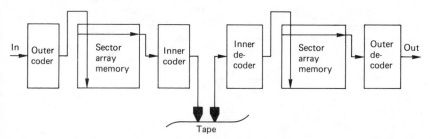

Figure 10.6 Basic interleave mechanism. Incoming data from columns in the array memory but are written to tape rows. Process is reversed on replay. Burst errors on tape are broken up by the de-interleave process and are more easily correctable

before the memory, and checked after the memory, and so these are called outer codewords, whereas the sync blocks contain codewords which are generated at the output of the memory and checked before the memory, so these are called inner codewords. A tape defect which causes the destruction of a sync block will result in only one sample being in error in a large number of outer codes, and this is the interleave mechanism.

Fig. 10.7(a) shows the sample sequence from the sector distributor. If samples in this sequence were made into an outer code and written in the sector array as a column, the effect would be as shown in Fig. 10.7(b). Samples relating to one pixel would appear in three different inner codewords, and so it would not be possible to update pixels properly if a single sync block is recovered in shuttle. The sector array has done an excellent job of interleaving the samples. Unfortunately it has done too well, and it is necessary to oppose some of the sector array interleave with a reverse interleave prior to the generation of outer codewords in order to get all samples relating to a pixel into one sync block.

Fig. 10.7(c) shows that the samples from the distributor are split into three blocks of one-third of a line which each contain 120 samples. These blocks are then subjected to a four-way interleave which produces four 30 byte blocks to which 2 bytes of Reed–Solomon redundancy are added to produce outer codewords. It will be seen from Fig. 10.7(c) that each codeword is formed entirely from the same type of sample. When these

Horizontal
Index →

Index →	0	1	2	3	4	5	6	7	8		356	357	358	359
Type of → symbol	CB_0	Y_0	CR_0	Y_1	CB_2	Y_2	CR_2	Y_3	CB_4		CB_{178}	Y_{178}	CR_{178}	Y_{179}

Figure 10.7(a) The output of the four channel distributor is a sequence of this kind in each channel. There will be 360 bytes in each line

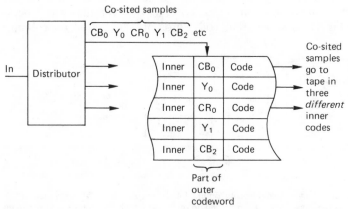

Figure 10.7(b) The result of interleaving the sample sequence of (a) is that co-sited samples appear in different inner codes and cannot be recovered in shuttle

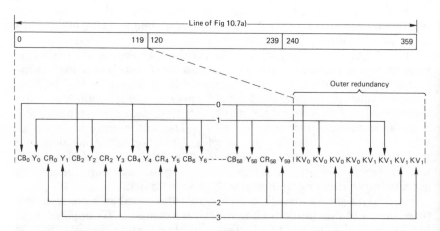

Figure 10.7(c) The line of (a) is split into three parts. Each is then made into four interleaved codewords as shown here. Each outer code has 30 data bytes and two redundancy bytes. Twelve such outer codes are needed to complete the line. Each code is formed from the same type of sample

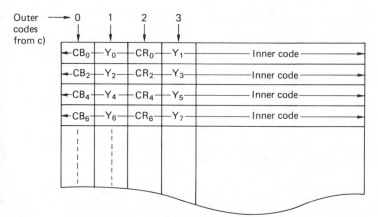

Figure 10.7(d) When the outer codes of (c) are used to form columns in a sector array as shown here, the inner codes will contain co-sited pixels due to the reverse interleave which was performed prior to generating the outer codes. Inner codes picked up at random in shuttle now can be used to update a framestore

outer codewords become adjacent columns of the sector array, it will be seen from Fig. 10.7(d) that all three samples relating to a given pixel will be in the same row of the array, and so will be recorded in the same sync block, permitting framestore updating in shuttle[5].

The process must be repeated three times to deal with the whole line, and this will result in 12 outer code blocks which occupy 12 adjacent columns in the sector array. As there are 50 lines in the segment, the sector array will need $12 \times 50 = 600$ columns.

10.7 Sync block generation

As was shown in Chapter 7, the inner codes of a product block are designed to correct one-byte random errors and to declare with high reliability the entire codeword to be in error in the case of dropout. This then generates erasure flags to enable correction to be performed by the outer codes.

If the inner codeword is too large, it will effectively magnify errors by declaring the whole codeword to be in error when only part of it is corrupt. A further consideration is that if synchronization is lost by the data separator due to a dropout, data will be lost until the next synchronization pattern is seen, again magnifying the effect of the error. Finally in shuttle it is also advantageous if the sync blocks are short, so that they will be more likely to be recovered when the heads cross tracks.

If an inner codeword were made from a complete row of the sector array, it would contain 600 bytes of data, but this is far too large, for the reasons stated[8]. Instead, the sector array is divided horizontally into ten product blocks, so that each inner codeword contains only 60 bytes of data. 4 bytes of Reed–Solomon redundancy are added to form a 64 byte codeword. Making each codeword into a sync block would introduce an

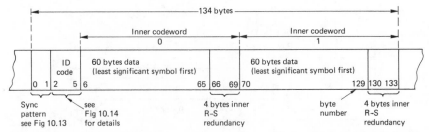

Figure 10.8 The D-1 sync block begins with synchronizing and identification, and contains two inner codewords each having four bytes of redundancy

excessive synchronizing overhead. Instead two codewords form a sync block, and 160 sync blocks will be necessary to contain the entire sector array.

Fig. 10.8 shows the details of a sync block. The two 64 byte inner codewords are preceded by a synchronizing pattern and a 4 byte identification code. This code uniquely labels every sync block over a four-field sequence and is especially useful in shuttle when tracks are crossed randomly. The generation of the ID codes is complex and will be treated separately.

Each sync block represents a track length of just less than half a millimetre.

10.8 The shuffling mechanism

It has been stated that there are two conflicting requirements for the shuffling scheme, and the solutions adopted in D-1 must therefore contain an element of compromise. Nevertheless a robust and practical format has resulted.

In normal play, an error which is too large to be corrected will have to be concealed. It can be seen from the sector array that two symbols can be corrected in each outer codeword using erasure. Since there are 600 columns in the sector array, and thus the same number of outer codewords, then a maximum 1 200 bytes of data can be lost from a sector and still be corrected. This corresponds to 20 inner codewords, ten sync blocks or a track length of about 4.8 mm. If this error condition is exceeded, total correction is no longer possible, and horizontal rows of erroneous data will appear in the sector array. The inner codewords detect these errors as before, but the erasure flags will now be used for concealment. The problem is that the eye is extremely adept at spotting regular arrays, and even if all of the failed samples were concealed, the regular shape of the concealment area would still be discernible.

The solution is to break up the regularity of the sector array using shuffling. The outer codes are generated as usual and fed to successive columns of the array, but when the array is full, it is subjected to a memory mapping process which permutes the row and column addresses when the array is read to form inner codewords and sync blocks. As a result, individual sync blocks contain pixels gathered from a 50 line screen area.

When the tape is played back, the same mapping process is initiated to generate write addresses when the sector array is filled with inner codewords off tape. The shuffle is thus reversed, and the sector array contains the same outer codewords in the same columns as before. However, uncorrectable errors will now result in a pattern of concealments which is the same as the shuffle pattern. These will then be much less visible.

In shuttle, sync blocks will be recovered at random, and the shuffle means that when a sync block is successfully read, the pixels it contains are spread widely, so the framestore will be updated all over instead of just in certain areas. This explains the twinkling effect observed in the shuttle picture of DVTRs.

For good concealment, the shuffle should disperse the pixels as far apart as possible over the whole picture, whereas for good shuttle performance, the shuffle should disperse the pixels randomly over a segment. This apparent contradiction is overcome by considering that the shuttle picture is actually made up of parts of many sectors, whereas concealment will take place within the same segment. The shuffle within the sector is designed primarily with dispersion in mind to give good concealment. If all sectors were the same, at certain tape speeds, parts of the track would never be read and stale samples would be read from the framestore. However, the shuffle is not constant; it changes between odd sectors and even sectors, and from field to field over a four-field sequence. This changing shuffle pattern generates the necessary spatial variability to reduce the probability of stale data in shuttle.

Address A	A × 11		A × 11 mod 16
0	0		0
1	11		11
2	22	(−16)	6
3	33	(−32)	1
4	44	(−32)	12
5	55	(−48)	7
6	66	(−64)	2
7	77	(−64)	13
8	88	(−80)	8
9	99	(−96)	3
10	110	(−96)	14
11	121	(−112)	9
12	132	(−128)	4
13	143	(−128)	15
14	154	(−144)	10
15	165	(−160)	5

Figure 10.9(a) The permuted addresses for a shuffle can be obtained by multiplication of the addresses by a number relatively prime to the modulo base

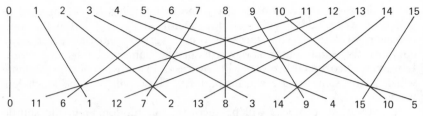

Figure 10.9(b) The shuffle which results from the calculations of (a)

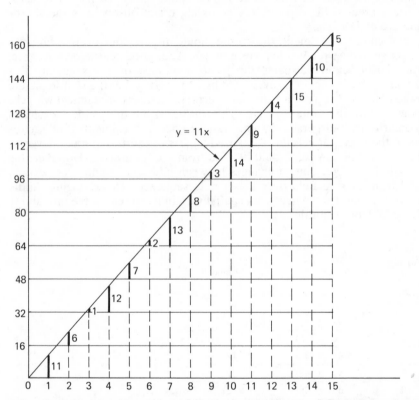

Figure 10.9(c) Modulo arithmetic is rather similar to quantizing. The results of Figure 10.9(a) can be obtained by quantizing the graph of y = 11x with the quantizing intervals of 16 units

The sector array is quite large, and it is not easy to implement a suitable shuffle because the goal is contradictary – repeatable irregularity. Whilst any shuffle desired could be implemented with an address lookup table, such a table stretching over four fields would be immense and unworkable. On the other hand an address relationship obtainable from a simple algorithm would not be irregular enough.

The solution adopted in D-1 is to obtain a good compromise by using address multiplication by a prime number in modulo arithmetic. This is easier than it sounds, as the simple example of Fig. 10.9(a) shows. In this example, 16 pixels are to be shuffled. The pixel addresses are multiplied by 11, which is relatively prime to 16, and the result is expressed modulo 16, which is to say that if the product exceeds an integer multiple of 16, that integer multiple is subtracted. It will be seen from Fig. 10.9(b) that an effective shuffle is created. Modulo arithmetic has a similar effect to quantizing. In fact a number expressed modulo is the quantizing error due to quantizing in steps equal to the modulo base as Fig. 10.9(c) shows. When the input has a large range, the quantizing error becomes random.

Fig. 10.10(a) shows the address generator which is used in the D-1 shuffle[5]. On recording, this device generates the read addresses to shuffle

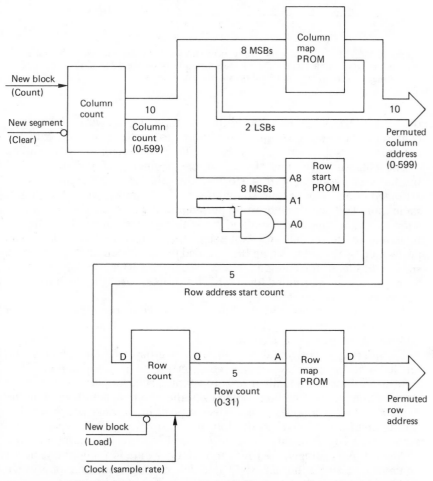

Figure 10.10(a) Shuffle address generator of D-1. The two least significant bits of the column count bypass the column Map PROM so that sets of four columns are permuted to keep co-sited samples adjacent. The row counter is loaded with a starting count from the Row Start PROM. When the two least significant bits of the column count are one, this corresponds to the last column of the set of four. This condition is detected by the AND gate which modifies the Row Start PROM address to shuffle the luminance only pixel in the last column relative to the co-sited samples in the other three columns

Row address

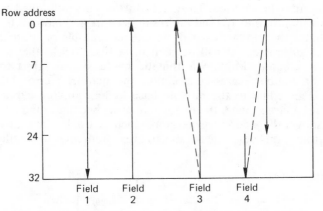

Field   Field   Field   Field
1   2   3   4

Figure 10.10(b) Modification of the row sequence from field to field improves randomness of shuffle for better shuttle picture. Field 1 reads forward from 0, Field 2 reads reverse from 32. Field 3 reads reverse from 7 and Field 4 reads forward from 24

the sector array before it is written to tape. On playback, the same configuration determines the write addresses, so that off-tape data are automatically subjected to a reverse shuffle as the sector array is written.

The column counter is cleared at the beginning of the sector, and produces a column count from 0 to 599. The columns in the sector array are arranged into groups of four, so that the co-sited samples will still be in the same inner codewords after group permutation. There are thus 150 group addresses, and these are shuffled by multiplying them by 41, which is relatively prime to 150, and expressing the product modulo 150. This is performed by the column map PROM, and it will be seen that the two least significant bits of the column address bypass the PROM so that groups of four columns are permuted together. This process results in the horizontal dimension of the shuffle.

The vertical dimension of the shuffle is obtained by performing a vertical address permutation on each column in the sector array, where the starting address of the process is also permuted.

Considering a horizontal row through a group of four columns, the left-hand three samples are the components of a co-sited pixel. The right-hand sample is a luminance-only sample. The row permutations must be the same for the first three columns of the group, again to maintain the presence of all components of a co-sited pixel in an inner codeword, but the luminance only pixel in the fourth column is physically near on the screen, and concealment would be better if it were in a different inner codeword. Accordingly, the row start count permutation stays the same for columns 0, 1 and 2, but an AND gate detects a column value of 3 which adds a constant to the row start address in the fourth column of the group. The column count is multiplied by 30 and expressed modulo 32 to give the starting address except when the last column of the group is encountered, when 5 is added to the product before being expressed modulo 32.

The row start count is loaded into the row counter which is clocked at sample rate. The row count runs from 0 to 31 since there are 32 symbols in an outer codeword and hence 32 rows in the sector array. The row count is multiplied by 7, which is relatively prime to 32, and the product is expressed modulo 32 to produce a permuted row address.

The pixels within a sector are now shuffled, but all sectors are not shuffled the same. The shuffle picture is improved by changing the shuffle over a four-field sequence, and this is shown in Fig. 10.10(b).

Since two heads work in parallel, a linear tape scratch could cause damage at the same place in two sector arrays and could therefore damage the concealment distribution strategy. This is prevented by rotating the row address by 16 between sectors written by adjacent heads and is simply implemented by inverting the MSB of the row address. Then, in different fields, the row address is rotated by differing amounts.

10.9 RNRZ channel coding

The need for channel coding was detailed in Chapter 6 and so this section will confine itself to those details specific to the implementation in D-1.

D-1 uses randomizing to break up uncontrolled run lengths in the raw data. Randomizing does not, however, result in run-length limiting; it only reduces the probability of longer run lengths. DC content is eliminated by randomizing, but low frequencies will still be present, resulting in long wavelengths on tape which cannot be fully erased by overwrite. The presence of low frequencies in the channel makes the system less suitable for azimuth recording which is not used and requires the presence of guard bands between the tracks. Residual tracking errors are prevented from modulating the replay signal by making the replay head a little narrower than the record head, as is done in stationary-head recorders. The lack of azimuth recording means that in shuttle either head of the parallel pair can pick up sync blocks from either track of the segment. This is an advantage for machines which have no track-following mechanism.

The possibility of long wavelengths on tape means that a separate erase process is necessary before recording, and, as with all helical scan video recorders, a stationary erase head cannot be used for editing, and erase heads must be mounted on the scanner. In order to reduce mechanical complexity in the scanner and the number of connections which must be

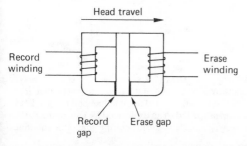

Figure 10.11 A separate erasehead is necessary with RNRZ recording, and this shares a common pole with the record head. Gaps between sectors must be large enough to accommodate the displacement between erase and record functions

brought to the rotating assembly, a combined erase and record head has been developed[9]. Fig. 10.11 shows that the erase and write gaps share a common centre polepiece. The record and erase drive circuits are both in the scanner, and can be enabled by the same signal. Only two signal connections are now needed to each record head. Erase is enabled whenever the record amplifier is activated by a third signal. This does, however, mean that writing and erasing begin and end at the same time, rather than in the same place on the tape. For example, at the end of writing a sector, the write head will be turned off, but at that time the erase gap will have erased ahead of the write gap, leaving a short length of erased track. Spaces between sectors have been deliberately left in the tracks so that editing of individual sectors can take place, for example when performing a frame insert, or where only one channel of audio is being recorded.

The tape used is an oxide type with a coercivity of 850 Oe, since at the time D-1 was standardized the higher coercivity metal powder tapes were not fully developed. It was found at the time of design that the best available heads could not saturate metal powder tape at the frequencies involved. The use of guard bands combined with tape of moderate coercivity means that the recording density achieved, although impressive in numerical terms, gives a tape consumption which is no better than that of an analog machine. The picture quality is of course above criticism.

The data randomizing is performed by recording the exclusive-OR function of the data and a Galois field. These were described in Chapter 7.

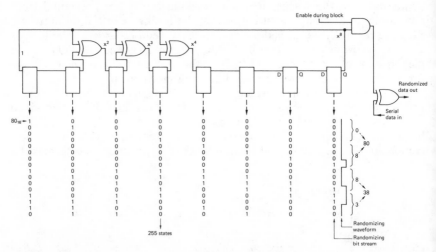

Figure 10.12(a) The polynomial generator (top) calculates $x^8 + x^4 + x^3 + x^2 + x^1$ and is preset to 80_{16} every 5 sync blocks at the addresses shown in (b). When the generator is clocked, it will produce a Galois Field having 255 states (see Chapter 7). The right hand bit of each field element becomes the randomizing bit stream, and is fed to an exclusive-OR gate in the data stream. Randomizing is disabled during the sync and ID patterns, but the generator continues to run.

It is also possible to randomize using a counter working at byte rate which addresses a PROM. Eight exclusive-OR gates will then be needed to randomize the byte in one clock period

The randomizing polynomial and one way in which it can be implemented are shown in Fig. 10.12(a). The polynomial is in fact the same one as is used for the generation of the inner and outer Reed–Solomon codes.

As the polynomial generates a maximum length sequence from an eight-bit wordlength, the sequence length is given by $2^8 - 1 = 255$. The sequence will repeat endlessly over this period, and could have been allowed to run over the entire length of a sector were it not for the requirement to have picture in shuttle. In order to recover the data from a randomized sync block, the sequence has to be recreated in the same relative phase as existed when the block was written. As the number of bytes in a sync block is not the same as the number of states in the sequence, each sync block would begin with a different state. This is of no consequence if the sector is played from end to end, but in shuttle only certain sync blocks will be recovered, and the correct starting state of the sequence will need to be preset into the sequence generator for each block. All of the starting values would have to be stored, raising the complexity of implementation. On the other hand, a sequence which is too short could raise the possibility of false sync detection.

A compromise is obtained by allowing the sequence to run for five sync blocks before resetting it. Since the audio sectors consist of five sync blocks, the sequence does indeed continue throughout audio sectors. However, in the video sectors there are 160 sync blocks, and this is conveniently a multiple of five, such that there 32 repeated sequences in each sector. If a sync block is picked up at random in shuttle, it is only necessary to decide which of five starting states is necessary. Fig. 10.12(b)

03	19	31	47	5D	75	8B	A3
08	20	36	4C	64	7A	92	A8
0D	25	3B	53	69	81	97	AD
14	2A	42	58	70	86	9C	B4

Figure 10.12(b) The above list shows the sync block ID codes at which the randomizer is reset. This is every five blocks for a sector length of 160 blocks (video sector). Note that the ID addresses are base 14 (see Figure 10.14a), and so it is possible to calculate the next address by adding 5 but treating the sum as a base 14 number. For example the third ID shown above is OD which is 13 decimal. Adding 5 makes 18 decimal which is 14 in base 14. The audio sectors are five sync blocks long, and so the reset will take place at the first block, which is C3 or D3. Some of the above IDs can be seen marked * in Figure 10.14(b)

shows the sync block numbers at which the sequence is reset, and Fig. 10.12(c) shows the randomizing sequence. The repeat after 255 states is marked. At the very beginning of each of these sync blocks, coincident with the first bit of the sync pattern, the cyclic circuit is preset to 80_{16} and generates the sequence shown. The first 6 bytes of the sync block are the sync pattern and the ID. Clearly these cannot be randomized, since this causes a Catch-22 situation where it is not possible to synchronize the sequence for replay until the ID is read, but it is not possible to read the ID until the sequence is synchronized!

To avoid this situation, the sequence is allowed to run, but it is not used until the first genuine data byte in the sync block. The sync pattern and the

Sequence A

80	38	D2	81	49	76										
82	DA	9A	86	6F	AF	8B	B0	F1	9C	D1	12	A5	72	37	EF
97	59	31	B8	EA	53	C8	3F	F4	58	40	1C	E9	C0	24	3B
41	6D	4D	C3	B7	D7	45	D8	78	CE	68	89	52	B9	9B	F7
CB	AC	18	5C	F5	29	E4	1F	7A	2C	20	8E	74	60	92	9D
A0	B6	A6	E1	DB	EB	22	6C	3C	67	B4	44	A9	DC	CD	FB
65	56	0C	AE	FA	14	F2	0F	3D	16	10	47	3A	30	C9	4E
50	5B	D3	F0	ED	75	11	36	9E	33	5A	A2	54	EE	E6	FD
32	2B	06	57	7D	0A	F9	87	1E	0B	88	23	1D	98	64	27

Sequence B

A8	AD	69	F8	F6	BA										
08	1B	CF	19	2D	51	2A	77	F3	7E	99	15	83	AB	3E	85
FC	43	8F	05	C4	91	0E	4C	B2	13	D4	D6	34	7C	7B	5D
84	8D	E7	8C	96	28	95	BB	79	BF	CC	8A	C1	55	9F	42
FE	A1	C7	02	E2	48	07	26	D9	09	6A	6B	1A	BE	BD	2E
C2	C6	73	46	4B	94	CA	DD	BC	5F	66	C5	E0	AA	4F	21
FF	D0	63	01	71	A4	03	93	EC	04	B5	35	0D	DF	5E	17
61	E3	39	A3	25	4A	E5	6E	DE	2F	B3	62	70	D5	A7	90
7F	E8	B1	80	38	D2	81	49	76	82	DA	9A	86	6F	AF	8B

↖ Sequence repeat

Sequence C

B0	F1	9C	D1	12	A5										
72	37	EF	97	59	31	B8	EA	53	C8	3F	F4	58	40	1C	E9
C0	24	3B	41	6D	4D	C3	B7	D7	45	D8	78	CE	68	89	52
B9	9B	F7	CB	AC	18	5C	F5	29	E4	1F	7A	2C	20	8E	74
60	92	9D	A0	B6	A6	E1	DB	EB	22	6C	3C	67	B4	44	A9
DC	CD	FB	65	56	0C	AE	FA	14	F2	0F	3D	16	10	47	3A
30	C9	4E	50	5B	D3	F0	ED	75	11	36	9E	33	5A	A2	54
EE	E6	FD	32	2B	06	57	7D	0A	F9	87	1E	0B	88	23	1D
98	64	27	A8	AD	69	F8	F6	BA	08	1B	CF	19	2D	51	2A

Sequence D

77	F3	7E	99	15	83										
AB	3E	85	FC	43	8F	05	C4	91	0E	4C	B2	13	D4	D6	34
7C	7B	5D	84	8D	E7	8C	96	28	95	BB	79	BF	CC	8A	C1
55	9F	42	FE	A1	C7	02	E2	48	07	26	D9	09	6A	6B	1A
BE	BD	2E	C2	C6	73	46	4B	94	CA	DD	BC	5F	66	C5	E0
AA	4F	21	FF	D0	63	01	71	A4	03	93	EC	04	B5	35	0D
DF	5E	17	61	E3	39	A3	25	4A	E5	6E	DE	2F	B3	62	70
D5	A7	90	7F	E8	B1	80	38	D2	81	49	76	82	DA	9A	86
6F	AF	8B	B0	F1	9C	D1	12	A5	72	37	EF	97	59	31	B8

Sequence E   — During sync + 1D — not used

EA	53	C8	3F	F4	58										
40	1C	E9	C0	24	3B	41	6D	4D	C3	B7	D7	45	D8	78	CE
68	89	52	B9	9B	F7	CB	AC	18	5C	F5	29	E4	1F	7A	2C
20	8E	74	60	92	9D	A0	B6	A6	E1	DB	EB	22	6C	3C	67
B4	44	A9	DC	CD	FB	65	56	0C	AE	FA	14	F2	0F	3D	16
10	47	3A	30	C9	4E	50	5B	D3	F0	ED	75	11	36	9E	33
5A	A2	54	EE	E6	FD	32	2B	06	57	7D	0A	F9	87	1E	0B
88	23	1D	98	64	27	A8	AD	69	F8	F6	BA	08	1B	CF	19
2D	51	2A	77	F3	7E	99	15	83	AB	3E	85	FC	43	8F	05

Figure 10.12(c) The sequence which results when the randomizer of (a) is allowed to run for five sync blocks. The first six symbols are not used, since they are generated when the sync pattern and ID patterns are being recorded. Five sync blocks exceeds the sequence length of 255 ($2^8 - 1$) and the repeats of the sequence can be seen underlined

ID code have to be rendered DC free in a way which does not require randomizing. Clearly the sync/ID information also has to be provided with its own error correction mechanism, since it is excluded from the main code words in the sync block.

10.10 Synchronization and identification

Each sync block contains two inner codewords, as was shown in Fig. 10.8. It is called a sync block because it is the smallest quantum of data on the track with which the playback channel can synchronize independently. Synchronizing occurs on three levels: to the bit, to the symbol, and to the sync block.

The recording density used in DVTRs is such that mechanical measurement of scanner phase is not sufficiently accurate to locate a given bit. Synchronization on playback is achieved by letting the heads rotate to a reasonable standard of accuracy and accepting the signals at the exact time they are replayed. A phase-locked loop in the replay circuitry must lock to the actual bit rate of the offtape signal so that the individual bits in the recording can be separated. At the beginning of a track a reference for the phase-locked loop, called a preamble, is recorded. This contains no data, but serves to set the frequency of the PLL the same as the offtape bit rate and thus achieve bit synchronism. Once the loop is locked, it can stay in lock by phase-comparing the location of data transitions with its own. In this way bit synchronism can be achieved at the beginning of the track, maintained throughout it, and even regained if it is lost due to a severe dropout, since the PLL can relock to data transitions.

Once bit synchronization is achieved, the serial bit stream has to be correctly divided up into 8-bit symbols to restore the original samples. This is word synchronization, and it is achieved with the help of a unique bit pattern which always occurs at the start of the sync block. The purpose of this sync pattern is to reset the divide-by-eight counter which deserializes the data into symbols. The sync pattern is extremely important, since detecting it 1 bit early or late would corrupt every symbol in the sync block, since the LSB of one sample would become the MSB of the next. The sync pattern of D-1 is a 16 bit code shown in Fig. 10.13 which carries a range of run lengths so that it differs from itself shifted by as many bits as possible.

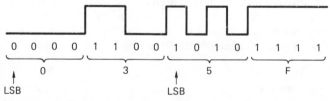

Figure 10.13 The sync pattern of D-1 carries a variety of run-lengths so that it is very difficult to detect sync with a bit shift in the presence of noise. Serialization is Least Significant Bit (LSB) first, so sync pattern is written 3OF5

Random errors are then less likely to produce a mistimed sync detection, and an accurate detection is still possible in the case of a random bit error. The sync pattern is DC free because it contains as many ones as zeros. In the body of a sector, sync patterns occur regularly every 134 bytes, so it is desireable for the replay circuitry to predict the position of a window in which the next sync pattern will be seen. This flywheel mechanism reduces the possibility of false sync detection.

Once symbol synchronizing is achieved, it is possible to read the sync block, and it remains to determine *which* sync block has been found. In normal play it will be the one after the previous one, but in shuttle the sequence is unpredictable. This is the third level of synchronization, and is the function of the ID pattern which occupies four bytes.

The correct identification of the sync block address is crucial, because a number of processes depend on it:

(a) It must be possible to distinguish reliably between audio and video sectors, so that audio does not end up on the screen in shuttle.

(b) There are five different states to which the pseudo-random sequence generator could be pre-set,only one of which is right.

(c) The shuffle permutation changes over a four-field sequence. The position in the sequence must be known, or the sync block cannot be deshuffled.

(d) There are four parallel channels of data and the picture cannot be demultiplexed correctly if the channel number of a sync block is not known.

The ID system carries the following parameters to meet the above requirements:

(a) A 2 bit field ID which repeats over a four-field sequence to reveal the shuffle permutation to be used. This sequence can become discontinuous at edits.

(b) A 3 bit segment ID which counts segments through a field. It will count 0–5 in 625 line systems and 0–4 in 525 line systems.

(c) The sector ID LSB which specifies which track of the two parallel tracks in a segment is being read.

(d) The sector ID MSB which alternates between audio and video sectors and between the first and second halves of the track.

(e) An 8 bit sync block number specifying the sync block address within a sector for video, within a sector pair for audio.

Using the above information, if the ID pattern is correctly recovered, it is possible to position the sync block precisely over a four field sequence. All of the mechanisms which depend on sync block position will then operate with a high degree of reliability even in shuttle.

Input ID	ID code	Input ID	ID code
0	1B	8	96
1	2E	9	A3
2	35	A	B8
3	47	B	CA
4	5C	C	D1
5	69	D	E4
6	72	(E) ⎫ Invalid code	
7	8D	(F) ⎬ Not dc free	

Figure 10.14(a) ID cannot be protected by codewords in the sync block due to use of RNRZ coding. Thus ID must have its own redundancy, and each 4 bits of Input ID is expressed as an eight-bit word which is a distance 4 BCH codeword. Codewords for E and F are not DC-free and are not used, so ID code is base 14

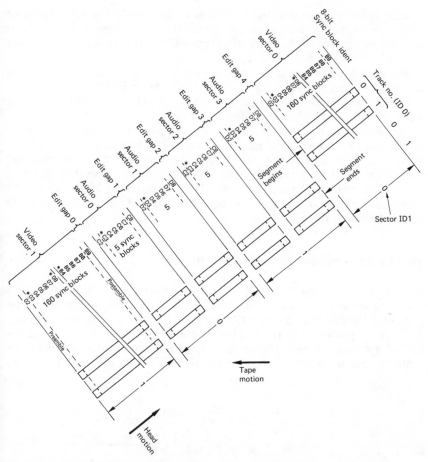

Figure 10.14(b) The relationship between ID codes and the position along the track. The sector ID is a two bit value comprising ID0 and ID1 shown here. These are combined with the segment and field ID to form the following:

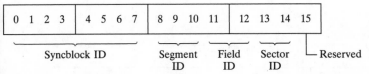

0 1 2 3	4 5 6 7	8 9 10 11	12 13 14 15
Syncblock ID		Segment ID	Field ID	Sector ID	Reserved

This is then mapped according to (a) from four bit symbols to eight bit symbols, to make a four byte ID pattern shown in Figure 10.8. The * symbol indicates IDs of sync blocks at which the randomizer of Figure 10.12 is reset

As the sync block ID is so important, it is protected against random errors by coding each 4 bits of ID address into an 8 bit codeword. This redundancy also allows the codewords generated to be DC free, since they cannot be randomized. The coding scheme used is a distance 4 BCH code and is implemented with lookup tables as shown in Fig. 10.14(a). Only 14 of the codes out of the 16 possible are DC free, and so the ID numbering system is base 14, so that the 8 bit sync block numbering has a range of 196_{10} (14^2) which is more than enough for the video sectors. The segment number never exceeds 5, and so the segment/field ID can also be expressed base 14.

With 4 bits of redundancy, correction of single-bit errors and detection of double-bit errors is possible using a 256 location PROM.

Fig. 10.14(b) shows the relationship between ID codes and sync block position over a complete segment.

In normal speed playback, sync blocks are played in sequence, and the player can predict what the next ID code will be and compare it with the value read to reduce further the probability of incorrect synchronization. In shuttle this is not possible, but it is quite likely in shuttle that if a complete sync block is recovered, the ID of the next sync block can also be read, and so a pair of inner codewords straddled by a pair of contiguous ID codes should be observed[10].

10.11 Gaps, preambles and postambles

A preamble has been seen to be necessary before the first sync block in a sector to allow the phase locked loop in the data separator to lock. The preamble also contains a sync pattern and an ID code so that the player can confirm the position of the head before entering the sector proper. At the end of a sector a postamble containing an ID code is written before the write current is turned off, so that the ID codes before and after the last

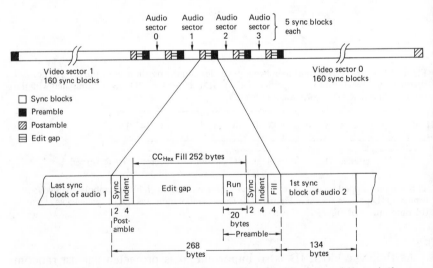

Figure 10.15 The position of preambles and postambles with respect to each sector is shown along with the gaps necessary to allow individual sectors to be written without corrupting others.

When the whole track is recorded, 252 bytes of CC_{Hex} fill are recorded after the postamble before the next sync pattern. If a subsequent recording commences in this gap, it must do so at least 20 bytes before the end in order to write a new run-in pattern for the new recording

sync block can still be compared. The preamble and postamble ID codes can be seen in Fig. 10.14(b). As the erase gap is ahead of the record gap, a short length of track will be left erased when recording stops. It is necessary to leave sufficient space along the track between sectors so that they may be written independently for editing. The sync block is the smallest data quantum which can be read, but the sector is the smallest data quantum which can be independently written.

Fig. 10.15 shows the position and structure of preambles and postambles. An edit gap is exactly the same length as two normal sync blocks so that it can be conveniently generated on record by allowing the sync block timing to continue and by simply switching to 'fill' data. At the end of the last sync block of a sector, the 6 byte sync pattern and ID are written, followed by 252 bytes of CC_{16}. This pattern causes data of 00110011... to be repeated, giving a replay signal at half the maximum bit rate which is the run-up pattern. Finally a 6 byte sync pattern and ID code for the preamble of the next block are recorded, followed by 4 more bytes of run-in code to act as a decision space for the player before the next sync block is entered.

During editing, recording may commence in the edit gap. There is some latitude for mechanical tolerance, but the new recording must not begin so early that the postamble of the previous sector is destroyed, and at least 20 bytes of new run-in must be recorded before the new preamble sync pattern, because it will not be possible to maintain bit phase through an edit, and the PLL will need to resynchronize when the track is subsequently played.

10.12 Block diagram of a D-1 machine

The video information to be recorded is specified by CCIR 601 and the layout of these data on tape is specified by the D-1 standard, but provided these requirements are met, there is no compulsion to use a particular mechanical design or circuit architecture.

Fig. 10.16(a) shows a typical block diagram of the record section of a D -1 machine, where the inputs will be component video and four audio channels. Audio and video inputs can be either analog or digital, and machines can incorporate converters which will be bypassed if a direct digital input is available. Whichever input form is used, the input video will always control the timing of the recording circuitry. In the case of a digital video input, the 27 MHz clock accompanying the data will be used to derive the symbol clock for much of the recorder. In the case of an analog input, the sync pulses will be fed to a phase-locked loop which produces a line-locked sampling rate which then will be used for the symbol clock.

The video data are distributed over four logical channels as was shown in Fig. 10.3. Only one of these is shown in full since they differ only in detail.

Following distribution, the mapping process of Fig. 10.4 is performed. The reverse interleave of Fig. 10.7 then takes place, and these data blocks then have two redundancy bytes added to make outer codes which are written into a sector array in columns. When the sector array is full, it is transferred to a second array memory, but the read addresses are

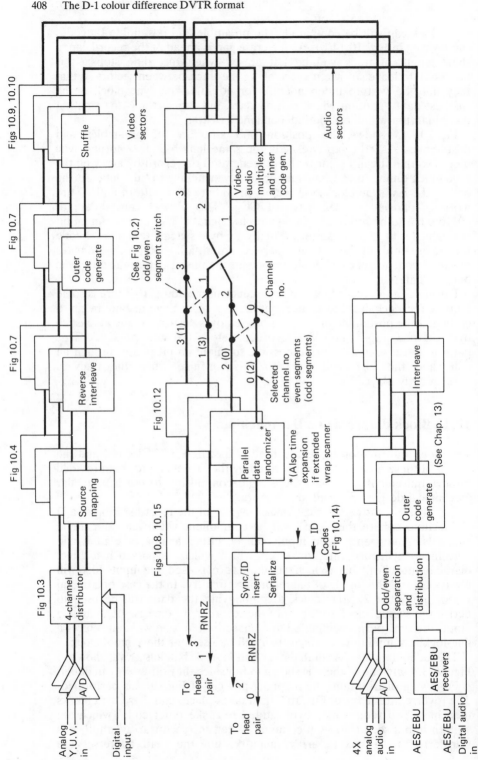

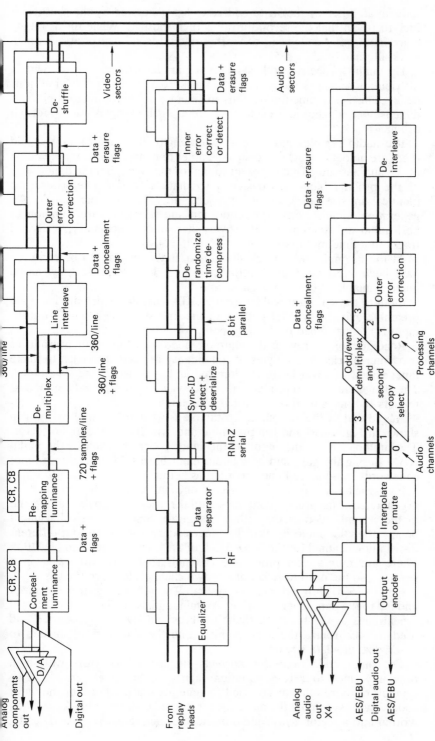

Figure 10.16(b) D-1 replay system. Note time decompression stage to allow data read in one head sweep to be processed in the time taken for the scanner to complete one revolution

sequential, whereas the write addresses are generated by the shuffler of Fig. 10.10, so that the second array is then shuffled. While this is taking place input outer codes will be written into a second pair of arrays which work alternately.

The audio processing takes place in parallel with the video, with a distribution scheme which spreads samples from all channels over all four heads. This is explained more fully in Chapter 13. Since audio is not two dimensional, no shuffle is necessary, and a regular array is used to form a product block.

The audio samples have longer wordlength than video samples, and there are no details such as co-sited samples to handle, so the outer coding of the audio is somewhat different to that of the video, but the dimensions of the product block are designed so that the audio inner codes are identical in size to video inner codes. In this way, the inner code generation, randomizing, ID generation and serializing are common to both audio and video, which effectively share the same circuitry, heads and tracks in a time multiplex.

At the beginning of a track, the audio and video data to be recorded have been interleaved and shuffled and are held in RAM so they can be made available at the appropriate time.

Input to the serializer will be from the ID generator which produces the preamble and the sync/ID pattern of the first sync block. The serializer input is then switched to the data path.

Reading along a row of the shuffled video sector array then produces two inner blocks, and 4 bytes of redundancy are added to each to make inner codewords which are randomized and recorded in the sync block. The ID generator then produces the next sync/ID pattern, and the process repeats 160 times until the sector is completed.

At the end of the sector the postamble is written followed by the gap shown in Fig. 10.15 and the preamble and sync/ID for the audio sector. The multiplexer on the input to the inner coder switched to the audio RAM during the gap, and now audio inner blocks are turned into inner codewords, randomized and recorded as before.

Five sync blocks are needed to record one audio sector, then another gap is generated. This process continues until the track is completed at the end of the second video sector with a postamble. Since the logical segment begins after the audio blocks, the inner coder must switch to a different distribution channel for the second half of the track, as shown in Fig. 10.2. There are four logical processing channels, but only two tracks in a segment, so the need to select one of two channels for each track is clear.

Fig. 10.16(b) shows the replay system. The offtape signal is equalized and fed to the data seperator which contains a phase-locked loop. This will synchronize to the bit clock. Sync patterns and IDs are recognized and used to synchronize the derandomizer and the shift register needed to deserialize the data stream.

The inner code processor corrects single symbol errors with high reliability since four R–S equations agree on the single error[10]. Two symbols or more in error are used to generate erasure flags for the outer codes. Every symbol in the inner code is flagged bad. Inner blocks are then written into a sector array, audio or video as determined by the ID code, and when it is full the contents are transferred to a second array. This time the read address comes from the shuffle generator, and the write address is sequential. The data are thus de-shuffled, and any burst errors are now dotted around the sector array.

The outer correction now uses the erasure flags which have come from the inner detection system. Two error symbols in each outer code can be corrected. If there are more, correction is not possible, and uncorrectable flags accompany the samples forward.

The reverse interleave is then opposed, and the four channels are combined. The recombination must reflect the changing relationship between head number and sector number. The video mapping is then reversed to restore the original sample values. Samples and uncorrectable flags now pass to the concealment system which can interpolate over different distances and in different directions depending on the nature of the errors to be concealed.

The samples are now in their original sequence and can be output digitally or fed to converters.

The audio samples are corrected by inner and outer codes in the same way, and as there are two copies of all audio data, any error-free data will be used to reassemble the output samples. The distribution of audio samples over all channels makes the audio demultiplexer more complex because it has to select any audio channel from any processing channel, and in the case of an uncorrectable error, it must select the second copy from a different channel. Although complex, this approach means that concealment in audio is extremely rare.

10.13 Variable speed

Track following is not easy in D-1 machines because of the high rotational speed of the scanner and the large distance the heads must jump. First-generation D-1 machines have no track following and the variable-speed range is restricted[11].

It is possible to obtain a small range of speeds around normal by changing the capstan and scanner speeds in proportion so that all tape tracks are still followed. There are limits to the range over which this can be used since the offtape frequencies change and the phase-locked loops find it harder to lock. The dynamics of the head–tape interface also change and the bit error rate will deteriorate. The disparity between offtape field rate and reference field rate is resolved by repeating or skipping fields in a store.

Beyond this limited speed range, the machine has no option but to unlock the capstan and scanner and cross tracks. The scanner peripheral speed can be controlled as a function of tape linear speed to make offtape frequencies the same as normal. Since the scanner speed dominates the head-to-tape speed this approach can be used over a surprisingly large speed range.

The track crossing causes guard band noise which makes a proportion of sync blocks unreadable. The read heads are narrower than the tracks, so there will be a short length of track where the replay signal is unimpaired.

Reading will also be possible with a certain degree of mistracking until the SNR becomes inadequate. It is possible to compute the percentage of time that data will be readable from the head and track geometry and from the mistracking tolerance of the signal channel. In fact this does not change with tape speed, and remains constant at 40–50%[12] as Fig. 10.17 shows.

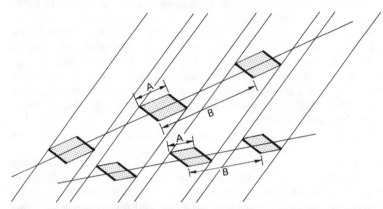

Figure 10.17 In shuttle, the heads cross tracks randomly, but the proportion of data which are readable is independent of the speed. If the sync blocks are shorter than the minimum track length played at the highest speed, then data can be recovered at all speeds. The angles here are exaggerated for the purpose of illustration. Even at 30× normal speed about 5 sync blocks can be recovered per track crossed. In practice the head can read for slightly longer than is indicated here because a slight tracking error will only reduce the signal to noise ratio

At speeds close to still, the scanner makes many revolutions in the same track area and virtually all of the sync blocks in a field can be retrieved over successive head sweeps. Inner correction can be used, but complete sector arrays cannot be assembled, so the outer code is powerless. Any sync blocks not recovered will not update the framestore and concealment must be used. At speeds close to normal, the proportion of data lost from each field is small, and good reproduction is also possible. As the speed rises, track crossings grow more frequent, and the proportion of a given field recovered falls to the geometrically derived limit and the use of interpolation becomes obvious. Whilst this quality of video cannot be used for production, it is perfectly adequate for locating scenes in shuttle.

10.14 Track following in D-1

Track-following VTRs must jump tracks to omit or repeat fields in variable speed. In the D-1 format there are only the audio sectors between the end of one field and the beginning of the next. This is a distance of only 13 mm which is covered by a typical transport in less than half a millisecond. In this short time the head pair has to jump 10 or 12 tracks, nearly half a millimetre.

A solution to this problem is to use additional heads so that the time available to jump is greater.

In an experimental machine demonstrated by Sony a D-1 transport had been modified by fitting a pair of track-following head assemblies at 180° to one another in place of the usual playback heads. Each head assembly carries an array of four heads, tracing four adjacent tape tracks, instead of the two heads of the regular machine. This necessitated extra rotary transformers, and these were on top of the scanner. The presence of the extra heads means that the effect of a jump of one segment can be had simply by switching from one pair of heads to the next. The actual head jump need not then take place during the audio blocks, but can be performed when the head is out of contact with the tape.

The Sony D-1 scanner uses an extended wrap to reduce the instantaneous bit rate, so each head assembly has about 100° of rotation in which to jump in variable-speed mode. This is a much larger angle than is available in the C-format, but the scanner speed is three times higher in D-1, so the actual time available is about the same. By way of contrast, a PAL D-2 scanner will be going at only twice the speed of a C-format scanner and has half a revolution in which to jump.

The g-forces on the heads rise with the square of the rotational speed, so in D-1 the heads are withstanding $5000\,g$. Nevertheless Sony have succeeded in deflecting them with a piezoelectric element basically similar to those used in their other track-following VTRs.

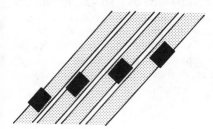

Figure 10.18 Four heads are fitted to one arm, but the spacing is not even. Two heads are offset to one side of the track, two to the other. A tracking error causes the level of the signals from one pair of heads to fall and the signal from the other pair to rise

The track-following system does not use dither like C-format or D-2, rather it relies on a relative displacement of the four heads on the moving arm. Fig. 10.18 shows that they are not evenly spaced, but slightly offset from the track centres. If the head assembly drifts off-track in one direction, one of the head pairs will show an increase in RF level, whereas the other will show a reduction. Movement in the opposite direction will cause the levels to change the other way. Thus the system can obtain the magnitude and the sense of the tracking error without dither. A feedforward mechanism is also used, which predicts the slope of the deflection ramp from the speed of the capstan.

Without deflection, the two head assemblies are at the same height in the scanner, and so at normal speed every track can be played by the inner pairs of heads only; the outer pairs are not needed. However, as the capstan speed increases, the heads will deflect to follow the tracks until a jump is necessary. Now one head pair jumps by two tape tracks. If only

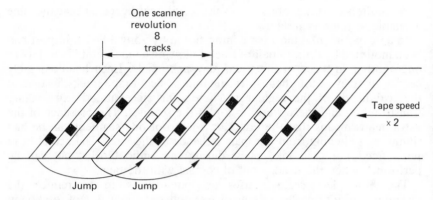

Figure 10.19 Since there are four heads per arm instead of two, all tape tracks can be read at ×2 speed. Each head arm must jump by two tracks while it is out of contact with the tape

pairs of heads were fitted, this would result in loss of information, but because each head arm is fitted with four heads, the tracks on both sides of the two main tracks are also read. Fig. 10.19 shows that this results in all tape tracks being read up to the maximum of 2× normal speed. Clearly with all tracks being read, the problem of trying to jump a pair of heads over a whole field during a quarter of a revolution does not arise. The penalty is that twice as much data as is needed comes off the tape, and duplicated replay channels are necessary, followed by a simple multiplexer which selects the information for the fields it intends to keep, and dumps that information for the fields it is jumping over.

It is also possible to go in reverse. By jumping back four tracks the beginning of the previous segment is reached, and so segments are played in reverse order. A modification of the memory addressing system restores the segments to the correct position in the picture.

References

1. European Broadcasting Union, Standard for recording digital television signals on magnetic tape in cassettes. *EBU Doc. Tech.*, 3252 E
2. Proposed American National Standard for Component Digital Video Recording – 19 mm Type D-1 cassette – Helical Data and Control Records, SMPTE 227M
3. HEITMANN, J. K. R., Electrical system design for the SMPTE D-1 DTTR. Presented at 20th SMPTE Television Conf. (Chicago, 1986), *SMPTE J.*, **95**, 1215–1221 (1986)
4. Proposed American National Standard for Component Digital Television Recording – 19 mm Type D-1 Cassette Format – Signal Content of Cue and Timecode Longitudinal Records, SMPTE 228M
5. BRUSH, R., Video data shuffling for the 4:2:2 DVTR. Presented at 20th SMPTE Television Conf. (Chicago, 1986), *SMPTE J.*, **95**, 1009–1016 (1986)
6. SLAVIN, K. R. and WELLS, N. D., The effects of random bit errors on YUV component video signals – II. *BBC Res. Dep. Tech. Memo.* no. ER-1526 (1985)
7. WATNEY, J. P., Picture quality criteria, error statistics and error correction for the D-1 format DVTR. *SMPTE J.*, **95**, 1222–1229 (1986)
8. GILLARD, C. H., Error correction strategy for the new generation of 4:2:2 component digital video tape recorders. Presented at 6th Video, Audio and Data Recording Conf. (Brighton, 1986), *IERE Publ.* no. 67, 165–175 (1986)

9. EGUCHI, T. and WILKINSON, J. H., The 4:2:2 component DVTR. An introduction to the world's first product. Presented at the 11th International Broadcasting Convention (Brighton, 1986), *IEE Conf. Publ.* 268 57–62 (1986)

10. WILKINSON, J. H., The SMPTE Type D-1 digital television tape recorder – error control. Presented at 20th SMPTE Television Conf. (Chicago, 1986), *SMPTE J.*, **95**, 1144–1149 (1986)

11. WILKINSON, J. H., and COLLINS, M. C., Replay of digital video recordings at non-standard tape speeds. Presented at 13th International Television Symposium (Montreux, 1983)

Many of the above references and numerous other relevant papers can be found in *Digital Television Tape Recording and Other New Developments*, Scarsdale, NY: SMPTE (1986)

The D-2 composite digital format

Although component recording has indisputable advantages, for the foreseeable future the majority of broadcasters will have a need to record composite video because of the tremendous investment in composite routing and other hardware.

The D-2 format is designed to bring the advantages of digital recording to the composite environment, and is the subject of this chapter.

11.1 History of D-2

The D-2 format began life as a development by Ampex. Some years ago, most manufacturers were building experimental digital recorders, and many of these were composite machines. It was then argued that component recording was superior to composite recording, which is not in doubt, and that the immediate need was for a digital format which recorded components, which does not actually follow. This led to the development of the D-1 format, which has been described in Chapter 10.

At the same time, Ampex were faced with the need to find a replacement for the venerable ACR-25 cartridge machine. This unit allows automated broadcasting of commercials and short spots using cassettes mechanically retrieved and automatically threaded. The quadruplex format is used on 2 inch tape, now well obsolete. The newer C-format could not be adapted to cassette operation because the extended scanner wrap needed to give field per scan virtually precluded mechanical threading.

It was clear that the replacement would have to be digital, but it was also clear that the purpose of the cart machine is to play back to air in a broadcast environment, and this demands composite recording in the majority of instances.

The composite digital recording research at Ampex was to turn into the ACR-225 automated broadcasting system.

Although the D-1 format was capable of higher technical quality, this would remain academic for those who could not afford to replace their entire installation with component equipment. What was needed by broadcasters was essentially a digital replacement for the C-format.

The composite digital format of the Ampex cart machine grew into that role, and became known as D-2.[1]

There is a world of difference between a laboratory curiosity which records digital video to prove a principle and a machine which has the facilities necessary to be used in a television system. Now that users have become accustomed to the facilities offered by C-format, no proposed replacement will succeed if it does not also offer all of those facilities. Even if it does so, it still will not succeed unless it offers a tangible advantage over any predecessor. Sheer technical quality is obviously an advantage of digital recording, but the C-format has been refined to such a high standard that it is virtually impossible for the eye to distinguish a first-generation C-format recording on a top-flight machine from a D-2 recording.

If it is to succeed, D-2 will do so partly because it takes nothing away operationally and gives a small quality advantage, but mainly because it will cost less to run. D-1 gave a quality advantage, but it took away operational features and cost more to run. It should be realized that D-2 is a more recent technology than D-1, and is in some respects developed from it. The application is quite different, and so a direct comparison is neither fair nor relevant. Both are tremendous technical achievements.

11.2 Introduction to D-2

The basic specification of D-2 is that it should provide composite recording in an analog or digital environment, quality audio, all of the stunt modes offered in C-format, and economy of tape use in a cassette which allows automated or manual operation.[2]

The composite digital recorder simply converts a composite video waveform into numerical information and stores the numbers. All of the characteristics of the original waveform are preserved in the digital domain. Accordingly a composite digital recorder will still have two line types if it is NTSC, four if it is PAL. It will still have a four- or eight-field sequence which must be maintained during editing, and so it will still need colour framing circuitry. In variable-speed operation, fields will be omitted or repeated, the subcarrier sequence will be broken, and colour processing will be necessary.

Although all of the characteristics of composite *video* are still present, all of the artefacts which are normally observed in composite *recording* are eliminated by the use of digital techniques.

Moiré is absent, differential gain cannot occur unless the converters are poorly engineered, and timebase error is zero. This is particularly important for composite signals, since timebase error in quantities which are invisible in monochrome can cause unacceptable degradation of the chroma, particularly over several generations. Analog composite recorders can never correct for chroma phase disturbances within a line, because the correction bandwidth is limited by the fact that the burst reference only occurs once per line.

The time and amplitude stability of composite digital recording are such that observing a vectorscope display of the replay of colour bars from tape leads one to believe that the vectorscope is being directly fed from a generator. Where such accurate timing is available, precision digital decoding of replay signals is possible, and the slow-motion performance of composite digital machines will exceed that of analog units, especially in PAL.

As has been stated in more than one chapter of this book, colour processing is easier to implement if the sampling rate is a multiple of the subcarrier frequency, and much easier, particularly in PAL, if it is four times the subcarrier frequency.

Four times subcarrier sampling is greatly in excess of the sampling rate necessary to satisfy sampling theory alone, and has to be classed as oversampling. This gives a number of advantages. When a D-2 machine is used in a composite analog environment, each generation of recording will necessitate a conversion to and from the digital domain.[3] The generation buildup of degradations will be less if $4 \times F_{sc}$ sampling is used because the anti-aliasing and reconstruction filters will not need such steep cut-off slopes, and so can be optimized for minimum passband ripple. It will be advantageous if these two filters are of slightly different response in a given machine to prevent buildup of correlated ripples.[4]

The use of oversampling also gives a noise advantage in that the quantizing noise is spread over the range up to half the sampling rate and will measure proportionately less in the normal video band.

There is a considerable difference between the subcarrier frequencies of PAL and NTSC, and a corresponding difference between the data rates which result from digitizing. As a result there are really two D-2 formats which leave different tape footprints, but which nevertheless have a lot in common in order to use the same circuitry and mechanical parts as much as possible. There is also a PAL-M version, which as far as the tape format is concerned is essentially NTSC with an eight-field control track.

As the D-2 format is cassette based, it made good sense to use the cassette shell developed for D-1, as this is reliable and protects the tape well. The ¾ inch tape, however, is not the same, as 1500 Oe metal powder tape 13 μm thick is used. This higher coercivity tape allows shorter wavelengths to be recorded, which contributes in part to the tape economy.

A further increase in efficiency is obtained by the use of azimuth recording. As was shown in Chapter 5, azimuth recording requires no guard band between tracks and allows a degree of immunity to mistracking, which makes possible the use of narrow tracks without putting excessive tolerance demands on the transport.

The azimuth effect fails at low frequencies, because the wavelengths are then too long for the head tilt to produce significant phase shifts. The solution is to use a channel code which contains no low frequencies. D-2 uses Miller[2], which is DC free and has a frequency range of 3:1 maximum. This narrow frequency range then means that erase can be achieved by overwrite, and no separate erase heads are necessary on the scanner[5]. This allows a significant simplification of the scanner construction, and also simplifies the system design because it is not then necessary to allow for the different timing of events due to the physical separation of erase and record heads. A full description of the Miller[2] code can be found in Chapter 6.

In many respects the D-2 format is a higher bit-rate version of the R-DAT digital audio recorder[6] as both use 1500 Oe tape and azimuth recording with a spectrally shaped channel code. R-DAT has, however, a higher recording density than D-2 for a number of reasons. D-2 is a professional format which has to be more conservative to withstand intensive use in automated systems. The high data rate of digital video results in greater losses in heads. The tracking error in a rotary-head transport is roughly proportional to the track length, and so R-DAT can use narrower tracks because they will be shorter. R-DAT uses a track-following servo as standard. In D-2 it is optional.

Azimuth recording demands at least two heads on the scanner, one of each azimuth type, but in any case the data rate is beyond the frequency capability of a single head. At any one time, two heads, one of each azimuth type, will be working together, sharing the data rate.

There is too much data in one field to be recorded on a single track pair, and so segmentation becomes necessary as was discussed in Chapter 9. Segmentation does not imply a potential quality loss as it does in the analog domain, owing to the discrete nature of the information[7].

One of the tenets of D-2 is that it will not take away any operational flexibility which exists in current analog formats. This means that a wide variable-speed range and recognizable pictures in shuttle are mandatory.

The implementation of variable speed is somewhat more difficult in a segmented format, because entire fields must be omitted or repeated. The tape format must take into consideration the mechanical difficulties and time constraints involved in moving heads across a number of tracks.

In D-2, the information to be recorded is a straightforward function of the relevant television standard, but the tape format is determined in strategy and in detail primarily by the need to offer operational flexibility.

The basics of the format are shown in Fig. 11.1. The audio blocks are placed at the ends of the tracks, and the fields begin and end with whole tracks. In a typical transport, two pairs of heads are positioned at 180°

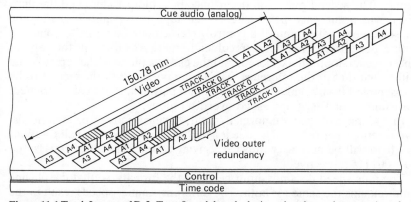

Figure 11.1 Track Layout of D-2. Type 0 track has clockwise azimuth rotation, type 1 track has anti-clockwise azimuth rotation. Note video outer redundancy at beginning of video sector. This can be omitted in some modes to give the heads more time to settle on track. Audio channels are in separate sectors with gaps so they can be independently edited. Note second copy of audio on opposite side of tape and on different head

apart on a scanner which uses a wrap of just over half a turn. The head pairs trace the tape alternately, so each has almost half a revolution in which to jump. As the tape speed increases, the audio will no longer be necessary, and the heads can begin to jump in the audio blocks at the end of the track and continue to settle during the audio blocks at the beginning of the track. The outer code redundancy is all recorded at the beginning of the video sectors. At normal speed this makes no difference. At shuttle speed the tracks are crossed and the outer codes are of no use, so again this makes no difference. At moderate speeds, however, correction can be by inner code only and the heads can continue to settle during the outer code blocks after jumping, and so track following is possible over a wider speed range.

11.3 Track layout and segmentation

The wide disparity between the subcarrier frequencies of NTSC and PAL leads to different segmentation being used in each case. The fundamental unit in the D-2 format is the segment, which consists of a pair of tracks, 0 and 1, one of each azimuth type. The first recorded track in a field is always a type 0 track, in which the azimuth is rotated clockwise by 14.97° from perpendicular when looking at the magnetic coating side of the tape. In a type 1 track, the azimuth is rotated 15.03° anticlockwise.

Fig. 11.2(a) shows that in PAL, four segments of 76 lines each record a total of 304 lines per field,[8] whereas in NTSC, shown in Fig. 11.2(b), three segments of 85 lines each record a total of 255 lines per field.[9] The segment and track numbering is also shown. The control track necessary for segmented operation must convey segment, colour frame and frame information. Fig. 11.2(c) shows that there is an event in the control track once per segment, and there are three positions in which a control track pulse can occur. A pulse is always present in the first position and is used to control the capstan servo so that the segments will be properly traced on replay. The second pulse will occur once per colour frame, and the third pulse will occur once per frame. When tape travel initially starts, the capstan speed will slip until a control track colour frame pulse coincides with a pulse from the reference colour framer. At this point the capstan phase-locked loop will be closed, and the chroma phase of the replay signal will match that of the reference. The frame pulses allow the picture to be reassembled from segments correctly when playback is not colour framed, for example in TSO (tape speed override) mode.

In a scanner of the type normally used, having opposing pairs of heads, two rotations per field will be needed in PAL, and one and a half rotations per field will be necessary in NTSC, giving scanner speeds of 100 Hz and 90/1.001 Hz respectively.

The tape speed does not differ between the formats, so that the playing time remains the same for both. The different scanner speeds result in the two formats having different track angles. The track widths are in inverse proportion to the scanner speeds, so the PAL track is 90% of the width of the NTSC track. A common transport can be used, having one helix angle, but the heads fitted will need to be specific to the format.

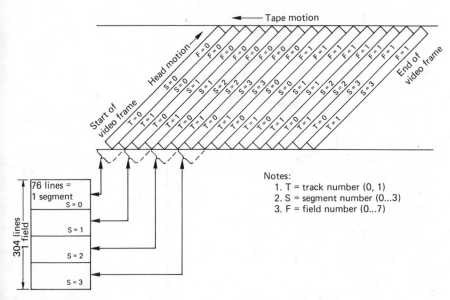

Figure 11.2(a) PAL segmentation in D-2. Four segments of 76 lines are necessary to record one field. The numbering scheme needed to re-create correctly framed pictures is shown here. The field number reflects the 8-field sequence of PAL. Audio blocks are omitted for clarity

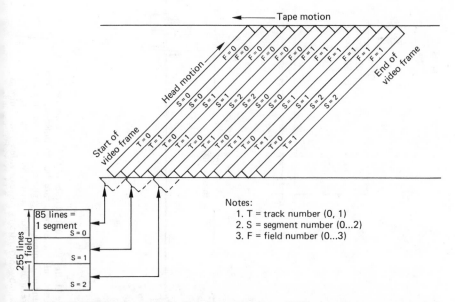

Figure 11.2(b) NTSC segmentation in D-2. Three segments of 76 lines are necessary to record one field. The numbering scheme needed to recreate correctly framed pictures is shown here. The field number reflects the 4-field sequence of NTSC. Audio blocks are omitted for clarity

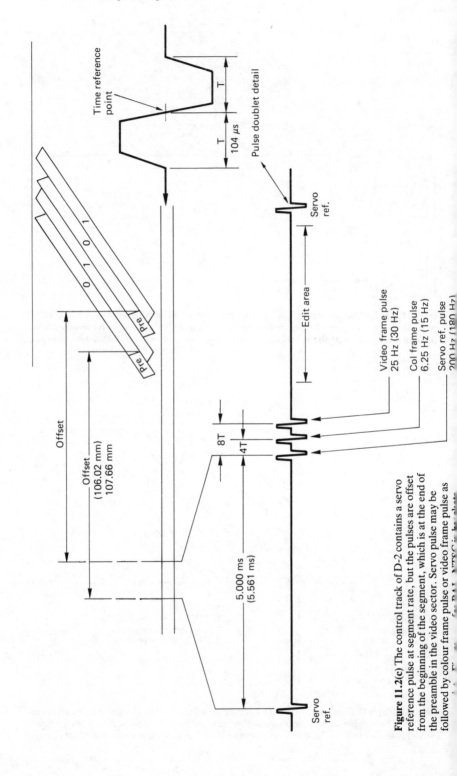

Figure 11.2(c) The control track of D-2 contains a servo reference pulse at segment rate, but the pulses are offset from the beginning of the segment, which is at the end of the preamble in the video sector. Servo pulse may be followed by colour frame pulse or video frame pulse as

The heads which record the track pairs are staggered 4.22° around the scanner, so that the trailing type 1 head partially overwrites the edge of the track written by the leading type 0 head. This is shown in Fig. 11.3(a). The leading head of the next head pair then trims the edge of the track written by the trailing head. In this way there can be no gaps between the tracks, and so it is not possible to replay unwanted signals from previous recordings while mistracking, a necessary condition because there is no separate erase process. Additionally, the tracks are narrower than the heads which wrote them, since the track width is controlled by the linear tape speed rather than the pole width of the head. The amount of overwrite is kept small so that tracks inserted in the centre of an existing recording in certain edit modes do not unnecessarily overwrite adjacent existing tracks. The longitudinal offset of 4.22° is necessary to allow the two heads physically to overlap, but it also means that the transverse displacement between the two heads is not equal to the track pitch. Fig. 11.3(b) shows that the longitudinal offset between the heads must take into account the fact that the tape is moving up the scanner as the heads pass. By the time the trailing head has reached a given point on a track made by the leading head, that track will be higher on the scanner than it was when it was written, and so the trailing head must be positioned higher on the scanner to put the next track in the correct place.

It is easy to calculate the adjustment necessary. In both formats, the tape rises by two track widths in half a rotation of the scanner. The correction is obtained by calculating the rise which takes place in 4.22° of rotation, as follows:

(1) for PAL

$$\text{tape rise} = \frac{35.2 \times 2 \times 4.22}{180} \mu m = 1.7 \mu m$$

(2) for NTSC

$$\text{tape rise} = \frac{39.1 \times 2 \times 4.22}{180} \mu m = 1.8 \mu m$$

Subtracting these correction factors from the track pitch results in the head displacement along the scanner axis which is necessary to produce the standard format. The displacement is 33.5 μm for PAL and 37.3 μm for NTSC.

The angular separation between the heads in a pair means that compensation is also necessary in the timing with which one head begins to write with respect to the other. In helical recording the start points of successive tracks are staggered, and the timing difference takes into account the track stagger and the head stagger. The data to be recorded by each head will be available in an interleave memory, and the timing difference is easily accommodated by reading the memory at different times for each head.

In most machines there will be a separate pair of replay heads 90° of scanner rotation away from the record heads. The use of azimuth recording allows the replay head width to be somewhat larger than both the record head and the track, so there is considerable immunity to tracking error on

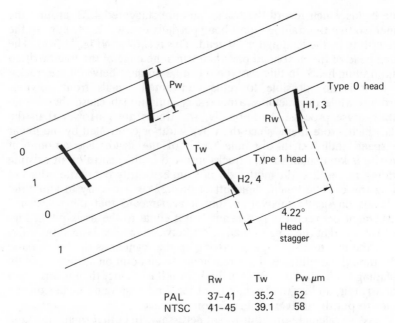

	Rw	Tw	Pw μm
PAL	37–41	35.2	52
NTSC	41–45	39.1	58

Figure 11.3(a) A pair of heads, one of each azimuth type follow one another across the tape. The resulting track width, T_w is less than the width of the record heads, R_w, because of partial overwrite. The replay head width, P_w, can be usefully made 50% greater than the track width

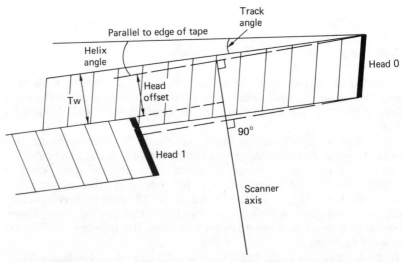

Figure 11.3(b) The movement of the tape causes the track angle to be different to the helix angle of the scanner. Thus the track width T_w, measured on the track angle, is not the same as the displacement between the heads which is measured at right angles to the helix angle – which is along the scanner axis. The compensation value is derived in the text

replay and a raised probability of recovering data when tracks are crossed in shuttle.

Prior to an edit, the machine will also play back with the record heads in order to arrive at the correct mechanical relationship with the existing recording when the new recording commences.

Pole widths for record heads are shown in Fig. 11.3 for the two formats, and considerable tolerance exists in this dimension owing to the nature of azimuth recording. The replay pole widths are suggestions, since the format only specifies the track width, and a manufacturer can choose any suitable replay head width which meets his requirements.

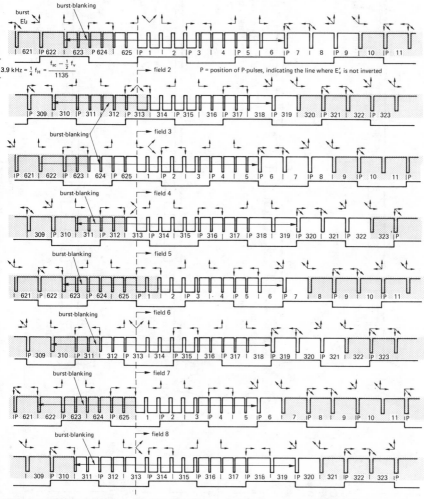

Figure 11.4(a) Each field recorded contains 304 lines in PAL D-2, but the actual lines recorded change from field to field so that the fields always begin with the same line type in the PAL sequence. This eases the production of a picture in shuttle since the colour processor then only needs to know the position in the field, since all fields off tape appear identical

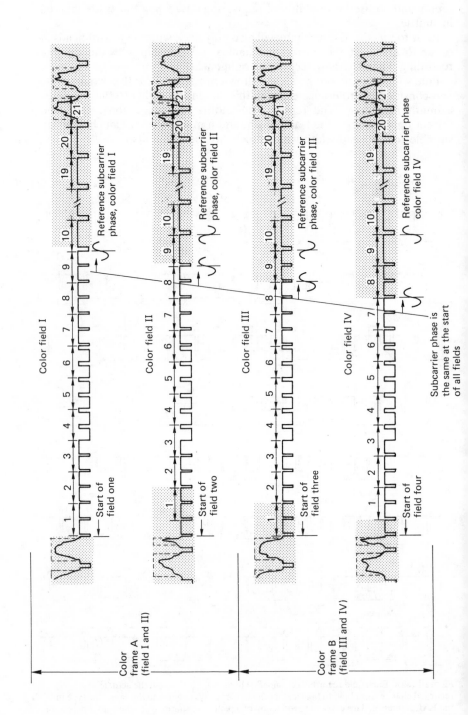

Color field I

Reference subcarrier phase, color field I

Start of field one

Color field II

Reference subcarrier phase, color field II

Start of field two

Color field III

Reference subcarrier phase, color field III

Start of field three

Color field IV

Reference subcarrier phase color field IV

Start of field four

Subcarrier phase is the same at the start of all fields

Color frame A (field I and II)

Color frame B (field III and IV)

It will be seen from Fig. 11.4 that the picture lines recorded differ from field to field. This is necessary to allow picture in shuttle. The recording is composite and contains an embedded chroma signal. Colour processing is necessary in shuttle to change the phase of the offtape signal to that of reference. When tracks are crossed in shuttle, sync blocks are picked up at random, and a frame-store is updated by information which has come from several different fields. This is only possible if samples off-tape can be colour processed. The necessary interleave and shuffle processes in a DVTR mean that each sync block contains samples which have come from various places within a field segment. When a frame-store is updated in shuttle, successive samples in a given line could have come from a different colour line type, and they would no longer represent the modulation of a continuous subcarrier. The colour processor would not be able to operate.

The solution adopted in D-2 is to record more lines than necessary, so that the first line of each field recorded can change over a four- or eight-field sequence. This ensures that all fields on tape have the same chroma phase at the same line number. At normal speed and in slow motion, the recorded lines are put back into the correct position in the reference fields and the normal chroma sequences result, but in shuttle, the colour processor now only needs to know the line number of recovered pixels and they can be correctly processed.

The offset of the line start causes a loss of vertical resolution in shuttle (four lines in PAL, two lines in NTSC), but this is acceptable since resolution falls in shuttle anyway due to movement in the picture.

11.4 The active line

Sampling in D-2 has been described in Chapters 2 and 8, where it was shown that in both line standards the sampling clock is derived from subcarrier. The very existence of the samples indicates the phase of subcarrier, so it is not necessary to record the burst. The subcarrier has a mathematical relationship with sync, which can easily be reconstructed on replay, and so it is not necessary to record syncs either.

Accordingly, D-2 only records the active line, along with sufficient positioning information so that syncs and burst can be regenerated on replay.

As a result, if a non-standard ScH signal is fed into a D-2 recorder, standard ScH will be automatically generated on playback.

PAL D-2 records 948 samples symmetrically disposed around the unblanked active line, and NTSC records 768 samples similarly. In each case, sample zero is the first sample to be recorded in each line.

The raw video data rate which must be sustained can now be derived.

For PAL, 948 samples in 304 lines at 50 Hz results in 14 409 600 samples per second, whereas for NTSC, 768 samples in 255 lines at 59.94 Hz results in 9 976 089.6 samples per second. Each sample is of 8 bit resolution.

In practice, these figures will need to be increased somewhat to allow for an error-correction overhead of about 15%, the presence of addressing or identification codes and for the double recording of four audio channels. Additionally, a proportion of each track will be used up with the preambles and sync patterns necessary to the operation of the channel coding, and tolerance gaps needed to allow independent editing of audio and video.

11.5 Distribution and concealment

Data to be recorded are divided equally between the two heads which are active at any one time. This process is called distribution, and is necessary because one head could not sustain the necessary data rate alone.

If the playback process could be guaranteed to be error free, the distribution scheme could be arbitrary, but in a practical machine it is necessary to take into account the fact that the error-correction system may be overwhelmed, albeit infrequently, by corruptions greater than those it was designed to handle. In this case the lost samples can be approximated in a concealment process, the success of which is partly determined by the distribution strategy.

Fig. 11.5 shows the concept of distribution, which ensures that in both rows and columns alternate samples are recorded by a different head. If

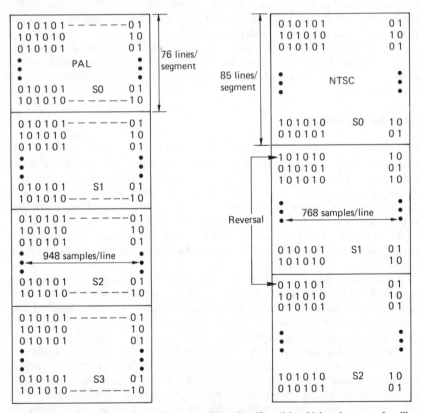

Figure 11.5 D-2 distribution, showing the track number (0 or 1) in which a given sample will be recorded. In PAL (left) there is an even number of lines in the segment so they are all the same. In NTSC there is an odd number, so the distribution reverses from segment to segment in order to maintain the pattern across segment boundaries

samples from a given head are lost for any reason, each lost sample is surrounded on four sides by samples from the other head. In the case of complete loss of signal from one head, due perhaps to clogging, it is still possible to produce a picture of reasonable quality from the remaining head because the quality will be as if the picture had originally been sampled at $2 \times F_{sc}$. The bandwidth available with one head out of action could, with suitable concealment circuitry, be greater than is available in slow motion in most C-format recorders.

As the recording is segmented, care must be taken to maintain the distribution pattern over segment boundaries. In PAL, there is an even number of lines in a segment, so the distribution in all segments is the same. In NTSC, there is an odd number of lines in a segment, and so it is necessary to reverse the distribution scheme on alternate segments. There are thus two distinct types of segment in NTSC, but this causes no difficulty since there are six segments in a frame, and so the same distribution will always be applied to the first segment in all frames. The distribution reversal is also shown in Fig. 11.5.

11.6 The error-correction strategy

Error correction in DVTRs is more complex than in other forms of recording because of the number of conflicting requirements. Chapter 7 showed that interleave is necessary to break up burst errors, and that a product code gives an efficient and reliable system. Unfortunately the product code produces a regular structure of rows and columns, and if such a system is overwhelmed, regular patterns of uncorrected errors are produced, and the effectiveness of concealment is reduced because the eye can perceive more easily the regular structure.

An irregular interleave, or *shuffle*, can be designed to disperse contiguous errors on the tape track over two dimensions on the screen, and the concealment is then more effective.

Clearly for the best concealment, the shuffle should work over the entire picture, but this is not possible because of the requirement to produce a picture in shuttle.

In shuttle the track-following process breaks down, and the heads cross tracks randomly so that the recovery of entire sectors is impossible. A picture of some sort is needed in shuttle, in order to assist in the location of wanted material, but the quality does not need to be as high as in other modes.

Fig. 11.6 shows that, in shuttle, the path of the head crosses tape tracks obliquely. The use of azimuth recording allows the replay head to be about 50% wider than the track, and so a useful replay signal results for a reasonable proportion of the head path, at the times where the head is near the centre line of a track of the same azimuth type, interrupted by noise when the head crosses tracks of the wrong azimuth type. The sectors are broken into short elements called *sync blocks* which are smaller than the length of track which can be recovered at typical shuttle speeds. Each sync block contains two Reed–Solomon codewords, and so it is possible to tell if the sync block was correctly recovered or not, without reference to any other part of the recording.

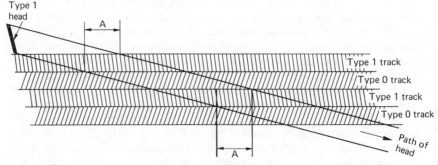

Figure 11.6 During shuttle, the heads cross tracks randomly as shown here (exaggerated). Owing to the use of azimuth recording, a head can only play a track of its own type (0 or 1) but as the head is typically 50% wider than the track (see Figure 11.3(a)) it is possible to recover normal signal for the periods above marked A. If sync blocks are shorter than this period, they can be picked up intact. In fact a slightly longer pickup will be possible because the replay system may tolerate a less-than-perfect signal. In any case the final decision is made by checking that the sync block recovered contains valid or correctable codewords

If a sync block is read properly, it is used to update a framestore which refreshes the picture monitor. Sync blocks which are not read correctly will not update the framestore, and so if concealment cannot be used, data from an earlier frame will be used to refresh the display.

Using this mechanism, the picture in shuttle is composed of data from many tape frames, and a frame-based shuffle would be extremely complex to implement, so that in practice the shuffle is restricted to operate only over one segment of the field.

A further concern is that at certain tape speeds the passage of tracks can beat with the head rotation, such that some parts of the track are consistently not recovered. If this were allowed to happen, parts of the framestore would never be updated, and the picture refreshed with stale data which is no longer representative of the recording. This problem is reduced if the shuffle is random, but a random shuffle is less effective for concealment, because it can result in variable density of uncorrected errors, which are harder to conceal than the constant error density resulting from a maximum distance shuffle.

Finally it is necessary to consider the likely cost of implementing shuffling schemes. Essentially the screen is considered to be a two-dimensional memory, and the shuffle is achieved by address mapping (see Chapter 5). The address generator used should not be unnecessarily complicated.

The product codes used in D-2 have 8 bytes of redundancy in the inner codes and 4 bytes in the outer codes. The inner codes are faced with essentially random data during dropouts and when crossing tracks in shuttle, and so their reliability has to be high. Although four random errors could be corrected, there is a significant probability that noise will produce what appears to be a codeword with a 4 byte error. If the inner code is only used to correct up to three random errors, the remaining 2 bytes of redundancy can be used to double-check, thereby avoiding the potential miscorrection. In the case of more than three errors, the inner code declares the entire block bad, and the outer code must correct by erasure. If the inner code were too large, this would effectively magnify burst errors to the size of the codeword. A further consideration is that if each sector were to be one long data block, loss of synchronization in the data separator due to a dropout would result in the loss of the rest of the sector, again magnifying the error.

Instead, one row of the sector array is made into six inner code blocks, and this reduces error magnification due to small bursts. To identify each inner block individually would result in an excessive overhead, so each sync block contains two codewords, which share a common ID.

11.7 The shuffling mechanism

The conflicting requirements mean that compromise is inevitable in the design of the shuffling process, to give a balanced performance in different operating modes.

Fig. 11.7(a) shows the sector array of D-2 PAL, and Fig. 11.7(b) shows the equivalent in NTSC. Outer codes are vertical columns, and six inner codes are formed along each row. In normal play, an error which is too large to be correctable will have to be concealed. Since the outer codes contain four redundancy symbols, each can correct four symbols by erasure. This corresponds to 4 bytes per column of the sector array. The largest data loss which can be handled will be when this damage is experienced in every column of the array, so the correctable burst error size is given by multiplying the number of columns in the sector array by four. The resulting figures are 1824 bytes for PAL and 2040 bytes for NTSC. These figures are for video data only; the actual size of the burst will be larger because the length of the track involved also contains sync and ID patterns and inner redundancy for 12 sync blocks. The maximum correctable burst corresponds to about 13 mm of track length, or a longitudinal tape scratch of about 1.4 mm width.

If this condition is exceeded, total correction is no longer possible, and rows of flagged erroneous data will appear in the sector array. Concealment will become necessary, but the eye is adept at detecting patterns and would perceive the shape of the concealment area if no steps were taken to reduce its visibility.

In fact the concealment patterns are made irregular by using shuffling. When the outer codes are generated, the symbols are assembled in a non-sequential order by address permutation. Successive outer codes are non-adjacent in the sector array owing to permutation of the column address. As a result, each inner code block contains one sample from each television line in the segment, but in a different place on each line. If an entire inner code block becomes uncorrectable, the concealments will then be scattered about the segment and will be much less visible.

In shuttle, sync blocks will be recovered at random, and the shuffle means that when a sync block is successfully read, the pixels it contains are spread widely, so the framestore will be updated all over instead of just in certain areas. The twinkling effect on the picture in shuttle is caused by the shuffle.

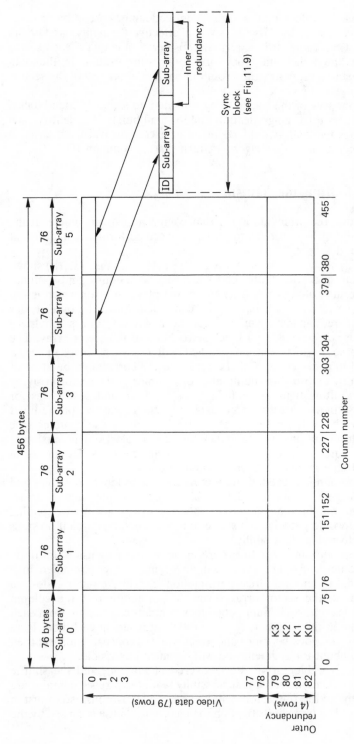

Figure 11.7(a) The sector array of D-2 PAL contains columns which are outer codewords. Rows are read, and two horizontal sub-arrays are used to construct a sync block by adding inner redundancy and ID codes. The video section of the track will thus contain $83 \times 3 = 249$ sync blocks. Array reading begins at the bottom so the outer redundancy appears at the beginning of the track. Data distributed over two such tracks (0 and 1) makes a segment. 4 segments make a field

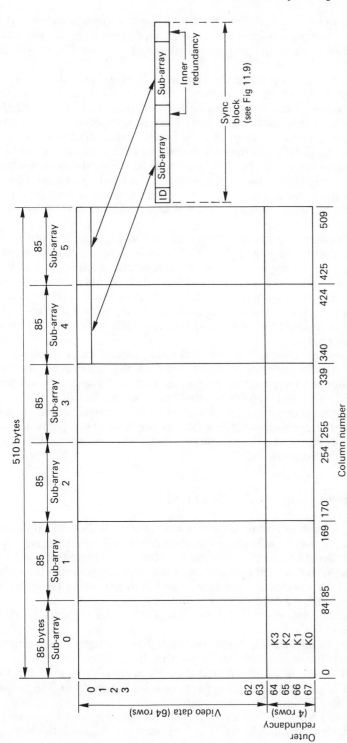

Figure 11.7(b) The sector array of D-2 NTSC contains columns which are outer codewords. Rows are read, and two horizontal sub-arrays are used to construct a sync block by adding inner redundancy and ID codes. The video section of the track will thus contain 68 × 3 = 204 sync blocks. Array reading begins at the bottom so that outer redundancy appears at the beginning of the track. Data distributed over two such tracks (0 and 1) makes a segment. 3 segments make a field

For good concealment, the shuffle should disperse samples widely and at even spacing, whereas to prevent patterns appearing in shuttle when the head rotation beats with the passing of tracks, the shuffle should be random.

The solution is to optimize the shuffle in a given track primarily for concealment, but with shuttle in mind, and to increase the randomizing effect for shuttle by changing the shuffle from track to track. In D-2 the two parallel channels feeding the pair of heads of different azimuth type have a different shuffle pattern. The two heads are mounted together, and so in shuttle both will find themselves able to read a section of track at about the same time. At certain shuttle speeds, where the rate at which tracks are passing the scanner is a multiple of the head passing rate, some parts of the track will never be read. By having a different shuffle pattern in each track of the segment, the presence of stale data in the framestore is reduced.

Clearly the shuffle process on recording has to be exactly reversed on replay. The shuffle mechanism is one of address mapping, where samples in each channel of a segment are given addresses which are sequential on the television line and in line number. The samples are selected non-sequentially by generating a suitable address sequence. In principle, the address sequence could be arbitrarily generated from a lookup table, but the sector arrays are large, and this approach would be extremely expensive to implement.

It is desirable that the address generation should be algorithmic to reduce cost, but an algorithm must be found which gives irregular results.

The solution is to use modulo arithmetic, and as this approach was also used in the D-1 format, reference should be made to Fig. 10.9.

Generating a randomizing effect with modulo arithmetic depends upon the terms in the expression being relatively prime so that repeats are not found in the resulting shuffle, and this constrains the dimensions which can be used for the codewords.[9]

11.8 Implementing the shuffle in PAL

The shuffle uses the same principles in both standards, but with different parameters. To avoid confusion, this section contains the PAL parameters, whereas Section 11.9 contains the same text but with the parameters for NTSC. The shuffle process falls into two main stages: permuting the order of samples within sector array columns, and then permuting the order of the columns. These will be dealt with in turn.

One possible implementation of the first shuffle stage is shown for PAL in Fig. 11.8(a).

The source of information is a memory which sequentially stores samples from the distributor. In each line it will thus have 474 samples. Samples from each line are to be distributed over six outer code blocks, but the distribution is permuted, and the permutation changes from line to line throughout the 76 lines of the segment.

An incoming byte rate clock controls the system. This clock operates a counter/divider which divides by 79 before resetting. As this is the number of samples in an outer block, it provides the block address, and the reset will increment a block count. The block counter/divider divides by six, the number of blocks in a line, and in turn the reset drives the line counter which counts the 76 lines in a segment.

Operation begins with all of the accumulators cleared. The byte accumulator adds 60 every time it is clocked, and so produces 60× the byte number. In the first block the other accumulators will remain zero, so only this value passes to the modulo 474 circuit which subtracts integer multiples of 474 until the output no longer exceeds 474. Part of the calculation sequence is shown in the diagram, where it will be seen that successive source addresses are six samples apart. The intervening five samples will go into other blocks. The source address is used to obtain a sample from the pixel memory, and the byte count is used to place the sample in the correct place in the block. In this way a permuted block is assembled.

At the end of the first block, the byte counter resets, clearing the byte accumulator and incrementing the block counter. This causes the block accumulator to add 79 to the previously cleared state. The source address now becomes 60× the byte address plus 79× the block address. The process continues until all six blocks of the first line are complete, when the block count will reset, clearing the block accumulator and incrementing the line count. This causes the line accumulator to add 83 to the previously cleared value, so the full source address is given by 60× the byte count plus 79× the block count plus 83× the line count. This process continues throughout the whole segment, until 456 blocks have been assembled.

The second stage of the shuffle is to permute the column number in the sector array. Fig. 11.8(a) also shows that the block rate clock also operates a second accumulator which multiplies the block number by 76. To the output of this is added the line number, and the result is taken modulo 456, since 456 is the number of columns in the sector array. This produces the column address into which the blocks produced by the mapping process are written. The row address is equal to the byte address within the block. The shuffle process is then complete. The outer redundancy can be added on the columns, and the inner redundancy and ID codes can be added to the rows. The array contents are then ready to be recorded.

11.9 Implementing the shuffle in NTSC

The shuffle process falls into two main stages: permuting the order of samples within sector array columns, and then permuting the order of the columns. These will be dealt with in turn.

One possible implementation of the first shuffle stage is shown for NTSC in Fig. 11.8(b).

The source of information is a memory which sequentially stores samples from the distributor. In each line it will thus have 384 samples. Samples from each line are to be distributed over six outer code blocks, but the distribution is permuted, and the permutation changes from line to line throughout the 85 lines of the segment.

An incoming byte rate clock controls the system. This clock operates a counter/divider which divides by 64 before resetting. As this is the number

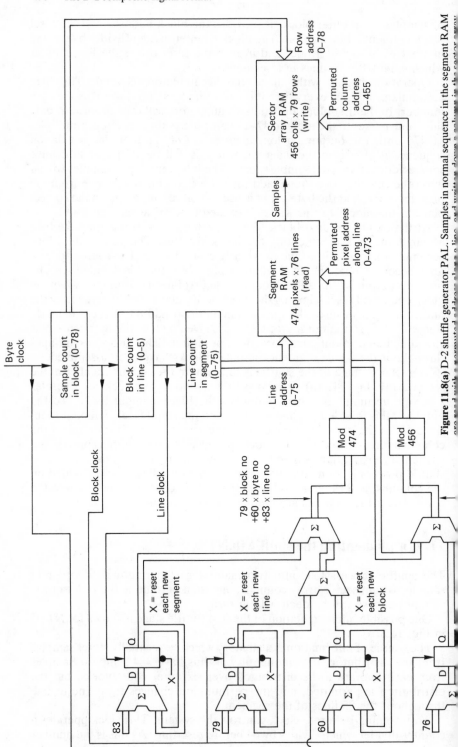

Figure 11.8(a) D-2 shuffle generator PAL. Samples in normal sequence in the segment RAM

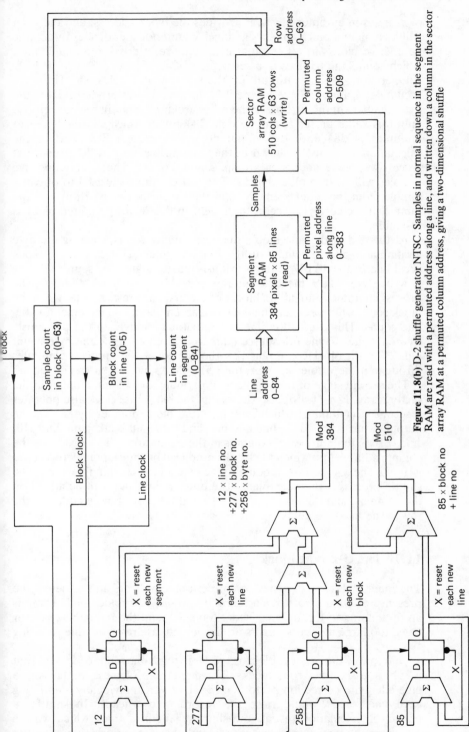

Figure 11.8(b) D-2 shuffle generator NTSC. Samples in normal sequence in the segment RAM are read with a permuted address along a line, and written down a column in the sector array RAM at a permuted column address, giving a two-dimensional shuffle

of samples in an outer block, it provides the block address, and the reset will increment a block count. The block counter/divider divides by six, the number of blocks in a line, and in turn the reset drives the line counter which counts the 85 lines in a segment.

Operation begins with all of the accumulators cleared. The byte accumulator adds 258 every time it is clocked, and so produces 258× the byte number. In the first block the other accumulators will remain zero, so only this value passes to the modulo 384 circuit which subtracts integer multiples of 384 until the output no longer exceeds 384. Part of the calculation sequence is shown in the diagram, where it will be seen that successive source addresses are six samples apart. The intervening five samples will go into other blocks. The source address is used to obtain a sample from the input memory, and the byte count is used to place the sample in the correct place in the block. In this way a permuted block is assembled.

At the end of the first block, the byte counter resets, clearing the byte accumulator and incrementing the block counter. This causes the block accumulator to add 277 to the previously cleared state. The source address now becomes 258× the byte address plus 277× the block address. The process continues until all six blocks of the first line are complete, when the block count will reset, clearing the block accumulator and incrementing the line count. This causes the line accumulator to add 12 to the previously cleared value, so the full source address is given by 258× the byte count plus 277× the block count plus 12× the line count. This process continues throughout the whole segment, until 510 blocks have been assembled.

The second stage of the shuffle is to permute the column number in the sector array. Fig. 11.8(b) also shows that the block rate clock also operates a second accumulator which multiplies the block number by 85. To the output of this is added the line number, and the result is taken modulo 510, since 510 is the number of columns in the sector array. This produces the column address into which the blocks produced by the mapping process are written. The row address is equal to the byte address within the block. The shuffle process is then complete. The outer redundancy can be added on the columns, and the inner redundancy and ID codes can be added to the rows. The array contents are then ready to be recorded.

11.10 The D-2 sync block

The inner codes are designed to correct random errors and to detect the presence of burst errors by declaring the whole inner block bad. There is an optimum size for an inner code: too small and the redundancy factor rises; too large and burst errors are magnified, as are errors due to losing sync.

One row of the product block is too large to be one inner code, and so it is split into six inner code blocks. The dimensions of these are chosen to give adequate correction performance. However, individually identifying each inner code would raise the recording overheads. In shuttle, a geometric calculation reveals the shortest length of track which will be recovered at maximum tape speed, and this determines that it is not necessary to identify every inner codeword. Accordingly one sync block contains two inner codewords, but only one ID code. Three sync blocks then form one complete row of the sector array.

Fig. 11.9(a) shows a PAL sync block. A 2 byte synchronizing pattern serves to phase the data separator and the deserializer. Following this is a 2 byte ID code which uniquely identifies this sync block in an eight-field sequence. The first data block of 76 bytes then follows, and the 8 bytes of inner redundancy are calculated over the ID code as well as the data, so a random error in the ID can be corrected. The first codeword is thus 86 bytes long. The second inner code block is 2 bytes shorter because it contains no ID. The entire sync block occupies just over half a millimetre of track.

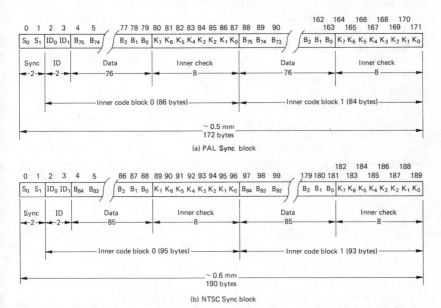

(a) PAL Sync block

(b) NTSC Sync block

Figure 11.9 The sync blocks of D-2 contain two codewords but only one ID code which forms part of the first codeword. As a result, the first code block is two bytes longer than the second

Fig. 11.9(b) shows an NTSC sync block. A 2 byte synchronizing pattern serves to phase the data separator and the deserializer. Following this is a 2 byte ID code which uniquely identifies this sync block in a four-field sequence. The first data block of 85 bytes then follows, and the 8 bytes of inner redundancy are calculated over the ID code as well as the data, so a random error in the ID can be corrected. The first codeword is thus 95 bytes long. The second inner code block is 2 bytes shorter because it contains no ID. The entire sync block occupies nearly two-thirds of a millimetre of track.

11.11 Miller^2 code in D-2

The need for channel coding has been shown in Chapter 6 and so this section confines itself to the implementation in D-2.

Miller^2 code has the same density ratio but half the jitter window of RNRZ, all other things being equal, and so might be thought inferior. In practice this turns out not to be the case because the narrow spectrum of Miller^2 is less stringent about equalization, the smaller ratio of run lengths causes less peak shift, and the higher clock content eases the task of the data separator. Thus in practice the performance of Miller^2 may be inferior under accurate tracking conditions, but the performance will not fall so rapidly with the onset of tracking error and may actually be better than RNRZ during mistracking.

The main advantage of Miller^2, however, is that it allows overwrite, eliminating erase heads, and makes guard-band-less recording possible, minimizing tape consumption.

The encoding rules of Miller^2 were explained in Chapter 6, but are repeated here briefly. A transition will be recorded in the centre of all data ones and between successive zeros, but in the case of an even number of ones between zeros, the transition of the last one is omitted.

These coding rules are used to generate a variety of patterns used for synchronizing the data separator and identifying the location of the head.

Fig. 11.10 shows that the run-up pattern or preamble is obtained by feeding alternating ones and zeros to the channel coder. This results in a frequency of half the maximum, since only the ones result in a transition. This frequency will suffer fewer losses, and so will be readily detectable on replay. The transitions all indicate the centre of the bit cell and the PLO can easily synchronize to them. This run-in pattern precedes nearly every sector.

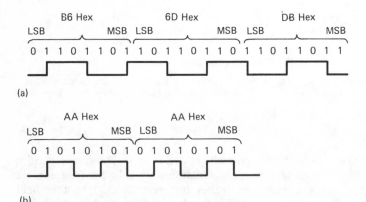

(a)

(b)

Figure 11.10 (a) Under the coding rules of Miller^2, the transition due to the last one in an even number of ones is omitted, so that a repeated sequence of data bits 011 will generate only one transition. This represents the lowest frequency possible in Miller^2, and is used to uniquely identify the first segment in a field. (b) The alternation of data ones and zeros produces a frequency of half the maximum which is ideal for bringing the phase locked loop in the data separator into lock

Fig. 11.10 also shows that if 011 repeated is presented to the channel coder, the last coding rule is invoked and the transition due to the second one is omitted, resulting in a frequency of one-third the maximum. This is the lowest frequency which Miller^2 code can generate, and is very easily detectable with a simple filter. This pattern is used only at the beginning of the first segment of a field. It is incorporated in order to simplify the construction of automated systems where several transports share a single signal system. Each transport need only have a simple preamplifier and tuned circuit to detect the field run-in, and so it can, in conjunction with the control track and timecode, synchronize the scanner and colour frame the capstan without the presence of a signal system. A cut between two tapes in two transports can thus be made by switching the input to a single signal system at the transport preamplifiers.

11.12 Synchronization and identification

Each sync block contains two inner codewords and is the smallest quantum of data on the track with which the playback channel can synchronize independently. Synchronization takes place on three levels: to the bit, to the symbol and to the sync block.

The recording density in DVTRs is such that it is not possible to position the heads mechanically with sufficient accuracy to locate an individual bit. The heads are rotated with reasonable accuracy, and the replay signal is accepted as and when it arrives. A phase-locked loop in the data separator must lock to the bit rate and phase of the recording. At the beginning of the track a reference for the phase-locked loop known as a preamble is recorded. This serves to set the frequency of the PLL the same as the offtape bit rate. Once the loop is locked, it can stay in synchronism by phase comparing the data transitions with its own. However, if synchronism is lost due to a dropout, it cannot be regained until the next synchronizing pattern is seen. This is one reason that the tracks are broken into short sync blocks.

Once bit synchronism has been achieved at the preamble, the serial data have to be correctly divided up into 8 bit symbols to restore the original samples. This is word synchronization, and it is achieved by the unique pattern which occurs at the beginning of every sync block. Detection of this pattern resets the divide by eight counter which deserializes the data. The sync pattern of D-2 is 30F5$_{16}$, and is in fact the same pattern as is used for D-1. Fig. 10.13(a) showed that this pattern differs from itself shifted by as many bits as possible to reduce the possibility of false sync generation. Within a sector, sync patterns occur at regular spacing, so it is possible for the replay circuitry to predict the arrival of the sync pattern in a time window.

Once symbol synchronizing is achieved, it is then possible to read the inner code blocks, and the first of these contains the ID code and reveals which sync block has been recovered. In normal play this will be the one after the previous one, but in shuttle the sequence will be unpredictable.

In shuttle, samples from any sync block properly recovered can be put in the correct place in a framestore by reference to the ID code.

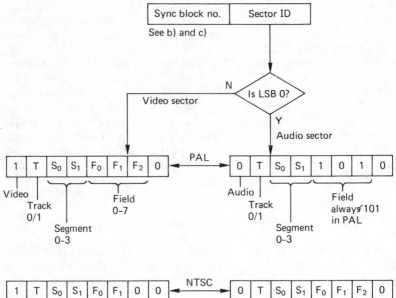

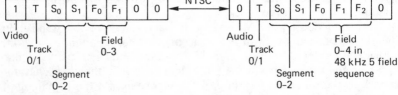

Figure 11.11(a) The ID code splits into two bytes, one of these is a number, the other describes the type of sync block and its position in the sequence. For video blocks the position in colour framing and segmentation sequences is shown. In PAL, the audio blocks only reflect the segmentation, whereas in NTSC the position in the 5-field audio sequence (see Chapter 13) is shown. ID code is protected because it is part of the first code word in the sync block

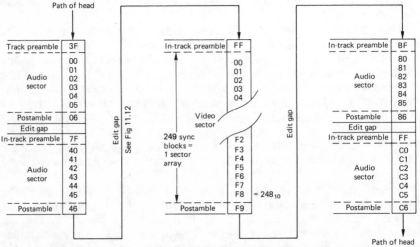

Figure 11.11(b) PAL ID numbering in the first byte of the ID code uniquely identifies every sync block in a sector. Second byte then determines which sector

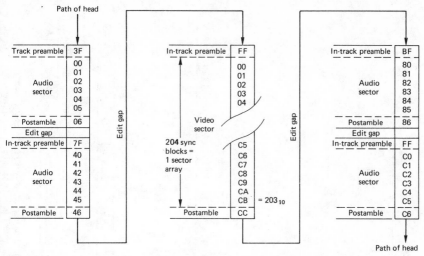

Figure 11.11(c) NTSC ID numbering in the first byte of the ID code uniquely identifies every sync block in a sector. Second byte then determines which sector

Fig. 11.11(a) shows that the information recorded in the ID code is split into two parts. The first byte is the sync block number in the track, the second identifies the sector. The V/A bit specifies whether the block is audio or video, and the T bit specifies which track of the parallel pair. The segment bits determine which segment out of four for PAL and three for NTSC is present, and the field bits specify the position in the eight- or four-field sequences to help colour framing.

Fig. 11.11(b) shows the sync block numbering within the segment for PAL, and Fig. 11.11(c) shows the equivalent for NTSC.

11.13 Gaps, preambles and postambles

Each slant track in D-2 is subdivided into five sectors, two of audio at each end and one of video in the centre. It is necessary to be able to edit any or all of the audio channels independently of the video. For this reason short spaces are left between the sectors to allow write current to turn on and off away from wanted data. Since the write current can only turn off at the end of a sector, it follows that the smallest quantum of data which can be written in the track at one time is a whole sector, although the smallest quantum which can be read is a sync block.

A preamble is necessary before the first sync block in a sector to allow the phase-locked loop in the data separator to lock. The preamble also contains a sync pattern and ID code so that the machine can confirm the position of the head before entering the sector proper. At the end of the sector a postamble containing an ID code is written before the write current is turned off. The pre and postamble details can be seen in Fig. 11.12.

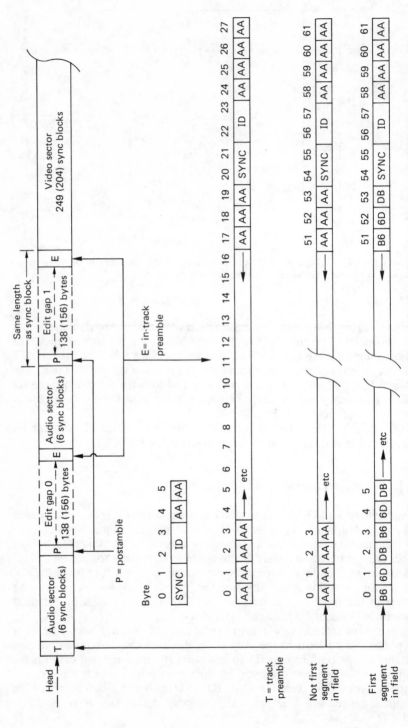

Figure 11.12 Edit gap begins with postamble of previous sector and ends with preamble of next. Remaining space is AA Hex fill which occupies 138 bytes PAL (156 bytes NTSC). Total length of edit gap is then the same as one sync block. Track preamble T is 54 bytes of run-in followed by preamble ID. In the first segment of a field, run-in pattern is changed to B6, 6D, DB sequence (see Figure 11.10).

The space between two adjacent sectors is known as an edit gap and it will be seen in Fig. 11.12 to begin with the postamble of the previous sector and end with the preamble of the next sector. Editing may result in a discontinuity nominally in the middle of the gap. There is some latitude, but the new recording must not begin so early that the postamble at the end of the previous sector is damaged, and at least 20 bytes of preamble must be written before the sync pattern at the beginning of the next sector, because it will not be possible to maintain continuity of bit phase at an edit, and the PLL must resynchronize.

In fact the length of the postamble, gap and preamble combined is exactly equal to the length of one sync block, which simplifies the design of the sequencer which controls the track recording. This is half the length of a gap in D-1, and is possible because there is no separate erase head in D-2.

11.14 Block diagram of a D-2 machine

The D-2 format specifies the dimensions and arrangement of the tape record, but provided these are met, there is no compulsion to use a particular mechanical design or circuit architecture.

Fig. 11.13 shows a typical block diagram of the record section of a D-2 machine, where the inputs will be composite video and four audio channels. Audio and video can be analog or digital, and most machines incorporate converters which can be bypassed if a digital input is available. Whichever input is used, the input video will always control the timing of the recording circuitry. In the case of a digital input, the $4 \times F_{sc}$ clock accompanying the data will be used to derive the symbol clock for much of

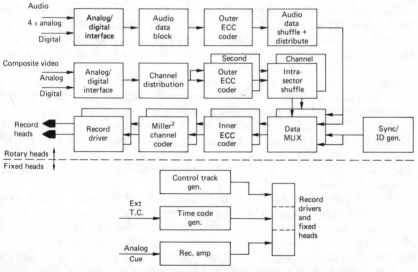

Figure 11.13 D-2 record section showing major stages. Note particularly the distribution of video over two channels, and the merging of the audio and video data into common inner coding circuits

the recorder. In the case of an analog input, the video burst will be fed to a phase-locked loop which generates the sampling clock locally.

The video data are distributed over two logical channels as was shown in Fig. 11.5. Only one of these channels is shown since they are identical. Unlike the D-1 format, there is no mapping stage, and samples are recorded unchanged.

The distribution process results in each logical channel having half of the original number of samples in each line, 474 in PAL and 384 in NTSC. Each of these lines will be interleaved into six outer codewords, such that samples in the same codeword are six samples apart in the channel, and 12 samples apart on the television line. This is done by calculating the sample address along the line as a function of the block number and the byte number within the block. The first stage of the shuffle is obtained by changing the address calculation from line to line so that samples in the same place in an outer block on an adjacent line will have come from a different position along the line. This interleave/shuffle process results in blocks of 79 samples in PAL and 64 samples in NTSC. Four bytes of Reed–Solomon redundancy are calculated on each block to make it into a codeword. The size of the outer codewords is equal to the height of the sector array memory, and outer codewords form columns in the sector array. Adjacent outer blocks do not form adjacent columns owing to the second stage of the shuffle. In this, the column number is a function of the line number as well as the block number.

Eventually the sector array will be filled with columns of outer codewords, and it is then read in rows which are used to form inner codewords.

Each row results in six inner codewords, and two inner codewords are used in each sync block. The first codeword in the sync block is extended to protect the ID code and so it is 2 bytes longer than the second codeword.

There will be 249 video sync blocks in a PAL track and 204 video sync blocks in an NTSC track. In both channels, the reading of the sector array begins at the bottom, so that the four rows of outer code redundancy are placed at the beginning of the track. In the case of channel 0, readout continues in descending row order, but the memory readout sequence is modified for channel 1 so that a linear tape scratch crossing both tracks in the same place does not result in an identical corruption pattern in the two channels and so that a more random shuffle is effected in shuttle.

This additional shuffle is implemented by permuting the sector memory row addresses in channel 1 when the memory is being read to tape. In PAL, 39 is added to the row address and the result is expressed modulo 79, whereas in NTSC, 32 is added to the row address and the result is expressed modulo 64.

The audio processing is shown in parallel with the video processing, and uses a distribution scheme to spread samples in all channels over both heads and double recording to compensate for the fact that the audio blocks are small. This is explained more fully in Chapter 13. Since audio is not two dimensional, no shuffle is necesary, and a regular array is used to form a product block. Audio samples have longer wordlength than video samples, so the outer coding of the audio is somewhat different to the video, but the dimensions of the product block are such that the audio inner codewords are identical in size to the video inner codewords, so that common processing can be used.

The inner code generation, ID generation, serializing and channel coding are common to both audio and video, which effectively share the same circuitry, heads and tracks in a time multiplex.

At the beginning of a segment, the audio and video to be recorded have been interleaved and shuffled and are held in RAM so that they can be made available at the appropriate time.

Input to the serializer will initially be from the sync generator which produces the preamble at the beginning of the track. The serializer input then receives audio sync blocks until the end of the first audio sector, when the edit gap will be written. Following the preamble at the end of the edit gap, the second audio sector will be written, followed by another edit gap. After this edit gap, video sync blocks will be written, followed by a second edit gap and the second pair of audio sectors.

Fig. 11.14 shows the replay system. Following the channel decoder, the sync detector phases the shift register in the deserializer so that the serial bit stream is correctly assembled into a parallel byte stream.

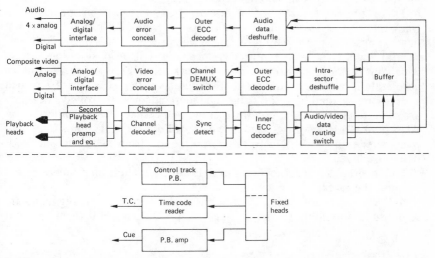

Figure 11.14 D-2 replay section. Two replay channels handle both audio and video as far as inner code error correction, and the data router then splits the audio and video to separate outer code processing

Inner blocks are checked by the inner decoder, which therefore also checks the ID code in the first inner block of a sync block. With 8 bytes of redundancy, the inner decoder could correct up to four random errors, but this would be at the expense of too many miscorrections. Accordingly, the inner code corrects up to three random errors, and a larger number are handled by declaring the entire inner code to be corrupt. An error flag is attached to every symbol in the block. Inner blocks are written into the sector array and de-shuffled, and any burst errors are converted to single byte errors dotted around the array. These are accompanied by the error flags from the inner decoder, and so the 4 bytes of redundancy in the outer codes can correct four errors by erasure. If there are more than four error flags in an outer code, the symbols will be flagged as uncorrectable, and concealment must be used. When the two channels are combined the concealment process takes place.

The samples are now in their original sequence and can be output digitally or fed to a converter.

The audio samples are corrected by the inner and outer codes as for video, but as there are two copies of all audio data, any error-free data will be used to reassemble output samples. This means that audio interpolation to conceal uncorrectable erors is extremely rare.

11.15 Variable speed in D-2

The variable-speed range of C-format machines has essentially become the yardstick by which competing formats will be measured. It is important for the success of D-2 that at least an equal speed range is available and the means to obtain this will be discussed here.

There are a number of issues to be addressed in providing a track-following system in D-2. The use of a segmented format means that head jumps necessary to omit or repeat one or more fields must jump over several segments. This requires a mechanical head-positioning system which has the necessary travel and will work reliably despite the enormous acceleration experienced at the perimeter of the scanner. Two such systems are needed, and they must be independently controlled since they are mounted in opposition on the scanner and contact the tape alternately. Also required is a control system which will ensure that jumps only take place at the end of a field to prevent a picture from two different fields being displayed.

The degree of accuracy required is much higher than in C-format because the tracks are much narrower.

In PAL, the track pitch is 35 μm, and eight tracks or four segments are required in one field. The heads must jump a distance of 0.28 mm to omit

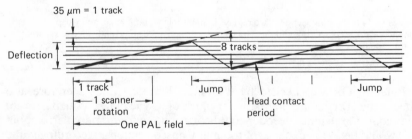

Figure 11.15 Head deflection waveform for PAL D-2 at +3× normal speed. This requires a jump of two fields between every field played, and this corresponds to 8 tracks. Since head pairs trace the tape alternately, the head has half a revolution in which to jump, so the actual jump is only 6 tracks. However, the vertical position of the above waveform is subject to an uncertainty of ±2 tracks because capstan phase is random during variable speed

or repeat a field. In NTSC the track pitch is 39 μm, and six tracks or three segments are required in one field. The corresponding jump distance is 0.23 mm.

When the tape speed is close to three times normal, most of the time a two-field jump will be necessary at the end of every field. Fig. 11.15 shows the resulting deflection waveform (for one head pair only). Since the control track phase is random, an offset of up to ±½ field will be superimposed on the deflection, so that if a two-field jump must always be possible, a total deflection of three fields must be available. This determines the mechanical travel of the heads, which will be 0.84 mm for PAL, which is the larger of the two.

11.16 The actuator

In Ampex D-2 machines, the piezo-electric actuators common in C-format were not considered adequate for the larger travel demanded in a segmented format,[10] and a moving-coil actuator has been developed. These had been used experimentally in certain analog recorders, but gave way to piezo-electric actuators in the C-format. Now that rare earth magnets are available, which offer high field strength with low mass, the moving-coil actuator becomes attractive again, because it allows a low-mass cantilever which has higher resonant frequencies and requires less force to deflect. The moving coil is inherently a low-impedance device requiring a current drive which is easier to provide than the high voltages needed by piezo-electric devices.

Fig. 11.16(a) shows the concept of the moving-coil head and Fig. 11.16(b) shows the appearance of the actual unit. The cantilever is folded from thin sheet metal which is perforated to assist the folding process. The resulting structure is basically a torsion box supported on a wide flexural

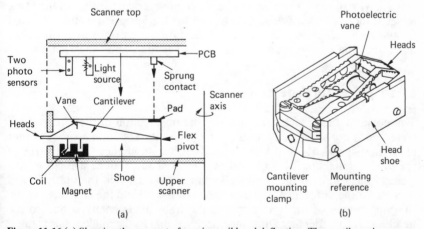

(a)   (b)

Figure 11.16 (a) Showing the concept of moving coil head deflection. The cantilever is flexurally pivoted at the opposite end to the heads, and position feedback is obtained from a vane on the cantilever which differentially varies the light falling on two photosensors. (b) Shows the appearance of an actual replaceable AST head assembly (courtesy AMPEX)

pivot. This means that it can bend up and down, but it cannot twist, since twisting would introduce unwanted azimuth errors. The cantilever carries the actuator coil and is supported in a metal shoe which carries the magnet.

Positional feedback of the cantilever deflection is obtained by a photo-electric system. This has one light source and two sensors between which moves a blade which is integral with the cantilever. When the cantilever deflects, a differential signal results from the sensors. The photo-electric sensor is mounted inside the scanner top and automatically aligns with the moving blade when the top is fitted.

11.17 Detecting the tracking error

The track-following system of D-2 uses dither or wobble which follows the principle described for the C-format in Chapter 4. The RF amplitude of the replay signal is examined whilst the head is wobbled up and down about the nominal track centre. Each cantilever carries two heads, one of each azimuth type, and the RF levels from the two heads are averaged together. This gives a 3 dB improvement in signal-to-noise ratio, as well as accommodating manufacturing tolerances in the elevation of the video tips. Only one detector or synchronous rectifier is then required per cantilever.

Dither cannot be used with analog VTRs employing azimuth recording because the transverse head motion interacts with the azimuth angle to give the effect of rising and falling head-to-tape speed. In FM recording, this introduces an unwanted signal into the video. The effect is still present in a digital recorder, but the result is that the instantaneous offtape data rate rises and falls slightly. This is accommodated by the phase-locked loop in the data separator, and has no effect on the data. A harmless dither component will be observed in the VCO control voltage.

The tracking error is averaged over the entire track to produce an elevation error, and it will also be sampled at several points down the track to see if there is a consistent curvature in the tracking. This can be reduced by adding a correction curve to the deflection waveform which will adjust itself until the best envelope is obtained over the whole track length.

11.18 The ramp generator

The positional feedback generated by the observation of the dithered RF envelope is not sufficiently accurate to follow the tracks unassisted except at normal speed where it can be used as an interchange aid. In variable speed the deflection of the head is predicted to produce a feedforward signal which adds to the head deflection. The feedback then only has to correct for the difference between the feedforward and the actuality. When the tape travels at the wrong speed, the track angle changes, and so the head needs to deflect by a distance proportional to the angle it has rotated in order to follow the track. The deflection signal will be in the form of a ramp, which becomes steeper as the tape speed deviates more from normal. The actual speed of the capstan can be used to generate the slope

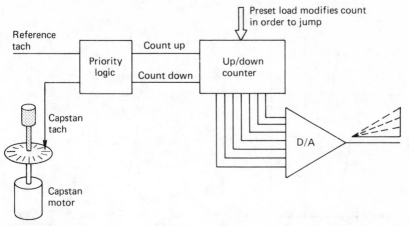

Figure 11.17 An up/down counter is fed with pulses from the capstan tach, and from a reference whose frequency is precisely that of capstan tach at normal speed. The counter will thus integrate speed deviation from units, and the D/A convertor will produce a range whose slope is proportional to speed difference. This is the feedforward signal which drives the head deflection system

of the ramp. One possible implementation of this is shown in Fig. 11.17. A counter has count-up and count-down inputs. The first of these is driven by the capstan tacho disk, and the second is driven by a clock whose frequency is exactly equal to that generated by the capstan tacho at normal speed. When the capstan runs at normal speed, the counter receives as many up clocks as down clocks, and remains unchanged. However, if the capstan speed is raised, the counter will begin to count up at a rate proportional to the speed difference. The counter drives a DAC which produces the deflection ramp. The dither detector will generate pulses which are also fed into the counter so that the elevation correction can be made.

The same deflection ramp slope will be fed to both head pairs so that they will read alternate segments for an entire field. At some point it will be necessary to jump the heads to reduce the deflection, and this requires some care. The heads are 180° opposed, and contact the tape alternately. The jump takes place while the head is out of contact with the tape. The two head pairs will have to jump at different times, half a scanner revolution apart. Clearly if one head jumps, the second head must also jump, otherwise the resulting picture will have come from two fields. As the jumps are half a revolution apart, it follows that the decision to jump must be made half a scanner revolution *before* the end of the current field. The decision is made by extrapolating the deflection ramp forwards to see what the deflection *will be* when the end of the field is reached. If the deflection will exceed half a field, it can be reduced by jumping one field. If the deflection will exceed one field, it can be reduced by jumping two fields. The jump can be executed by adding or subtracting a number of pulses in the ramp counter.

Tape tension changes can cause the track width to vary minutely. This is normally of no consequence, but when taken over all of the tracks in a segment the error may be significant. It is possible to compare the tracking

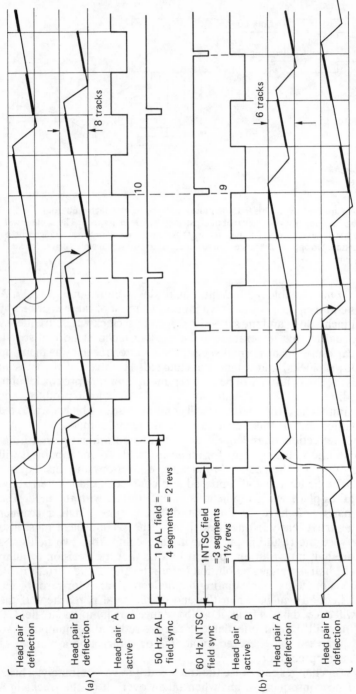

Figure 11.18 The timing and deflections necessary at a speed of $+2\times$ in D-2 for (a) PAL and (b) NTSC. Note the segment ratio of 9:10 between the two formats, which is also the ratio of scanner speeds. In order to play entire fields, jumps must take place about the field boundary, so that if one head pair jumps, the other must follow (serpentine arrow). In NTSC there are three segments per field, so the jumping follows a two field sequence, where the head fails to jump in one field, but jumps twice in the next

error before and after a jump, and if the error becomes greater, the jump distance was inappropriate for the tape being played. It is possible to modify the distance jumped simply by changing the number of pulses fed to the ramp counter during the jump command. In this way the jump distance can optimize itself for the tape being played.

Fig. 11.18(a) shows the ramping action for the two moving heads in PAL with the tape stopped. It will be seen that when one head jumps, the other one will also jump, so both heads always play the same field. The timing shift due to the heads being separated by half a revolution can be seen. As there are four segments per field in PAL, corresponding to two scanner revolutions, all fields will contain the same sequence. Fig. 11.18(b) shows the equivalent sequence of events for NTSC. As there are three segments per field and two moving heads, the action differs between odd fields and even fields. During one field, a given head may jump twice, but in the next field it will not jump at all.

11.19 Track-following block diagram

Fig. 11.19 shows a typical D-2 track-following system. There is an inner feedback loop which consists of the head actuator, the position feedback sensor and an amplifier. This loop is a position servo which makes the head

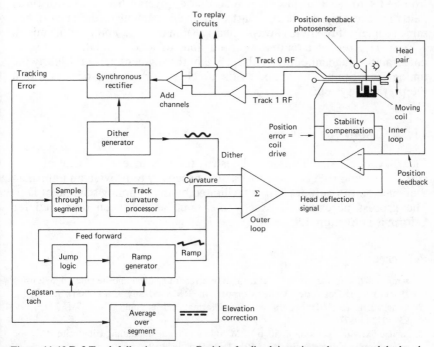

Figure 11.19 D-2 Track following system. Position feedback in an inner loop around the head positioner linearizes and damps positioner so that mechanical deflection is proportional to head deflection signal from outer loop. Dither generator wobbles the head and drives synchronous rectiver to obtain tracking error which is used to correct the head elevation and to compensate for track curvature. Feedforward system generates ramps

deflection proportional to the input voltage. Like any position servo it is provided with compensation to prevent oscillation and maximize frequency response. The inner loop is driven by the sum of four signals. These are:

(a) The dither signal, which is a sinusoid designed to wobble the head either side of its average elevation.
(b) The elevation correction obtained by averaging the tracking error over the entire track.
(c) The track curvature compensation which is a segment rate curve obtained by sampling the tracking error at several points along the track.
(d) The feedforward ramp and jump signal. The slope is obtained from capstan speed difference and the jumps are initiated by analysing the deflection.

There are two moving heads and so two of these systems are necessary. They are largely independent except for a common jump control system which ensures that when one head jumps during the last segment of a field the other head will follow once it has played that segment.

When a head jumps, it will move to a track which began at a different place along the tape, and so the timing in that track will not be the same as in the track which the head left. In a segmented format, the effect is magnified by the number of tracks in a field. To support a speed range from $-1\times$ to $+3\times$, it has been seen that an overall head travel of three fields is necessary. From the start of a given segment to the start of the same segment three fields away is nearly 8 mm in PAL, and over 6.5 mm in NTSC. The replay circuitry must be able to accommodate the timing uncertainty which amounts to about 5% of the segment period. Clearly the timing error can be eliminated by the timebase correction processes within the playback system.

11.20 Colour processing

Clearly variable-speed mode will destroy the subcarrier sequences of PAL and NTSC, and so a colour processor is necessary to provide an unbroken sequence on the output. This is facilitated by the sampling scheme of D-2. The process necessary is exactly the same as has been described for C-format in Section 4.9.

References

1. Ampex digital format for video and audio tape recording of composite video signals using 19 mm type D-2 cassette. Ampex Corporation, Redwood City, CA (1988)
2. ENGBERG, E. *et al*. The composite digital format and its applications. *SMPTE J.*, **96**, 934–942 (1987)
3. DEVEREUX, V.G., Tests on 8 video PCM codecs in tandem handling composite PAL and monochrome video signals. *BBC Res. Dep. Rep.* 1982/19
4. MORRISON, E.F., Multi-generation performance of a digital composite DVTR. *IEE Conf. Publ.*, no. 293, 391–394 (1988)
5. MORRISON, E.F., Tape format for a PAL DVTR. Presented at 15th Int. Television Symposium (Montreux, 1987)

6. KOSAKA, M., Report of the DAT conference. *J. Audio Eng. Soc.,* **34**, 570–576 (1986)
7. SAWAGATA, K., TAKAYAMA, J. and IVE, J.G.S., Format considerations for composite digital video tape recording. *IEE Conf. Publ.* no. 293, 381–386 (1988)
8. BRUSH, R., Design considerations for the D-2 PAL composite DVTR. *IERE Conf. Publ.* no. 79, 141–148 (1988)
9. BRUSH, R., Design considerations for the D-2 NTSC composite DVTR. Presented at SMPTE Technical Conference (Los Angeles, 1987)
10. OLDERSHAW, R., Design of an automatic scan tracking system for a D-2 recorder. *IEE Conf. Publ.* no. 293, 395–398 (1988)

Chapter 12

Disk drives in digital video

Disk drives came into being as random access file-storage devices for digital computers. Now that high-density technology in disk drives has advanced, the rapid access of disk drives is finding applications in digital video for still stores, animation and editing.

12.1 Types of disk drive

Once the operating speed of computers began to take strides forward, it became evident that a single processor could be made to jump between several different programs so fast that they all appeared to be executing simultaneously, a process known as multiprogramming. Computer memory remains more expensive than other types of mass storage, and so it has never been practicable to store every program or data file necessary within the computer memory. In practice some kind of storage medium is necessary where only programs which are running or are about to run are in the memory, and the remainder are stored on the medium. Punched cards, paper tape and magnetic tape are all computer media, but suffer from the same disadvantage of slow access. The disk drive was developed specifically to offer rapid random access to stored data. Fig. 12.1 shows that, in a disk drive, the data are recorded on a circular track. In floppy disks, the magnetic medium is flexible, and the head touches it. This restricts the rotational speed. In hard-disk drives, the disk rotates at several thousand rev/min so that the head-to-disk speed is of the order of one hundred miles per hour. At this speed no contact can be tolerated, and the head flies on a boundary layer of air turning with the disk at a height measured in microinches. The longest time it is necessary to wait to access

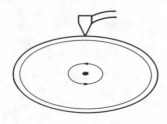

Figure 12.1 The rotating store concept. Data on the rotating circular track are repeatedly presented to the head

456

a given data block is a few milliseconds. To increase the storage capacity of the drive without a proportional increase in cost, many concentric tracks are recorded on the disk surface, and the head is mounted on a positioner which can rapidly bring the head to any desired track. Such a machine is termed a moving-head disk drive. The positioner was usually designed so that it could remove the heads away from the disk completely, which could thus be exchanged. The exchangeable-pack moving-head disk drive became the standard for mainframe and minicomputers for a long time, and usually at least two were furnished so that important data could be 'backed up' or copied to a second disk for safe keeping.

Later came the so-called Winchester technology disks, where the disk and positioner formed a sealed unit which allowed increased storage capacity but precluded exchange of the disk pack. This led to the development of high-speed tape drives which could be used as security backup storage.

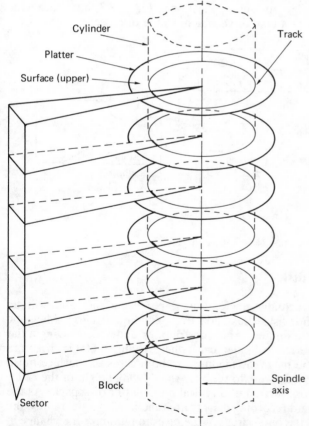

Figure 12.2 Disk terminology. Surface: one side of a platter. Track: path described on a surface by a fixed head. Cylinder: imaginary shape intersecting all surfaces at tracks of the same radius. Sector: angular subdivision of pack. Block: that part of a track within one sector. Each block has a unique cylinder, head and sector address

Optical disk storage has also emerged in computer peripherals, with earlier devices offering enormous capacity by magnetic disk standards, but being unable to erase or alter a recording once made. These are known as write once read many (WORM) devices. Later disks offered the ability to erase through the adoption of thermomagneto-optic technology. The positioners of optical disks are still rather slow when compared with those of magnetic drives, and the data rate is still too low for real-time video use.

These technologies will all be explained in this chapter and followed by a treatment of the applications of disks in actual digital video machines.

12.2 Disk terminology

In all technologies there are specialist terms, and those relating to disks will be explained here. Fig. 12.2 shows a typical multiplatter disk pack in conceptual form. Given a particular set of coordinates (cylinder, head, sector), known as a disk physical address, one unique data block is defined. A common block capacity is 512 bytes. The subdivision into sectors is sometimes omitted for special applications. Fig. 12.3 introduces the essential subsystems of a disk drive which will be discussed.

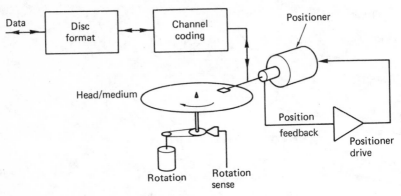

Figure 12.3 The main subsystems of a typical disk drive

12.3 Structure of disk

The floppy disk is actually made using tape technology and will be discussed later. Rigid disks are made from aluminium alloy. Magnetic oxide types use an aluminium oxide substrate, or undercoat, giving a flat surface to which the oxide binder can adhere. Later metallic disks are electroplated with the magnetic medium. In both cases the surface finish must be extremely good owing to the very small flying height of the head. Fig. 12.4 shows a cross-section of a typical multiplatter disk pack. As the head-to-disk speed and recording density are functions of track radius, the data are confined to the outer areas of the disks to minimize the change in these parameters. As a result, the centre of the pack is often an empty well. Removable packs usually seat on a taper to ensure concentricity, and elaborate fixing mechanisms are needed on large packs to prevent the pack

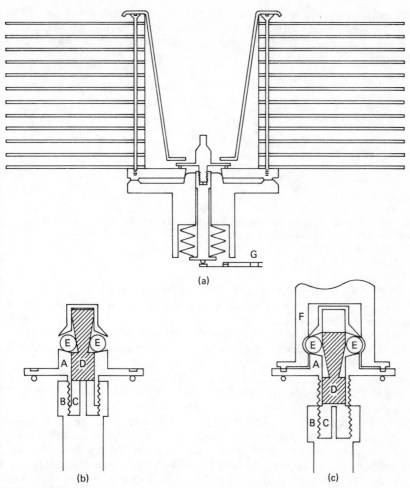

(a)

(b)

(c)

Figure 12.4 (a) Typical construction of multiplatter exchangeable pack. The pack weighs about 20 lb (9 kg) and turns at up to 3600 rev/min. The hold-down mechanism must be faultlessly reliable, to resist the forces involved, and must centre the pack precisely to allow proper track alignment and balance. In (b), the hold-down screw A is fully engaged with the lockshaft B, and the pin C lifts the ramp D, retracting the balls E. In (c), the hold-down screw is withdrawn from the lockshaft, which retracts, causing the ramp to force the balls into engagement with the cover F. The lockshaft often operates a switch to inform the logic that a pack is present (G)

from working loose in operation. Smaller packs are held to the spindle by a permanent magnet, and a lever mechanism is incorporated in the cartridge to assist their removal.

12.4 Principle of flying head

As was mentioned in Chapter 6, disk drives permanently sacrifice storage density in order to offer rapid access. The use of a flying head with a deliberate air gap between it and the medium is necessary because of the high medium speed, but this causes a severe separation loss which restricts the linear density (Fig. 12.5). The construction of disk heads was also illustrated in Chapter 7.

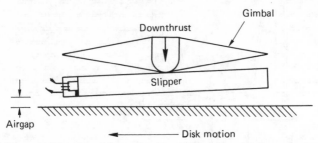

Figure 12.5 Disk head slipper develops lift from boundary layer moving with disk. This reaches equilibrium with the downthrust at the designed flying height. Resultant air gap prevents head wear but restricts storage density

Early disks used FM coding, which was easy to decode but had a poor density ratio. The invention of MFM revolutionized hard disks and was at one time universal. Further progress led to run-length-limited codes such as 2/3 and 2/7 which had a high density ratio without sacrificing the large jitter window necessary to reject peak shift distortion. Partial response is also suited to disks but is not yet in common use.

Typical drives have several heads, but in a disk drive intended for use with a computer, only one head will be active at any one time, which means that the read and write circuitry can be shared between the heads, and the unit cost will be minimized. Where high data transfer rates are needed, for example in real-time digital video, special purpose disk drives can be made which have one data channel per head. These parallel transfer machines are made in small quantities and are accordingly expensive. For still stores, rapid access is more important than data rate, so most of these machines work with standard computer-type disks. For real-time video, it is also possible to use several conventional drives in parallel to obtain throughput rather than parallel transfer drives.

12.5 Reading and writing

Fig. 12.6 shows the system which selects the active head in a conventional drive. It can be seen that the centre-tapped heads are isolated by connecting the centre tap to a negative voltage, which reverse-biases the matrix diodes. The centre tap of the selected head is made positive. When reading, a small current flows through both halves of the head winding, since the diodes are forward biased. Opposing currents in the head cancel but read signals that are due to transitions on the medium can pass through the forward-biased diodes to become differential signals on the matrix bus. During writing, the current from the write generator passes alternately through the two halves of the head coil. Further isolation is necessary to

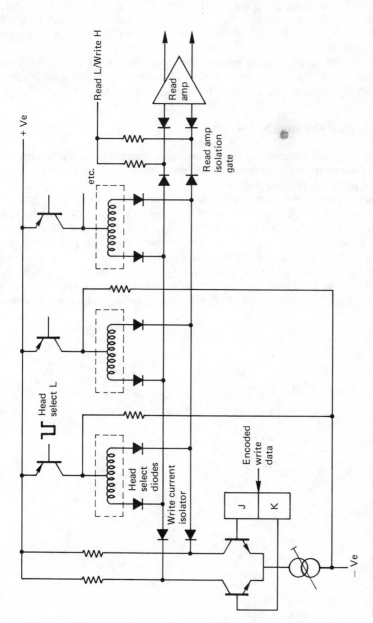

Figure 12.6 Representative head matrix

prevent the write-current-induced voltages from destroying the read preamplifier input.

The read channel usually incorporates AGC (automatic gain control), which will be overridden by the control logic between data blocks in order to search for address marks, which are short, unmodulated areas of track. As a block preamble is entered, the AGC will be enabled to allow a rapid gain adjustment.

The high bit rates of disk drives, owing to the speed of the medium, mean that peak detection in the replay channel is usually by differentiation. The detected peaks are then fed to the data separator.

12.6 Moving the heads

The servo system required to move the heads rapidly between tracks, and yet hold them in place accurately for data transfer, is a fascinating and complex piece of engineering.

In exchangeable-pack drives, the disk positioner moves on a straight axis which passes through the spindle. The head carriage will usually have preloaded ball races which run on rails mounted on the bed of the machine, although some drives use plain sintered bushes sliding on polished rods.

Motive power on early disk drives was hydraulic, but this soon gave way to moving-coil drive, because of the small moving mass which this technique permits. Lower-cost units use a conventional electric motor as shown in Fig. 12.7 which drives the carriage through steel wires wound

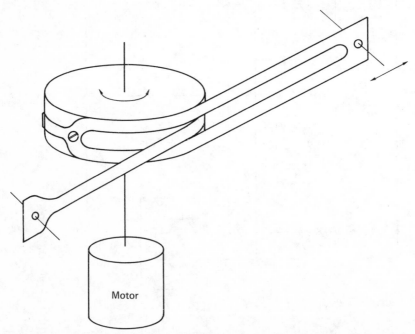

Figure 12.7 A low-cost linear positioner can be obtained using a drum and split-band drive, shown here, or with flexible wire. The ends of the band are fixed to the carriage

around it, or via a split metal band which is shaped to allow both ends to be fixed to the carriage despite the centre making a full turn around the motor shaft. The final possibility is a coarse-threaded shaft or leadscrew which engages with a nut on the carriage. In very-low-cost drives, the motor will be a stepping motor and the positions of the tracks will be determined by the natural detents of the stepping motor. This has an advantage for portable drives, because a stepping motor will remain detented without power. Moving-coil actuators require power to stay on track.

When a drive is track following, it is said to be detented, in fine mode or linear mode depending on the manufacturer. When a drive is seeking from one track to another, it can be described as being in coarse mode or velocity mode. These are the two major operating modes of the servo.

With the exception of stepping-motor-driven carriages, the servo system needs positional feedback from a transducer of some kind. The purpose of the transducer will be one or more of the following:

1. to count the number of cylinders crossed during a seek
2. to generate a signal proportional to carriage velocity
3. to generate a position error proportional to the distance from the centre of the desired track.

Sometimes the same transducer is used for all of these, and so transducers are best classified by their operating principle rather than by their function in a particular drive.

The simplest transducer is the magnetic moving-coil type, with its complementary equivalent the moving-magnet type. Both generate a voltage proportional to velocity and can give no positional information, but no precise alignment other than a working clearance is necessary.

Optical transducers consist of gratings, one fixed on the machine base and one on the carriage. The relative position of the two controls the

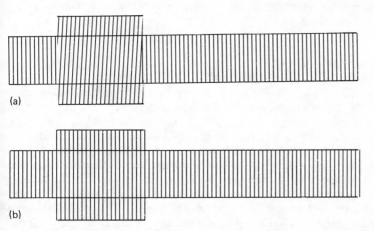

Figure 12.8 Glass-grating transducers work by modulating a light beam with the interaction of moving and stationary bars. It is vital that these units are correctly adjusted both mechanically and electrically, and this is often a time consuming process. (a) Moiré-grating transducer has non-parallel bars, and the resulting fringe patterns generate a sinusoidal output. (b) Parallel-bar grating transducer generates triangular waveform

amount of light which can shine through on to a sensor. Reference to Fig. 12.8 will show that there are basically two categories of grating transducer: the moiré-fringe device and the parallel-bar type.

In a moiré-fringe transducer, the two sets of bars are not parallel, and relative movement causes a fringe pattern which travels at right angles to the direction of carriage motion. This results in sinusoidal modulation of the light beam. In the parallel-bar type, the moving grating acts as a simple shutter, and the output is a triangle wave. In both types, the spacing between the two parts of the grating is critical. Both types give the same performance for counting cylinder crossings, as the waveform is not of any consequence for that application. The choice of which type to use is determined by whether positional information for track following or velocity feedback for seeking is needed. The slope of a sine wave is steeper in the zero region than an equivalent triangle wave, and so the moiré type is preferable for position sensing. Conversely, the constant slope of the triangle wave is easier to differentiate to give a velocity signal.

As the differential of a triangle wave changes sign twice per cycle, a two-phase optical system is often used to give a continuous output. The stationary grating has two sets of bars with a 90° phase relationship, and the resultant two output signals are invariably called sin and cos even if they are triangular waves. Fig. 12.9 shows that the two waveforms and their complements are differentiated, and then the four differentials are selected at times when they have no sign change. This process of commutation is achieved by analog switches controlled by comparators looking for points where the input waveforms cross. The result is a clean signal proportional to carriage velocity.

Where one transducer has to generate all three signals, the moiré type is better as the position sensing is more important, and ripple on the velocity signal has to be accepted.

Optical transducers usually contain additional light paths to aid carriage-travel limit detection and to provide an absolute reference to the incremental counting.

12.7 Controlling a seek

A seek is a process where the positioner moves from one cylinder to another. The speed with which a seek can be completed is a major factor in determining the access time of the drive. The main parameter controlling the carriage during a seek is the cylinder difference which is obtained by subtracting the current cylinder address from the desired cylinder address. The cylinder difference will be a signed binary number representing the number of cylinders to be crossed to reach the target, direction being indicated by the sign. The cylinder difference is loaded into a counter which is decremented each time a cylinder is crossed. The counter drives a DAC which generates an analog voltage proportional to the cylinder difference. As Fig. 12.10 shows, this voltage, known as the scheduled velocity, is compared with the output of the carriage-velocity transducer. Any difference between the two results in a velocity error which drives the carriage to cancel the error. As the carriage approaches the target cylinder,

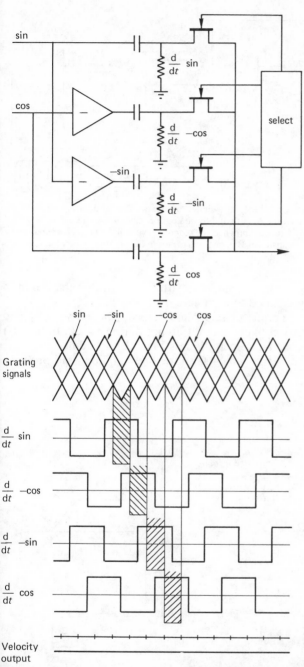

sin

cos

select

$\frac{d}{dt}$ sin

$\frac{d}{dt}$ −cos

−sin

$\frac{d}{dt}$ −sin

$\frac{d}{dt}$ cos

sin   −sin   −cos   cos

Grating
signals

$\frac{d}{dt}$ sin

$\frac{d}{dt}$ −cos

$\frac{d}{dt}$ −sin

$\frac{d}{dt}$ cos

Velocity
output

Figure 12.9 Optical-velocity transducer. Four quadrature signals are produced from the
two-phase transducer. Each of these is differentiated, and the four derivatives are selected
one at a time by analog switches. This process results in a continuous analog output voltage
proportional to the slope of the transducer waveform, which is itself proportional to carriage
velocity. In some drives one of the tranducer signals may also be used to count cylinder
crossings during a seek and to provide a position error for detenting

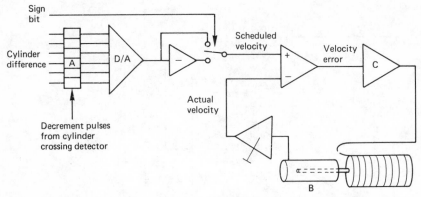

Figure 12.10 Control of carriage velocity by cylinder difference. The cylinder difference is loaded into the difference counter A. A digital-to-analog converter generates an analog voltage from the cylinder difference, known as the scheduled velocity. This is compared with the actual velocity from the transducer B in order to generate the velocity error which drives the servo amplifier C

the cylinder difference becomes smaller, with the result that the run-in to the target is critically damped to eliminate overshoot.

Fig. 12.11(a) shows graphs of scheduled velocity, actual velocity and motor current with respect to cylinder difference during a seek. In the first half of the seek, the actual velocity is less than the scheduled velocity, causing a large velocity error which saturates the amplifier and provides

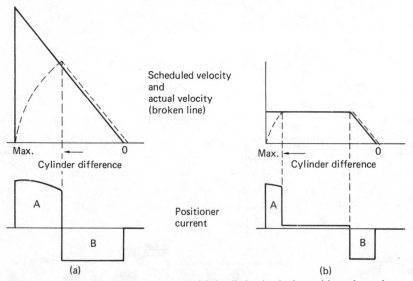

Figure 12.11 In the simple arrangement at (a) the dissipation in the positioner is continuous, causing a heating problem. The effect of limiting the scheduled velocity above a certain cylinder difference is apparent in (b) where heavy positioner current only flows during acceleration and deceleration. During the plateau of the velocity profile, only enough current to overcome friction is necessary. The curvavature of the acceleration slope is due to the back EMF of the positioner motor

maximum carriage acceleration. In the second half of the graphs, the scheduled velocity is falling below the actual velocity, generating a negative velocity error which drives a reverse current through the motor to slow the carriage down. The scheduled deceleration slope can clearly not be steeper than the saturated acceleration slope. Areas A and B on the graph will be about equal, as the kinetic energy put into the carriage has to be taken out. The current through the motor is continuous and would result in a heating problem. To counter this, the DAC is made non-linear so that above a certain cylinder difference no increase in scheduled velocity will occur. This results in the graph of Fig. 12.11(b). The actual velocity graph is called a velocity profile. It consists of three regions: acceleration, where the system is saturated; a constant velocity plateau, where the only power needed is to overcome friction; and the scheduled run-in to the desired cylinder. Dissipation is only significant in the first and last regions.

A consequence of the critically damped run-in to the target cylinder is that short seeks are slow. Sometimes further non-linearity is introduced into the velocity scheduler to speed up short seeks. The velocity profile becomes a piecewise linear approximation to a curve by using non-linear feedback. Fig. 12.12 shows the principle of the shaper or profile generator.

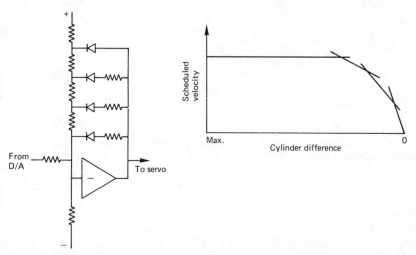

Figure 12.12 The use of voltage-dependent feedback around an operational amplifier permits a piecewise-linear approximation to a curved velocity profile. This has the effect of speeding up short seeks without causing a dissipation problem on long seeks. The circuit is referred to as a shaper

In small disk drives the amplifier may be linear in all modes of operation, resembling an audio power amplifier. Larger units may employ pulse-width-modulated drive to reduce dissipation, or even switched-mode amplifiers with inductive flywheel circuits. These switching systems can generate appreciable electromagnetic radiation, but this is of no consequence as they are only active during a seek. In track-following mode, the amplifier reverts to linear mode; hence the use of the term linear to mean track-following mode.

The input of the servo amplifier normally has a number of analog switches which select the appropriate signals according to the mode of the servo. As the output of the position transducer is a triangle or sine wave, the sense of the position feedback has to be inverted on odd-numbered cylinders to allow detenting on the negative slope. Sometimes a separate transducer is used for head retraction only. A typical system is shown in Fig. 12.13.

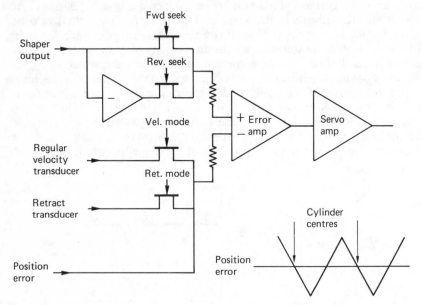

Figure 12.13 A typical servo-amplifier input stage. In velocity mode the shaper and the velocity transducer drive the error amp. In track-following mode the position error is the only input

12.8 Rotation

The rotation subsystems of disk drives will now be covered. The track-following accuracy of a drive positioner will be impaired if there is bearing run-out, and so the spindle bearings are made to a high degree of precision. On larger drives, squirrel-cage induction motors are used to drive the spindle through a belt. The different motor speeds resulting from 50 Hz and 60 Hz supplies are accommodated by changing the relative sizes of the pulleys. As recording density increases, the size of drives has come down, and the smaller units incorporate brushless DC motors with integral speed control. In exchangeable-pack drives, some form of braking is usually provided to slow down the pack rapidly for convenient removal. This can be done by feeding DC to an AC motor, which causes it to act as an eddy current brake.

In order to control reading and writing, the drive control circuitry needs to know which cylinder the heads are on, and which sector is currently under the head. Sector information is often obtained from a sensor which detects slots cut in the hub of the disk. These can be optical, variable-reluctance or eddy current devices. Pulses from the transducer increment the sector counter, which is reset by a double slot once per revolution. The desired sector address is loaded into a register, which is compared with the sector counter. When the two match, the desired sector has been found. This process is referred to as a search and usually takes place after a seek. Having found the correct physical place on the disk, the next step is to read the header associated with the data block to confirm that the disk address contained there is the same as the desired address. In the vast majority of disk drives, the rotation of the disk is uncontrolled, and it turns at whatever speed the motor naturally runs. The data transfers are synchronized to the rotation of the disk, rather than the other way round. An exception to this system is where the disk drive is used for real-time video storage, when the disk rotation can be phase locked to video timing to reduce latency. In this case, the disk motors need to be powered by amplifiers driven by phase comparators, similar to the approach used in VTR scanners.

12.9 Cooling and filtration

Rotation of a disk pack at speed results in heat buildup through air resistance. This heat must be carried away. A further important factor with exchangeable-pack drives is to keep the disk area free from contaminants which might lodge between the head and the disk and cause the destructive phenomenon known as a head crash, where debris builds up on the head until it ploughs the disk surface.

The cooling and filtration systems are usually combined. Air is drawn through an absolute filter, passed around the disk, and exhausted, sometimes cooling the positioner motor and circuitry on the way. This full-flow system is fine for environmentally controlled computer rooms, but for the office or studio environment a closed-circuit filtration system can be used, where the same air goes round the pack and through the blower and filter endlessly. This results in extended filter life in adverse environments, but requires a heat exchanger in the loop to carry away the heat developed by disk rotation.

12.10 Servo-surface disks

One of the major problems to be overcome in the development of high-density disk drives was that of keeping the heads on track despite changes of temperature. The very narrow tracks used in digital recording have similar dimensions to the amount a disk will expand as it warms up. The cantilevers and the drive base all expand and contract, conspiring with thermal drift in the cylinder transducer to limit track pitch. The breakthrough in disk density came with the introduction of the servo-surface drive. The position error in a servo-surface drive is derived from a head reading the disk itself. This virtually eliminates thermal effects on head positioning and allows great increases in storage density.

In a multiplatter drive, one surface of the pack holds servo information which is read by the servo head. In a ten platter pack this means that 5% of the medium area is lost, but this is unimportant since the increase in density allowed is enormous. Using one side of a single-platter cartridge for servo information would be unacceptable as it represents 50% of the medium area, so in this case the servo information can be interleaved with sectors on the data surfaces. This is known as an embedded-servo technique. These two approaches are contrasted in Fig. 12.14.

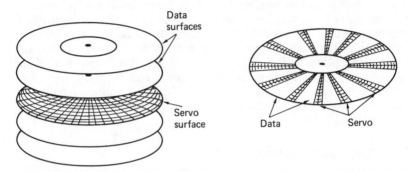

Figure 12.14 In a multiplatter disk pack, one surface is dedicated to servo information. In a single platter, the servo information is embedded in the data on the same surfaces

The servo surface is written at the time of disk pack manufacture, and the disk drive can only read it. The key to the operation of the servo surface is the special magnetic pattern recorded on it. In a typical servo surface, recorded pairs of transitions, known as dibits, are separated by a space. Fig. 12.15 shows that there are two kinds of track. On an A track, the first transition of the pair will cause a positive pulse on reading, whereas on a B track, the first pulse will be negative. In addition the A-track dibits are shifted by one half cycle with respect to the B-track dibits. The width of the magnetic circuit in the servo head is equal to the width of a servo track. During track following, the correct position for the servo head is with half of each type of track beneath it. The read/write heads will then be centred on their respective data tracks. Fig. 12.16 illustrates this relationship.

The amplitude of dibits from A tracks with respect to the amplitude of dibits from B tracks depends on the relative areas of the servo head which are exposed to the respective tracks. As the servo head has only one magnetic circuit, it will generate a composite signal whose components will change differentially as the position of the servo head changes. Fig. 12.17 shows several composite waveforms obtained at different positions of the servo head. The composite waveform is processed by using the first positive and negative pulses to generate a clock. From this clock are derived sampling signals which permit only the second positive and second negative pulses to pass. The resultant waveform has a DC component which after filtering gives a voltage proportional to the distance from the centre of the data tracks. The position error reaches a maximum when the

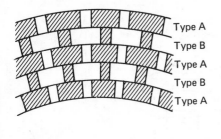

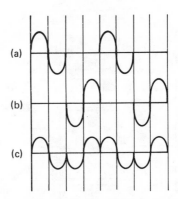

Figure 12.15 The servo surface is divided into two types of track, A and B, which are out of phase by 180° and are recorded with reverse polarity with respect to one another. Waveform (a) results when the servo head is entirely above a type A track, and waveform (b) results from reading solely a type B track. When the servo head is correctly positioned with one half of its magnetic circuit over each track, the waveform of (c) results

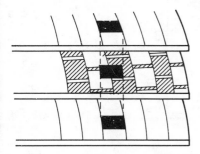

Figure 12.16 When the servo head is straddling two servo tracks, the data heads are correctly aligned with their respective tracks

servo head is entirely above one type of servo track, and further movement causes it to fall. The next time the position error falls to zero will be at the centre line of the adjacent cylinder.

Cylinders with even addresses (LSB = 0) will be those where the servo head is detented between an A track and a B track. Cylinders with odd addresses will be those where the head is between a B track and an A track. It can be seen from Fig. 12.17 that the sense of the position error becomes reversed on every other cylinder. Accordingly, an inverter has to be switched into the track-following feedback loop in order to detent on odd cylinders. This inversion is controlled by the LSB of the desired cylinder address supplied at the beginning of a seek, such that the sense of the feedback will be correct when the heads arrive at the target cylinder.

Seeking across the servo surface results in the position-error signal rising and falling in a sawtooth. This waveform can be used to count down the cylinder difference counter which controls the seek. As with any cyclic transducer there is the problem of finding the absolute position. This difficulty is overcome by making all servo tracks outside cylinder 0 type A and all servo tracks inside the innermost cylinder type B. These areas of identical track are called guard bands, and Fig. 12.18 shows the relationship between the position error and the guard bands. During a

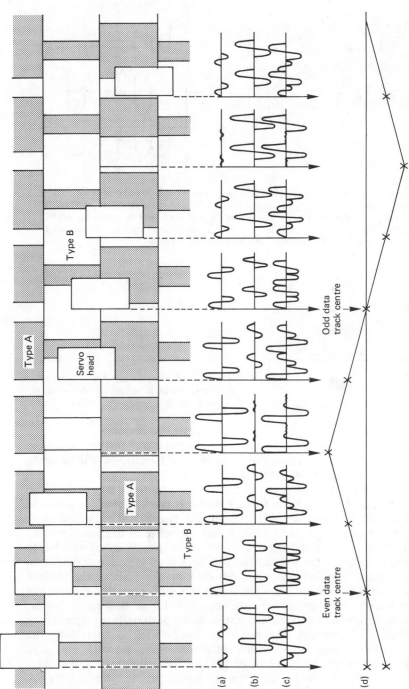

Figure 12.17 Waveforms resulting from several positions of the servo head with respect to the disk. At (a) and (b) are the two components of the waveforms, whose relative amplitudes are controlled by the relative areas of the servo head exposed to the two types of servo track. Because the servo head has only one magnetic circuit, these waveforms are not observed in practice, but are summed together, resulting in the composite waveforms shown at (c). By comparing the magnitudes of the second positive and second negative peaks in the composite

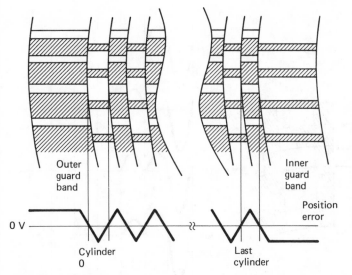

Figure 12.18 The working area of the servo surface is defined by the inner and outer guard bands, in which the position error reaches its maximum value

head load, the servo head generates a constant maximum positive position error in the outer guard band. This drives the carriage forward until the position error first falls to zero. This, by definition, is cylinder 0. Some drives, however, load by driving the heads across the surface until the inner guard band is found, and then perform a full-length reverse seek to cylinder 0.

An alternative form of servo surface for exchangeable-pack drives is shown in Fig. 12.19. In this type, there is a common sync bit in all tracks, and subsequent servo bits at different times afterwards. The position error is derived by opening sampling gates at different times after the sync bit. As three distinct pulses can be seen in the waveform, the result is called a tribit signal.

12.11 Soft sectoring

It has been seen that a position error and a cylinder count can be derived from the servo surface, eliminating the cylinder transducer. The carriage velocity could also be derived from the slope of the position error, but there would then be no velocity feedback in the guard bands or during retraction, and so some form of velocity transducer is still necessary.

As there are exactly the same number of dibits or tribits on every track, it is possible to describe the rotational position of the disk simply by counting them. All that is needed is a unique pattern of missing dibits once per revolution to act as an index point, and the sector transducer can also be eliminated.

Unlike the read-data circuits, the servo-head circuits are active during a seek as well as when track following and have to be protected against

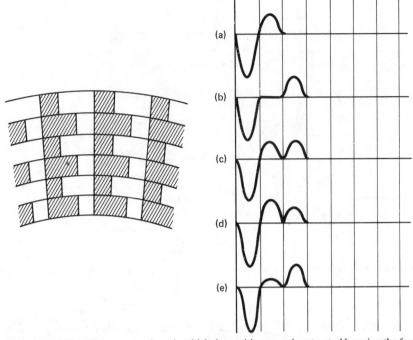

Figure 12.19 The tribit servo surface, in which the position error is extracted by using the fact that pulses from the two types of track occur at different times after the common negative sync pulse. Waveforms (a) and (b) are obtained when the servo head is entirely over one or other of the tracks, and (c) is the correct on-track waveform. (d) and (e) show typical off-track waveforms

interference from switching positioner drivers. The main problem is detecting index, where noise could cause a 'missing' dibit to be masked. There are two solutions available: a preamplifier can be built into the servo-head cantilever, or driver switching can be inhibited when index is expected.

The advantage of deriving the sector count from the servo surface is that the number of sectors on the disk can be varied. Any number of sectors can be accommodated by feeding the dibit-rate signal through a programmable divider, so the same disk and drive can be used in numerous different applications.

In a non-servo-surface disk, the write clock is usually derived from a crystal oscillator. As the disk speed can vary owing to supply fluctuations, a tolerance gap has to be left at the end of each block to cater for the highest anticipated speed to prevent overrun into the next block on a write. In a servo-surface drive, the write clock is obtained by multiplying the dibit-rate signal with a phase-locked loop. The write clock is then always proportional to disk speed, and recording density will be constant. In synchronized rotation drives for real-time recording, the servo surface will be the source of rotational feedback for the spindle drive, where index will have the same function as the once-around pulse generator in a VTR scanner.

Most servo-surface drives have an offset facility, where a register written by the controller drives a DAC which injects a small voltage into the track-following loop. The action of the servo is such that the heads move off track until the position error is equal and opposite to the injected voltage. The position of the heads above the track can thus be program controlled. Offset is only employed on reading if it is suspected that the pack in the drive has been written by a different drive with non-standard alignment. A write function will cancel the offset.

12.12 Embedded servo drives

In drives with a small number of platters, the use of an entire surface for servo information gives an excessive loss of data-recording area. In the embedded-servo drive, servo information is interleaved with data on the same surface, causing a smaller loss of storage area.

The embedded-servo drive heads will be reading data at some times and alignment information at others as the disk rotates. A sector transducer is required to generate a pulse which is true when the head is over servo information. Fig. 12.20 and Fig. 12.21 show the principle. On all disk

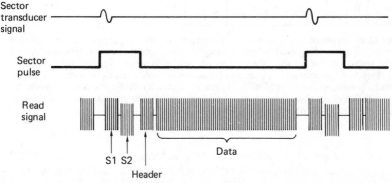

Figure 12.20 The same head is used on the embedded servo drive for both servo information and read/write data. During a sector pulse, the read signal is treated as servo information

drives, the width of the head pole is less than the track pitch to prevent crosstalk. As the servo head is also the read/write head in an embedded-servo drive, it is slightly narrower than the servo-information pitch. This has the harmless effect of rounding off the peaks of the position-error waveform. During the pulse from the sector transducer, the head sees alignment information and develops a position error in much the same way as any servo drive. Within the servo area are two sets of patterns, the second giving a position error of zero when the first is a maximum, i.e. there is a 90° phase shift between them. The two bursts of information are known as S1 and S2. Sample-and-hold circuitry is used to carry over the position errors whilst the head is reading and writing in the data area.

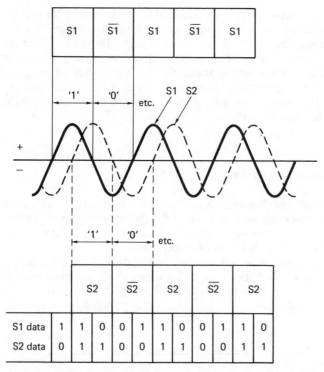

| S1 data | 1 | 1 | 0 | 0 | 1 | 1 | 0 | 0 | 1 | 1 | 0 |
| S2 data | 0 | 1 | 1 | 0 | 0 | 1 | 1 | 0 | 0 | 1 | 1 |

Figure 12.21 There are two basic types of servotrack, S_1 and S_2, but these are recorded at two different places, in a staggered fashion. During S1 time, a position error is generated from the relative areas of the two types of track under the head as in the conventional servo-surface drive. This position error is maintained with sample-and-hold circuitry. For track counting, the position error is compared with 0 V to generate a data bit. At S2 time another position error and another data bit are generated. The four possible combinations of the two bits are shown here in relation to the two position errors

The discontinuous nature of the servo information means that cylinder crossings cannot be counted directly during a seek as the positioner is fast enough to cross several tracks between bursts. With reference to Fig. 12.22, this problem is overcome as follows. During the S1 period, the position error is compared with zero volts to produce a single data bit, whose state depends upon whether the head was inside or outside the track centre. A similar process takes place for the S2 period, and the position of the head relative to the track centre is then described to the accuracy of one-fourth of the track pitch by the two data bits. These bits are stored, and at the next servo burst, two further bits are computed, describing the new position of the head. Fig. 12.22 shows that there can be many cases which can satisfy the same initial and final conditions. The only difference between the cases is the carriage velocity, so the output of the velocity transducer is digitized and used to resolve the ambiguity. At every sector pulse, 2 bits from the previous burst, 2 bits from the current burst and the digitized velocity are fed into a ROM which is preprogrammed to return the number of cylinders which must have been crossed for all combinations

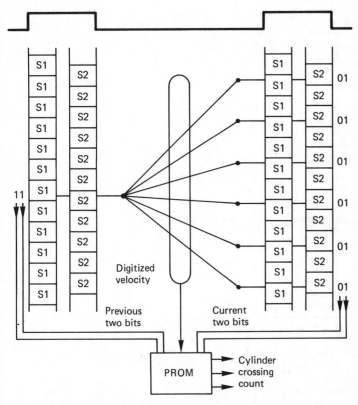

Figure 12.22 For the same initial and subsequent data bits, there can be several possible head trajectories. The ambiguity is resolved by using the carriage velocity in digital form

of inputs. This number is then subtracted from the cylinder-difference counter which is controlling the seek. The calculation will only be valid for one disk rotational speed, and so the disk motor requires close control. This is conveniently done by counting cycles of a reference clock between sector pulses to produce a speed error. As the cylinder count is deductive, there will be the odd occasion where the count is in error and the positioner comes to the wrong cylinder. In a conventional disk drive this would result in a mispositioning error which would warrant maintenance. In the embedded-servo drive, however, the condition is handled differently. Fig. 12.23 shows a flowchart for control of the drive, which has no absolute cylinder-address register and in which all seeks are relative. The system only knows where the heads are by reading headers. In order to reach a particular cylinder, the program has to read the first header it sees on the current cylinder and calculate the cylinder difference needed. This is used to perform a deductive seek. When this is complete, a further header will be read. Most of the time this will indicate the correct cylinder, but in the occasional condition where the positioning was in error, the program simply loops and calculates a new cylinder difference until the correct cylinder is finally reached.

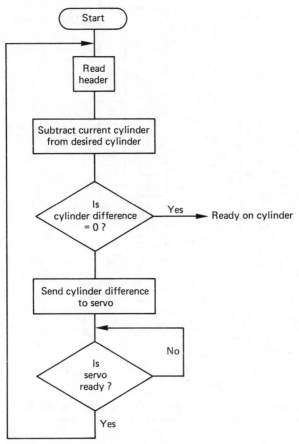

Figure 12.23 Flowchart for the control of an embedded-servo positioner. All seeks are relative, and seek errors are transparent, as they simply cause an extra execution of the loop

Since each surface has its own alignment information, some exchange-able-pack drives using this principle need no head alignment during manufacture at all. When switching between heads, a repositioning cycle will be necessary because all of the heads will not necessarily be on the same cylinder. In fact the definition of a cylinder is indistinct in such drives.

12.13 Winchester technology

In order to offer extremely high capacity per spindle, which reduces the cost per bit, a disk drive must have very narrow tracks placed close together, and must use very short recorded wavelengths, which implies that the flying height of the heads must be small. The so-called Winchester technology is one approach to high storage density. The technology was developed by IBM, and the name came about because the model number of the development drive was the same as that of the famous rifle.

Reduction in flying height magnifies the problem of providing a contaminant-free environment. A conventional disk is well protected whilst inside the drive, but outside the drive the effects of contamination become intolerable.

In exchangeable-pack drives, there is a real limit to the track pitch that can be achieved because of the impossibility of engineering head-alignment mechanisms to make the necessary minute adjustments to give interchange compatibility.

The essence of Winchester technology is that each disk pack has its own set of read/write and servo heads, with an integral positioner. The whole is protected by a dust-free enclosure, and the unit is referred to as a head disk assembly, or HDA.

As the HDA contains its own heads, compatibility problems do not exist, and no head alignment is necessary or provided for. It is thus possible to reduce track pitch considerably compared with exchangeable-pack drives. The sealed environment ensures complete cleanliness which permits a reduction in flying height without loss of reliability, and hence leads to an increased linear density. If the rotational speed is maintained, this can also result in an increase in data transfer rate.

The HDA is completely sealed, but some have a small filtered port to equalize pressure. Into this sealed volume of air, the drive motor delivers the majority of its power output. The resulting heat is dissipated by fins on the HDA casing. Some HDAs are filled with helium which significantly reduces drag and heat buildup.

An exchangeable-pack drive must retract the heads to facilitate pack removal. With Winchester technology this is not necessary. An area of the disk surface is reserved as a landing strip for the heads. The disk surface is lubricated, and the heads are designed to withstand landing and take-off without damage. Winchester heads have very large air-bleed grooves to

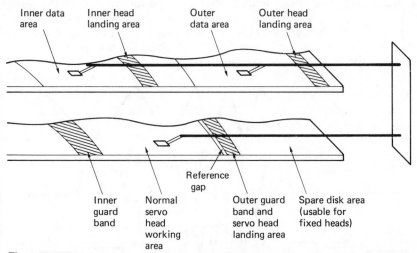

Figure 12.24 When more than one head is used per surface, the positioner still only requires one servo head. This is often arranged to be equidistant from the read/write heads for thermal stability

allow low flying height with a much smaller downthrust from the cantilever, and so they exert less force on the disk surface during contact. When the term retraction is used in the context of Winchester technology, it refers to the positioning of the heads over the landing area.

Disk rotation must be started and stopped quickly to minimize the length of time the heads slide over the medium. A powerful motor will accelerate the pack quickly. Eddy current braking cannot be used, since a power failure would allow the unbraked disk to stop only after a prolonged head-contact period. A failsafe mechanical brake is used, which is applied by a spring and released with a solenoid.

A major advantage of contact start/stop is that more than one head can be used on each surface if retraction is not needed. This leads to two gains: first, the travel of the positioner is reduced in proportion to the number of heads per surface, reducing access time; and, second, more data can be transferred at a given detented carriage position before a seek to the next cylinder becomes necessary. This increases the speed of long transfers. Fig. 12.24 illustrates the relationships of the heads in such a system.

12.14 Servo-surface Winchester drives

With contact start/stop, the servo head is always on the servo surface, and it can be used for all of the transducer functions needed by the drive. Fig. 12.25 shows the position-error signal during a seek. The signal rises and falls as servo tracks are crossed, and the slope of the signal is proportional to positioner velocity. The position-error signal is differentiated and rectified to give a velocity feedback signal. Owing to the cyclic nature of the position-error signal, the velocity signal derived from it has troughs where the derivative becomes zero at the peaks. These cannot be filtered out, since the signal is in a servo loop and the filter would introduce an additional lag. The troughs would, however, be interpreted by the servo driver as massive momentary velocity errors which might overload the amplifier. The solution which can be adopted is to use a signal obtained by integrating the positioner-motor current which is selected when there is a trough in the differentiated position-error signal.

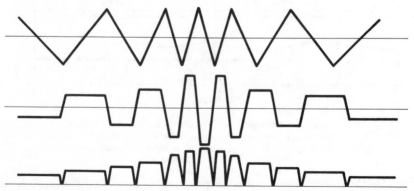

Figure 12.25 To generate a velocity signal, the position error from the servo head is differentiated and rectified

In order to make velocity feedback available over the entire servo surface, the conventional guard band approach cannot be used since it results in steady position errors in the guard bands. In contact start/stop drives, the servo head must be capable of detenting in a guard band for the purpose of landing on shutdown.

A modification to the usual servo surface is used in Winchester drives, one implementation of which is shown in Fig. 12.26, where it will be seen that there are extra transitions, identical in both types of track, along with the familiar dibits. The repeating set of transitions is known as a frame, in which the first dibit is used for synchronization, and a phase-locked oscillator is made to run at a multiple of the sync signal rate. The PLO is used as a reference for the write clock, as well as to generate sampling pulses to extract a position error from the composite waveform and to provide a window for the second dibit in the frame, which may or may not be present. Each frame thus contains one data bit, and succesive frames are read to build up a pattern in a shift register. The parallel output of the

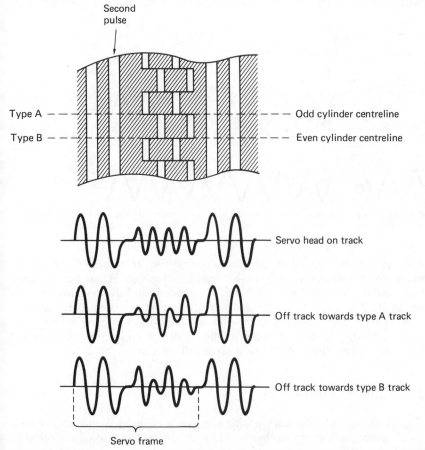

Figure 12.26 This type of servo surface pattern has a second pulse which may be omitted to act as a data bit. This is used to detect the guard bands and index

shift register is examined by a decoder which recognizes a number of unique patterns. In the guard bands, the decoder will repeatedly recognize the guard band code as the disk revolves. An index is generated in the same way by recognizing a different pattern. In a contact start/stop drive, the frequency of index detection is used to monitor pack speed in order to dispense with a separate transducer. This does mean, however, that it must be possible to detect index everywhere, and for this reason index is still recorded in the guard bands by replacing the guard band code with index code once per revolution.

A consequence of deriving velocity information from the servo surface is that the location of cylinder 0 is made more difficult, as there is no longer a continuous maximum position error in the guard band. A common solution is to adopt a much smaller area of continuous position error known as a reference gap; this is typically three servo tracks wide. In the reference gap and for several tracks outside it, there is a unique reference gap code recorded in the frame-data bits. Fig. 12.27 shows the position error which is generated as the positioner crosses this area of the disk and shows the plateau in the position-error signal due to the reference gap. During head

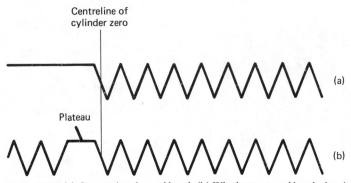

Figure 12.27 (a) Conventional guard band. (b) Winchester guard band, showing the plateau in the position error, known as the reference gap, which is used to locate cylinder zero

loading, which in this context means positioning to cylinder 0, the heads move slowly inwards away from the head landing area. When the reference code is detected, positioner velocity is reduced, and the position error is sampled. When successive position-error samples are the same, the head must be on the position-error plateau, and if the servo is put into track-following mode, it will automatically detent on cylinder 0, since this is the first place that the position error falls to zero.

12.15 Rotary positioners

Fig. 12.28 shows that rotary positioners are feasible in Winchester drives; they cannot be used in exchangeable-pack drives because of interchange problems. There are some advantages to a rotary positioner. It can be placed in the corner of a compact HDA allowing smaller overall size. The

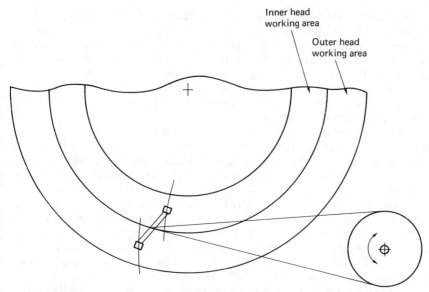

Figure 12.28 A rotary positioner with two heads per surface. The tolerances involved in the spacing between the heads and the axis of rotation mean that each arm records data in a unique position. Those data can only be read back by the same heads, which rules out the use of a rotary positioner in exchangeable-pack drives. In a head disk assembly the problem of compatibility does not arise

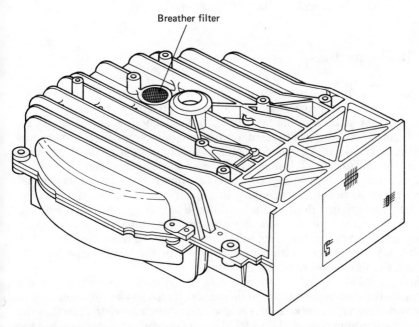

Figure 12.29 Head disk assembly with a rotary positioner. The adoption of this technique allows a very compact structure

manufacturing cost will be less than a linear positioner because fewer bearings and precision bars are needed. Significantly, a rotary positioner can be made faster since its inertia is smaller. With a linear positioner all parts move at the same speed. In a rotary positioner, only the heads move at full speed, as the parts closer to the shaft must move more slowly. Fig. 12.29 shows a typical HDA with a rotary positioner. The principle of a rotary positioner is exactly that of a moving-coil ammeter, where current is converted directly into torque.

One disadvantage of rotary positioners is that there is a component of windage on the heads which tends to pull the positioner in towards the spindle. In linear positioners windage is at right angles to motion and can be neglected. Windage is overcome in rotary positioners by feeding the current cylinder address to a ROM which sends a code to a DAC. This produces an offset voltage which is fed to the positioner driver to generate a torque which balances the windage whatever the position of the heads.

When extremely small track spacing is contemplated, it cannot be assumed that all the heads will track the servo head because of temperature gradients. In this case the embedded-servo approach must be used, where each head has its own alignment patterns. The servo surface is often retained in such drives to allow coarse positioning, velocity feedback and index and write clock generation, in addition to locating the guard bands for landing the heads.

Winchester drives have been made with massive capacity, but the problem of backup is then magnified, and the general trend has been for the physical size of the drive to come down as the storage density increases. Early drives used 14 in disks; later 8 in and 5¼ in became common, helped by the expanding market in desktop computers.

12.16 Floppy disks

Floppy disks are the result of a search for a fast yet cheap non-volatile memory for the programmable control store of a processor under development at IBM in the late 1960s. Both magnetic tape and hard disk were ruled out on grounds of cost since only intermittent duty was required. The device designed to fulfil these requirements – the floppy-disk drive – incorporated both magnetic tape and disk technologies.

The floppy concept was so cost-effective that it transcended its original application to become a standard in industry as an online data-storage device. The original floppy disk, or diskette as it is sometimes called, was 8 in in diameter, but a 5¼ in diameter disk was launched to suit more compact applications. More recently Sony introduced the 3½ in floppy disk which has a rigid shell with sliding covers over the head access holes to reduce the likelihood of contamination.

Strictly speaking the floppy is a disk, since it rotates and repeatedly presents the data on any track to the heads. It also has a positioner to give fast two-dimensional access, but it also resembles a tape drive in that the magnetic medium is carried on a flexible substrate which deforms when the read/write head is pressed against it.

Floppy disks are stamped from wide, thick tape and are anisotropic, because the oxide becomes oriented during manufacture. On many disks this can be seen by the eye as parallel striations on the disk surface. A more serious symptom is the presence of sinusoidal amplitude modulation of the replay signal at twice the rotational frequency of the disk, as illustrated in Fig. 12.30.

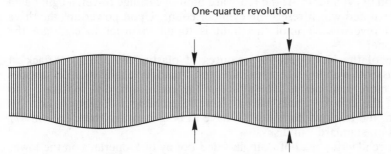

Figure 12.30 Sinusoidal amplitude modulation of floppy disk output due to anisotropy of medium

Floppy disks have radial apertures in their protective envelopes to allow access by the head. A further aperture allows a photoelectric index sensor to detect a small hole in the disk once per revolution.

Fig. 12.31 shows that the disk is inserted into the drive edge-first and slides between an upper and a lower hub assembly. One of these has a fixed bearing which transmits the drive; the other is spring loaded and mates with the drive hub when the door is closed, causing the disk to be centred and gripped firmly. The moving hub is usually tapered to assist centring. To avoid frictional heating and prolong life, the spindle speed is restricted when compared with that of hard disks. Recent drives almost universally use direct-drive brushless DC motors; older machines used an

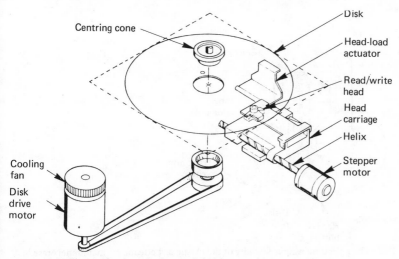

Figure 12.31 The mechanism of a floppy disk drive

induction motor and belt drive. Since the rotational latency is so great, there is little point in providing a fast positioner, and the use of leadscrews driven by a stepping motor is universal. The permanent magnets in the stepping motor provide the necessary detenting, and to seek it is only necessary to provide a suitable number of drive pulses to the motor. As the drive is incremental, some form of reference is needed to determine the position of cylinder 0. At the rearward limit of carriage travel, a light beam is interrupted which resets the cylinder count. Upon power-up, the drive has to reverse-seek until this limit is found in order to calibrate the positioner.

One of the less endearing features of plastics materials is a lack of dimensional stability. Temperature and humidity changes affect plastics much more than metals. The effect on the anisotropic disk substrate is to distort the circular tracks into a shape resembling a dog bone. For this reason, the track width and pitch have to be generous. There are only 77 tracks on standard 8 in disks.

The read/write head of a single-sided floppy disk operates on the lower surface only and is rigidly fixed to the carriage. Contact with the medium is achieved with the help of a spring-loaded pressure pad applied to the top surface of the disk opposite the head. Early drives retracted the pressure pad with a solenoid when not actually transferring data; later drives simply stop the disk. In double-sided drives, the pressure pad is replaced by a second sprung head.

Because of the indifferent stability of the medium, side trim or tunnel erasing is used, because it can withstand considerable misregistration.

Fig. 12.32 shows the construction of a typical side-trimming head, which has erase poles at each side of the magnetic circuit. When such a head writes, the erase poles are energized and erase a narrow strip of the disk either side of the new data track. If the recording is made with misregistration, the side trim prevents traces of the previous recording from being played back as well (Fig. 12.33).

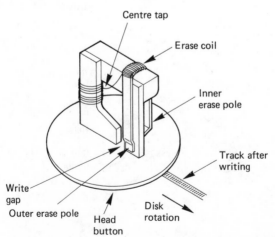

Figure 12.32 The poor dimensional stability of the plastic diskette means that tunnel erase or side trim has to be used. The extra erase poles can be seen here

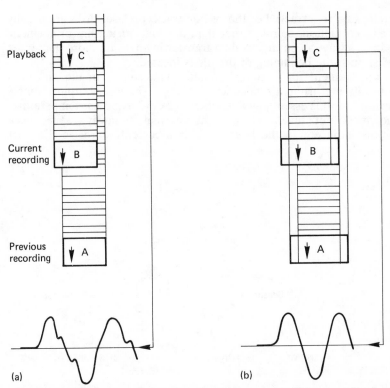

Figure 12.33 The effect of side trim is to prevent the traces of a previous recording from interfering with the latest recording: (a) without side trim; (b) with side trim

As the floppy-disk drive is intended to be a low-cost item, sophisticated channel codes are never used. Single-density drives use FM and double-density drives use MFM. As the recording density becomes higher at the inner tracks, the write current is sometimes programmed to reduce with inward positioner travel.

The capacity of floppy disks is in the range of hundreds of kilobytes to a few megabytes. This virtually precludes their use for digital video sample storage, but they find application in edit-list storage, effects storage for DVEs, and as a software-loading medium for computer-based equipment.

12.17 Structure of optical disk drives

The optical principles behind laser drives were discussed in Chapter 6. A typical laser disk drive resembles a magnetic drive in that it has a spindle drive mechanism to revolve the disk and a positioner to give radial access across the disk surface. The positioner has to carry a collection of lasers, lenses, prisms, gratings and so on, and in early units could not be accelerated as fast as a magnetic-drive positioner. A penalty of the very small track pitch possible in laser disks, which gives the enormous storage capacity, is that very accurate track following is needed, and it takes some time to lock on to a track. For this reason tracks on laser disks are usually made as a continuous spiral, rather than the concentric rings of magnetic disks. In this way, a continuous data transfer involves no more than track following once the beginning of the file is located.

The requirement for a monochromatic light source in the pickup is economically met using a semiconductor laser. The laser output requires stabilization, as it is essentially a regenerative device and has temperature-dependent output level. To prevent thermal runaway, a feedback photodiode adjacent to the laser controls a current source in the laser power supply.

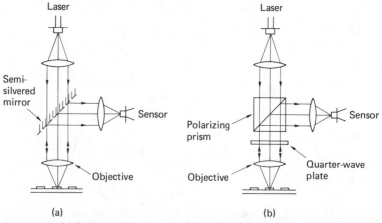

(a)   (b)

Figure 12.34 (a) Reflected light from the disk is directed to the sensor by a semisilvered mirror. (b) A combination of polarizing prism and quarter-wave plate separate incident and reflected light

In order to extract a signal, the pickup must be capable of separating the reflected light from the incident light. Fig. 12.34 shows two systems. In (a) a semi-silvered mirror reflects some of the returning light into the photosensor. This is not very efficient, as some of the light is lost by transmission straight on. In the example at (b) separation is by the plane of polarization. A polarizing prism passes light from the laser which is polarized in a plane at right angles to the plane of the page. This light is passed through a quarter-wave plate, which rotates the plane of polarization through 45°. Following reflection from the disk, the light passes again through the quarter-wave plate and is rotated a further 45°, such that it is now polarized in the plane of the page. The polarizing prism reflects this light into the sensor.

12.18 Focus systems

Since the channel frequency response and the amount of crosstalk are both a function of the spot size, care must be taken to keep the beam focused on the information layer. Disk warp and thickness irregularities will cause focal-plane movement beyond the depth of focus of the optical system, and a focus servo system will be needed. The depth of field is related to the numerical aperture, which is defined, and the accuracy of the servo must be sufficient to keep the focal plane within that depth, which is typically $\pm 1\,\mu$m.

The focus servo moves a lens along the optical axis in order to keep the spot in focus. Since dynamic focus changes are largely due to warps, the focus system must have a frequency response in excess of the rotational speed. A moving-coil actuator is often used owing to the small moving mass which this permits. Fig. 12.35 shows that a cylindrical magnet assembly almost identical to that of a loudspeaker can be used, coaxial with the light beam.

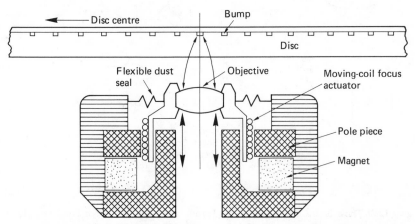

Figure 12.35 Moving-coil-focus servo can be coaxial with the light beam as shown

A focus-error system is necessary to drive the lens. There are a number of ways in which this can be derived, the most common of which will be described here.

In Fig. 12.36 a cylindrical lens is installed between the beam splitter and the photosensor. The effect of this lens is that the beam has no focal point on the sensor. In one plane, the cylindrical lens appears parallel sided and has negligible effect on the focal length of the main system, whereas in the other plane, the lens shortens the focal length. The image will be an ellipse whose aspect ratio changes as a function of the state of focus. Between the two foci, the image will be circular. The aspect ratio of the ellipse, and hence the focus error, can be found by dividing the sensor into quadrants. When these are connected as shown, the focus-error signal is generated. The data readout signal is the sum of the quadrant outputs.

Fig. 12.37 shows the knife-edge method of determining focus. A split sensor is also required. At (a) the focal point is coincident with the knife edge, so it has little effect on the beam. At (b) the focal point is to the right of the knife edge, and rising rays are interrupted, reducing the output of the upper sensor. At (c) the focal point is to the left of the knife edge, and descending rays are interrupted, reducing the output of the lower sensor.

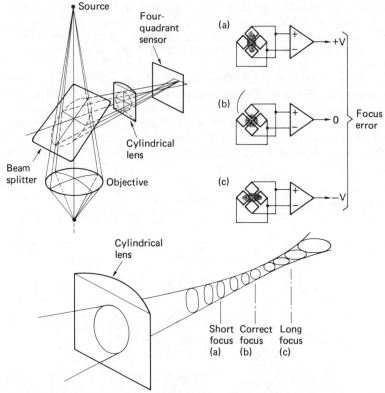

Figure 12.36 The cylindrical-lens focus method produces an elliptical spot on the sensor whose aspect ratio is detected by a four-quadrant sensor to produce a focus error

The focus error is derived by comparing the outputs of the two halves of the sensor. A drawback of the knife-edge system is that the lateral position of the knife edge is critical, and adjustment is necessary. To overcome this problem, the knife edge can be replaced by a pair of prisms, as shown in Fig. 12.37(d)–(f). Mechanical tolerances then only affect the sensitivity, without causing a focus offset.

The cylindrical lens method is compared with the knife-edge/prism method in Fig. 12.38, which shows that the cylindrical lens method has a much smaller capture range. A focus-search mechanism will be required, which moves the focus servo over its entire travel, looking for a zero crossing. At this time the feedback loop will be completed, and the sensor will remain on the linear part of its characteristic.

12.19 Tracking systems

The track pitch of a typical laser disk is only 1.6 μm, and this is much smaller than the accuracy to which the player chuck or the disk centre hole

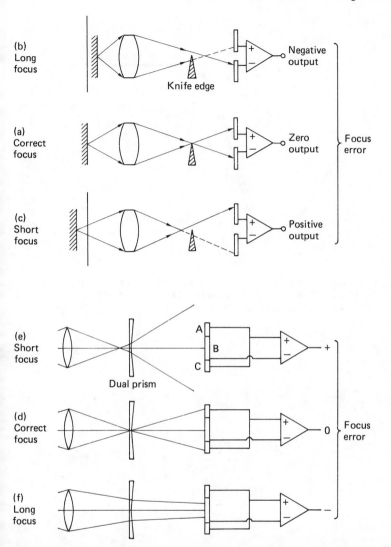

Figure 12.37 (a)–(c) Knife-edge focus method requires only two sensors, but is critically dependent on knife-edge position. (d)–(f) Twin-prism method requires three sensors (A, B, C), where focus error is (A + C) − B. Prism alignment reduces sensitivity without causing focus offset

can be made; on a typical player, run-out will swing several tracks past a fixed pickup. In addition, a warped disk will not present its surface at 90° to the beam, but will constantly change the angle of incidence during two whole cycles per revolution. Owing to the change of refractive index at the disk surface, the tilt will change the apparent position of the track to the pickup, and Fig. 12.39 shows that this makes it appear wavy. Warp also results in coma of the readout spot. The disk format specifies a maximum warp amplitude to keep these effects under control. Finally, vibrations

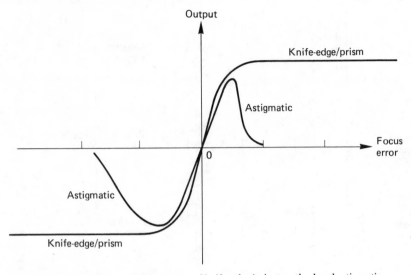

Figure 12.38 Comparison of captive range of knife-edge/prism method and astigmatic (cylindrical lens) system. Knife edge may have range of 1 mm, whereas astigmatic may only have a range of 40 micrometres, requiring a focus-search mechanism

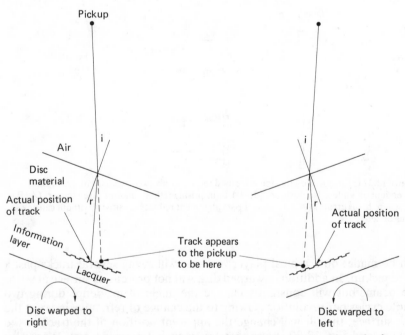

Figure 12.39 Owing to refraction, the angle of incidence (i) is greater than the angle of refraction (r). Disk warp causes the apparent position of the track (dotted line) to move, requiring the tracking servo to correct

induced in the player from outside, will tend to disturb tracking. A track-following servo is necessary to keep the spot centralized on the track in the presence of these difficulties. There are several ways in which a tracking error can be derived.

In the three-spot method, two additional light beams are focused on the disk track, one offset to each side of the track centre line. Fig. 12.40 shows that, as one side spot moves away from the track into the mirror area, there is less destructive interference and more reflection. This causes the average

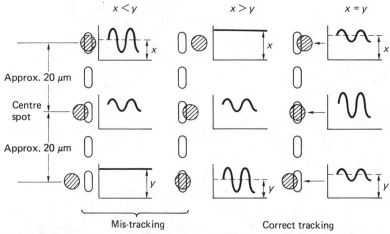

Figure 12.40 Three-spot method of producing tracking error compares average level of side-spot signals. Side spots are produced by a diffraction grating and require their own sensors

amplitude of the side spots to change differentially with tracking error. The laser head contains a diffraction grating which produces the side spots and two extra photosensors on to which the reflections of the side spots will fall. The side spots feed a differential amplifier, which has a low-pass filter to reject the channel-code information and retain the average brightness difference. Some players use a delay line in one of the side-spot signals whose period is equal to the time taken for the disk to travel between the side spots. This helps the differential amplifier to cancel the channel code.

The alternative approach to tracking error detection is to analyse the diffraction pattern of the reflected beam. The effect of the spot being off centre is to rotate the radial diffraction pattern about an axis along the track. Fig. 12.41 shows that if a split sensor is used, one half will see greater modulation than the other when off track. Such a system may be prone to develop an offset due either to drift or to contamination of the optics, although the capture range is large. A further tracking mechanism is often added to obviate the need for periodic adjustment. Fig. 12.42 shows this dither-based system, which resembles in many respects the track-following method used in the C-format and described in Chapter 4. A sinusoidal drive is fed to the tracking servo, causing a radial oscillation of spot position of about $\pm 50\,\text{nm}$. This results in modulation of the envelope of the

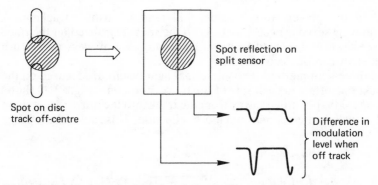

Spot on disc
track off-centre

Spot reflection on
split sensor

Difference in
modulation
level when
off track

Figure 12.41 Split-sensor method of producing tracking error focuses image of spot onto sensor. One side of spot will have more modulation when off track

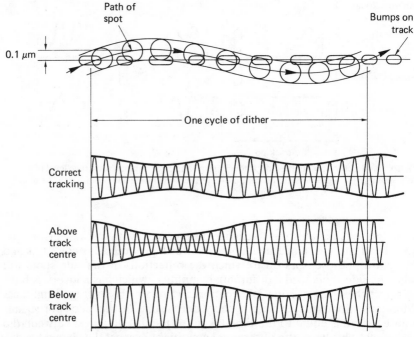

Figure 12.42 Dither applied to readout spot modulates the readout envelope. A tracking error can be derived

readout signal, which can be synchronously detected to obtain the sense of the error. The dither can be produced by vibrating a mirror in the light path, which enables a high frequency to be used, or by oscillating the whole pickup at a lower frequency.

12.20 The disk controller

A disk-based system will have some kind of control computer that determines where and when frames will be stored and retrieved, sends instructions to the disk controller which causes the drives to read or write, and transfers samples between them and the memory. When recording, the disk must be supplied with data at exactly the correct rate, or the disk format cannot be properly laid down. The disk data will have to share the system bus with other transactions which may cause the data rate to fluctuate. In the same way, on replay, data from the disk have to be accepted at the speed which the disk decides. The solution is to incorporate a silo or FIFO memory in the disk controller. The operation of these devices was described in Chapter 3.

The essentials of a disk controller are determined by the characteristics of drives and the functions needed, and so they do not vary greatly. For digital video use, it is desirable for economic reasons to use a commercially available disk controller intended for computers. The controller, disk buses and drives are all then readily available parts, and only the video-specific circuitry needs to be specially built. For parallel transfer drives, this approach cannot be adopted because of the enormous throughput. A special controller integrated with the video system will need to be constructed.

A disk controller consists of two main parts: that which issues control signals to and obtains status from the drives; and that which handles the data to be stored and retrieved. Both parts are synchronized by the control sequencer.

The execution of a function by a disk subsystem requires a complex series of steps, and decisions must be made between the steps to decide what the next will be. There is a parallel with computation, where the function is the equivalent of an instruction, and the sequencer steps needed are the equivalent of the microinstructions needed to execute the instruction. The major failing in this analogy is that the sequence in a disk drive must be accurately synchronized to the rotation of the disk.

Most disk controllers use direct memory access, which means that they have the ability to transfer disk data in and out of the associated memory without the assistance of the processor. In order to cause a file transfer, the disk controller must be told the physical disk address (cylinder, sector, track), the physical memory address where the file begins, the size of the file, and the direction of transfer (read or write). The controller will then position the disk heads, address the memory, and transfer the samples. One disk transfer may consist of many contiguous disk blocks, and the controller will automatically increment the disk address registers as each block is completed. As the disk turns, the sector address increases until the end of the track is reached. The track or head address will then be incremented and the sector address reset so that transfer continues at the beginning of the next track. This process continues until all of the heads have been used in turn. In this case both the head address and sector address will be reset, and the cylinder address will be incremented, which causes a seek. A seek which takes place because of a data transfer is called an implied seek, because it is not necessary formally to instruct the system to perform it. As disk drives are block-structured devices, and the error correction is codeword based, the controller will always complete a block even if the size of the file is less than a whole number of blocks. This is done by packing the last block with zeros.

The status system allows the controller to find out about the operation of the drive, both as a feedback mechanism for the control process, and to handle any errors. Upon completion of a function, it is the status system which interrupts the control processor to tell it that another function can be undertaken.

In a system where there are several drives connected to the controller via a common bus, it is possible for non-data transfer functions such as seeks to take place in some drives simultaneously with a data transfer in another.

Before a data transfer can take place, the selected drive must physically access the desired block and confirm this by reading the block header. Following a seek to the required cylinder, the positioner will confirm that the heads are on track and settled. The desired head will be selected, and then a search for the correct sector begins. This is done by comparing the desired sector with the current sector register, which is typically incremented by dividing down servo-surface pulses. When the two counts are equal, the head is about to enter the desired block. Fig. 12.43 shows the structure of a typical disk track. In between blocks are placed address

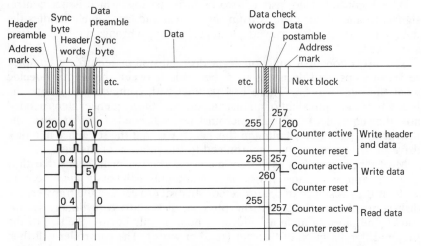

Figure 12.43 The format of a typical disk block related to the count process which is used to establish where in the block the head is at any time. During a read the count is derived from the actual data read, but during a write, the count is derived from the write clock

marks, which are areas without transitions which the read circuits can detect. Following detection of the address mark, the sequencer is roughly synchronized to begin handling the block. As the block is entered, the data separator locks to the preamble, and in due course the sync pattern will be found. This sets to zero a counter which divides the data-bit rate by eight, allowing the serial recording to be correctly assembled into bytes, and also allowing the sequencer to count the position of the head through the block in order to perform all the necessary steps at the right time.

The first header word is usually the cylinder address, and this is compared with the contents of the desired cylinder register. The second header word will contain the sector and track address of the block, and these will also be compared with the desired addresses. There may also be bad-block flags and/or defect-skipping information. At the end of the header is a CRCC which will be used to ensure that the header was read correctly. Fig. 12.44 shows a flowchart of the position verification, after which a data transfer can proceed. The header reading is completely automatic. The only time it is necessary formally to command a header to be read is when checking that a disk has been formatted correctly.

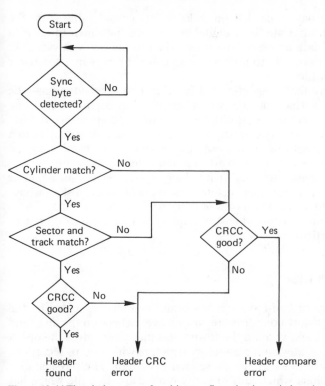

Figure 12.44 The vital process of position confirmation is carried out in accordance with the above flowchart. The appropriate words from the header are compared in turn with the contents of the disk-address registers in the subsystem. Only if the correct header has been found and read properly will the data transfer take place

During the read of a data block, the sequencer is employed again. The sync pattern at the beginning of the data is detected as before, following which the actual data arrive. These bits are converted to byte or sample parallel, and sent to the memory by DMA. When the sequencer has counted the last data-byte off the track, the redundancy for the error-correction system will be following.

During a write function, the header-check function will also take place as it is perhaps even more important not to write in the wrong place on a disk. Once the header has been checked and found to be correct, the write process for the associated data block can begin. The preambles, sync pattern, data block, redundancy and postamble have all to be written contiguously. This is taken care of by the sequencer, which is obtaining timing information from the servo surface to lock the block structure to the angular position of the disk. This should be contrasted with the read function, where the timing comes directly from the data.

12.21 Defect handling

The protection of data recorded on disks differs considerably from the approach used on other media in digital video. This has much to do with the intolerance of data processors to errors when compared with video. In particular, it is not possible to interpolate to conceal errors in a computer program or a data file.

In the same way that magnetic tape is subject to dropouts, magnetic disks suffer from surface defects whose effect is to corrupt data. The shorter wavelengths employed as disk densities increase are affected more by a given size of defect. Attempting to make a perfect disk is subject to a law of diminishing returns, and eventually a state is reached where it becomes more cost-effective to invest in a defect-handling system.

There are four main methods of handling media defects in magnetic media, and further techniques needed in WORM laser disks, whose common goal is to make their presence transparent to the data. These methods vary in complexity and cost of implementation, and can often be combined in a particular system.

12.22 Bad-block files

In the construction of bad-block files, a brand new disk is tested by the operating system. Known patterns are written everywhere on the disk, and these are read back and verified. Following this the system gives the disk a volume name and creates on it a directory structure which keeps records of the position and size of every file subsequently written. The physical disk address of every block which fails to verify is allocated to a file which has an entry in the disk directory. In this way, when genuine data files come to be written, the bad blocks appear to the system to be in use storing a

	1	1	1	1	1	1	1	1	1	1	1	0	0	0	0	0	A
A	0	0	0	0	0	0	1	1	1	1	1	1	1	1	1	1
	1	1	1	1	1	1	1	1	1	1	1	1	1	1	1	1
	1	1	1	1	1	1	1	0	0	0	0	1	0	0	0	0	B
	0	0	1	1	1	1	1	1	1	1	1	1	1	0	0	0
	0	0	0	0	0	0	0	0	e	tc.						

Figure 12.45 A disk-block-usage bit map in sixteen-bit memory for a cluster size of eleven blocks. Before writing on the disk, the system searches the bit map for contiguous free space equal to or larger than the cluster size. The first available space is the second cluster shown at A above, but the next space is unusable because the presence of a bad block B destroys the contiguity of the cluster. Thus one bad block causes the loss of a cluster

fictitious file, and no attempt will be made to write there. Some disks have dedicated tracks where defect information can be written during manufacture or by subsequent verification programs, and these permit a speedy construction of the system bad-block file.

In association with the bad-block file, many drives allocate bits in each header to indicate that the associated block is bad. If a data transfer is attempted at such a block, the presence of these bits causes the function to be aborted. The bad-block file system gives very reliable protection against defects, but can result in a lot of disk space being wasted. Systems often use several disk blocks to store convenient units of data called clusters, which will all be written or read together. Fig. 12.45 shows how a bit map is searched to find free space and illustrates how the presence of one bad block can write off a whole cluster.

12.23 Sector skipping

In sector skipping, space is made at the end of every track for a spare data block, which is not normally accessible to the system. Where a track is found to contain a defect, the affected block becomes a skip sector. In this block, the regular defect flags will be set, but in addition a bit known as the skip-sector flag is set in this and every subsequent block in the track. When the skip-sector flag is encountered, the effect is to add one to the desired sector address for the rest of the track, as in Fig. 12.46. In this way the bad block is unused, and the the track format following the bad block is effectively slid along by one block to bring into use the spare block at the end of the track. Using this approach, the presence of single bad blocks does not cause the loss of clusters, but requires slightly greater control complexity. If two bad blocks exist in a track, the second will be added to the bad-block file as usual.

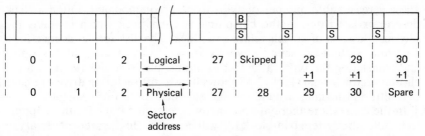

Figure 12.46 Skip sectoring. The bad block in this example has a physical sector address of 28. By setting the skip-sector flags in the header, this and subsequent logical blocks have one added to their sector addresses, and the spare block is brought into use

12.24 Defect skipping

The two techniques described so far have treated the block as the smallest element. In practice, the effect of a typical defect is to corrupt only a few bytes. The principle of defect skipping is that media defects can be skipped over within the block so that a block containing a defect is made usable. The header of each block contains the location of the first defect in bytes

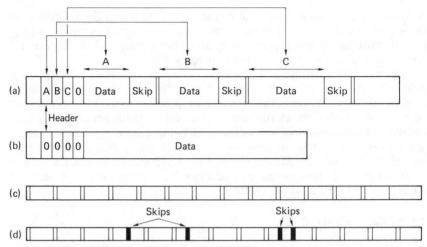

Figure 12.47 Defect skipping. (a) A block containing three defects. The header contains up to four parameters which specify how much data is to be written before each skip. In this example only three entries are needed. (b) An error-free block for comparison with (a); the presence of the skips lengthens in the block. To allow for this lengthening, the track contains spare space at the end, as shown in (c), which is an error-free track. (d) A track containing the maximum of four skips, which have caused the spare space to be used up

away from the end of the header, and the number of bytes from the first defect to the second defect, and so on up to the maximum of four shown in the example of Fig. 12.47. Each defect is overwritten with a fixed number of bytes of preamble code and a sync pattern. The skip is positioned so that there is sufficient undamaged preamble after the defect for the data separator to regain lock. Each defect lengthens the block, causing the format of the track to slip round. A space is left at the end of each track to allow a reasonable number of skips to be accommodated. Often a track descriptor is written at the beginning of each track which contains the physical position of defects relative to index. The disk format needed for a particular system can then be rapidly arrived at by reading the descriptor and translating the physical defect locations into locations relative to the chosen sector format. Fig. 12.48 shows how a soft-sectoring drive can have two different formats around the same defects using this principle.

In the case where there are too many defects in a track for the skipping to handle, the system bad-block file will be used. This is rarely necessary in practice, and the disk appears to be contiguous, error-free, logical and physical space. Defect skipping requires fast processing to deal with events in real time as the disk rotates. Bit-slice microsequencers are one approach, as a typical microprocessor would be too slow.

12.25 Revectoring

A refinement of sector skipping which permits the handling of more than one bad block per track without the loss of a cluster is revectoring. A bad block caused by a surface defect may only have a few defective bytes, so it

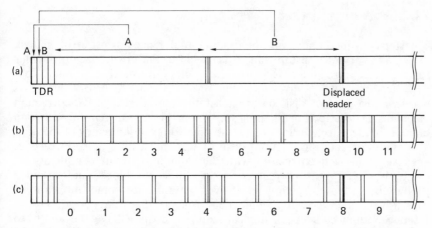

Figure 12.48 The purpose of the track descriptor record (TDR) is to keep a record of defects independent of disk format. The positions of the defects stored in the TDR (a) are used by the formatter to establish the positions relative to the format used. With the format (b), the first defect appears in sector 5, but the same defect would be in sector 4 for format (c). The second defect falls where a header would be written in (b) so the header is displaced for sector 10. The same defect falls in the data area of sector 8 in (c)

is possible to record highly redundant information in the bad block. On a revectored disk, a bad block will contain in the data area repeated records pointing to the address where data displaced by the defect can be found. The spare block at the end of the track will be the first such place and can be read within the same disk revolution, but out of sequence, which puts extra demands on the controller. In the less frequent case of more than one defect in a track, the second and subsequent bad blocks revector to spare blocks available in an area dedicated to that purpose. The principle is illustrated in Fig. 12.49. In this case a seek will be necessary to locate the replacement block. The low probability of this means that access time is not significantly affected.

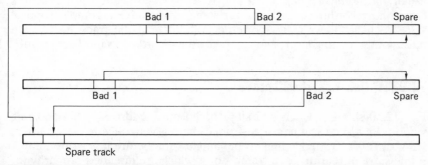

Figure 12.49 Revectoring. The first bad block in each track is revectored to the spare block at the end of the track. Unlike skip sectoring, subsequent good blocks are unaffected, and the replacement of block is read out of sequence. The second bad block on any one track is revectored to one of a number of spare tracks kept on the disk for this purpose

12.26 Error correction

The steps outlined above are the first line of defence against errors in disk drives and serve to ensure that, by and large, the errors due to obvious surface defects are eliminated. There are other error mechanisms in action, such as noise and jitter, which can result in random errors, and it is necessary to protect disk data against these also. The error-correction mechanisms described in Chapter 7 will be employed. In general each data block is made into a codeword by the addition of redundancy at the end. The error-correcting code used in disks was, for a long time, Fire code, because it allowed correction with the minimum circuit complexity. It could, however, only correct one error burst per block, and it had a probability of miscorrection which was marginal for some applications. The advances in complex logic chips meant that the adoption of a Reed–Solomon code was a logical step, since these have the ability to correct multiple error bursts. As the larger burst errors in disk drives are taken care of by verifying the medium, interleaving is not generally needed.

In some systems, the occurrence of errors is monitored to see if they are truly random, or if an error persistently occurs in the same physical block. If this is the case, and the error is small and well within the correction power of the code, the block will continue in use. If, however, the error is larger than some threshold, the data will be read, corrected and rewritten elsewhere, and the block will then be added to the bad-block file so that it will not be used again.

12.27 Defect handling in WORM disks

In erasable optical disks, formatting is possible to map out defects in the same way as for magnetic disks, but in WORM disks it is not possible to verify the medium because it can only be written once. The presence of a defect cannot be detected until an attempt has been made to write on the disk. The data written can then be read back and checked for error. If there is an error in the verification, the block concerned will be rewritten, usually in the next block along the track. This verification process slows down the recording operation, but some drives have a complex optical system which allows a low-powered laser to read the track in between pulses of the writing laser, and can verify the recording as it is being made.

12.28 A disk-based still store

Fig. 12.50 shows a video still store based on disk drives. The incoming video from a slide scanner or rostrum camera is generally decoded into Y, U, V or R, G, B, depending on the application, before it is written into a frame store in real time. In frame stores which are intended primarily for still pictures, advantage can be taken of the phase change of subcarrier from field to field to cancel subcarrier in luminance and vice versa. The frame store can be used as a delay line to make a comb filter which combs

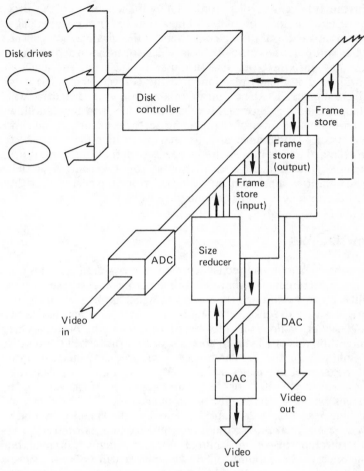

Figure 12.50 Architecture of a simple frame store showing converters, disk controller and the size reducer needed to generate browsing files

over four fields (PAL). As the subcarrier inverts after four fields, digital addition of these fields results in luminance only; subtraction results in chroma only. Where it is necessary to grab from moving video, a lower performance mode will be adopted.

Once the frame is in memory it can be repeatedly accessed and sent to a DAC which will produce a continuous video signal suitable for viewing on a monitor. The monitor image can be assessed for suitability, and if necessary the capture can be repeated with a slight repositioning of the camera, for example. If the image in the frame store is suitable for storage, the operator will key in a command to the control processor to file the image to disk. The operator must assign a name or code to the image, and the system will then add that name to the directory of known images. A suitable vacant area on the disk will also be determined, and the disk addresses used will be added to the directory entry so that the image can be retrieved in the future. The disk controller will then be told the disk address to use and the location of the data within the frame stores. The appropriate frame store will then be accessed by the disk controller. The disk controller will read the array of pixels which form the image and will re-format the data into the block structure used on the disk. The selected disk drive will have its heads positioned to the correct block, and data transfer will commence. The transfer rate of a conventional disk drive will be slower than the data rate of real-time digital video, and the data flow will be discontinuous because of the discrete sector structure of the disk surface. This is not a problem because the image is fixed in the frame store and can be accessed at leisure. The only necessity is that the frame store must be fast enough to interleave read requests from two sources, so that the displayed monitor image can be refreshed from the memory at the same time as the disk controller is reading it.

12.29 Browsing files

Once a large library of stills has been assembled on a disk database, it is not humanly possible to remember what each still looked like. It is necessary to have a facility to browse through the images to select appropriate material by eye. The fact that the disk drive works at rather less than real time means that retrieving many images for browsing is a lengthy process. One way of accelerating this process is to create browsing files when the disk is written. In addition to the regular image, a reduced-size image is also stored. If, for example, the image is reduced by a linear factor of four, this results in one-sixteenth the storage requirement. In other words, 16 reduced images can be stored in one regular image disk file. The ability to access many images at once dramatically increases the speed with which browsing can be undertaken, since the reduced-size images need only be written into different places in a frame store and many can then be displayed at once on the monitor. The size reducer can be seen in Fig. 12.50. The full-size image is accessed by the size reducer via the lower bus and reduced in size by FIR filtering using the principles of manipulation dealt with in Chapter 5. The hardware needed will differ from that of a real-time effects machine, since much more time is available to carry out the transform. The number of fast multipliers needed can be drastically reduced. A further asset is that the size reduction is by an integer factor, so no fancy work with coefficient phases is needed. Essentially the size reduction performs FIR filtering and decimation along each line of the image, but places the decimated lines into a recirculating memory so that several decimated lines then become available in parallel for the vertical decimator to operate on. The output of the size reduction process is then written back into spare space in the frame store, so that it can be accessed by the disk controller. The directory will now contain a further entry specifying where on the disk the browse (reduced-size) file can be found. Browsing files are the disk drives' equivalent of pictures in shuttle in VTRs.

A large still collection on disk will need facilities for simultaneous access in a broadcast environment. More than one user might want to retrieve stills at once, perhaps one user is using captions on air, whereas another is retrieving images to be incorporated in a post-production. Yet another user may be busy adding new images to the database. Such an application can be accommodated by adding more frame stores to the central unit. Requests for files are then dealt with in turn by the disk controller. In some cases, each user may require two frame stores and two DACs, since in an on-air application, one will be producing the live output and the other will be producing a preview of the next still, or be used for browsing to locate the next one. A small complication is that identical timing of video signals from such disparate sources as transmission and post-production cannot be guaranteed, so each DAC and frame store is generally configured to use timing from a different reference signal.

12.30 Editing in a disk system

When video samples are fed into a disk-based system, from a digital interface or from an ADC, they will be placed in a memory, from which the disk controller will read them by DMA. The continuous input sample stream will be split up into disk blocks for disk storage. Time code from an external source or a local generator will also enter the system, and this will be used to assemble a table which contains a conversion from real time to the physical disk address of the corresponding video files. Wherever possible, the disk controller will allocate incoming samples to contiguous disk addresses, since this eases the conversion from time code to physical address.

The table of disk addresses will also be made into a disk file and stored in a different area of the disk from the video files. Several recordings may be fed into the system in this way, until the capacity of the disks is reached.

If it is desired to play back one or more of the recordings, then it is only necessary to specify the starting time code and the file name, and the system will look up the physical address of the first and subsequent sample blocks in the desired recording and begin to read them from disk and write them into the memory. The disk transfers must by definition be intermittent, because there are headers between contiguous sectors. Once all the sectors on a particular cylinder have been read, it will be necessary to seek to the next cylinder, which will cause a further interruption to the reading sequence. If a bad block is encountered, the sequence will be interrupted until it has passed. The instantaneous data rate of a parallel transfer drive is made higher than the continuous video data rate, so that there is time for the positioner to move whilst the video output is supplied from the FIFO memory. In replay, the drive controller attempts to keep the FIFO as full as possible by issuing a read command as soon as one block space appears in the FIFO. This allows the maximum time for a seek to take place before reading must resume. Fig. 12.51 shows the action of the FIFO during reading. Whilst recording, the drive controller attempts to keep the FIFO as empty as possible by issuing write commands as soon as a block of data is present, as in Fig. 12.52. In this way the amount of time available to seek is maximized in the presence of a continuous video sample input. In order to edit the raw video files fed into the system, it is

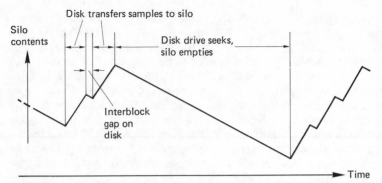

Figure 12.51 During a video replay sequence, silo is constantly emptied to provide samples, and is refilled in blocks by the drive

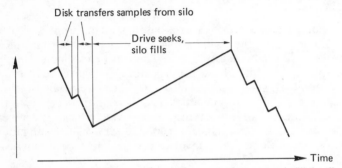

Figure 12.52 During video recording, the input samples constantly fill the silo, and the drive attempts to keep it empty by reading from it

necessary to determine the position of edit points. This can be done by playback of the whole file at normal speed, but this neglects the random access capability of a disk-based system. If an event list has been made at the time of the recordings, it can be used to access any part of them within a few tens of milliseconds, which is the time taken for the heads to traverse the entire disk surface. This is far superior to the slow spooling speed of tape recorders.

Once the rough area of the edit has been located, the video files from that area can be played to locate the edit point more accurately. Video frames in the area of the edit point can be transferred to memory and accessed in either direction by deriving the memory addresses from a hand-turned jog wheel.

Using one or other of these methods, an edit list can be made which contains an in-point, an out-point and a video file name for each of the segments of video which need to be assembled to make the final work, along with a crossfade period which will be needed if a switcher is used to make a fade or pattern wipe rather than a cut between the two segments. This edit list will also be stored on the disk. When a preview of the edited work is required, the edit list is used to determine what files will be necessary and when, and this information drives the disk controller.

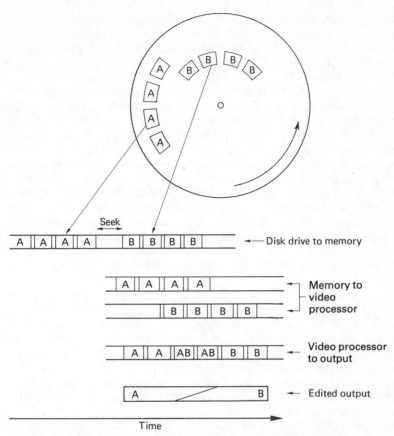

Figure 12.53 In order to edit together two video files, they are brought to memory sequentially. The audio processor accesses file pages from both together, and performs a crossfade between them. The silo produces the final output at constant steady-sampling rate

Fig. 12.53 shows the events during an edit between two files. The edit list causes the relevant video blocks from the first file to be transferred from disk to memory, and these will be read by the signal processor to produce the preview output. As the edit point approaches, the disk controller will also place blocks from the incoming file into the memory. It can do this because the rapid data transfer rate of the drive allows blocks to be transferred to memory faster than real time, leaving time for the positioner to seek from one file to another. In the memory there will be simultaneously the end of the outgoing recording and the beginning of the incoming recording. Before the edit point, only samples from the outgoing recording are accessed, but as the crossfade or wipe begins, samples from the incoming recording are also accessed, multiplied by the gain parameter, and then mixed with samples from the outgoing recording according to the crossfade period required, or switched according to the output of the wipe pattern generator. The output of the signal processor becomes the edited preview material, which can be checked for the required subjective effect. If necessary the in- or out-points can be trimmed, or the crossfade period or wipe pattern changed, simply by modifying the edit-list file. The preview can be repeated as often as needed, until the desired effect is obtained.

Once the editing is finished, it will be necessary to transfer the edited material to some external storage, since the Winchester drives in the editor have fixed media. It is only necessary to connect the digital output of the signal processor to a digital VTR, and then the edit list is executed once more. The edit sequence will be performed again, exactly as it was during the last preview, and the results will be recorded on tape. It is important to realize that at no time during the edit process were the original video files modified in any way. The editing was done solely by reading the files. The power of this approach is that if an edit list is created wrongly, the original recording is not damaged, and the problem can be put right simply by correcting the edit list. The advantage of a disk-based system for such work is that location of edit points, previews and reviews are all performed almost instantaneously, because of the random access of the disk. This can reduce the time taken to edit a program to a quarter of that needed with a tape machine.

During an edit, the disk drive has to provide files from two different places on the disk simultaneously, and so it has to work much harder than for a simple playback. If there are many close-spaced edits, the drive may be hard pressed to keep ahead of real time, especially if there are long crossfades, because during a crossfade the source data rate is twice as great as during replay. A large buffer memory helps this situation because the drive can fill the memory with files before the edit actually begins, and thus the instantaneous sample rate can be met by the memory's emptying during disk-intensive periods.

Disk formats which handle defects dynamically, such as defect skipping, will also be superior to bad-block files when throughput is important. Some drives rotate the sector addressing from one cylinder to the next so that the drive does not lose a revolution when it moves to the next cylinder. Disk-editor performance is usually specified in terms of peak editing activity which can be achieved, but with a recovery period between edits. If an unusually severe editing task is necessary where the drive just cannot access files fast enough, it will be necessary to rearrange the files on the disk surface so that files which will be needed at the same time are on nearby cylinders. Spare cylinders called caching areas will be spread throughout the disk so that the drive can get data from the cache after a very short seek if it is deduced that there is not time to get it from the original file. An alternative is to spread the material between two drives so that overlapped seeks are possible.

Where synchronized spindle drives are used, an increase in speed can be had by intelligent layout of the data on disk. The disk block becomes the equivalent of a sync block on tape, and each track becomes the equivalent of a segment. The use of revectoring or defect skipping becomes almost mandatory to avoid the structure being upset by a bad block.

Chapter 13

Digital audio with video

Television without sound would not be television, but for a long time the sound aspects of television were considered unimportant, and the audio quality of the average television set was mediocre, not just because of its own performance, but also because the quality of the signal reaching it was undistinguished. Fortunately this picture is changing. The advent of the Compact Disc made high-quality audio extremely affordable and raised the expectations of the consumer. Rented videocassettes with stereo soundtracks, CD–Video disks, and the advent of stereo sound with terrestrial and satellite television have all served to raise the profile of audio in the television context. Digital technology made inroads into audio a little before it transformed video, and much of that technology has been absorbed into video equipment.

13.1 Typical digital audio equipment

Once audio has been converted to the digital domain, it becomes data which do not differ in principle from any other. A detail difference is that a high-quality digital audio channel will require only 1 megabit per second, which is considerably less than the data rates which have been seen in video. Although the frequency range of audio is much less than that of video, the dynamic range is much greater, and sample wordlengths of 16 bits and greater will be found. Video converter technology is inadequate for these wordlengths, and the special techniques developed for audio will be described here.

Since data can be stored in many ways, digital audio recorders have been made using many technologies. Early units known as PCM adaptors converted the digital audio data to a black-and-white checkerboard video-like signal which could be recorded on a VCR. Later, direct digital rotary-head recorders such as RDAT[1] appeared. Digital audio can also be recorded on open-reel tape with stationary heads, and certain of these formats actually supported cut-and-splice editing.[2]

Disk drives have also been successfully employed for audio, because the low data rate compared with video allows a realistic recording time yet with rapid access for editing.

Many of these machines incorporate timecode facilities so that synchronization with video recorders is possible. This is, however, a complex subject which will also be treated here. Digital video recorders invariably have rotary heads in order to support the substantial data rate. The presence of several channels of digital audio causes an increase in data rate of only a few per cent, and it is common to record the audio with the same heads as the video by allocating small audio blocks at specified places along the main recorded tracks. This simplifies the construction of the machine tremendously, since there are no separate audio heads, and the same RF and coding circuitry is timeshared between audio and video, and sometimes part of the error-correction circuitry can also be common.

Standards exist for the interconnection of audio machines in the digital domain, not the least important being the AES/EBU interface which has found wide acceptance as is fully detailed here.

Although most broadcast television sound is analog, and is thus outside the scope of this book, there is a major exception in the shape of the NICAM 728 digital stereo system, itself a close relative of the MAC/packet system developed for satellite work. A full description of NICAM 728 will also be found here.

13.2 Choice of sampling rate for digital audio

In Chapter 2 it was seen that sampling theory demanded a sampling rate of at least twice the baseband frequency to be carried, and then the rate had to be raised a little to allow the use of filters with finite slope. All of this applies equally to audio; indeed it would be most surprising if it did not. This does not, however, mean that only one sampling rate is necessary for audio: there are a number of rates which have different purposes.

For consumer products, the lower the sampling rate the better, since the cost of the medium is directly proportional to the sampling rate: thus sampling rates near to twice 20 kHz are to be expected. For professional products, there is a need to operate at variable speed for pitch correction. When the speed of a digital recorder is reduced, the offtape sampling rate falls, and Fig. 13.1 shows that with a minimal sampling rate the first image frequency can become low enough to pass the reconstruction filter. If the sampling frequency is raised without changing the response of the filters, the speed can be reduced without this problem. It follows that variable-speed recorders, generally those with stationary heads, must use a higher sampling rate.

In the early days of digital audio research, the necessary bandwidth of about 1 megabit per second per audio channel was difficult to store. Disk drives had the bandwidth but not the capacity for long recording time, and attention therefore turned to the video recorder. As has been stated, these were adapted to store audio samples by creating a pseudo-video waveform. The sampling rate of such a system is constrained to relate simply to the field rate and field structure of the television standard used, so that an integer number of samples can be stored on each usable TV line in the field. Unfortunately there are two standards – 525 lines at 59.94 Hz and 625 lines at 50 Hz – and it is not possible to find a frequency which is a common multiple of the two and low enough to use as a sampling rate.

The allowable sampling rates in a pseudo-video system can be deduced by multiplying the field rate by the number of active lines in a field

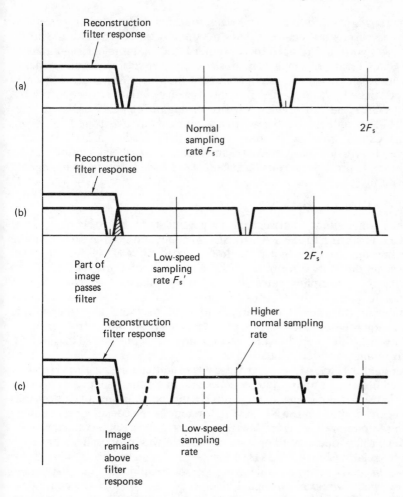

Figure 13.1 At normal speed, the reconstruction filter correctly prevents images entering the baseband, as at (a). When speed is reduced, the sampling rate falls, and a fixed filter will allow part of the lower sideband of the sampling frequency to pass. If the sampling rate of the machine is raised. But the filter characteristic remains the same, the problem can be avoided, as at (c)

(blanked lines cannot be used) and again by the number of samples in a line. By careful choice of parameters it is possible to use 525/59.94 or 625/50 video with only a slight difference in sampling rate.

In 59.94 Hz video, there are 35 blanked lines, leaving 490 lines per frame, or 245 lines per field for samples. If three samples are stored per line, the sampling rate becomes

$$59.94 \times 245 \times 3 = 44.0559 \text{ kHz.}$$

In 50 Hz video, there are 37 lines of blanking, leaving 588 active lines per frame, or 294 per field, so the sampling rate becomes

$$50.00 \times 294 \times 3 = 44.1 \text{ kHz}$$

There is a 0.1% difference between these two rates, which means that for some purposes a recording made at one rate can be played at the other.

These two rates are used by consumer PCM adaptors corresponding to the EIAJ format,[3] which record six samples per line to allow stereo operation, and allow the use of a VCR of the video format of the country of sale, since it was expected that the consumer would require to use the same VCR either for regular video recording or for PCM audio.

44.1 kHz came to be the sampling rate of the Compact Disc. Even though CD has no video circuitry, the equipment used to make CD masters is video based and determines the sampling rate. Oddly enough, the VCRs used for CD production run at 525/60.00 *not* 59.94 Hz, so the sampling rate is given by

$$60 \times 245 \times 3 = 44.1 \text{ kHz}$$

The strange situation arises that it is possible to lock a 60 Hz based VCR for CD mastering to the PAL or SECAM video system at 50 Hz via the sampling rate, but it is not possible to lock to 59.94 Hz NTSC, although with some difficulty a form of synchronization can be arranged.

With these sampling rates having been established so early, it was natural to suggest higher rates for professional use which had a simple relationship to them. The argument was that digital sampling-rate conversion is eased if the rates are related. The professional frequencies of 50.349 65. . .kHz and 50.4 kHz are obtained by multiplying the pseudo-video frequencies derived earlier by 8/7.

For landlines to FM stereo broadcast transmitters having a 15 kHz audio bandwidth, the sampling rate of 32 kHz is more than adequate, and has been in use for some time in the United Kingdom and Japan. This rate has also been adopted for the NICAM 728 system. Some consumer camcorders use a sampling rate of twice line rate for their digital audio channels.

The professional sampling rate of 48 kHz was proposed as having a simple relationship to 32 kHz, being far enough above 40 kHz for variable-speed operation, and having a simple relationship with PAL video timing which would allow digital video recorders to store the convenient number of 960 audio samples per video field. The important work done on variable sampling-rate converters demonstrated that there was no longer a need to have simple relations between sampling rates, and so 48 kHz came to be the accepted sampling rate for professional audio. This rate is supported by both D-1 and D-2 DVTR formats.

Although in a perfect world the adoption of a single sampling rate might have had virtues, for practical and economic reasons digital audio now has essentially three rates to support: 32 kHz for NICAM/broadcast, 44.1 kHz for CD/CD–V/EIAJ, and 48 kHz for professional/digital VTR record/play.[4]

13.3 Audio quality considerations

The acuity of the human ear is astonishing. It can detect tiny amounts of distortion and will accept an enormous dynamic range. The only criterion for quality that we have is that if the ear cannot detect impairments, we must say that the reproduced sound is perfect. Usually, people's ears are at their most sensitive between about 2 kHz and 5 kHz, and although some people can detect 20 kHz at high level, there is much evidence to suggest that most cannot tell if the upper frequency limit of sound is 20 kHz or 16 kHz.[5,6] For a long time it was thought that frequencies below about 40 Hz were unimportant, but it is becoming clear that reproduction of frequencies down to 20 Hz improves reality and ambience.[7] A digital system can deliver a response down to DC if necessary. The dynamic range of the ear is obtained by a logarithmic response and certainly exceeds 100 dB. At the extremes of this range, the ear is either straining to hear or is suffering pain, neither of which can be described as pleasurable or entertaining, and it is hardly necessary to produce recordings of this dynamic range for consumers since, among other things, they are unlikely to have anywhere to listen to them.

Probably more important than dynamic range is the sensitivity of the ear to distortion. The ear behaves as a kind of spectrum analyser, with frequency bands about 100 Hz wide below 500 Hz and from one-sixth to one-third of an octave wide, proportional to frequency, above this. In the presence of a complex spectrum, it appears to protect itself from information overload by failing to register energy in some bands when there is more energy in a nearby band. This is the phenomenon of auditory masking, defined as the decreased audibility of one sound in the presence of another. The information reduction achieved is considerable; masking can take place even when the masking tone ceases before the masked sound appears. Another example of the slowness of the ear is the Haas effect, in which the source of a sound is attributed to the first arriving wavefront even though a later echo is much louder. Since distortion results in energy moving from one frequency band to another, a knowledge of masking is essential to estimate how audible the effect of distortion will be. Before digital techniques were used for high-quality audio, it was thought that the principles of digitizing were adequately understood, but the disappointing results of some early digital audio machines showed that this was not so. The ear could detect the minute imperfections of filters and converters, which could be neglected in, for example, instrumentation applications. A more rigorous study of digitization was soon applied, and the essentials of it can be found here. The important topic of oversampling which was shown in Chapter 2 to be useful in video is also extremely relevant to audio and will be described in that context.

13.4 Types of digitization

There are several methods of converting an audio waveform to a bit stream, and it is more useful to compare them than to contrast them because they are related; in advanced conversion systems it is possible to move from one system to another to combine the advantages of both. Fig. 13.2 introduces the major techniques involved in conversion.

In digital video, the sampling process produces pulses whose amplitude is an analog quantity. When the height of these pulses is quantized and expressed as a number code, the result is known as pulse code modulation,

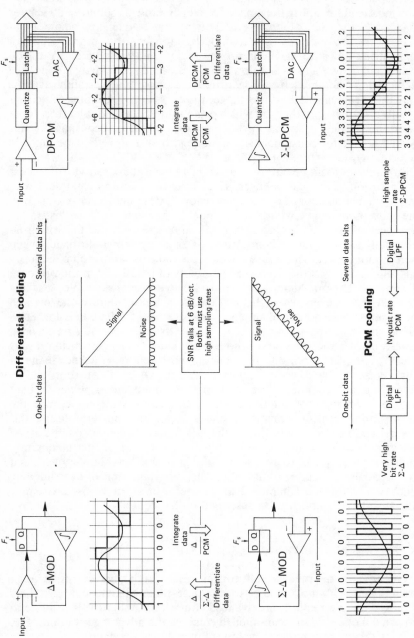

Figure 13.2 The four main alternatives to simple PCM conversion are compared here. Delta modulation is a one-bit case of differential

again better known by the abbreviation PCM. The frequencies involved in video virtually preclude any other approach, but this is not the case for audio.

The amplitude of the signal which can be conveyed by PCM only depends on the number range of the quantizer and is independent of the frequency of the input. Similarly, the amplitude of the unwanted signals introduced by the quantizing process is also largely independent of input frequency.

In differential pulse code modulation (DPCM), the parameter which is quantized is the difference between the previous absolute sample value and the current one. This process limits the maximum rate at which the input signal voltage can change, and thus the permissible signal amplitude falls at 6 dB per octave. The unwanted signal amplitude is constant again, so as input frequency rises, ultimately the signal level available will fall down to it.

It is possible to produce a DPCM signal from a PCM signal by simply subtracting successive samples; this is digital differentiation. Similarly the reverse process is possible by using an accumulator to compute sample values from the differences received. The problem with this approach is that it is very easy to lose the baseline of the signal if it commences at some arbitrary time, and a digital high-pass filter is necessary to prevent unwanted offsets.

If DPCM is taken to the extreme case where only a binary output signal is available then the process is described as delta modulation. The meaning of the binary signal is that the analog input is above or below the accumulation of previous bits. The characteristics of the system show the same trends as DPCM, except that there is severe limiting of the rate of change of the input signal. Since the decoder must also accumulate all the difference bits to provide an analog output, this function can be performed by an integrator.

If an integrator is placed in the input to a delta modulator, the integrator's response loss of 6 dB per octave parallels the amplitude limit of 6 dB per octave, and thus the system amplitude limit becomes independent of frequency. This integration is responsible for the term delta sigma modulation, since in mathematics sigma is used to denote summation. The transmitted signal is now the amplitude of the input, not the slope; thus the receiving integrator can be dispensed with, and all that is necessary is an LPF to smooth the bits. Unfortunately the removal of the integration stage now means that the unwanted signal amplitude rises at 6 dB per octave, ultimately meeting the level of the wanted signal.

This principle of using an input integrator can also be applied to a true DPCM system and the result should perhaps be called sigma DPCM. The dynamic range improvement over delta sigma modulation is 6 dB for every extra bit in the code. Because the level of the unwanted signal rises at 6 dB per octave, just as in delta sigma modulation, the system is sometimes referred to as a 'noise-shaping' converter, although it will be seen later in this chapter that the use of the word 'noise' is not wholly appropriate. The output of a sigma DPCM system is again the absolute signal amplitude, and a DAC will be needed to receive it, because it is a binary code.

As the differential group of systems suffer from a wanted signal that

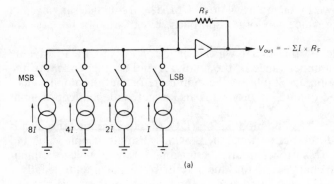

(a)

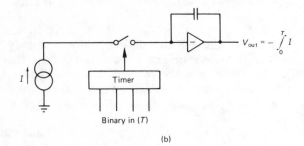

(b)

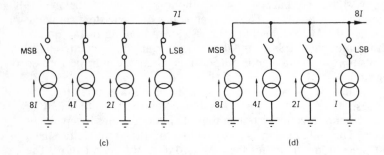

(c)   (d)

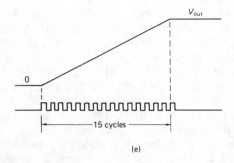

(e)

Figure 13.3 Elementary conversion: (a) weighted current DAC; (b) times integrator DAC; (c) current flow with 0111 input; (d) current flow with 1000 input; (e) integrator ramps up for fifteen cycles of clock for input 1111

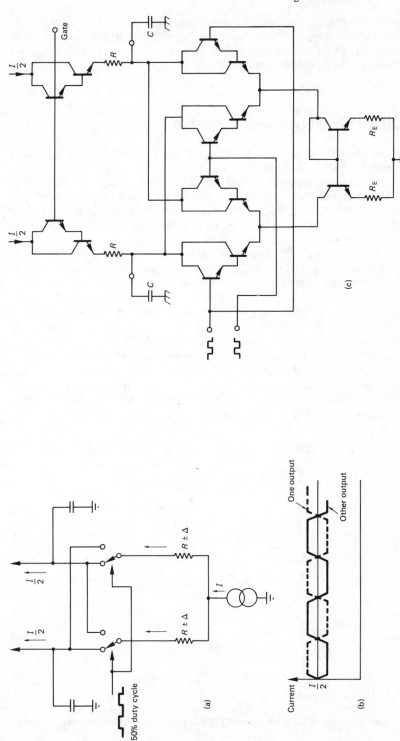

Figure 13.4 Dynamic element matching. (a) Each resistor spends half its time in each current path. (b) Average current of both paths will be identical if duty cycle is accurately 50%. (c) Typical monolithic implementation. Note clock frequency is arbitrary

converges with the unwanted signal as frequency rises, they all must use high sampling rates.[8] It is possible to convert from sigma DPCM to conventional PCM by reducing the sampling rate digitally. This has some advantages which will become evident when oversampling is discussed (Section 13.7).

13.5 Basic digital-to-analog conversion

The reverse of the quantizing process will be discussed first, since ADCs often use DACs in feedback loops.

There are two main ways of obtaining an analog signal from PCM data. One is to control binary-weighted currents and sum them; the other is to control the length of time a fixed current flows into an integrator. The two methods are contrasted in Fig. 13.3. They look simple, but are of no use for audio in these forms because of practical limitations. In Fig. 13.3(c), the binary code is about to have a major overflow, and all the low-order currents are flowing. In Fig. 13.3(d), the binary input has increased by one, and only the most significant current flows. This current must equal the sum of all the others plus one least significant current to an accuracy of rather better than one least significant current. In this simple 4 bit example, the necessary accuracy is only one part in 16, but for a 16 bit system it would become one part in 65 536, or about 0.0015%. This degree of accuracy is almost impossible to achieve, let alone maintain in the presence of ageing and temperature change.

The integrator-type converter in this 4 bit example is shown in Fig. 13.3(e); it requires a clock for the counter which allows it to count up to the maximum in less than one sample period. This will be more than 16 times

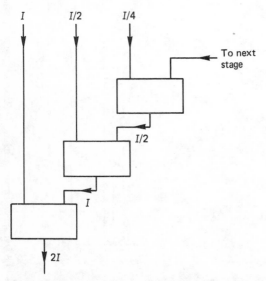

Figure 13.5 Cascading the current dividers of Figure 13.4 produces a binary weighted series of currents

the sampling rate. However, in a 16 bit system, the clock rate would need to be 65 536 times the sampling rate, or about 3 GHz. Clearly some refinements are necessary to allow either of these converter types to be used in audio applications.

One method of producing highly accurate currents is *dynamic element matching*.[9,10] Fig. 13.4 shows a current source feeding a pair of nominally equal resistors. The two will not be the same owing to manufacturing

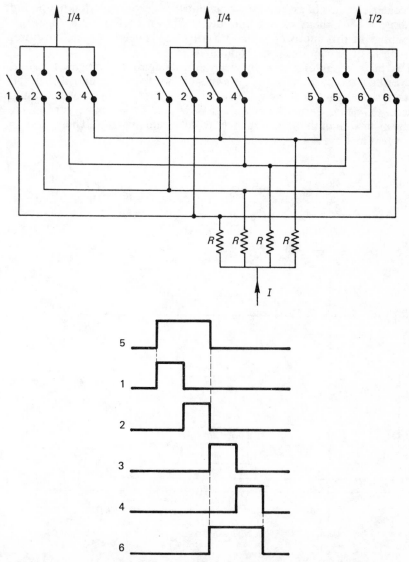

Figure 13.6 More complex dynamic element matching system. Four drive signals (1, 2, 3, 4) of 25% duty cycle close switches of corresponding number. Two signals (5, 6) have 50% duty cycle, resulting in two current shares going to right-hand output. Division is thus into 1:1:2

tolerances and drift, and thus the current is only approximately divided between them. A pair of change-over switches places each resistor in series with each output. The average current in each output will then be identical, provided that the duty cycle of the switches is exactly 50%. This is readily achieved in a divide-by-two circuit. Current averaging is by a pair of capacitors which do not need to be of any special quality. By cascading these divide-by-two stages, a binary-weighted series of currents can be obtained, as in Fig. 13.5. In practice, a reduction in the number of stages can be obtained by using a more complex switching arrangement. This generates currents of ratio 1:1:2 by dividing the current into four paths and feeding two of them to one output, as shown in Fig. 13.6. A major advantage of this approach is that no trimming is needed in manufacture, making it attractive for mass production.

To prevent interaction between the stages in weighted-current converters, the currents must be switched to ground or into the virtual earth by change-over switches. The on resistance of these switches is a source of error, particularly the MSB, which passes most current. A solution in monolithic converters is to fabricate switches whose area is

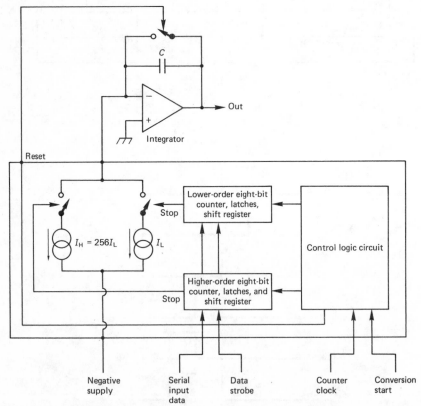

Figure 13.7 Simplified diagram of Sony CX-20017. The high-order and low-order current sources (I_h and I_L) and associated timing circuits can be seen. The necessary integrator is external

proportional to the weighted current, so that the voltage drops of all the switches are the same. The error can then be removed with a suitable offset. The layout of such a device is dominated by the MSB switch since, by definition, it is as big as all the others put together.

The practical approach to the integrator converter is shown in Fig. 13.7 and Fig. 13.8 where two current sources whose ratio is 256:1 are used; the the larger is timed by the high byte of the sample and the smaller is timed by the low byte. The necessary clock frequency is reduced by a factor of 256. Any inaccuracy in the current ratio will cause errors, but tracking is easier to achieve in a monolithic device. The integrator capacitor must have low dielectric leakage, and the operational amplifier must have high input impedance to prevent non-linearity.

The output of the integrator will remain constant once the current sources are turned off, and an analog switch will be closed during the

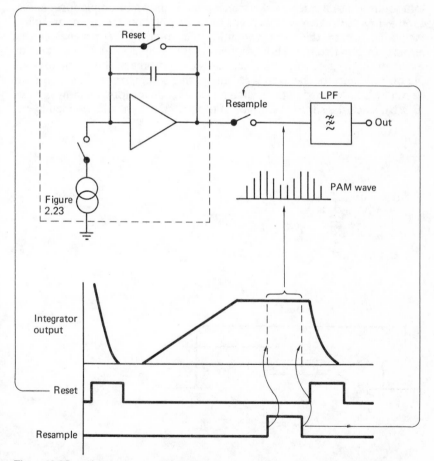

Figure 13.8 In an integrator converter, the output level is only stable when the ramp finishes. An analog switch is necessary to isolate the ramp from subsequent circuits. The switch can also be used to produce a PAM (pulse amplitude modulated) signal which has a flatter frequency response than a zero-order hold (staircase) signal

voltage plateau to produce the resampled output. Clearly this device cannot produce a zero-order hold output without an additional sample–hold stage, so it is naturally complemented by resampling. Once the output pulse has been gated to the reconstruction filter, the capacitor is discharged with a further switch in preparation for the next conversion. The conversion count must take place in rather less than one sample period to permit the resampling and discharge phases. A clock frequency of about 20 MHz is adequate for a 16 bit 48 kHz unit, which permits the ramp to complete in 12.8 μs, leaving 8 μs for resampling and reset.

13.6 Basic analog-to-digital conversion

Many of the ADCs described here will need a finite time to operate, whereas an instantaneous sample must be taken from the input. The solution is to use a track/hold circuit, which is shown in simple form in Fig. 13.9. When the switch is closed, the output will follow the input, and when the switch opens the capacitor holds the voltage of the signal at that instant. In practice, the shortcomings of this simple arrangement are too great for audio use. In particular, the time constant of the capacitor with the on resistance of the switch results in long settling time. The effect can be minimized by putting the switch inside a feedback loop as shown in Fig. 13.9(b), since the series resistance of the switch will then be divided by the

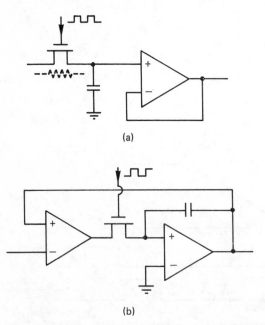

(a)

(b)

Figure 13.9 (a) The simple track-hold circuit shown has poor frequency response as the resistance of the FET causes a roll-off in conjunction with the capacitor. At (b) the resistance of the FET is now inside a feedback loop and will be eliminated, provided the left-hand op-amp never runs out of gain or swing

open-loop gain of the buffer. The specification of the buffer amplifier is stringent, since it requires adequate open-loop gain well beyond the audio band to ensure that the operation is always controlled by feedback. When the switch opens, the slightest change in the input will cause the buffer to saturate, and it must be able to recover from this condition rapidly. The feedback eliminates the switch on resistance, but the off resistance must be high enough to prevent the input signal from affecting the held voltage. The impedance seen by the capacitor must be high enough to keep droop of the sample voltage within rather less than one quantizing interval.

The clock which drives the switch must have very low jitter, or noise may be superimposed on the sample values. The mechanism was illustrated in Chapter 2 and is equally relevant to audio. The mistiming due to clock jitter causes the wrong voltage to be sampled. Worst-case assumptions demand an accuracy within about 100 ps!

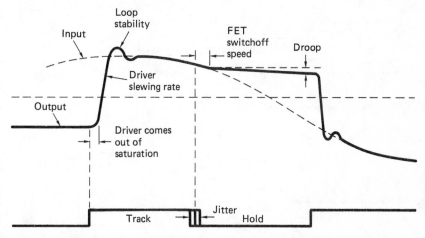

Figure 13.10 Characteristics of the feedback track/hold circuit of Figure 2.25 (b) showing major sources of error

Fig. 13.10 shows the various events during a track/hold sequence and catalogues the various sources of inaccuracy. The track/hold stage is extremely difficult to design because of the accuracy required in audio applications. In particular it is difficult to meet the droop specification for a system of more than 16 bits' accuracy. Whenever such performance bottlenecks are found, it is tempting to look for an alternative method which avoids the problems. This alternative will be found in oversampling.

The general principle of a quantizer is that different quantized voltages are compared with the unknown analog input until the closest quantized voltage is found. The code corresponding to this becomes the output.

The flash converter is probably the simplest technique available for PCM and DPCM conversion. The principle was shown in Chapter 2. The threshold voltage of every quantizing interval is provided by a resistor chain which is fed by a reference voltage. As one comparator is necessary for each quantizing interval, a 16 bit device would need a ridiculous 65 535 comparators, and thus these converters are not practicable for direct audio conversion, although they will be used in DPCM and in oversampling converters. The analog signal has to drive a lot of inputs, and a low-impedance driver is essential to avoid restricting the slewing rate of the input. The extreme speed of a flash converter which makes it suitable for video use is a distinct advantage in audio where large oversampling factors can then be used. Because computation of all bits is performed simultaneously, no track/hold circuit is required, and droop is eliminated.

Reduction in component complexity can be achieved by quantizing serially. The most primitive method of generating different quantized voltages is to connect a counter to a DAC as in Fig. 13.11. The resulting

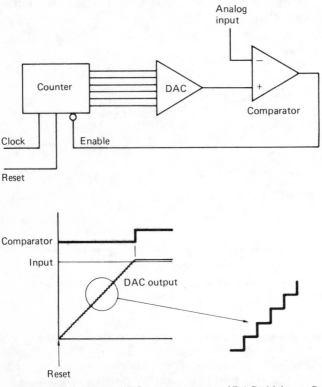

Figure 13.11 Simple ramp ADC compares output of DAC with input. Count is stopped when DAC output just exceeds input. This method, although potentially accurate, is much too slow for digital audio

staircase voltage is compared with the input and used to stop the clock to the counter when the DAC output has just exceeded the input. This method is painfully slow and is not used, as a much faster method exists which is only slightly more complex. Using successive approximation, each bit is tested in turn, starting with the MSB. If the input is greater than half range, the MSB will be retained and used as a base to test the next bit,

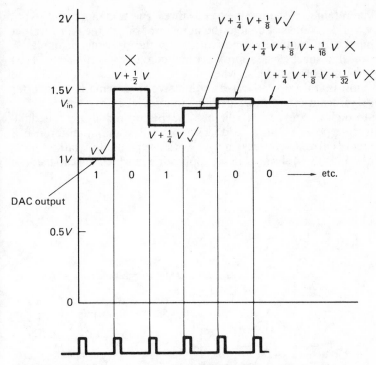

Figure 13.12 Successive approximation tests each bit in turn, starting with the most significant. The DAC output is compared with the input. If the DAC output is below the input ($\sqrt{}$) the bit is made 1; if the DAC output is above the input ($\times$) the bit is made zero

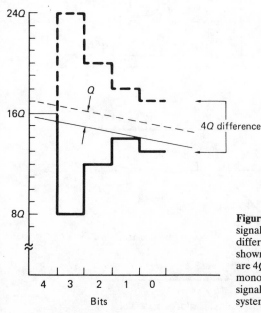

Figure 13.13 Two drooping track/hold signals (solid and dotted lines) which differ by one quantizing interval Q are shown here to result in conversions which are $4Q$ apart. Thus droop can destroy the monotonicity of a converter. Low-level signals (near the midrange of the number system) are especially vulnerable

which will be retained if the input exceeds three-quarters range and so on. The number of decisions is equal to the number of bits in the word, rather than the number of quantizing intervals, as in the previous example. A drawback of the successive approximation converter is that the least significant bits are computed last, when droop is at its worst. Fig. 13.12 and Fig. 13.13 show that droop can cause a successive approximation converter to make a significant error under certain circumstances.

Anolog-to-digital conversion can also be performed using the dual-current-source-type DAC in a feedback system; the major difference is that the two current sources must work sequentially rather than concurrently. Fig. 13.14 shows a 16 bit application in which the capacitor of

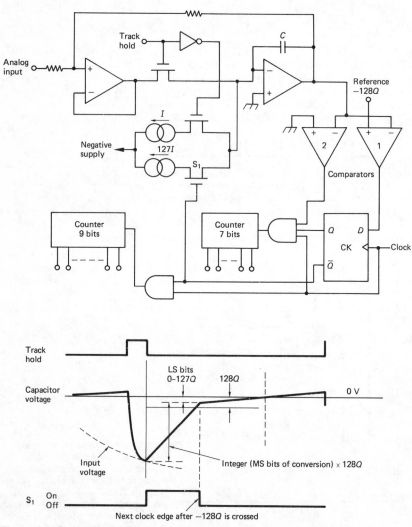

Figure 13.14 Dual-ramp ADC using track/hold capacitor as integrator

the track/hold circuit is also used as the ramp integrator. The system operates as follows. When the track/hold FET switches off, the capacitor C will be holding the sample voltage. Two currents of ratio 128:1 are capable of discharging the capacitor. Owing to this ratio, the smaller current will be used to determine the least significant seven bits, and the larger current will determine the nine most significant bits. The currents are provided by current sources of ratio 127:1. When both run together, the current produced is 128 times that from the smaller source alone. This approach means that the current can be changed simply by turning off the larger source, rather than by attempting a change-over.

With both current sources enabled, the high-order counter counts up until the capacitor voltage has fallen below the reference of $-128Q$ supplied to comparator 1. At the next clock edge, the larger current source is turned off. Waiting for the next clock edge is important, because it ensures that the larger source can only run for entire clock periods, which will discharge the integrator by integer multiples of $128Q$. The integrator voltage will overshoot the $128Q$ reference, and the remaining voltage on the integrator will be less than $128Q$ and will be measured by counting the number of clocks for which the smaller current source runs before the integrator voltage reaches zero. This process is termed residual expansion. The break in the slope of the integrator voltage gives rise to the alternative title of gear-change converter. Following ramping to ground in the conversion process, the track/hold circuit must settle in time for the next conversion. In this 16 bit example, the high-order conversion needs a maximum count of 512, and the low order needs 128, a total of 640. Allowing 25% of the sample period for the track/hold circuit to operate, a 48 kHz converter would need to be clocked at some 40 MHz. This is rather faster than the clock needed for the DAC using the same technology.

An ADC cannot be more accurate than the DAC it contains, and because of the higher operating speed, and the imperfections of the track/hold process, ADCs are generally responsible for more signal degradation than DACs. The two devices have the same transfer function, since they are only distinguished by the direction of operation, and therefore the same terminology can be used to classify the shortcomings of both. The major converter errors were shown in Chapter 2 in connection with video conversion and do not differ in audio converters except for the magnitude of allowable error.

Offset error has no effect on sound quality, unless the offset is gross, when the symptom would be premature clipping. DAC offset is of little consequence, but ADC offset is undesirable since it can cause an audible thump if an edit is made between two signals having different offsets. Offset error is sometimes cancelled by digitally averaging the converter output and feeding it back to the analog input as a small control voltage. Alternatively, a digital high-pass filter can be used.

The gain stability is probably the least important factor in a DAC, since ears, meters and gain controls are logarithmic.

For audio the absolute accuracy is rather less important than linearity. For example, if all the current sources in a converter have good thermal tracking, linearity will be maintained, even though the absolute accuracy drifts.

13.7 Oversampling

The information in an analog signal is two-dimensional; it was shown earlier that the number of levels which can be resolved unambiguously represents one dimension, and the bandwidth represents the other dimension. Fig. 13.15 shows that it is an area which is the product of bandwidth and signal-to-noise ratio expressed linearly. The figure also

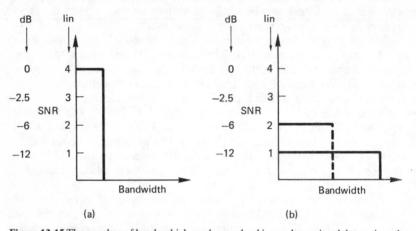

(a)   (b)

Figure 13.15 The number of levels which can be resolved in a voltage signal determines the amount of information at any instant. The bandwidth determines the rate at which that information can be conveyed; hence the overall information capacity is the product of linear SNR and bandwidth. If a given input signal at (a) is modulated in some perfect way, it may be conveyed down a channel with one-half the signal-to-noise ratio ($-6\,dB$) if the bandwidth is doubled, or with one-quarter the signal-to-noise ratio ($-12\,dB$) if the bandwidth is quadrupled

shows that the same amount of information can be conveyed down a channel with 6 dB less SNR if the bandwidth used is doubled, with 12 dB less SNR if bandwidth is quadrupled, and so on, provided that the modulation scheme used is perfect. This theory predicts that if an audio signal is spread over a much wider bandwidth by, for example, the use of an FM broadcast transmitter, the SNR of the demodulated signal will be higher than that of the channel it passes through, and this is clearly the case. The theory also predicts that stereo FM will have more hiss; since two channels of audio are now using the same transmitter bandwidth, each one can have only half the information capacity, so it will lose 6 dB of SNR. In practice things are slightly worse, because the process is not perfect.

The information in an analog signal can be conveyed using some analog modulation scheme in any combination of bandwidth and SNR which yields the appropriate channel capacity. In digital audio, a signal having only two states, known as a binary channel, will be used, needing only a poor SNR but a correspondingly high bandwidth.

It is useful to examine information capacity in the digital domain. Fig. 13.16 shows several examples. A single binary digit can only have two states; thus it can only convey two pieces of information, perhaps 'yes' or

	0 = No 1 = Yes	00 = Spring 01 = Summer 10 = Autumn 11 = Winter	000 do 001 re 010 mi 011 fa 100 so 101 la 110 te 111 do	0000 0 0001 1 0010 2 0011 3 0100 4 0101 5 0110 6 0111 7 1000 8 1001 9 1010 A 1011 B 1100 C 1101 D 1110 E 1111 F	0000 FFFF	Digital audio sample values
No of bits	1	2	3	4	16	
Information per word	2	4	8	16	65536	
Information per bit	2	2	≈3	4	4096	

Figure 13.16 The amount of information per bit increases disproportionately as wordlength increases. It is always more efficient to use the longest words possible at the lowest word rate. It will be evident that sixteen-bit PCM is 2048 times as efficient as delta modulation. Over-sampled data is also inefficient for storage

'no'. Two binary digits together can have four states and can thus convey four pieces of information, perhaps 'spring summer autumn or winter', which is two pieces of information per bit. Three binary digits grouped together can have eight combinations and convey eight pieces of information, perhaps 'doh re mi fah so lah te or doh', which is nearly three pieces of information per digit. Clearly the further this principle is taken, the greater the benefit. In a 16 bit system, each bit is worth 4000 pieces of information. It is always more efficient, in information-capacity terms, to use the combinations of long binary words than to send single bits for every piece of information. This is one reason why PCM is more popular than delta modulation, despite the simplicity of implementation of the latter. PCM simply makes more efficient use of the capacity of the binary channel.

Information theory is necessary to understand oversampling. The storage or transmission system is usually going to be PCM, where the sampling rate is a little more than twice the audio bandwidth. In the converters, the sampling rate will be higher, because of the advantages stated earlier in the construction of the analog filters. There are other advantages because, when the sampling rate is raised, information theory suggests that the wordlength of the samples can be reduced. Fig. 13.17 shows the reverse case of Fig. 13.16. The information rate is held constant, and as the sampling rate doubles, one bit can be removed from the wordlength. Thus by using oversampling, not only can the problems of

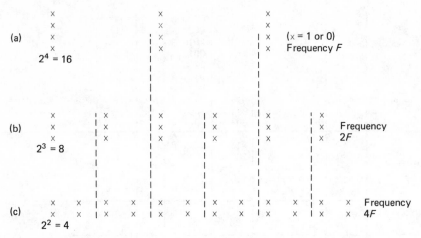

Figure 13.17 Information rate can be held constant when frequency doubles by removing one bit from each word. In all cases here it is 16F. Note bit rate of (c) is double that of (a). Data storage in oversampled form is inefficient

analog filters be overcome, but also the wordlength of the converters is reduced, making them easier to construct. Note that the theory only predicts what is possible; it is not a guarantee of success. Oversampling simply means raising the sampling rate. Further mechanisms are needed to take advantage of the wordlength reduction.

13.8 An oversampling DAC

Consider a system which oversamples by a factor of four. Starting with 16 bit PCM, the 4 × oversampling will permit the use of a 14 bit converter, but only if the wordlength is reduced optimally. Simple truncation of wordlength gives the same result as if the original audio had been quantized into fewer levels in the first place. For every bit lost, the same amount of distortion will be obtained with a level 6.02 dB higher. Simple truncation, then, does not allow the results predicted by information theory.

The roundoff mechanism used in oversampling spreads the distortion products owing to truncation over the entire oversampling spectrum; thus distortion power within the baseband is only a fraction of the total. The fraction is the reciprocal of the oversampling factor. Thus in our 4 × example, removing 2 bits raises the distortion by 12 dB, but this is spread over a spectrum four times as great, thus reducing the distortion by the same 12 dB. The wordlength is reduced by an extension of the technique of rounding up. The error caused by the previous truncation is carried over to the next, so that the average error of the two is smaller. As the sampling rate is much higher than normal, the averaging process will have taken place by the time the signal has returned to baseband audio. Fig. 13.18 shows that the accumulated error is controlled by using the bits which were

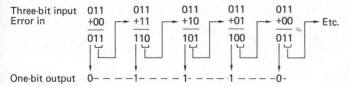

Figure 13.18 By adding the error caused by truncation to the next value, the resolution of the lost bits is maintained in the duty cycle of the output. Here, truncation of 011 by two bits would give continuous zeros, but the system repeats 0111, 0111, which, after filtering, will produce a level of three quarters of a bit

neglected in the truncation and adding them to the next sample. In this example, with a steady input, the roundoff mechanism will produce an output of 01110111 . . . . If this is low-pass filtered, the three ones and one zero result in a level of ¾ of a bit, which is precisely the level which would have been obtained by direct conversion of the full digital input. Thus the information capacity is maintained even though 2 bits have been removed. This process is often referred to as noise shaping, but this is a misnomer, as failure to perform these steps results in harmonic distortion. The term time averaging is also used to describe this kind of resolution extension.

In the oversampling system used in Philips Compact Disc players[11] the aperture effect in the DAC is used as part of the reconstruction filter response, in conjunction with a third-order Bessel filter. Equalization of the frequency response is by the digital filter which produces the oversampled data. The operation of digital filters is described in Chapter 5, where it will be seen that their frequency response is proportional to the sampling rate. If a digital recorder is played at a reduced speed, the response of the digital filter will reduce automatically and prevent images passing the reconstruction process. If oversampling were to become universal, there would then be no need for the 48 kHz sampling rate.

13.9 Oversampling ADCs

The use of oversampling to extend the resolution of ADCs is subject to the same limits set by information theory, but it is harder to approach the limit in ADCs than in DACs.

If a perfect quantizer is used, no amount of oversampling will increase the resolution of the system, since a perfect quantizer is blind to all changes of input within one quantizing interval, and looking more often is of no help. It was shown earlier that the use of dither would linearize a quantizer, so that input changes much smaller than the quantizing interval would be reflected in the output. Dither must be employed to minimize distortion in conventional quantizers. Resolution cannot be extended in ADCs unless some signal is added to the analog input.

Fig. 13.19 shows the example of a white-noise-dithered quantizer, oversampled by a factor of four. Since dither is correctly employed, it is valid to speak of the unwanted signal as noise. The noise power extends over the whole baseband up to the Nyquist limit. If the baseband width is

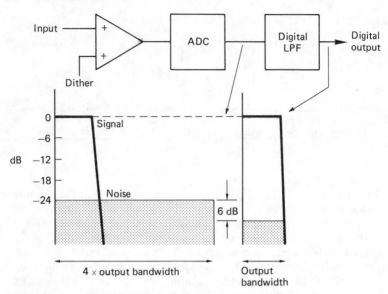

Figure 13.19 In this simple oversampled converter, 4× oversampling is used. When the converter output is low-pass filtered, the noise power is reduced to one quarter, which in voltage terms is 6 dB. This is a sub-optimal method and is not used

reduced by the oversampling factor of four back to the bandwidth of the original analog input, the noise bandwidth will also be reduced by a factor of four, and the noise power will be one-quarter of that produced at the quantizer. One-quarter noise power implies one-half the noise voltage, so the SNR of this example has been increased by 6 dB, the equivalent of one extra bit in the quantizer. Information theory predicts that an oversampling factor of four would allow an extension by 2 bits, so it can be concluded that this method is suboptimal.

The division of the noise by a larger factor is the only route left open, since all the other parameters are fixed by the signal bandwidth required. The reduction of noise power resulting from a reduction in bandwidth is only proportional if the noise is white, i.e. it has uniform power spectral density (PSD). If the noise from the quantizer is made spectrally non-uniform, the oversampling factor will no longer be the factor by which the noise power is reduced. The goal is to concentrate noise power at high frequencies, so that after low-pass filtering in the digital domain to the audio input bandwidth, the noise power will be reduced by more than the oversampling factor. The sigma DPCM converter has a natural application here; as seen earlier its noise spectrum rises at 6 dB per octave. Fig. 13.20 shows an oversampling system using a sigma DPCM converter and an oversampling factor of four. The sampling spectrum shows that the noise is concentrated at frequencies outside the audio part of the oversampling baseband. Since the scale used here means that noise power is represented by the area under the graph, the area left under the graph after the filter shows the noise–power reduction. Using the relative areas of similar triangles shows that the reduction has been by a factor of 16. The

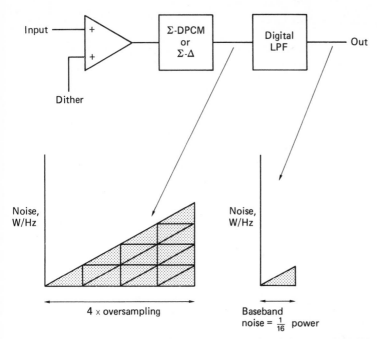

Figure 13.20 In a Σ-DPCM or Σ–Δ converter, noise amplitude increases by 6 dB/octave, noise power by 12 dB/octave. In this 4× oversampling converter, the digital filter reduces bandwidth by four, but noise power is reduced by a factor of sixteen. Noise voltage falls by a factor of 4 or 12 dB

corresponding noise–voltage reduction would be a factor of four, or 12 dB, in a white-noise system, being exactly that permitted by four times oversampling, but because of the rise of 6 dB per octave in the PSD of the noise, the SNR will be 3 dB worse at the edge of the audio band. This 3 dB loss remains the same whatever the oversampling factor; therefore the greater the oversampling factor, the less significant the loss. The noise injected by the vital dither process will be of the same order anyway, and the digital low-pass filter will introduce some noise, so that the slope of 6 dB per octave will not continue back to the origin; it will level out. The performance of such a system is thus not far short of the information theory limit for a dithered converter. A 16 times oversampling system using this technique allows a resolution extension of 21 dB. The number of bits needed to express this greater resolution will be four; thus the effective quantizing intervals of the system have been made one-sixteenth the size of the quantizer steps. The amount of white-noise dither on the analog input must be reduced accordingly. Adams[12] has described a system based on these principles using an oversampling factor of 128 to achieve a true 18 bit accurate conversion with exceptional phase linearity. At the time of writing this probably represents the state of the art in audio converters.

13.10 Spectral coding

There have been studies and proposals made on the subject of spectral recording, but it can be said to be in its infancy at the moment. The basic principle of spectral recording is that instead of trying to record the pressure waveform, which changes at frequencies up to 20 kHz, the sound spectrum is recorded because it changes much less frequently.[13] The recording process consists of periodically calculating the spectrum or Fourier transform of the input and storing it digitally as a series of centre frequencies and levels. On replay the spectral information is used to control frequency synthesizers which reproduce the sound pressure waveform. In practice the masking characteristics of the ear are exploited so that low-level spectral entries which are present in the waveform but which could not be perceived by the ear are omitted from the recording; the storage requirement is thus greatly reduced compared with that of conventional digital audio recording. The data reduction offered is most promising, as it is several orders of magnitude, but the current problem to be overcome is the sheer amount of computation required in a traditional digital computer to derive the Fourier transform.[14] Spectral recording cannot currently be done in real time, since several hours of CPU time are required for a few minutes of sound waveform. If new methods of calculating transforms, perhaps using optical techniques, become available, then spectral recording will become more significant.

13.11 Digital audio interconnection

Although digital audio recorders and the audio sections of digital video recorders can be connected to an analog world by the use of converters, many of the advantages of the digital domain are lost if transfer of audio between digital machines has to be via analog signals. The importance of direct digital interconnection was realized early, and numerous incompatible methods were developed by various manufacturers until standardization was reached in the shape of the AES/EBU digital audio interface.

13.12 AES/EBU interconnect

In all of the digital interconnects which were independently devised by various manufacturers there is enough similarity owing to the common purpose to make interfacing possible with a little extra hardware, but enough difference to be irritating.

The AES/EBU digital audio interface[15] was proposed to embrace all the functions of existing formats in one standard which would ensure interconnection independent of the manufacture of equipment at either end. For consumer use, a corresponding standard has been arrived at which offers different facilities yet retains compatibility with the professional interface so that, for many purposes, consumer and professional machines can be connected together.[16]

Many of the older interconnects for professional use have separate lines for bit clocks and sampling-rate clocks, which is acceptable for the short distances required for simple dubbing, but causes problems in the broadcast environment where long lines might be needed in a studio complex. It was desired to use the existing analog audio cabling in such installations, which would be 600 ohm balanced line screened, with one cable per audio channel, or in some cases one twisted pair per channel with a common screen.

If a single channel is to be used, the interconnect has to be self-clocking and self-synchronizing, i.e. the single signal must carry enough information to allow the boundaries between individual bits, words and blocks to be detected reliably. To fulfil these requirements, the AES/EBU interconnect and the consumer equivalent both use FM channel code (see Chapter 6) which is DC free and strongly self-clocking. Synchronization is achieved by violating the usual encoding rules.

Using FM means that the channel frequency is the same as the bit rate when sending data ones. Tests showed that in typical analog audio-cabling installations, sufficient bandwidth was available to convey two digital audio channels in one twisted pair. The standard driver and receiver chips for RS-422A[17] data communication (or the equivalent CCITT-V.11) are

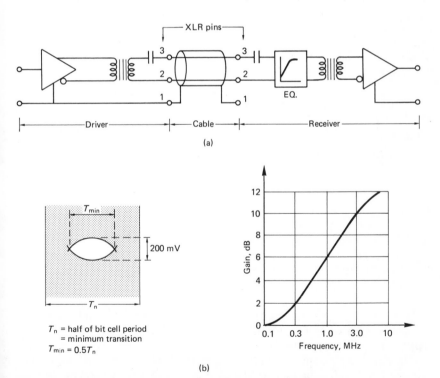

(a)

(b)

Figure 13.21 The configuration of the AES/EBU interface which is suggested for long cables. XLR pin connections are the same as balanced-line audio cables, which can be used. At (b) the minimum eye pattern which a receiver must be able to detect, and a suggested equalization response

employed for professional use, but work by the BBC[18] suggests that equalization and transformer coupling are desirable for longer cable runs, particularly if several twisted pairs occupy a common shield. Successful transmission up to 350 m has been achieved with these techniques. The use of the transformer is mandatory in the equivalent EBU specification.[19] Fig. 13.21(a) shows a typical configuration. The output impedance of the drivers will be about 110 ohms, and the impedance of the cable used should be similar at the frequencies of interest. The driver should produce between 3 and 10 V p–p into such an impedance.

The receiver impedance is high at 250 ohms, which allows up to four receivers to be driven from one source. The number of loads may need to be reduced if long cables are used. In Fig. 13.21(b), the specification of the receiver is shown in terms of the minimum eye pattern (see Chapter 6) which can be detected without error.

The purpose of the standard is to allow the use of existing analog cabling, and as an adequate connector in the shape of the XLR is already in wide service, the recommendations of IEC 268 Part 12 have been adopted for digital audio use. Effectively, existing analog audio cables having XLR connectors can be used without alteration for digital connections. The standard does, however, require that suitable labelling should be used so that it is clear that the connections on a particular unit are digital.

The need to drive long cables does not generally arise in the domestic environment, and so a low-impedance balanced signal is not necessary. The electrical interface of the consumer format uses a 0.5 V peak single-ended signal, which can be conveyed down conventional audio-grade coaxial cable connected with phono plugs.

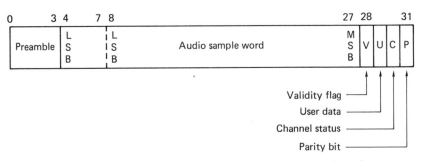

Figure 13.22 The basic subframe structure of the AES/EBU format. Sample can be twenty bits with four auxiliary bits, or 24 bits. LSB is transmitted first

In Fig. 13.22 the basic structure of the professional and consumer formats can be seen. One subframe consists of 32 bit cells, of which four will be used by a synchronizing pattern. Up to 24 bit sample wordlength can be used, which should cater for all conceivable future developments, but normally 20 bit samples will be available with four auxiliary data bits, which might be used for a voice-grade channel in a professional application. In a consumer RDAT machine, subcode can be transmitted in bits 4–11, and the 16 bit audio in bits 12–27.

In contrast with preceding formats, this format sends the least significant bit first. One advantage of this approach is that simple serial arithmetic is then possible on the samples because the carries produced by the operation on a given bit can be delayed by one bit period and then included in the operation on the next higher-order bit.

Four status bits accompany each subframe. The validity flag will be reset if the associated sample is reliable. The parity bit produces even parity over the subframe, such that the total number of ones in the subframe is even. This allows for simple detection of an odd number of bits in error and improves the probability of detection of sync. The user and channel-status bits are discussed later.

Two of the subframes described above make one frame, which repeats at the sampling rate in use. The first subframe will contain the sample from channel A, or from the left channel in stereo working. The second subframe will contain the sample from channel B, or the right channel. At 48 kHz, the bit rate will be 3.072 MHz.

In order to separate the audio channels on receipt the synchronizing patterns for the two subframes are different.

The channel-status and user bits in each subframe form serial data streams with one bit of each per audio channel per frame. It is in the use of these bits that the differences between the professional and consumer interface standards are most pronounced. The channel-status bits are given a block structure and synchronized every 192 frames, which at 48 kHz gives a block rate of 250 Hz, corresponding to a period of 4 milliseconds.

In professional applications, users are free to assign any desired format to the user bits, but it is recommended that the same block size is used, so that the user-block boundaries align with the channel-status block boundaries. This would minimize problems if the data structure was upset during synchronizing operations between systems with non-phased sampling clocks. It has been suggested that the user data are employed for labelling.[20] Labelling information is assembled into one or more 48 bit words which begin with a uniquely identifiable synchronizing pattern. Suggested uses of the labelling structure include:

Time and date of program origin
Program and identification number
Take number
Programme duration
Cue information
Act or scene number
Timecode-related information
Network information
Radio data information
Generation number (for recording)
Copyright ownership code
Editing information
Signal source information (e.g. originating microphone)

In order to synchronize the channel-status blocks, the channel A sync pattern is replaced for one frame only by a third sync pattern. These three sync patterns are shown in Fig. 13.23. As stated, there is a parity bit in each

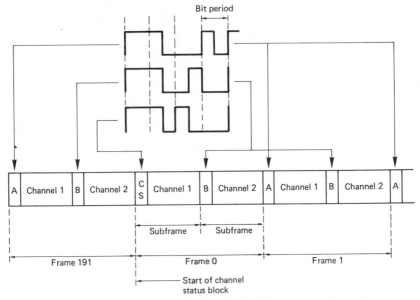

Figure 13.23 The A and B channels are distinguished by different sync patterns. Once every 192 blocks, the A sync is replaced by channel status block sync. Inverse of sync patterns is also valid; system is not polarity-conscious

subframe, which means that the binary level at the end of a subframe will always be the same as at the beginning. Since the sync patterns have the same characteristic, the effect is that sync patterns always have the same polarity and the receiver can use that information to reject noise. The polarity of transmission is not specified, and indeed an accidental inversion in a twisted pair is of no consequence, since it is only the transition that is of importance, not the direction.

In the professional format, the sequence of channel-status bits over 192 subframes builds up a 24 byte channel-status block, shown in Fig. 13.24. The first byte determines the use of emphasis and the sampling rate, with details in Fig. 13.25. The second byte determines the channel usage, i.e. whether the data transmitted are a stereo pair, two unrelated mono signals or a single mono signal. Fig. 13.26 gives details. The third byte determines wordlength as in Fig. 13.27.

There are two slots of 4 bytes each which are used for alphanumeric source and destination codes. These can be used for routing.

Bytes 14–17 convey a 32 bit sample address which increments every channel-status frame. It effectively numbers the samples in a relative manner. Bytes 18–21 convey a similar number, but this is a time-of-day count, which starts from zero at midnight. With a sampling rate of 48 kHz, the binary count represents the number of 4 millisecond intervals from midnight and can easily be converted into, for example, EBU timecode by dividing by ten to obtain a count of 40 ms video frames. At other sampling frequencies, the division ratio would need to be modified appropriately.

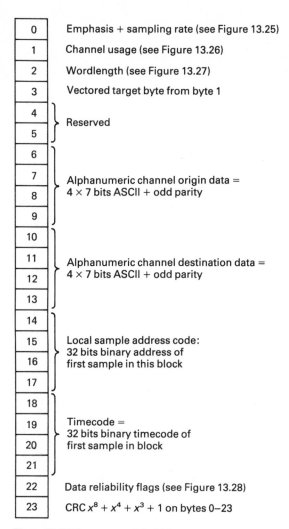

0	Emphasis + sampling rate (see Figure 13.25)
1	Channel usage (see Figure 13.26)
2	Wordlength (see Figure 13.27)
3	Vectored target byte from byte 1
4 5	Reserved
6 7 8 9	Alphanumeric channel origin data = 4 × 7 bits ASCII + odd parity
10 11 12 13	Alphanumeric channel destination data = 4 × 7 bits ASCII + odd parity
14 15 16 17	Local sample address code: 32 bits binary address of first sample in this block
18 19 20 21	Timecode = 32 bits binary timecode of first sample in block
22	Data reliability flags (see Figure 13.28)
23	CRC $x^8 + x^4 + x^3 + 1$ on bytes 0–23

Figure 13.24 The content of the 24-byte sequence of channel-status data in the AES/EBU format

The penultimate byte contains four flags which indicate that certain sections of the channel-status information are unreliable (see Fig. 13.28). This allows the transmission of an incomplete channel-status block where the entire structure is not needed or where the information is not available. For example, setting bit 5 to a logical one would mean that no origin or destination data would be interpreted by the receiver, and so they need not be sent.

The final byte in the message is a CRCC which converts the entire channel-status block into a codeword (see Chapter 7).

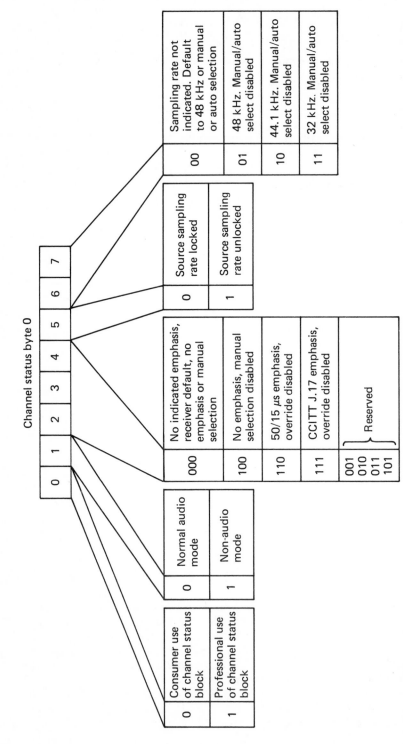

Figure 13.25 The first byte of the channel status information in the AES/EBU standard deals primarily with emphasis and sampling rate control

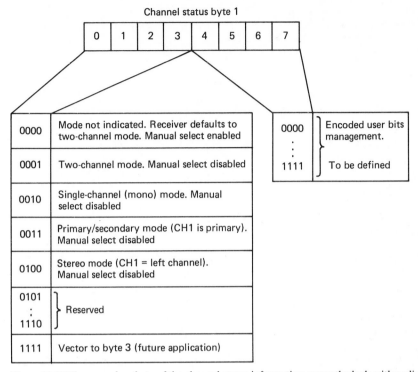

Figure 13.26 The secondary byte of the channel-status information currently deals with audio channel usage, but will be extended in the future to manage user bits

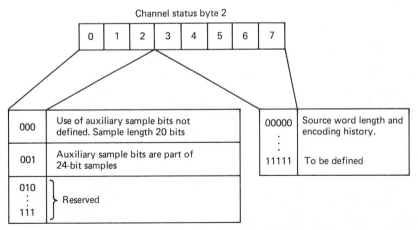

Figure 13.27 Byte 2 of channel status determines whether all 24 bits of the word slot are used for audio samples, or just 20 maximum

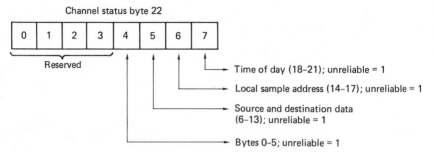

Figure 13.28 Byte 22 of channel status indicates if some of the information in the block is unreliable

13.13 Fibre-optic interfacing

Whereas a parallel bus is ideal for à distributed multichannel system, for a point-to-point connection, the use of fibre optics is feasible, particularly as distance increases. An optical fibre is simply a glass filament which is encased in such a way that light is constrained to travel along it. Transmission is achieved by modulating the power of an LED or small laser coupled to the fibre. A phototransistor converts the received light back to an electrical signal.

Optical fibres have numerous advantages over electrical cabling. The bandwidth available is staggering. Optical fibres neither generate, nor are prone to, electromagnetic interference and, as they are insulators, ground loops cannot occur. The disadvantage of optical fibres is that the terminations of the fibre where transmitters and receivers are attached suffer optical losses, and while these can be compensated in point-to-point links, the use of a bus structure is not really feasible. Fibre-optic links are already in service in digital audio mixing consoles.[21] There is a fibre-optic standard for the AES/EBU/IEC interface.

13.14 Parallel interfacing

The AES/EBU interface and the consumer derivative are ideal for a small number of audio channels. In some professional applications, such as DVTRs which have four audio channels, it is more convenient to convey them together. The use of a parallel interface has some advantages for this application, since the distances involved are usually short, and the cost of the cable is not an issue.

In the parallel digital audio format devised by Ampex for the D-2 format,[22] the audio data have been packed into a format where they can be conveyed by the same electrical and mechanical interface as the parallel digital video interconnect. Fig. 13.29(a) shows that one of the spare signals of the 8 bit parallel interface has become a square wave at 48 kHz. Between falling edges of this sync signal, audio data for the four channels are multiplexed. Each audio channel is of 32 bits, so that the whole of the

Contact	Signal line	Contact	Signal line
1	Clock	14	Clock ret.
2	System ground	15	System ground
3	Data 7 (MSB)	16	Data 7 ret.
4	Data 6	17	Data 6 ret.
5	Data 5	18	Data 5 ret.
6	Data 4	19	Data 4 ret.
7	Data 3	20	Data 3 ret.
8	Data 2	21	Data 2 ret.
9	Data 1	22	Data 1 ret.
10	Data 0	23	Data 0 ret.
11	Spare	24	Spare ret.
12	Sync	25	Sync ret.
13	Chassis shield		

(a)

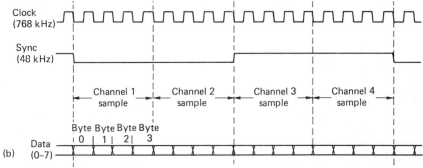

(b)

Figure 13.29 In the Ampex four channel parallel digital audio interconnect, four byte channel samples are sent serially in one sample period. The same connections are used as for the video interconnect except that an additional signal, SYNC, shown at (a) is needed to specify which samples correspond to which channel as in (b)

	Data 0	1	2	Bit number in a) 3	4	5	6	Data 7
0	A	A	A	A	A	A	A	A MSB audio
Byte order in b) 1	A	A	A	A	A	A	A	A
2	WM_1	WM_2	WM_3	SM	A_0 / C	A_1 / U	A_2 / V	A_3 / R
3	EM_0	EM_1	EM_2	V_D	V_J	CH_1	CH_2	CH_3

A = Part of audio sample.
SM = Sync mark. This sample is the first of an AES block.
WM = Word mode
CH = Channel usage.

EM = Pre emphasis mode.
C, U, V, R = Channel status bits,
V_D = 1 if sample was interpolated, else 0..
V_J = 1 if any of C, U, V, R bits unreliable.

Figure 13.29(c) The four bytes corresponding to each audio channel are assembled as shown here

AES/EBU information is conveyed and split into 4 bytes, such that 16 timeslots are necessary in one audio sample period. Each timeslot is clocked by the main 768 kHz clock as shown in Fig. 13.29(b). The byte contents are shown in Fig. 13.29(c), where it will be seen that the beginning of the AES/EBU channel-status block is specified by the SM bit.

13.15 Audio in the scrambled serial video interconnect

In this interconnect, which was described in Section 8.8, there is provision for auxiliary data to be sent during vertical and horizontal sync pulses. Fig. 13.30(a) shows that following the usual TRS-ID, there will be an auxiliary data flag whose value must be $3FC_{16}$. Following this is a code which identifies the kind of data which are being sent. In the case of digital audio, this will be all ones. Next, a symbol count parameter specifies how many

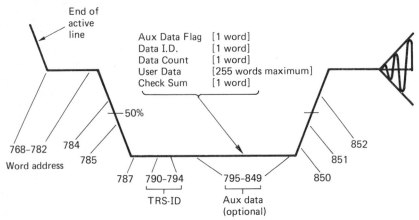

Figure 13.30(a) In the scrambled serial digital video interface, auxiliary data, including digital audio, can be sent during sync pulses (shown) and during equalizing pulses. The auxiliary data must be preceded by the Auxiliary Data Flag and followed by a checksum as shown

Address ⟍ Bit	x3	x3 + 1	x3 + 2
B9	$\overline{B8}$	$\overline{B8}$	$\overline{B8}$
B8	A (2^5)	A (2^{14})	P
B7	A (2^4)	A (2^{13})	C
B6	A (2^3)	A (2^{12})	U
B5	A (2^2)	A (2^{11})	V
B4	A (2^1)	A (2^{10})	A MSB (2^{19})
B3	A LSB (2^0)	A (2^9)	A (2^{18})
B2	CH (MSB)	A (2^8)	A (2^{17})
B1	CH (LSB)	A (2^7)	A (2^{16})
B0	Z	A (2^6)	A (2^{15})

Figure 13.30(b) AES/EBU data for one audio sample is sent as three nine-bit symbols. A = audio sample. Bit Z = AES/EBU channel status block start bit

symbols of user data are being sent in this packet. The audio data proper follow, and at the end of the packet a checksum is calculated.

Fig. 13.30(b) shows that the system wordlength is 9 bits and that three 9 bit symbols are used to convey all of the essential bits of the 32 used in the AES/EBU subframe. Since DVTRs have four audio channels, there are two channel bits which specify the channel number to which the subframe belongs. A further bit, Z, specifies the beginning of the 192 sample channel-status message. V, U and C have the same significance as in the normal AES/EBU standard, but the P bit reflects parity on the three 9 bit symbols.

The exact positions of the packets in the video structure are not specified, but it is only necessary to provide a little RAM buffering at both ends of the link. The receiver can determine the sampling rate from the video timing and demultiplex the channels according to the symbol labelling.

13.16 Synchronizing

When digital audio signals are to be assembled from a variety of sources, either for mixing down or for transmission through a TDM system, the samples from each source must be synchronized to one another in both frequency and phase. The source of samples can often be fed with a reference sampling rate from some central generator and will return samples at that rate. In a video environment there will already be a master timing generator which provides reference synchronizing pulses and subcarrier phase, and it will be necessary for the audio sampling rate to be derived from this. Some digital audio recorders can be fitted with an accessory which allows the sampling rate to be generated from a video reference. DVTRs will do this internally.

When making a digital audio recording in conjunction with video recorders, it is vital that the video frame rate, the sampling rate and the timecode to be recorded on both machines are synchronous. If this is not the case, problems will occur on playback. For example, if the audio sampling rate free-runs on recording, it will slip with respect to timecode. If the recording is subsequently to be digitally transferred to a DVTR, that DVTR will send a sampling-rate reference to the audio recorder which it has derived from video timing. If the audio recorder plays back locked to that sampling rate, the timecode lock will slip. If it plays back with timecode lock, the sampling rate will slip and produce noise.

In some cases synchronization will not be possible, and extra hardware will be necessary to accommodate slippage. In a satellite transmission, it is not really practicable to genlock a studio complex half-way round the world to another. Outside broadcasts may be required to generate their own master timing for the same reason. When genlock is not achieved, there will be a slow slippage of sample phase between source and destination owing to such factors as drift in timing generators. This phase slippage will be corrected by a synchronizer, which is intended to work with frequencies which are nominally the same. It should be contrasted with the sampling-rate converter which can work at arbitrary frequency relationships. Although a sampling-rate converter can act as a synchronizer, it is a very expensive way of synchronizing. A synchronizer can be thought of as a lower-cost version of a sampling-rate converter which is constrained in the rate difference it can accept.

In one implementation of a digital audio synchronizer,[23] memory is used as a timebase corrector as was illustrated in Chapter 3. Samples are written into the memory with the frequency and phase of the source and, when the memory is half-full, samples are read out with the frequency and phase of the destination. Clearly if there is a net rate difference, the memory will either fill up or empty over a period of time, and in order to recentre the address relationship it will be necessary to jump the read address. This will cause samples to be omitted or repeated, depending on the relationship of source rate to destination rate, and would be audible on program material. The solution is to detect pauses or low-level passages and permit jumping only at such times. The process is illustrated in Fig. 13.31(a). Such synchronizers must have sufficient memory capacity to absorb timing differences between quiet passages where jumping is possible, and so the average delay introduced by them is quite large, typically 128 samples. They are, however, relatively inexpensive.

An alternative to address jumping is to undertake sampling-rate conversion for a short period (Fig. 13.31(b)) in order to slip the input/output relationship by one sample.[24] The delay caused by the unit

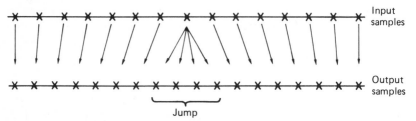

Figure 13.31(a) In jump-synchronizing, input samples are subjected to a varying delay to align them with output timing. Eventually the sample relationship is forced to jump to prevent delay building up. As shown here, this results in several samples being repeated, and can only be undertaken during program pauses, or at very low audio levels. If the input rate exceeds the output rate, some samples will be lost

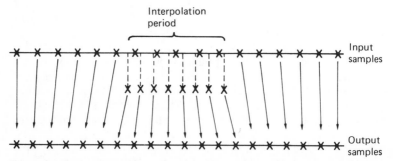

Figure 13.31(b) An alternative synchronizing process is to use a short period of interpolation in order to regulate the delay in the synchronizer

can be smaller than that of a timebase corrector, because it will be determined by the window length of the digital filter, but the device is now constructionally similar to a sampling-rate converter and would be more expensive to implement. The result of interpolation is a small momentary pitch change.

The difficulty of synchronizing unlocked sources is eased when the frequency difference is small. Proposals have been made[25] for a standard of accuracy for timing generators for various purposes.

13.17 Introduction to NICAM 728

This system was developed by the BBC to allow two additional high-quality digital sound channels to be carried on terrestrial television broadcasts. Performance was such that the system has been adopted as the UK standard, and it is recommended by the EBU to be adopted by its members, several of whom have done so.[26]

The introduction of stereo sound with television cannot be at the expense of incompatibility with the existing monophonic sound channel. In NICAM 728 an additional low-power subcarrier is positioned just above the analog sound carrier, which is retained. The relationship is shown in Fig. 13.32. The power of the digital subcarrier is about one-hundredth that of the main vision carrier, and so existing monophonic receivers will reject it.

Since the digital carrier is effectively shoehorned into the gap between TV channels, it is necessary to ensure that the spectral width of the

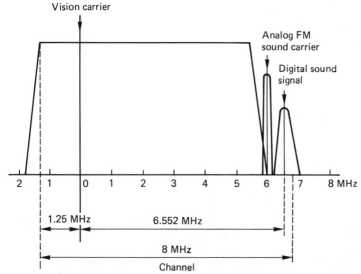

Figure 13.32 The additional carrier needed for digital stereo sound is squeezed in between television channels as shown here. The digital carrier is of much lower power than the analog signals, and is randomized prior to transmission so that is has a broad, low level spectrum which is less visible on the picture

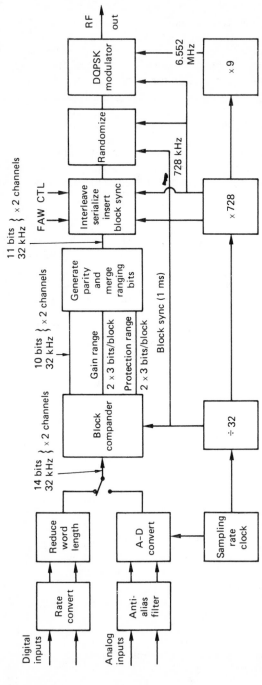

Figure 13.33 The stages necessary to generate the digital subcarrier in NICAM 728. Audio samples are block companded to reduce the bandwidth needed

intruder is minimized to prevent interference. As a further measure, the power of the existing audio carrier is halved when the digital carrier is present.

Fig. 13.33 shows the stages through which the audio must pass. The audio sampling rate used is 32 kHz which offers similar bandwidth to that of an FM stereo radio broadcast. Samples are originally quantized to 14 bit resolution in two's complement code. From an analog source this causes no problem, but from a professional digital source having longer wordlength and higher sampling rate it would be necessary to pass through a rate converter, a digital equalizer to provide pre-emphasis, an optional digital compressor in the case of wide dynamic range signals, and then through a truncation circuit incorporating digital dither as explained in Chapter 3.

The 14 bit samples are block companded to reduce data rate. During each 1 millisecond block, 32 samples are input from each audio channel. The magnitude of the largest sample in each channel is independently assessed and used to determine the gain range or scale factor to be used. Every sample in each channel in a given block will then be scaled by the same amount and truncated to 10 bits. An eleventh bit present on each sample combines the scale factor of the channel with parity bits for error detection. The encoding process is described as a near instantaneously companded audio multiplex, NICAM for short. The resultant data now consist of $2 \times 32 \times 11 = 704$ bits per block. Bit interleaving is employed to reduce the effect of burst errors.

At the beginning of each block a synchronizing byte, known as a frame alignment word (FAW), is followed by five control bits and 11 additional data bits, making a total of 728 bits per frame, hence the number in the system name. As there are 1000 frames per second, the bit rate is

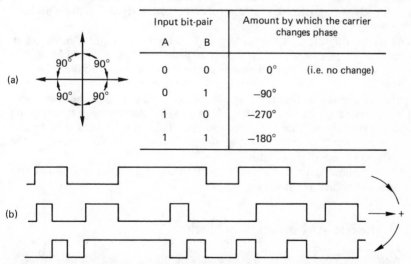

	Input bit-pair		Amount by which the carrier changes phase	
	A	B		
(a)	0	0	0°	(i.e. no change)
	0	1	−90°	
	1	0	−270°	
	1	1	−180°	

Figure 13.34 At (a) the carrier has four possible phases 90° apart. Two bits can thus be carried in the angle by which the phase changes. The absolute phase has no significance; only the changes count, hence the name of Differential Quadrature Phase Shift Keying. At (b) the input to the modulator is randomized by an exclusive-OR function with a pseudo-random sequence. The same sequence must be generated at the receiver to recover the original data

728 kbits/s. This is multiplied by nine to obtain the digital carrier frequency of 6.552 MHz.

The digital carrier is phase modulated. It has four states which are 90° apart, as shown in Fig. 13.34(a). Information is carried in the magnitude of a phase change which takes place every 18 cycles, or 2.74 μs. As there are four possible phase changes, 2 bits are conveyed in every change. The absolute phase has no meaning – only the changes are interpreted by the receiver. This type of modulation is known as differentially encoded quadrature phase shift keying (DQPSK), sometimes called four-phase DPSK. Reference to Fig. 13.34(a) will show that in the case of continuous zeros (audio mute) there would be no phase change, the receiver could lose lock with the bit clock, and all transmitted energy would be in the carrier. In order to provide consistent timing and to spread the carrier energy throughout the band irrespective of audio content, a RNRZI coding (see Chapter 6) is performed on the data. Fig. 13.34(b) shows that the channel data are the exclusive–or function of the real data and the output of a synchronized pseudo-random sequence generator, except during the Frame Alignment Word. On reception, the FAW is detected and used to synchronize the pseudo-random generator to restore the original data.

13.18 NICAM 728 frame structure

Fig. 13.35 shows the general structure of a frame. Following the sync pattern or FAW is the application control field. The application control bits determine the significance of following data, which can be stereo audio, two independent mono signals, mono audio and data or data only.

Control bits C_1, C_2 and C_3 have eight combinations, of which only four are currently standardized. Current receivers are designed to mute audio if C_3 becomes 1.

The frame flag bit C_0 spends eight frames high then eight frames low in an endless 16 frame sequence which is used to synchronize changes in channel usage. In the last 16 frame sequence of the old application, the application control bits change to herald the new application, whereas the actual data change to the new application on the next 16 frame sequence.

The reserve sound switching flag, C_4, is set to 1 if the analog sound being broadcast is derived from the digital stereo. This fact can be stored by the receiver and used to initiate automatic switching to analog sound in the case of loss of the digital channels.

The additional data bits AD_0 through AD_{10} are as yet undefined and reserved for future applications.

13.19 The NICAM sound/data block

The remaining 704 bits in each frame may be either audio samples or data. The two channels of stereo audio are multiplexed into each frame, but multiplexing does not occur in any other case. If two mono audio channels are sent, they occupy alternate frames. Fig. 13.35(a) shows a stereo frame, where the A channel is carried in odd-numbered samples, whereas Fig.

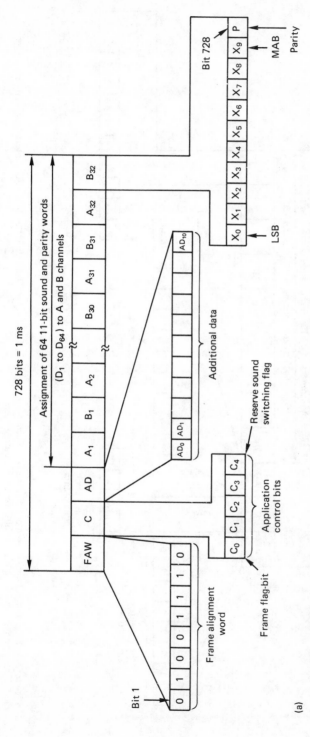

Figure 13.35(a) The block structure of a stereo signal multiplexes samples from both channels (A and B) into one block

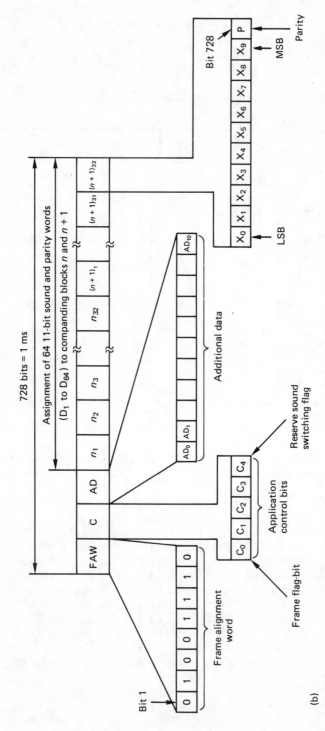

(b)

Figure 13.35(b) In mono, samples from one channel only occupy a given block. The diagrams here show the data before interleaving. Adjacent bits shown here actually appear at least 16 bits apart in the data stream

13.35(b) shows a mono frame, where the M1 channel is carried in odd-numbered frames. The format for data has yet to be defined.

The sound/data block of NICAM 728 is in fact identical in structure to the first-level protected companded sound signal block of the MAC/packet systems.[27]

13.20 Companding, scaling and parity

These three subjects are intimately related in NICAM 728. Fig. 13.36(a) shows how the companding works. The 14 bit samples are examined to extract the sample magnitude. Clearly the sign bit plays no part in determining magnitude, and so the diagram has a certain vertical symmetry. The most significant nine of the remaining 13 bits will be used, along with the sign bit, to produce a 10 bit mantissa. As there are only five shifted positions in which 9 bits can reside within 13 bits, clearly there are only five scaling factors. 3 bits are required to describe five scaling factors, and 3 bits actually allows eight combinations.

The error-protection strategy of a companded channel is subtle. In NICAM 728 there is no error correction. The channel is sufficiently reliable that errors are rare. If an error occurs, it is not corrected, but it is detected so that concealment can be used. The subjective effect of a bit error is roughly proportional to its significance in the companded sample, and so it is only necessary to detect errors in the most significant bits, as errors in the low-order bits only will experience the same masking effects which allow the use of companding in the first case. In NICAM 728, the six most significant bits of each companded sample are protected by an additional parity bit. This works perfectly until the lowest-magnitude samples occur in the fifth coding range. When the sample is 6 dB below the fifth coding range, the MSB of the companded sample will no longer be active, and when the sample is 12 dB below the fifth coding range the two most significant bits will not be active. It makes more sense to slide the 6 bits which are protected by parity down by 1 or 2 bits respectively, giving an improvement in SNR on quiet signals in the presence of errors of up to 12 dB. This explains the fact that although there are only five different scale factors, there are seven different protection ranges.

In order to convey the scale factor to the receiver during a stereo broadcast, 3 bits must be transmitted for each channel of each block. These data are actually merged with the parity bits. In the case of the most significant scale factor bit R_2, reference to Fig. 13.36(b) will show that when R_2 is 1, the parity bits of samples 1, 7, 13, 19, etc. are inverted, but when R_2 is 0 they are left unchanged. Similarly if R_1 is 1, the parity bits of samples 3, 9, 15, 21, etc. are inverted, and so on for bit R_0. As stated, errors in transmission are relatively few, and so on reception the presence of an apparent parity failure in bits 1, 7, 13, 19, etc. is interpreted as R_2 being set to 1. An actual error would cause the parity check to succeed, but this would still be interpreted as an error because if, for example, sample 7 had no parity error yet samples 1, 13, 19, 25, etc. did, it is more likely that R_2 is 1 and sample 7 has a parity error than that sample 7 is correct, R_2 is 0 and all the other samples are wrong. The receiver requires majority

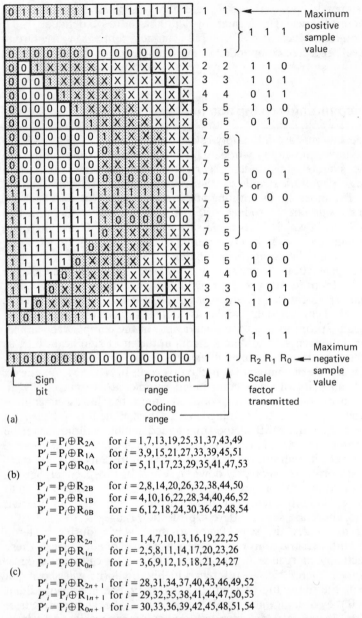

(a)

(b)

$$P'_i = P_i \oplus R_{2A} \quad \text{for } i = 1,7,13,19,25,31,37,43,49$$
$$P'_i = P_i \oplus R_{1A} \quad \text{for } i = 3,9,15,21,27,33,39,45,51$$
$$P'_i = P_i \oplus R_{0A} \quad \text{for } i = 5,11,17,23,29,35,41,47,53$$

$$P'_i = P_i \oplus R_{2B} \quad \text{for } i = 2,8,14,20,26,32,38,44,50$$
$$P'_i = P_i \oplus R_{1B} \quad \text{for } i = 4,10,16,22,28,34,40,46,52$$
$$P'_i = P_i \oplus R_{0B} \quad \text{for } i = 6,12,18,24,30,36,42,48,54$$

(c)

$$P'_i = P_i \oplus R_{2n} \quad \text{for } i = 1,4,7,10,13,16,19,22,25$$
$$P'_i = P_i \oplus R_{1n} \quad \text{for } i = 2,5,8,11,14,17,20,23,26$$
$$P'_i = P_i \oplus R_{0n} \quad \text{for } i = 3,6,9,12,15,18,21,24,27$$

$$P'_i = P_i \oplus R_{2n+1} \quad \text{for } i = 28,31,34,37,40,43,46,49,52$$
$$P'_i = P_i \oplus R_{1n+1} \quad \text{for } i = 29,32,35,38,41,44,47,50,53$$
$$P'_i = P_i \oplus R_{0n+1} \quad \text{for } i = 30,33,36,39,42,45,48,51,54$$

Figure 13.36 The companding of NICAM 728 is shown here. As the program material becomes quieter, the high order bits no longer play any part, since they become the same as the sign bit. In a companded sample, the sign bit and nine other bits are transmitted, as the heavy lines indicate. There are only five gain ranges (1–5) possible. However, parity is only generated on the six most significant bits of the sample, except at low levels where the bits checked are slid down one or two places. Thus there are five gain ranges but seven protection ranges which are conveyed for each block by the scale factor bits $R_0 – R_2$. Scale factor is transmitted by reversing parity at predetermined bit positions. These are shown at (b) for stereo and at (c) for mono

decoding logic correctly to interpret the received parity and ranging bits. It is possible to convey two more bits in the same way using the parity modification of samples 55–59 and 60–64, although this is not needed in the NICAM 728 application.

Fig. 13.36(c) shows how the scale factor is merged with the parity on a mono transmission. In mono, each frame contains two blocks from one audio channel and needs a separate scale factor for each. Note that some of the samples (28–32) from the first block are used to carry the scale factor of the second block. This causes no concern, as a frame can never be transmitted without both blocks present, and it allows samples 55–64 to be used for other purposes as before.

The interleaving is performed as follows: columns of an array are assembled, each of which contains four 11 bit samples. 16 columns are necessary to hold the 64 samples of each frame. The data bits are read out in rows and transmitted. As a result, bits in the same sample are never closer together than 16 transmitted bits. (See Chapter 7 for a further discussion of interleaving.)

13.21 Digital audio in production DVTRs

Digital audio recording with video is rather more difficult than in an audio-only environment. The special requirements of professional video recording have determined many of the parameters of these formats and have resulted in techniques not found in audio-only recorders. Professional video formats must permit different degree of flexibility in audio editing, allowing at one extreme simple circuits for portable recorders and at the other extreme complex post-production recorders. These will perform track bouncing, synchronous recording and split audio edits with variable crossfade times. A further requirement is the ability to unlock the audio sampling rate from the television frequencies.

13.22 Problems of analog audio in VTRs

The audio performance of video recorders has traditionally lagged behind that of audio-only recorders. In video recorders, the use of rotary heads to obtain sufficient bandwidth results in a wide tape which travels relatively slowly by professional audio standards. The most common professional analog video recorders today use formats where the audio tracks are longitudinal. The audio performance is limited by the format itself and by the nature of video recording. In all rotary-head recorders, the intermittent head contact causes shock-wave patterns to propagate down the tape, making low flutter figures difficult to achieve. This is compounded by the action of the capstan servo which has to change tape speed to maintain control-track phase if the video heads are to track properly.

The requirements of lip-sync dictate that the same head must be used for both recording and playback, when the optimum head design for these two functions is different. When dubbing from one track to the next, one head gap will be recording the signal played back by the adjacent magnetic circuit in the head, and mutual inductance can cause an oscillatory loop if extensive antiphase crosstalk cancelling is not employed. Placing the tracks on opposite sides of the tape would help this problem, but phase errors between the channels can then be introduced by tape weave. This can mean the difference between a two-channel recorder and a stereo recorder. Crosstalk between the timecode and audio tracks can also restrict performance. Whilst the number of analog machines in use speaks for the current adequacy of performance, the modern trends are towards stereo audio and extensive post-production where multigeneration work is essential.

The adoption of digital techniques essentially removes these problems for the audio in VTRs just as it does for audio-only recorders. Once the audio is in numerical form, wow, flutter and channel-phase errors can be eliminated by timebase correction; crosstalk ceases to occur and, provided a suitable error-correction strategy is employed, the only degradation of the signal will be due to quantizing. The most significant advantages of digital recording are that there is essentially no restriction on the number of generations of re-recording which can be used and that proper crossfades can be made in the audio at edit points, following a rehearsal if necessary.

13.23 Track sectoring

The audio samples in a DVTR are binary numbers just like the video samples, and although there is an obvious difference in sampling rate and wordlength, this only affects the relative areas of tape devoted to the audio and video samples. The most important difference between audio and video samples is the tolerance to errors. The acuity of the ear means that uncorrected audio samples must not occur more than once every few hours. There is little redundancy in sound, and concealment of errors is not desirable on a routine basis. In video, the samples are highly redundant, and concealment can be effected using samples from previous or subsequent lines or, with care, from the previous frame. No analog VTR corrects dropouts. All dropout compensation in analog recording is by concealment; a section of a previous line is typically substituted for the dropout. Major differences can be expected between the ways that audio and video samples are handled in a DVTR. One such difference is that the audio samples have 100% redundancy: every one is recorded twice with a physical separation. Apart from data-integrity considerations, this double recording is also necessary to support simple audio editing, as will be discussed later. In both D-1 and D-2 formats the audio samples are carried by the same channel as the video samples. The audio could have used separate stationary heads, but this would have increased tape consumption and machine complexity. In order to permit independent audio and video editing, the tape tracks are given a block structure. Editing will require the heads momentarily to go into record as the appropriate audio block is reached. Accurate synchronization is necessary if the other parts of the recording are to remain uncorrupted. The concept of a head which momentarily records in the centre of a track which it is reading is the normal operating procedure for all computer disk drives, as described in Chapter 12. There are in fact many parallels between digital helical recorders and disk drives. Perhaps the only major difference is that in one the heads move slowly and the medium revolves, whereas in the other the medium moves slowly and the heads revolve. Disk drives support their heads on an air bearing, achieving indefinite head life at the expense of linear density. Helical digital machines must use high-density recording, and so there will be head contact and a wear mechanism. With these exceptions, the principles of disk recording apply to DVTRs, and some of the terminology has migrated.

One of these terms is the sector. In moving-head disk drives, the sector address is a measure of the angle through which the disk has rotated. This translates to the phase of the scanner in a rotary-head machine. The part of a track which is in one sector is called a block. The word 'sector' is often used instead of 'block' in casual parlance when it is clear that only one head is involved. However, as DVTRs have at least two heads in action at any one time, it is necessary to be quite clear which one is involved, and the use of the word 'sector' in the SMPTE/EBU D-1 documents unfortunately reflects the casual definition.

Fig. 13.37 and Fig. 13.38 show the structure of the audio portions of the tape tracks of D-1 and D-2 respectively. As there are four independent audio channels, there are four audio sectors, since for reasons which will become clear it is only possible to edit complete blocks. In D-1 the audio is in the centre of the track, so there must be two video sectors and four audio sectors in one head sweep, and since there are two active heads, in one sweep there will be four video blocks written and eight audio blocks. In D-2 there are also two active heads in each sweep, but the audio blocks are at the ends of the tracks, so that there are only two video blocks in the centre.

There is a requirement for the DVTR to produce pictures in shuttle. In this case, the heads cross tracks randomly, and it is most unlikely that complete video blocks can be recovered. To provide pictures in shuttle, each block is broken down into smaller components called sync blocks. These contain their own error checking and an address, which in disk terminology would be called a header, which specifies where in the picture the samples in the sync block belong. In shuttle, if a sync block is read properly, the address can be used to update a frame store. Thus it can be said that a write block is the smallest amount of data which can be written and is that part of a track within the same sector address, whereas a sync block is the smallest amount of data which can be read. Clearly there are many sync blocks in a write block. In D-1, one video-write block contains 160 sync blocks, and one audio-write block contains five sync blocks. In D-2 there are 204 (NTSC) or 249 (PAL) sync blocks in a video-write block and six (PAL and NTSC) sync blocks in an audio-write block. The sync block structure continues in the audio because the same read/write circuitry is used for audio and video data. Clearly the address structure

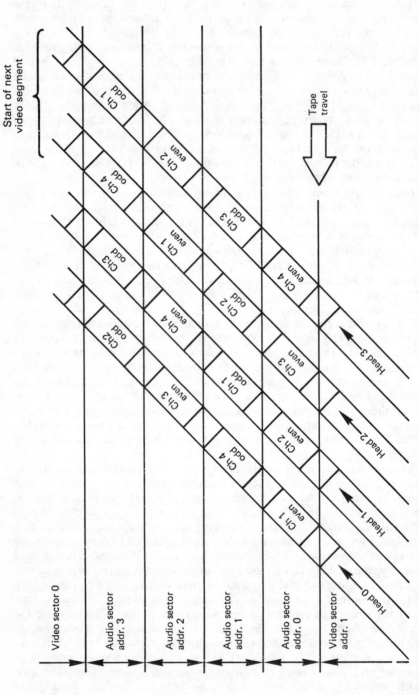

Figure 13.37 The structure of the audio blocks in D-1 format showing the double recording, the odd/even interleave, the sector addresses, and the distribution of audio channels over all heads. The audio samples recorded in this area represent a 6.666 ms timeslot in the audio recording

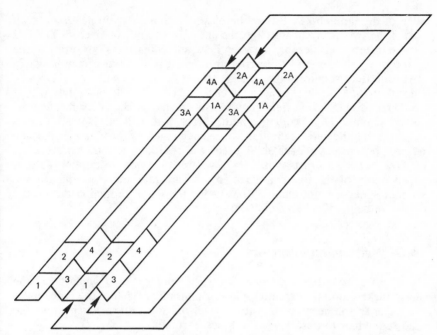

Figure 13.38 In the composite digital format, data from each audio channel are recorded twice, so that the copy is at the opposite edge of the tape, and read by a different head. This gives immunity to head clogs and linear tape scratches

must also continue through the audio. To prevent audio samples from arriving in the frame store in shuttle, the audio addresses are different from the video addresses. In both formats, the arrangement of the audio blocks is designed to maximize data integrity in the presence of tape defects and head clogs.

In D-1, but not in D-2, the audio is separated into odd and even samples, which are recorded in physically different places. If uncorrectable errors occur, interpolation can be used to conceal the errors.

As stated, every sample is recorded twice at different sector addresses. Continuing the example of D-1, if a linear tape scratch damages the data in audio-sector zero, the data can be found in sector two, albeit in a different order. It will also be seen that the relationship of the audio channels to the physical tracks rotates by one track against the direction of tape movement from one audio sector to the next. The effect of this is that, if a head becomes clogged, the errors will be distributed through all audio channels, instead of causing severe damage in one channel. In a four-headed D-1 machine, one head can fail completely, and all channels are fully recoverable owing to the distribution strategy and the double recording. There are 16 audio-write blocks in one sequence, which requires two segment periods to complete. As the segment rate is 300 Hz in D-1 the audio sequence will have a rate of 150 Hz or a period of 6.6666. . .ms.

In D-2 the audio blocks are at the ends of the head sweeps; the double recording ensures that the second copy of an audio block is at the opposite edge of the tape and that it will be played with a different head, and so if one of the two active heads clogs the audio is still fully recovered. The D-2 format differs considerably between PAL and NTSC versions owing to the difference between the subcarrier frequencies of the two standards. In PAL one field requires eight tracks, so the track rate will be 400 Hz, and since there are four audio blocks in each track, the audio block rate will be 1600 Hz. In NTSC one field requires six tracks, so the track rate will be 360 Hz (minus 0.1%) and the audio block rate will be 1440 Hz (minus 0.1%). Since the audio sampling rate is unchanged by the video format, the number of samples in each audio block will be different in the two versions of D-2. This contrasts with D-1, where the video sampling rate is independent of the line standard, so the data rate and consequently the scanner speed do not change (except for the 0.1% reduction due to the field rate being 59.94 Hz not 60 Hz).

13.24 Writing audio sectors

Each audio write block commences with a preamble to synchronize the phase-locked loop in the data separator on replay. Each of the sync blocks begins, as the name suggests, with a synchronizing pattern which allows the read sequencer to deserialize the block correctly.

At the end of a write block, it is not possible simply to turn off the write current after the last bit, as the turnoff transient would cause data corruption. It is necessary to provide a postamble such that current can be turned off away from the data. It should now be evident that any editing has to take place a sector at a time. Any attempt to rewrite one sync block would result in damage to the previous block owing to the physical inaccuracy of replacement, damage to the next block due to the turnoff transient, and inability to synchronize to the replaced block because of the random phase jump at the point where it began. Owing to the difficulty of writing in exactly the same place as a previous recording, it is necessary to leave tolerance gaps between sectors where the write current can turn on and off to edit individual write blocks. The tolerance gaps need to be about the same length as two sync blocks. The first half of the tolerance gap is the postamble of the previous block, and the second half of the tolerance gap acts as the preamble for the next block. The tolerance gap following editing will contain, somewhere in the centre, an arbitrary jump in bit phase and a certain amount of corruption due to turnoff transients. Provided that the postamble and preamble remain intact, this is of no consequence. Fig. 13.39 shows the structure of the preamble, postamble and the tolerance gap in the D-1 format.

13.25 D-1 audio error correction

The error-correction system of D-1 uses product codes as described in Chapter 7. Codewords are formed prior to interleaving – the so-called outer code – and further codewords are formed after interleaving, known as the inner code. The inner code is optimized to correct random errors, so

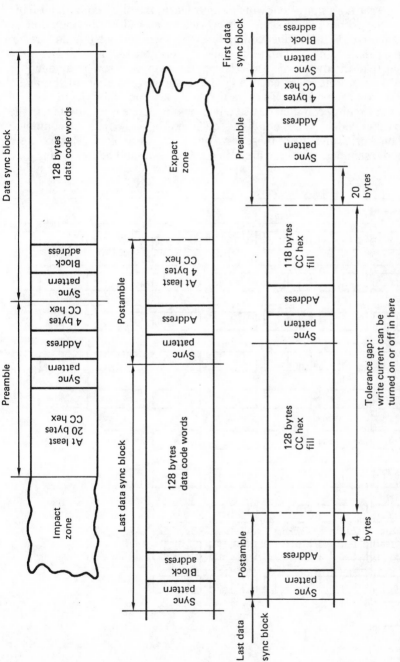

Figure 13.39 The preamble and postamble in D-1 format are shown here to be the same as the ends of the tolerance gap. The tolerance gap allows writing to begin with a physical position error without corrupting adjacent data. It is intended that the address in the centre of the tolerance gap can be destroyed by an edit. This is no problem, provided that the preamble and postamble remain intact

that these will not be seen by the outer code. Burst errors will overwhelm the inner code; it will simply declare all data in the codeword as bad and attach error flags to it. Following de-interleave, the outer code can use the error flags to perform erasure correction, which will not be impaired by random errors. The product coding is done by writing data into an array in columns and adding column redundancy to form the outer code. The array is then read in rows, which interleaves the data, and row redundancy is added to form the inner code. Fig. 13.40 shows the details of the audio product-code generation. The inner code is the same as for video, because common circuitry can then be used, but the outer code is different from the video outer code which is not discussed here. The audio data are contained in 20 bit words, and 168 of these form one audio-write block. Most of these are audio samples, but there are also control words and housekeeping data

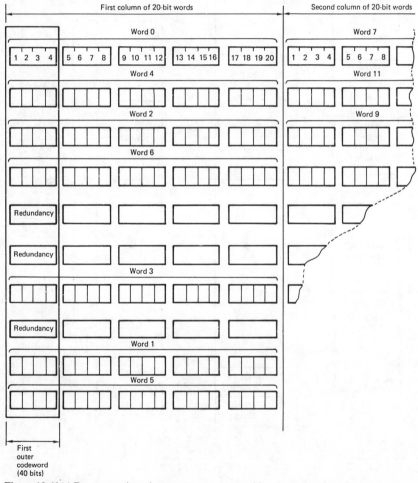

Figure 13.40(a) Data are written into an array as twenty-bit columns, and read out as rows. The column redundancy is produced in four-bit wide columns, and forms the outer codewords of 40 bits each

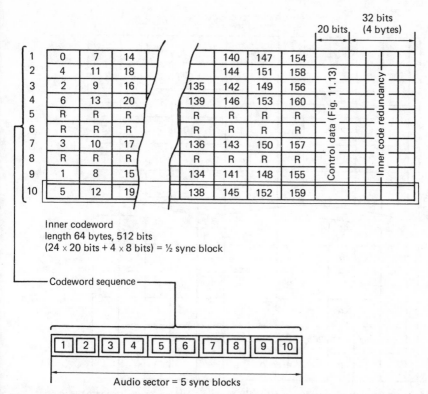

Inner codeword
length 64 bytes, 512 bits
(24 × 20 bits + 4 × 8 bits) = ½ sync block

Codeword sequence

Audio sector = 5 sync blocks

Figure 13.40(b) The row redundancy forms the inner code, as four check bytes are added to the data to produce ten codewords of 64 bytes each. The relationship to the tape track is such that two inner codewords occupy one sync block. Five sync blocks can hold the entire interleave block

which will be detailed later. The data are written into columns which are seven words high. The columns are written non-sequentially to produce the maximum distance between adjacent samples after interleave; 24 columns are necessary. Each column is then treated as five columns of 4 bits each, and three nibbles of redundancy are added to each column, so that there are now ten rows. Redundancy is now produced along each row, and 4 bytes are added, making the total length of a row 64 bytes. One sync block holds 128 bytes; thus the rows are written sequentially and can be accommodated in five sync blocks, which is one audio-write block. The use of 4 bit symbols in the error correction means that PROM decoders can be used as a result of the short symbol lengths.

13.26 D-2 audio error correction

In the composite-digital format, each audio channel is recorded independently as in D-1. A product code is used, and the interleave is generated by the usual memory array, as Fig. 13.41 illustrates for NTSC.

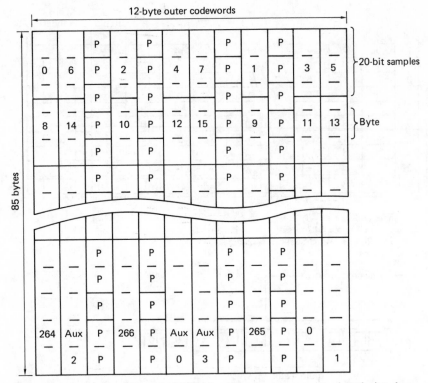

Figure 13.41 In the composite digital VCR, the audio samples are written into the interleave array in rows to produce outer codewords, and read out in 85-byte columns to form sync blocks as shown in Figure 13.42

The 20 bit audio samples are written into the array in rows, where 2½ rows of bytes are needed for one row of samples. Each row of the array is loaded with eight samples, and then 4 bytes of Reed–Solomon redundancy are added to form a 12 byte outer code. Reading the array in columns and adding 8 bytes of R–S redundancy produces inner codewords. Two of these inner codewords can be accommodated in one sync block as shown in Fig. 13.42. Accordingly six sync blocks are necessary to record one audio block.

Sync	1D	Data	Inner check	Data	Inner check
2 bytes	2 bytes	85 bytes	8 bytes	85 bytes	8 bytes

Inner codeword (95 bytes)   Inner codeword (93 bytes)

Figure 13.42 One sync block of the composite digital format contains two inner codewords formed from columns of Figure 13.41. Six sync blocks are necessary to hold the entire interleave block, and form one audio sector (NTSC)

In PAL, the audio block rate is higher, so each block contains fewer samples. The interleave block remains the same except that the columns are only 76 bytes tall instead of 85 bytes.

13.27 Audio functions in DVTRs

The contents of the audio blocks of the DVTR formats can now be detailed in relation to the various audio functions.

A large number of digital audio recorders can run at more than one sampling rate, with many supporting both 44.1 and 48 kHz. Unfortunately neither D-1 nor D-2 offer the option of recording at 44.1 kHz, which is the rate used by the majority of professional music recording organizations, simply because that is the rate used on Compact Disc. As the various technologies of audio, video and computation continue to move closer, this inflexibility may prove to be a drawback.

13.27.1 AES/EBU compatibility

In order to comply with the AES/EBU digital audio interconnect, wordlengths between 16 and 20 bits can be supported, but it is necessary to record a code in the sync block to specify the wordlength in use. Pre-emphasis may have been used prior to conversion, and this status is also to be conveyed, along with the four channel-use bits. As was seen in Section 13.12, the AES/EBU digital interconnect uses a block-sync pattern which repeats after 192 sample periods corresponding to 4 ms at 48 kHz. Since the block size is different to that of the DVTR interleave block, there can be any phase relationship between interleave-block boundaries and the AES/EBU block-sync pattern. In order to recreate the same phase relationship between block sync and sample data on replay, it is necessary to record the position of block sync within the interleave block. It is the function of the interface control word in the audio data to convey these parameters. There is no guarantee that the 192 sample block-sync sequence will remain intact after audio editing; most likely there will be an arbitrary jump in block-sync phase. Strictly speaking a DVTR playing back an edited tape would have to ignore the block-sync positions on the tape and create new block sync at the standard 192 sample spacing.

13.27.2 Synchronization between audio sampling rate and video field rate

Clearly the number of audio sync blocks in a given time is determined by the number of video fields in that time. It is only possible to have a fixed tape structure if the audio sampling rate is locked to video. This is the preferred mode of the DVTR, and results, for 625/50, in exactly 160 audio samples in every write block.

For use on 525/60, it must be recalled that the 60 Hz is actually 59.94 Hz. As this is slightly slow, it will be found that in 60 fields, exactly 48 048 audio samples will be necessary. Unfortunately 60 will not divide into 48 048 without a remainder. The largest number which will divide 60 and 48 048 is 12; thus in 60/12 = 5 fields there will be 48048/12 = 4004 samples.

In D-1, the channel distribution operates over a four-track sequence, as was shown in Fig. 13.37. Since there are ten tracks in a field in 525/60, the four-track channel distribution sequence can only complete after a whole frame. As there is an odd/even sample interleave, putting in a single extra sample would also reverse the definition of odd and even. The solution is that the five-field sequence derived above has to be extended to become a five-frame sequence. Fig. 13.43 shows that over the five-frame period, extra samples are inserted by changing the number of samples in the even block from 160 to 161, whereas the odd blocks are left unchanged. A code is present in each block which denotes the number of useful samples in the block, and this will be read on replay to synchronize the audio correctly. The five-frame sequence is one of the items carried in the linear control

Frame no	Segment no	Audio sample count		
		Even block	Odd block	Frame
	00	160	160	
	01	161	160	
0	02	160	160	1602
	03	161	160	
	04	160	160	
	05	160	160	
	06	160	160	
1	07	161	160	1601
	08	160	160	
	09	160	160	
	0A	160	160	
	0B	161	160	
2	0C	160	160	1602
	0D	161	160	
	0E	160	160	
	0F	160	160	
	10	160	160	
3	11	161	160	1601
	12	160	160	
	13	160	160	
	14	160	160	
	15	161	160	
4	16	160	160	1602
	17	161	160	
	18	160	160	

Figure 13.43 In 525/60 Format D-1, the slip between audio sampling rate and field rate is accommodated by varying the number of samples in the even block over a five frame sequence. The beginning of this sequence is conveyed by the control track

track by an extra pulse doublet (see Chapter 10), and the sequence must remain unbroken after audio editing.

In D-2 a similar principle is applied. There are six tracks in a field in NTSC, and so in a given audio channel there will be 30 audio blocks in a five-field period. There are no odd and even blocks as in D-1, but double recording is implemented, so that there are 15 audio blocks repeated twice. In 14 of these blocks there are 267 audio samples and the remaining block contains 266 samples. The D-2 format does not indicate the audio five-field sequence in the control track, only in the status words of the helical tracks, but again the sequence must remain unbroken after editing.

Although only the use of synchronous audio is deemed to meet the format standard for interchange, the D-1 format permits non-synchronous operation. There will be cases where it is not possible to make a synchronous recording, for example where a digital audio mixing desk is responsible for the audio sampling rate, but the recorder cannot genlock to the desk because it has to lock to network for a simultaneous broadcast. In these cases, the variable-size block concept is extended. A further code pattern allows the use of 159 samples per block in addition to the use of 160 and 161, and the synchronous status bit is changed. The DVTR locks to its video reference and simply varies the block content according to how many audio samples are received. In 625/50, if every block has 159 samples, this corresponds to the audio sampling rate being about 0.6% slow, whereas if every block has 161 samples, the sampling rate is 0.6% fast. In 525/60, the sampling rate is already 0.1% fast relative to the 59.94 Hz field rate, so the speed range will be +0.5% to −0.7%. These ranges are adequate to provide recordings which are not synchronized, where only a slow phase drift takes place. It is not intended to support the use of a non-standard sampling rate. D-2 does not offer this mode of operation.

Fig. 13.44 shows the status words of D-1 and D-2 which control these operations.

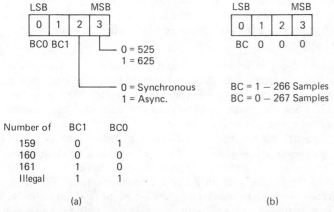

(a)   (b)

Figure 13.44 At (a) the Block Count (BCNT) parameter of D-1 allows for slip between 48 KHz and 59.94 Hz, and also for asynchronous operation in 525 or 625 lines. At (b) the Block Count in D-2 only appears in NTSC. Asynchronous mode is not supported

13.27.3 Variable-speed replay

Variable-speed operation really falls into two categories: speeds close to normal, and more extreme speeds. At extreme speeds, the heads cross tracks too frequently, and the digital audio system is overwhelmed by errors and lack of data and gives up. If audio is required, the analog linear track at the edge of the tape must be used.

At speeds close to normal, used for example to squeeze the length of a programme to insert a newsflash, the highest possible video and audio quality are required. One way in which this can be obtained is by changing capstan and scanner speed by the same amount, to allow the heads to follow the tape tracks correctly. The incorrect video field rate will be corrected by a suitable frame store. Clearly if the head-to-tape speed is changed, the audio sampling rate will change also. If the audio samples are simply being fed to a DAC for immediate conversion to the analog domain, this is of no consequence except for a pitch change, but if the samples have to be fed at standard rate into a fully digital studio, a sampling-rate converter will be necessary to avoid the degradation due to reverting to analog.

13.27.4 Editing

It has been explained that the audio-write blocks can be individually written with the use of tolerance gaps to protect adjacent data. There is, however, rather more to editing than that. The D-1 and D-2 formats support three levels of audio editing, all of which leave a standard formatted tape, but which deliver different performance according to the complexity of the recorder. The reader should take care to distinguish between that which the format permits and that which is implemented on a given model of recorder. Assemble editing, insert editing and split audio/video editing are all supported to achieve maximum flexibility; however, a machine which can only record audio and video together is still capable of meeting the format. In other words a machine can still achieve interchange without supporting every possible edit feature. These features will be described in turn.

1. Split audio/video editing is achieved in the overall control system of the DVTR. As video and audio data occupy different sync block addresses on tape, they can be written quite independently, and it is only a matter of supplying different timecodes to the video and audio record enables and the split edit will be performed automatically.

2. Assemble and insert recording of audio are a little more complex because the tape tracks are shared between audio and video. The block structure of the tracks must always be maintained; therefore it is not possible to record only video or only audio on a blank tape. When an assemble is made, the tape beyond the assemble point is assumed to be blank, and a new control track will be written. If only video is supplied to the machine after an assemble, the audio blocks will still be written, filled, most likely, with zero samples, and including the content count

which allows the sampling rate to be established. If only audio is supplied after an assemble point, the video blocks will still be written, filled with black. The major difference between assemble and insert is that the control track is read in insert, such that at the end of the insert the original recording carries on without loss of synchronism. During an insert any or all of the audio channels may be changed, by having the heads record during audio sectors, and/or video may be changed, by having the heads record during the video sectors. In practice, once a tape has been recorded, all future work on that tape can be in insert mode as, in digital recording, the format of the tape has a separate existence to the programme material.

3. The actual mechanism of video editing is simply to start recording the new data at a field boundary, the result appearing as a cut in the picture. This is also the most basic way of editing the audio; at an interleave block boundary the new recording is substituted for the old. It is to be expected that this will result in step discontinuities of the audio waveform, audible as clicks, but this may well be acceptable in a portable machine whose tapes will be the raw material for post-production. As all audio data are recorded twice in different blocks, there is a possibility of performing a more satisfactory edit by initially updating only half of the blocks with new data. During this overlap period, the end of the previous recording and the beginning of the new will both be present, and the DVTR can perform a crossfade in the digital domain between the two sample streams. At the end of an insert, the reverse crossfade would take place. The overlap period is flexible, because the best crossfade time varies subjectively with the material recorded. Clearly, on performing the edit, the crossfade period is simply the time for which only half of the sample blocks are recorded. On replay, the crossfader needs to know how its coefficients should vary with time to match what has been recorded. This is neatly solved by incorporating a gain parameter in the audio blocks, which will change during the overlap period and control the replay crossfader. The format is such that machines which do not support this mode record zeros in the parameter position, and this code results in no action in any player. There is an imperfection in this simple crossfading approach because the 100% redundancy is absent during the overlap period, and large dropouts during crossfades could cause the machine to interpolate using the odd/even interleave. At first sight, the accuracy to which an audio edit can be made appears subject to the position of the nearest block boundary. However, the actual state of the crossfade is determined by the crossfade code carried in the sync blocks, and this can be used to position the crossover point anywhere. In fact this mode of operation is available only in the D-1 format; D-2 does not support it. The AES/EBU user bits complete the necessary audio block contents, and a diagram of the block content in excess of the sample data appears in Fig. 13.45.

4. For post-production, it will be seen that audio editing can be carried out to the same standards of accuracy and fidelity as in the best digital audio-only recorders, albeit with some hardware complexity. The use of interleaving is a powerful tool against dropouts, but it makes editing to

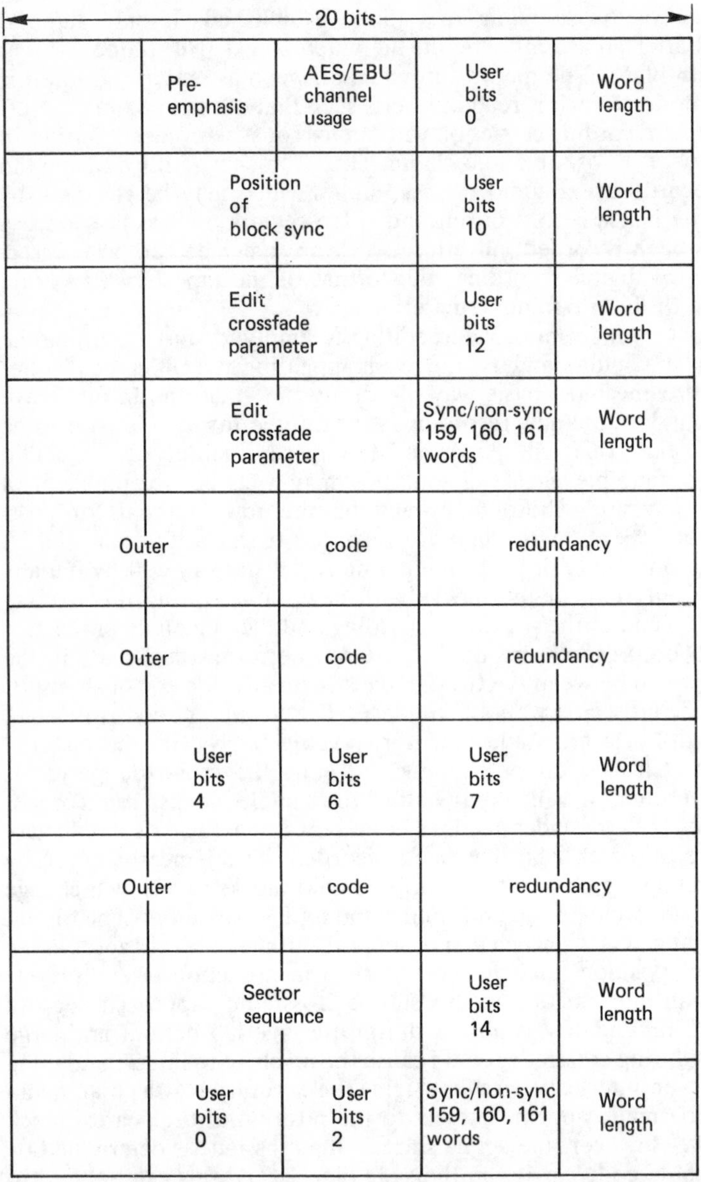

←		20 bits		→
	Pre-emphasis	AES/EBU channel usage	User bits 0	Word length
	Position of block sync		User bits 10	Word length
	Edit crossfade parameter		User bits 12	Word length
	Edit crossfade parameter		Sync/non-sync 159, 160, 161 words	Word length
	Outer	code	redundancy	
	Outer	code	redundancy	
	User bits 4	User bits 6	User bits 7	Word length
	Outer	code	redundancy	
	Sector sequence		User bits 14	Word length
	User bits 0	User bits 2	Sync/non-sync 159, 160, 161 words	Word length

Figure 13.45 The audio block also contains various user and control bits, with positions as shown here. Note that many of them are repeated. This diagram is an enlargement of the rightmost column of data in Figure 13.40 (b) (D-1 only)

sample accuracy much more difficult. The principles involved are exactly those of a digital audio-only machine. Because of the structure of the codewords, only entire blocks can be recorded without error, whereas crossfades need to be performed on de-interleaved data. In

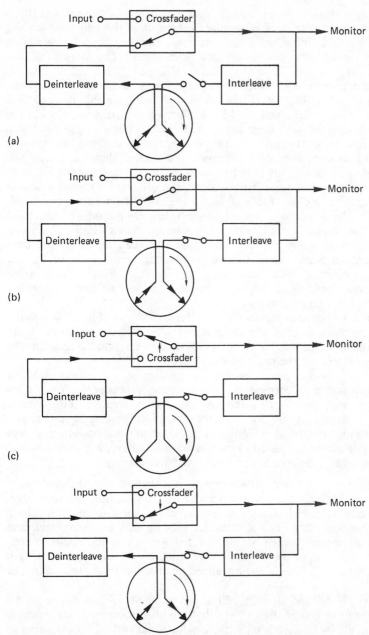

(a)

(b)

(c)

Figure 13.46 In the most sophisticated version of audio editing, there are advanced replay heads on the scanner, which allow editing to be performed on deinterleaved data. An insert sequence is shown. At (a) the replay head signal is decoded, and fed to the encoder which, after some time, will produce an output representing what is already on the tape. In (b), at a sector boundary, the write circuits are turned on, and the machine begins to rerecord. In (c) the crossfade is made to the insert material. At (d) the insert ends with a crossfade back to the signal from the advanced replay heads. After this, the write heads will once again be recording what is already on the tape, and the write circuits can be disabled at a sector boundary. An assemble edit consists of the first three of these steps only

order to perform a true crossfade edit with sample accuracy and 100% redundancy, the existing recording in the area of the edit must first be played back, de-interleaved and corrected, and then digitally crossfaded at any point with the insert/assemble audio. The output of the crossfader has then to be re-interleaved, and the result has to be recorded in the blocks which were played back earlier to update them. The problem is that, until the block has been played, the contents cannot be de-interleaved, and by the time the correction, crossfading and re-interleave have been performed, the block has long gone. There are two solutions to this. The first is that the area of the edit point is played into a memory on a first pass of the tape; then the machine is backed up, and the crossfade to new material and the re-recording take place on a second pass. This is slow, but allows the use of a simple DVTR. The second method is to use an advanced replay head, separated by the decode/correction–encode delay period. In the DVTR this would require extra heads on the scanner and an additional amount of memory to delay the data from the advanced replay by the time between the heads minus the decode/encode delay. However, if the machine is fitted with track-following heads to allow variable-speed operation, these heads could be made to deflect so that they would become the advanced replay heads.

The sequence of events in such a system is shown in Fig. 13.46. As the complete audio structure of the channel to be edited is rewritten, there is no loss of redundancy at the edit crossfade point, and the resistance to corruption will be the same as elsewhere.

5. In order to dub one channel to another (track bouncing) the de-interleave and correction process must precede the record interleave, and, clearly, to avoid loss of lip-sync, an advanced playback head is necessary as for the most sophisticated edit technique. Synchronous recording is similar in principle to track bouncing, except that a performer can listen to the playback of an existing recording and play along to it to record another track in synchronism.

There are some further possibilities with such a multiheaded post-production machine. In conjunction with a digital sampling-rate converter, such a machine could convert a non-synchronous D-1 recording to a synchronous recording. The advanced replay heads would play back into the rate converter, which would be fed with a synchronous output reference. The output could then be recorded on the same tape before it left the scanner. The use of the advanced head ensures the preservation of lip-sync.

As a DVTR can individually edit audio channels, it does not require a great leap of the imagination to see that a multitrack audio-only machine could be made by filling the tape tracks with audio sectors. The number of channels this would permit is staggering, and it may be more useful to incorporate a reduced-resolution or monochrome video channel. The high recording density of helical scan means that the tape speed would be much lower than any other kind of multitrack audio recorder, and the apparent rewinding speed would be much higher, making possible a workstation approach as is currently implemented with hard disks.

References

1. ARAI, T., NOGUCHI, T., KOBAYASHI, M. and OKAMOTO, H., Digital signal processing technology for R-DAT. *IEEE Trans. Consum. Electron.*, **CE-32**, 442–452 (1986)
2. WATKINSON, J.R., Splice handling mechanisms in DASH format. Presented at 77th Audio Engineering Society Convention (Hamburg, 1985), preprint 2199(A-2)
3. ISHIDA, Y., *et al.* A PCM digital audio processor for home use VTRs. Presented at 64th Audio Engineering Society Convention (New York, 1979), preprint 1528
4. ANON., AES recommended practice for professional digital audio applications employing pulse code modulation: preferred sampling frequencies. AES5-1984 (ANSI S4.28-1984), *J. Audio Eng. Soc.*, **32**, 781–785, (1984)
5. MURAOKA, T., IWAHARA, M. and YAMADA, Y., Examination of audio bandwidth requirements for optimum sound signal transmission. *J. Audio Eng. Soc.*, **29**, 2–9 (1982)
6. MURAOKA, T., YAMADA, Y. and YAMAZAKI, M., Sampling frequency considerations in digital audio. *J. Audio Eng. Soc.*, **26**, 252–256, (1978)
7. FINCHAM, L.R., The subjective importance of uniform group delay at low frequencies. Presented at the 74th Audio Engineering Society Convention (New York, 1983), preprint 2056(H-1)
8. ADAMS, R.W., Companded predictive delta modulation: a low-cost technique for digital recording. *J.Audio Eng. Soc.*, **32** 659–672 (1984)
9. V.D. PLASSCHE, R.J., Dynamic element matching puts trimless convertors on chip. *Electronics*, (16 June 1983)
10. V.D. PLASSCHE, R.J. and GOEDHART, D., A monolithic 14 bit D/A convertor. *IEEE J. Solid-State Circuits*, **SC-14**, 552–556 (1979)
11. V.D. PLASSCHE, R.J. and DIJKMANS, E.C., A monolithic 16 bit D/A conversion system for digital audio. In *Digital Audio*, ed. B.A. Blesser *et al.*,, New York: Audio Engineering Society, pp. 54–60
12. ADAMS, R.W., Design and implementation of an audio 18-bit A/D convertor using oversampling techniques. Presented at the 77th Audio Engineering Society Convention (Hamburg, 1985), preprint 2182
13. RANADA, D., New hi-fi horizons. *Stereo Rev.* 68–70, 117 (Dec. 1984)
14. SCHROEDER, E.F. and VOESSING, W., High-quality digital audio encoding with 3 bits/sample using adaptive transform coding. Presented at the 80th Audio Engineering Society Convention (Montreux, 1986), preprint 2321
15. Audio Engineering Society, AES recommended practice for digital audio engineering – serial transmission format for linearly represented digital audio data. *J. Audio Eng. Soc.*, **33**, 975–984 (1985)
16. Draft standard for a digital audio interface. IEC report 84/WG11
17. EIA RS-422A. Electronic Industries Association, 2001 Eye St N.W., Washington, DC 20006, USA
18. SMART, D.L., Transmission performance of digital audio serial interface on audio tie lines. *BBC Des. Dep. Tech. Memo.*, 3.296/84
19. European Broadcasting Union, Specification of the digital audio interface. *EBU Doc. Tech.*, 3250
20. LAGADEC, R. and MCNALLY, G.J., Labels and their formatting in digital audio recording and transmission. Presented at 74th Audio Engineering Society Convention (New York, 1983), preprint 2003
21. LIDBETTER, P.S. and DOUGLAS, S., A fibre-optic multichannel communication link developed for remote interconnection in a digital audio console. Presented at the 80th Audio Engineering Society Convention (Montreux, 1986), preprint 2330
22. Ampex Digital Format for Video and Audio Tape Recording of Composite Video Signals using 19mm Type D-2 Cassette. Ampex Corporation (1988)
23. GILCHRIST, N.H.C., Digital sound: sampling-rate synchronization by variable delay. *BBC Res. Dep. Rep.*, 1979/17

24. LAGADEC, R., A new approach to sampling rate synchronisation. Presented at 76th Audio Engineering Society Convention (New York, 1984), preprint 2168
25. SHELTON, W.T., Progress towards a system of synchronization in a digital studio. Presented at the 82nd Audio Engineering Society Convention (London, 1986), preprint 2484(K7)
26. ANON., NICAM 728: specification for two additional digital sound channels with System I television. BBC Engineering Information Dept, London (1988)
27. ANON., Specification of the system of the MAC/packet family. *EBU Tech. Doc.* 3258 (1986)

Index